The history of

Maine. 1661-1900

Edwin Emery

Alpha Editions

This edition published in 2019

ISBN : 9789353862633

Design and Setting By
Alpha Editions
email - alphaedis@gmail.com

THE

HISTORY OF SANFORD,

MAINE.

1661 — 1900.

BY

EDWIN EMERY, A. M.

COMPILED, EDITED AND ARRANGED BY HIS SON,

WILLIAM MORRELL EMERY, A. M.

➤✳✳◄

FALL RIVER, MASS. :

PUBLISHED BY THE COMPILER,

1901.

Salem Press:
THE SALEM PRESS CO., SALEM, MASS.
1901

PREFACE.

The author of the following pages devoted the leisure of twenty years, until within a few weeks of his death in the autumn of 1895, to gathering and arranging facts for a narrative history of the town of Sanford. With no thought of gain, without hope of reward other than that which comes from the consciousness of duty faithfully performed, he set himself to the task, bringing to it not only a love for historical research, but (the compiler, through filial regard, will be pardoned for saying) a mind well adapted, both by nature and habit of thought, for the prosecution of the work in a logical, discriminating and methodical manner. Conscientious and painstaking, he sought to make his history reliable and thorough, deeming no detail too trivial for the most careful and ofttimes laborious verification. Possessed of that robust health which apparently betokened a long life, there never occurred to him the need of hastening the work, which, when his fatal illness overtook him, was still uncompleted.

Having been asked to prepare the History of Sanford for publication, the compiler found, upon examination, that it was comprised within several volumes of bulky note books, and that while the major portion was written *in extenso* and arranged by subject matter, in other instances there were merely notes, unclassified memoranda, copies of old documents, or additional data gathered subsequent to the writing of the earlier sections. Use has been made of all this material. Inasmuch as it was desired to preserve the original manuscripts intact, it has been necessary to transcribe the work entire for the printers, a task in itself of no small magnitude, and increased by attendant circumstances and conditions. Care has been taken, except where necessity existed for a condensation of material, to retain the author's exact text; and for this reason and because of the obvious enumeration of events since the author's death, it has not been deemed requisite to make formal distinction between the work of the author and the compiler. An exception should be noted, however, in Chapters II and III, interwoven as they are with material obtained by the compiler from original sources, namely, the Proprietors' Records, for which the author sought diligently through a score of years, and the existence of which was brought to his attention only a short time before his death. These valuable records (much of them, it may be said in passing, in the handwriting of the famous Samuel Adams, proprietors' clerk) are in the possession of Mr. George W. Johnson, of Somersworth, N. H., in whose family they have been for about seventy-five years; by him they were kindly placed at the convenience of the compiler, who found them of the utmost service in tiding over gaps in the narrative and settling a number of disputed questions.

Of the merits of this volume, the compiler fain would leave the reader to judge, yet cannot forbear reference to the author's evident intention not merely to chronicle the events of the town, but, by presenting as well that which indicates clearly the trend, growth, and development of public sentiment in the community on all the great questions of the day, to deal in some measure with the true philosophy of history. Such will be found in the chapters on the Revolution and the events immediately succeeding it; the action with reference to adoption of the Constitution, the Embargo, separation from Massachusetts, and surplus revenue; the temperance movement; and the Civil War; while the votes for President and Governor, set forth in dry figures though they be, bear interesting witness to frequent changes in the manifestation of political principles, in the expression of which, we cannot doubt, the greatest freedom has always been permitted.

It is a matter of pride to the compiler to be enabled to present to the public the author's history of his native town,—a life-work. Without the aid, advice, and encouragement of a host of willing friends, however, the task would have been difficult of accomplishment. The compiler's hearty thanks are due to Hon. Frank A. Allen, Hon. E. M. Goodall, Hon. Sumner I. Kimball, Mr. George E. Allen, Mr. Charles B. Allbee, Mr. Harry E. Bryant, Mr. Frank H. Dexter, Mr. Fred B. Averill, and Mr. Edwin R. Champlin (the latter of Fall River), among others, for courtesies extended, and for friendly suggestions and criticisms. Laboring under the disadvantage of being at so great a distance from the scene, the information relating to affairs of the last five years, as supplied principally by Mr. George E. Allen, has been especially helpful. To the many who were of assistance to the author during his period of research, and who cannot here be called by name, the compiler also would extend his sincere thanks.

Within a few hours the midnight chimes will ring out the old, ring in the new. The dawn of the twentieth century is bright with hope and encouragement. "The great gain on an occasion like the present," as has been so well said by an eminent son of Maine, "is that we stand for the moment in the focus of two great lights. We see ourselves in the light of the past and in that of the future. We judge the past, and we know as we judge the past, so the future will judge us. We stand thus in the presence of an ideal partially fulfilled. . . . . Today we lift the heroism of the fathers of our town up from the obscurity in which their lives were passed, and honor it. Let it be an inspiration to our own lives; so that when the great light of the future is turned back upon our memories, as we turn back the light of the present upon theirs, we, in the peace and comfort of our homes, shall be seen to be no unworthy successors of those whose strong arms and brave hearts conquered for us in the wilderness."

WILLIAM MORRELL EMERY.

FALL RIVER, MASS.,
December 31, 1900.

CONTENTS.

CHAPTER 1.

DESCRIPTION.

CHAPTER II.

PURCHASE FROM THE INDIANS.

CHAPTER III.

PHILLIPSTOWN.

CHAPTER IV.

FRENCH AND INDIAN WARS.

CHAPTER XXII.

THE TEMPERANCE MOVEMENT.

CHAPTER XXIII.

SURPLUS REVENUE.

CHAPTER XXIV.

BUSINESS.

CHAPTER XXV.

THE MEXICAN WAR.

CHAPTER XXVI.

LAW AND MEDICINE.

CHAPTER XXVII.

ROADS.

CHAPTER XXXIII.

MEMORABLE OCCURRENCES.

CHAPTER XXXIV.

THE FRATERNAL ORDERS.

CHAPTER XXXV.

CEMETERIES AND GRAVEYARDS.

CHAPTER XXXVI.

LATTER DAY SCHOOLS.

CHAPTER XXXVII.

MUNICIPAL MATTERS.

CHAPTER XXXVIII.

ODDS AND ENDS OF HISTORY.

PORTRAITS.

ERRATA.

Page 48, line 14.   For " seem " read " seen."

Page 81.   Peter Nasson was born in 1766.

Page 195.   As will be noted by statements on pages 195 and 484, traditions regarding the Nasson house fail to agree in all details. Assuming that General Jotham Moulton was born in 1740, the house, if erected by him, must have been built later than the date mentioned on page 195. It may be that the original structure was built by his grandfather, Colonel Jeremiah Moulton, in 1740–41 (having been possibly a block-house), and that General Moulton built only the upper story.

Page 201, line 21.   For " Goodwin's " read " Goodrich's."

Page 213, line 10.   David Morrison came to Sanford about 1785.

(xvi)

CHAPTER I.

DESCRIPTION.

Situation — Size — Topography — Hills — Mousam River — Water powers — Brooks — Ponds — Trees — Soil — Mineralogy and Geology — Villages.

SANFORD is situated in latitude 43° 25' north, and in longitude 6° 13' east from Washington, or 70° 47' west from Greenwich. It is about four miles south from the Court House, Alfred, thirty-one west-southwest from the City Hall, Portland, and eighty-two southwest from the State House, Augusta. These are air-line distances. It is bounded on the north by Acton and Shapleigh, on the northeast by Alfred, on the southeast by Kennebunk and Wells, and on the southwest by North Berwick and Lebanon. Owing to its irregular boundaries, a part of Shapleigh lies west, of North Berwick, southeast, and of Lebanon, northwest, of Sanford. Its length is nearly twice its breadth, averaging about ten miles by five. Its lower boundary is nearly six and three-quarters miles. Its greatest length, from the corner of Acton, Lebanon and Sanford to the Wells line, is about eleven and a half miles. A straight line from that corner through the pond at Sanford to the Kennebunk line near the Mousam River measures nearly twelve miles. Its area is approximately 64,000 acres.

The lower part of the town is sandy and marshy. Its low and level surface is relieved by two hills only, Oak and Lyon. The upper part is diversified by hills and valleys — the hills, generally called ridges, bearing the names of early settlers, as Low's or Shaw's ridge, Hanson's or Plummer's ridge, and Deering's ridge. Oak Hill received its name from the large and abundant oaks which covered it when first settled. Though a slight elevation its summit affords a good view of the White Mountains. More than a century ago, President Dwight, of Yale College, visited it that he might obtain a view of the famous hills. In his "Travels," Volume I, page 427, he informs us that he was at Rogers's inn, eight miles from Portsmouth Bridge,

(1)

Thursday, October 6, 1796, and then briefly describes the appearance of the mountains as seen from the hill.

" Our host, having informed us that, at Sanford, four miles north-west from his house, the White Mountains were visible, we took our horses and rode to an eminence named Oak Hill; the spot where, as he told us, this interesting object might be seen. The day was bright and clear; and Mount Washington, the highest of these summits, was in full view. The computed distance, not far from the real one, is ninety miles. The color of this summit was a blue, approximating to white. It was misty and dim, but easily distinguishable. Immediately before a storm it is said *to loom* in an extraordinary manner, *i. e.* to rise, apparently; to seem nearer; and to become more distinct to the eye than at other times."

One suggestion in regard to the origin of the name of Lyon Hill is, that it is a corruption of Lyman's Hill, named for Doctor Job Lyman, who was a land owner in Sanford during the latter part of the last century. Another suggestion is a similar corruption of Liron's Hill, Liron being the name of one of the heirs of Elisha Sanford's thousand acres. And still another that the name of Lion Hill was applied to this region, whence, in the days of the early settlers, came the howlings of wolves and an occasional catamount, making it a region of terror.

The writer has this origin of the name, which seems more reasonable than the other explanations of it, from one (Deacon Stephen Dorman) who had it from an early settler (William Bennett) : The hill was so called because one Captain Lyon encamped thereon, with a company of soldiers, when on an expedition toward the eastern frontier. (Captain Henry Lyon was in Roxbury in 1711, and in York in 1714.)

Beaver Hill, in the northeast part of the town, derives its name from the beaver, whose haunts were in the neighboring pond. From its summit, six hundred and twenty-six feet above the level of the sea, a fine view can be had of the valley of the Mousam.

The highest elevation of land is Mount Hope, six hundred and eighty-five feet above the sea level. This was formerly Annis's Hill, from its first settler, Charles Annis. The name Mount Hope is found recorded in 1806, but what reason can be given for the change is wholly a matter of conjecture. A magnificent view is presented from Mount Hope. Toward the west and north stretch the hills of New Hampshire, terminating in the White Mountains. Toward the east and south lies the valley of the Mousam with low hills beyond, and with apparently higher land near the ocean. Woods and fields interspersed spread out a beautiful landscape, beyond which the Atlantic rolls as far as eye can see. The white sails of vessels going hither and thither skirt the horizon, and occasionally a passing steamer may be traced by a thread of black smoke gradually dissipated into the atmosphere.

The Mousam River, western branch, enters Sanford about midway of the northern boundary, flows in a southeasterly direction nearly nine miles, and then east till it unites with the eastern branch, and forms the boundary between Sanford and Alfred to the Kennebunk line. It is from two to four rods wide in its natural course, but where dammed as at Willard's, Sanford and Springvale, forms ponds of considerable width. Near Morrison's Mill privilege there is a natural curiosity called the "Gulf." It is a narrow cut through a ledge, about fifty feet long, twenty high and ten or twelve wide, through which the water rushes with much force. There is a tradition that a Littlefield, chased by an Indian, leaped across this chasm, and escaped from his fleet-footed pursuer.

In his "Summary," Douglass says: "Mausom River comes from some Ponds near the famous Lovell's Pond, about 40 miles above Piscataqua Harbour; at these Ponds Bryant the Surveyor began to set off the N. 8d. E. Line between the Province of Main and New Hampshire: this river falls into the Ocean in the Township of Wells." Says Williamson: "The Mousam, formerly called Cape Porpoise River or Maguncook, which issues from ponds of that name in Shapleigh, twenty miles remote, turns several mills, but has no good harbor by nature." Sullivan adds, "and is increasing in its use and consequence."

The Mousam River (three branches, eastern, middle and western) is about twenty-five miles long, drains one hundred and twenty square miles of territory, and has an estimated yearly discharge of 4,680,-000,000 cubic feet. It is supplied by the Shakers', Bunganut, Mousam, Square and Loon Ponds, whose approximate area is four and eighty-five hundredths square miles. At the railroad crossing it is two hundred and fourteen feet above the level of the sea, and its descent from about the level of Springvale to tide water is two hundred and sixty-two feet. According to the United States Coast Survey, the depot is three hundred and twenty-eight feet above the level of the sea.

At some remote period the course of the river near Morrison's Corner seems to have been changed. Holes worn in the rocks by the attrition of water would indicate that the river flowed nearer the Corner than its present channel. It has also been conjectured that, by some great upheaval of the earth's crust, the lower course was turned toward the east from its original basin. The chain of ponds extending toward the south from South Sanford seems to indicate that the waters found their way to the ocean through the valley of the Piscataqua. It is a noticeable fact, that, since the forests have been cleared away, a less quantity of water than formerly flows in the channel.

The following brooks are tributaries of the Mousam: A small brook which rises in Shapleigh, flows through the Welch neighborhood and empties into that river below Morrison's; Frost's brook, which crosses the road just below Butler's Corner above Springvale and flows easterly; Chapman's brook, which rises west of Springvale, and crosses the road between there and Sanford; Beaver Hill brook, which drains the swamps east of the depot, and Muddy brook, which drains those south of Shaw's ridge; the Birch-log brook and Thompson brook are small water courses, crossing "Hardscrabble;" Boston's brook east of Jonas C. Littlefield's; Perkins's brook at East Sanford, which runs east, and has its outlet below Whitcher's grist mill.

The Hay Brook, so called on account of the large number of meadows along its banks which it drains, rises southeast of Beaver Hill, forms a part of the boundary between Sanford and Alfred, and empties into the eastern branch of the Mousam. Its tributary is Cane's brook, which rises below the late residence of Stephen H. Moulton.

According to the returns made by Moses W. Emery and James O. Clark, in 1868, to Walter Wells, superintendent of the Hydrographic Survey of Maine, there were sixteen water powers on the Mousam within the limits of the town having an aggregate fall of two hundred and four feet. According to a subsequent survey reported in 1890, there are nineteen mill-privileges with an aggregate fall of three hundred and six feet. We are indebted to the same excellent authority for a description of the same. "Commencing with the upper end and following the river down," says Mr. Emery, "we find first the fall at Jellison's bridge, that a survey makes 62 feet; then Jordan's saw-mill, fall 10 feet; next the Churchill fall 12 feet; then George K. Gibbs, 18 feet; next the Morrison mill privilege owned by Sumner I. Kimball, fall 25 feet; then Springvale mills, fall 17 feet; first shoe factory, fall 10 feet; second shoe factory, 14 feet; Shackley's grist mill, 9 feet; next a water privilege owned on the east by S. D. Tibbetts, and on the west by Sumner I. Kimball, fall 15 feet; then come the three water privileges of the Sanford Mills, aggregate 36 feet. Then there was, so long ago that none but the very old people remember it, a mill privilege opposite the Jotham Moulton place, owned and occupied by a man named Cane, fall said to be 8 feet. Below is the Cram, or Willard mill privilege, fall 8 feet Next is the Linscott mill, fall 20 feet; then Estes mill, fall 10 feet; Morse mill, fall 14 feet, and last Hill's mill, with a fall of 18 feet, making in all 19 mill privileges, with an aggregate of 306 feet. The fact that there are these good water privileges within very short distances of each other, at both Springvale and Sanford Corner, and also the lands adjoining the same were favorable to build upon, furnishes the reason for the two prosperous villages in this town. Seven of the water privileges enumerated are occupied by saw and grist mills, six are unoccupied, and among them are some of the very best of all, but their location has so far prevented their use, while those at Springvale and Sanford Corner are not equal to the amount of business done, so that it is sometimes said that these places have about made their natural growth as manufacturing places.''

Willis says that the name Mousam is of Indian origin, but Judge Bourne has a different opinion. In his " History of Wells and Kennebunk," he gives an account of the change from Cape Porpoise to Mousam, but sees no reason why the appellation should have been used. Henry Sayward completed a saw-mill at the falls, at Kennebunk, in 1672, and then built a grist-mill, to which establishment as a whole he gave the name Mousam mills. " Previous to this period, the river had been known by the name of Cape Porpoise; soon after, it was called Mousam. The change was probably wrought by this designation of the works on it. It would be natural, in referring to the Mousam mills, as common in the intercourse of life, to give the same name to the territory about it and to the river on which the business of the mill was done." But why Sayward gave it the name Mousam neither record nor tradition reveals to us.

The Great Works River, or brook, as it is frequently called, rises between Hanson's ridge and Mount Hope, flows in a southerly direction, forms a part of the boundary between Sanford and North Berwick and empties into Bauneg Beg Pond. Among its tributaries are Cold Spring brook, which rises west of the Corner, and flows through the bed of the " Old Pond," of which it was formerly the outlet; Shepherd's Machine brook, the outlet of Fishing Pond; the Bean brook and Walnut brook at the foot of Mount Hope; and Allen's Marsh brook near Oak Hill. At one time, it furnished water-power a part of the year for four mills: Hobbs's, Gowen's, Bennett's and Johnson's.

A brook rising near the Worsters flows easterly, then southerly near the Carrolls, and empties into a branch of Little River. The outlet of Deering Pond, called the "Branch," with its tributaries, empties into Little River. On an old plot of Lydston's grant, the Indian name of the pond is given as Tombegewoc, and the name of its outlet, Salmon Falls River.

The Red brook, so called, on the Hanson's ridge road, received its name from the red loam or ochre found in its bed and in early days used for painting.

The Branch River has its sources in the swamps and lowlands, southwest of the Wells road, through which the "Long Causey" is built, and flows southeasterly through Wells into the Atlantic ocean. Merriland River rises in the swamps east of Oak Hill.

According to the plan of Sanford as surveyed in 1794, there were thirteen ponds in town, having an estimated area of two hundred and eighty-five acres, and two lying partly in town, of one hundred and thirty acres: Deering, twenty acres; Cold Spring, thirty acres; Fishing, twenty acres; Curtis, eighteen acres; Picture, twenty acres; Sand, forty acres; Duck and Eel, ten each; four nameless ponds, ten each; and one of eighty acres near the southwest boundary of Wells. Thirty acres of Beaver Hill Pond and one hundred of Bauneg Beg Pond were in Sanford. The latter lies at the foot of Bauneg Beg Hills. Its name is undoubtedly of Indian origin, but what it means, or its correct orthography, Bonny Bigg, Bonny Beag, Benepeag, or Bauneg Beg, we have been unable to determine.

The name of Picture Pond came from the "Picture Tree" standing on its shore, which received its name from the following circumstance: About 1754, "a daughter of Peter Morrell, a Quaker, on the northeast side of Berwick, went out on a Sunday morning into the woods, near her father's house, to gather hemlock bows (boughs) for a broom; the savages shot her and carried away her head, not having time to take off her scalp." When they reached Picture Pond they engraved an image of the child upon an old pine tree, which for years was a noted landmark in that vicinity.

Cold Spring Pond has disappeared. Whether these estimates of a century ago hold good as to the other ponds, we have no means of knowing.

The surveyor of the eight miles square in 1720, indicated on his plan the character of the territory surveyed. Between the Kennebunk and Mousam Rivers there was " good land ;" on the southwest side of the Mousam along the Wells head-line, " much clear level land and a good soil," beyond which was " The head of Merriland Marshes." On the northeast side of the Mousam, western branch, about the confluence of the two branches, "pine timber " was abundant; along the Berwick boundary, near Bauneg Beg, " much white ash timber," and near the Great Works River, " beech and pine." Of the land in general, Surveyor Preble thus writes November 10, 1720, after having taken possession of the land : " It is a tract of very good land, plain flatt level land, good soil as far as we could judge, fat land, and well meadowed upon every part ; and for timber the best that ever I saw or those that were with me ; yet we saw but the least part ; white pine in abundance fit for sawing into boards and not difficult to transport ; white oak and red oak in abundance and a great deal of large pitch pine suitable for to saw, or for turpentine, or making tar, and of white ash Timber enough to supply the Kingdom many years. And I am credibly informed that there is a great quantity of very good and large white Cedar. The rivers will be very serviceable to transport your lumber, &c., the way from Wells thither is very good & plain and not more than six or seven miles to Wells Township and from the Westward part I believe not more than seven or eight miles to Berwick meeting house."

The forests of pine, of which Surveyor Preble writes, disappeared, and the white ash, in large quantities, seems to have been a tree of the past. Cedar has been abundant in the cedar swamp at South Sanford. Oak covered the hill which derived its name from the tree. That part of the town now Alfred, was well covered with pitch-pine and white oak. North of Bunganut Pond was broken white oak. Across the Coxhall line white oak and pitch-pine, along the upper course of the eastern branch, and pitch-pine along the lower course. Between that branch and the highway from Wells to Massabesec, much pitch-pine, both above and below Eastman's Pond and its surrounding heath. On the other side of the road, near the junction of the eastern and middle branches, white oak flourished, between which and the pitch-pine above, was a sharp dividing line, and still above the large tract of pitch-pine, another marked division between pine and white oak. Broken pitch-pine, heaths and rocky land lay between the middle and western branches. It was the tract between these two branches that furnished a weighty reason for dividing the town. It was described as a barren pitch-pine plain and large spruce swamp unfit for settlements between the two parishes, and some years rendered unfit for passage from one parish to another without great difficulty, on account of the flow of water. Scrub-oak and scrub-pine are found on the plains, while the more hardy soils grow white, red and yellow oak, white and pitch-pine, beech, maple, birch, spruce, cedar and hemlock. Willow is found in small quantities, and a few walnut trees stand out by themselves near Deacon Samuel Nowell's on the North Berwick road, at the foot of Mount Hope. In our day, a few large, tall Norway pines stood, like giant sentinels, near the Hay Brook on the lower road to Alfred.

The lower parts of the town are sandy plains or marshes. Oak Hill and Lyon Hill are good strong soil, as are the other hills or ridges in the northeast and northwest parts. Mount Hope was formerly covered with pine growth, but now with hard-wood growth, maple, birch, beech, and has a strong ledgy soil. Deering's ridge has a rich loam to support its hard-wood growth, and produces hay, wheat, corn and potatoes. Hanson's ridge, Plummer's ridge, Shaw's ridge and the Beaver Hill neighborhood, have productive soils, which yield good crops under skilful cultivation and favorable conditions of the weather.

A complete analysis of the mineralogy and geology of the town has never been made. Granite, gneiss and mica slate abound in the western counties of Maine, and there are several fine granite quarries in Sanford, the stone being said to be equal to that of Quincy. In 1772 there was in town an iron works erected for the purpose of smelting ore and forging iron, the ore being obtained in the northerly part of Sanford and in Shapleigh. This venture did not prove successful. Professor John W. Webster, in the summer of 1848, discovered vesuvianite, or idocrase, on the land of the late Solomon Allen, the bed being upwards of two hundred feet in length. Professor Webster relates that he also found molybdenum, epidote, albite and calc spar. Of the vein of idocrase, Kunz, in his "Gems and Precious Stones of North America" (1890) says, it "occurs in unlimited quantities, one ledge, fully thirty feet wide, being made up entirely of massive idocrase, associated with quartz, and occasionally with calcite, which fills the cavities containing the crystals. Some of the crystals are seven inches long and occasionally the smaller ones would afford fair gems." It was thought a few years ago that copper had been discovered in a granite ledge on the farm now owned by

Willard Littlefield, but a superficial examination showed pyrites of iron, with slight traces of gold and copper. Some beautiful specimens of feldspar of various hues were also found. There are two villages in the town, Sanford, or Sanford Corner, as it was long known, and Springvale. The latter name is also applied to the station of the Portland and Rochester Railroad. South Sanford can hardly be called a village, though a post-office is established there. Moultonborough is a part of South Sanford extending along the eastern side of the river. Mouse Lane, in the eastern part, is said to have been a term of reproach. The early settlers kept a breed of very small cattle whose coming and going out of the narrow wood roads were suggestive of mice darting here and there through the almost hidden approaches of their burrows. The Pèrkins neighborhood, the Branch, and Getchell's Corner are in the lower part of the town; the Littlefield and the Deering neighborhoods in the upper part. Morrison's Corner is a mile above Springvale. "Grammar Street" is the road leading from Shaw's ridge to the lower Alfred road. Its name was said to have been given because a large number of teachers had their homes on that road. Another reason is also ascribed for this name. A school-house stood above the woods not far from Samuel Shaw's barn. It was burned before 1822. In that school-house, about 1817, a class of grown-up scholars began the study of grammar, the first time it was studied in any school in town. Thereupon some of the scholars began to call the road "Grammar Street."

According to the Postal Register, there are fourteen other Sanfords in the United States: in Alabama, Colorado, Connecticut, Florida, Georgia, Michigan, Mississippi, Montana, New York, North Carolina, Pennsylvania, South Carolina, Tennessee and Virginia. There are also Sanford Corners, New York; Sanfordtown, Kentucky; Sanfordville, Illinois; and Sandford in Indiana and Kentucky. There are eight other Springvales in the United States: in Georgia, Kansas, Michigan, Minnesota, Oklahoma, Pennsylvania (York County), Tennessee and Virginia. Some are towns, while others are merely post villages.

CHAPTER II.

PURCHASE FROM THE INDIANS.

The Province of Maine—Fluellin's Deed to Major William Phillips, 1661—Tract of Nineteen Thousand Acres Given to Nineteen Heirs—Survey of 1720—Action of Proprietors—Efforts at Colonization—Grants—Life and Character of Major Phillips.

THE name "Province or Countie of Maine " was first used by King Charles I of England, in 1639, in chartering the territory lying between the Kennebec and Piscataqua Rivers to Sir Ferdinando Gorges, a leading spirit in the Plymouth Company. This tract was claimed, in 1652, by the General Court of the Colony of Massachusetts Bay, as a part of that colony, and the Province of Maine was thereupon erected into a county called Yorkshire, most of the inhabitants acknowledging themselves as subject to Massachusetts. Sir Ferdinando had meanwhile died, and after the Restoration, his grandson and heir, Ferdinando Gorges, began to agitate his claim to the territory of his grandfather. In 1664 Charles II recognized the claimant, and ordered the colony to make restitution of his lands, or to " show us reasons to the contrary." Troubles arose between the adherents of the two parties, two governments were established, and a bitter contest was waged. The party of Gorges was obliged to yield, though he did not relinquish his claim until 1677, when Massachusetts purchased his right for twelve hundred and fifty pounds sterling. The indenture transferred all the territories granted by charter to Gorges in 1639, " excepting all leases, grants and conveyances made by the original proprietor or his agents, engaged in planting the Province, especially all grants to William Phillips."

The Province of Maine constituted one county, York, until 1760, when the counties of Cumberland and Lincoln were established. These three counties formed the northern district of Massachusetts, when the state was divided into three districts, in 1778, acquired a distinctive name, and was thereafter, until the separation, known as the District of Maine.

William Phillips, in whose favor exception was made by Gorges, was a prominent man in the early history of Saco and Biddeford. He owned extensive mills at Saco, and large tracts of land inland, which he had purchased of the native chiefs. One of these was deeded to Lieutenant Phillips, then residing in Boston, by Hombinowitt, *alias* John Rogomock, Indian, of Saco, and lay on the west side of Saco River, from Salmon Falls to Captain Sunday's Rocks, and " so upward in ye country to his furthest extent." Another tract was purchased of Fluellin, son of Sosowen, and particularly concerns us, since it embraced the territory about which we are writing. His deed, recorded according to the original, July 31, 1717, by Joseph Hammond, Register, volume eight, folio two hundred and twenty (Vol. 8, p. 220), registry of deeds, Alfred, is as follows:

Know All men by these presents that I Fluellin Sometimes residing at Saco, Indian, for & in Consideration of Satisfaction have & by these presents do sell all my land from Saco Pattent bounds Southward beyond Cape porpus river for breadth & from ye head of Wells and Cape porpus Townships hed, up into the Countrey to his furthest Extent with all ye appurtenances & priviledges whatever Excepting four miles Square Sold to bush, Sanders & Turbut,[1] to Lieut. Wm Phillips of Boston in ye County of Suffolk his heirs & Assigns forever To have & To hold & peaceably to Enjoy from any other Indians as witness my hand this thirtieth day of March in ye year of Our Lord 1661.

FLUELLIN ⟩ his mark

Subscribed & Delivered with the
words appurtenances y^r of
In ye presence of us
RICHARD R F FOXELL
   his mark
HAR : SYMONDS
JOHN ALDEN

Fluellins Extent above
mentioned was Intended
to Captⁿ Sundays rocks as is
Inserted in Rogomocks deed
written by me
JOHN ALDEN.

Captain Sunday, *alias* Meeksombe, was an Indian chief of Newichewanack (Newichawannock). The rocks referred to were described as " three hills of rocks," and from their shining appearance were supposed to be impregnated with silver. It is supposed that they contained mica, and were situated in Limington.[2]

---

[1] Lieutenant John Bush, John Sanders and Peter Turbet, who in 1660 had purchased of Sosowen (the grant being afterwards confirmed by Fluellin) that tract of land which later comprised Coxhall (Lyman).

[2] Folsom's " History of Saco and Biddeford."

Whatever may have been the price of this land deeded by Fluellin, it is evident that the grantee recognized the claim of the natives, and that the Indians, through their chief, received satisfaction therefor. In fact, Fluellin is, in various instruments, acknowledged to be "the true Indian proprietor," whose rights were paramount to those of the crown. Among these is the confirmation of Gorges, in 1670, to Nathaniel Phillips, of the several tracts of land purchased of the Indians. Nathaniel Phillips, a merchant of Saco, was the oldest son and heir of Lieutenant William Phillips. Early in 1670 Gorges confirmed to him, " for and in consideration of Several good & acceptable service & mutch time which the sd Nathaniel Phillips hath done & spent for the sd Ferdinando gorges in England and for other good causes," the tracts of land embraced in the original Phillips purchase. Four years later Nathaniel mortgaged these lands to Sir Francis Watson of Jamaica for thirty pounds. This sum, with twenty-four pounds for interest, was paid in 1689, by Elisha Hutchinson of Boston, to Thomas Betterton, the agent of Watson, and the mortgage was transferred to him, he making a release in 1716 to Eliphal Stretton, only surviving daughter and child of Bridget, widow of William Phillips.

As early as 1676 a project was formed of laying out a township within the Fluellin grant. It was designed to be eight miles square on the westernmost side of Kennebunk River, and eight miles from the sea, adjoining the inland head of Wells. Major Phillips, by deed having date June 15, 1676, conveyed nineteen thousand acres of the proposed township to nineteen persons, one thousand acres to each, reserving the remainder for his own disposal. This land was given, granted, bequeathed, and enfeoffed, " For diverse good causes," as he says, "A^d Considerations mee thereunto moving, a^d espetially for the love A^d tender affection which I beare unto my children, A^d the children of my now beloved wife," to the following: Samuel Phillips, his eldest son; William Phillips, his youngest son; Mary Field, eldest daughter; Martha Thurston, second daughter; Rebecca Lord, third daughter; Elizabeth Alden, fourth daughter; Zachary Gillnm, son-in-law; Sarah Turner, youngest daughter; Eliphal Stretton, daughter of his wife, formerly Bridget Sanford; Peleg Sanford, her eldest son; John Sanford, second son; Elisha Sanford, third son; Robert Lord, London, mariner, son-in-law; John Jollife, Boston, merchant; John Woodmansy, Boston, merchant; Elisha Hutchinson, Boston, merchant; Theodore Atkinson. Boston, felt-maker; John Sanford, Boston, writing-school master; and William Hudson, Boston, vintner. It was a provision of the deed that this land should be taken up in the most convenient place for settling a town, and the donors were to have and to hold the said parts " with all the woods & underwood trees timber mines quarries rivers & water courses with all rights privlleges and advantages of fishing fowling hawking and hunting within the limits of the sd Tract of Lands." None of the donees were to take up their parts or portions without the consent of a majority of the parties, " that so the Intent of Settling a town may not be frustrated."

By his will of February, 1682, Major Phillips gave his lands in Maine to his wife and two sons, Samuel and William, the latter of whom was then a captive among the Spaniards. Mrs. Phillips outlived her husband, and by her will of September 29, 1696, bequeathed to Peleg Sanford, Samuel Phillips, William Phillips and Eliphal Stretton, one-fourth part of her lands in the tract of eight miles square. The other three-fourths were reserved for the payment of the debts of her husband, deceased. If there were no debts, then that part was to be divided among her four children (presumably those before mentioned in her will) with the exception of one thousand acres given to her grandson, William, son of William and Eliphal (Sanford) Stretton.

It would appear that, during the lifetime of Phillips and his immediate heirs, no steps were taken toward the laying out of the proposed township — it had an imaginary existence far away in the " forest primeval," but had not even been projected on paper. It was not until several years after the death of the principal and his sons, that any definite action was taken in regard to the matter. On the 15th of June, 1720, however, Samuel Tyley of Boston, and Theodore Atkinson were appointed attorney and assistant attorney, respectively, of the proprietors, the major part, at least, of the heirs of Phillips, of nineteen thousand acres above Wells, with power "to survey and make a division of the land belonging thereto." That they might avail themselves of any advantage arising from such a division, and that their lands might be offered for sale under more favorable conditions, the following parties were interested in the survey and division :

Theodore Atkinson, owner of one thousand acres ; Simeon Stoddard, Boston, assignee of John and Elizabeth Alden, whose share was mortgaged to Stoddard, January 19, 1690 ; Samuel Adams maester, for himself, Edward Bromfield, Junior, merchant, and Thomas Salter, cordwainer, all of Boston, assignees of the heirs of

Samuel Phillips, deceased, by whom, viz., Sarah Phillips, widow, John Merryfield, cordwainer, and Bridget, his wife, and Anne Phillips, single woman, of Boston, the right and title to Samuel Phillips's thousand acres was sold December 1, 1718, to Bromfield and his copartners; Thomas Hutchinson, for himself and the rest of the heirs of Elisha Hutchinson; W. Allen, attorney to Edward and Mary Muckett, only child of Martha Thurston, deceased; John Jenkins, attorney to Mary Newell and Susannah (Flegg) Flagg the two only surviving heirs of William Hudson, deceased; Brattle Oliver, for the heirs of Zachary Gillum, deceased; Margaret Claxton, only child of John Woodmansy; Samuel Tyley, in behalf of William Sanford, only son and heir of Peleg Sanford, deceased, and also in behalf of Eliphal Stretton; Martha Balston, as heir of John Jolliffe (Joyliffe).

Peleg Sanford died in 1701, having bequeathed by will all the lands which he had received from his mother, Bridget Phillips, to his son Peleg. He left two sons and three daughters. By the provisions of the will, probated September 1, 1701, the surviving son, if one should die, was to have the other son's property by paying his sisters or their heirs three hundred pounds. Peleg died under age and unmarried, in consequence of which, William, the surviving son, became heir to a part of the eight miles square.

Acting under the authority of the proprietors' attorney, Abraham Preble surveyed their land, and made a plan thereof. His report, entered at the registry of deeds, May 12, 1722, was recorded by himself, at that time serving as register:

"November ye 1th 1720 by the desier of Mr. Sam^ll Tyley jn^r of Boston for him selfe and attorney for the Maj^or Part of the Propriators of a Tract of Land of Eight Miles Square; Joyning upon the Northwest End or Inland head of Wells Towuship upon the Southwest side of Kennebunk river Clamed by Said Tyley and Partnors by vertue of the Will of Maj^r William Phillips dec^d as by his deed bareing date June the 15th 1676: on Record in the County of York With Sundry Other Pappers and writings Referance thereunto being had may more at larg appear and is butted and bounded as followeth viz: Beginning at a small Pine Tree Standing upon ye North corner of said Wells Township and on the Southwest side of said Kennebunk river upon the north end of a rockey hill which tree is Marked on four sids and from thence Southwest by Wells Bounds (being assisted by the selectmen of Wells) eight miles: to a pitch Pine tree marked on four sides & markt with: N upon the North Side: which Tree Standeth upon the west side of a Marsh or fresh

Meadow called Meriland Meadow; and Runs from thence northwest
Eight Miles to a Greate hemlock tree marked on four sids standing
three Miles to the northward of Bonnebeag hills and runs from thence
Northeast eigt Miles to a Great white oak tree Marked on four Sids
and Runs from thence South East Eight Miles to the Pine Tree Began at: Justly Measured by two men sworn for that Purpose: the
bounds hereof being More Perticarally set forth in the Platt on the
Other side Laid out.

" p me ABRA^m PREBLE Surua^t

"I have also taken Possession of above said land by cuting and
felling Trees and Bulding Tents and Lodging therein &c.

" p me ABRA^m PREBLE above sd."

The "Platt on the other side" is not found on the records at Alfred, but another copy shows that the eastern boundary of the nineteen
thousand acres began where the Mousam crosses the head-line of
Wells, and extended northwest eighteen hundred and ten rods; and
that the southern boundary extended southwest from the river five
and a quarter miles along the head-line of Wells.

In a letter to the proprietors dated at York, Nov. 10, 1720,
Preble reports on his unpleasant experiences in surveying the land.
"I have spent eight days myself & five men with me; the Beaver
have so drowned the low ground and dammd the rivers that we have
bin forced to wade every day while in the woods above the knees,
which hath satisfied my rambling ambition at present." Regarding
the expense of the survey, Preble reports that he paid the five men
who were with him "forty shillings apiece & two shillings each in
Rum," and he says in the letter at its close: "I should be glad that
you will send the Ballance of this Accompt by our representative
Mr. Samuel Came, for I am something considerable out of pocket."
The expense of this survey was about nineteen pounds, and at a meeting of the proprietors, held at the Green Dragon Tavern in Boston,
December 1, 1720, the proprietors present subscribed a sum of money
to settle Preble's claim.

Two years before this survey and three years after, three transfers
of land were made, but the names of the grantees do not appear upon the earliest plan in our possession, which must have
been made about 1730, or subsequently thereto. Eliphal Stretton
deeded to Anne Atkins, Bridget Ladd, Boston, and Katherine Liron,
wife of Lewis Liron, Milford, her daughters, one thousand acres in
Yorkshire, and her right in one thousand acres of Elisha Sanford,

tree markt on the northeast of a great hill & then running Southwest five miles & a quarter to a great hemlock tree markt & then running Southwest down to a Pine tree mark'd on the westerly Side of merryland marishes, & then running on a northeast Point on wells line to Mousam River to an Elm tree markt where we first began and as for laying out the Lots we think it will be best to lay out a four rod way thro Sd Land & butt one home lot upon each Side of Sd way; and we are of opinion that the land is very good & capable of makeing of a very good Settlement, as may more plainly appear by the plans.

"JOHN WHEELWRIGHT
"JER MOULTON   } comite"
"JOHN JONES

It was voted that Moulton and Jones, with Charles Frost of Kittery, be a committee to adjust the boundary lines with surrounding towns; to lay out highways four rods wide through the nineteen thousand acres; to lay out lots with meadows for each of the proprietors; to lay out two one hundred acre lots, "one for the Minister and the other for the ministry, and a commodious tract of land for a meeting house;" and also to lay out forty settlers' lots of one hundred acres each. The latter were to include a house lot of fifty acres, and fifty acres besides, with five acres of meadow, and were to be granted "to forty able bodied men," provided, under penalty of forfeiture, that each should build a house eighteen feet long, sixteen feet wide, and seven feet stud, and break up and fence in four acres of land within three years, and live upon and improve the land for ten years. The settlers were also to have the use of the proprietors' meadow land. At the same meeting the proprietors voted to pay twenty pounds per annum for seven years towards building a meeting house, and supporting the first orthodox Gospel minister. The proprietors also granted to Edward Bromfield, Junior, in consideration of one hundred pounds, one twentieth part of their land, and subsequently, as will appear later, Jeremiah Moulton received a proportional part, one twenty-first.

It seemed necessary to have men of character and enterprise, like Bromfield and Moulton, to aid in the work of settling a wilderness. Bromfield was an eminent merchant of Boston, "distinguished for frankness of disposition, urbanity of manners, undeviating rectitude, and for great benevolence." He died in 1756. Moulton was born in York, in 1688. He was taken by the Indians when they attacked York in 1692, but was returned shortly after to one of the garrison-

2

houses with others, women and children, — an instance of Indian gratefulness. He was one of the four captains in the successful expedition against the Indians at Norridgewock, and twenty years later served as colonel — the third in command — in the expedition against Louisburg. He was representative two or three years, county treasurer, sheriff, a justice of the Common Pleas, a member of the Provincial Council, 1735–1752, and Judge of Probate, 1745–1765. As a military commander, he was prudent, skilful, and brave ; as a man, unassuming in disposition and manners, of sound judgment, and of uncommon excellence of character. Though " never a restless aspirant for office," few men of his time " had a greater share of public confidence, or were called to fill so many places of official trust and responsibility."[1] Having become an extensive landowner, he was interested in the early settlement of the town, and helped build the mills known as Moulton's Mills. He died July 20, 1765.

On the 23d of September, 1729, Edward Muckett and Mary, his wife, formerly Mary Thurston, daughter of Martha Thurston, deeded the one thousand acres to which she became heir, to Nathaniel Alden and Mary, his wife, late Mary Smith, granddaughter of Mary Muckett.

December 22, 1730, the proprietors made an allotment of their land, drawing lots for the same. Without being officially so designated, the territory gradually came to be " commonly called " Phillipstown, as appears by the first mention of the name in the record of the proprietors' meeting of November 23, 1733.

At a meeting held February 22, 1736, Sir William Pepperrell, of Kittery, and Jeremiah Moulton, of York, were granted five hundred acres each of the undivided land, in consideration for undertaking to secure forty settlers within six years. Colonization being slow, however, the proprietors finally decided to increase the settlers' lots to one hundred and thirty acres each, the grantee to dwell thereon seven years, except in case of war with the Indians, when a return within three years after conclusion of a peace was required. Another inducement was held out in the offer of concessions for the construction of a saw mill and a grist mill.

The proprietors granted to Dr. David Bennett, of York, January 23, 1738, a mill privilege and fifty acres of land on both sides of the Mousam in the southern part of the town, and in 1742, another tract in the same vicinity, as appears from their vote at an adjourned meeting held at the Exchange Tavern, Boston, December 16 :

1 Williamson's " History of Maine,' Vol. II.

" Voted unanimously that there be and hereby is granted unto Dr. David Bennett of York, and his heirs forever one hundred acres of timber land in Phillipstown in a square body adjoining to the grant to him made of the mill privilege between the branches of Mousam River where Jeremiah Moulton, Esquire, shall judge most convenient to supply him with timber for building a meeting-house and the accommodation of the inhabitants with boards at a reasonable rate, so as not to interfere with the proprietors' or settlers' lots : and the clerk is hereby impowered to pass a deed to him for the same, he paying giving bond to pay twenty shillings an acre old tenor for the same to the clerk, sixty pounds whereof to be applied in purchasing glass and nails for the meeting-house intended to be built in the said town and the remainder as the proprietors shall order."

This lot began at the head and northerly corner of the mill privilege about two hundred rods from the mill.

Inasmuch as Pepperrell and Moulton had met with but little success in colonizing, their grant was, on June 18, 1739, declared null and void. Moulton, however, was at once admitted as a proprietor, on condition of procuring forty settlers. He was also given leave to "remove the meeting house lot, as he shall think most convenient." Within twenty months all but twelve of the settlers' lots had been disposed of. From time to time, the proprietors granted the rights of cutting trees on their land, first to Dr. Bennett, for supplying the inhabitants with boards ; later to Moulton, who was to sell the trees for the proprietors ; and finally to Colonel John Storer. Among the grants to Moulton was one of a water privilege, for a grist mill ; and, in December, 1740, another of two lots whereon to erect " a good substantial Garrison." A year later, two hundred acres were granted to Sir William Pepperrell, who was to build thereon, within two years, " a good block-house, and carry to and keep in it two great Guns, with powder and ball at his own charge."

Various grants of land within the present limits of the town were made by the General Court. December 6, 1734, a tract of four hundred acres near Phillipstown and the new settlement above Berwick, for his four sons, was granted to Captain Joseph Bean. The grant was confirmed some twenty years later, as appears from the Massachusetts Archives, Vol. 46, pp. 393–6. Joseph Bean was born about 1675. He was taken captive by the Indians, and lived several years among them, learning their language, and becoming acquainted with their customs. He lost a hand in the service of the government and was pensioned. The following is a copy of an order which came into possession of the author :

" Sir,

" I do hereby direct you to proceed forthwith in the Transport Sloop Massachusetts to the Truck House upon St Georges River under the Command of Cp^t Andrew Robinson where you are to officiate as Interpreter to the Indians & the Said Cp^t Robinson is directed to receive you accordingly.

" Boston April 20, 1742.   " Your Servant
" To Mr. Joseph Bane.   " W. Shirley."

It was for this and similar service that the land above mentioned was granted. His sons surviving in 1755 were John, husbandman, and James, mariner, of York, and David, gentleman, of St. George's. The last named moved to Sanford and settled upon his inherited lands. In 1791, a portion of his lot, two hundred and one acres, was set off by a committee in answer to his petition to the General Court.

Another similar grant was made to Jonathan Bean in June, 1748. He obtained three hundred acres from the province, in consideration for the services of his father in raising companies of soldiers yearly, and marching with them and helping kill about fifty Indians during the ten-year war. He first applied in 1736, but the council did not concur with the house in granting the land. The elder Bean was probably Captain Jonathan Bean, whose company of scouts in 1747–48 contained ten or twelve Phillipstown men.

In December, 1736, Samuel Green received two hundred acres between Phillipstown and Bauneg Beg Pond and about this time Tobias Leighton had two hundred acres near the same pond.

In November, 1791, the Commonwealth of Massachusetts granted to Solomon Allen two hundred and eighty acres near Oak Hill, formerly belonging to Sir William Pepperrell.

The Lydston grant, of three hundred and twenty-four acres, was in the west part of the town. It was granted to John Lydston, in 1744, for his services in the Indian wars, and especially because his thigh was broken in the War of 1693. Within the grant was a pond, the Indian name of which was Tombegewoc, now known as Deering's Pond, and from which flows one branch of the Salmon Falls River.

In July, 1784, the Commonwealth of Massachusetts granted to Samuel Dennett six hundred acres between Lydston's grant and Shapleigh town line.

William Frost, Junior, purchased a part of the Lydston grant, and also about three hundred and sixty acres from the Commonwealth, which, with several other grants, among them Joseph Bean's, were set off from Sanford in 1785, and annexed to Shapleigh. Subsequently, they must have been re-annexed, in part, at least, for they now lie within the present bounds of Sanford.

Major William Phillips, for whom Phillipstown was named, was a resident of Charlestown, but removed to Boston in 1646, where he was a vintner. Moving to Saco he became a large land proprietor and engaged extensively in lumbering operations. He owned mills upon the Saco, at Saco Falls, which were on what was then considered the frontier, and were exposed to the attacks of the Indians. Phillips fortified these, and in 1675 defended them with a courage and valor that gave him his well-earned title. His mills were burned and he removed to Boston soon after. In Hubbard's "Indian Wars," a graphic description of the fight is given, in which Phillips received a wound in his heroic defence. He was an officer and magistrate in 1663 and was confirmed by royal commissioners in 1665. At one time a lieutenant, he was promoted to be a major in 1675. He died in Boston in 1683. Major Phillips had three wives : Mary, by whom he had one son and two daughters ; Susanna, widow of Chris. Stanley, by whom he also had one son and two daughters, probably ; and Bridget, widow of John Sanford, by whom he had three sons. His third wife survived him. At the time of her marriage to Phillips she had three sons and one daughter. One of Phillips's daughters, Elizabeth, married for her first husband Abiel Everill, and second, in 1660, John, son of the famed John and Priscilla (Mullins) Alden, of the old Plymouth Colony.

CHAPTER III.

Settlement — Forty Settlers' Lots — Names of First Settlers — Lots Improved by Them — The First Houses — The First Mill — County and Other Roads laid out — Early Litigation — First Innholder and First Retailer.

THE settlers' lots, to which reference is frequently made, were in two ranges, at the head of the proprietors' lots laid out above the head-line of Wells. They are designated as the middle and western ranges, the eastern range being allotted to the proprietors. In each range were twenty lots, numbered consecutively to twenty in the middle range, and from twenty-one to forty in the western. Number one lay just below the present site of Willard's mill, and number twenty just below Elm Street, formerly the " mill lane." Number twenty-one[1] abutted upon the " Old Pond," and number forty was on the opposite side of the proprietors' road between the ranges, from number one. The middle range extended five hundred and twenty rods to the eastern range, and the western, the same distance to Berwick line. Each lot was laid out forty rods front, and contained one hundred and thirty acres, fifty acres of which were designated as the " home lot," and eighty, " additional." The writer has been informed that the lots averaged about forty-four rods front, making each lot measure thirteen acres more. It is true, undoubtedly, that the early surveyors and chainmen were less particular than those of to-day, for they were measuring land of comparatively little value, — a whole lot being worth less than a house-lot to-day. In addition to these settlers' lots were three other important lots : the church lot, for the first Congregational church ; the minister's lot, for the first settled Congregational minister ; and the school lot, for the first grammar schoolmaster. The church lot was below number one, the minister's, below number forty — exchanged for number eleven — and the school lot, below the original minister's lot. This will appear from the plan on page 23.

---

[1] Number twenty-one is now owned by Hon. Thomas Goodall.

(22)

MILL LOT.

21		20	
22		19	1 Mary Field
23		18	
24		17	2 Elizabeth Alden
25	Settlers' Lots.	16	
26		15	8 Edward Bromfield
27		14	
28	130 acres	13	4 Theodore Atkinson
29		12	Settlers' Lots
30		11	5 Peleg Sanford
31	50 plus 80 acres.	10	
32		9	6 William Phillips
33		8	
34	40 rods front	7	7 Rebecah Lord
35		6	
36		5	8 Samuel Phillips
37		4	
38		3	9 Elisha Sanford
39		2	
40		1	10 Martha Thurston

100 rods to Berwick Line. (left margin, opposite rows 32–36)

Range line running on southwestern side of Mousam River. (vertical, center)

924 rods from Wells line to Settlers' Lots. (vertical, far left)

Road 4 rods wide. (vertical, right)

Minister's Lot. 42	Church - - - - -	11 Sarah Turner
1 School lot	1 Rebecca Lord	12 Robert Lord
2 John Woodmansay	2 Robert Lord	126 Bennett's 100-acre lot 126
3 Theodore Atkinson	3 Theodore Atkinson	
4 John Jolife	4 Edward Bromfield	13 Esborn Sanford
5 Elizabeth Alden	5 Elisha Sanford	
6 Elisha Sanford	6 Mary Field	14 John Sanford
7 Esborn Sanford	7 Sarah Turner	
8 Eliphal Stretton	8 William Phillips	15 John Jolife
9 Elisha Hutchinson	9 Samuel Phillips	
10 Mary Field	10 Jeremiah Moulton [XXI]	16 Zachariah Gillam
11 Robert Lord	11 Eliphal Stretton	
12 Edward Bromfield [XX]	12 John Woodmansay	17 William Hutson
13 Peleg Sanford	13 Esborn Sanford	
14 Sarah Turner	14 Peleg Sanford	18 Eliphal Stretton
15 Samuel Phillips	15 William Hutson	
16 William Phillips	16 Martha Thurston	19 John Woodmansay
17 William Hutson	17 Zach. Gillam	
18 John Sanford	18 John Sanford	20 Jeremiah Moulton
19 Martha Thurston	19 Elisha Hutchinson	
20 Zachariah Gillam	20 John Jolife	21 Elisha Hutchinson
21 Rebecah Lord	21 Elizabeth Alden	

520 rods.　　　　520 rods.

Wells.

PROPRIETORS' AND SETTLERS' LOTS.

This plan, obtained by the author from Joseph Shaw of Sanford, indicates how the proprietors of Phillipstown, prior to 1739, had allotted their land, the eastern range and lower half of the middle and western ranges, twenty-one lots in each range, to themselves, Edward Bromfield and Jeremiah Moulton, reserving the upper half of two ranges for forty settlers' lots.

Fifteen of these lots, at least, were deeded May 1, 1739 and, it is supposed, that the summer following found men improving them. Who was the first settler? Where did he live? are natural questions arising in our mind. We wish he had left some tangible evidence of his right to be called the first settler of that little community which endured the hardships and braved the dangers of the first two decades of the plantation. We wish that we could answer these questions beyond a reasonable doubt, and establish a date that might be regarded as the birthday of the town. There must have been temporary residents when the first mill was built, and, perhaps, the earliest settlement was near that mill. Knowing the dangers to which the early settlers were exposed, especially from the Indians, it seems to us the most natural thing for them to do would have been to remove hither in a company at the same time for mutual protection and safety. All this is a mere matter of conjecture.

We have, however, one record of importance, which presents an almost conclusive answer to the foregoing questions. In his interleaved copy of " Ecclesiastical Sketches," the author, Rev. Jonathan Greenleaf, pastor of the First Congregational Church in Wells, 1815–1828, makes this note on a leaf opposite the page upon which a short sketch of Sanford is given :

" Samuel Wilson was the first settler. He began a farm on the county road about half a mile north of the present Congregational meeting-house, which is now owned by Amos Goodwin."

Samuel Willson took up lot number twenty-five May 1, 1739, and Amos W. Goodwin, who afterwards lived upon it, died in 1838. Rev. Mr. Greenleaf's note was made between the publication of his work in 1821, and the death of Mr. Goodwin, probably prior to 1828. We do not hesitate to express the opinion that he obtained his information during his pastorate at Wells, from one of the early settlers, if not one of the first, and that Samuel Willson, who settled on the west side of the county road, one mile below the Corner, upon the farm owned and occupied in late years by John Lord, deceased, and at present by Bert Goodrich, has the honor to be called the first settler.

As far as we have been able we have found the names of the original grantees of the settlers' lots, and the early residents of the town. The settlers' lots were granted to the following persons on the dates noted :

Church lot. John Stanyan, Hampton, N. H., shipwright, March 1, 1741.

No. 1. John Stanyan, Hampton, N. H., shipwright, March 1, 1741.

No. 2. Mary Donnell, York, widow, January 1, 1745.

No. 3. Jacob Perkius.

No. 4. Joshua Adams, Wells, laborer, May 1, 1742.

No. 5. Alexander Bulman, York, chirurgeon, May 1, 1739.

No. 6. Thomas Donnell, Biddeford.

No. 7. Nicholas Cane, York, husbandman, May 1, 1739.

No. 8. Daniel Moulton, York, gentleman, November 18, 1742.

No. 9. Jeremiah Moulton, Jr., York, gentleman, November 18, 1742.

No. 10. Rev. Samuel Chandler, York, November 18, 1742.

No. 11. Minister's lot after exchange, by vote of proprietors, August 13, 1744.

No. 12. Joshua Cane, York, tanner, May 1, 1739.

No. 13. Jonathan Adams, York, laborer, May 1, 1739.

No. 14. William Standley, Kittery, blacksmith, May 1, 1739.

No. 15. Samuel Chadbourn, Kittery, husbandman, May 1, 1739.

No. 16. John Frost, son-in-law of Samuel Willson, Phillipstown, laborer, March 2, 1741.

No. 17. Thomas Fernald, May 1, 1739.

No. 18. Tobias Leighton, Kittery, yeoman, a settler, January 1, 1741.

Nos. 19 and 20. James Chadbourn, Kittery, yeoman, May 1, 1739.

Nos. 21 and 22. Jeremiah Moulton, Jr., York, gentleman, November 18, 1742.

No. 23. William Standley, Kittery, blacksmith.

No. 24. Charles Annis, Wells, husbandman, May 1, 1739.

No. 25. Samuel Willson, Wells, husbandmau, May 1, 1739.

Nos. 26, 27, and 28. Dr. David Bennett.

No. 29. Edward Whitehouse.

No. 30. Dr. David Bennett.

No. 31. William Curtis, Wells, husbandman, May 1, 1739.

No. 32. Alexander Bulman, York, chirurgeon, May 1, 1739

No. 33. Spencer Bennett.

No. 34. Benjamin Holt, York, coaster, November 18, 1742.

No. 35. Daniel Moulton, York, gentleman, November 18, 1742.

No. 36. William Babb, York, laborer, March 2, 1741.

No. 37. Jonathan Johuson, York, husbandman, May 1, 1739.

No. 38. Jeremiah Bragdon, York, coaster, May 1, 1739.

No. 39.   Christopher Pottle, York, tanner, March 15, 1743.

No. 40.   Joseph Simpson, Jr., York, felt maker, March 1, 1741.

The names of the settlers from 1739 to 1780, arranged by years, are as follows:

1739.   Samuel Willson, Wells, husbandman; Jonathan Adams, York, laborer; Charles Annis, Wells, husbandman; Jeremiah Bragdon, York, coaster; Joshua Cane, York, tanner; Nicholas Cane, York, husbandman; James Chadbourn, Kittery, yeoman; Samuel Chadbourn, Kittery, husbandman; William Curtis, Wells, husbandman; Thomas Fernald; Jonathan Johnson, York, husbandman; William Standley, Kittery, blacksmith.

1741.   William Babb, York, laborer (later a tailor); John Frost, husbandman; Tobias Leighton, Kittery, yeoman; John Stanyan, Hampton, N. H., shipwright.

1742.   Joshua Adams, Wells, laborer; Benjamin Holt, York, coaster; Samuel Staples, laborer.

1743.   Christopher Pottle, York, tanner.

1745.   Mary Donnell, York, widow.

1745/6.   Robert Allen, Kittery.

1747.   Ephraim Low (probably 1742).

1748.   John Low, Wells, weaver.

1749.   John Garey, Jr., York, laborer; Robert Miller, Hampton, N. H.; John Thompson, York, husbandman.

1750.   Moses Fowler, sawyer; John Urin, Greenland, N. H., cordwainer and tanner.

1751.   Thomas Wastgatt, laborer; William Bennett (had lived in town 58 years in 1809).

1752.   James Urin, Greenland, N. H.

1753.   Benjamin Wittum, clothier; Daniel Wittum, laborer.

1754.   Benjamin Harmon, York, gentleman; Naphtali Harmon, York.

1755.   Samuel Willard, York, cordwainer.

1757.   John Frost, Wells, mariner.

1758.   Solomon Allen.

1762.   Joseph Swett; Moses Tebbetts (?).

1763.   Elijah Allen, Kittery.

1764.   Joseph Linscott; Phinehas Thompson, Gorhamtown, blacksmith.

1768.   Thomas Walter Powers.

1770.   Jacob Linscott, mill man.

1773. Caleb Emery, Berwick, cordwainer.

1778. Josiah Paul.

1780. Jonathan Tebbets, Berwick, joiner.

In 1754, at the desire of the proprietors, Jonathan Johnson prepared a list of these lots, having especial reference to the fulfilment
of the provisions upon which they were granted. He reported that
in thirty-two instances the conditions were either being complied with
or wholly fulfilled; and of the lots owned by the following he said:
"Jacob Perkins, a frame but no Person — his son will fulfill directly;
Capt. Thomas Donnell, nothing done; Rev. Mr. Chandler, an house
built but burnt down; William Bab, not fulfilled, small house and
some land improved; Jer. Bragdon, now Benj. Wickham, not fulfilled, no family there; Joseph Simpson, Jun., now James Urin,
unfulfilled." On number eight there was "an house with small improvements by Samuel Lane;" on number nine Jeremiah Moulton,
Junior, had a tenant, and on twenty-one and twenty-two, "a small
frame on each and small improvement;" James Chadbourn had purchased number eighteen; Samuel Staples occupied numbers twenty-
six and twenty-seven; and Jon. Howard, twenty-eight; and other
new occupants of lots reported by Johnson were Jonathan Swett,
Thomas Waistcott, Joseph Standley, John Harmon, Benjamin Har-
rald (Harmon?), John Thompson, Ed. Standley, Eph. Low, John
Wilson, John Gerry, John Low, Moses Fowler, Michael Brawn, and
James Miller. Concerning number two there seems to have been
some confusion. Johnson's final endorsement is: "Jas. Berry, not
fulfilled, small improvements by Jno Thompson, since gone."

In consequence of this report, the proprietors voted that Rev. Mr.
Chandler "be indulged with one year more to complete the settlement of his lot;" that lot number six "be sued for;" that "all
other settlers be indulged one year more by paying forty shillings
for such indulgence, and no further time allowed them;" and that
"the money raised as aforesaid be applied towards settling the Gospel in Phillipstown." Four years previously the proprietors had
considered the matter of a subscription "toward the support of the
Gospel," but the money had evidently not been raised. In 1763 the
proprietors appropriated a lot for the support and maintenance of a
school.

In the vicinity of the Leighton grant, near Bauneg Beg Pond,
Colonel, afterward Sir William Pepperrell owned a large tract of
land. Jeremiah Moulton, who had bought of Tobias Leighton,

sold, in 1742, one-half of two hundred acres, to Jacob Perkins, and May 6, 1743, Samuel Green, Leighton and Moulton sold to Robert Allen, of Berwick, one-half of two hundred acres. Allen and Perkins, in 1745-6, divided their land, Allen taking the lower half near his land bought of Pepperrell, and Perkins the half between Phillipstown and the pond. This Robert Allen was the first settler on Oak Hill, from whom, through Solomon and Elijah Allen, and perhaps others, the numerous Allen family of the south part of the town descended.

The first houses, built in accordance with the conditions imposed on the grantees, were known as block-houses. They were rudely constructed of timber and some were undoubtedly of logs. Not far from 1742, a few years later, probably, Dr. David Bennett built the first "proper house" in Sanford, according to a deposition made by Ephraim Low in 1797. Dr. Bennett fenced in his three lots, numbers twenty-six, twenty-seven and twenty-eight, and somewhere on his land (on number twenty-seven, as stated in a deposition made by Edward Standley in 1803) built a house to which he brought, it is said, the first minister that ever preached in town, "and the people generally attended the said meeting in the said Dr. Bennett's house." Dr. Bennett also sowed a nursery for apple trees. In 1751 Daniel Moulton had a frame for a dwelling house erected. In 1764, the first settler of the Alfred district lived in an Indian wigwam, and not long after, Daniel Lary built a frame-house near Emerson's bridge, which is supposed to have been the first of the kind in that part of the town. Log- and block-houses slowly gave place to frame houses, generally one story in height.

Mills were necessary before much progress could be made in settling the town. The first mill was built in 1739. In January, 1738/9, the proprietors deeded to Dr. David Bennett, of York, fifty acres of land on both sides of the western branch of the Mousam River, with the first mill privilege above the junction of the two branches. On April 6, 1739, Dr. Bennett, Jacob Perkins and John Winn of Wells, Jeremiah Moulton and Daniel Moulton of York, agreed to build, before the first of September following, a double mill to go with two saws, "on the westernmost branch of the Mousam river, at the first falls above the crotch thereof." Bennett's share was one-half ; each of the others was to have one-eighth. Prior to October 15, the mill was completed ; for on that day three-eighths of it were deeded to the Moultons, in consideration for work done by them in the erection and fitting thereof. In January following Doctor Bennett sold one-eighth to James Littlefield of Wells, a millwright, whom we shall find interested at a later day in other mills in town. In 1742 Daniel Moulton sold his right to Jeremiah Moulton for two hundred and fifty pounds sterling. The work had at that time reached such a magnitude that eight oxen were required to haul the logs to the mill and the boards and planks from it. Perkins also sold his eighth to Jeremiah Moulton. In later years the Linscotts, John and Jacob, came into possession of the larger part of the mill. It had been known as " Moulton's mill," but was afterward designated, and is frequently mentioned in the records, as " Linscott's mill." It was rebuilt several times. In 1807 John Linscott remarked, at a rebuilding, " This is the fourth mill I have seen built here." A mill as built then would stand about twenty years. One mill was burnt.

The second saw mill in town was built by James Chadbourn just below the Corner. This and subsequent mills will be more fully described in another portion of this work. Probably the earliest grist mills were those set up in the corner of the kitchen for family use. They were quite common before mills were built to go by water power. The Chadbourns had one, the stones of which were formerly seen in the stone wall east of Nelson A. Bennett's house. The mill is said to have been brought from Berwick (Kittery?) and the upper stone to have weighed about one hundred and fifty pounds. Cane's saw mill, probably the third in the town, was built at South Sanford about 1756. It was burned October 29, 1764.

Indian paths and hunters' trails were the first travelled ways. They lay along the Mousam and the ponds where fishing and camping grounds were found, and in the forests where game was abundant. The first roads, however, were wood-roads and " mast-ways," which, as their names indicate, were used for the transportation of wood and timber. In some places these logging roads were crooked and hilly ; in others comparatively straight and level. By the charter of Massachusetts, in 1691, certain trees were reserved to the crown, and in 1743, white pine growing upon any soil or tract not granted to any private person, and measuring twenty-four inches and upward in diameter at twelve inches above the ground, was protected by a special law, and reserved for masting the royal navy. Such trees for the royal navy were hauled along the " mast-ways " to Berwick and Kittery and Wells. One of these roads extended from the pitch-pine plains in the south part of the town along the southeast side of Bauneg Beg hills. Another probably extended from the southeast part of the town to Wells, and was used when Moulton's mill was built.

When the proprietors divided their lands and laid out lots for settlement, they made provision for two four-rod roads, one between
the eastern and middle ranges, the other between the middle and
western ranges. The former was laid out from the head-line of Wells
below Mouse Lane northwest, terminating at the upper settlers' lot
near the residence of Edgar Wentworth; the latter began near the
Branch Brook and ran northwest near Willard's mill, a few rods
northeast of the residences of late Abiel H. Johnson and Horace
Bennett, and, crossing the present highway near Bert Goodrich's,
terminated in "Cold Spring Pond," at the head of the "mill lot."
When the settlers' lots were taken up, and the lands above occupied,
rough cart-paths were the main thoroughfares of the pioneers.

A county road running through Phillipstown was laid out in 1744,
agreeably to the following petition of Nathaniel Donnell and twenty-
seven others :

"To the Honb^{le} his Majest^s Justices of the Court of General Sessions of the Peace now holden at York within and for the County of
York on the first Tuesday of Jany A. D. 1743.

"The Petition of Us Subscribers Inhabitants of the County of
York

" Humbly Shews

" that the Lands lying between Saco Salmon Falls and Pesumpscotte River near the Center of the Settlement called Goreham Town
and also between the said Salmon Falls and Phillips Town & from
thence thro' Berwick to Nechewannick River above the Saltwater, are
verry convenient for laying out a Road or highway which Road your
Petition^s humbly Conceive would be of great Service to the Said
Towns and Settlement & Likewise to the County for Travelling from
Casco Bay (thro Exetor) to Boston making the said Road much
shorter then the present Road & almost clear of Ferries but more
especially the Said Road would be quite Necessary for marching of
Scouts and other forces along the Frontier in Case of Warr Your
Petitioners therefore Humbly pray Your Honours would be pleased
to appoint a Committee to View the Said Lands from Saco Salmon
Falls to Pesumpscotte River and from the Said Salmon Falls to
Phillips Town and from thence to Newichwannick River and to Consider the Necessity & Conveniency of laying out a Road or Highway
thro' the Same lands and to Report thereon to this Honb^{le} Court as
Soon as may be in order to the Speedy Laying out the Said Road adjudged Necessary as soon as the Season of the Year will admit of it
and Your Petitioners (as in Duty bound) shall ever pray &c."

The court at once appointed Benjamin Nichols, of the Saco

truck house, and Jacob Bradbury, of Biddeford, as the committee asked for. More than a year later, March 29, 1744, this committee made its report, laying out the highway as follows :

" Beginning at Pesumpscot River, about the Centre of Gorham Town, & opposite to the Block House at New Marblehead & running thence about West by South as the Road now Goes, by the Southerly Side of Mr. John Phinney's House, & thence about South West, by a line of Marked Trees to the Fresh Meadow so called — thence the Same Course, by a Line of marked Trees, & on the North West Side of Stroudwater Pond, to the Mast Road, & keeping the Same Course along the Mast Road on the South Easterly Side of the Block House at Narrhaganset Town No. 1 — to Saco Salmon Falls — & Crossing sd Saco River, at the Head of the Steep Falls, thence down the West Side of sd Falls, & crossing the Mouth of Cook's Brook, to a Ridge of High Land on the South Westerly Side of it — Or to go from the last mentioned Block House down the Easterly Side of Sd Salmon Falls to Pleasant Point, & there crossing Sd Saco River, & thence about South West, on sd Ridge of Land passing on the South East Side of Morrill's Hill so called, going over ye Head of the Great Plain & between the Swan Ponds & by the South East End of ye Highest Mousom Pond, & by the North West Side of Kennebunk Pond & over Two Branches of Mousom River to the Western Branch of it, & crossing the Same, at the Ripling Falls, near Mr. Chadbourn's Block House in Philips Town — thence about South by West on the Eastern Side of s^d Chadbourn's Block-House — & by the Western side of Mr. Wilson's Block House to the Western side of Mr. Johnson's Dwelling House in s^d Philips Town — & thence about South South West — along the Mast Road, by the South Easterly side of Bonny = Beag Hill & Bonny-Beag Ponds, & by the South Easterly side of Mr. Hobbs's House, near the Great Works Landing — & thence near the Same Course along Berwick Town Road, to Newichwannick River above the Salt Water."

At the July term of the court of sessions, James Chadbourn and others, inhabitants of Phillipstown, petitioned the court " that they Labour under Great inconveniency and Discouragement in their Infant Settlement in not having Convenient highways or Roads laid out and maintained thro' the Towns of Wells and Berwick to Phillips Town," and therefore prayed the court to order the required roads laid out. Richard Cutts of Kittery and Jeremiah Moulton of York, who were appointed a committee to view the ground, reported in 1750 the necessity of the roads petitioned for. A warrant was issued to the sheriff or his deputy to summon a jury to lay out such ways, and accordingly, a jury of twelve men, viz., Simon Lord, Jos: Hearl, Caleb Emery, Noah Emery, Samuel Shaw, Jos: Junkins, Jos: Leavit, Jn? H? Bartlet, Nathan Bartlet, Abel Moulton, Hen? Simpson and Jn? Frost, was summoned March 25, 1751. The jury was at work three days that month, and at the April term, 1751, the deputy sheriff made his return. The roads laid out were : One from the highway in Berwick, near Peter Morrell's mill on the Great Works River, over Oak Hill, by Allen's marsh, through the pitch-pine plain, along a " mast-way " to the east, on the ridge (South Sanford) into the proprietors' way (between the middle and western ranges) to the Commons (above Sanford) ; also another road west of the pond (Cold Spring) to the Commons ; also another from the " mast-way" above mentioned down by the foot of Lyon Hill, as straight as may be to Wells, to the " Great mill at Meriland." The roads were to be four rods wide in every place. In 1763 the highway from Wells line to John Stanyan's inn was miry and in want of bridges (old bridges were in decay), so that the inhabitants could not pass and repass with their carriages without great damage to themselves and their goods.

Litigation began early in Phillipstown. The first to sue was John Stanyan, who, in July, 1744, brought a writ of ejectment against Joseph Stanyan of Hampton, to recover settler's lot number one, conveyed to John Stanyan three years previous. The plaintiff won his case, whereupon the defendant appealed to the next superior court of judicature, but as no further record is found, it is to be assumed that the appeal was not pressed. A few years later John Stanyan again appears as a plaintiff, this time in a suit against Henry Rines of Berwick, instituted in April, 1749. The verdict was for the defendant, and an appeal was taken to the next superior court of judicature.

Although as late as 1752 the town contained only something like twenty families, numbering about one hundred souls, a demand for a public house arose at an earlier date. In 1749 the aggressive John Stanyan was the first licensed innholder of whom we have record. His license gave him authority not only to provide entertainment for man and beast, but also to engage in selling the chief intoxicating beverage of the day, New England rum. Stanyan probably kept tavern nearly twenty-five years, though licensed only about twenty. His inn stood near the site of John Fletcher's house at South Sanford. There is a tradition, however, that Ephraim Low

STILLMAN B. ALLEN.

was the first innholder, but he was not licensed until twenty years after Stanyan began to keep tavern.

While the settlement existed for only ten years without an inn, it remained for over twenty without a trading place. Daniel Coffin was the earliest trader of record. He was in town in 1763, and bought of Naphtali Harmon forty acres of land lying along the Mousam. The same year he was licensed as a retailer, and probably traded in the Moulton neighborhood at South Sanford. Under the provisions of his license he could sell groceries, of which the three prime articles were fish, New England rum and molasses.

Olive, daughter of Ephraim Low, who lived one mile below the Corner, is said to have been the first child born in town of white parents, June 28, 1742.

3

CHAPTER IV.

FRENCH AND INDIAN WARS.

Exposure of Frontier Settlements to Attack — The Aborigines of
Phillipstown — Scouts and Garrison Houses — Names of Soldiers Serving in French and Indian Wars, 1744–1762.

THE frontier settlements of Maine were exposed to attacks from
the Indians, and suffered more or less from their depredations
until the treaty between the French and English was made in 1763.
At first it was the seaboard towns which became a prey to the savage,
and then, as the more hardy explorer and adventurer moved back into
the forests, the second tier of towns suffered at his revengeful hand.
The Indians were unceasing in resisting the encroachments of the
English, and were spurred on by the French, whenever hostilities
arose between the two rival European governments claiming jurisdiction over American territory.

Block-houses were erected for defence and refuge at convenient intervals ; scouts were employed to guard against the approach of the
wily red men ; and every precaution was taken to prevent a surprise.
The loaded flint musket was the constant companion of the laborer
in the field, or stood, like a sentinel, near the door of the house, or
hung upon wooden hooks in its accustomed place over the mantel,
when danger was not apprehended.

Though Phillipstown was not an especial sufferer, the people were
on the alert, and were frequently called into active service. The
preserved records of those times are few, but are enough to show
that the early settlers found military service in the line of their duty.
Meagre indeed are the accounts given of the aborigines dwelling upon this territory, or roaming over it. There is circumstantial evidence that the Indians dwelt here a part of the time, and, later,
passed through here on their excursions toward the south. The
streams and ponds abounded in fish, game was plenty, and there were
places favorable for encamping and preparing for sudden incursions
upon the inhabitants of the towns below, Berwick, York, Wells, and

Saco, upon which they fell with savage cruelty. They had camping grounds along the Mousam, near the ponds, and, it is said, on the north side of Cold Spring Pond, the "Old Pond" of a generation or more ago, a little southeast of Sanford. Various implements of Indian manufacture and warfare, stone hatchets and arrow-heads, have been found. It is thought the Indian burial ground was near the brook in the rear of Bert Goodrich's residence. What is believed to have been an Indian gristmill or mortar, where they ground, or rather pounded their corn, can be seen about three rods from the road opposite the grand stand on the fair grounds. The Indian names Bunganut, Massabesec, Tombegewoc, Towwoh (Lebanon), Benapeag (Bauneg Beg), Mousam, according to the late Hon. William Willis, and Maguncook, a former name of the river, which appropriately signifies "ponds at head," furnish inferential evidence that the Indians dwelt in this vicinity.

A few Indians lived in town after it was settled, but were quite peaceable. The great trouble which they gave the whites was their constant begging. In his "History of Alfred," Dr. Usher Parsons informs us that, as late as 1764, "a few Indians still lingered about Massabesec and Bunganut Pond, one family being in a wigwam where the present house of Shaker worship stands; but soon all the aborigines disappeared." These Indians were the Abnakis (Abenakis, Abneaques, or Wanbanakkie, more properly), of which there were several tribes, four or eight. One tribe, the Sosokis, or Sockhigones, as Gorges calls them, had their residence on the Saco, and upon the islands near the falls, a few miles from the sea. They were numerous before the tribe divided, but were greatly reduced by the Indian war of 1675. The chiefs before mentioned belonged to this tribe. Receding from the tide of civilization, the tribe divided into two lodgments, the one at Fryeburg, the other on the Great Ossipee River, fifteen or twenty miles below, and took the names Pequawkets (or Pigwackets) and Ossipees.

There is a tradition that Captain Lovewell of the ill-starred expedition against the Pequawkets at Fryeburg, fought one of his bloodiest battles on the territory of Phillipstown. The killing of Peter Morrell's daughter by Indians on the northeast side of Berwick has already been referred to in a previous chapter.

The precautionary measures of scouting and garrisoning were early resorted to. In 1723 Jeremiah Moulton of York made a report of a scouting party under his command, watching for the Indians between Berwick and Saco. On the 23rd of May he reported that he was

scouting "on the Littel River and mousam River and Kennebunk
River and camped at Kennebunk falls."

In 1743, the General Court appropriated twelve hundred and eighty
pounds to be disbursed from the public treasury and expended among
the eastern settlements for their defence. "To Phillips-Town £100
were granted in order to erect a Garrison or Garrisons of Stockade, or
of Square Timber around some dwelling house or houses, or otherwise,
as will be most for the security and defence of the whole inhabitants
of the town."[1] In November of that year William Pepperrell, Jeremiah Moulton, Moses Butler, Tobias Leighton, Samuel Moody, James
Skinner, and Jacob Perkins, with others, were authorized to lay out
the sum raised for garrisons in the most prudent manner. "The
charge of fortifying the several places aforesaid," so reads the order
to Pepperrell and Moulton, " you must proportion according to the
several sums allowed by the Gen. Court for fortifying each of the
places aforesaid, and be sure not to exceed those sums, but take care
that they be lay'd out with all prudence and frugality. The several
Garrisons or Fortifications you may judge necessary to be erected
in those places, must be built of Stockade or square timber as you
shall apprehend will be most suitable for defence. The particular
places in said settlements for erecting those works must be such as
will best accommodate the whole body of the inhabitants in those
settlements, and so far as that end may be attained, I direct you to
erect those works in such a situation as may convene any other of
his Majesty's subjects settled in the exposed parts of the frontiers
within this district, and that they may be placed at such a distance
from one another as may be most convenient for the reception and
accommodation of such scouts as may from time to time be employed
in ranging the woods and forests as in case of war, may be sent
out for the annoyance of the enemy in any of those settlements."
Subsequently Pepperrell and Moulton were empowered to commission
officers needed for four companies of fifty men each, and to supply
them with the proper munitions of war.

It is not known whether the Phillipstown block-house was a stockade or of square timber, nor precisely where it was erected. Tradition locates it on top of the hill below Bert Goodrich's house,
near the residence of Joseph Breary, where the late John Lord, who
owned the farm, found several bullets, stone arrowheads, gouges and
other evidences of the presence of the Indians. Another tradition
locates it on the other side of the road in a pasture, and a little fur-

[1] Journal of the House, 1743, p. 134.

ther down. In either case, it seems quite reasonable; for the settlers in the upper part of the town would be the first to be troubled by the Indians, and with a garrison house near, would be the better protected. In case of an attack they could flee to it, and send out an alarm to those dwelling below. The scouts from Newichawannock (Berwick) could easily cross over from the foot of Bauneg Beg, above the pond, near which the Indians encamped, and follow their trail to the Saco truck-house, near Salmon Falls in Buxton. From a petition dated March 29, 1744, we know that two block-houses were then standing; namely, James Chadbourn's and Samuel Willson's. We are of the opinion that these were private property, and that a public block-house was provided according to law.

In 1743, four hundred men were ordered to be detached or enlisted in the county of York, and organized into four companies, as minute-men, to be in constant readiness, with every equipment, and prepared to march at the shortest notice. Besides a good gun and sufficient ammunition, every one of them was to provide himself with a hatchet, an extra pair of shoes, or a pair of moccasins, and even a pair of snow shoes. A small stipend was to be paid to them for these preparations, and their wages from the time they left home, should they be called into active service.

On the 19th of April, 1744, Governor Shirley ordered Jeremiah Moulton, colonel of the Third Massachusetts regiment, to take perfect lists of all persons in his command obliged by law to appear under arms upon any alarm. On the 14th of May following, Colonel Moulton wrote from Kittery to John Hill, Esq., Judge, in regard to the matter. In his letter he says: "My Desire is to meet you at Berwick Tomorrow morning. If you think it will not be safe to go to Phillips Town without the Troop with their Pistols & Guns you may give Capt Shapleigh orders to meet us accordingly."

In 1744, December 2, all drafted men were ordered to be discharged, and one hundred effective men to be enlisted out of Colonel Pepperrell's regiment, and formed into eight guards — to be stationed at suitable distances from one another, and at convenient places between Berwick and St. Georges, whence they were severally to scout as far as the next station. Each guard was under the command of a sergeant. Twelve men were stationed at Newichawannock, to scout to the block-house at Phillipstown, and twelve at Phillipstown to scout to Saco truck-house. (Truck-houses or trading-houses were established, according to the French-English treaty of 1726, at convenient places where the Indians could exchange furs and kindred commodities for the goods of civilized countries.)

In 1745 four hundred and fifty men protected the frontier from Berwick to Brunswick, and ranged in scouting parties between the forts and block-houses at which they were stationed. Phillipstown had its quota, as it did in 1747, when three hundred and seventy men were employed in similar work, scouting as far east as Damariscotta. More than twenty-five large and noted block-houses then stood in Maine. In 1748 there were seventeen persons doing guard duty at the Wells and Phillipstown garrisons. From a muster roll of Captain Jonathan Bean's company, dated October 27, 1748, we know that James Chadbourn, Joshua Chadbourn, Jonathan Adams, Joshua Cane, Ephraim Low, Edward Whitehouse, John Stanyan, Samuel Willson, John Frost, William Holt, and John Chadbourn were scouts between December 10 and March 9, 1747/8. They were probably stationed at the Phillipstown block-house. All except Frost and Holt served thirteen weeks and received each five pounds, one shilling, seven pence. Frost served to February 27, eleven weeks and three days, for four pounds, nine shillings, three pence, and Holt to December 22, one week and six days, for fourteen shillings, seven pence. All except the same two served in the company, March 10-15.

In 1745 Pepperrell's memorable expedition against the French at Louisburg occurred. Four hundred men enlisted from York County, among whom are several Phillipstown names. Jonathan Adams, Joshua Adams, and William Curtis were among the early settlers. Curtis died at Cape Breton. Charles White was in the North Parish in 1766, and James Jepson in Sanford in 1789. Benjamin Harmon, who was a lieutenant in the sixth company, First Massachusetts regiment, Captain John Harmon, presumably his father, came into town in 1754. Robert Miller moved into town in 1749. He lost an arm near the shoulder, at the assault on the island battery. About eight years after, he was pensioned three pounds annually, and in 1766, on account of his advanced age, six pounds. Dr. Alexander Bulman of York, the grantee of settlers' lots numbers five and thirty-two, was one of the surgeons of His Majesty's forces at Cape Breton, and died there.

In 1754, money was appropriated for repairing the block-houses or fortified habitations at Towwoh (Lebanon), Phillipstown, etc. Sir William Pepperrell used every means in his power to have that part of the province in which his command was, well prepared to defend itself, and to meet any emergency. In the wars with the Indians, sudden demands were made, emergencies of such a nature arose that only great foresight, judgment, and precaution could have been exercised to meet them successfully. Colonel Moulton, to whom reference is frequently made in this history, was active and vigilant. It was enjoined upon him to see that ammunition was provided, as the following notice to John Storer of Wells will show ·

"March 14, 1754. Sir, I this day received from Sir William Pepperell, to take Cair and see that the town of York is well Proved with Ammunition in their Town Stock, and also that the men be well provided with arms and ammunition; and direct me to writ to you to see likewise that Wells and the Towns to the Eastward of Wells and Phillipstown be all likewise well provided as above.

"I am, Sir, your humble Servant,

"JERE MOULTON."

In 1755, fifty men were employed to scout between Lebanon and Saco River. Every recruit who furnished his own gun received eighteen shillings bounty; also the statute reward for captives and scalps. Enlistments were made for five months from June 20. In 1758, eighteen scouts were stationed at Phillipstown. The muster roll for that year contains the names of several Phillipstown men. Naphtali Harmon, sergeant, Robert Miller, Samuel Cane, Joshua Wittum, Joseph Stanley, Michael Bran (Brawn), John Thompson, Joseph Rounds, James Geare, James Chadbourn, John Willson, and John Staples, sentinels, were on duty in His Majesty's service at Phillipstown, August 29–October 31, nine weeks and one day. Amount due for said service, thirty-seven pounds, eight shillings, nine pence. William Babb was in Captain Jonathan Bean's company, at the Saco block-house, October 17–29, 1756, and also in 1757–8. In imagination we see these men scouting through the woods, far out on the border of civilization, — sturdy men inured to hardships and exposed to danger, who, in after years, enjoyed the comforts and happiness that come from peace.

Meanwhile (1755–8), there were urgent calls for soldiers for the expedition against Crown Point, and for the reduction of Canada, and later for the eastern frontier, to which Phillipstown nobly responded. It is known that the infant settlement sent out during seven years some twenty-five men, among whom no casualty seems to have occurred, but Joseph Stanley, Edward Whitehouse, and John Whitehouse contracted the small pox, and died soon after their return home. These soldiers were as follows:

1756.

Samuel Staples, house carpenter, corporal, aged forty-nine years, born in Kittery, and Joseph Ayers, laborer, private, aged eighteen years, born in Gorhamtown, residing in Phillipstown, were in Captain Joseph Holt's company, Colonel Ichabod Plaisted's regiment, May 7, 1756, in the expedition against Crown Point, and were at Lake George. They were in camp at Fort William Henry, August 7 and October 11. Their terms of service were from April 22 to December 1 and 8, respectively, thirty-two and thirty-three weeks.

1758.

Ebenezer Staples, son of Samuel, aged eighteen years, Jesse Thompson and Joshua Wittum were in Captain James Littlefield's company, Colonel Jedediah Preble's regiment for the reduction of Canada, April 7-November 18, eight months and two days, including twenty days' travel. They were at Lake George. John Staples, corporal, April 5-December 18, eight months, four days, twenty days' travel, and James Garee (Garey), April 12-November 18, were in the same company. John Willson was in Captain Ichabod Goodwin's company, same regiment, May 2-November 18, seven months, five days ; allowed twenty miles' travel. Edward Harmon, son of Benjamin Harmon of York, was in Captain James Gowen's company, same regiment, April 13-November 18. The Lake George campaign, in which Colonel Preble's regiment participated, was a disastrous one. There were two battles, on July 6 and 8, in which the army lost nearly two thousand men. For over three months Colonel Preble's regiment remained at Fort William Henry, arriving at home in November. "The advance of this army down Lake George, July 5, was probably one of the grandest spectacles ever seen in this country. There were nine hundred batteaux, one hundred and thirty-five whaleboats, and a large number of heavy flat boats bearing the artillery." Parkman has made the scene the subject of a glowing pen picture.

1759.

Samuel Staples and Ebenezer Staples enlisted April 2, 1759, in Sir William Pepperrell's command, under General Jeffrey Amherst, commander-in-chief, to whom the reduction of Ticonderoga was assigned. John Chadbourn, sergeant, James Chadbourn, Ephraim Low, Joshua Chadbourn, Joseph Stanlee (Stanley), Edward Stanlee, James Garee, John Staples, Samuel Willson, Robert Miller, Jonathan Johnson, Jonathan Johnson, Jr., John Willson, and Edward Harmon, sentinels, were in Captain Gerrish's company, called marching company, May 24-September 12. This company consisted of fifty men, of whom the captain was from Berwick, the lieutenant and one sentinel from Gorhamtown, twelve men from Narragansett, eight from Lebanon, thirteen from Pearsontown, and fourteen from Phillipstown. Edward Harmon, Kittery, aged seventeen years, servant to Nathaniel Clarke, was in Pepperrell's expedition, April 6. He was also in Captain Joshua Moody's company, November 2, 1759–January 12, 1761. There is much doubt as to whether he was the Phillipstown Harmon.

1760.

A company of thirty-one men, William Gerrish of Berwick, captain, and ten men each from Phillipstown, Narragansett and Lebanon, was on the eastern frontier, April 10–September 11, twenty-two weeks. The Phillipstown quota was: John Chadbourn, sergeant, Sampson Johnson, Stephen Johnson, Robert Miller, Joshua Chadbourn, James Garee, John Willson, Edward Stanlee, Jesse Thompson and Edward Harmon, sentinels. The following were in Captain Simon Jefferds's company, enlisted for the total reduction of Canada : Joseph Stanley, Edward Whitehouse, John Whitehouse, Obadiah Whitehouse, servant of Naphtali Harmon, and Jonathan Adams, serving from March until the middle of December, a period of thirty-seven or thirty-eight weeks. Edward Whitehouse, aged forty-nine years, was born in Dover, and John, his son, aged nineteen years, in Kittery.

1762.

Ebenezer Staples was in Captain James Sayward's company, April 10–November 1.

Alphabetically arranged, we have the following who served His Majesty between 1756 and 1762. The numbers on the right indicate the times of their service. Others probably bore arms, but their names have not appeared in any record or roll examined :

Jonathan Adams	1	Edward Harmon	3
Joshua Ayers	1	Naphtali Harmon, sergeant	1
William Babb	1	Jonathan Johnson	1
Michael Bran (Brawn)	1	Jonathan Johnson, Jr.	1
Samuel Cane	1	Sampson Johnson	1
James Chadbourn	2	Stephen Johnson	1
John Chadbourn, sergeant	2	Ephraim Low	1
Joshua Chadbourn	2	Robert Miller	3
James Garee	4	Joseph Rounds (York)	1

Edward Stanley	2	Edward Whitehouse	1
Joseph Stanley	3	John Whitehouse	1
Ebenezer Staples	3	Obadiah Whitehouse	1
John Staples, corporal	3	John Willson	4
Samuel Staples, corporal	2	Samuel Willson	1
Jesse Thompson	2	Joshua Wittum	2
John Thompson	1		

To these should be added the name of another, who moved into town in 1773, and for fifty years was among the foremost men in Sanford, — Caleb Emery. In 1758, when seventeen years of age, he was at Lake George from April 13 to September 25, in Captain James Gowen's company, Colonel Jedediah Preble's regiment; April 2, 1759, enlisted in Pepperrell's expedition; corporal in Captain Joshua Moody's company, November 2, 1759 to January 12, 1761; and sergeant in Captain Simon Jefferds's company, December 13, 1761 to May 27, 1762.

CHAPTER V.

INCORPORATION.

Two Ineffectual Petitions — Increase in Population — The Act of 1768 — Name of the New Town — Biographical Sketch of Governor Peleg Sanford, in Whose Honor it was Named — First Town Meeting — Early Votes.

PHILLIPSTOWN was incorporated as Sanford February 27, 1768, and was the twenty-fifth town in Maine. Sixteen years previous, however, the inhabitants of the plantation had petitioned the General Court to incorporate them into a township, and an act of incorporation had passed the house of representatives, and there rested. Four years later, they had again petitioned, urging the same reasons for incorporation, but their prayer was not answered.[1] Let the records tell the story of these ineffectual attempts, and the result of subsequent legislation, by which Phillipstown became Sanford:

"To His Hon[r] Spencer Phipps Esq[r] L[t] Govern[r] & Commander in Chief in and over His Majesty's Province of the Massachusetts Bay

"The Hon[ble] His Majesty's Council & the Hon[ble] House of Representatives in Gener[l] Court Assembled May 27th 1752

"The Subscribers most humbly shew, That the Prop[rs] of a Large Tract of Land of Eight Miles Square situate at the Inland head of the Town of Wells commonly called by the Name of Phillips-town beginning at a small Pine Tree standing upon the North Corner of said Wells Township & on the South West Side of Kennebunk River upon the North End of a Rockey Hill which tree is mark'd four sides thence South West by Wells bounds Eight Miles to a Pitch Pine Tree mark'd four Sides & with the Lett[r] N. upon the North side & being upon the West Side of a Marsh or Fresh Meadow called Merryland Meadow & runs from thence North West Eight Miles to a great Hemlock Tree marked on four Sides standing three Miles to the Northward of Bonnebeege Hills, thence North East Eight Miles to a Large White Oak Tree mark'd on four Sides & thence South

---

[1] In 1755 and 1761 the proprietors contemplated petitioning for incorporation, but took no definite action.

East Eight Miles to the Pine Tree began at — in Ord. to bring forward the settlement thereof for a Township (agreeable to the intent of Maj. William Phillips in his first Granting the same) did Grant to Forty Persons One Hundred & Thirty Acres each being part of said Tract upon certain Conditions of their settling the same That there are now in consequence thereof some of our Families to the Numb. of more than Twenty settled upon the said Tract & upwards of one hundred souls most of whom thro' the Assistance & protection afforded them by this Province have stood it out all the last War without the loss of men so much as One Person to the great encouragement of not only your Petitioners but many Others who frequently are coming to settle In the said place & building there which give hopeful prospects of a Flourishing settlement in a Few Years if still Suitably encouraged and would in process of Time not only be of service to the Neighbour Towns as a Barier to them in Case of an Indian War but 'tis hop'd to the Province in General, That their greatest Difficulties at present is their being under no proper regulation of an Incorporated Town or Precinct and so no pow. or Priviledge of Raising Money and Obliging the Non-resident Settlers & Prop. to pay their proportion for the Support and Maintenance of the Gospel among them so necessary for the prevention of Irreligion & Profaness as well as for the Edification of such as are Religious and well dispos'd and such other necessary Charges arising in making & keeping in Repair necessary and convenient Highways &. c.

" Wherefore your Petitioners pray this Court to take the Promises into consideration & of their wonted goodness & Parental care for such Infant Settlements Incorporate them into a Town or Precinct & Grant y.^m such Powers & Priviledges as have been usual for such — or Provide such other way & means for the effectual redress of their Inconveniencies aforesaid And Incouraging the s.^d Settlem.^t as this Court in their Wisdom shall Judge most fit & reasonable &

" Your Petitioners as in duty bound
shall ever pray ——

" John Frost	John Stanyan
" James Chadbourn	Sam :ll Staple
" James Chadbourn Jun	Sam :ll Willson
" Moses Fowler	John Garey
" John Chadbourn	Joshua Cane
" Joshua Chadbourn	Jonathan Adams
" Thomas Donnell	Jeremiah Dunham

" Jeremiah Moulton ter[ts]
" Daniel Moulton
" Benja. Holt
" Jos : Simpson Ju[n]

Thomas Wasgatt
Eph Low
Nicolas Cane
Sam[ll] Cane
John Low
Edward Whitehouse
Jonathan Jonsun
Robert Miller
John Urin —— "

On the reverse the petition is briefed :

" Pet[n] of John Frost and others   " Petition of Phillips
May 29, 1752. Capt Plaisteed   Town men "
Mr Wells Mr Gerrish to prepare a
Bill to Erect them into a Township."

The bill, granting the " inhabitance " of Phillipstown what they desired, was duly prepared and reported in the house. On June 4 it was passed to be engrossed in the house of representatives and sent up for concurrence. No further record is found regarding it.

The petition of 1756 was of the same tenor, and in nearly the same language as that of 1752. There were then about thirty families and " upwards of one hundred and fifty souls." Most of the inhabitants had fulfilled the conditions of settlement, or were in a fair way to do so. The petition was signed by

Daniel wittum	Naphtali Harmon	John Harmon
Joshua wittum	Jonathan Adams	Joshua Cane
Robert Miller	John Garey	Sam[ll] Wilson (?)
Nicolas Cane	Jos Stanley	Jonathan Johnson
John miles	John thompson	Sam[l] Cane
(or miler)	John thompson Jun	John Stanyan
	Eph Low	John Chadbourn
	John Calark	Joshua Chadbourn
	Benja Harmon	Thomas Wasgatt
	Benjamin Harmon Jun	Jesse Thompson
	Edward Harmon	Edward Whitehouse
	John Staple	Jonn : Johnson
	Eben Staple	Samson Johnson
	Benj : Wittum	James Garey
		Jonathan Swett

The petition was read in the house of representatives June 4, 1756, and it was ordered that the non-resident proprietors be notified to show cause, if any, on the second Wednesday of the next sitting of the General Court, why the prayer should not be granted. In this the council concurred, and later the whole matter was referred to the next session of the General Court.

It is to be noted that these petitions fix the population of Phillips-town in 1752 and 1756, and furnish us with the names, in part at least, of the early settlers. All except four or five of the first list, were actual settlers, though it is doubtful whether the descendants of more than half a dozen can be found in town to-day. It is to be noted also that in accepting and settling lots, the petitioners had voluntarily become a barrier against the Indians, for the neighboring towns, but would be a more effectual barrier in case the settlement increased, and at the same time would be a stronger defence unto themselves. They had the wisdom, too, to discern that the Gospel is a power, and that the preaching thereof conduces to the general good. More than this, that the improvement of one part of a town generally enhances the value of other parts, and that in justice, one should not bear all the burden of improvement and others reap the advantages thereof.

The second Wednesday of the next sitting of General Court came and passed, but no hearing seems to have been held. The order was unnoticed, either because the province was in a state of excitement attendant upon the fitting out of expeditions for the French and In-dian War, or because the petition was deemed of too little consequence to be attended to at that time. We do not find any reference to the subject of incorporation until twelve years later, when the house of representatives took the initiative in the matter. The successive steps were as follows : February 13, 1768, " Upon a Motion made, *Ordered*, 'That Major *Chadburn* bring in a Bill to incorporate a Place called *Phillipstown* into a Town." February 19, bill read first time, and ordered that it be read again at 3 o'clock. February 20, bill read second and third times, and passed to be engrossed. February 23, Engrossed bill read and passed to be enacted. March 4, signed by the Governor.

The engrossed bill thus reads :

" An Act for erecting a Tract of Land eight miles square called Phillipstown joining upon the Northwest end of the Town of Wells in the County of York into a Town by the name of Sanford.

" *Anno Regni Regis Georgii tertii octavo.*

" Whereas the Erecting of that Tract of Land called Phillipstown

into a Town will greatly contribute to the growth thereof, and remedy
many inconveniences to which the Inhabitants and Proprietors may
be Otherwise subject :

" Be it Enacted by the Governor, Council, & House of Representatives That the Tract aforesaid Bounded as followeth — vizt Lying
on the Northwest end of the Town of Wells, West of Kennebunk
River, East of the Town of Berwick and North by Province Grants
in part and in part by unappropriated Lands, Be and hereby is erected
into a Town by the name of Sanford, and that the Inhabitants thereof be and hereby are invested with all powers, privileges and Immunities which the Inhabitants of the Towns within this Province do
enjoy.

" And be it further Enacted That Benjamin Chadbourne, Esqr be
& hereby is impowered to issue his warrant directed to some principal Inhabitant of said Town requiring him to warn the Inhabitants
of said Town who have an Estate of Freehold according to Charter
to meet at such time and place as shall be therein set forth to chuse
all such officers as are or shall be required by Law to manage the
affairs of said Town.

" February 23, 1768. This Bill having been Read three several
times in the House of Representatives Passed to be Enacted.

" THOMAS CUSHING Spk^r

" February 23, 1768. This Bill having been Read three several
times in Council Passed to be Enacted.

" A OLIVER Sec^t

" February 27, 1768. By the Governor.
" I consent to the Enacting of this Bill.

" FRA BERNARD."

We are not bound to account for every discrepancy that may
appear in the records consulted, but we may suggest that this act
was not published until March 5, nearly a week after the Governor's
signature was affixed, and that in all probability the house of representatives had no official knowledge of his consent before the 4th of
March, when it is recorded in the Journal of the house that the bill
was signed by the governor.

The engrossed bill only contains the name Sanford. This would
indicate that. the name was not given until the act had reached the
Governor ; and, if so, would corroborate the statement, we know not

upon what authority made, that it was the practice of the General
Court of the Province of Massachusetts Bay, previous to the Revolution, out of courtesy to the Governor, to send bills for the incorporation of towns to him with blanks left for the names. This gave
him an opportunity to compliment his friends by filling the blanks
with their names, when he signed the bills, or with names suggested
by them. The Lieutenant-Governor, Thomas Hutchinson, and the
Secretary, Andrew Oliver, had married granddaughters of Peleg
Sanford, in honor of whom the town received its name.

In a list of towns in Massachusetts at the state house, Boston, appears this record : " Sandford 27 Feb. 1768. Original name, Phillipstown or Benapeag." The latter name is undoubtedly of Indian origin,
and may have been a form of the familiar Bauneg Beg, or Bonny
Beag. Phillipstown, as we have seem, took its name from the original grantee, Major William Phillips. Peleg Sanford, whose name was
ultimately given to the town, was the son of John and Bridget Sanford, and by the marriage of his widowed mother became the stepson
of Major Phillips. He was a useful, energetic, and prominent citizen of his day. Born in Portsmouth, R. I., May 10, 1639, he was
admitted freeman of that colony in 1666, and resided at Newport.
He served as assistant in the General Assembly six years, and at the
age of forty-one was elected Governor, to which office he was thrice
re-elected. The third time he declined to be inaugurated, for " sufficient reasons." Sanford was also General Treasurer at times both
during and previous to his governorship, and held other offices under
the colonial government and the crown. He inherited a large part
of the nineteen thousand acres, or otherwise came into possession of
it, so that as late as 1768, three thousand six hundred and fifty acres
adjoining Coxhall, were set off to three of his heirs. He died in
1701. We may safely assume that Governor Sanford always honored
the office to which he was chosen, and served his day and generation
with faithfulness and zeal. Governor Sanford was twice married.
By his second wife he had three sons and four daughters. His youngest son, William, had three daughters, Mary, who became the wife
of Andrew Oliver, Margaret, the wife of Thomas Hutchinson, and
Grizzel (Griselda), unmarried.

It is noticeable that Sanford was the only town incorporated in
Maine during a period of nearly four years, from June 25, 1767,
when Lebanon was incorporated, to April 26, 1771, when Hallowell
and three other towns were added to the list. The reason for this
has been assigned to the opposition of the royal Governor to the en-

FRED B AVERILL.

largement of the house of representatives, by which the power and influence of the popular branch would be increased. In this action we have indications of that conflict of opinion and authority which ended when the mother country formally acknowledged the independence of the colonies.

Sanford having been incorporated, no time was lost in calling a town meeting for the transaction of the public business. Following is a copy of the warrant for the first town meeting:

" York ss To Mr John Stanyan of Sanford in the County of York Yeoman Greeting

" In his majestys name, you are Required to warn the Inhabitants of Said Town of Sanford that have an Estate of Freehold in Said Town Quallified by Charter to vote in Town meetings, To meet at the Dwelling House of Mr John Stanyans inholder in Said Sanford on Wednesday the Thirtyeth day of March Currant at one of the Clock in the afternoon, Then and there, to Chuse a Moderator for Said meeting, And to Chuse all such Officers as are or shall be by Law Required to mannage the Affairs of said Town,

" And make Return of this Warrant with your doings Thereon at the Time and place appointed for Said meeting——

" And for your so doing this shall be your Sufficient Warrant given under my hand and Seal this 11th day of March In the Eighth year of his Majestys Reign annoque Domini 1768.

" BENJ^A CHADBOURN Jus peace "

The record of this town meeting is lost, but we know from other records that Benjamin Harmon, Naphtali Harmon and John Stanyan were chosen selectmen, and William Bennett, collector of taxes and constable.

The records of subsequent early town meetings throw an interesting light upon the doings of those days:

1769. March 22 (?) " Voted that William Bennett late constable should deliver up the Warrant and Tax Bill for the year 1768," which was accordingly done.

" Voted that Hogs go at large except they do mischief." (A pertinent vote, when we consider that much land was lying in common, and swine would make much havoc among the growing crops. It was probable that they were yoked and ringed according to the act of 1693, under William and Mary, which required swine to be yoked from April to October 15, and ringed all the year.)

March 27, an adjourned meeting was held at Samuel Willard's

4

house. " Voted that there be raised on the Polls and Estates of the Inhabitants of this Town the sum of Fifty Pounds lawful money for defraying the Town charges the year ensuing."

1770. Annual meeting. March 21. " Voted that Hoggs shall goe at large with yoking and ringing untill they Do mischief.

"Voted that the fifty Pounds that was voted the Last year and was not Raised should be Raised this year to Support the gospel and other insedent Charges."

On May 9th the selectmen issued a warrant to the freeholders and others " That have an Estate of Freehold in Land within this Province or Territory, of Forty Shillings p^r annum at the least, or other Estate to the Value of Forty Pounds Sterling," for a town meeting on May 22 to elect one or more persons " to Serve for and Represent you in the great and general Court or Assembly appointed to be Convened held and kept for his Majesty's Service at Harvard Colledge in Cambridge," on May 30. There is no record extant that this meeting took place. The first representative was not elected until a number of years later.

1771. Annual meeting at the dwelling house of Lieutenant Jonathan Johnson, innholder, Thursday, March 21. " Voted to give Mr. Nathaniel Bennet Constable one Shilling on the Pound for gathering the Rates for the year Past and his Rates for the Same year.

" Voted that Swine Should Run at Large untill they Do Mischief." (Similar vote, March 18, 1772.)

1772. March 18. Voted not to raise any money.

May 1   Met at " the Meting House." Voted not to send any representative.

1773. March 16. William Bennet was chosen to serve on the grand jury.

May 21. Voted not to send a representative this year.

Dec. 20. " Voted that William Bennet Daniel Gile James Geary and John Stanyan be a Committy to Prefer a Pertition to the Great and General Court that the Court of Genera Sessions of the Peace and Court of Common Pleas holden at Bideford may be Removed to the Town of Wells as it Near the Centor of the County."

1774. Annual meeting at the house of John Stanyan, innholder, Monday, March 21, 1774. " Voted to have Two Constable Edward Harmon Constable in the Town and Ebenezar Hall Constable for that part of the Township called massabeseck.

" Voted that a committee be chosen to examine the accounts of the former Selectmen and make Report thereof to this meeting on the adjournment thereof and Massrs Caleb Emery Enoch Hale and morgain Lewis were chosen accordingly."

Sept. 27. Met at the house of Jonathan Johnson. No reference is made to His Majesty in the warrant for this meeting.

1775. March 14. " Voted by the Town to chooes three men to see who are or not (voters) & they Brought in if a man paid six shilling one singal Rate shall be a Voter for this Presant year." Adjourned to May 22 : " To chouse a Committee of Safty; To see where the town will agree to hier a ministre to preach sum part of the time ; To see where the Town will chouse a Town Treasury ; To see whare the Town will alow James Jackson for his portison."

What is now Alfred formed the northern part of the original town of Sanford. Within its limits lay a portion of the territory known as Massabesec. This is the Indian name of the pond from which the eastern branch of the Mousam flows, and gave name to the upper part of Alfred and lower part of Waterborough. According to Judge C. E. Potter, Massabesec means " much-pond-place ;" Massa, much, nipe, pond, ni omitted and s put in for sake of the sound; and auke, place. But, according to Mary, daughter of the old chief Neptune of the Penobscot tribe of Indians, it is formed by combination and contraction as follows : Mad, great; om, am, or um, suckers ; which with the besec or betticks, according to Potter, would make it signify " Great-sucker-pond-place." We assume that our Massabesec is of the same origin as the Thomaston Massabesec, and has the same signification.

CHAPTER VI.

SANFORD IN THE REVOLUTION.

Names of Soldiers Furnished, Terms of Service, and Interesting
Facts in Regard to Them—Votes of Town—Money Raised.

THE first seven years of the history of the town were eventful
ones in colonial times, scarcely less eventful than the second
seven. Then was the period of agitation and discussion of the question, "Shall the American Colonies be compelled to bear their proportion of the expenses of the home government, and have no voice
in that government?" The men of the frontier towns, although far
from the centres of discu ssion and agitation, were alive to any emergency that might arise. The immediate action of the people of York
County, when the first call to arms resounded in 1775, shows how
ready they were, and how thoroughly in earnest.

The news of the battle of Lexington reached Lebanon on the morning of the 20th of April, 1775, at four o'clock,[1] and not many hours
later aroused the inhabitants of Sanford. The "minute-men" had
watched with intense interest the progress of events, and were then,
at a moment's warning, called upon to shoulder their muskets and
leave their firesides and friends. The Lebanon company was sent
off on the 21st, and without doubt, the Sanford company did not long
delay marching. However that may have been, it is evident that
thirty-eight men marched sixty miles, and did three days' service
prior to April 28, at which date their muster roll was made out. The
following are names of those who "Marched on the Alarum upon Lexington Battle:"

Captain—Morgan Lewis.

Lieutenant—Benjamin Tripe.

Ensign—Nathaniel Bennett.

Sergeants—Andrew Burley, Jeddiah Peabody, Samuel Jalison.

Corporals—Paul Giles, Henery Hambleton.

Privates—John Adams, John Barrons, Isreal Hibbard, Jonathan

---

[1] Parson Hasey's Diary.

Adams, Moses Pette, Samuel Harmon, Samson Johnson, Henery Nutter, Abraham Barrons, Josiah Harmon, John Cram, Joshua Batchelder, William Tripe, Henery Tibbets, Ephraim Gile, Isaac Coffin, Daniel Lary, Thomas Kimble, Timothy Silver, Joseph Thompson, Benjamine Lord, Joseph Giles, Benjamine Norton, Joshua Taylor, Eliflit Taylor, Jonathan Low, Jonathan Boston, Stephen Hatch, Phinas Thompson, Seth Peabody.

There were minute-men in other companies, some of whom are known. Joseph Horn and Samuel Whitehouse were privates in Captain Noah M. Littlefield's company, Colonel Moulton's regiment. Ebenezer Guptail was a sergeant, aud Stephen Perkins, John Clarke, Joseph Giles, Jr., Jeremiah Smith, Nathaniel F. York, Israel Smith, and Daniel Giles, privates in the " Massabesick " company, Captain John Smith, which marched April 22.

War had actually begun, and other soldiers than minute-men, hastily equipped and poorly furnished, were needed. As soon as Captain Lewis's company returned home, Captain Joshua Bragdon, of Wells, who had enlisted two days after the Lexington and Concord fight, raised a company of eight months' men, in Sanford, Wells, and Berwick. It numbered fifty-seven men, of whom thirty-three were from Sanford. We give the names of the company entire, as they appear on the first muster-roll, August 1, 1775. The numbers (106) and (100) show the distances in miles from their homes to place of muster-in, from which we see that twenty-three were from what was afterwards the North Parish, or Alfred, and ten from the South Parish, or Sanford :

Captain— Joshua Bragdon, Wells.

Lieutenant — Morgan Lewis, Sanford, (106).

Ensign — Moses Sweet, Sanford. (106).

Sergeants — Abraham Barens, Wells ; Enoch Hale, Sanford, (100) ; William Patton, Wells ; Jerediah Pebody, Sanford, (106).

Corporals — Simeon Hatch, Wells ; Samuel Cluff, Sanford, (106) ; Peter Cram, Wells ; Ephraim Gile, Sanford, (106).

Drummer — Joseph Thompson, Sanford, (106).

Fifer — Josiah Harmon, Sanford, (100).

Privates — John Adams, Sanford, (100) ; Jonathan Adams, Sanford, (100) ; William Burks, Sa nford, (106) ; Nathaniel Butland, Wells ; William Boston, Wells ; Elijah Boston, Wells ; Daniel Bos_ ton, Sanford, (100) ; Richard Blabon, Wells ; John Clarke, San_ ford, (106) ; Isack Coffin, Sanford, (106) ; John Emons, Sanford, (106) ; Pentleton Emons, Wells ; Nathaniel Edward, Wells ; Stephen

Edward, Wells ; Daniel Eastman, Sanford, (106) ; James Ford, Wells ;
Samuel Harmon, Sanford, (100) ; Jeams Hall, Wells; Joseph Hibbard, Sanford, (106) ; Isac Jones, Sanford, (106) ; Thomas Jepson,
Wells; Samuel Jelson, Stanford (Sanford), (106) ; Charles Jell-
son, Berwick; Abram Kimble, Sanford, (106) ; Joseph Knight,
Berwick; Jeddiah Low, Wells ; John Lord, Sanford, (106) ; Thomas
Neele, Wells ; Abr Pribel, Sanford, (100) ; Moses Pettey, Sanford,
(100) ; William Powers, Sanford, (100) ; Jeremiah Smith, Sanford,
(106) ; Jeremiah Steward, Wells; Marsters Tredwell, Wells ; Nath-
aniel Tredwell, Wells ; Samuel Whitehouse, Wells ; Charles White,
Sanford, (106) ; George Whales, Sanford, (100) ; Nathaniel Folsom
York, Sanford, (106) ; Paul Giles, Sanford, (106) ; Daniel Giles,
Sanford, (106) ; Israel Smith, Sanford, (106) ; Noah Merrill, Wells ;
Israel Hibbard, Sanford, (106).

Another muster-roll subsequent to September 17, does not have
thereon the names of Jerediah Pebody, Isack Coffin, and Moses
Pettey, but the names of Caleb Clark, Wells, sergeant, and Daniel
Coffin and Jonathan Powers, Sanford, privates, appear.

This company, most of whom enlisted May 3, was in Colonel
James Scammans's (Thirtieth) regiment, of which Samuel Nasson of
York, afterwards of Sanford, was quartermaster, and marched to
Cambridge under the command of Lieutenant Lewis. They were at
least four days on the road and were in camp on May 23. Owing to
what seems to have been a misunderstanding of orders, this regiment
did not take part in the battle of Bunker Hill, but assisted in cover-
ing the retreat of the exhausted men under Prescott. " Colonel
Scammans was ordered to go where the fighting was, and went to
Lechmere's Point. Here he was ordered to march to the hill, which
he understood to mean Cobble Hill, whence he sent a messenger to
General Putnam to inquire whether his regiment was wanted. This
delay prevented it from reaching the field in season to do any good."
. . . " His regiment did not advance nearer the battle than Bunker
Hill. (It should be borne in mind that the battle was fought on
Breed's Hill, and that Bunker Hill was some seven hundred yards
nearer Charlestown Neck, over which the retreat was made.) The
colonel was tried for disobedience of orders, but acquitted."[1] From
the fact that Lieutenant Lewis, before the court-martial, " deposed
and said, ' I saw nothing of cowardice or backwardness in Colonel
Scammans that day,' "[2] it is inferred that he commanded the company

Frothingham's " Siege of Boston."
The Historical Magazine, June, 1868.

at that time. On August 19, Captain Bragdon resigned and returned home, and Lieutenant Lewis became captain of the company. There is conclusive evidence that the company served during the eight months' campaign of that year, for thirty-four names, at least, of which Captain Lewis's is one, appear in the "Pension Index, Eight months' Service," "Coat Rolls, 1775."

There were in the possession of the company, fifty-five guns, thirty-nine cartridge-boxes, two bayonets, one drum, and one fife. The captain and ensign furnished bayonets (swords seemed to have been wanting), and fifty-two men furnished their own muskets. Three guns were taken from the store, of which Enoch Hale's was valued at two pounds, and eight shillings, and William Burks's, at two pounds, two shillings, and eight pence.

After Washington took command of the army Colonel Scammans's regiment manned a fort at Cambridge. "The service of the regiment . . . . was not an eventful one. There were no battles. The firing between the lines was desultory, and the encounters with the enemy were in the nature of skirmishes."[1] The men served until December 31, 1775.

Other soldiers enlisted in 1775, mostly May 3 : Stephen Johnson, corporal, Joseph Kilgore, fifer, Abraham Barnes, Jonathan Baston. Timothy Baston, John Cram, Joseph Horn, Nason Lord, Pelatiah Penney, Salathiel Penny, Allen Perry (Christian name variously written Allen, Allin, Alex. and Hen [?]), Eliphalet Taylor, and Henry Tebbetts, privates, in Captain Samuel Sayer's (Sawyer's) company ; Daniel Adams, James Davis, and Joshua Emery, privates, in Captain Samuel Leighton's company ; Robert Williams of Mast Camp (Massabesec), private in Captain Jeremiah Hill's company ; William Tripe, corporal, and Peter Nasson (said to have been a drummer boy), in Captain Jonathan Nowell's company; Seth Peabody, private, in Captain Jesse Dorman's company, all of Colonel Scammans's regiment ; Jethro Smith of Massabesec, private in Captain William Hudson Ballard's company, Colonel Fry's regiment, at Cambridge, October 6 ; William Faye, John Penney, and Stephen Perkins, privates, in Captain Hubbard's company, Colonel Doolittle's regiment, at Winter Hill, Cambridge, now Somerville, October 10 ; Matthew Lassell, corporal, and Gatnsby Witham, private, in Captain Benjamin Hooper's company, raised to defend the seacoast, at Biddeford, July 17–December 31.

[1] "Col. James Scammans's Thirtieth Regiment of Foot, 1775," by Nathan Goold, Maine Historical Society Collections.

There are traditions among their descendants that James Chadbourn and Ephraim Low, Jr., were at the battle of Bunker Hill, and that Low had the end of his nose shot off. He was also in sight of Washington and Howe when they concluded the terms for the evacuation of Boston, and was present when the British fleet sailed out of that harbor.

Daniel Giles, Paul Giles, Nason Lord, and Israel Smith are borne on the muster rolls, as having " enlisted in the train, June 3." Paul Giles and Smith are borne on another roll as having enlisted June 10 in Captain Samuel Gridley's company, Colonel Richard Gridley's matross (artillery) regiment.

James Davis, who was also a minute man in the Wells company, in April, was reported as a deserter, May 31; but we incline to the opinion that, after an absence without leave, he completed his term of service; for his name appears on the " Coat Rolls," and those entered there received, at the expiration of their term of enlistment, a coat each in addition to their pay, and were entitled to a pension from the United States, after the formation of our government.

Nathaniel Bennett was sergeant in Captain Moses Merrill's company, Colonel Edmund Phinney's regiment, from May 15 to July 5.

The Committee of Safety for this year, chosen May 22, was James Gare, Daniel Giles, Walter Powers, Benjamin Tripe, and Elisha Smith. This committee was chosen, as were other similar committees in other towns, for the purpose of " consulting, upon any emergency, the safety, peace, and prosperity of the town, as well as of the whole government and continent."

1776.

The term of enlistment of most of the eight months' soldiers expired in the early part of this year. Probably some re-enlisted, but not enough to fill the quota of the town. On the 19th of January, Colonel Sawyer of Wells, Mr. Sullivan of Biddeford, afterward Governor of Massachusetts, and Major Goodwin of Berwick, were appointed a committee to raise men for York county. Only two hundred and thirty-eight were required from the ten towns then incorporated, of whom Sanford was to furnish twelve. The number was undoubtedly raised, though we are unable to give the names of the men, as documentary proof is lacking from the archives. For some unexplained reason, there are fewer rolls for service during 1776 than of any other year during the period covered by the Revolutionary war.

William Tripe did service from January 17 to August 31, in Captain Philip Hubbard's company, stationed at Kittery Point and "Old York."

Eliphalet Taylor was in Captain John Wentworth's company, Colonel Aaron Willard's regiment, and was discharged at Fort Edward in July. He appears subsequently to have been allowed pay for three hundred and twelve miles' travel from Bennington, in the vicinity of which he had been campaigning under the same officers. It also appears that he and William Martine (?) were in Captain Joseph Ilsley's company, Colonel Cogswell's regiment, from September 30 to November 16, and were allowed pay for thirteen days to reach home, two hundred and sixty miles distant, and mileage at the usual rate, a penny a mile.

John Giles and John Lord were in Captain Samuel Leighton's company, at Dorchester Heights, in August, and were credited with one hundred and twenty-five miles' travel. Michael Brown (Brawn) was also in the same company at Dorchester.

John Clarke and Joseph Kimble (Kimball) were in Lieutenant Daniel Wheelwright's company prior to August 31, and had marched from home, or were distant therefrom, one hundred and twenty miles, as it appears from a "marching or billeting roll of part of a company." Undoubtedly they were two of the "six men from the town of Sanford and Smith's company, of thirty-six men with Wheelwright and Lane as first and second lieutenants," who, "agreeably to resolve of July 10, 1776, marched for the heights of Dorchester as supernumerary men, the 12th of August." A report to this effect is dated at Watertown September 5, and signed by Joseph Storer, committeeman.

Benjamin Evans, William Martin, and Joseph Kimball were allowed for one hundred and twenty-five miles' travel home from Dorchester in November. They were in Captain Isaac Tuckerman's company, Colonel Ebenezer Francis's regiment.

On the 6th of September (1776?), Captain Ichabod Goodwin certified that eight men from Sanford and Smith's company ("Massabesick") joined the regiment raised in the counties of Essex and Cumberland, and marched July 22, under his command. Perhaps some of the twelve required were among them. On a roll of the travel of Captain Jedediah Goodwin's company, Colonel Edward Wigglesworth's regiment, discharged at Albany, N. Y., November 30,—made up from thence to their respective towns, at one penny per mile, and one day's pay for each twenty miles,—are the following names:

Josiah Harmon, sergeant, John Knight, Abel Getchel, Thomas Gubtail, Samuel Mereal, Daniel Brown, and Samuel Henderson, privates.

Nathaniel Bennett's name appears as lieutenant in Captain Edward Harmon's ninth (Sanford) company, Colonel Ebenezer Sayer's (First York County) regiment, in a list of officers of the Massachusetts militia, commissioned June 25 ; in a list of militia officers, returned by Brigadier General Jotham Moulton, dated Providence, December 24, he is rated as first lieutenant of Captain Daniel Littlefield's company, Colonel John Frost's regiment.

During a session of the Provincial Congress, April 26, 1775, it was ordered that powder be supplied for the use of the towns, but with what limitation, and at whose expense, the records do not show. It would seem, however, from a vote of the town March 26, 1776, that some action had been taken, prior to that time, in regard to supplying the soldiers with ammunition, and from another vote, at a later day, that all expenses were to be borne by the town :

"Voted that James Gare shall pay back that money that was drawn out of Jonathan Johnson, Jr. Constable hand for to buy powder."

James Gare was first on the Committee of Safety in 1775, and would be naturally invested with power to receive money drawn for that purpose, and to expend what was necessary to purchase powder.

July 8, 1776 : "Voted to have a Town Stock of Powder led and flints. Voted to get half Berrel Powder half hun^d led & 1 grose flints. Voted M^r. John Stanyan & William Person are the two men chosen to go and buy s^d Town Stock. Voted Mr John Stanyan & Nathl Conant are the two men chosen to take the Town Stock till it tis Call for."

William Person, Walter Powers, and Nathaniel Bennett were Committee of Safety.

1777.

This year long term men were called for. The following are known to have enlisted from Sanford for three years, or during the war : Thomas Barnes, Daniel Brawn, Samuel Bridges, William Burks, Dominicus Gray, Thomas Gubtail, Josiah Harmon, Samuel Harmon, Joseph Hibbard, Thomas Hutchings, Levi Hutchins, Stephen Johnson, Stephen Kent, Joshua Kimball, Jonadab Lord, John Lord, Nason Lord, John (or Jonathan) Mooney, Thomas Smith, William Straw, Obadiah True, Samuel Whitehouse.

Barnes was mustered in by Nathaniel Wells, muster master, and served from June 15 as private in Captain John Reed's company, Colonel Ichabod Alden's (afterwards Colonel John Brooks's) regiment. He died in the service, probably about January 1, 1778. Barnes was a recipient of state bounty.

Brawn was in Captain James Donnell's company, Colonel Samuel Brewer's regiment. He marched to Bennington, having twenty-nine rations furnished him from February 19 to March 20. He was at Valley Forge, January 22, 1778. He is reported as having deserted from the Colonel's company (Ebenezer Sprout succeeded Brewer in command of the Twelfth regiment after the latter was cashiered, September 29, 1778), after having served nineteen months and twenty-two days. He was also reported dead. He returned from desertion July 20, 1780, as shown by the returns of that year, and served until December 31, 1780.

Gray enlisted in Captain Daniel Wheelwright's company (subsequently Captain Thomas Francis's), Colonel Ebenezer Francis's regiment. He was mustered in as a resident of Wells, February 7, 1777, but the next January was reported from Sanford.

Josiah Harmon was at first in Captain Wheelwright's company, Colonel Francis's regiment. On June 13 he received state and continental bounties. He was a sergeant in Colonel Sherburne's regiment, July 15, 1777, to February 1, 1779. On the latter date he deserted, but returned by proclamation as certified by Lieutenant Phelon of Colonel Henry Jackson's regiment.

Hibbard, Levi Hutchins and Nason Lord were mustered in January 1, 1777. They were in Captain Daniel Merrill's (afterwards Captain Luke Hitchcock's) company, Colonel Brewer's regiment. They marched to Bennington, two hundred and eighty miles, and are credited with ninety days' service to March 17. Hutchins was a sergeant, and served three years. Hibbard is reported as a deserter, after a service of thirty months and seven days. On another muster roll he is borne as having served to July 7, 1779, and been discharged. Lord deserted in four months, but was not returned, though apprehended. "N. B. The above Nason Lord now resides in Sanford, has been taken as a deserter, and brought before Nath. Wells, Esq., muster master for the County of York, who has dismissed him and let him go."[1]

Corporal Johnson enlisted March 17 in Captain Thomas Francis's company, Colonel Ebenezer Francis's (Eleventh) regiment (Colonel Benjamin Tupper's, after Colonel Francis was killed, July 7, 1777),

[1] Muster Rolls, Boston, Vol. 21, p. 115.

and was discharged May 27, 1778.   Term of service, fourteen
months, ten days.   He was furnished with firearms.

Kent was in the same company with Johnson from May 2, 1777,
to December 31, 1779, thirty-one months, twenty-nine days.   He
was a fifer.   On April 17, 1777, he received state and continental
bounties.

John Lord was in Captain Peter Page's company, Colonel Calvin
Smith's regiment, and died after serving seven months and sixteen
days.

True was in Captain Francis's company, Colonel Francis's regiment, from March, 1777, to December 31, 1779, serving thirty-three
months and thirteen days.   He was the recipient of state and continental bounties but was not furnished with firearms.   He was at the
surrender of Burgoyne.

Whitehouse enlisted March 14, and served till December 31, 1779.
He was in Captain John Mills's company, Colonel Joseph Vose's
regiment.   Credited to Wells in 1780, he served that entire year, a
total of forty-five months and seventeen days.

Bridges, Gubtail, Thomas Hutchings, Kimball, Jonadab Lord,
Mooney and Smith, all of Massabesec, or Mast Camp, served in Colonel Calvin Smith's (late Colonel Edward Wigglesworth's) regiment,
the group with the exception of Lord being credited to Captain Peter
Page's company, which was at Valley Forge in 1778 and at Providence in the spring of 1779.   On another muster roll these men,
Kimball excepted, are credited to Captain Matthew Fairfield's company, Colonel Wigglesworth's regiment, and all received state bounty.
Lord was also the recipient of continental bounty.

It is probable that Eliphalet Taylor, Jonathan Webber, Stephen
Weymouth, Thomas Wright, and Joseph Young enlisted for three
years.   Taylor was at the surrender of Burgoyne, and declared that
it was the happiest day he ever saw.   The names of the others, with
the exception of Weymouth, appear on the muster roll of Captain
Wheelwright's company, January 25, 1778.

Abram Pribble, January 18, and John Huston, April 2, were in
Captain Daniel Wheelwright's company, Colonel Francis's regiment,
but it is uncertain how long they were in the service.   On one muster
roll it appears that Pribble marched April 26 and served ninety-nine
days.   He was not furnished with arms.

In December, 1776, the governor of Rhode Island solicited the aid
of Massachusetts in defence of that state, and on several occasions
she responded to similar appeals for assistance.   During the follow-

ing spring and summer many troops were sent to Providence and
vicinity for a few weeks, or months at most, partly as a protection
to Rhode Island, and partly as a precautionary measure of defence,
because fears were entertained that the enemy at Newport would
march through the country and attack Boston. It would appear that
nine men, at least, from this town, responded to one call. Joseph
Thompson, drummer, Stephen Gowen, Ezekiel Gowen, John Gowen,
Caleb Emery, Stephen Perry, James Davis, Daniel Adams, William
English, Jonathan Gooding, Richard Tinan, and Noah Cluff, privates,
served between May 19 and July 18, in Captain Abel Moulton's
company, Colonel Jonathan Titcomb's regiment, and were allowed
three hundred and twenty miles' travel. Though the last three are
credited to Sanford, it is doubtful whether they belonged to the town,
for Gooding does not appear to have been a resident, Tinan is elsewhere enrolled from Wells, and Cluff from Arundel.

Another record states that Gershom Boston, William Worster,
Jabez Perkins, Jedediah Jellison, James Davis, Junior, Stephen
Gowen, William Bennett, Junior, and Joseph Miller Thompson were
drafted for service in Rhode Island, May 8, 1777, for two months.
In another place Boston is credited with service from May 19, 1777
to July, 1778.

Paul Giles was hired to serve eight months from July 2, joined
Captain Merrill's company, and was discharged January 11, 1778.
Others hired at that time refused to march until their mileage was
paid to them.

Although Sanford had a large number of men in the field, it was
included in the order of August 9 for a draft to form a York County
battalion under Lieutenant Colonel Joseph Storer to aid in re-enforc-
ing the northern army. There were two companies, one of fifty-four
men, from the First Parish of Wells and Sanford, "being a sixth
part of the able-bodied effective men drafted from the brigade,"
James Littlefield, Captain, Samuel Gooch, Lieutenant, Tobias Lord,
Second Lieutenant; and the other, forty-eight men, from Wells,
Second Parish, Arundel, and Massabesec, Thomas Nason, Captain,
Issacher Damm, Lieutenant. Lieutenant Lord, son of Captain Tobias, of Arundel, was drafted while residing at Moulton's Mills. He
was at the capture of Burgoyne's army in October.

William Burks, Benjamin Evans, Samuel Harmon, John Stevens,
William Straw, and Joseph Thompson were drafted out of the militia,
or hired by those who were drafted, to serve eight months from Sep-

tember 4. They were mustered into Captain Nicholas Blaisdell's company, Colonel Wigglesworth's regiment.

Burks and Straw are returned as privates in Captain Joseph Fox's company, Colonel Henry Jackson's regiment (Sixteenth), from September 1. Both enlisted for three years. Both deserted ; the former, May 6, 1779; the latter, November 14, 1777, but returned or was retaken, May 6, 1779, the day upon which his comrade left. On another roll Straw is reported as serving his full twenty-eight months from September 1, 1777, to December 31, 1779, and also the entire year 1780.

Evans joined Colonel David Henley's regiment, one of the three additional infantry regiments. His residence seems to have been at Coxhall, incorporated after the draft.

Harmon probably enlisted August 14, was transferred after his muster-in to the company of Captain William North, Colonel Henry Jackson's regiment (Sixteenth), and was promoted to be corporal, September 1, 1778. Note is made of the fact that his family was at "Old York," and Straw's at Kennebunk, with the view, probably, of rendering them the assistance promised as an inducement for a three years' enlistment. Three of the six drafted or hired for eight months enlisted for three years.

It is not improbable that John Gowen, after returning from Rhode Island, again entered the service for three years.

Joseph Kimball of Massabesec was in Captain Fairfield's company, Colonel Wigglesworth's regiment. He received state bounty February 8.

James Davis, after his return from Rhode Island, served in Captain Thomas Bragdon's company (late) Colonel Storer's regiment, from August 14 to November 30. He was with the Northern army and was discharged at Queman's Heights. Jonathan Baston (Boston) was in the same company for an equal length of time on the same service.

On December 2, 1777, John Smith of Massabesec was allowed mileage, twenty-eight pounds, sixteen shillings, to Saratoga.

The following letter from Major Osgood needs no explanation :

" ANDOVER Sep^t 22^d 1777

" Gentlemen

    " I haye deliv^d Two fire Arms to the Melitia of your Town Lieu^t Lord certifying that it was your intention that s^d Men should receive s^d arms must therefore request pay for the same & am ready

to deliver the Remainder of your Towns Proportion when called for
which is 48 Pounds of Lead 40 flints & two gun Locks

" I am Gentlemen

" Your humble serv^t

" SAMUEL OSGOOD."

" (Selectmen of Sanford) "

The archives show that in October of this year the selectmen were
allowed mileage to Bennington, forty pounds, and in December, for
rations, eight pounds, ten shillings.

John Stanyan, Naphtali Harmon, and William Person were Committee of Safety.

1778.

This year Michael Brawn was in a company stationed at Kittery,
eight months, and Daniel Lary did service in Captain Simeon Brown's
company, Colonel Nathaniel Ward's regiment, for six months and
eight days. He was discharged at East Greenwich, R. I., July 1,
one hundred and sixty miles from home.

Israel Smith, Daniel Eastman, Daniel Goodrich, Nathan Powers,
William Powers, Joshua Cane, John Huson, and Charles Smith
were in Captain Samuel Waterhouse's company, Colonel Jacob Ger-
rish's regiment, on guard at Winter Hill, from April 2 to July 3.
James Gary, Ruke Stillings, and John Gowen were also at Winter
Hill, in Captain Esaias Preble's company, same regiment, undoubt-
edly for the same term of service. Ezekiel Eastman also served at
Winter Hill for four months in Colonel Gerrish's regiment.

From a return made by Nathaniel Wells, muster master, between
April 9 and 27, we learn that Joseph Horn and Stephen Peary were
hired to fill the quota of the town of Wells, and were assigned to
Captain Merrill's company, Colonel Brewer's battalion. " Stephen
Peary was mustered to go in the room of Allin Peary, mentioned in
my last return as belonging to Wells or Sanford, and it since appears
certainly that he belongs to Sanford and so could not be entitled to
receive a bounty from the town of Wells as was engaged him by the
person who enlisted him; said Allin returned his bounty. Horn being very poor has liberty from his Capt. as I am informed to enlist
and serve as one of the quota of the Town of Wells." Other returns
show that Allin Peary (or Perry), Captain Daniel Wheelwright's company, Colonel Benjamin Tupper's regiment, received state and continental bounties, April 9; that the same soldier served in Captain
Hitchcock's company, Colonel Sprout's regiment, April 1, 1778–

April 1, 1780; that Stephen Peary served in the same company and
regiment, April 1, 1778 – December 31, 1779, and subsequently re-
enlisted for one year; and that Joseph Horn was in Captain J. Pray's
company, Colonel Sprout's regiment, April 10, 1778 – December 31,
1779.

Tobias Cole, Daniel Getchel, Joshua Gutterage (Goodrich) and
Joseph White marched under the command of Captain Samuel Leighton to Fish Kill, June 1, 1778, and were to report to Brigadier Jonathan Warner. Cole and Getchel seem to have dropped out by the
way. Gutterage and White arrived at Fish Kill, June 4, and are returned as forming a part of the fifteen battalions raised for nine
months, Rufus Putman, Colonel.

William English was also drafted from Massabesec to serve nine
months. He was at Fish Kill, June 23. Three more of the men
drafted for Fish Kill were Thomas Clerk (Clark), Daniel Scribner,
and John Sills, who were in Captain Smith's company, Third regiment.
Clark was returned as received of John Frost, superintendent for
York County, by Captain Samuel Leighton at Kittery June 1, 1778,
to be conducted to Fish Kill and delivered to Brigadier Warner.
Jonathan Baston (Boston) was also in the Fish Kill contingent.

During this year two of the men who enlisted in 1777 were heard
from. They were at Valley Forge, and in deep distress they sent
the following letter to " Captain Morgan Lewis, Sandford, Massachusetts State, To be left at Captain Merrill's:"

                                        " PENSYLVANIA STATE
" Camp at Valley Forge, Aprill 15th 1778
    " For In as much as we are the only two Men that belongs to
your Company & Prefink that continue in the Army for the term of
three years & have Suffered the lofs of all our cloathing laft year in
the Retreat from Ticonderoga & Suffered Everything Else but Death
itt Self and have had a hard fateanguing Campain last year & a very
uncomfortable Winter & no clothes except some Shews & Stokings
or a shirt & Tie no prospect of having any, unless sent by the town,
And as ye other towns in that state are Dayly Sending Cloathes to
their men, we can therefore only send our Request which we Pray you
to take into Consideration & do your Endeavour to help us if you can ;
as we have no relations to apply to must apply to the Town or Prefink by sending to you as a father & a friend in time of need We are
both of us Exceeding Poorly out for cloathing we Cnt Purchase any
here unlefs it be old ones of the Virginia or Coneticut troops & Then

COLONEL NEHEMIAH BUTLER.

the price will be 4 or 5 times ye valley of new cloathing: Joseph Hebbard is Lame with his old Rheumatizm pains and has been for 4 weeks paſt & we have as much to do, as we can do to support our-ſelves here with our Rations & Wages both. Levi Hutching haſs a family he Expects at home, but how they are Supported or how they are to live I cannot tell But Pray they may not be left Deſtitute of friends So as to Suffer while in a christian land an He cannot get leave to come home & If he could, not Save anything to help his family We remain your Dutifull & Suffering Servants

> " Levi Hutchings
>
> " Joseph Hebberd "

August 28 the selectmen were allowed mileage and baggage to Pix-hill and Fish Kill, forty pounds. December 5 they were allowed thirteen pounds for mileage of four men to Providence and Boston, although it does not appear who these men were.

The fourth article in the warrant for a town meeting to be held at the school house, December 1, was : " To see if the Town will ad-vance money for the Fire arms in the hands of the Board of Wars at Boston, or Give liberty to any one or more of the Town Inhabi-tants to take them." At that meeting the town voted not to raise any money for the firearms, and to give liberty to any one or more per-sons to buy the said firearms.

John Stanyan, Naphtali Harmon, and Samuel Friend were Com-mittee of Safety.

1779.

James Chadbourn, Joshua Cane, and Nathan Powers were in Cap-tain Samuel Sawyer's company, Major Littlefield's detachment (York County) in the expedition against Penobscot, July 7 – September 6, 1779.

Michael Brawn (Brown) served in the Second regiment at Spring-field for nine months during this year.

Ebenezer Hall, Elisha Smith, and John Thompson were Committee of Safety.

September 6. " Votᵈ not to raise solgers by a Rate. Votᵈ the method that the Town has agreed upon to Suply the solgers families is by Superscription."

1780.

A number of the three years' men of 1777 are found in the service this year, but as to whether they re-enlisted the records are not

5

always clear. Some of them undoubtedly did re-enlist, being induced, perhaps, by the bounty of three hundred dollars offered, when a committee, sent out for that purpose late in 1779, just before the expiration of the term of service of some of the three years' men, visited the army.

Samuel Bridges, who deserted in 1779, was certified May 6, 1780, as having returned and re-entered Colonel Calvin Smith's regiment, Captain Woodbridge's company. He served until December 31. Thomas Gubtail, Thomas Hutchings, and Joseph Kimball, were also in Colonel Smith's regiment, Captain John Towle's company, serving through January, and Kimball further remained with the command during February.

In Colonel Sprout's regiment was Daniel Brown (Brawn) who returned from his desertion.

Samuel Harmon and William Straw were in Colonel Henry Jackson's regiment on December 1, 1779. Harmon served as a corporal from January 1 to August 14, 1780, and Straw remained in the army throughout the year.

Josiah Harmon, who had been a deserter, was a sergeant in July, and Obadiah True, private six months, and corporal six months, in Captain Thomas Francis's company, Tenth (Eleventh?) regiment. True is also credited to Captain Peter Page's company in 1780. Samuel Whitehouse served from January 1 until December 31. All of the foregoing were three years' men of 1777.

Stephen Perry was in Captain J. Pray's company the entire year.

Jacob Brown, of Massabesec, enlisted January 21, at Providence, as a private in the Colonel's company, Colonel Ebenezer Sprout's regiment. A week later he was at West Point. He served until December 31. Brown is also credited to Captain Henry Sewall's company, Second Massachusetts regiment.

The Tories who had moved into Lincoln County caused the patriotic settlers there some trouble. To inspire the people of the eastern counties with union and a spirit of resistance, the requirements upon them of men to reinforce the Continental army were somewhat relaxed. It was determined, however, in March, that a detachment of six hundred men be taken from the three eastern brigades and organized into companies of a single regiment, and distributed at Falmouth, Camden, and Machias. Three hundred were to be stationed at Falmouth.[1] A town meeting was called to be held June

---

[1] Williamson's " History of Maine. "

20, at the house of Jonathan Powers, " To see if the town will Give any incouragement to Raise Soldiers for falmouth, and for the Southern Department." One would naturally suppose that soldiers for home defence would be more easily raised than those for a distant field of action ; but for some reason not recorded, the town

" Voted not to give any encouragement to the soldiers desired for fallouth from this town.

" Voted to give the men desired for the southward an encouragement.

" Voted to choose a committee to agree with two men to go to the southward, and a committee of three was chosen to hire two soldiers for southward."

On the 21st of July, the town " Voted to raise £3150 for the use of paying the six months soldiers bounty. Also to be raised £450 as a bounty to hire a soldier for the term of three months." It seems as if James Gare was then and there hired for three months, for he served as a private in Captain Andrew P. Fernald's company, from July 21 to October 10, and was discharged three hundred miles from home. He was allowed pay for three months and five days.

One of the six months' soldiers was Nathan Powers, who served in the thirty-third division from July 28, 1780, to February 5, 1781. He arrived at Springfield August 4, and on the next day marched thence with Captain Samuel Carr.

" Agreeable to a Resolve of October the 5th 1781. For making out a Pay Roll for the Six Month Soldier, which went from Sanford. he marched the twenty eight Day of July 1780 and was disbanded at West Point the 5 of Feby 1781. Nathan Powers was the man we find that from West Point [to] Sanford is three hundred and forty [miles] Time of Service 6 months 26 days @ 2 Pound Per month

" Due £13–14–8

  " (Signed) " JAMES GARE   Selectmen
               of
      " ELEAZAR CHADBOURN Sanford."

On the 11th of March, 1782, the town " Voted to see where they allow Edward Harmon anything on account of hiring Nathan Powers for six months soldier."

On a list of men mustered by Nathaniel Wells, muster master, to serve eight months for the defence of Eastern Massachusetts, appear the names of Asa Lassel and John White, Sanford, Moses Deshon, Massabesec, and Joseph Chaney, Jr., Wells. They were certified

June 6. Deshon was engaged for Biddeford. He became a private
in Captain Josiah Davis's company, Colonel Joseph Prime's (York
County) regiment, which he joined May 9, and was discharged at
Arundel, December 8. Michael Braun (Brown) was in Captain
Thomas Bragdon's company, Colonel Prime's regiment, from May 7
to October 30.

Dominicus Gray also served eight months during the year in the
defence of the eastern parts of the state.

On November 6, 1780, the following allowances were made to the
selectmen of Sanford :

" For mileage for two men to Springfield
   " Being 200 miles at 6/ P^r mile   £120
" Also to two men to Clavernack it
   " Being 330 miles at 6/ P^r mile   198
" Also to two men to falmouth it
   " Being 40 miles at 3/ P^r mile   12
                                             £330
" Redus to New Money   8–5–0 "

Towns were required not only to furnish soldiers, but also clothing
and subsistence. At one time Sanford was required to furnish ten
coats.[1] A town meeting for the purpose of raising thirty-two hundred
and ten pounds of beef for the army, agreeably to an act of the General Court, was held October 23, at which the people

" Voted to be Raised on the poles and Estates of the Inhabitants
of this town five thousands pounds to purchase said beef and the
charges arising thereby.

" Voted to Let out said Beef to the Lowest Bidder.

" Voted Capt Morgan Lewis & Mr. Elezer Chadbourn messers a
Committee to purchase said beef as Cheep as Possable and to Deliver
the same to the County agent appointed for that purpose."

It was also " Voted not to make up any depreciation of money."

Jonathan Tebbets, Benjamin Tripe, and John Stephens were Committee of Safety.

1781.

This year began with large requisitions and increased burdens. At
a town meeting, January 8, adjourned from December 28, 1780, and
called " To Vote and Raise a Sum of money sufficient to purchase
6165 pounds of beef for the army," and " To see what method the

---

[1] Journal of Provincial Congress.

town will take to Raise the Soldiers now demanded To fill up the Continental army and furnish them," it was

"Voted to raise £9248 lawful money for that purpose.

"Voted to class the poles and estates of this town according to the directions of the general court to procure the 8 soldiers now demanded.

"Voted Mr. Samuel Willard to be paid out of the town money for a pr. men's shoes delivered for encouraging soldiers."

The eight soldiers were soon raised. Ebenezer Low, Jr., was the first to respond, as may be seen from the following receipt:

"SANFORD February 7, 1781

"then & there Received of Capt. Morgan Lewis the proper Security for nine Cows paid me as a bounty for inlisting to Serve in the Continental army for the term of three years

"(Signed) "EBENEZER X Low, Jr."
his
mark

"Attest. CALEB EMERY."

John Giles enlisted February 12, for sixty pounds in silver; Samuel Gowen, Wells, and Andrew Walker Pugsley, were hired February 13, for two hundred and eighty-eight dollars each in specie; William Staples and Robert Tripe, same day, for two hundred dollars in specie; Thomas Jellison, March 27, for sixty pounds in produce, corn at four shillings per bushel, or its equivalent at standard prices; and Thomas Gown of Berwick for sixty-two pounds, six shillings, six pence; all were returned May 10.

The General Court relieved towns somewhat, and lightened the burdens, by offering a bounty of fifty dollars for each soldier enlisted, to be allowed on the settlement of their taxes; and no tax was laid on the polls and personal estate of soldiers thus enlisted.

On the 17th of May, the town "Voted this account that the committee brought in against Daniel Lary be taken out of his bounty." We are unable to determine whether or not the bounty thus referred to was promised to him for his service in 1778. We conjecture, however, that he was one of the six months' soldiers of 1780.

On July 1 the selectmen were allowed the mileage of eight men to Boston, five pounds.

There is no record showing that there was opposition to raising money, though the hard lot of the inhabitants made it difficult for the town to act as readily as it could wish. Pecuniary means, not patriotic motives, seem to have been wanting. However, on the 10th of July, the town "Voted and raised £42 7s and 6d to purchase two thousand five hundred and forty three lbs. beef, to be paid in silver. Also £27 3s for to purchase soldiers' clothing." This latter was undoubtedly to meet the tax specifically assessed for shoes and hose. The beef tax on Maine was 236,120 pounds, and the shoe and hose tax one thousand and sixteen pairs.[1] On the 2nd of August, Morgan Lewis and Caleb Emery were chosen a committee to hire six three months' soldiers at the cheapest rate, and to make their report in twelve days ; and on the 16th, fifty pounds were raised, to be paid in silver, to hire those six men.

In Volume 141 of Massachusetts Archives appears the following memorandum of clothing furnished by Sanford in 1781 :

10 shirts	12s	£6
8 shoes	10s	£4
10 hose	6s	£3
4 blankets	£1 4s	£4 16s.
30 miles' travel ⎫ 3 days ⎭		£2 0s. 6d.

£19 16s. 6d.

Brigadier General Frost sent a detachment under Captain John Evans, September 24, to the relief of Sudbury-Canada (Bethel) on "Amorescoggin" River. Of these men, several were from Sanford : Sergeant George Wales, and Privates William Chadbourn, Ezra Thompson, Bodwell Coffin, Daniel Warren, Thomas Burke, Joseph Henderson, Daniel Coffin, Joseph Moody, and Christopher Chiffener. They served September 16 – December 3.

Though the surrender of Cornwallis virtually closed the war, endeavors were made to fill up the army by the enlistment of men for three years or during the war. No pressing demands, however, were made, and men relaxed their efforts.

1782.

For the purpose above mentioned, towns were divided into classes, and each class was to furnish a man, or to pay a sum sufficient to employ a man to serve in the Continental army. We have no evidence that this requirement was fulfilled, or that the town made any effort

[1] Massachusetts Resolves, Vol. 5.

in that direction. A Committee of Safety, consisting of Caleb Emery, Samuel Nasson, and Ebenezer Hall, was chosen, and the year following David Bane, Nathaniel Bennett, and Daniel Giles filled that office, rendered unnecessary after the treaty of peace, September 3, 1783, and the disbanding of the army two months later, November 3.

One vote more, pertaining to the war, was passed, January 5, 1784 : " Voted to choose a committee to settle the affairs respecting the beef."

It is a matter of surprise that the inhabitants of the town were able to meet the demands placed upon them for provisions, and so willingly contributed of their small resources the large amounts which they were assessed. They were constantly struggling to reclaim the soil, and gain a livelihood. Agriculture was their main support, markets were few and distant, money was scarce. The wages and bounties of the soldiers brought in some money, but husbandmen were not at home to till the soil and clear the land as in days of peace. It is true indeed, that when the amount raised to be expended for beef is reduced to the standard of silver then in use, the Spanish milled dollar, it is small compared with the thousands of pounds assessed. But such calculation, if made at that time, would not have afforded relief to the people, when their means of subsistence were slender, and the scarcity of money prevented them from complying, except under extreme pressure, with the urgent demands of the time.

We can readily understand why the following vote should have been passed at a town meeting, January 18, 1782 : " Agreed upon and Vot^d to chuse a Committe^e to Draw up Petion to send to the general court for to see wyther they abate any part of our taxes or Delay the Execution for a longer time." The request was not that of beggars, impoverished and destitute through misconduct and improvidence. It was the request of patriotic men, desirous that justice might be done them, struggling against adverse circumstances, and exercising their utmost endeavors to fulfil the requirements of the government, and to aid in securing to themselves the rights of freemen and the privileges of self government, both of which were more than life to them.

The paper money of the colonies depreciated during the war, and at one time the ratio to specie was ninety to one. Stephen Gowen, a Sanford soldier, is said to have received a sixty dollar note for six months' service, which became so nearly worthless that he retained it in his possession almost threescore years, and transmitted it as an

heirloom to his son, Walter, who in recent years held it in a good
state of preservation, though tender by age. The tradition that Aaron
Witham paid, at one time, eleven hundred dollars for a cow and her
calf, contains more truth than fiction.

Brief sketches of Revolutionary Soldiers who served from Sanford,
and from other towns, who were subsequently residents of Sanford :

ADAMS, DANIEL. He is supposed to have been the son of Jonathan or Joshua Adams, who took up settlers' lots in the south part
of the town, but what became of him, whether he died in town or removed, is not known. Poverty seems to have been his lot. One of
his neighbors, a kind hearted woman, frequently gave him food. At
one time, she was trying to teach one of her little daughters a hymn,
a free version of the thirteenth chapter of I Corinthians. Coming to
the line about feeding the poor, the artless child insisted on making
the version still freer, rendering it, "Feed Daniel Adams."

ADAMS, JOHN. He was probably a son of the foregoing. In 1783,
he lived on the east side of the county road leading to Shapleigh,
just below where Ira Witham now lives. He died February 22, 1800,
in his fifty-third year.

ADAMS, JONATHAN. There were two of this name in town, father
and son. If the former was in the service, he must have been sixty-
three years of age, and have had experience as a scout in Captain
Jonathan Bane's company in 1747-8, and in the French and Indian
War in 1760, in Captain Simon Jefferds's company. He died March
21, 1791, aged seventy-nine. We think the son was the Revolutionary
soldier. He lived, in 1783, near where Ira Witham lives, was designated by the title "Junior" in 1788, and was a voter in 1805.

BARNES (BARRONS), ABRAHAM. It is quite probable that he was
one of the five sons of Benjamin Barnes, who came from York, and
settled at the foot of Shaker Hill, and then moved to the top of it.
He removed to Francisborough, now Cornish, and was one of the
members of the branch of the Sanford Baptist Church organized there
in 1788. He died in Cornish, October 24, 1819.

BARNES, JOHN. Another of the five sons; lived on Shaker Hill
and belonged to the "Merry Dancers." He was one of the most disorderly at the meetings of the Congregationalists at Mast Camp. Of
him and one John Cotton, Dr. Parsons says : "One of their practices was to hoot the devil, as they called it, in which they would
march around the Shaker Pond, raving like maniacs. Barnes would
wear a baize jacket over his clothes, a wig upon his head, with a
cow's tail attached to it, and Cotton, an untanned cowhide, and in

these garbs would scream ' Woe! woe!! woe!!!' audible in the stillness of the evening nearly the distance of one mile. Barnes's explanation of his conduct in hooting the devil, drinking to excess, and indulging in indecent and immoral practices was that they were a sort of carnal slough through which he was doomed to pass, preparatory to spiritual regeneration." [1]

BARNES, THOMAS. Another of the five sons, probably, and an original member of the Baptist Church. He died in the service, January 1, 1778.

BATCHELDER, JOSHUA. "Colonel" Batchelder was born in Kensington, N. H., May 19, 1749, old style, and married Abigail Hazeltine, of Buxton, Me., said to have been a niece of Governor Hancock. He moved into town in early life, was a bloomer by trade, and worked in the bloomery, "Iron Works," then standing near the bridge across the Mousam at the Corner. When or for what reason he acquired the title of "Colonel," we have no knowledge. He died February 7, 1826.

BENNETT, NATHANIEL. Lieutenant Bennett was born in York about 1741. He came into town about 1770, lived at South Sanford, and was a leading man. His wife was a Tripp. He was first lieutenant of the Eleventh Matross Company, of which Samuel Nasson was captain. He was one of the original members of the Congregational Church, and served one year, 1780-1, on the board of selectmen. He died January 23, 1804, in the sixty-third year of his age. The several Bennett families in town are his descendants.

BOSTON (BASTON), DANIEL. He came into town from Wells prior to 1772, and was one of the original members of the Baptist Church. He removed to Francisborough (Cornish), and was a member of the Baptist Church there in 1792.

BOSTON, JONATHAN. Either Daniel or Jonathan lived in the Moulton neighborhood. The latter was in town in 1789. He lost his wife, Abigail, March 2 of that year, and married Mehitable Weston of Coxhall (Lyman) December 10.

BOSTON, TIMOTHY. He lived in 1792 on Shaw's ridge. None of this name resided in town in 1805.

BOSTON, WILLIAM. A Wells soldier, who was a first lieutenant in Colonel Edmund Phinney's regiment throughout 1776. He was at the Evacuation of Boston, and saw service at Ticonderoga and Fort George. Also served in the Penobscot Expedition, 1779.

BRIDGES, SAMUEL. Also credited to Pepperrellborough. On a list

---

[1] Parsons's "History of Alfred."

of deserters in 1779 his age is given as 38 years; height, five feet, seven inches; complexion, light; residence, "Mascamps."

BROWN (BRAWN), DANIEL. He received two-thirds pension in 1776.

BROWN, JACOB. On a descriptive list of enlisted men he is given as five feet ten inches in height, and of light hair and complexion.

BROWN (BRAWN, BRAN), MICHAEL. He was on duty at the garrison-house, August 29–October 31, 1757, and was deer informer in 1769.

BURK (BURKS), WILLIAM. He received a pension of thirty dollars a year from October 10, 1808.

BURLEIGH (BURLEY), ANDREW. He was the son of Andrew Burley, a graduate of Harvard, 1742, and was born in Ipswich, Mass., where he was baptized December 2, 1744. His second wife was Rhoda White, whom he probably married after his removal into town about 1773. He was in town in May of that year, and lived at Massabesec, or near the Gore, where he built a saw-mill. He was in command of a small quota, sent at one time from Massabesec. Though an unsuccessful potash-maker, he was an influential man in the early history of Waterborough. He was justice of the peace, selectman, and clerk of the courts while they were held in that town. One of his daughters married a Bean, a second, a Hasty, both of Waterborough, and a third, Simon Ross of Shapleigh.

CANE, JOSHUA. He was the son of Joshua Cane, who took up a settler's lot in 1739. After his father's death, and mother's second marriage, he moved to Wells. Though his name appears among Sanford names on a muster-roll of 1778, he lived in Wells in November of that year.

CHADBOURN, JAMES. He was a son of John Chadbourn, an early settler, and was born February 4, 1758. He married Deborah, daughter of Naphtali Harmon, and had five sons and five daughters: Benjamin, Lucy, Nathaniel, Levi, Mehitable, Anna, George, Mary, Theodate, and William. At one time he owned a pottery on the side of Nasson Hill. His farm was on Hanson's ridge. He died May 18, 1839.

CLARK (CLARKE), JOHN. He came into town as early as 1756, and may have been the grandfather of Abner Clark, who took up land at Mouse Lane.

CLUFF (CLOUGH), SAMUEL. He came from Kittery, and settled on "Back Street," near a bend in the road, upon a farm owned in late years by the Fergusons. He was an ensign in the militia in 1788, captain in 1792, and major.

COFFIN, DANIEL. He was born August 17, 1737, removed from Newbury in 1765, and lived in the North Parish. His wife was Mehitable Harmon. In 1772 he was chosen deacon of the Baptist Church.

COFFIN, ISAAC. He was one of the Coffins that settled in Massabesec, in 1764-5.

COLE, TOBIAS. He was in town in 1805.

CRAM, JOHN. From all that we can gather, he was Captain John Stanyan Cram, father of the Cram families in town. He was an ensign in the militia in 1788, and captain in 1792. His second wife, whom he married November 30, 1808, was Jerusha, daughter of Captain Enoch Hale, born 1749. He was a pensioner. When he took oath, July 4, 1820, he was sixty-six years old, his wife seventy-one years, and his daughter Sarah twenty-four years. He died in Waterborough not long after.

EASTMAN, DANIEL. He was probably one of the sons of Daniel Eastman, who came from Concord, N. H., with six sons, and settled just above Alfred Corner.

EASTMAN, EZEKIEL. He was brother of the foregoing, and lived half way between Lary's bridge (now Emerson's) and the Brooks house.

EMERY, JOSHUA. He occupied a house a quarter of a mile south of Shaker bridge; started a pottery as early as 1791, joined the Shakers; left them and returned; left and returned a second time.

EMONS, PENDLETON. He served from Wells, but on the " Coat Rolls " he is credited to Sanford.

GAREY (GARY, GARE), JAMES. He was the son of John Garey, a settler in the south part of the town prior to 1750, and was born about 1737. He had experience in the French and Indian War, serving as a guard at Phillipstown in 1757, in Captain James Littlefield's company, Colonel Jedediah Preble's regiment in 1758; in Captain William Gerrish's company, " a marching company," in 1759 ; and in the last-named company on the eastern frontier, in 1760. He was selectman, 1773-7, 1781-3, eight years, and town treasurer, 1775. He was an original member of the Congregational Church, a deacon thereof twenty-four years, and the last survivor of the original members, except Caleb Emery, who had withdrawn from the church. He died March 22, 1824, aged eighty-seven years.

GETCHELL, DANIEL. He was in town in 1805.

GILES (GILE), DANIEL. He was a native of Plaistow, N. H., and came into town in 1765. In 1766 he removed to the North Parish, and settled a quarter of a mile north of Coffin's wigwam, on the bank of the brook, near the site of the potash manufactory, subsequently established. He built the first two-story house in what is now Alfred. He was selectman 1772-6 and 1778, six years.

GILES, EPHRAIM, JOHN, JOSEPH, JOSEPH, JUNIOR, and PAUL. These five were all undoubtedly residents of the same neighborhood with Daniel Giles. Prior to 1782, Daniel, John, Joseph, and Joseph, Junior, had settled in the east part of Shapleigh.

GOODING, JONATHAN. It is questionable whether he was a Sanford man, although so credited on the rolls.

GOODRICH (GUTTERAGE), DANIEL. One Daniel Goodrich is mentioned by Dr. Parsons as one of the successors of Cooley and Jewett, Shakers.

GOODRICH, JOSHUA. He came from Berwick in 1774 or 5, settled near the eastern branch of the Mousam, just below Alfred Corner, and subsequently moved to the Gore. He was a blacksmith.

GOODWIN, AMOS W. He was born in 1755, was a Berwick soldier, and came to town about 1796. He owned the Willson lot a mile below the Corner. His death occurred March 20, 1838. His widow, Eunice, drew a pension in 1840, and died May 2, 1845, aged seventy-seven years and three months.

GOODWIN, ——. There is a tradition that a Goodwin of this town was on the " Bon Homme Richard," under John Paul Jones.

GOWEN, EZEKIEL. William Gowen, of Kittery, accompanied by his two sons, Ezekiel and Stephen, came into town about 1770. Ezekiel lived on the homestead on the farm now owned by C. F. Tebbets, on Lebanon street, half a mile from the Corner. He was grandfather of Samuel, Daniel and Frank Gowen.

GOWEN, JOHN. In 1788 there was a John Gowen living at Mouse Lane, but his identity is doubtful. He occupied a house in the field, a short distance back of the residence of the late Abner Clark. He probably died March 18, 1792, and his widow, after living in that vicinity some time, removed and joined the Shakers.

GOWEN, SAMUEL. He belonged in Wells and was hired by Sanford in 1781. He had seen service in 1780.

GOWEN, STEPHEN. This son of William Gowen, above-mentioned, was born in Kittery, June 17, 1753, and came to town about 1770. From a memorandum in his handwriting, we learn that he worked on the " Iron Works " dam in 1771. He was constable and collector several years, selectman, 1799, town treasurer 1804-6, 1810-15, and 1820, justice of the peace 1811, 1820-9, and postmaster from January

18, 1816 to December 13, 1817. In 1791 he built, across the river, the two-story house now owned by Edgar Wentworth, and in 1815, a grist-mill at the Gowen privilege, a mile above the Corner. About 1818, in company with his sons, James and Walter, he built a saw-mill in connection with the grist-mill. He raised a large family, among whom were "Old Master Gowen," Timothy, James, George, and Walter. He died March 14, 1846.

GOWEN, WILLIAM. He served from Wells.

GRAY, DOMINICUS. At first he was enrolled from Wells, and then from Sanford. The Baptist society bought their parsonage of him. He lived, or owned land, on Mount Hope, and was in town in 1789. He died in Groton, Vt., in 1829, aged seventy-one years.

HALE, ENOCH. He lived below Butler's bridge on the. Willard C. Littlefield place. He was captain of the militia in 1788, and died May 13, 1805.

HAMILTON (HAMBLETON), HENRY. "Old Master Hamilton," a Scotchman by birth, was born about 1748. He was coroner, 1782-5. He married Eunice Lord, in 1780, taught school many years, and died in Harrison, Me., February 21, 1819.

HAMILTON, JONATHAN. He lived in Sanford in 1835 or 6, enlisted from Berwick.

HARMON, JOSIAH and SAMUEL. The Harmons were descendants of the York Harmons. One of Samuel's ancestors, Captain Harmon, was distinguished in the Indian wars, and took a prominent part in the destruction of the Indian settlement at Norridgewock in 1724. Samuel Harmon came to town about 1754. He was one of the original members of the Baptist Church. He left town prior to 1788, and in 1835 or 6, lived in Dixmont. Some of his descendants were among the early settlers of Harrison.

HASKELL, EZRA. There is a tradition that he did service at Sudbury-Canada in 1781.

HATCH, SIMEON. His name is borne on the "Coat Rolls" as from Sanford, but it is undoubtedly a mistake, for he resided in Wells.

HATCH, STEPHEN. He came from York and settled near the Hay Brook. He was a brickmaker, and owned the second brickyard in town. He was grandfather of Stephen Hatch, formerly of Sanford.

HENDERSON, JOSEPH. He served from Coxhall; enlisted in 1778 for the remainder of the war.

HIBBARD, ISRAEL. He was one of the Hibbards that attended the meetings of the "Merry Dancers" at Mast Camp, and resided near Shaker Hill.

HIBBARD, JOSEPH.   Probably another of the "Merry Dancers."

HILL, NELSON.   He was born in Kittery (now Eliot), in 1755, served as a soldier three years, beginning January 1, 1777, in Colonel Sprout's regiment; married a Miss Abbott, and prior to 1788, settled on the hill beyond Hanson's ridge, where he died, leaving several children.

HUSTON (HUSON), JOHN.   In 1840, John Huston, a pensioner, aged seventy-seven, lived with his son John in the south part of the town.   He was probably a son of John Huston, who died in 1827; and, born in 1763, must have been only fourteen, if he was the soldier of 1777.   He married Sarah Estes, June 12, 1796, and in 1820 had eight children.

HUTCHINS, EASTMAN and LEVI.   These two were cousins.   The former came from Arundel, and settled at the north end of "Back Street."   He was sergeant in Colonel Sprout's regiment from March, 1777, to December 31, 1780.   He served as town clerk and selectman.   At the time of his death, May 8, 1826, he was living in Alfred.   His wife's name was Betsey.   Levi came from Cape Porpoise, but was in town before his cousin Eastman, who belonged to Arundel as late as 1778.   Levi resided near John Plummer's.   In 1835 or 6 he lived in Alfred.   His wife's name was Olive.   Both men were pensioned.

JACOBS, GEORGE.   Lieutenant Jacobs was of the fourth generation from that venerable martyr, George Jacobs, who was executed at Salem for witchcraft, August 19, 1692, and was the fifth George in succession.   He served as lieutenant in Captain Robert Davis's company, Colonel Joseph Vose's regiment, through 1777.   He married Hephzibah Bourne, of Wells, where he resided, and long after the war removed to Lyon's Hill, where he died June 4, 1831, at the age of seventy-nine years.   In 1840, his widow was living with her son, Theodore Jacobs; and drew a pension.

JELLISON (JALISON), JEDEDIAH, SAMUEL, and THOMAS.   The Jellisons came from Berwick (South Berwick).   Jedediah settled a mile southwest of Swett's bridge, and his son Thomas, opposite him.   Samuel, brother of Jedediah, settled in Mouse Lane, and at length removed to Shapleigh.

KILGORE, JOSEPH.   He was the son of Joseph Kilgore, who lived in the south part of the town.

KIMBALL, THOMAS.   He was one of the builders of Conant's mill, and dwelt a quarter of a mile above it.

KNIGHT, JOHN.   He came from Kittery Shore, near Portsmouth, purchased land of Isaac Coffin, built a barn, resided in one part of it, and entertained travellers, from which he acquired the sobriquet, "Barn Knight." It was in that barn that a town meeting was held May 25, 1780, to examine the several articles in the new form of government. At one time, religious meetings were held there, and were much disturbed by the "Merry Dancers." Knight moved to the hill, now Yeaton's, and was in 1801 succeeded by Dr. Hall.

LARY, DANIEL. Lary was a tanner by trade, and had a tanyard by the brook, near his house, built between the bridge and Ezekiel Eastman's. It is supposed to have been the first frame dwelling house built in Alfred, and was finally moved to the Corner, where Griffin's brick hotel stood, and was used many years as a schoolhouse. In felling a tree near the late Colonel Lewis's, he accidentally killed Daniel Hibbard.

LASSELL (LASDEL), ASA. He received a pension in 1835 or 6. At one time he lived in Alfred.

LASSELL, CALEB. He came from Arundel, and in 1835 or 6 was living in Waterborough. He served in two regiments from February 1, 1777 to December 31, 1779. He was a pensioner. His wife's name was Dorcas.

LEAVITT, DANIEL. He was in Captain John Smith's company of minute-men from Massabesec. In 1840, a Betsey Leavitt, possibly his widow, was a pensioner. She lived with her daughter, Mrs. Daniel L. Littlefield.

LEWIS, MORGAN. Major Lewis, a native of York, came to town from "Scotland Parish," in 1772, and settled in "York Street," on the hill east of the river, near where John Lewis used to live. He was a prominent man in town affairs, serving on various committees of importance, and on the board of selectmen seven years, 1774-9, and 1781. He took a deep interest in the conflict between the colonies and the mother country, espousing the cause of the former with all his soul. After the service of which we have made mention, he became captain of the Eleventh Matross Company (militia), and was subsequently promoted to be major. He was the first militia captain in Alfred. He married Sarah Tripp, and their children were: Jeremiah, Daniel (who became colonel in the militia), Morgan, Jr., John, Sarah, married Jeremiah Trafton, Dorcas, married David Bean, Katherine, married Benjamin Trafton, Patience, Abigail and Dolly. Major Lewis died November 17, 1784, aged forty-seven years; his widow, surviving him thirty-five years, died October 28, 1819, aged seventy-nine. Both were buried in the Alfred cemetery,

the former being the first person there interred. Major Lewis's estate amounted, according to the inventory, to eight hundred and thirty-
eight pounds, two shillings, two pence, and included two cartridge
boxes, valued at three shillings, and a powder horn at eight pence.

LINSCOTT, THEODORE.   He was born in 1756.   Enlisted from
York; lived in Sanford 1835 or 6. His wife's name was Dorcas.
He was a pensioner.

LORD, BENJAMIN. He was the son of Benjamin Lord, Senior, who
came into town with Major Lewis, and settled, about 1772, near
Conant's mill.

LORD, JOHN.   Died in the service.

LORD, TOBIAS.   Lieutenant Lord, son of Captain Tobias Lord, of
Arundel, was born about 1748. When a boy of fourteen or fifteen
years of age, he went to live with a relative at Moulton's Mills, Sanford, and was there employed principally in getting lumber from the
mills to the house, situated some distance away. This work was attended with peril, especially when, at night, he drove his oxen to the
barn half a mile from the road leading to Wells (Kennebunk). "The
wolves were always on the watch, though they were great cowards. The
only way in which he could reach his home was by riding one of the
oxen, and keeping them back with a club or some kind of a bludgeon.
They came around him in flocks night after night, but he was able
successfully to defend himself."[1] He was drafted from this town,
commissioned lieutenant, and served under Captain James Littlefield.
In 1778, he went to Wells (Kennebunk), built a house and a store,
and engaged in ship-building. He transferred his business from the
Mousam to the Landing, enlarged his operations, but, having lost
several vessels by shipwreck, he became embarrassed. "Under these
depressing circumstances he went to William Gray, of Salem, and
told him his condition. So high an opinion had Mr. Gray of his
integrity, that he told him to go on with his ship-building and he
would take care of him. He did so, and again prosperity attended
him; and though some of his vessels were taken by the French, he
still maintained a safe pecuniary standing."[1] His hospitality to
teamsters from the country became proverbial, and burdensome to
his family; and to alleviate their labors, he abandoned his business
and removed to Alfred in 1803. In 1808, he returned to Kennebunk,
and on the 16th of January, died suddenly, aged fifty-nine years.

LOW, EBENEZER, JUNIOR, EPHRAIM, JUNIOR, JEDEDIAH, and JONA-
THAN. The Lows came from Wells. Ephraim, Junior, was the son

[1] Bourne's "History of Wells and Kennebunk."

FRANK H. DEXTER.

of Ephraim, who lived where Bert Goodrich now lives, and was born March 14, 1748. He married a Miss Littlefield, of Wells, and moved before 1777, on to the ridge, which, from him, received the name Low's ridge (now Shaw's). He was a noted bear hunter, and is said to have killed one year as many bears as there were days in that year. He had six children, five daughters and one son. We think that he must have had two wives, because Ephraim Low, Junior, of Sanford, married Esther Lewis, of Berwick, June 15, 1788. One of his daughters, Lucy, was the first wife of General Shaw. His son, Ephraim, 3rd, was commissioned lieutenant in 1811, served in the War of 1812, and was adjutant of the Third Regiment, first brigade, first division (after separation), from 1818 to 1826. In the latter year Ephraim and Ephraim, Junior (the first Ephraim had long been dead), removed to Mercer, Me., where the former died March 14, 1834, and the latter, February 1, 1859, aged seventy-five. Jedediah Low, a brother of the first Ephraim, came from Wells during the war, or soon after, and settled on a farm above Springvale. In 1785, having received from the agents of Massachusetts, a deed of the land upon which he lived, concerning which there was a famous lawsuit, years later (Allen vs. Littlefield), he sold the same and removed to Shapleigh. His son, Jeremiah, was the father of the late Asa Low, Esquire, of Springvale. Jonathan Low was in town in 1788-9. There is a tradition that the Ephraim who served in the Revolution was shot in the nose at the battle of Bunker Hill.

MERRILL (MEREAL), SAMUEL. Perhaps it was this Samuel Merrill that married Miriam Rankins, November 14, 1793.

NASSON, PETER. He was born about 1763, and served as a drummer boy at the age of twelve. He was the son of Major Samuel Nasson, and probably came into town with his father's family. He died in December, 1784.

NASSON, SAMUEL. He enlisted from York, May 2, 1775, in Colonel Scammans's regiment, where he served eight months as quartermaster, and was ensign and quartermaster in Colonel William Prescott's Seventh Continental regiment during the year 1776. He served through the siege of Boston and took part in the Long Island campaign. There is a tradition that he crept three miles on his hands and knees to set Boston on fire when held by the British.

NORTON, NATHANIEL. He died in Limington November 22, 1831. His wife, named Hannah, survived him.

NUTTER, HENRY. He was one of the original members of the Baptist Church.

6

PATTEE (PETTE), MOSES. He lived in the Moulton neighborhood, removed to Fryeburg, and was one of the original members of the branch of the Sanford Baptist Church there.

PEABODY (PEBODY), JEDEDIAH. Sergeant Peabody was born in Boxford, Mass., April 11, 1748, and removed to Sanford, North Parish, where, in 1776, he married Alice Howlet. In 1781, he removed to Henniker, N. H., with his ox-team. He arrived at Hopkinton on a Saturday night, and the next morning yoked up his oxen and proceeded on his journey. He soon met some tything-men, who informed him that he could not go any farther. As he was anxious to reach his destination, he remonstrated, but it was of no avail. He was obliged to put up his team until Monday morning. His residence was in Warner, near the Henniker line. He died in East Lebanon, N. H., about 1825.

PEABODY, SETH. He was the son of Matthew and Sarah (Dorman) Peabody, and was born in Topsfield, Mass., November 27, 1744. He came to Alfred, where he married Abigail Kimball, in 1771. He was one of the builders of Conant's mill, and lived some thirty rods west of his brother-in-law, Thomas Kimball. He was in Captain Jesse Dorman's company in 1775 from Wells, and later enlisted for Topsfield, but was mustered in Boxford. From May, 1777 to December 31, 1779, he was in Captain Hitchcock's company, Colonel Sprout's regiment, and also served in 1780. He died in Canaan, Me., in 1827.

PENNEY, PELATIAH, and SALATHIEL. They served from Wells in 1775. Salathiel was also a three years' man from Wells in 1777. After the war Pelatiah lived on "Grammar Street," and sold his place to Samuel Shaw. He died in Barnstead, N. H., in 1842, aged eighty-five years. Salathiel married Margaret Grant, December 28, 1788, and was then living in town.

PERRY, STEPHEN. He was in town in 1788-9. In 1805 or 6 he lived at Denmark.

POWERS, JONATHAN, NATHAN and WILLIAM. These were sons of Elder Thomas W. Powers. Jonathan was a Baptist elder, and preached in "Back Street." Nathan lived on "Grammar Street," and was a deacon of the Baptist Church nearly twenty-six years. William lived where Daniel Garey owned a farm on "Grammar Street."

QUINT, JOHN. He was in town in 1788, and a pensioner living with John Quint, in 1840. He was born about 1761. He was a privateersman, and died in 1856.

RICHARDSON, ELDER ZEBADIAH. He served nine months in the Revolution, prior to becoming pastor of the Sanford Baptist Church.

ROBINSON, ELDER OTIS. He was also a pastor of the Baptist Church. In 1778, at the age of fourteen, he enlisted in the Continental army from Attleborough, Mass., and served through the war.

SHACKFORD, SAMUEL. He was born about 1761, served eight months in 1780 in the eastern part of the state, married Eunice Day, November 15, 1787, and lived at Mouse Lane. He was a pensioner, living with Christopher Shackford, in 1840.

SHAW, SAMUEL. He was born in York, August 7, 1757, and was a soldier from that town. He was among those who enlisted for the defence of Rhode Island in 1777, as attested by his receipt for fourteen pounds "as bounty for serving as a soldier for Providence." In 1788 he came into town, moving into a log house between the Hay Brook and the site of the house in which he afterward lived, upon the place bought of Pelatiah Penney. He occupied that for eight years, and then built a one-story house, subsequently raised another story by his son, General Timothy Shaw. He was a lieutenant in the militia in 1800, was pensioned eight dollars per month from February 13, 1808, and continued a pensioner until his death, June 28, 1840. His wife, Patience, died September 2, 1840, aged eighty-five.

STAPLES, WILLIAM. He was in town in 1788–9. He died in Bethel, February 15, 1832.

STRAW, VALENTINE. "Vol" Straw married Sarah Coffin, and settled near the site of the Shaker saw mill. He became a "Merry Dancer." Abiel H. Johnson told the writer that the quota of Sanford, at one time, met at his grandfather's inn to start for the front, and that among them was "Vol" Straw.

SWETT (SWEET), MOSES. Lieutenant Swett came from New Hampshire about 1772, and lived in a small house thirty rods east of Swett's bridge. About 1795, he built a two-story house opposite, which was moved in 1801 a mile north.

TAYLOR, ELIPHALET. "Life" Taylor, as he was called, married Martha Lord, March 8, 1787, and lived on the Linscott mill privilege. He was a very intemperate man, and once, when not quite himself, threatened to kill his wife, whom he accused of being a witch. He quoted the Mosaic law, "Thou shalt not suffer a witch to live," to prove that he would be justified in taking her life. His neighbor, Mr. Clark, turned him from his purpose by offering to "swap" wives with him for thirty wooden tubs "to boot." Taylor, who was a cooper, accepted the offer in good faith, but was not ready for the exchange. Clark never heard any more about "swapping" wives, nor did Mrs. Taylor suffer death at her husband's hands. Taylor was wont to tell an interesting story of his experience at Saratoga, the day before Burgoyne was taken, when Gates's men, of whom he was one, were ordered to lie on their backs in a hollow in front of the British works. Of course they growled somewhat, being inclined to think the misery of lying there was more than the danger of rising. At last one man near "Life" asked the comrade next to him : "Tom, what do you suppose Molly would say if she knew where you are now?" "Humph! I don't know," replied Tom, popping up his head. At that instant a cannon ball whizzed by, and poor Tom's head went with it. A thrill of horror ran through his fellows, and after this every soul kept still until the firing ceased at night. "It was the longest day I ever lived," declared Taylor afterwards. The American troops were surprised the next morning, he said, to see that Burgoyne was ready to surrender on the first invitation to do so.

TAYLOR, JOSHUA. His name appears on tax lists of 1788 and 9, and on voting list of 1805.

TAYLOR, NOAH, and OBADIAH. There is a tradition that Obadiah Taylor lost a leg in the service, and another that Noah also lost a leg Whether or not the two have been confounded, we cannot say. Noah was in Captain Merrill's company at Bennington in 1777, enlisting from Wells, and in Captain Hitchcock's company, in 1780. He died in the hospital, December 1, 1780.

TEBBETS, HENRY. He was the son of Moses Tebbets, a centenarian of South Sanford. He joined the Baptist Church, having been baptized at Massabesec, November 22, 1772, by Elder Pelatiah Tingley.

THOMPSON, JOSEPH. He probably removed to Francisborough (Cornish), and was one of the members of the branch Baptist Church there, 1788.

THOMPSON, PHINEHAS. The ancestors of Deacon Thompson lived in York. He married Martha, daughter of Samuel Willard, of York, in 1762, and removed from Gorhamtown (Gorham) to Sanford about 1765. He was a farmer and a blacksmith, and lived near Thompson's, now Butler's bridge. He was one of the original members of the Baptist church, and for many years one of its deacons. He was the father of Ezra, Samuel, Isaac, John, Martha, Hannah, Mary and Phinehas Thompson. Deacon Thompson died March 6, 1815, aged about seventy years.

TRAFTON, BENJAMIN. He came from York after the war, and settled in York Street. He was a sergeant, was in the battles of Bunker Hill and Monmouth, and in the retreat under General Lee. He was lieutenant of militia in 1792.

TRIPP (TRIPE), BENJAMIN. Lieutenant Tripp was one of the builders of Conant's mill, and lived a short distance north of it. He removed to Lyman.

TRIPP, ROBERT. He was the son of Samuel Tripp, who settled back of Lyon's Hill. In 1840 he was a pensioner, living with Robert Tripp. He died at Solomon Allen's, August 28, 1845. Two of his children were Olive and Robert.

TRIPP, WILLIAM. He was born in Kittery, January 17, 1750, and died in Sanford, March 12, 1828. His first wife was Dorcas, daughter of Ephraim Low, by whom he had five children, Jotham, William, Thomas, Nathaniel and Catherine. His second wife was Keziah Thompson, who bore him three sons, William, Richard and Robert, and nine daughters, Dorcas, Catherine, Sarah, Keziah, Mary, Eunice, Margery, Margaret, and Anna. William became a minister, and Robert lived and died on the old homestead. In 1777, William owned a lot on the east side of the Mousam River, but subsequently removed to " Grammar Street, " where he lived and died.

TRUE, OBADIAH. He was born in 1758. He entered the army at seventeen, and practically served all through the war. After the surrender of Burgoyne he came home on a furlough, and shipped for his return at Portsmouth, N. H., on a schooner bound for Boston. The first day out she was captured by a British cruiser, and True was taken prisoner and carried to England, where he remained in prison a year or more. He was released in season to take part under General Wayne at the storming of Stony Point in July, 1779. He enlisted in the War of 1812, though not from Sanford, and served until its close. These facts are contained in statements made to the writer by Joseph Bennett and Abiel H. Johnson. True left town before 1805, removed to Denmark, Me., and lived there to a good old age, dying in November, 1844. Though he could neither read nor write, he had a retentive memory, and could relate with much force the incidents of his soldier life.

WADLIA (WADLEY, WADLEIGH), DANIEL. A native of Berwick, he served from that town as a private, in Captain Philip Hubbard's company, Colonel Scammans's regiment, in 1775, as a sergeant in Captain Samuel Derby's company, Colonel John Bailey's regiment, and also in Captain Jedediah Goodwin's company, Colonel Joseph Prime's regiment, under General Wadsworth, from May 3 to November 20, 1780. Prior to 1788, he came into town, and owned a house and farm on the Lebanon road, near the site of the old Baptist meeting house. His grandson, Hiram Witham, said of him : " He

took his first lesson at Bunker Hill, and received his diploma at York-
town. He was with Wayne in the assault on Stony Point, was in
Lafayette's division in the battle of Brandywine, and was one of the
army under Washington, when he wintered at Valley Forge. When
Lafayette visited this country in 1824, he went to Kennebunk and
saw his old commander. They recognized each other, although they
had been separated more than forty years."

WALES (WHALES), GEORGE. " He was at a place at the head of
Sanford, and bordering thereon, not in any town, parish, or village,"
in 1777. In 1784 he was at Ossipee. In December, 1780, one George
Whales was living in Shapleigh.

WEBBER, DANIEL. Lieutenant Webber moved into town after the
war, and prior to 1788, and bought the lot lying along the Mousam,
formerly owned by William Tripp. He was an ensign, afterward
second lieutenant in Colonel Bailey's regiment, commissioned first
lieutenant April 30, 1782, and was in Colonel Sproat's regiment in
1783. He was adjutant of Colonel Caleb Emery's regiment of militia
from 1790 to 1794, when he removed to Hancock County, where he
was living in 1818, when pensioned by act of Congress; but, returning to Sanford, he died February 1, 1827. He was a member of the
Massachusetts Society of the Cincinnati.

WEBBER, PAUL. After the war he came from Cape Neddock, and
was hired on the farm of the widow of Samuel Friend, who became
his wife; he built the George W. Came house, and about the year
1795 erected a large house at Alfred village ; for many years he kept
a hotel and grocery store ; was captain of the militia. He returned
to the Came house in 1808, and there died, leaving one son, Paul.

WEYMOUTH, STEPHEN. He lived in 1781 near the Great Works
brook, on the Lebanon road, in part then laid out.

WHITE, CHARLES, and JOHN. In 1766, Charles White, son of
Robert, of York, came into town from Kennebunkport, where his
father had settled in 1740. His wife was Sarah Lindsey. He lived
two or three years about a hundred rods west of the brick house
built by Andrew Conant, in the White field. Charles and his brother,
John, erected half of a double saw-mill, which with their land
they exchanged for another tract of land half a mile south on the
Mousam road. Charles was succeeded by his son, Deacon Samuel
White, while John was succeeded by his son, John, Junior.

WITHAM, AARON. He was born May 4, 1750, and died July 14,
1841.

WITHAM, GATNSBY. He was in town in 1783, and lived above the

Corner on the west side of the road, but whether he moved into town subsequently to the Revolution, we have no knowledge.

WITHAM, JEREMIAH. These three Withams probably descended from the York family of that name. More than a century ago, Jeremiah Witham bought 300 acres of land lying east of "Grammar Street" (most of it in the present town of Alfred), and moved his family from Berwick. A part of the land was subsequently owned by Hiram Witham, and was retained in the Witham family until a comparatively few years ago. Jeremiah Witham was a soldier in the French and Indian War, was wounded in one shoulder, and carried the bullet to his grave. While the army was at Cambridge in 1775, under Putnam, he received a furlough bearing General Putnam's signature, which was cherished for more than a century as a relic by the family. Witham's five children, four daughters and one son, lived to mature age, and died leaving no children. He died May 12, 1806, aged seventy-five years.

WITHAM, JONATHAN. There is a tradition that he served on the "Bon Homme Richard," under John Paul Jones, before he came to Sanford.

WITHAM, SIMEON. He resided near the Haleys in York Street, and also at the grist-mill that once stood a quarter of a mile west of the late Aaron Littlefield's.

WORSTER, THOMAS. He came from Berwick. Died in Sanford, March, 1822 (?). He left a widow named Susan.

WORSTER, WILLIAM. Born in Berwick in 1754, he was in his boyhood apprenticed to a blacksmith of Portsmouth, Chadbourn by name, with whom he learned his trade. He enlisted and served eighteen months during the war, and then, as tradition runs, several months longer at the request of General Washington. After that service, he sailed in a privateer, so goes the story, was taken prisoner by the English, and kept till the war closed. Soon after the war he came into this town, settling above the Deering neighborhood. He began his blacksmith business near his house, and then moved his shop into the hollow where the same business was continued for so many years by his son Samuel and grandson Fernald. He was a pensioner. He died August 7, 1842, aged eighty-eight years. His first wife, Susannah, died April 26, 1802, aged thirty-five, and his second, Eleanor, November 24, 1852, aged one hundred years and six months.

YORK, NATHANIEL F. He lived in the Gore, and built a mill there.

We have dwelt thus long upon this portion of the town's history, because we have felt that the memory of our heroes should be perpetuated. They left their homes, imperilled their lives, performed weary marches, endured the severities of winter campaigns, and passed through the terrible ordeal of battle, that independence for themselves and their posterity might be won. We take pride in the foregoing list, because it contains so many names, and reveals the spirit of our ancestors. But there are others worthy of commendation. The men and women who remained at home, and engaged in peaceful pursuits that they might support those in the field, suffered and sacrificed much. We honor those noble men, soldiers and civilians, and praise the patriotic women of the Revolution, to each of whom should be attributed a part of the glory of achieving our national independence.

CHAPTER VII.

AFTER THE REVOLUTION.

Establishment of New Form of Government — Division into Parishes — Alfred Set off and Incorporated — Boundary Troubles — Disputed Land Titles — Fryeburg and Groton — First Direct Tax.

THE subject of establishing a form of government by the people had been discussed in Massachusetts even before the Declaration of Independence was passed, but no decisive action was taken until September of 1776, when a committee of the General Court recommended that the Representatives elected thereto be empowered to act for the establishment of a new government. The action of the town of Sanford in this matter was not so decisive and pronounced as upon other public questions. The inhabitants stood aloof, simply expressing a willingness on their part, and passively waiting for other men to act. In accordance with the foregoing recommendation, they voted on the 14th of October to send a Representative vested with the powers desired, but on the 22nd the vote was reconsidered, and it was simply "Voted that this Town are willing for the house of Representative and Counsel to form a state government."

A constitution drafted by delegates chosen on recommendation of the General Court in 1777 being rejected by the people in 1778, a call for another convention was issued the following year. Instructed again to lay the subject before the town, the selectmen of Sanford issued a warrant for a meeting to be held at the house of Nathaniel Conant, May 24, 1779: (1) "To see whether they chuse at this time to have a new Constitution or form of Government made;" and (2) "To see whether they will impower their Representatives for the next year to vote for the calling a State Convention for the Sole Purpose of forming a new Constitution." Nothing seems to have been done at that meeting, or no record of action taken was made. The majority of the people, however, were desirous of having a convention called, and the General Court issued precepts for delegates to be chosen to meet at Cambridge on the first Wednesday of September, 1779. This town again did nothing in regard to it, except to vote on the 21st of August, " not to send any delegate to represent them in said convention. "

The delegates convened at the time and place aforesaid, and framed a constitution, which, early in 1780, was ordered to be printed. A copy was sent to each town and plantation for approval or disapproval. A town meeting was called in Sanford May 25, to examine the several articles in the new form of government, at which the following action was taken :

" Voted to Chouse a committee to make Remarks on a number of the ortacles in said form ; Voted to make Remarks on the third ortacle ; Voted the Said Committee to take under consideration the ortacle of the Governor Sinneters and Councellors that shall be Prodistants ; Voted the 7 ortacle to be taken under consideration ; Voted Walter Powers Ebenezer Bussel Daniel Gile Jonathan Tibbetts and Nath[l] Cunnant Be a Committee for the above Purpose, and make Report the next meeting."

The third article referred to is the Bill of Rights and provides for the religious instruction of the people. Throughout the state, alterations relating to that article were proposed. Satisfied of the importance of religious teachers to the welfare of society and the morals of the people, all, undoubtedly, desired perfect toleration. No one was to be molested on account of his religious opinions, and no denomination was to have exclusive or peculiar privileges. Those sects inferior in number and in wealth were opposed to anything that seemed, by implication even, to discourage their existence or to limit their resources. The Baptists especially were inclined to complain, because they were obliged to apply for special license to leave one society to join another.[1] The seventh article, to which reference is made, is the seventh article either of the second chapter, which relates to the powers and duties of the Governor as commander-in-chief of the militia, or of the sixth chapter, which contains provisions respecting the privilege and benefit of the writ of *habeas corpus*, both of which were objected to and quite fully discussed. As there is nothing in any section with regard to officers being Protestants, we cannot understand why the town should discuss a point settled in the convention, when the word " Protestant" was rejected. Perhaps, however, the term " Christian " was regarded by the inhabitants as

---

[1] Bradford's " History of Massachusetts," Vol. II.

synonymous with "Protestant," and they desired a free and full opinion of the declaration to be made by the Governor, Lieutenant Governor, Councillor, Senator, or Representative, before entering upon the duties of his office: "I, A. B., do declare that I believe the Christian religion, and have a firm persuasion of its truth." The more probable construction to put upon it is that they wished a religious qualification or test, and desired that their chief magistrate and representatives should be Protestants, in the literal acceptation of the term.

When the town met at the adjourned meeting, in John Knight's barn, June 1, they "Voted not to Except the Report of the Committee Brought in Concerning the several ortacles Brought in against the form of Government; not to act anything upon the new form of Government; not to Except the Committee's Report Brought in Concerning the 7th ortacle." Thus they dismissed the important subject, leaving other towns to accept or reject the new constitution. They seem to have overcome the difficulty by having nothing to do with it, though they virtually accepted the constitution by their non-acceptance of the report of the committee against the new form of government.

On the 16th of June, 1780, the convention having decided that the constitution as submitted to the people had been accepted, passed a resolution that the first election of Governor, Lieutenant Governor, Councillors and Senators should be held in September, and for Representatives in October. On the 4th of September the town cast fourteen votes for Governor, all of which "the Honorable John Hancock, Esqr.," received. No Representative was chosen in October, nor was the town represented in the General Court until 1785, when Caleb Emery was chosen to fill the office.

According to the early laws, the parish embraced the whole town. In process of time, divisions arose on account of the formation of different societies or churches, and the inconveniences arising from an extensive parish. As parish matters were town matters, any question concerning a division must be acted upon by the town, and then by the General Court. On the 11th of March, 1782, the town chose a committee to see where the town should be divided into two parishes so as to accommodate all, and when on the 2nd of April they reported favorably, another committee was appointed to draw up a petition to send to the General Court, with reference to the division. The result was the formation of two parishes, the first step toward a division into two towns. The act of the General Court was passed July 1. This act provided that the parishes should be known respectively as the South Parish and the North Parish; that the division should be by a line beginning " at the head of the township of Wells, at Mousam River, so called; thence running up the eastern branch thereof, to the mouth of a certain brook, called the Hay Brook; then up said brook to a certain place known by the name of Staple's Marsh; then northwest to the head of the said town of Sanford;" that the two parishes should be vested with "all the powers, rights, privileges and immunities " enjoyed by other parishes in the commonwealth; and that meetings should be called to choose officers to manage the affairs of the parishes.

In 1790 Samuel Nasson, William Parsons and Henry Smith, selectmen (?) of Sanford, petitioned the General Court that the town be incorporated into two districts, the north and the south, the former to be called Smithfield, and to have all the privileges of a town without the privilege of sending a Representative to the legislature. The reasons for this petition were that a barren pitch-pine plain and a large spruce swamp unfit for settlement lay between the two parishes, and some years passage was very difficult from one parish to the other on account of the flow of water. A bill to divide passed the house February 18, 1791, but was rejected in the senate three days later.

In 1791 a petition signed by Parsons and Smith, selectmen, and one hundred and nine others, stated that the sense of the town was misrepresented in 1790. There was a very full meeting, and the vote was carried by a large majority of the principal inhabitants.

From the petition, it appears that the signers, for the most part, lived in the North Parish, and the objection to the division arose in the other parish. In 1793 (June 10), however, the town " Vot^d that the North Parish Shall be set of as a District and to have all the Preveledges as the other Town has: forty-two for it & four against it. Vot^d Wm Parson and Caleb Emery Esq and Henry Smith Chosen a Committee to draw a Petion to Send to the General Court and they are to Prosecute the Same at there Discretion." The opposition at this time was so small and powerless that there was no great difficulty in securing the desired legislation, and on the 4th of February, 1794, the North Parish was incorporated, by an Act of the General Court, into a district by the name of Alfred, with all the privileges of a town, except that of sending a Representative. The Representative was to be chosen by Sanford and Alfred jointly, at elections held in the town and district alternately.

The history of the North Parish henceforth ceases to be a part of the history of Sanford. By the act of 1794 Alfred was virtually made a town united with Sanford in the formation of a Representative district, though it retained the name of district and was recognized as such in all of its official acts, until it received the rank and privileges of a town by act of February 25, 1808.

This was done upon the petition of William Parsons and others, in May, 1807, and the vote of the town of Sanford, December 14, 1807, expressing a willingness for Alfred to be incorporated into a distinct town. The petition of Parsons and others declared, in part, that " the opposite interests of the two incorporations make it extremely inconvenient for us who are the minority to enjoy that right of suffrage which is so wisely secured to us by the constitution." What "the opposite interests " were, we have no definite means of knowing. For ten years the town and district had no representation at the General Court. Two years they were represented by the strongest man they could send, — John Holmes, then a Federalist, — though the first year the selectmen were to give him directions. Two years they sent two Representatives, Nathaniel Conant, Junior, of Alfred, and Thomas Keeler, of Sanford. One year Keeler's seat was contested by John Sayward, of Alfred, but unsuccessfully. We surmise, however, that " the opposite interests " were political interests, because Sanford was strongly Anti-Federal, giving an overwhelming majority for Jefferson in 1804. This idea is strengthened by the fact that when the town voted twice, in 1804, to send no Representative, John Holmes and nineteen others petitioned the selectmen to call a meeting to choose a Representative.

The first settler of Alfred was Simeon Coffin, who dwelt, in November, 1764, " in an Indian wigwam, that stood a few rods south of the present residence of Colonel Ivory Hall." The next year several others came in, and for ten years a large accession was made.

Williamson informs us that the town was named for Alfred the Great, and says : " Alfred (eighty-fourth town), when incorporated into a district, was vested with all town privileges, except it continued united to Sanford, in the choice of a Representative, till large enough to choose one. The village is on a plain ; the side of which, and the territory about two miles square, were claimed under the Governor's right (Hutchinson and Oliver) and was long in dispute. The title to the residue of the town is the same as in Sanford. Alfred has been a shire-town since September, 1803. A post-office was established here in 1800."

Although Alfred had become a town, it seems not to have been separated ecclesiastically from Sanford; or at least not to have been independent of the parent society; for on the 2nd of May, 1808, Sanford " Voted the petition from Alfred praying they may be incorporated into a Society by the name of the first parish in Alfred be granted."

The early days of the incorporate town were not free from disputes with adjacent towns over the boundary lines. The proprietors had previously, on several occasions, appointed agents to perambulate the lines, but evidently the latter were not definitely settled. Soon after Lyman, or Coxhall, was incorporated in 1778, there was a dispute with Sanford regarding the boundary, arising, apparently, out of the indefinite terms of Fluellin's deed to Major Phillips. Sanford, in town meeting, " Voted and agreed we Give no part of the Town (the eight miles square) away to that part called Coxhall." The matter was finally settled by the joint action of committees from both towns.

After the claim of the heirs of Nicholas Shapleigh to a tract of land above Sanford had been established by the General Court, a question arose about the boundaries of the Shapleigh township and the Phillips tract. This dispute was settled by the legislature in favor of Sanford. When Shapleigh was incorporated, March 5, 1785, all " Gores " adjoining Sanford, not belonging to any other incorporated town, except those belonging to the plantation of Massabesec, were annexed to Sanford. This annexation was repugnant to some of the inhabitants of the " Gores," who petitioned that the tracts be made a part of Shapleigh, because they were " fearful that Sanford being an old town was in debt," and they wished to be taxed in one town. A committee from Sanford investigated the matter, and reported that signatures to the petition had been obtained through the influence of " designing men," and that certain signers had been coerced because " they were under embarrassments to some persons," and that the petition did not represent the real sentiment. The General Court, however, repealed in part the annexation act of 1785, and annexed five hundred acres to Lebanon, and twenty-seven hundred acres to Shapleigh. This encouraged further Sanford petitioners for annexation to Shapleigh, on the ground of lower taxes, in 1792, but this time the Sanford protest proved availing. In 1795 another unsuccessful attempt was made to annex a portion of Sanford to Shapleigh.

Meanwhile, in 1779, trouble had arisen with regard to the Berwick line. By the original survey, the boundary was very indefinite, being largely fixed by a certain hemlock tree. The failure of committees from the two towns to agree resulted in years of controversy and litigation, recourse being had to the General Court and to the law courts. Suits were instituted by Nathaniel Bennett, John Thurston and others of Sanford, against Reuben Chadbourn and Simon Tebbets of Berwick, to recover for alleged trespass in the cutting of timber on lands claimed by the plaintiffs. During 1802 decisions in these cases were given in favor of the inhabitants of Sanford, but the boundary question was finally settled in 1804 in favor of Berwick.

Disputes over land titles were frequent in the early days. In 1761, on petition of the proprietors of the common and undivided lands in Phillipstown, the General Court passed a bill annulling the division made in 1730, in order that the proprietors might be enabled to proceed to a new division of the lands held in common, the provision being made that the bill should not affect the right or title of any person actually settled upon lands assigned him before the division of 1730. This petition was brought because no plan of the ancient division could be found.

In 1791 the courts were called upon to establish the title of Frances Shirley Western, widow, residing in England, daughter and sole heir of William Bollan, of Boston, deceased, to a tract of about fifteen hundred acres lying along the head-line of Berwick. Bollan had bought the land in 1738 of William Phillips, grandson of Major William, and long after his death, no claimant appearing, the tract was sold for taxes, subject to the right of redemption. It had meanwhile, in part, been occupied and improved. In 1793 it was sold in small lots, under constable and collector sales, to some thirty grantees. One of these, Samuel Willard, had bought of Eleazer Chadbourn in 1780, to pay taxes, but paid one hundred and fifteen pounds additional in 1793. We can easily account for the tradition, " My grandfather paid for his land twice."

The lands conveyed to Edward Bromfield in 1718 and 1730 gave rise to controversy and trouble. Between 1804 and 1812 Bromfield's heirs took steps to recover the estates of their ancestor, with the result that a large tract, already occupied by supposed grantees, was divided among them. These settlers had bought their lands in good faith, but the prior claims, not having been satisfied, still existed. Several of the grantees repurchased their rights of the Bromfield heirs. A number of lawsuits were instituted. There was also a controversy over the Governor Hutchinson lands, claimed by the heirs of Peleg Sanford.

To us judging from records and plans, it seems that the majority of the early occupants of the territory above the nineteen thousand acres settled thereon without any title, but subsequently came into lawful possession by actual purchase, though the right of redemption remained with those whose lands were sold to pay taxes.

Sanford seems to have been a point of departure for the early settlers of Fryeburg, and to have entertained relations of friendship with that frontier town. It was also a centre of trade. In his "Centennial Address," Rev. Mr. Souther notes the fact that, in 1763, "there were no settlements between Fryeburg and Sanford, a distance of sixty miles, and no bridges across the rivers and streams." A county road was laid out between the two towns in 1783. In 1788, seven persons residing in Fryeburg became members of the Sanford Baptist Church, and two years later were embodied into a church, to which Elder Richardson ministered after leaving Sanford. New centres of enterprise and business sprang up, and the intimate relations ceased to exist.

After the Revolution, a number of the inhabitants of Sanford removed to Groton, Vt., and became prominent in the affairs of that town. Among them were Deacon Josiah Paul, and Sarah, his wife, Captain William Frost, Dominicus Gray, Captain Ephraim Gary, Captain Stephen Roberts, Foxwell Whitcher, Moses, Moses, Junior, and Samuel Plummer, and Obadiah Low.

Although there was previous taxation, the first direct tax was laid in 1798. Sanford, Lebanon and Shapleigh comprised the sixteenth district of the second division of the District of Maine. Caleb Emery was the principal assessor, and Samuel Nasson, Eleazar Chadbourn, Thomas M. Wentworth, Andrew Rogers, and Jeremiah Emery, assistant assessors. They received one dollar and fifty cents a day. The tax list bears date October 1, 1798.

CHAPTER VIII.

THE FIRST CHURCH.

Organization of the Baptist Church, 1772, and Ordination of Rev. Pelatiah Tingley—Sketch of his Life—Growth of the Church— Incorporation of the Society—First Meeting-House and Subsequent Places of Worship—Pastors and Deacons.

TWO objects of prime importance engaged the attention of the early settlers,—the church and the school. The proprietors well understood the needs and demands of a young community, and were far-sighted enough to endeavor to meet them, as we have already seen, although their offers of land and money did not result in the formation of a church.

At first, missionaries occasionally passed through the township on their eastern tours. and held religious meetings in dwelling-houses and barns, or even the open air. The Rev. Messrs. Daniel Little, of Wells (Kennebunk), Matthew Merriam, of Berwick, and Abial Abbott were among those who visited the town and awakened deep interest.

As soon as the town was incorporated, the people began to raise money for preaching the Gospel. In 1770 and 1771 it was voted to hire a minister three months, and in 1772 to raise thirty pounds to defray the expenses of preaching and other incident charges. The next year it was decided to petition the General Court to tax the non-resident land owners toward building a meeting-house and hiring an orthodox minister. In 1778, one hundred pounds, and in 1779, five hundred, were raised for preaching. All of these votes, and others of a similar character, were in accordance with the laws of the Commonwealth, which made it compulsory for the people to provide for preaching, by an " able, learned orthodox minister."

Although matters tended so strongly to promote the interests of the Congregationalists, of whom there were a number in the plantation, the Baptists were the first to organize a church in the town. How did this happen? Some had embraced the Baptist doctrine

7   (97)

before coming to Sanford, and others soon after. The Coffins, who settled in the northeast part of the town in 1764 and 1765, came from Newbury, Mass., where they had heard Elder Hezekiah Smith preach. They were his coadjutors when his missionary labors called him to Maine. He visited Sanford in 1766, 1768, and 1771, preaching at the houses of Daniel and Simeon Coffin, and during one of his journeys an extensive revival occurred in the new township. But the Coffins were not the only Baptists in the settlement. There was in town, in 1768, a minister of the same faith with Elder Smith, Elder Thomas Walter Powers. In 1755, he was ordained as pastor of a Baptist Church organized at Newtown (now Newton), N. H. Removing to Sanford, he settled in the south part of the town, and there he was somewhat instrumental in building up a society of Baptists. Some of his sons helped nurture the growing society in its infancy. Walter, Jonathan, and Timothy Powers followed in the footsteps of their father in proclaiming their views.

There was an influence from the Berwick church that pervaded the neighboring towns. In 1768, that church, the first of the Baptist denomination in Maine, was organized, and began its aggressive work. " As a result," says Worth, in his " Centennial Discourse," " a church was gathered in Sanford in 1772," the third Baptist Church in Maine.

Another person may be named in addition to those already mentioned, who was an active supporter of the church formed, and perhaps, the prime mover in the organization. Rev. Pelatiah Tingley, at first a Congregationalist, having been attracted to the Baptist faith by the preaching of Elder Hezekiah Smith at Haverhill, came to Sanford to labor among "the scattered brethren," and, under his personal influence, steps were taken towards the embodying of his followers into a church.

There is a tradition that eighteen persons, on August 17, 1772, held a preliminary meeting east of the John Powers house, near the Mousam River, at which it was decided to constitute a Baptist Church. This tradition is corroborated, in part at least, by the words of a vote passed at a church meeting, July 3, 1773: "Before our Begining which was voted to be Augt 1772." The organization, however, was effected on the 16th of September, and five weeks later, October 21, on a large rock in a field some rods southwest of the residence of Charles P. Moulton, Pelatiah Tingley was ordained as elder. A council had previously been called, composed of "messengers " from the churches in Haverhill, Stratham, Brentwood, Deerfield, and Berwick. The records say:

" Then (according to the agreement of said messengers or chosen men), being congregated, Elder E. Smith officiated in prayer; Elder S. Shepherd preached a sermon suitable to the solemn occasion; Elder Shepherd also gave the charge ; Elder Hovey the right hand of fellowship — but after the teaching Elders and two of the private brethren had laid on hands, and one prayed. Then after prayer, singing, etc., Deac. Sleeper gave an excellent caution and exhortation to the church not to lean on ministers, etc. Then returned from the open air into the Wid° Powers's, and the house seemed in a few minutes space to be filled with the glory of the Lord.

" Then the solemn ordinance of Baptism was administered by Eld[r] Shepherd to eight persons, Moses Tebbets, Benj[a] Harmon, and Catherine his wife, Sarah Linscot, Susanna Haselton, Eunice Merril, Mary Sanbourn (Ruth Haselton was baptized by him next day at Berwick) and Anna Harmon. At night also (at Hale's), the power of God's love, etc., flowed very sweetly."

Who constituted the original church we cannot tell, but from the records we know that the following persons must have been among the number : Naphtali Harmon, Daniel Coffin, Walter Powers, Phineas Thompson, Eleazar Chadbourn, Stephen Johnson, Edward Harmon, John Powers, Timothy Powers, Daniel Hibbard, Joshua Chadbourn, Henry Nutter, Daniel Boston, Samuel Harmon, and Thomas Barnes. Thomas Bussel was probably an original member, while the other two, if tradition be correct in regard to the number, may have been wives of two male members. There is evidence that Elder Tingley was not included in the membership. Samuel Scribner was admitted into church fellowship a few days later. Naphtali Harmon and Daniel Coffin were chosen deacons.

Among the early church votes were those passed in regard to unnecessary apparel. " Dec[r]. 5th, 1772. Church met and voted That it shall be esteemed a matter of offence, 1, For a brother to wear more buttons on his clothes than are needful or convenient for ye body. 2, To wear a silken ribband on his hair. Also, for a sister, 1, To wear ruffles. 2, To bow ribbands. 3, To wear laces on their cloaks." On the first of March following, however, it was voted that " the sisters may wear the laces that are now on their cloaks." Alongside of these should be placed another : " Voted that ye deacons should endeavor to procure a coat and surtout and other smaller things for Elder Tingley as said deacons may think he needs."

Differences of opinion in regard to raising money for the support of the minister caused hard feeling in the young church, resulting in the withdrawal of one prominent officer and a "long declension," from which, however, the church successfully emerged. The rules of the society provided that the minister's "liberality" should be collected "by an equality according to that a man has and not according to that he has not, that there may be no oppressions amongst us." There seemed to be a disposition to have the "equality" bear as lightly as possible upon all. One member had his "equality" abated three pounds, old tenor, and the church voted, "That such as cannot so conveniently make up their equality otherwise, should be employed by the deacons to work on Brother Tingley's land." The trouble arose over the question of the time at which the "equality" should begin.

In July, 1773, sixteen baptized persons in Lebanon (of whom Philip Door was later chosen deacon) were received into the fellowship of the Sanford church, being a year later embodied into a church by themselves. One of the members, Tozier Lord, was licensed to preach, and ministered to the church in Lebanon. He was ordained in 1776, but three years later left the Baptists and joined in the Freewill Baptist movement. Elder Lord appears to have preached in Sanford in 1793–4.

In 1774, the church felt the need of a ruling elder, and made choice of Deacon Walter Powers. He began to preach probably, as early as 1780, for in 1783 the society voted "to raise a sum for Elder Powers and others" that had "improved their gifts with this society during the two years past." Subsequently he was pastor of the Baptist church of Gilmanton, N. H., for about twenty years.

A conference, embracing three churches, viz., Berwick, Sanford, and Brentwood, N. H., was formed in 1776, on the initiative of the Sanford body. In 1785 the New Hampshire Baptist Association was organized.

The records of the church from July 7, 1777, to November 18, 1786, are lost. The records of the society begin in 1783. Elder Tingley probably preached until 1780, though he did not leave town until 1782, perhaps later.

Elder Tingley's career was an interesting one. The second son of Ensign Timothy and Ruth (Patridge) Tingley, he was born in Attleborough, Mass., January 3, 1734/5. His father was a Representative from that town to the General Court in 1735. At the age of sixteen Pelatiah experienced religion, and united with the Congregational Church. He was graduated at Yale College, in 1761, and received the degree of Master of Arts in 1765. Meanwhile he studied theology two years, and was licensed to preach in 1762. We are told that, when he entered the ministry of the " standing order," he was " sadly backslidden in heart.[1]" In 1764 he was preaching in the West Parish of Haverhill, Mass., and during the next two years in Gorham, Maine. He declined a call to settle as pastor of the Congregational Church in the latter place, for the probable reason that, under the influence of Elder Hezekiah Smith at Haverhill, his doctrinal belief was undergoing a change, and he was in the valley of indecision. By November, 1767, the change had taken place, and he received the rite of baptism by immersion at the hand of Elder Smith, and united with the Baptist Church of Haverhill. Although he was permitted to " improve his gift," a license to preach was withheld until he should become firmly grounded in his new faith. In 1768, he was preaching in Weare, N. H., but whether with or without a license, we cannot say. We lose all traces of him from that time until he appears in Sanford. Our first introduction to him there is through a warrant in our possession, dated June 28, 1771, issued by the selectmen, by whom he is warned forthwith to depart out of the town, and disowned for an inhabitant.

The Chadbourns, Harmons, Thompsons, Coffins, and Powerses had preceded him, and his friend and co-laborer, Elder Smith, had, in his journeys into Maine, visited them several times. It is presumed that Elder Tingley was invited by them or sent among them to preach, or selected this frontier town as his field of labor, because it promised an abundant harvest. He so commended himself to the people that he was unanimously chosen " To be Ordained or Set apart to ye Work of an Elder, or Office of a Bishop," and was publicly ordained. For probably eight years he exercised the functions of pastor, and was zealous in his calling. His work extended beyond his own parish, his labors in a degree being those of a missionary; in fact, his church was a missionary church. In 1773 and 1780, we find him in Lebanon, preaching and baptizing converts; in 1775, receiving persons into the church at Gilmanton, N. H.; and in 1777, preaching at the North Church, Barnstead, N. H.

When the doctrine of election and atonement was discussed in Calvinistic churches, in 1780, he took the Arminian side, and was one of the founders of the Freewill Baptist denomination. He became a coadjutor of Elder Benjamin Randall, and took a prominent part in the organization of churches, travelling and preaching Free-

---

[1] Stewart's " History of the Freewill Baptists."

will doctrines. That he was second to Randall is evident, though Elder Tozier Lord seems to have been the first Baptist minister to preach to an anti-Calvinistic church. There are various authorities to show that Tingley was the first to unite with Randall in the Free-will movement. In 1781, through the efforts of these two elders, there were churches established in Woolwich, Georgetown, Hollis, Edgecomb, New Gloucester, and Parsonsfield.

Elder Tingley remained in Sanford until 1782. Though his views had changed, it is quite certain that the Baptist society had not given him up, even at a later period; for, on the 5th of July, 1783, they gave him an invitation to preach for them, which he declined to accept. According to Stewart, "the line of demarcation between the Calvinistic and Arminian Baptists was but faintly drawn for several years."

"I have a tradition from the Hibbard family," writes Rev. Hosea Quinby, "that in October, 1783, Randall, Tingley, and Hibbard met as strangers in Gorham (Hollis), had a season of prayer together, and held a conference for interchanging views, in which they found themselves in unison on doctrine, and the general principles of Christian enterprise, then and there agreeing upon the system of Quarterly Meetings, the first of which was in that place, December of the same year. Ever after Tingley stood as Randall's right-hand man." Tradition is true thus far at least: Elder Tingley was present at the organization of the Quarterly Meeting in Hollis, December 6, 1783. He was chosen clerk of that body, and had much to do with drawing up the covenant. It was a matter of special importance to him to attend Quarterly Meeting, and of the thirty-four sessions held prior to June, 1792, he was moderator once, and clerk twenty-four times.

In 1790 he was at Waterborough, where he organized a church. For twenty years he was actively engaged. He travelled among many frontier settlements in Maine, preaching and organizing churches, also visiting New Hampshire and Vermont. Many times he encountered strong opposition and even malicious persecution in the work of his denomination.

Elder Tingley was a delegate from Waterborough to the convention at Boston in 1788 which assented to and ratified the Constitution of the United States. He voted "nay" on the question of ratification.

Of his marriage we have no knowledge, except that he had a wife and one daughter; the former died before him, and the latter, Mrs.

Burrows, did not long survive him. On his farm in Waterborough he spent the declining years of his life. Even before "three-score years and ten" his appearance entitled him to the epithet "venerable," by which he was described, and he well deserved the title, by common usage conferred upon him, "Father" Tingley. At the age of eighty-six he attended the Quarterly Meeting at Waterborough, where he preached one of his short sermons of eight or ten minutes. "A few months after this he requested a visit from several of his brethren in the ministry, and a few other friends. The interview was one of great satisfaction to the good old man, now coming down to the grave, and rising from the bed, he stood in his sick-dress, divinely supported, and preached for a few minutes from the text, 'Render, therefore, unto Cæsar the things which are Cæsar's, and unto God the things that are God's.' He failed fast after this, and died early in the autumn, full of years and good works."[1]

In 1854, the Freewill Baptists erected a small, plain granite monument over his grave, at Waterborough, bearing this inscription: "Rev. Pelatiah Tingley, Died Sept. 3, 1821, Ae. 83. Mary, his wife, Died May, 1797, Ae. 51." If the date of his birth, as furnished by the historian of his native town, is correct, Elder Tingley was eighty-six years and eight months old on the day of his death.

Elder Tingley was a good man, though fond of innovation, and too much given to change. Zealous in his work, he was frequently impetuous. He spoke with power, and his words made an impression. He was quick-witted, and ready to reprove. One cold, blustering day, a rough fellow entered the public room in which Elder Tingley was seated, leaving the door open. Bantering, he accosted the unassuming preacher with the question, "Well, Elder, what did you learn in college?" "I learned to shut the door," was the timely answer. He usually spoke pointedly and incisively. "He was a man of short prayers, short sermons, and short speeches." Of the seven early prominent leaders of the Freewill Baptist denomination, Elder Tingley was the only one liberally educated. He was learned, understood the languages, and was useful in instructing his brethren. Especially was his power acknowledged when any letter or report was to be prepared. The tact and caution sometimes exercised, when matters of a delicate nature were to be disposed of, reveal the wisdom of a teacher, to whom had been given the power of a disciplined mind as well as the grace of a renewed heart. Precious, indeed, to the denomination whose early history is so closely connected with his life, should be the memory of " Father " Tingley.

Prior to 1783, or early in that year, a society of Baptists was formed in Sanford, and a constitution adopted. One of the articles provided that " all persons that offer themselves to join this society be examined of the motives they have in so doing." The reason for this was, that the Baptists, among other denominations, having been exempted from taxation for the support of the Congregational clergy, there were some persons who sought the protection of the society in order to evade payment of their taxes for supporting a minister, a proceeding which was not countenanced by the Baptists.

In 1786 a Mr. Webster was invited to " improve his gift" half the time for four months, and Elder Eliphalet Smith, formerly of Deerfield, N. H., received a similar invitation to preach the other half of the time. At this period meetings were held at the house of a Mr. Taylor, to whom the society paid one shilling per day for a room. On the 5th of October, 1786, Elder Zebadiah Richardson was called by vote of the society to preach part of the time, for which he was to receive " twenty-four shillings per Lord's Day when he improves with society." An endeavor was made to arrange for him to serve Coxhall in conjunction with Sanford, although Coxhall had a pastor, Elder Simon Locke. Perhaps, however, there was need of assistance in that portion of the town adjoining Sanford, and one minister could supply the wants of both societies. Thirty pounds were raised for the support of Elder Richardson's family, and ten, afterward reduced to six, for moving his family. That the society had to struggle to support him, and that he had to undergo the inconveniences of an unsettled life, are evident from the records.

" Voted that Indian corn (when contributed for Mr. Richardson's support) be 4/ per bushel, rye, 5/ per b., pork 2d. per lb., and other things in proportion. W. India and English goods at the market price."

" The society agreed to work on said Mr. Richardson's house upon the first Monday in October next." (1788.)

Elder Richardson closed his labors in 1790. It was at his request that the church and society paid him the amount due for his preaching, moved " his family to Plymouth (N. H.), or elsewhere as far distant," and gave " him a full fair discharge."

A few months prior to Elder Richardson's invitation to preach with the society, measures had been taken for building a meeting-house. The frame was raised in 1786, and, in June of that year, it was voted "to move it up to Mr. John Powers, and set it on his land at the corner near his dwelling-house, fronting to the southwest, said Powers giving said privilege to set it on, said house to be fitted for a society meeting-house, at the cost of the society from the stump." A committee of three was appointed to carry on the work, and forty pounds lawful money were to be proportioned by "equality" to enable them to complete the house.

At a subsequent meeting, a change of location was decided upon, and the society voted "to set the meeting-house on the N. E. of said Powers house, fronting to the S. E." Edward Stanley was selected as master of the underpinning, and Deacon Eleazar Chadbourn as master-workman to finish the house. In the fall of 1788, the society voted to convert the meeting-house frame to a dwelling-house for Elder Richardson. At the annual meeting, in April, 1789, by adjournment, all votes respecting the society meeting-house were reconsidered, and it was decided to fix the house for Elder Richardson, as previously mentioned. The forty pounds voted June 20, 1786, were to be used to finish the house and to pay Mr. Powers for ten acres of land for Elder Richardson. In view of the indecision, and of the fact that Elder Richardson had no permanent abiding place, there are good grounds for the tradition that Mrs. Richardson thought they better set the house on wheels so as to move it about easily, when he preached from place to place. It is quite satisfactory to know that the society voted "That Dea. Chadbourn's conduct in selling the house meant for Mr. Richardson was for the best."

It was during the ministry of Elder Richardson that two branch churches, one at Francisborough (Cornish), the other at Fryeburg, were organized, the former with twenty-two members, and the latter with seven. In 1790, the Fryeburg branch was constituted a separate church. The organization of the church at Francisborough came in 1792. Of this church John Chadbourn and William Sayer were deacons. Some of the members had removed to Cornish and Hiram from Sanford.

While Elder Tozier Lord was preaching in 1794, it was proposed by the society to build a meeting-house to be set near Deacon Chadbourn's. The site selected was at the forks of the roads leading over Hanson's ridge and Mount Hope. The structure was raised in the spring of 1794, and the lower part completed during the summer and fall. In October, 1794, the lower pews—twenty-two in number, with twelve half pews—were finished and sold at vendue. In 1797-8 the sixteen gallery pews were completed, and also sold by auction.

When this house was first occupied, " it was a two-story building, with outside porch, and high galleries inside : for years it was without plastering or means for a fire. Aged people a few years ago told how rich was the carving of the old-fashioned square pews, and of the quaint sounding-board high over the pulpit, that was itself even with the galleries." These extended nearly around the house. The lower pews were entered from a broad aisle, extending from the porch to the pulpit, and from narrow aisles forming on each side of the broad aisle three sides of a rectangle. The meeting-house stood near the present residence of Mrs. James Thompson. In 1795, the society purchased land and buildings of Dominicus Gray, for a parsonage, but after improving the land one year without a minister to occupy the dwelling, it was deemed advisable to sell the same.

Ebenezer Kinsman, a licentiate, preached for the society in 1796. After various attempts to obtain the services of a minister, in 1798, Otis Robinson, of Livermore, having supplied the pulpit, was called to the pastorate. The society raised seventy dollars for him, and paid the expenses of moving his family. Later his salary was fixed at one hundred dollars a year. His home was in the Deering neighborhood. On June 7, 1798, he was ordained to the ministry in the new church. This was the beginning of the flow of the tide, which had reached its lowest ebb. A general revival commenced with Elder Robinson's ministry, which, in two years, enlarged the church from thirty to one hundred and forty-four. This revival continued several years, and Elder Robinson during the first seven years of his ministry, baptized one hundred and fifty-nine persons. He was dismissed at his own request, after one request had been denied, March 3, 1810. The ministry of this good and useful man had not been without its troubles, and even dissensions.

In 1798 a number of Baptists at Lebanon were received as members of the church in Sanford, and a year or two later constituted a church by themselves.

The society formed as early as 1783 was not a body corporate. Several petitions to the General Court were brought, year after year, to secure incorporation, but without success. Finally the town gave its consent, and on June 23, 1806, the society was incorporated.

Elder Jonathan Powers, a member of the church, supplied the pulpit for a time during 1811. In 1815 there was quite an extensive revival, during which, Elder Gideon Cook, of Dixmont, Maine, was among those participating. He was then " in the prime of his strength, full of zeal and energy," and proved himself so acceptable to the people that he was called to the pastorate. Accepting the invitation, Elder Cook was installed December 27, 1815. His ministry lasted for nearly ten years, during which about forty were added to the church. Between 1825 and 1832 the pulpit was supplied by Elders Otis Robinson, John Chadbourn, Nathaniel G. Littlefield, John Sanders, William Johnson, and Philander Hartwell.

Sins of omission seemed to have weighed down upon the church members in 1830, when they accused themselves of remissness in discipline. The ancient records were read. The children called to remembrance what their fathers did more than half a century before, and judged that their action was worthy to be followed. The old articles of faith and covenant, as adopted in 1798, were read aloud, reaffirmed, and ordered to be recorded in a book.

In March, 1832, Elder Cook was called to his second pastorate, which continued until his dismissal, April 7, 1838. Following him, Elder Paul S. Adams labored here. About this time several persons residing on Mount Hope withdrew from this meeting, and set up one by themselves. Though nearly all returned, and were received into full membership, another church, consisting of seventeen members, was formed on Mount Hope in 1841. Elder Adams was succeeded by Elder H. W. Strong in a short pastorate.

Singular as it may seem at the present day, intemperance had made sad inroads upon the church. The practice of drinking ardent spirits was for a long time common even among members. The church, however, took no action in regard to it until April 11, 1840, when a vote was passed not to receive any person into the church unless he took the temperance pledge, and this was to be inserted in the church covenant. This was one step in the right direction. But there were members not affected by this; they had not pledged themselves to abstain from spirituous liquors. How should they be reached? Another step was taken, when, on the 11th of December, 1841, it was "Voted this church become a temperate church, and each member abstain from all distilled spirituous liquors except in case of sickness."

Elder Joseph Gilpatrick preached one year, 1841–2, and Elder John Boyd most of the time from 1842 until 1846. The title "Elder" gave way to "Reverend" during his ministry, and was applied to him at its close.

In 1847, the old meeting-house, which had stood for more than fifty years, with scarcely an alteration after Joshua Hanson finished the lower part in 1803, was entirely remodelled. It was cut down to one story, made smaller, and refitted with modern pulpit, pews and choir. It was moved back a short distance from the original site, and turned so as to front eastward toward the village. In 1848 it was rededicated.

Rev. William H. Copeland began to labor among the people in the summer of 1848, and continued his service until the spring of 1850. He was followed the next year by Rev. B. F. Hubbard, who preached one year. Rev. Thomas Jameson supplied the pulpit two years, 1853–5, and was succeeded by Rev. Walter T. Sargent, whose labors with the church closed in 1857. During the summer of 1853, Rev. Mr. Jameson prepared a history of the church, which, with amendment, was accepted. Rev. Gideon Cook was secured, in 1858, to preach at the Corner and Mount Hope, and he remained two years. Subsequently Rev. John Hubbard, Senior, preached a short time.

"From 1860 to 1870, the prospect for better days was almost hopeless. The total membership was reduced to twenty-two. But during this darkness a little gleam of light was seen in the springing up of a new business life in the village which pointed to a growth of the population. The brethren of the association saw it, and began to advocate the removal of the meeting-house from its old site, more than a third of a mile west of the post-office, into the village. Rev. James A. Ferguson, as the county colporteur, was directed to labor among them, with this object in view. He was successful . . . . . . and upon the first sufficient snow of the succeeding winter (1870–1), the almost forlorn house was moved upon its present convenient lot (which Brother Goodel, a student from Newton, who preached here during his vacation, was largely instrumental in securing), and fitted up, and dedicated in June, 1871, nearly free of debt."[1]

From 1871 to 1873, Rev. Sumner Estes was pastor. In 1872, the church and society entertained the association the sixth time, the first being in 1803, at which Rev. George B. Ilsley, pastor of the Springvale Baptist Church, delivered a centennial address.

The exercises of the one hundredth anniversary of the organization of the church were of an interesting character. The house was well filled with attentive listeners. The services, conducted by the pastor, Rev. Mr. Estes, included the delivery of the "Centennial Discourse" by Rev. Mr. Ilsley; remarks and reminiscences by Rev. Edmund Worth of Kennebunk, on the character and labors of Elder Otis Robinson; by Rev. G. W. Gile, respecting "Father" Cook (the labors

[1] Ilsley's "Centennial Discourse."

of these two men covered nearly a third of a century) ; by Rev. W. H. Copeland, of Wells, the only ex-pastor present, on his ministry with the church; by Deacon J. H. Gowen, of Saco, a former member; and by Deacon Goodwin, of Lebanon, on church-going of years before. A few earnest words were spoken in behalf of the church by the pastor.

The meeting-house was burned in the great fire of 1878. There was no insurance upon it, so the loss was total, except for the furniture saved from the burning building. In July, 1880, a notice, signed by Jonathan Tebbets, Samuel Nowell, and Jeremiah Moulton, called for a meeting of those interested in rebuilding the Baptist meeting-house. At that meeting Messrs. Nowell and Moulton were appointed a building committee, and work was begun in September. Captain Jonathan Tebbets had generously offered two hundred dollars towards the project, but his eyes were never gladdened by the sight of the new church, for on Sunday morning, September 5, within a week after work was begun, he died suddenly of heart disease, in his eighty-sixth year. The new house of worship was completed and ready for occupancy in the spring of 1882, the dedication occurring Tuesday, March 14, of that year. The sermon of the afternoon was preached by Rev. T. C. Russell, of Springvale, and the dedicatory prayer was by Rev. J. L. Sanborn, of South Waterborough. In the evening Rev. H. M. Sawtelle of East Lebanon preached. The structure cost about fifteen hundred dollars, of which two hundred dollars was indebtedness at the time of dedication.

Rev. T. C. Russell supplied the pulpit for a few months from the Sabbath following the dedication, and was succeeded by Rev. A. Sherwin, during the year 1883. Rev. Frank S. Bickford was pastor from 1884 to March, 1888. Rev. Samuel H. Emery was settled in April following for a pastorate of three years. About this time the growth of the society was so rapid that the need of a more commodious structure became necessary, and in the summer of 1888 the church building was sold to the Methodists (subsequently coming into the possession of the Catholics), to make room for a new place of worship. This building was erected and furnished at a cost of eight thousand five hundred dollars, from plans of John Calvin Stevens, architect, of Portland. Three thousand five hundred dollars were furnished by the Baptist State Convention Board, and the remainder by members of the church and their friends. The new edifice was dedicated free of debt on Thursday, April 4, 1889. Previous to the ceremonies Rev. Mr. Emery announced that an indebtedness of something over eighteen hundred dollars was to be removed, and this amount was immediately secured in the congregation, the subscriptions pouring in at the rate of one hundred dollars a minute for fifteen minutes. W. H. Nason, George H. Nowell, S. J. Nowell, and Rev. Sumner Estes each doubled their previous subscriptions, and others gave generously. Rev. A. T. Dunn, of Portland, offered the prayer of dedication, and an original hymn, written by Samuel R. Robinson, of Sanford, to the music of " Old Hundred," was sung.

Since 1890 the pastors have been: Rev. C. C. Speare, 1891–1897; Rev. Arthur Twain Belknap, January 24, 1897–October, 1898; Rev. A. N. Dary, October, 1898–July, 1900; Rev. George M. Stilphen, from July, 1900, to the present time.

The present membership of the church is one hundred and sixty-nine.

The deacons of the church have been: Naphtali Harmon, 1772–1783; Daniel Coffin, 1772–1774; Walter Powers, 1772–1774; Philip Door (Lebanon branch),1773–1774; Eleazar Chadbourn,1780–1788; Phinehas Thompson, 1783 – (?); Joshua Goodwin, 1783 – (?); John Chadbourn, Junior, 1788–1792; Samuel Charles (Fryeburg), 1788–1790; Nathaniel Gubtail (Lebanon branch), 1798–1800; Nathan Powers, 1801–1827; John Libby, 1815–1831; Benjamin Beal, 1831–1866; Daniel Wadlia, 1831–1835; Gideon Dearing, 1831–1843; Daniel Plummer, 1836-1842; William Chadbourn, 1836–1850; George Moulton, July 5, 1851, to his death, November 21, 1884; W. H. Nason, 1883 to date; Samuel Nowell, 1883 to date.

Deacon Samuel Nowell has been clerk of the church from 1861 to the present time, and George H. Nowell has been superintendent of the Sunday School for the past thirteen years. There has been, for some time, a Young People's Society connected with the church, of which Miss Sarah Nutter is now president.

CHAPTER IX.

OTHER BAPTIST CHURCHES.

Second Baptist Church, Mouse Lane—Mount Hope Church—Spring-vale Baptist Church.

THE Second Baptist Church was organized at Mouse Lane, July 27, 1830. Prior to that date it had existed as a branch of the Baptist Church in Kennebunk. It was probably the branch established in the Getchell house, known as "Pilgrims' Tavern." Elder Roberts came up from "Alewive" to preach before the church was organized, and it is said that Elder John Chadbourn, son of Eleazar, preached there in 1826.

Elder Philander Hartwell, ordained in 1830, supplied the church one year, during which it increased to forty members, the original number being seventeen. Elder Hartwell was succeeded by Elder John Chadbourn in 1832, who remained as pastor two years, and afterward preached in Hiram. Elder Chadbourn was originally a member of the First Baptist Church. For three years after he left the Mouse Lane Church, it was without a minister. But in 1837, under the preaching of the neighboring ministers,—perhaps Elder Cook, then in Sanford, was one, for he preached there once at the time of an extensive revival,—the church awoke from its slumber, active and zealous work followed, and twenty-one were added to the membership. The church was too weak, however, to employ a pastor, and soon relapsed into its former condition. It is related that, when an erring sister was under discipline, one of its members, sympathizing with her, uttered these words : " If you turn her from the church, as sure as God liveth, the church will go down." They seem like prophetic words ; for, after her excommunication, not a member was ever added to the church.

The small meeting-house at the forks of the road between Goodwin's and Linscott's was burned about 1850, and in 1855 most of the members in good standing joined with the church in Alfred on the " Back Road," in building a meeting-house at Littlefield's Mills, and forming the church worshipping there.

About the year 1838, several members of the First Baptist Church,. residing at Mount Hope, or in that vicinity, withdrew from that organization, and set up a meeting by themselves. They had become disaffected for various reasons, one of which undoubtedly was that the main body of the church was not in accord with them on the temperance question agitating the community. Such a proceeding could not be overlooked, and accordingly the parent church took action on the matter. September 1, 1838, it was " Voted to enter a complaint against those persons that had left our meeting, and set up one in opposition to the gospel, Daniel Johnson, Nehemiah Littlefield, Thomas Merrill, Ebenezer Libby, Royal Morrison, Samuel Worster, Enoch Littlefield, and chose Deacon Plumer and Deacon Chadbourn to notify those persons to attend our next meeting." Their method of separation, not being in accordance with the usage of the denomination, undoubtedly had much to do with this vote.

At various times during the year, until September 14, 1839, the case of these offending members was brought up, and finally on that day disposed of. Two of them had been restored to good fellowship, but on that day it was " Voted that the difficulty between the church and Br. Nehemiah Littlefield and others be settled forever." But a new difficulty apparently arose, for, in 1840, Daniel Johnson, Nehemiah Littlefield, and Enoch Littlefield were dropped at their own request.

In the meantime, those friendly to the Mount Hope project were not inactive. They decided, partly owing to the distance at which they lived, to have a house of worship of their own, and contributed generously toward that object. A plain structure, without tower or spire, was erected, and in 1840, completed for worship. On the 6th of February, 1841, the First Baptist Church dismissed seventeen members to organize the new body, and chose Deacons Beal, Plummer, and Chadbourn, to sit in council. But these men did not take their seats, thereby revealing the antagonism of the old church to the new. The council convened February 25, with Elder O. Barron, of Wells, as moderator, and Elder Gideon Cook, of Cape Neddock, as scribe, and the following brethren and sisters were organized into a church : John Nowell, Daniel Johnson, Nathan Goodwin, Samuel Worster, Thomas Merrill, Royal Morrison, Tabitha Butler, Philena Johnson, Mary Nowell, Martha Nowell, Lois Butler, Betsey More, Lydia Gowell, Abigail Wise, Susannah Worster, Olive Merrill, Mary Johnson, Ann Goodwin. The sermon was preached by Elder Barron, the inaugurating prayer was offered by Elder Cook, and the hand of fellowship was given by Elder Hayden, of Dover, N. H.

PRESCOTT EMERY.

At a church meeting, March 2, it was "Voted that the church be called by the name of the Mount Hope Church." On April 25, Elder Gideon Cook was voted pastor of the church. He preached until the fall of the next year, when the church granted him his dismission at his own request. In 1843 Elder John Boyd was pastor, but how long he remained there is no evidence. In March, 1847, it was "Voted that Br. B. F. Hubbard shall be ordained pastor of this church." A council was accordingly held on March 30, at which Rev. N. G. Littlefield, of Acton, was moderator, and Rev. John Peacock, of Springvale, scribe. The examination of the candidate proving satisfactory, Mr. Hubbard was duly ordained the following day.

In May, 1849, the church voted to give Rev. Mr. Hubbard his dismission from the pastorate, although it was not until 1852 that he and his wife withdrew from membership in the church. Up to August, 1849, he had preached most of the time. After that, the young church, finding out that to sustain preaching theoretically was far easier than to support a minister practically, began to devise means to have a meeting part of the time only. They chose " a committee to meet the Baptist old church in Sanford, to see if they can agree to get a minister to preach to them in both places." This proposition failed, the old church not being disposed to render assistance to the new. There was afterwards occasional preaching for a few years. The last church meeting was held August 17, 1857, when it was "Voted to disorganize the church."

The meeting-house, unoccupied for years, was fast going to decay and ruin, when one of its owners sold it. It was moved a short distance from its original site, adjoining the graveyard on the southwest side of the road, and converted into a barn.

The total membership of the church in its short existence was thirty-nine. There were two deacons, Daniel Johnson, 1841–1857, and Enoch Frost, 1842–1850.

The Baptist Church at Springvale was organized in 1843. The improvement of the water power at that village some three years previous, and the building of a mill at the upper fall, had brought into town several Baptists, who were desirous of forming a permanent union. Among them were Danforth White, Ivory M. Thompson, William Gage, Benjamin F. Hodgdon, and John Montelius, Junior, who met at the house of Mr. Gage on the 23rd of May, 1843, and organized in the choice of Mr. Gage as chairman, and Mr. Montelius as secretary. After some conversation relative to the object for which they had convened, they appointed Messrs. Hodgdon, White

8

and Thompson a committee " to confer with Rev. Eleazar Robbins, of Waterborough, and extend to him an invitation to preach, and to make every necessary arrangement for carrying the same into effect."

A few weeks later, the committee reported that they had engaged Rev. Mr. Robbins to preach every other Sabbath for five dollars a Sabbath. When he came to preach, he was to spend a few days among them, and perform the duties of a pastor. A constitution and by-laws for the government of the church were duly adopted. Several articles therein deserve more than a passing notice. The temperance question had been before the people a few years, and many churches had taken a decided stand against the use of intoxicating drinks. The slavery question was in the first stages of its agitation, and men were timorous when it arose before them. The new church was outspoken in its opinion upon those two great moral questions, and bold in its denunciation of slavery, against which a few only in the town had taken a firm stand. The articles referred to declared:

" No individual can retain membership with this church without abstaining strictly from all intoxicating liquors, as an article of luxury, drink or entertainment, and no individual shall be received into membership without fully embracing the first clause of this article."

" This church will not hold fellowship nor communion with slavery in any form, directly nor indirectly, neither admit into its pulpit, as a minister, a slaveholder, nor an abettor of slavery, knowing him to be such."

" As this church views slavery as a great and daring sin against the law of God, and against the liberty and right of our fellow creatures, and trampling on the poor and down-trodden, and violating every personal right, and as the practice of this sin leads to every vice and outrage which characterizes the slave-holding community, we must, in all conscience, denounce this sin, against which the Lord God has frowned, and opposed His law, and, viewing it in this light, we cannot recommend a member of this church to have any fellowship with a slaveholding church."

Preparations to hold a council were made, and a covenant and articles of faith were adopted. John Montelius, Junior, was chosen clerk of the proposed church, and as a committee to prepare an address to be presented to the council, setting forth the reasons for proceeding to the organization of a church at Springvale. The address spoke of the advantages of the new field of labor, and declared that " your petitioners made every exertion with the Baptist Church located at Sanford to change its place of worship to this village, and having been unsuccessful in all their exertions to accomplish an object so desirable, now think it their solemn duty . . . . to form a church here."

Although there were already three churches of the same faith and order in town, the council, meeting on July 27, 1843, with Rev. O. Barron, of Wells, as moderator, and Rev. J. Richardson, of South Berwick, clerk, organized the petitioners into the Baptist Church of Springvale, with twelve members, as follows: John Montelius, Junior, William Gage, Julia Gage, Julia Ann Gage, Ivory M. Thompson, Eleanor Thompson, Dorcas Ham, Benjamin F. Hodgdon, Apphia Hodgdon, Danforth White, Lucy White, and Caroline Emery, all of whom presented letters of dismissal from other Baptist churches in various parts of New England. Rev. J. Richardson preached the sermon of the occasion, Rev. Eleazar Robbins gave the right hand of fellowship to the church, and Rev. John Boyd, of Sanford, gave the charge to the church.

Rev. Mr. Robbins served the new church until October 22, when he resigned to accept a position with the Domestic Missionary Society. During the fall a beautiful communion service was received as a gift from two ladies of Cambridge, Mass., Ellen M. Freeman, and a Mrs. Farwell. Rev. J. M. Wedgewood supplied the pulpit, following Rev. Mr. Robbins, one-half the time until March, 1844. Meetings were held during this period in the Methodist meeting-house, on the south side of the county road to Lebanon. In the summer of 1844 measures were taken for the erection of a house of worship, but after the committee appointed to secure a site, and to draft a plan of a church edifice had reported, it was voted " to postpone the erection of our house for the present, on account of funds."

Silas Pearsons and Benjamin F. Hodgdon were chosen the first deacons, on December 20, 1843. Four years later Pearsons was disciplined by the church and excluded. Deacon Hodgdon served the church for a long period, during almost twenty years being also clerk.

Rev. John Boyd, who had preached or lectured weekly at the house of Ivory M. Thompson early in 1845, was invited to become pastor of the church, a call which he at first declined, but later accepted in part, preaching one-half of the time, the services being held in the Congregational vestry, engaged for that year. In 1846 the church was again without a pastor and place of worship, meetings were omitted, and the Home Missionary Society espoused its cause, voting two hundred dollars for preaching for the year ensuing, a fact which indicates that the Baptists of Maine regarded Springvale as an important position to be maintained. Rev. John Peacock, a preacher of considerable success, then at Fitzwilliam, N. H., was invited to take the pastorate. Having accepted the call and entered upon his duties in September, 1846, a revival of deep interest soon began. This work continued during the year, the church being greatly strengthened by accessions.

In 1847, a meeting-house was built, on the road leading to Shapleigh, now Maple street, just above the residence of Deacon Hodgdon. It was all paid for by the church and society with this exception : Two dollars were contributed by two persons outside of Rev. Mr. Peacock's congregation. The building was ready for occupancy by the first of August, and was dedicated on the third day of that month. Rev. J. Richardson, of South Berwick, preached the sermon ; Rev. N. W. Williams, of Saco, offered the dedicatory prayer ; and Rev. H. G. Nott, of Waterville, delivered an address to the church. This commemorative occasion was rendered especially attractive by the York Baptist Quarterly Meeting, which was in session on the three succeeding days.

Rev. Mr. Peacock closed his labors September 2, 1849. During his three years of service he had received fifty-two members into the church. Rev. Austin Robbins supplied the pulpit from October 7, 1849, to July 18, 1852 ; Rev. Nicholas Branch, October, 1852–October, 1853 ; Rev. Albert Dunbar, May, 1854–January, 1856 ; Rev. Mr. Storer, a short time in 1856 ; and Rev. Henry Stetson, May 4, 1856–May, 1860 (?). In August, 1861, W. T. Emerson, a licentiate of the Baptist Church, Saco, accepted a call to preach one year, and in October was ordained to the ministry. The following summer he asked for his dismission, and enlisted in the army. Rev. B. F. Hubbard and Rev. James Ferguson, of Alfred, were his successors in the pulpit supply.

In the spring of 1864 William Willard Boyd began to preach, though without a license. He had been a member of a Congregational Church, but had adopted immersion views after his removal to Springvale. On July 3 he was baptized and received into the church, to which he ministered, by license, two years and five months, closing his labors, August 26, 1866. Fifty-seven were received into the church during this time.

George B. Ilsley, a graduate in theology, began to preach on the following Sabbath, September 2. Two months later, by a council called by the church, he was ordained to the ministry, the exercises occurring on November 21. On the same day, the meeting-house having been enlarged and remodelled, through the efforts of Rev. Mr. Boyd, " it was rededicated to the worship of Almighty God." Rev. Mr. Ilsley resigned in 1873, preaching his farewell sermon June 29. During his pastorate, and by his exertions, a parsonage, costing eighteen hundred dollars, was built, and two-thirds of the debt upon the church was paid. His services, which had warmly endeared him to the people, were commemorated in complimentary resolutions adopted at the close of his pastorate.

Edward P. Roberts was ordained to the ministry at the church October 23, 1873, and remained as pastor until August 1, 1875. Rev. Amasa Bryant was pastor from August 22, 1875 to October 6, 1878, resigning on account of ill health. During his last year the meeting-house was again remodelled and repaired, and on the 18th of August, 1878, for the second time, rededicated.

Rev. John E. Dame preached from November 17, 1878, to July 25, 1880. Succeeding pastors have been : Rev. L. D. Hill, 1880 ; Rev. T. C. Russell, 1881 to October 1, 1883 ; Rev. Frank G. Davis, October, 1883, to October, 1889 ; Rev. George S. Chase, January, 1890, to October, 1894 ; Rev. W. B. Shumway, December, 1894, to October 1, 1899 ; and Rev. James Edward Cochrane, November 1, 1899, to the present time. The church has enjoyed a good degree of prosperity under these able and faithful pastors.

The deacons have been : Silas Pearsons, 1843–1847 ; Benjamin F. Hodgdon, 1843–1895 ; Jotham Moulton, 1848–1868 ; William F. Hanson, 1868–1883 ; Lewis Chadbourn, 1868–1869 ; Ferdinand A. Butler, 1869–1878 ; Loammi K. Moulton, 1869 to date ; Silas B. Ridley, 1880–1889 ; James Sayward, 1885–1900 ; Clarence Butler, 1895–1898 ; George W. Hanson, 1895 to date ; Henry S. Packard, 1898 to the present time.

The present church officers include : Charles M. Abbott, clerk ; Edmund E. Goodwin, treasurer ; Clarence E. Taylor, collector ; George W. Hanson, superintendent of the Sunday School. A Young Peoples' Society of Christian Endeavor was organized August 3, 1886, of which Mrs. Jeanette Wentworth is now president. The number of church members at present is one hundred and thirty-four.

CHAPTER X.

CONGREGATIONAL CHURCHES.

Early Orthodox Worship —Church in the South Parish Organized—
Rev. Moses Sweat — A Primitive Meeting-House — Church Edi-
fices at the Corner — Pastors and Deacons — The South Sanford
Church.

THE votes of the town already referred to were passed to meet
the wants of a portion of the people. Such votes were necessary, also, to satisfy the demands of the law, which a town could not
transgress with impunity. It was an old law, enacted in 1692–3,
during the reign of William and Mary, and remained in force more
than a century. One of its requirements was, " That the inhabitants
of each town within the province, shall take due care, from time to
time, to be constantly provided of an able, learned orthodox minister
or ministers, of good conversation, to dispense the word of God to
them ; which minister or ministers shall be suitably encouraged, and
sufficiently supported and maintained by the inhabitants of such
town." The services rendered by " orthodox ministers " from time
to time, were for a few months only, and for twelve years no steps
were taken, as far as records show, towards the formation of a Congregational church. In 1780, however, a church was organized in
the northeast part of the town, by Rev. Messrs. Daniel Little, of
Wells (Kennebunk), and Matthew Merriam, of Berwick.

"The first beginnings of this church were the gatherings of a few
who loved the truth, to listen to the reading of a sermon."[1] It consisted of twelve or fifteen members, and, two years later, when the
town was divided into two parishes " for the greater convenience
of attending the public worship of God," constituted the church of
the North Parish. " The religious interest of 1780, which centered
at the newly made parish, continued and increased. Some individuals
were strangely affected, and seem to have turned religious enthusiasts.
Though for a time they attended worship at the Congregational parish, eventually they left and formed the society of Shakers, yet of

[1] " Semi-Centennial of York County Conference, 1872."

(118)

this town."[1] According to another,[2] " The ministrations of Mr. Little and Mr. Merriam wrought some conversions, but their zeal soon engendered extravagancies, and some became strangely affected and disorderly, which gave them the name of ' Merry Dancers ; ' most of them seceded and joined those on Shaker Hill."

In the spring of 1784, a meeting-house was built, but it does not appear that the church organization was kept up. It is highly probable that the church became extinct, or was reduced so low as not to maintain public worship, prior to August, 1788; for, at that time, Doctor Abiel Hall and wife united with the church in the South Parish. The parish, indeed, began to act independently in 1787, and to make efforts to procure a pastor. " They invited several preachers as candidates, among whom were Rev. David Porter, Isaac Babbit, and Mr. White,"[3] none of whom accepted a call to preach for the struggling society. But in February, 1791, Mr. John Turner accepted a call, and was ordained in September following, at which time the present Alfred Church was re-organized, or rather organized. Referring to the church of 1780, Greenleaf says : " It does not appear that the church thus formed at Alfred ever received any accessions. Neither is it now known whether they kept any records, or performed any church act. It is most probable they did neither, for at the subsequent settlement of ministers, both in Alfred and Lyman, no church could be found, and the ordaining council proceeded to organize one in each place." That the organization and ordination did not take place, September 7, or September 8, is evident from the record of the church in the South Parish, the 18th of that month. " In public service read to the church a letter from the North Parish in Sanford requesting assistance in gathering a church there, and in ordaining Mr. John Turner to the work of the ministry." The church voted to send Elder David Bean, Deacon Caleb Emery, and Deacon Samuel Nasson. " Also voted, That a recommendation and dismission be given to Abiel Hall and his wife, upon their joining in the church about embodying in the North Parish of Sanford, if requested of them. One week later, September 25, Parson Sweat adds to the record : " Being called upon by Mr. Hall, in behalf of himself and wife, I gave a certificate agreeably to the above vote of the church." The organization was probably effected on the 28th of September.

Rev. John Turner was from Randolph, Mass., and graduated at

[1] " Semi-Centennial of York County Conference, 1872."
[2] Usher Parsons, M.D.
[3] Parsons's " History of Alfred."

Brown University in 1788. Ordained, as above mentioned, he served the church and society twelve or thirteen years, and was dismissed May 18, 1804. He was installed as pastor of the Second Congregational Church, Biddeford, March 1, 1805, from which he was dismissed in 1818. Thence he removed to Kingston (New Hampshire or Massachusetts?), though he was stated supply at Sebec in 1834–5. He died in Dorchester, Mass., October 2, 1839, aged seventy-one years.

Deacon Moses Stevens, who died June 14, 17.0, was probably an officer of the original church, and Deacons Daniel Gile and Ebenezer Hall, of the new organization. In 1797, when trouble with Rev. Mr. Turner arose, Deacon Hall requested to be excused from the office to which he had been chosen, and Thomas Williams was chosen deacon in his place.

Although the South Parish had enjoyed preaching from time to time, and a few had cherished the hope that a church would be formed, yet no definite steps were taken with that end in view, until early in 1786. At an adjourned meeting of the parish on Tuesday, March 28 (no records of first meeting or former meetings appear), it was voted, "That Captain David Bean, James Gare, James Heard, William Bennett, and Captain Samuel Nasson be a committee to form some proposals to offer Mr. Moses Sweat in regard to his settling with us in the work of the gospel ministry." There can be no doubt but that Mr. Sweat had supplied the parish the preceding season, as Rev. Mr. Hall had, in 1783, surveyed the field, learned what was proposed to be done, and given encouragement to those desiring of forming a church.

The proprietors had set apart one lot for the ministry, and one for the first settled minister. As an inducement to Mr. Sweat, who would be the recipient of one lot, if he should accept a call to settle, the committee reported, "That it is their (our) opinion that it is necessary to him as a settlement, to clear, fence, and plough nine acres of land on the minister lot, that is three acres in a year till it is completed, and also to help him in boards, timber and labor, to the amount of forty-five pounds towards his buildings, and eighty pounds as a salary during his continuance with us in the ministry."

Messrs. David Bean, Caleb Emery, Samuel Nasson, James Heard, and Nathaniel Bennett were a committee to present the proposals and invitation to Mr. Sweat. On the 17th of April, the candidate gave his acceptance in writing, and the parish appointed the 19th of July following for the day of ordination.

The ecclesiastical council invited by letters missive convened on the day specified, at the house of Captain Samuel Nasson, which stood on the brow of the hill known as Nasson's Hill. Rev. Daniel Little, of Wells, was chosen moderator, and Rev. Nathaniel Webster, of Biddeford, scribe. The council having examined the candidates, embodied Moses Sweat, David Bean, Ephraim Low, Caleb Emery, Nathaniel Bennett, John Stanyan, Samuel Nasson, James Gare, and Daniel Morrison, as a Church of Christ, agreeably to the covenant by them subscribed, which was presented by the council.

The church having been incorporated gave a call to Mr. Sweat, which he accepted. The council examined the candidate, and voted to proceed to his ordination, which was done. Rev. Elihu Thayer, of Kingston, N. H., preached the ordination sermon, Rev. Mr. Little gave the charge, and Rev. Moses Hemmenway, D.D., of Wells, gave the right hand of fellowship.

At the first church meeting, held on the 19th of August, it was voted that there should be one elder and two deacons in the church. David Bean was chosen elder, and Caleb Emery and Samuel Nasson first and second deacons. The first votes of the church were purely and wholly orthodox and Congregational. But there follows a vote which savors otherwise. It was probably introduced through the influence of the pastor, and is one reason why some regarded Parson Sweat as weak in the faith, not strictly orthodox; an Arminian. The vote read thus : "That if any person shall present himself to the church, and desire to join in covenant with it, and yet shall not see his way clear to partake of the Lord's Supper, he may be admitted as a member, and have the privilege of Baptism for his children, the church being satisfied with him in other respects." This was essentially the "half-way covenant" which found favor a century or more ago, and prevailed in many Congregational churches. As long as Parson Sweat lived, this vote stood unchanged, but before his successor, Rev. Mr. Marsh, was ordained, at the request of the pastor-elect, the church voted to erase said vote from their records.

During his ministry of thirty six years, thirty-three members were added to the church. At the time of his death, there were nine members,—the same as the original number. Peace and harmony seemed to have prevailed, though there were seasons of discipline and discouragements. Serious differences arose between individual members, which happily were settled without causing disruption. Members were disciplined for non-attendance upon public worship, and other offences. In 1794, a serious trouble is indicated in a letter from Henry Hamilton to Elder Bean, but whether it grew out of trouble between prominent members, or was the result of general dissatisfaction in church and society, the language of the letter does not say.

These facts are patent: The Baptists made inroads upon the society, and drew off a large number, and even attracted some members of the church. One of its deacons had threatened to hurt the parish, and was accused of attending a Baptist society meeting, when a meeting of his own society was to be held, at which he was expected to be present. One woman, wife of a prominent man, had joined the church in 1790, but for some time had absented herself from meeting. A committee appointed to converse with her reported "that she was not allowed to attend with the church." The first deacon became offended for some cause, unknown, and said " that he should do no more concerning the parish." Two years later he became a member of the Baptist society.

Two years after the organization of the church, during which meetings were held in school- and dwelling-houses, the parish began work upon a meeting-house. Illustrative of the custom of the time, and furnishing evidence of the date of raising the frame of the house, is a peculiar vote passed on the second Monday in April, 1788. " Voted to procure and order for Mr. Cram to provide 1 berrell $\frac{1}{2}$ of N. E. Rum, 2 quintals $\frac{1}{2}$ of fish and 10 Gallons of Molasses, and hogsfat if he can get it,"—all of which was to be paid for out of the meeting-house tax. Caleb Emery, William Bennett, and Nathaniel Bennett were appointed a committee that year, to carry on the work, and the parish voted to procure stuff as far as they could, and underpin the house. The building went slowly on, and the first intimation we have of its occupancy is the record of March 15, 1792, at which time the parish meeting was held in the meeting-house. The house was then ready (however poorly) for use, for on the 28th of May following, the parish voted to " give up the old school-house to the main district to move it when they see fit."

The house stood on the northeast side of the county road then leading from the south part of the town over Mount Hope, just above the house lately owned by Horace Bennett. It was two stories in height, and fronted toward the south. When it was first occupied, there were no desk, no pews, and but three or four glass windows. Parson Sweat read his sermons over a chair, the congregation listening to his fifteen minute discourse, on rough seats, made by placing planks or boards upon logs or rocks, which had been carried in for that purpose. At length a pulpit was put in, over which, like a monstrous toadstool, hung the uncouth sounding-board. Square pews and galleries were necessary accompaniments. They were similar to those in the Baptist Church, two miles above.

To this central locality, came the people from all parts of the town. Men and women came on horseback, "double-behind," while the young people and those unable to keep a horse came on foot, all unmindful of the weather. An aged lady[1] told the writer that she used to walk from her father's on Shaw's ridge down to Parson Sweat's meeting-house, through rain and sunshine, heat and cold, and sit during the hour of service without minding it. In the coldest weather, there was no fire, and ofttimes, with wind whistling through the cracks, the rain or snow would beat in upon the people. Some of the more fortunate carried warming-pans or foot-stoves, but none escaped the hardships of those cold winters, if they ventured out to church.

For years, only male voices were heard in singing. Early in this century Nathaniel Bennett, Timothy Shaw, John Frost, Benjamin Sweat, and Moses Sweat, were "chief singers," and Ebenezer Garey and Jeremiah Moulton players on the bass-viol. The voice of Rose Garey was the first voice of woman heard in public worship in the old Congregational meeting-house.

In 1809, either because new glass was needed, or window-panes had been broken, money received was expended for putting in glass. So much injury was done on public days, town meeting days, or muster days, that it was a matter of necessity for the parish to adopt means of protection. Accordingly, in 1811, Rufus Bennett was chosen agent to take charge of the meeting-house to prevent any damage being done to it on public days.

In 1813, suits were commenced by the assessors of the parish, against Solomon Welch, Aaron Gowen, and others, testing whether the parish could tax parties in town not belonging to any other society. After several years of expensive litigation, the assessors were sustained in their action in the premises. Hon. John Holmes and Hon. Cyrus King were counsel in these suits. In 1818, the parish voted to prosecute Holmes for money in his hands. As no further action was taken, we suppose the demand against him was cancelled.

Parson Sweat's ministry closed with his life on the 30th of August, 1822.

Rev. Moses Sweat, or Parson Sweat, as he was generally called, was a remarkable personality. Although not college-bred, he became

---

[1] "Aunt Nabby" Gowen.

a linguist of high attainments, and at the age of thirty-six was honored by Harvard College with the degree of Master of Arts. He was born in Kingston, N. H., on Sunday, December 23, 1754, the son of Benjamin and Abigail Sweat. His father was a farmer, and, for many years, one of the deacons of the Congregational Church, dying in 1787, in the eightieth year of his age. His mother was nearly ninety-one at the time of her death. The advantages of education received by him in boyhood were limited. He was obliged to assist his father on the farm, and permitted to attend public school only a short season of the year. He enjoyed the opportunity, however, of reciting to his father at stated hours of the day, when not pressed with work in the field or forest. There is a tradition that his brothers were inclined to shirk their lessons, and ofttimes induced him to recite for them while they did his work on the farm; no irksome task for one eager for knowledge. He was fond of books, and took special delight in the study of the dead languages, in which he progressed quite rapidly under the instruction of Parson Moody, preceptor of Dummer Academy, Newbury, Mass. A farmer in early manhood, he taught school occasionally, in winter, and, it is said, kept up with a class in college, while farming and teaching.

Of his early religious instruction and experience, we have no knowledge. In the twenty-fourth year of his age, on the 19th of July, 1778, he united with the Congregational Church of his native town, on profession of his faith. His own belief was that he was regenerated and called to preach, a belief which led him to prepare for the ministry by reading theology with Rev. Elihu Thayer, D.D., pastor of the church to which he belonged.

On October 21, 1783, he married Hannah, daughter of Ensign Edward Eastman, of Hawke (now Danville), with whom he lived thirty-nine years. They had five children, three sons and two daughters, viz.: Homer, born December 2, 1784; Hannah, May 6, 1789; Moses, July 9, 1792; Sarah, January 23, 1795; Benjamin, January 26, 1799. His wife and children all survived him.

Becoming pastor of the South Parish of Sanford in 1786, he began his ministerial labors, which lasted for more than a generation. Not only must sermons be written (two a week during his early ministry), church meetings held, and preparatory lectures delivered, but parochial visits among a people widely scattered in a large parish must be made. Wherever there was sickness, his voice was heard in prayer, and it was his duty to minister to the wants of the needy. For several years, his duties called him into the North Parish. Nor were these all. He took possession of the "ministerial lot," granted by the proprietors to the first settled Congregational minister, erected a small dwelling-house, and did the usual work of a farmer in a new settlement, clearing, fencing, and reducing the wild land to a state of cultivation. With this double duty to perform, there is no wonder that "he thought it hard to be a farmer and a minister."

Interested in the common schools, and pre-eminently qualified "to inspect" them, he was always one of the committee for that purpose. In the winter of 1807, he taught school at South Sanford, proving himself a capable instructor. He had, at various times, private pupils, who desired to pursue the classics. They recited to him at his house, but frequently found him at work in his field, and there recited. Prominent among his pupils may be mentioned Usher Parsons, George Heard, and Ezra Thompson.

Parson Sweat was pastor of the church thirty-six years, during which he labored among his people constantly with the exception of about one year. On account of ill health, some ten years subsequent to his settlement, he suspended labors about a year. He united two hundred and nine couples in marriage, attended two hundred and forty-seven funerals, baptized one hundred and twelve persons, many of whom were infants, received thirty-three into the church, and prepared nine hundred and forty sermons. His sermons may have numbered more than that, but it is the number given in the inventory of his property at his death. He probably wrote more, for he exchanged but little. He held no prayer meetings, had no Sabbath School, but punctually held church meetings and preparatory lectures, and sacredly observed the Sabbath services of the sanctuary.

The hard and constant labor to which he was subjected impaired his health, and undermined his constitution, and consumption gradually fastened upon his system. He preached his last sermon in the church on the last Sabbath in May, 1822, but attended one funeral after that. For days and weeks before his death he suffered great pain of body, yet his mind was unclouded and his spirit calm. He retained until the end the same cheerful disposition that characterized his life. Elder George Heard describes a visit to him about two hours before the good man's death. "He asked me to shave him, saying in his usual pleasant manner, ' Do not strike the bones.' After a short conversation, being in much pain, turning over in his bed, he asked to be excused from saying more." He died on Friday, August 30, 1822. It was a beautiful afternoon upon which his numerous sorrowing friends assembled in the meeting-house, to pay

their last tribute of respect to him whom they had so highly esteemed and honored. The services were conducted by Rev. Messrs.
Calef, of Lyman, Douglass of Alfred, Greenleaf of Wells, and Hil-
liard of Berwick.   Rev. Mr. Calef preached the funeral sermon.
His remains were interred in the town burying ground about a mile
below the Corner, where a plain slate headstone was set to mark his
resting-place.

Temperate in his habits, he seldom used spirituous liquors, and did
not pass the decanter when he had company.   Sometimes, in haying
season, he furnished his hands with liquor.   He made use of much
cider, with which his productive orchards furnished him.   Owing to
his hard labor upon his farm, he partook of great quantities of substantial food five or six times a day.

Parson Sweat was a good neighbor ; was a peace-maker ; was a
kind husband and indulgent father.   He was punctual in his business, and was shrewd and prudent in money matters.   Moral in
every respect, his example was a help to the community.   Possessed
of a vein of humor, and a ready gift of anecdote, he was a genial
companion with all.

By close application to study and untiring perseverance, often remaining at his books until late in the night, Parson Sweat became
conversant with eleven languages, most of which he could read with
ease.   In his small library of eighty volumes, there were works in
eight different languages, in addition to a large Polyglot Bible, six
volumes, containing eight versions of the Scriptures.   A favorite
study was Euclid, which he regarded as the foundation of reason.
His master's degree from Harvard, in 1790, was in recognition of
his fine scholarly attainments and classical learning.

One of the early presidents of Bowdoin College, Appleton, or
Allen, having heard of Rev. Mr. Sweat, came up from Kennebunk
with a friend to see him.   It was in haying time, and the Parson
was at work in his field.   At the call of Mrs. Sweat, he made his
appearance in tow breeches.   Taking his guests into his house, he
was asked by the President to read from his Polyglot Bible.   He
complied, and read with such ease, and showed so much knowledge
of the several versions therein, that the astonished visitor remarked,
" It is a wonder that one of your education should settle down in
such a place.   You are buried alive."   " It is better," replied Parson
Sweat, " for a large man to get into a small field, than for a small
man to get into a large field."   The President then tried to purchase
the Bible, but without success.   " I can't sell my books," was the

reply. " It would be a poor plan for a carpenter to sell the tools with which he worked. Without his tools he would be without employment." President Appleton, on leaving, was constrained to exclaim, " I don't know anything in comparison with that man ! "

The Polyglot Bible was procured from London by Parson Sweat at a cost of about one hundred and fifty dollars, for which sum he toiled and kept school of winters. It was bequeathed to his son Moses, who probably sold it to Prof. Thomas C. Upham, and thereby it found its way into the library of Bowdoin College.

Rev. Mr. Sweat's sermons were written in haste, but were " faultless in style in every particular, even to punctuation." While he devoted about ten hours to writing a sermon, it is probable that his mind was busy during his hours of manual labor. " There was nothing impassioned about his discourses, but simply appeals to reason and common sense." In 1805, he published a discourse of about one hundred pages, duodecimo, entitled, " A Critical Investigation of the Mode of Baptism, as performed by the Primitive Churches," in which he traced out the words *bapto* and *baptizo* in several of the Oriental languages. It was a scholarly production, highly appreciated by the learned. The only other publication was a discourse preached at Alfred, on the occasion of its separation from Sanford.

Parson Sweat was gifted in prayer, but nothing in exhortation. The fervency with which he prayed one Sabbath morning during a severe drought was long remembered. A deep impression was made, when, a little later, it rained powerfully. The devout felt that his prayer was answered when naught save the beating of the rain against the house was heard as the pastor read his sermon.

So liberal was he in his views, that many regarded him as a Unitarian, a suspicion, however, wholly groundless.

Dr. Usher Parsons said of him that " in all the graces of a Christian gentleman and model pastor," he never saw his equal. As long as the Congregational Church of Sanford exists, his name will be held in grateful remembrance.[1]

On the 4th of April, 1823, the church voted unanimously to give Christopher Marsh, of Kennebunkport, a call to settle over the church, which he accepted. Rev. Mr. Marsh was ordained on June 4, and filled the pastorate four and a half years. During his ministry nine

---

[1] In 1863, at the suggestion of Prof. Alpheus S. Packard, of Bowdoin College, the writer prepared for the Maine Historical Society a sketch of Parson Sweat's life, from which much of the foregoing has been taken.

persons on profession and three by letter were added to the church. A Sabbath School was established the first year of his pastorate, and subsequently Mrs. Marsh opened one at the Corner, over Morrill's store. The attendance was small, but increased when the advantages of a small library became apparent. Through Rev. Mr. Marsh's personal influence, "the church agreed," on the 10th of April, 1827. "to meet weekly for prayer at such places as should be agreed from time to time." This was the beginning of the weekly prayer meeting in Sanford. Mr. Marsh was dismissed at his own request, in December, 1827. It appears that he felt his salary was inadequate, and he saw no encouraging prospects for the future. He was destined, however, to minister again to the church some thirty years later.

Elisha Bacon, a graduate of Bowdoin College, where he had been the classmate of Longfellow and Hawthorne, was the third pastor. He was ordained May 6, 1829, and was dismissed in September, 1834. It was during his pastorate that the temperance question agitated the church, and the town. Like his predecessor, he was a staunch temperance man, and did not believe in the then prevalent custom of using intoxicating liquors. The church became a temperance society, and none could become members without adopting the principles of temperance.

Soon after Rev. Mr. Bacon's ordination, the society began to contemplate building a new meeting-house at the Corner. The old house stood too far from the centre of business, and population. Several years before, during Rev. Mr. Marsh's ministry, a new school district had been formed at the Corner, and a school-house built, in Deacon Frost's field, opposite the present residence of Hon. Thomas Goodall. At that "Congregational school-house," as it was called, meetings were frequently held, and a Sabbath School formed in 1830, by Deacon Stephen Dorman, and John Skeele. These facts, together with another important one, namely, that men of means and disposition to build lived at the Corner, induced many to favor the enterprise, and Rev. Mr. Bacon gave his assistance to it. The site selected was on the west side of the county road leading to Shapleigh, on a lot adjoining Dr. Dow's. It was given by Deacon Frost, to belong to the society as long as a Congregational meeting-house stood thereon, but to revert to him or his heirs in case the house was removed or became other than a Congregational meeting-house. Deacon Frost, William Emery, Junior, John Storer, and Timothy Shaw, Senior, took hold of the work, and, in the summer and autumn of 1831, erected a neat and commodious place of worship. In due time it was finished, with

SAMUEL B. EMERY.

steeple and vane surmounting a belfry. In the latter, a small bell was hung, the first in the town. This was purchased by subscription, large numbers contributing their twenty-five cents to help raise the required amount. The bell was cracked during a fire at the Corner, and was replaced by another of nine hundred pounds weight. The church was dedicated December 29, 1831.

After Mr. Bacon came into town he taught a singing school and the singing in church greatly improved. The clarinet and violin were sometimes used.

During the ministry of Mr. Bacon seventy-two persons were received into the church. At Springvale, considerable religious interest was manifest, and he assisted in conducting services in the " dry shed " at the print works, in 1831, and later in the church built there.

For five years various attempts were made to obtain a minister, Rev. Josiah Carpenter supplying from 1835 to 1837, and calls were extended to Rev. Mr. Marsh, Rev. Jacob C. Goss, Rev. Mr. Bacon, Rev. Mr. Goss, a second time, and Rev. George W. Bourne, who accepted. Meanwhile difficulties arose in the church and society in regard to a place for holding public worship. Those in the neighborhood of the two meeting-houses claimed that any pastor ordained or installed should supply both, but as to time in each they could not agree. Some thought, even, that services should be held at the lower house all the time ; others, that the Corner being a central locality, and the people at Springvale having some claims, it would be better to give up the old meeting-house, and use the new one altogether. The parish could not settle the difficulties at their meeting in the spring of 1835, and in June the church called a council, which was likewise unable to adjust the trouble.

Mr. Bourne had labored several weeks in the church before invited to settle. There was unanimity of feeling in both parts of the town, but means of support could not readily be raised, and a committee was appointed to ask aid of the Maine Missionary Society. Funds were soon forthcoming, and the way was opened for a settlement of Mr. Bourne. He was installed February 6, 1840.

In 1840, the church took action again in regard to temperance, and voted that the church be a " Temperance Church." It was necessary, for intemperance was making sad work among the members. The pastor was appointed to draft a pledge, which members were required to sign. In 1842, the church voted " That when it can be procured, the pure juice of the grape be used at communion. instead of common wine."

9

Fifty-three persons were added to the church during Rev. Mr. Bourne's ministry. In 1842, the pastor was dismissed, and Rev. William Davenport was secured as stated supply for one year. Rev. Jacob C. Goss, after a long delay, accepted a call which was tendered him, and began to preach in November, 1843, although he was not installed until 1846. The church was strong, and the prospect of a continued prosperous condition was favorable. Services were held at the Corner, though some meetings were held in the new house, built in 1841, on the east side of the road, a few rods south of " Powers's Corner," and occasionally at the vestry at Springvale, built in 1844, a few rods above the store known as the " Factory Store." But the old trouble between the two sections broke out afresh. Six members living in the lower part of the town withdrew from the meetings, and contributed to the support of a minister of another denomination. A committee appointed to consider the matter effected an arrangement which averted further trouble for a time. In June, 1847, however, several members residing in the lower part of the parish, under the leadership of Rev. Clement Parker, then residing at Springvale, assumed to be the " South Church of Sanford," chose a clerk and a deacon, and requested the " North Church " to concur with them in their opinion. As a result, a council was called, at which the aggrieved parties were advised to ask for dismission, and organize a church regularly, and the church was further advised to encourage such organization. Following this advice, fourteen members asked to be dismissed from the church, and on November 9, with others, were organized as the South Congregational Church, Sanford.

Rev. Mr. Goss terminated his labors August 21, 1850. From that time on, for many years, the church had no settled minister, but the pulpit was occupied most of the time by a stated supply. These included Rev. Albert Cole, 1851–1853 ; Rev. Stephen Bailey, 1853–1854 ; Rev. Edmund Burt, 1855 ; and Rev. George L. Becker, 1856–1857. Rev. Christopher Marsh, the second settled minister, became acting pastor early in 1858, and a great revival occurring during his ministry, thirty-two were received into the church. He preached his last sermon March 13, 1859, and died a few montns later. The pulpit was then supplied by Rev. Theodore Wells, 1860–1862 ; Rev. John U. Parsons, 1864–1865 ; Rev. James Richards, D.D., 1869 ; Rev. William V. Jordan, 1870–1871 ; Rev. Elias Chapman, 1871–1874.

At one time Rev. Mr. Bailey had some trouble with Samuel Tompson, who thereupon had his pew covered with a plank and the door nailed up.

The meeting-house was thoroughly repaired outside and remodelled inside in 1871 and 1872, at an expense of about fourteen hundred dollars. The choir was directly behind the pulpit, the old seraphine, of Rev. Mr. Goss's pastorate, gave place to a small organ, and modern pews, neatly carpeted, took the place of the old. The church was rededicated Wednesday, June 19, 1872. Rev. Albert Cole, of Cornish, preached the sermon, and an original hymn was written for the occasion by Miss Abbie G. Clark.

After Loren F. Berry, a student of the Theological Seminary, New Haven, had spent four months among the people, in 1875, Rev. Thomas N. Lord served as acting pastor from October, 1875, to July, 1877.

In the spring of 1878, Henry J. Stone, a licentiate, began his labors, which continued until 1884. He occupied the pulpits of the two churches, at the Corner and South Sanford. On the 1st of July, 1878, the meeting-house was destroyed by fire. The pulpit, chairs, Bible and a few cushions were saved.

" The smoke had not ceased to ascend from the ashes of the Congregationalist Church, when it was declared that another must be built. The people met and chose a building committee, consisting of George Gowen, Octavius Allen, C. O. Emery, E. K. Bennett and H. J. Stone, advising them to build such a house as they could free from debt. The committee pushed their work vigorously. Many who had spent their younger days in our village remembered us in our distress, and rendered us valuable aid in the shape of funds. Among the most prominent were William Emery, of Alfred ; Messrs. Stillman B. and Frank A. Allen, Salter Emery, Albert D. Kilham, and Dr. Albert Day, of Boston ; Edwin Emery, New Bedford ; heirs of John Storer, Portland ; Miss Rebecca Weld, Lebanon. At home, there was scarcely a person, even to a child, who did not do something to help. While we were wonderfully cheered, and had received more than we dared to expect, yet we had not enough to place a bell in the tower. At this time, Mrs. Daniel P. Stone, of Malden, Mass., made us a generous offer of a nice new bell, if we would complete our church free from debt. The committee accepted the offer, and received a fine-toned bell, which weighed about fifteen hundred pounds. This, with the mountings, cost over four hundred dollars. The windows, which are of ground and colored glass, were presented by the following parties : Our Sunday School, George H. Frost, Charles H. Frost, Captain George Nasson, E. P. Kimball, William Miller, Chelsea Friends, Alfred Congregational Sunday School, High Street Congregationalist church, Portland, and a United States Representative, who did not wish his name to appear, and at whose suggestion the names of Deacon William L. Emery and William Emery, who had been prominently connected with the church, but have passed away, were put in place of his. The pews were given mostly by members of the Congregationalist Churches of Maine. After about eighteen months of hard labor on the part of the committee, and helped by the noble efforts of the people, we have been able to secure a neat, comfortable and pretty church, which we can dedicate to the worship of Almighty God, who has 'supplied all our needs according to His riches in glory by Christ Jesus,' and we are free from debt."[1]

It may be truly said, we think, that much credit is due to Mr. Stone, without whose constant labors and earnest solicitations the meeting-house would not have been built. While the church was in process of erection, services were held in Goodall's Hall, through the kindness of Hon. Thomas Goodall, and also in the school-house. The dedication services took place December 25, 1879, on which occasion Mr. Stone was also ordained to the ministry. The dedication sermon was by Rev. Jonathan E. Adams, D.D., of Bangor, and the prayer by Rev. B. P. Snow, of Alfred, while another original hymn by Miss Abbie G. Clark was sung.

Rev. J. C. Osgood, the Freewill Baptist pastor of Springvale, supplied the pulpit in 1884-5 ; Rev. E. C. Cook, also a Freewill Baptist, 1885-1887 ; Rev. W. G. Wade was acting pastor from April, 1887, to August, 1889 ; Rev. H. S. Ives, September, 1889, to September, 1891 ; Rev. E. P. Allen, October, 1891, to February, 1893 ; Rev. F. A. Poole was pastor in 1893-4, for a few months prior to his ordination acting as supply ; and Rev. C. L. Woodworth was pastor from November, 1894, to November 1, 1899. Rev. Andrew L. Chase, the present pastor, was installed January 31, 1900.

During Rev. Mr. Cook's ministry, on July 19, 1886, the church celebrated the one hundredth anniversary of its organization with a centennial sermon by Mr. Cook. At the time there were forty-nine members, a total of two hundred and fifty-nine since the formation.

There have been one elder and fourteen deacons : Elder, David Bean, 1786-1800. Deacons, Caleb Emery, 1786-1801 ; Samuel Nasson, 1786-1800 ; James Garey, 1800-1824 ; Joshua Gatchell, 1801-1802 ; John Frost, Second, 1824-1839 ; Stephen Dorman, 1831-1837, 1853-1884 ; Joshua Hobbs, 1839-1841 ; Obadiah Littlefield, 1839-

[1] Rev. Henry J. Stone's report.

1853 ; William L. Emery, 1841-1876 ; George Gowen, 1878-1895. The present deacons, with dates of election, are: Freeman C. Watson, September 6, 1887 ; Edward H. Emery, March 4, 1889 ; Howard L. Thyng, June 11, 1895 ; John J. Merrill, January 12, 1897.

Miss Ellen M. Emery is clerk of the church, and Freeman C. Watson, treasurer ; W. O. Emery is clerk of the parish, and Miss Inez M. Merrill, treasurer. The present membership of the church is one hundred and seventy-six.

Fred W. Cousins is superintendent of the Sunday School. A Young People's Society of Christian Endeavor was organized February 7, 1892, of which the present president is Miss Clara Burroughs.

As has been shown, the departure from the long-established custom of holding meetings at the south part of the town, a portion of the time at least, resulted in the establishment of the South Congregational Church in 1847. The members thereof asserted that they were the original church, and that those at the Corner had left them, and were the real seceders. This claim was not recognized by the church at the Corner, nor by a mutual council which was proposed for the settlement of all difficulties. In accordance with the recommendation of that council, Joel Moulton, Joseph Young, John Parsons, Mary Cram, Mercy Moulton, Sarah Moulton, Ednah Young, Anna Bennett, Deborah Cram, Shuah Johnson, Margaret Johnson, Jerusha Moulton, Caroline E. Moulton, and Dorcas Clark asked for and received their dismission from the original body, in order to form the new church at South Sanford. On November 9, 1847, a council, which was duly called, set apart these fourteen persons as a church by prayer and the expression of the fellowship of the churches. Rev. Clement Parker was installed as pastor. His ministry continued until 1859, with an intermission of one year which the pastor spent in Acton, and during which Rev. Isaac Weston was stated supply for a limited time. In 1858, feeling the infirmities of age, Rev. Mr. Parker resigned.

Rev. Noah Cressey, of Portland, supplied the pulpit a part of the time, 1859-1860. Rev. Messrs. Daniel Kendrick and James Carruthers, and others, supplied occasionally. Rev. Jonas Fiske was acting pastor from 1861 to 1863. For four years the church was without preaching, and then for three years had the services of theological students, a few months only, during each year. From April, 1870, to April, 1871, Rev. William V. Jordan supplied this church and that at the Corner. In 1872, Albert Bushnell, from Andover Seminary, in 1873, Albert H. Thompson, from Union Seminary, New York, and from May 1, 1874, to October, 1876, Rev. George S. Osborn, a Christian minister, were acting pastors. During the pastorate of Rev. Henry J. Stone at Sanford Corner, he also served the South Church. Of late years, services have been discontinued.

Up to 1880, there had been forty-six members of the church since its organization. There have been three deacons, John Parsons, Ebenezer L. Hobbs, and James L. Tripp.

The town was divided into two parishes by an act of the legislature, approved March 5, 1858, the parishes to be known respectively as the North and South Congregational. The act provided that the ministerial fund should be equally divided between the two, and be held by boards of trustees to be invested in real estate for the exclusive support of a Congregational minister in each parish. The trustees for the North Parish were Timothy Shaw, John Powers, William Emery, Samuel Lord, and Samuel B. Emery; and for the South Parish, Nathaniel Bennett, Horace Bennett, Theodore Tripp, Stephen H. Moulton, and John Parsons.

For years the two Congregational churches received aid from the Maine Missionary Society.

CHAPTER XI.

OTHER DENOMINATIONS.

Freewill Baptists — Elder Stewart's Church — Methodists — Christians — Adventists.— Catholic Churches.

THE first Freewill Baptist Church was organized in 1810, in Rodolphus Young's house, on "Grammar Street." There were fourteen (or fifteen) members, one of whom, William Tripp, became a Methodist minister, and died in Ripley, Maine. Humphrey Goodwin, who had been ordained as an elder, three years before, became their pastor. There are no records of this church, but there are strong evidences of its organization, possibly as a branch of the Freewill Baptist Church of Shapleigh (Acton). Its existence was not long continued, probably because when Elder Goodwin removed to Hollis from Acton, in 1814, he left them destitute of a leader, and was unable to return at stated intervals.

In 1815, when a powerful revival occurred in Lebanon and Acton, "Elder David Blaisdell was invited into Sanford from the latter place, and many were there converted, and a branch of the Lebanon church was there constituted."[1] Elder Blaisdell and his brother, Edward, came as evangelists, and held meetings in a school-house. According to Rev. C. E. Blake, the brothers Blaisdell came into town in 1817, and organized a branch church of fifteen members. A certificate filed with the town clerk, on September 3, 1817, on behalf of persons desirous of avoiding payment of the legal ministerial tax for the support of a Congregational minister, shows that on that date, Francis Pugsley, Elias Littlefield, Solomon Littlefield, and Theodore Emery (clerk), of Sanford, Benjamin Webber and Edward Standley, of Shapleigh, and James Ridley and John Beedle, of Alfred, were members " of the religious society in sd. town of Sanford called by the name of the first freewill Baptist Church and Society in sᵈ town of Sanford."

[1] Stewart's "History of the Freewill Baptists."

The two Blaisdells, Henry Hobbs, and others, labored with considerable success among this scattered flock. Their meetings were held in private dwellings and school-houses, sometimes at a distance north of Springvale, in Alfred. Elder Ephraim Stinchfield, also preached occasionally for the "New Lights," and frequently spent a week or two in the Littlefield neighborhood. After sustaining the relation of a branch of the Lebanon church several years, the members assumed the functions of a separate church, August 29, 1829. The meeting for organization was held at the house of Elias Littlefield, and Theodore Emery was chosen clerk. It is stated that the number of original members was fourteen, of whom Deacon Hiram Lord was the last survivor. From the records we can give but thirteen names: Theodore Emery, John Bedell, Edward Standley, Jedediah Storer, Hiram Lord, Stephen Webber, Polly Emery, Betsey Emery, Molly Littlefield, Ruth Littlefield, Susan Chatman, Polly Bedell, Sarah Goodwin. It is possible that one name was omitted, and entered on the list after others had joined, and that this member was Polly Morrison.

The following year the church sent Theodore Emery and Stephen Webber as messengers to the Parsonsfield Quarterly Meeting, held at Acton, by which they were cordially received, and the church in whose behalf they appeared, recognized as a duly organized body.

Elder David Blaisdell ministered to the church from 1829 to 1833; at first one-fourth of the time, and later, one-eighth. During his ministry, meetings were held at the house of Elias Littlefield, and in a school-house at Springvale. In May, 1834, Elder Samuel L. Julian came from Limerick to reside at Springvale, and to labor half the time in the gospel. Under his direction new life was infused into the church. A covenant was adopted July 1, 1834, which, in its essential features, was retained for many years.

In a few months the church grew strong in spirit, and on the 16th of November, 1834, "established a constant meeting of worship at Springvale on the Sabbath." Prior to this, however, the church voted to build a house of worship, which was completed the following year, at a cost of twelve hundred dollars. This house was situated on a rise of land, on the county road from Mount Hope to Alfred, on the east side of the Mousam River. It was dedicated August 13, 1835, Elder Arthur Caverno preaching the dedicatory sermon.

Elder Julian went west as a home missionary, and was succeeded by Elder Samuel Burbank. In 1837, Elder David H. Lord began his labors with this church and people, and the following year a great interest was awakened.

Notwithstanding the church had taken strong grounds in favor of temperance, and against the sale of intoxicating liquors, there appears to have been some doubts as to the propriety of ministers advocating temperance from the pulpit, or preaching against the use of ardent spirits. The church, however, took no step backward, but planted itself on higher ground. In 1842 a vote was passed endorsing the position of clergymen in their stand for temperance. A new covenant was adopted in October, 1843, into which were incorporated anti-slavery sentiments. A committee, however, appointed to draft resolutions on the subject of anti-slavery, never reported. There was a steady growth of the church during several pastorates, although there were a number of setbacks. Trouble arose in regard to the dismissal of Elder N. K. George, but the breach was healed when a Quarterly Meeting council, consisting of Elders Theodore Stevens, E. A. Stockman, and G. W. Bean, met and advised the disaffected members.

During the pastorate of Rev. A. J. Davis, the old meeting-house was replaced by a more commodious structure, costing seven thousand dollars. John Merrill, merchant, gave a bell weighing fifteen hundred pounds. That desirable gift was accepted at a public meeting of the society, held on March 31, 1866. After appropriate remarks by Rev. Mr. Davis, Mr. Merrill was introduced. He remarked that, a good while before, he made up his mind that a man ought not to undertake what he could not accomplish. He could not make a speech, but he could give a bell, which he did cheerfully, this proviso only being made : " It should be rung and tolled, when required, at the funeral services of any one, rich or poor, high or low, black or white."

The following have served as pastors of the church : Elder David Blaisdell, 1829–1833 (or 4) ; Elder Samuel L. Julian, 1834–1836 ; Elder Samuel Burbank, 1836–1837 ; Elder David H. Lord, 1837–1840 ; Elder Alvah Buzzell, 1840–1842 ; Elder Theodore Stevens, 1842–1845 ; Elder Gorham P. Ramsay, 1845–1847 ; Elder A. R. Bradbury, 1848–1849 ; Elder C. B. Mills, 1849–1851 ; Elder W. H. Waldron, 1852–1855 ; Elder Theodore Stevens, 1855–1857 ; Elder N. K. George, 1858–1860 ; Rev. Edwin Mason, 1860–1863 ; Rev. J· M. Brewster, 1863–1864 ; Rev. A. J. Davis, 1864–1868 ; Rev. J. H. Mason, 1868–1869 ; Rev. W. H. Yeoman, 1869–1875 ; Rev. C. E. Blake, 1875–1877 ; Rev. A. H. Hanscom, April, 1877–June, 1878 ;

Rev. B. G. Blaisdell, August, 1878–April, 1882; Rev. F. P. Wormwood, October, 1882–April, 1883; Rev. J. C. Osgood, May, 1883–April, 1885; Rev. R. D. Frost, June, 1885–April, 1886; Rev. A. M. Freeman, April, 1886–April, 1889; Rev. J. D. Waldron, April, 1889–April, 1893; Rev. B. M. Osgood, April, 1893–May, 1896; Rev. J. Manter, September, 1896–March, 1897; Rev. W. A. W. Hardey, April, 1897–September, 1898; Rev. E. M. Trafton, from December 25, 1898, to the present time.

The deacons have been as follows: Hiram Lord, 1836–1877; John Bedell, 1838–1866; Edwin J. Reed, 1864–1883; Silas B. Ridley, 1877–1880; Howard Gowen; Lyman Hooper, December 4, 1881, to present time; Ephraim Mills, 1892–1895; Joseph Ridley, November 2, 1897, to present time.

The present church officers include: Clerk, Frank Low; executive committee, Deacon Joseph Ridley, Freeman Goodwin, and Joseph Howe; superintendent of Sunday School, F. H. Dexter; president of Christian Endeavor Society, Miss Fannie Hobbs. The church membership is one hundred and forty-three, and that of the Sunday School, one hundred and forty.

In 1830 or 31, John Chadwick built a small meeting-house on the hill back of Captain Murray's house, which was afterwards used as a Congregational vestry. Elder Stewart of North Berwick preached in this meeting-house, and a church was there formed. The only record that we have been able to find in regard to it is the following vote from the First Baptist Church records, of date of December 3, 1831: "Voted, to exclude Deacon John Libby and wife, and Nathaniel More and wife from the fellowship of this church, as they have withdrawn themselves by joining Springvale church some months before."

We infer from a vote of the Congregational Church, September 22, 1811, that Elder Warren Bannister of the New England Methodist Episcopal Conference was in town, making efforts to form a church of his denomination. It seems to have been of no avail. In 1834, when Rev. Nathan D. George came into town, he found a small class formed at Springvale by Rev. J. W. Atkins, preacher in charge at Alfred. As long as the class had an existence, the Springvale Methodists remained a part of the Alfred charge, and received the ministrations of the Alfred pastor every fourth Sunday for two years. Rev. Mr. George was a shoemaker by trade, but was a licensed local preacher when he came into town. He worked half of the time at the bench, and devoted the rest to the church in embryo.

In his work he was ably assisted by Ichabod Frost, Dr. Jefferson Smith, Jotham Wilson, William Lord, and a Mr. Wheeler. In 1835 they built a small meeting-house on the south side of the county road to Lebanon, on Mr. Frost's land, which was used as a place of worship for some years. Rev. Mr. George moved away in 1836, and the class began to weaken, and finally disbanded. In 1848, the meeting-house was used for a private school, taught by Rev. Ammi R. Bradbury. A few years later, it was moved a few rods toward the east, used for a carriage manufactory, and burned in 1852.

The beginning of the present Methodist Episcopal Church was on June 27, 1887, when the first class meeting was held in the home of Mrs. Edna Whidden, on School Street. Calvert Longbottom was chosen leader. The class had preaching for the first time on Sunday, October 16 of that year, when Rev. Gilbert I. Lowe of Milton Mills, N. H., conducted services in Goodall's Hall. Other clergymen of the denomination followed him, and the first Quarterly Conference was held January 22, 1888, with the presiding elder of the Portland District, Rev. W. S. Jones, in the chair. The church was organized, and the following members were received by cards: Sarah W. Gowen, Mrs. Edna Whidden, Mary A. Whitaker, John J. Merrill, Mrs. John J. Merrill, Rose (Littlefield) Pike, Calvert Longbottom, and John Potter. Messrs. Longbottom and Merrill were elected stewards; Sarah W. Gowen, recording steward; and Mary A. Whitaker, treasurer. May 16, 1888, Rev. Gilbert I. Lowe was appointed pastor, and served the church for two years. The room underneath Goodall's Hall was fitted up and loaned to the church by Hon. Ernest M. Goodall, and here the Methodists worshipped until December, 1889, when the Good Templars' Hall in the Nowell block was occupied. Subsequently services were held in the old Baptist church on Church Street, then called Jones's Hall.

Rev. John M. Woodbury was appointed pastor May 4, 1890, and during the summer and fall the present handsome and convenient church structure on Bodwell Street was built. It was occupied for the first time on Sunday, September 28, 1890, Presiding Elder Jones preaching in the afternoon, and Rev. Henry E. Allen, of Concord, N. H., in the evening. The church was not formally dedicated until the 16th of April following, on which occasion Rev. J. O. Knowles, D.D., of Worcester, Mass., preached the dedicatory sermon. Three hundred dollars were raised by subscription during the afternoon and evening services.

On May 3, 1891, Rev. George F. Millward was appointed pastor, and served the church for five years. During his pastorate, October 19, 1892, the Millward Chapter, No. 8942, of the Epworth League, was organized. The present president is Mrs. Violet McCrellis. April 13, 1896, Rev. Thomas Whiteside was appointed pastor of the church, and during his ministry the parsonage, a two-story building at the rear of the church, on Bodwell Street, was erected.

The present pastor, Rev. Alphonso K. Bryant, was appointed to this charge on May 1, 1898. In the first year of his pastorate the church building was raised, and a basement constructed, in which pleasant and convenient vestries were finished off for the Sunday School and Epworth League. Extensive repairs were likewise made in the auditorium, the total cost being over one thousand dollars.

The church officers now serving include : Recording steward and treasurer, George Harding; district steward, Dr. R. S. Gove; treasurer of trustees, Calvert Longbottom ; class leader, John Wadsworth ; superintendent of Sunday School, Leroy D. Glass.

The Sanford and Lebanon Christian Church was organized in 1832, by Elder Paul Reynolds, of Acton, who was pastor for several years. A meeting-house was erected in the Deering neighborhood at a cost of one thousand dollars, and dedicated June 12, 1850. The sermon was preached by Rev. Mr. Pike of Newburyport, Mass. Among the pastors have been Rev. Messrs. Thomas Bartlett, Levi Eldridge (who was in town in 1844), Charles E. Goodwin (in town in 1854), Lemuel Goodwin, Samuel McCann, Joseph Whitney (in town in 1863), George S. Osborn, and J. H. Mugridge, who began his work in Sanford in 1872.

The church has been without a settled paster for more than twenty years, although there is occasional preaching by pastors of other Springvale churches. In the Year Book of the Christian denomination, the church is still borne on the rolls, with George L. Stillings as clerk, and is credited with forty-six members.

Advent meetings have been held in Springvale, more or less, for thirty years. No church edifice has ever been erected. A church of twenty-six members was organized June 16, 1895, in an unused school-house on Mill Street, with Elder C. M. Willand as pastor, Benjamin B. Hill and Leroy P. Goodwin, deacons, and Moses E. Lowd, church clerk. There is no settled pastor at present.

Up to the year 1887 there is no record of Catholic service in Sanford,[1] the spiritual needs of the few Catholic families being with those

---

[1] The major portion of the account of the Catholic Churches was written by Rev. John J. McGinnis.

of the Springvale Catholics, looked after by priests residing in nearby places, particularly Rochester, N. H., and Westbrook, Maine. In 1887 about twelve French-Canadian Catholic families had settled in Sanford. Already a few English-speaking families had preceded them. For these mass was celebrated in the home of Mr. Henry Gautier on Main Street. About this time Rev. Moise Denoncourt became pastor at Springvale. The Sanford people attended services, in common with the people of Springvale, in a hall at the latter village. Rev. Alexandre Dugree succeeded to the pastorate of Springvale, in due time built a church, and there the people from Sanford and Springvale continued to worship in common.

Rev. Father Dugree began his pastorate in February, 1889. The Church of Our Lady of Lourdes, on Pleasant Street, was opened for services in the fall of that year. On the 30th of June, 1890, it was dedicated by the Rt. Rev. James A. Healy, D.D., bishop of Portland, who preached the dedicatory sermon in both French and English. He was assisted in the services by Fathers Linehan, of Portland, Bradley, of Rochester, Gorman, of Brunswick, Decelle, of Saccarappa, and Harrington and Bergeron, of Biddeford. In 1894, Father Dugree built a parochial residence near his church. The entire value of the church property in Springvale is estimated at six thousand dollars.

In 1891 the number of Catholic families in Sanford was about thirty. Provision had to be made for services in the village. Father Dugree purchased the old Baptist Church on Church Street, fitted it up for Catholic worship, and there the little congregation, for the first time gathered together, began to hold parish services. The church took the name of St. Ignatius, Martyr. The number of Catholics increasing, Father Dugree thought it well to separate Sanford from Springvale, and a petition to that effect was sent to Bishop Healy. The petition was favorably received, and Rev. M. J. Healy came as the first resident pastor, in 1892. Father Healy began the work of organizing the people into a parish body, holding regular services every Sunday, establishing a Sunday School, and forming societies to attach the people the more strongly to the church. He also purchased a house on Elm Street to be used as a residence by the pastor. Father Healy remained as pastor until July, 1895. During his pastorate the work of formation was done. The societies flourished. The Catholic families numbered about one hundred.

In July, 1895, Rev. John J. McGinnis came from St. Mary's Church, Bangor, where he had been assistant, to assume charge of the parish at Sanford. The work of organization continued. The societies established were kept up, and provision made by the establishment of a private school, for the instruction of the children both during the day and in the evening. In the course of a few months the debt on the old church was paid off. The arrival of new families continued, and the two morning services hardly sufficed for the accommodation of the worshippers.

In March, 1897, the bishop transferred Father McGinnis to the parish at North Whitefield, Maine, and made Father Dugree resident pastor of Sanford, the depression in the cotton industry at Springvale having driven many of the Catholic families to look for employment elsewhere. In October, 1897, Father Dugree's health failed, and he was obliged to seek rest and change in Florida. He resigned the care of the Sanford church, but retained his pastorate at Springvale.

Father McGinnis was recalled to Sanford. The need of a more commodious church had become apparent. After long searching for a suitable location, the Increase S. Kimball place, between upper Main Street and the river, was purchased September 15, 1898, the house to be used as a parochial residence, and the lower end of the lot for a church site. Work on a church with brick basement and wood superstructure, from plans by F. H. and E. F. Fassett, architects, of Portland, was begun immediately. The building was finished and the basement made ready for occupancy February 1, 1899. On that day, the feast of the patron of the parish, St. Ignatius, Martyr, the church was solemnly blessed by Rt. Rev. Bishop Healy, who was assisted by Rev. T. P. Linehan of Biddeford, Rev. Fathers M. C. McDonough, E. F. Hurley, John O'Dowd, and D. J. O'Brien, of Portland, and Rev. J. W. Houlihan, of Dexter. The basement seats four hundred. With the two morning services, it no longer suffices for the convenience of the parishioners, and the upper church is now being made ready for use. The main church will seat five hundred on the floor and about one hundred in the gallery.

The parish now numbers about two hundred and twenty Catholic families. The attendance at the two morning services is seven hundred and fifty, and the Sunday School attendance, one hundred and eighty. The old church building on Church Street is now being used for school purposes, and there one hundred and twenty children are receiving instruction under the care of the Misses Clara and Margaret Bissonnette.

Rev. Father Dugree, in addition to his work at Springvale, has charge of the missions at Milton Mills, Kennebunk and Kennebunkport, having the spiritual direction, in all, of about five hundred Catholics.

CHAPTER XII.

EARLY EDUCATION.

The First Schools — Town Votes — Money Raised — Teachers — Mode of Teaching — School-Houses — Districts and Divisions — " Masters " Clark, Hamilton, Gowen, Thompson, Shaw, and Others.

THE importance of public instruction was early recognized in the " Colony of the Massachusetts Bay." The necessity of free schools was felt, and their preserving influence acknowledged; and early laws relative to the establishment of schools were passed. These laws were in force during the growth of the plantation of Phillipstown, though not binding upon the inhabitants thereof, until they were incorporated into a town. The early settlers, however, appreciated, in some degree, at least, the advantages of learning, and were not backward in fostering a spirit of improvement. If the parents among the first settlers could read and write, they taught their children themselves, as far as their knowledge and means went. When several families had settled sufficiently near together, the best educated person in the neighborhood would open a school for a few weeks, at his own house or at the house of a neighbor, and give rudimentary instruction. This was the only means available for several years, to teach the young. With few books, and those for the most part uninteresting, and with home-made ink and quills, the primitive methods were not fruitful in great results; yet there were learned the lessons of perseverance, self-reliance, and independence, which gave strength in manhood when emergencies arose.

In 1768, the year of incorporation, the selectmen state, in a petition to the Governor, council, and house of representatives, that the town " is destitute of a school-master which by law they are now obliged to be provided with," but no action in regard to the matter appears to have been taken that year or the next, to comply with the requirements of the statutes. The earliest votes recorded were passed June 12, 1770, when the town " Voted to hier a School-master three months," and appointed Naphtali Harmon, Jonathan Johnson, and John Stanyan as a committee for that purpose; the town also "Voted to fix the Schoole-house comfortable to meet in and that mr Samuell Willard and mr William Bennet and mr James Geary be a Commity to fix the Schoole-house." From this it appears that a school-house had been erected, but whether by individuals in their private relations before the incorporation, or by the town in its corporate capacity, we have no means of knowing.

In 1771, a committee, consisting of William Bennett, Ephraim Low, and Jonathan Johnson, was appointed to hire a school-master for three months, and the year following twenty pounds were raised for a school. At the annual meeting in March, 1773, the following votes were passed : " Voted to Rais Sum money. Voted to Rais twenty Pounds of Money. Voted that the said sum be for the use of a School. Voted that the Selectmen be a Committy to Hier a minister and school master." Three years intervened between these votes and the next recorded in regard to schools. In 1776, the people voted not to have a school, but the next year raised forty pounds for the use of a school, and left it with " the selectmen to appoint a place of keeping the schools." In 1778, one hundred pounds lawful money were raised for a similar object, and Samuel Emmons was chosen "to join with the selectmen to provide the places to keeping schools at." At an adjourned meeting, however, one half of the money raised for schools was "dropped." No money was raised the next year, though it was " Vot^d to leave it under the Direction of the Selectmen Chosen as a Committee to Provide a school and the Places of keeping." From these votes it would seem that more than one place was required for accommodating the pupils, and we infer that schools were established in different parts of the town.

We know of a certainty that a school-house at South Sanford had been occupied after 1770, and we learn from Dr. Parsons that Mrs. Ruth Hibbard, widow of Daniel Hibbard, and her daughter Dolly, taught about that time (1770) in the Ezekiel Eastman house, just above the site of Alfred Corner. The subjoined order shows that the scholars at Mouse Lane were provided with a school-teacher in 1780 :

" SANDFORD OCTOBER ye 3th 1780.

"to You Slectmen of Sanford Gentlemen We the Scribers do Hearby Send you these few Lins to notifi you that we Have Hired thankfull Taylor to Keep School as Much as comes to one Hundred ninty Five pound and we would be Glad if you will See it paid

" JOSHUA GOODWIN DANIEL GRAY
" JOHN GRAY."

WILLIAM L. EMERY.

According to a vote of March 7, 1780, school was to be taught six months, and nine hundred pounds were raised for school and town charges. At a later day, six hundred pounds additional were raised. In 1781, " Voted and raised £43 14s for schools to be paid in silver or paper equal thereto."

The second school-house was built in the North Parish, and was standing in 1787; for the warrant for a town meeting to be held December 10 of that year designated the school-house in that parish as the place of meeting. It is probable that the building was erected in 1782, soon after the town was divided into two parishes; for, prior to 1783, " the school-house " was designated, several times at least, as the place of meeting, but in that year, and in several years following, as if by way of distinction, " the school-house in the South Parish " was specified as the place of assembling.

About the time of the organization of the two parishes, the town contained one hundred families or householders, and was required by law to " set up " and maintain a grammar school. Accordingly, a grammar school was established, and Josiah Clark, of Wells, engaged to take charge of the same, and give instruction. He was, undoubtedly, the first master employed by the town, and was " of good conversation, well instructed in the tongues," but whether always a " discreet person," and " sober," may be questioned; for the masters of his time (and he was not an exception) were not morally sensible of the degrading influence of intoxicants, and did not live in a state of constant sobriety. It is known that " Master" Clark taught (probably his first school in town) in 1783, was in town in 1784, had wages due in 1788, was taxed in 1789, and taught in the North Parish. He had considerable intellectual ability, but was lacking in energy. He had a fund of stories which he related to his scholars, and of descriptions of all parts of the globe with which he entertained them, for, although a graduate of Harvard College, he had thereafter shipped on a whaling voyage, and had followed the sea some ten or twelve years. In his later days, he was fond of repeating hymns. " Master" Clark died in Waterborough, November 6, 1819. During his residence in Sanford he laid claim to the lot, given by the proprietors, and known as the " school lot," because he was the first grammar school-master. He finally sold all his right and title to the lot to William Emery.

In the North Parish, Dolly McDonald, or McDaniel, succeeded Mrs. Hibbard and her daughter. "The earliest school-master was John Dennie, grandson of Rev. Dr. Coleman, of Boston, who taught

10

one session among the Gileses." [1]   He preceded "Master" Clark in that part of the town.

In 1784, forty-five pounds were raised for schools, and it was "Voted to district the money that is for a school." "Schools were to be kept in each district long enough to take up the money in said district." It does not appear that any action was taken on the fifth article of the warrant for the annual town meeting, namely: "To See if the town will take the School Lot in the South Parish and Appropriate the Same to the Use of a School." In 1785, seventy pounds lawful money were raised for a school or schools, and it was "Agreed upon and Vot^d that the Selectmen are Chosen to Regulating the School or Schools in this town." In 1787, the inhabitants "Voted not to raise any money for schools, but to pay it out of the money in the bank," and also not to sell the school lot.

The following year it was decided to "Destrick" the schools, and in April it was "Vot^d the first Destrict for Schools in the South Parish Shall have amendment that is all ye Inhabitants on the Eastern side of mousam River Shall be Sot off by them Selves." About that time it was "Agree^{td} upon and Vot^d the Selectmen Shall Prosecut Mr Jonth Tebbets constable if he dont pay Master Clark." For several years, one hundred pounds per annum were appropriated for schools. In 1789 there appears to have been some trouble over the school in "the Gore," and it was voted that "the Selectmen are to overhaul ye school money to see where the Inhabitants on the Gore got there part." In 1790 it was voted to district the two parishes.

Though the school-house in the South Parish served the threefold purpose of a school-house, a town-house, and a meeting-house, it was wholly under the control of the parish; but having completed a meeting-house, the society voted May 28, 1792, "to give up the old school-house to the main district to move it where they see fit." It was probably moved to Powers's corner, and later was bought by John Bennett, who moved it and lived in it on the county road leading over Mount Hope, only a short distance from the old meeting-house. In May, 1793, it was "Vot^d that the Shackers Shall have there School money by themselv," thus virtually making a district of that young and peculiar community.

Some of the school-masters referred to by Dr. Parsons as having taught prior to 1800, John W. Parsons, Joseph Emerson, John Giles, Rev. John Turner, Daniel Smith, Robert Harvey, and Robert Jenkins, may have taught prior to 1794; and there is a possibility that

---

[1] Parsons's "Centennial History of Alfred."

the school-house, used for town purposes as early as 1787, was "the old frame house first raised in Alfred by Daniel Lary," and "finally moved to the Corner, where the brick hotel built by C. Griffin stood, and was used many years as a school-house."

School matters seem to have been in a state of constant agitation for ten years, and the best means to be employed to accommodate the people was frequently discussed, for every tax payer and every head of a family desired that no other resident have greater advantages than he. It therefore required tact on the part of those having a controlling influence to arrange the schools to the satisfaction of the majority. The custom that had prevailed for several years, of districting the schools annually, seems to have given way to a better method inaugurated in 1796, when, at the annual town meeting, a special committee was appointed to consider the alteration of the school districts, and other school matters in general. This committee reported, among other things, that the schools in the future be under the direction of a committee, to consist of seven members, who should be "men of learning," chosen annually in March or April. This committee, whose functions corresponded with those of the school committee of the present day, was to serve gratuitously, "Said Sarvice to be performed only for the Good of the Youth in Said Town So that they may have Learning, which is the support of Republican Government." The report was accepted, and the first school committee was chosen, consisting of the selectmen with Rev. Moses Sweat, Caleb Emery, Major William Frost, and Joshua Gatchell.

Thus far schools had been maintained in different parts of the town for the accommodation of the several neighborhoods, but only one permanent place, the parish school-house, had been provided. Dwelling-houses had been secured, from time to time, in the best room of which, or in some unfurnished apartment, the scholars met for daily instruction. These temporary rooms were so inconvenient, that it became necessary to have better accommodations. Consequently, in March, 1797, the people, in town meeting assembled, "Voted that Each School Destrict Build a Comfortable School house in the most proper place for Keeping the School in their Destrict." It was about this time, probably, that Major Samuel Nasson gave a piece of land for a school-house lot. The frame of a house was raised, but, owing to some trouble, was not boarded. The house occupied so many years, near the Baptist meeting-house, and after its removal, at the Corner, was built soon after.

On the 8th of March, 1798, seventeen persons residing in the vicinity of Linscott's mill petitioned for a new school district, and the district at Mouse Lane was accordingly divided. The first notice that we find of a district at what is now Springvale is in 1805. The school-house built that year stood at the forks of the road leading from the Province mill to Beaver Hill and to the Littlefield neighborhood. The next school-house was built on the western side of the Mousam, and was burned December 11, 1837. Betsey, daughter of Dr. Linscott, taught at one time in the former, and Mehitable Clark and Theodore Willard were among the teachers in the latter.

The town records for more than twenty years contain but few references to schools. The report of 1796, so far as it related to a school committee of seven, was entirely ignored after two years, and only six times prior to 1820, was any committee chosen. That report was not binding any longer than the town accepted it, and it was optional with all towns until after the separation to appoint a school committee, or leave the care of the schools to the selectmen. Appropriations, varying somewhat, however, were annually made.

We have, fortunately, the recollections of a few scholars of those early days, and are able to give a brief description of the schools of the olden time.

" The first school that I remember to have attended was kept in one room of my father's house, and that unfinished. For seats we had blocks of wood with planks laid across ; for writing desks, one large rough bench somewhat like those our carpenters use, only not quite so steady and well finished. The teacher had but one arm, and that was his left. The next one of which I have any remembrance, was a mile away. It was kept in a small, unfinished attic with two small windows, and was furnished like the former room. It was in the summer, and the room was so close and warm that I played truant whenever I could. The teacher was a nervous man—we never had any female teachers—so nervous that when he punished one of his scholars, he became much excited, turned all sorts of colors, and finally said, ' Come up here old times and taste of it.' In school and out, he thereafter went by the name ' old times.' When I was about ten or twelve years old, I went one winter near the old Baptist meeting-house. That school was also in a dwelling-house (Eleazar Chadbonrn's). It was kept in a back room about fifteen feet by eight. In one corner was a bed, and all the best clothing of the family, together with the week's ironing, was hung round the walls.   Our books were the testament and the spelling book ; our writing books consisted of a sheet of paper, each, folded once; our pens were made of goose quills. If we got two or three months' schooling in a year, we thought ourselves well off. I attended about six weeks in a school-house."[1]

One of the old-time masters, at South Sanford, was Henry Hamilton, Senior. He was a Scotchman by birth, tall, spare and with a palsied hand. He lived on a farm, near Parson Sweat's, and at such a distance from the school-house as to prevent his going home and returning during the usual intermission at noon. He was wont to resort to the tavern, probably Colonel Emery's, for his dinner. It did not vary in kind, though it did frequently in quantity, and yet he never tired of it. A gill of rum constituted his dinner, a glass, half a dinner. He was always served with it. "Master" Hamilton pretended to know much about law, and often tried cases in school, some of which continued nearly half a day. Among the boys that attended his school were Stephen Willard, William Taylor, and William Emery. One day during the progress of a spelling match, Willard crowded Emery against Taylor, who retaliated by striking Emery. The result was an out-of-door fight, in which Emery got the better of Taylor, who came off with a bloody nose. A trial was at once ordered. The master sat as judge. After the witnesses had been heard, sentence was pronounced and summarily executed. Taylor feruled Emery in the presence of the school, and then Emery feruled Taylor.

Some of "Master" Hamilton's punishments were severe; occasionally they were peculiar. For instance, one unruly girl was kept some time with her head between the master's knees, that she might be humbled and brought into subjection. The school-house in which he taught was furnished with long, narrow tables, or desks, and weak benches that creaked and trembled under their restless load. The girls occupied the seats on one side, and the boys, those on the other. Reading, writing, arithmetic, and spelling were taught.

"Aunt Nabby" Gowen informed the writer that Mrs. Esther, wife of Ephraim Low, and "Master" Ezra Thompson taught in a house on Shaw's ridge, where boards on rocks were used for seats. The first "Grammar Street" school-house stood in a field a short distance from the Samuel Shaw house. "Master" Thompson taught there many terms, and had the Gowens, Shaws, Thompsons, Willards and Lows for pupils. The building, which, when used for school purposes, was a rough unfinished affair, was occupied temporarily, by a family in 1819, and took fire and burned down.

[1] Related by Mrs. Sophia Webster, in 1857.

" Master " William Gowen began to teach in town about 1800, and
continued his work in several districts for some thirty years in winter,
though mostly in the school-houses near the Baptist meeting-house.
Often there were a hundred scholars, from the abecedarian to men
and women grown.   As there were but few printed arithmetics, he
carried most of his pupils, in his early schools, through the fundamental rules, by putting examples down on a piece of slate, and giving the rules orally.   At the same time, he gave to the young men who
so desired, lessons in wood and land surveying, teaching them to
make, from the wood pile at the door, with axe and jack-knives, the
instruments with which they worked.   He delighted in astronomy,
and studied it with his older scholars, as far as his limited means
would allow, drawing diagrams showing the positions of the planets
with chalk on his kitchen floor by firelight.   He frequently made
ciphering books for his pupils, some of which, preserved for more than
two generations, were unfaded and readable as print, though he made
his ink of maple bark and copperas, and his pens of goose quills.[1]
    Rev. Moses P. Webster thus writes :   " I remember when I began
to attend school.   The school-house, near the Baptist meeting-house,
was then an old and somewhat dilapidated building, with a large fire-
place on one side, and the seats all on the other.   In the winter, we
were either nearly frozen with the cold, or scorched with the heat.
The district then included nearly half the town, with about one hundred scholars in attendance, many of them men and women grown.
Some of the young men would weigh more than two hundred pounds,
and we should call them now rather a rough, though generally, a
good natured and peaceably disposed set of boys.   The school in
winter was often taught by ' Master Bill ' Gowen, as he was called.
He was very easy, and had but little government, and the school was
quite noisy." (Another says :   " He was stern and unsparing of
the rod in school government.") "Yet somehow he was apt to teach,
and would make the scholars learn.   But one winter I recollect that
a young lawyer from Alfred, by the name of Goodenow, and I think
afterward Judge Goodenow, was engaged to teach, and he could do
nothing with them ; and so, after a week or two, while I was reading
in the old ' American Preceptor,' he told me to stop, saying, ' The
school is dismissed,' and then caught his hat and cane, and ran as if
for life, with the whole school hooting at his heels.   The district was
afterward divided into six districts."
    Some of the most popular and competent masters of the early days
gave private lessons, among them Parson Sweat.   From him, William

[1] Miss Carrie Hatch.

Gowen learned grammar, that he might give instruction therein. At one time, Ezra Thompson spent two evenings a week with him in the study of Latin and Greek,—he began the latter at the age of fifty-two years—that he, too, might disclose their rich and varied treasures. "Master" Thompson, in turn, had private pupils in surveying and navigation.

In the Deering neighborhood, Abraham Carroll and Joseph Dam were early teachers. At a later period, John Hanson, Daniel Gowen, William B. Merrick, Tobias Emery, and Ivory M. Thompson taught there. Evat Willard taught in the Samuel Nowell district in 1829. When he was examined, John Hanson, of the committee, asked him a ninepence for examining him. Willard taught at the Corner in 1836, and again in 1860. William C. Allen, afterward Judge of Probate, was employed to teach in the school-house above Naphtali Chadbourn's. He was carried out by the large boys, and compelled to give up the school. George W. Hussey and Daniel Gowen also taught in this district. The "Grammar Street" school district was long noted for the large number of teachers brought up within its limits, or employed therein. The names of Ezra Thompson, Timothy Shaw, John Shaw, Theodore Willard, Daniel P. Shaw, Hosea Powers, John Thompson, Robert Tripp, George Chadbourn, William Gowen, James H. Chadbourn, Joseph L. Tripp, N. Powers Chadbourn, Lewis W. Gowen, Sally Powers, Clarissa Powers, Joanna Thompson, Elizabeth Chadbourn, Lucy H. Chadbourn, Betsey Shaw, Judith Ann Shaw, and Laura J. Shaw, are a guaranty that the reputation of the district was well merited. In that district, schools were taught in Daniel Garey's house, Ezra Thompson's, and John Thompson's. "Master" Timothy Shaw taught at one time in "Master" Thompson's house. He was regarded as a handsome man, but was considered by his pupils as stern and severe Town business frequently called him from the school, which pleased the scholars ; for, during his absence, "Master" Thompson supplied in his place. "Master" John Shaw was strict and dignified. He was a surveyor, and gave instruction outside of the school-room, in surveying.

Regarding the old school-house already alluded to, originally located near the Baptist meeting-house, and afterwards at the Corner, the records of the meeting of the first school district on January 18, 1802, say : "Voted and raised two hundred dollars to be assessed on the polls and estates of this district to be appropriated toward building a school-house. Voted the said school-house be twenty-six by twenty-six, and eleven feet post. Voted and let the said house

to Moses Chick to build and finish, including painting the trimmings
of said house, for two hundred and fifty dollars. Voted and raised
fifty dollars in addition to the two hundred to be appropriated toward
building the said school-house."

We have evidence showing that schools had been established in
eight districts prior to 1820 : South Sanford, Mouse Lane, two districts, " the Gore" (Deering neighborhood), Sanford Corner, the
Bean district, Shaw's ridge, and the Frost district (Springvale) ; and
we have reason to believe, in two other districts : Oak Hill and
Mount Hope. In 1821, school agents were chosen by the town for
the ten districts then established, as follows :

No. 1, Sanford Corner, Elisha Allen ; No. 2, South Sanford, John
Powers ; No. 3, Oak Hill, Jabez Perkins ; No. 4, Springvale, John
Morrison ; No. 5, Shaw's ridge, Stephen Gowen, Junior; No. 6,
Mount Hope, Abner Hill ; No. 7, Bean district, Nathaniel Bennett ;
No. 8, Deering's ridge, Stephen Fernald ; No. 9, Mouse Lane, David
Clark ; No. 10, Mouse Lane, Joshua Getchell.

At the same time, September 10, a new district was formed, and
Zebulon Beal was chosen agent. It was formed from the first district, and included residents of Hanson's ridge, the Hobbs road, and
Lebanon road. On the 19th, the twelfth district, embracing those
dwelling in the Hobbs neighborhood and on the Lebanon road, was
organized, and Sheldon Hobbs was chosen agent. The thirteenth
district was formed in April, 1822. In May of that year, the districts were bounded anew, and accepted July 20. The names were
practically the same as in 1821, although the fifth was called the
" Grammar Street " district, and the tenth, the Perkins. The eleventh
was the Plummer's ridge district, the twelfth, Hanson's ridge, and the
thirteenth, Shaw's ridge. In another month, a fourteenth district,
the " Hardscrabble," was formed.

It was about the time of redistricting the town that school-houses
were built in different localities where they were needed. In some
parts of the town, schools were taught in dwelling-houses. The
brick school-house, which stood for about fifty years at the intersection of the roads leading from the Corner and Springvale to Alfred,
was then erected. The wooden school-house that stood at the forks
of the road leading from the Corner to Hanson's ridge and the Hobbs
neighborhood, and did twenty-five years' service, was built in 1822.
It is highly probable that William Gowen, Junior, taught the first
school in that house in the winter of 1822-3.

Within a year or two, a division arose in the first district. It was proposed to move the school-house, to which objections were made. The vote was carried ; the school-house was started, but the first night only reached the foot of the hill on its way to the proposed site at the Corner. There the shoes were cut off, as it stood in the road, and a short delay was caused. The trouble may have arisen, in part, or have been aggravated, by the appointment of a meeting by Rev. Mr. Marsh, to be held in the school-house, near the Baptist meeting-house, at which Elder Cook and his friends presented themselves. Although the school-house was moved, the trouble grew so rife that a new district (the fifteenth) was formed, and a new house, known as the Congregational school-house, was built. It stood in Deacon Frost's field, opposite to the present site of the residence of Hon. Thomas Goodall. It was dedicated by Rev. Mr. Marsh. Following the example of Parson Sweat, Mr. Marsh taught a public school in that house. More than twenty years later, the house was moved to South Sanford, and converted into a dwelling for Rev. Mr. Parker. The establishment of the fifteenth district was followed, November 1, 1824, by the formation at Lyon Hill, of the sixteenth district. In 1826, the seventeenth district, below Oak Hill, was formed ; in 1830, the sixth district was divided and the eighteenth formed, which, in the year following, was annexed to the sixth ; in 1833, the eighteenth, Moulton's, nineteenth, Littlefield's, and twentieth, Colonel Butler's, were established ; in 1839, number four was divided ; and in 1846, the Beaver Hill district was established.

In 1847 a committee was appointed to redistrict the town, but for some reason unknown, no progress was made until 1849, when sixteen districts were established, in the following consecutive order : Springvale, Sanford Corner, South Sanford, above Springvale, " Grammar Street," Mouse Lane, Kennebunk line, Lyon Hill, Deering's, Hanson's ridge, Nowell's, Johnson's mill, Oak Hill, below Oak Hill, Moulton's, Mount Hope. Changes were made from time to time, one of which, as late as 1875, the consolidation of numbers thirteen and fourteen, occurred because the school committee reported that, " in number fourteen it has, cost the town fifty-six dollars to give two scholars nine weeks' school."

The erection of a new school-house, in 1852, in the " Grammar Street " district, near the residence of Timothy Gowen, resulted in the refusal of several persons to pay their taxes on the ground that the money was illegally raised. Their property was accordingly sold for taxes, and the matter was tested in court, judgment being rendered against the town. Several years elapsed before the cases were finally settled, and meanwhile another school-house had been built in the lower part of the district, so that, at one time, there were three school-houses within the limit of number five.

Graded schools were unknown in town prior to 1855. In that year, the first two-story school-house was erected at Springvale, at a cost of twenty-seven hundred dollars. It was designed and arranged for two grades, grammar and primary. Four years later, two grades of schools were established at the Corner, the lower one of which was taught in the vestry of the Congregational meeting-house. In 1868, a new house, the second two-story school-house in town, was built at the Corner, in which two grades were maintained, as at Springvale.

Elder George Heard, Daniel P. Shaw, Caleb Emery, Valentine Meader, Pelatiah Hussey, Charles Hill, Moses M. Butler, Titus S. Emery, John M. Ames, Abner Mitchell, William H. Wiggin, Joseph T. Nason, Hubbard Fogg, John M. Stanton, Levi W. Stone, Gershom Ricker, John Derby, and Edwin Emery, were among the teachers at the Corner in former years. In the summer, women taught, among whom were Rachel Humphrey, Nancy Moulton, and Mary T. Barker.

Sanford Academy was incorporated February 12, 1834. Gideon Cook, John Storer, John Skeele, Elisha Bacon, Charles Emerson, Daniel Wood, and Abner Flanders were trustees. Funds were wanting to make the new enterprise a success, and so the corporation existed only in name. This attempt to provide a higher course of instruction and mental training than the public schools afforded, is a revelation of the earnest desire of the people of the early part of the century for greater intellectual improvement, a desire which was met and satisfied, in a degree, by the private schools conducted by Elder George Heard, Rev. Mr. Goss, Moses M. Butler, Rev. Ammi R. Bradbury, Abner Morrill, John H. Goodenow, William Gowen, Ann Maria Hussey, and Albert L. Cleaves, in most of which instruction in Latin and the higher English branches was given. In 1831 or 2, Rev. Elisha Bacon, with the cause of education deeply at heart, introduced a new teacher into town, Miss Rachel Humphrey, of Freeport, whose improved methods, founded upon principles somewhat similar to those of the modern kindergarten, attracted scholars from a wide range, and the inspiration of her teaching was productive of lasting results.

An account of the schools of Sanford of the present day will be found in a subsequent chapter of the History.

CHAPTER XIII.

LIFE OF THE EARLY DAYS.

Agriculture — Spinning and Weaving — Customs of the People —
Wild Animals — Bear Stories — A Mink Climbs a Tree — Fish.

ONE of the conditions upon which the settlers' lots were granted,
was that four acres should be broken up and fenced in within
three years of the date of the deed conveying the same. When the
early settlers took up farms the land was cleared and burnt over,
much of the growth being burnt on the ground. Corn was planted
without ploughing, and rye sowed and " hacked " in with hoes. The
new ground yielded large crops, and an abundance of corn fodder and
rye straw was cured. Wild grass, bushes, and brakes were cut and
cured for fodder, upon which, and the hay hauled from Wells and
York, cows and oxen were kept during the winter in numbers sufficient for the comfort and convenience of the people. At first, however, only a few oxen were brought into town, and one of the greatest
wants of those early days was oxen to haul timber and to plough land
for planting.

Sheep and swine were a necessity, the former for wool, the latter
for food. One necessity produced another. Only a few potatoes
were planted at first. To keep hogs, farmers must have more corn
and potatoes. The forests themselves furnished one kind of food
spontaneously, which sheep and swine could eat. Acorns were abundant where oak growth flourished, so that in the fall these animals
found food enough to render them quite fat. Some farmers gathered
fifteen or twenty bushels of acorns in the fall, and fed them out during the winter. All the family, male and female, old and young, engaged in the work of gathering acorns.

The worth of a man was estimated from the number of cattle kept
and not the number of acres owned. There was a commendable pride
in having as many cattle as could possibly be kept during the winter
upon the fodder cured. Cattle and hogs were small. Oxen that
measured six feet in girth were rarely seen, and a kept-over hog that

weighed two hundred and fifty pounds was a great hog. Some farmers killed two hogs in the fall, and five or six shoats, the latter weighing from eighty to one hundred pounds apiece. Pork was the principal meat. Beef was eaten during the early part of the winter, pork in the spring and summer. Wild game furnished some families with nearly all the meat. Many families lived chiefly on bread and butter, or bread and milk (milk always for supper). Corn and rye bread was in general use; wheat bread was a great luxury. Beans and peas stewed with beef made most palatable bean and pea soup. Many families knew nothing for weeks at a time of the luxury of tea and coffee.

Cider was a favorite beverage, and New England rum was freely used. The first nursery of apple trees was sowed about 1742, by Dr. Bennett. Before orchards produced apples in abundance for cider, the farmers joined together, and sent teams to York to buy their stock of cider. There is a tradition that the first cider ever made in Sanford was made by Eunice Tripp and Mary Johnson. The apples were pounded in a long trough by them, and pressed by Jonathan Johnson. In connection with this it is interesting to notice that Lieutenant Jonathan Johnson was the only person in town 1771, that returned in the valuation any cider—eight barrels.

Flax was raised for clothing. Tow and linen cloth were often worn for shirts. Cotton was rarely worn, except by women and girls, and then only when they could afford to buy calico for gowns. Wool was carded, spun, and woven into cloth, which was made into clothes by the women in their houses. Almost every family had a large spinning-wheel for spinning wool, a foot wheel for spinning flax, and a loom for weaving. In 1810, there were one hundred and sixty looms in town, and twenty-nine thousand, three hundred sixty-nine yards of cloth were manufactured.

General Moulton was extensively engaged in farming, having at one time thirty acres in corn and rye. For years, to encourage wheat raising, there was a bounty on wheat. The same may be said of corn. In 1837, four hundred and eighty-five bushels of wheat were raised, on which the bounty was forty-two dollars and seventy-three cents; in 1838, six hundred and forty-nine bushels with a bounty given of sixty-three dollars and thirty-seven cents, and twenty thousand eight hundred and ninety-six bushels of corn with a bounty of eight hundred and seventy-four dollars and eighty-eight cents; in 1840, seventeen thousand and eighty-four bushels of wheat, rye, barley, etc., twenty-nine thousand one hundred and seventeen of potatoes, and two thousand and forty-seven tons of hay raised. According to the valuation of 1771, only one thousand three hundred and twenty-two bushels of grain were raised, and one hundred and sixty-seven tons of hay. Captain Jonathan Tebbets of Mount Hope informed the writer in 1877, that he had raised all his flour in fifty years, except one year when the wheat crop was killed by rust.

One spring, Master Gowen could not get any rum or potatoes, owing to the scarcity of those commodities in Sanford, so the reason is given. He travelled to York, brought home a bushel of small potatoes (rum of course was not wanting), and raised therefrom sixty bushels.

Grass grew very sparsely on some of the new clearings, and the want of it was a real privation to the neat housewife. One woman was much troubled for a place for drying clothes. Calling upon some neighbors whose lot had been cleared several years, she received on her return as many grass roots as she could carry. She cultivated them with the choicest care until she had a patch of grass large enough for drying her clothes and bleaching her linen. Clothes lines and clothes pins were almost unknown in those days.

The forests were mostly pine, and pine lumber was cut in considerable quantities. Before mills were numerous, clapboards and shingles were made at the farm houses, and even afterwards, because timber and boards were the principal articles manufactured at them. Logs were cut into the proper lengths, then split into suitable thickness to be shaved. These splits were taken to the kitchen and shaved in the long winter evenings or on stormy days. That kind of lumber was quite easily taken to market because of its lightness, and brought a good price. But there was much oak, which was used also. Oak Hill appropriately received its name from the oak which covered it.

Not until the beginning of the present century were nails in common use. All spikes and nails, large and small, were made by the blacksmith on the anvil. Shingle nails were worth from two to three shillings a pound. Poor people could not buy at that price, and were under the necessity of making oak pegs with which to fasten boards and shingles. For boards, the pegs were nearly as large as a rake tooth. Holes were bored through into the timber, and the peg, driven home, held quite fast. In shingling, a large awl was used, and a man shingled his house much as a shoemaker pegs on his soles. The barn that stood in the writer's boyhood, back of Mrs. Eliza Bodwell's small house on Washington Street, was so shingled. Moses Witham built the barn shortly after the close of the Revolution, and when it was taken down in 1845, and hauled to the Corner, some of the shingles were then sound, and the pegs as good as new.

Harvesting was followed frequently by two festal occasions, the husking and the apple bee. These evening gatherings for work were enlivened with song and laughter, jokes, repartee, and stories, alike entertaining to old and young, who were invited to be in attendance. Huge stacks of corn filled the barn, over which, suspended from pitchforks stuck securely into the hay-mow, were the old-fashioned tin lanterns, shedding their dim, flickering light. The huskers sat along one side, and threw their husks into the tie-up. When that red ear for which every one had been looking was found, and the huskers had "washed up," they sat down to tables loaded with hearty and substantial food, baked beans, Indian pudding, roast beef or lamb, spare rib, potatoes, doughnuts, pies, tea and coffee. These were consumed in large quantities, and the host and hostess seldom had occasion to express their fear that their food was not palatable. Rum and cider were often served, and always without stint, until public opinion began to change, and the habitual use of these was condemned by the best men in the town. Following the supper came a dance, on the threshing floor cleared for the occasion, or in the kitchen after the tables had been removed. If no fiddler (the term violinist was unknown) was present, some one sang for the dancers, as they " tripped the light (heavy) fantastic toe " in Virginia reels and country dances.

Apple bees were of a similar character, but more quiet and free from the rough, boisterous sports of huskings. Apples were pared, quartered, cored, and strung or sliced, for family use or the peddler, after they had been thoroughly dried in the sun. A supper, dancing, and games followed. Huskings and apple bees were often prolonged until the early morning. These gatherings were the natural results of the social nature of the people, although the pastime served the double purpose of getting work done, in addition. That the early settlers were of a very social disposition, is known from the fact that they would often travel two or three miles for a family visit, and tarry until a late hour at night before returning home. The quilting parties of housewives, preparatory to the marriages of their daughters, or for increasing their bedding, also disclose the character of our ancestors. The work was prepared ; the quilting frame, or poles, got in readiness ; the guests, if helpers may be so called, were invited. Deft fingers swiftly plied the needle, ready tongues glibly told the latest bits of news or gossip. Sometimes envious men, who were invited to tea that they might be present to accompany the women home, would intimate more in earnest than in jest, under the guise of pleasantry, that the women, while making with their hands a durable fabric for comfort, were tearing in pieces or destroying with their words the character of their neighbor.

In 1814 or 15 there had not been any Baldwin apples raised in town, though a few trees had been grafted. About that time, a young man who had been working in Massachusetts, brought home as a present to his betrothed, a few Baldwins in his pack.

From the earliest settlement of the town, hunting and trapping formed an important business, and sometimes a source of revenue. Furs were in demand, and sold quickly at good prices. Beavers, otters and minks were found near the brooks and ponds, and foxes, wild-cats, wolves and bears were plenty in the forests. A bounty was frequently paid for destroying some animals, and when money was scarce, peltry was taken for taxes. When beavers became scarce, and their skins sold for a high price, a single skin of good size and quality would hire a man for a month. Bear meat was eaten freely, so there was a double inducement to kill bears, sometimes triple, their meat, skins and bounty. It must be stated, however, that young men, fond of sport, often spent more time than was profitable in their frequent hunting expeditions.

There were beaver dams below Moulton's mill in 1741, as witnesses a deed of ten acres of meadow from David Bennett to James Littlefield. Beaver Hill and Beaver Hill Pond received their names from the beaver whose homes were numerous in that vicinity. In 1771, the pond of Sanford head-line was known by that name. There was a beaver dam a few rods below where the bridge is on the "new road."

We cannot reconcile the following with the town records, but copy it as showing the bounty allowed for each wolf killed and the course of procedure to prevent deceptions and the payment of a double bounty:

" Mr. Treasurer

" This may certify, that there has been paid out of the Town Stock of Sanford for five Grown Wolves, and —— Wolves Whelps, killed in and near this Town, since the 15 of february last past, and the Heads thereof brought unto our Constable or Constables, and the ears thereof cut off in the Presence of our Selves, as the Law directs, and so certified unto us, in the whole the Sum of ten *Pounds;*

which Sum we desire you to allow to our Town, by paying the same
unto Mr. Stunells our Town Treasurer.

"Dated in Sanford aforesaid, the first Day of July, Anno Dom.
1774.

"Benj^M Harmon) Selectmen
"Will^M Bennett } and
"John Stunells) Town Treasurer."

The town voted September 6, 1789, not to raise any money for
killing wolves. On the 8th of March, 1785, it was voted "To give
20 shillings lawful money for every wolf's head that is killed within
this town." This bounty and the worth of their skins caused them
to be hunted and killed in large numbers. We do not wonder at
this, for the torn and lacerated bodies of domestic animals killed by
wolves, and the dead carcasses of many farmers' sheep and hogs,
bore witness to the ferocity of the wolves.

At a later period bounties were given for crows and wildcats.
June 17, 1805, the town "Voted to give ten cents per head for
crows," and in 1807, twelve cents. In 1831, Elisha Allen was paid
seventeen dollars and fifty-two cents bounty for two hundred and
nineteen crows; in 1832, Francis A. Allen, nine dollars and thirty-
six cents for one hundred and seventeen crows, fifty-six cents for
eight crows, and one dollar for one wildcat; in 1833, nine dollars and
eighty-four cents for one hundred and twenty-three crows. Thirty
wildcats were killed in the county that year, and in 1834 four wildcats
and six crows were killed —where? The total state bounty for crows
in 1831 was three thousand, two hundred and forty dollars, and five
cents.

Many interesting stories of adventures with bears have been
handed down from the original settlers.

At one time, Mrs. Hanson, of Hanson's ridge, was on her way,
with her child, to visit a neighbor on Low's ridge, four miles distant,
when she met a bear in the road. Deeming discretion the better part
of valor, she turned and hastened home as fast as she could go.

Mrs. Batchelder, the "Colonel's" wife, with her infant in her arms
(born July, 1782), and with a Mrs. Waterhouse for company, started
by a path through the woods to visit a neighbor. Presently, on going
up a little rise, they saw a big brown bear, sitting in the path as if
he had taken possession of it. "Throw Sammy down, and let's run!"
exclaimed Mrs. Waterhouse, what courage she had thoroughly frightened out of her. "Sammy and I will live and die together," answered

HOWARD FROST.

Mrs. Batchelder, fixing her eyes on the bear, and walking slowly backward. When she was well out of sight, she ran with her baby as fast as she could, until she considered herself out of danger.

There is a tradition in the Low family, that Ephraim Low, Junior, was engaged after the Revolution in cleaning the forests of bears, and one year killed as many as there were days in the year. One was shot on Low's ridge.

At one time, the wife of one of the early settlers asked her husband to get a roast for Thanksgiving. Taking his oxen and sled, axe and gun, he went into the woods for game, from which he returned with a load of bears — nine large and small, — saying to his wife, "Here's your Thanksgiving."

At South Sanford, Mrs. Hale, widow of Captain Enoch Hale, went into the pasture one evening after her cows, when she ran across two cubs. They were frightened, and took to a tree where she attacked them. As they were not very expert climbers, they fell to the ground when she struck them. She killed them both with a pitch-pine knot.

One night a bear came to Major (?) Bennett's barn after his swine. The disturbance called out the Major with his gun. It was so dark that he could not see anything, but intending to frighten away whatever there was, he fired in the direction of the noise which he heard. Hearing nothing more he went to bed. In the morning, he found bruin dead, shot through the body by the random shot in the dark, and the indications were that the bear was quite near when the Major fired.

When Elsie Powers, who married Thomas Willard, was a girl she had a young lamb given to her. As was the custom of her early days, the barn door or entrance was fenced up in part, with a space left open above. One winter's night, the snow drifted about the door so that a wolf, which came prowling around, easily jumped into the barn, and killed the lamb. It was evident from the marks made that he jumped out only after repeated attempts.

The late Mrs. Sarah Allen told the writer that her grandfather on Hanson's ridge, used to go hunting in winter, leaving his wife alone with their child. Many a night her grandmother remained at home, with door barred, while the wolves came howling around. "Aunt Nabby" Gowen also told the writer that there were woods everywhere when she came into town in 1788. There were wolves enough then. "Wolves came around the house so you could hear them breathe," was her expressive language. She remembered that a young domestic animal was killed by them in a yard near by.

11

A man was on his way home, at Mouse Lane, from South Sanford. He carried a gallon rundlet filled with molasses. The wolves scented him and followed. He had heard that, if the attention of the leader of the pack could be diverted, or if he acted like a coward, the rest would turn upon him. Throwing his rundlet back among them, he ran, and, while they were fighting among themselves, reached his home in safety. The next morning, he returned to the scene of his evening adventure, and found his molasses, all right, but one wolf, supposably, the leader, was completely torn into pieces.

Whatever may be the fact, it used to be currently reported and believed that, if the wolves saw anyone put anything over his shoulder, like a gun, they would leave him unmolested. Colonel Emery was at one time travelling up into the country through the woods, when he heard a pack of wolves behind him. He shouldered a stake, and they passed by. At one time when returning to his camp in the woods from another to which he had been, shoeing oxen, he came near losing his life by wolves, but managed with the dextrous use of a large club to escape safely to his camp.

" Alpha," in the Sanford News, a few years ago, related the following bear stories :

" Solomon Allen and son, the latter the father of David and Solomon Allen, were out in the woods cutting logs, and had just finished loading, when the old man accidentally stuck his goad into the snow, and found there was a hollow place there, and upon digging away the snow, they found the den of a large black bear, and bruin was there, fast asleep. The first thought was, to capture him ; and the second was, ' How shall it be done?' As ' necessity is the mother of invention,' they were not long in devising a method to secure him. The old gentleman took a long stick and poked the bear in the nose to divert his attention, while his son fastened an ox chain around his hind leg. They had considerable difficulty in getting the cattle near enough to fasten the chain to them, as they smelled the bear and were afraid ; but by dint of coaxing and driving, they, at last, succeeded. The old gentleman then seized the axe and told his son to start the oxen and when the bear came out of the hole he would kill him. For once they ' reckoned without their host;' the cattle started and only succeeded in drawing the bear's leg out straight, when he drew it back with apparent ease, cattle and all. This went on for some time, until the snow had become beaten down around the den sufficiently to allow Mr. Allen to strike the bear in the head and kill him. He was then drawn out and put upon the load of logs and hauled home, and dressed; and they had fresh meat enough all winter. He weighed nearly eight hundred pounds.

" At another time, Mr. Allen was returning home from his work, with an axe on his shoulder, when he met a bear in his path, and as soon as bruin saw him, he arose on his hind legs and walked towards him with huge paws opened, with the intention, no doubt, of giving him a friendly hug; but Mr. Allen met him half way and saluted him with the axe on the head, killing him at once."

" A Story Teller " in the Sanford News, gives us " Reminiscences of Olden Time," in which he alludes to some of the courageous women of the early days, who occasionally visited their neighbors, although it was dangerous so doing. " Among the number were Aunt Nabby and Aunt Polly, who, each with a child in her arms, started one bright afternoon to visit a neighbor on the hillside, all in sight of where our village now stands. As they walked along a well beaten path, through the whispering pines, their ever watchful ears were sometimes startled by the wild cry of a bird or the crackling of a dry twig, broken by the leap of a squirrel, or some other strange sound in the dense thicket. Suddenly their attention was attracted by a huge bear that strolled leisurely from the woods and seating himself on his haunches in the path, only a few rods in front of them, gravely awaited their approach. Of course they were frightened, but not so terrified, as those less accustomed to such visitors might suppose. They neither screamed nor ran, but retreated slowly and silently, walking backwards with their eyes fixed on those of bruin, while they clasped their little ones more closely in their arms. Old bruin had doubtless dined sumptuously, for without insisting upon a fat baby for dessert or upon accompanying them home, he sat quietly, evidently amused at their discomfiture. As soon as Aunt Nabby and Aunt Polly escaped from his sight, they turned and ran home.

" A few years later Aunt Polly, one day, sent her two oldest children to a spring for water. While walking along the same path where their mother had before met this adventure, they were startled at the sight of another great bear greedily devouring one of their father's sheep. He looked steadily at them but, seeming to prefer the mutton he had to the children he had not, left the frightened little folks to scamper home as fast as their trembling legs could carry them. You may guess they were not allowed to go that path again unguarded. Their father on his return from work, being informed of the loss of his sheep, was so enraged that, armed with gun, he plunged alone into the thicket and by the light of the moon searched for hours for the thief, which was doubtless sleeping soundly in some hollow log or cave.

"Not many months after the loss of his sheep, Uncle Stephen started out early one frosty morning, axe in hand, to cut some timber near the river. The snow was nearly three feet deep, obliging him to wear his snow shoes. Having just left the clearing and gone a few rods into the woods, he espied a large bear running directly towards him. For Uncle Stephen to run was impossible, to climb a tree useless; all that remained for him to do was to 'fight it out on that line.' He instantly struck a defensive attitude with uplifted axe in his firm grasp, and awaited the approach of bruin, who seemed determined upon a hearty morning's meal. The bear rushed upon him with glaring eyes and open mouth, and extended his arms for the fatal hug. Nothing daunted, Uncle Stephen with no uncertain aim buried his axe in the head of his enemy, who fell at his feet; with a few well directed blows the contest was ended. Uncle Stephen then returned home and sent one of his boys for Uncle Joshua to come and help in hauling the bear home. When dressed the carcass weighed nearly four hundred pounds."

"Ben," in the Springvale Reporter of March 4, 1876, tells two stories concerning one of Sanford's early settlers, whose name he pretends to conceal. "A man whom we will call Real, made his way from old York to the foot of Lyon Hill by road, from thence up the Mousam about five miles, spotting trees as he went, thence westward about one mile to the side of the ridge, where he commenced a cutdown. His first business after locating was to put up a shanty. Here he heard the first whippoorwill, which scared him nearly out of his wits, thinking the cry was ' Whip poor Real, whip poor Real,' which to him meant that he was surrounded by enemies who intended to whip him and drive him away at break of day. He made tracks back the way he came, by spotted trees to the nearest house at the foot of Lyon Hill. There telling his night's experience he was informed it was only a bird that came to sing his song of welcome to the knight of the axe."

Whether whippoorwills were ever heard in York we may question, but we know that the nearest house to the Hobbs neighborhood, one hundred years before the foregoing story was written, was not further down than Ephraim Low's, a mile below the Corner.

"Every Saturday he walked home to old York for a fresh supply of food, which he carried back Monday on his back. On one of his home visits he came in contact with an old sea captain who, in course of conversation, introduced the article of coffee as one of the finest things in the world, and finally persuaded Mr. R. to take a small quantity and try it, whereupon a pound was procured and added to the already ponderous load. In due season he arrived at his shanty, and prepared for the duties of the next few days. ' Now,' he soliloquized, ' for some of that coffee for supper.' He put about one half of the coffee in a pot, built up a rousing fire under it, and it soon began to boil. Occasionally he would try it, but as it was not cooked soft, on would go a fresh lot of wood; in due season it was again tried but with like result. Thus he continued for three days, faithfully boiling his coffee early and late, after which time it was all thrown away as a ' humbug.' As usual Saturday found him beneath the paternal roof, relating his sad experience in ' bilin that coffee.' After a hearty laugh Mr. R. was informed of the *modus operandi*. Ever after coffee was his drink until his hand became so tremulous he was obliged to abandon its use."

It was in the fall of 1809 that the last bear of which we have any knowledge was killed in Sanford. There was then in the cedar swamp in the south part of the town a well-known cave, designated as the '' bear's den." One Saturday, two brothers, Jotham and Robert Johnson, were on their way to work, near the swamp, when it occurred to them to visit the den to see whether there was a bear in it or not. It has not come down to us whether there had been any bear in it for years before, or any tracks of one during that season or the preceding summer. It was probably an idle, visionary suggestion that entered the mind of one of the brothers, and led him to say, " Let's go to the ' bear's den ' to see if there's a bear in it." '' Yes, let's go to the ' bear's den ' to see if there's a bear in it," was the reply of the other; for these brothers, always together, had the peculiar habit of repeating each other's words without variation. So the two men made their way through the woods to the den, where to their surprise they found a bear. Her body was within the cave, and she so lay that her nose only stuck out. They were frightened at first, but on second thought decided to do something to injure, perhaps to kill, the bear. Jotham struck at her with his axe, but succeeded only in wounding her nose slightly. Thereupon she rose upon her hind legs, caught Jotham, downed him, bit him in the wrist, and ran away. The brothers were terribly frightened,—so was the bear—and hurried away in an opposite direction. Coming out into the cleared land they descried several young men, to whom Robert shouted, at the top of his voice, "A bear! a bear! we must raise a crew and go and catch her." Repeated by Jotham, whose loss of blood and fright had not completely unnerved him, the cry greatly excited the young men, and when Robert, with short, quick breath, and in broken sentences, told the story, it created the wildest enthusiasm among them. The report that Jotham had been bitten by a bear spread like wildfire, and a crew of ten or twelve men, armed with muskets, started in hot pursuit after the bear. They proceeded to the den, knowing that they could thence track her by the blood of her wound, as it fell upon the snow, which had recently fallen. From the cave her track was easily disclosed in a south-southeasterly direction down through the swamp to the road leading to Doughty's Falls. When the men reached there it was quite dark, and they could not go further, so they agreed to meet at that place early the next morning. About twenty stalwart fellows assembled at their rendezvous on Sunday morning, and continued their pursuit. In a short time they discovered the bear lying near a fence only a short distance from their place of meeting. Without any leader or systematic organization, they did nothing, allowing the bear to escape before a shot was fired. Following her towards the "great swamp" in the direction of Wells, William Emery and another came up within a few feet of her, having distanced all the rest of their companions. Emery had broken through the ice in a swampy place, and so wet his gun that it was entirely useless; the other had raised his gun, but it had missed fire. For a few moments they had a most exciting time; they were within six feet of bruin; she had turned and shown her teeth; their guns would not go off; their companions were too far back to render assistance; they were inclined not "to bulge an inch;" it would not be prudent to go forward. In this dilemma, Emery told the other to prime his gun, while he watched the movements of the bear. She soon eluded them, and was lost to sight among the bushes.

Once during the chase, Robert Johnson caught sight of her, and, though there were several directly in range of her, raised his gun, and shouted, "Fire! fire!" But he had scarcely got his words out of his mouth, when he fell backward, thus preventing a serious accident. In his excitement, he had made so violent an execution that he lost his equilibrium, his feet slipped from under him, his gun was thrown up, and he himself stretched at full length on the ground. Again they lost sight of her; again they were on her track. The nearer they approached, the more intense became their enthusiasm. Emery ran around a clump of bushes or trees to head her off, caring no more for her than a hog. She turned only to meet another, and in trying to escape ran along the whole length of a tree which had fallen. Henry Hamilton came up to the top of the tree as she was running, took aim, fired, and she fell across the butt. Some were afraid that she was not dead, but one of the most active and courageous of the company stepped up and took her by the ear. Her throat was cut, but owing to the loss of blood from the wound received from Johnson she bled but little. The ball that killed her entered her hip and passed to her shoulder. Upon poles bound together with withes, they carried her through the woods three-quarters of a mile to the road leading to Wells, and thence on a team home. They gave her skin to Jotham, who had been bitten, and he in turn gave it to Dr. Hall, of Alfred, for dressing the wound. The doctor used it for years as a carriage-robe. The meat was divided, and sent round among the neighbors. So numerous were they, that some of the principal actors in the drama got only three or four pounds. The writer's father, then a babe, had a taste of the meat, which may account for his delight in recounting the incidents of the story to his children. The particulars here given came from one of the actors, directly to the writer.

Many years ago, William H. Scribner taught writing-schools at Springvale and the Corner. He made Springvale his headquarters, and came to the Corner two or three evenings a week. One evening, he entered the school-house at the Corner under great excitement, and astonished his pupils with his adventure. As he was coming past Hanson's woods, above Mrs. Gowen's, he heard a loud noise, a screech or a howl, and the crackling of dried limbs and bushes, as if a ferocious animal was rushing through the woods towards him. He ran as fast as his feet could carry him, and reached the Corner out of breath. At the close of the session, the young men and boys accompanied him above the woods, but heard nothing save the noise which they themselves made. It was currently reported that a loup cervier was heard and seen in the woods, and some wonderful adventures were related, though nothing definite in regard to the size and appearance of the wild beast could be learned. A Canada lynx might have found his way so far from home, but it was a question whether the noise heard was not the hooting of a screech-owl, and the crackling that followed only a slight movement of the nocturnal bird which developed under his excited imagination into the tread of a rapacious quadruped.

It has now been more than forty years since the writer with a companion enjoyed an autumnal day, hunting in the woods to the

south and west of the Corner. A double-barrelled gun, a flask of
powder, a pouch of bullets, a box of percussion-caps were our arms
and munitions. A small, short-legged dog, whose slowness of loco-
motion and general make-up disclosed the fact that he was better
adapted for domestic duty on the hearth than for scenting game in
the forest, accompanied us on our predatory excursion. Through
Gowen's woods, across the Witham lot, toward the Paul Tebbets
place we wended our way. Now and then a chattering blue-jay attracted our attention, or a " lightning chipper " darted before us, and
escaped into his hole in the wall. Our dog ran as fast as his stumpy
legs could carry him, and barked as if he had something sure, and
we guess he had, for whatever he started up was surely safe from
harm. Occasionally the peculiar call of the red squirrel would draw
us toward a tree, from the branches of which we could see him jump
with wonderful agility, and ofttimes elude us by his rapid movements.
Across the Bean and Welch farms we wandered, and strolled along
the Great Works Brook at the foot of the hill near Rufus Welch's,
and up across the Witham field, then owned by " Uncle Bill." What
our fare was during the day, we have not the slightest recollection,
but we are safe in assuming that we got apples from the orchards
through which we passed, and perhaps, came as near the Corner as
Gowen's cider mill to get a little new cider.

Along in the afternoon, we were descending the hill from the Red
Brook toward the Springvale road, and had got nearly through the
woods, when our dog barked with noticeable earnestness. We hurried
in the direction from which the sound came. At the foot of an oak
standing on the edge of the road near John C. Gowen's, stood our
canine friend, still vigorously barking; while, at the top of the
almost leafless tree, appeared an animal, which, from its size and
color, we concluded must be a black squirrel. Our companion had
the gun, or took it, for we deferred to his skill in handling the weapon,
and used it. Our black squirrel did not fall at once. At the second
or third discharge of the musket, however, down dropped our game.
The dog showed a wonderful degree of activity, and could not re-
frain from shaking up well the dead victim, and left him in a sorry
looking plight.

Our black squirrel turned out to be a mink. He had evidently
been suddenly surprised, and could find refuge only in that solitary
tree. We have often wondered how he climbed up the trunk, and
reached the tip of a topmost branch. When we told the story at the
Corner, much incredulity was manifested, for no one had ever heard

of a mink climbing a tree before, and all doubted whether such a feat could be performed by that animal. Some may be incredulous now, but the fact remains, however strange it may seem, that a mink can climb a tree.

In former days the rivers and ponds were well stocked with fish, but in later years the number has been greatly reduced. The pickerel, perch, shiner, horn-pout, eel, chub, sunfish, barbel, and trout were abundant, and, probably, the salmon, shad and alewife came up the Mousam, within the town limits.

It is amusing to read, in the light of modern knowledge and experience, a remonstrance of the town, in 1816, against the construc-of a passage-way in the Mousam River, for salmon, shad and ale-wives. It appears that Dr. Jacob Fisher and others petitioned the General Court for such a fish-way, but the town thought it would be an injury to the water power of the river, and consequently sent in the following counter-petition :

" To the Hon. the Senate and the House of Representatives in General Court assembled,

" Humbly shew The inhabitants of the town of Sanford, in the County of York, that they have seen with no little astonishment, a petition of Jacob Fisher and others, praying that a passage-way may be made and laid open in Mousam River, in the County of York, for Salmon, Shad and Alewives.

" There are on said river and its branches four factories, seven grist-mills and seventeen saw-mills. The property is of vast importance to the owners, and utility to the public.

" The oldest inhabitant of this town has never known a Salmon, Shad or Alewive to have been caught in the river adjoining.

" There is not, we humbly conceive, the remotest probability that ever a Salmon, Shad or Alewive could be induced or persuaded to enter the river — What *good* motive could have induced the petitioners to make this extraordinary request, is beyond our comprehension. All *rational* men must deem the project the most crazy and outrageous.

" We therefore confidently hope that the Hon. legislature will give the petitioners leave to withdraw their extraordinary petition — and as in duty bound will ever pray.

" Presented by the Town.

" Nov. 4, 1816."

In contrast with this remonstrance is a report of Nathan W. Foster and Charles G. Atkins, fish commissioners of Maine, January, 1868.

After studying the characteristics of the river and the country through which it flows, the commissioners say: "The Mousam is eminently a salmon stream. . . . . . When unobstructed its whole extent nearly, must have been suitable spawning ground for salmon. . . . . . The natural aspect of the river promises salmon, and tradition accords with it. From Judge Bourne of Kennebunk we learn that the Mousam was once 'full of salmon.' Dr. Emerson informed him that one Wakefield once loaded a cart with salmon in a little while at the foot of his garden in Kennebunk. There were, also, shad and alewives; the shad still come into the river, but the salmon come no more. . . . . . There are between Mousam Pond and the sea, eighteen mill dams and one reservoir dam. There is no special obstacle to the construction of a fish-way over any of them. None of them are now provided with fishways, and we did not learn that they ever were. . . . . . Were it undertaken to restock this river, salmon should be the kind selected, but it might at the same time be found practicable to increase greatly the amount of shad, and to breed alewives here to a certain extent. It would further be necessary to breed salmon from the egg in the river, they being now entirely exterminated." The report concludes by suggesting that owing to the changed conditions of the Mousam "not so many salmon could be bred in the river as originally, unless resort should be had to artificial breeding."

In further support of the contention that salmon were once found in the Mousam River and within the limits of Sanford, is a communication from an old resident published in the Sanford News some years ago, in which he says that in his boyhood days, when fishing in the river between the mills and Butler's bridge, "once in a while, I used to catch what 'we boys' called a 'red-meated shiner.' They were usually about a foot long, bright light color, meat red as a cherry, and would weigh from a pound to a pound and a half. At that time I had never, that I know of, seen a salmon; but since then, having seen them by the hundreds just as they came out of the water, I have become entirely satisfied the 'red-meated shiners' we used to catch were nothing more or less than young salmon. This opinion is backed up by other boys of Sanford."

CHAPTER XIV.

CONVENTIONS.

Adoption of the United States Constitution — Opposition of Major Samuel Nasson — Alien and Sedition Acts — Hostility to the Embargo — Letter of Thomas Jefferson — Separation from Massachusetts — Removal of the Courts.

AFTER the adoption of the Federal Constitution by the convention in 1787, the General Court of Massachusetts provided that towns should choose delegates in the same manner in which Representatives were elected, to meet in Boston, in January, 1788, to consider the expediency of ratifying the Constitution. Sanford at first voted not to send a delegate, but, upon petition of some of the legal voters, a meeting was called December 10, 1787, to reconsider the former vote, and to choose one or more fit persons to attend the convention. At that meeting, Major Samuel Nasson was elected as a delegate. Whether or not he was authorized to oppose the ratification of the Constitution, we are not informed, but we think there is evidence for the presumption that he was selected as delegate on account of his well-known opposition to it. We can but regard him as the exponent of the town, and his action, whether by speech or vote, as an expression of the sentiment of the majority of the inhabitants, of which he was the mouth-piece. He was prominent in the convention, and took an active part in the proceedings.

Regarding the action of Sanford, David Sewall wrote from York a month later, to Hon. George Thatcher, member of Congress, from Massachusetts: "Sanford had one meeting and Voted not to send any (delegate) —But Mr. S. come down full charged with Gass and Stirred up a 2nd Meeting and procured himself Elected, and I presume will go up charged like a Baloon."

In a letter bearing date, New York, January 14, 1788, General Knox refers to three parties in Massachusetts, of which the second is in the Province of Maine. "This party are chiefly looking towards the erection of a new state, and the majority of them will adopt or

(171)

reject the new Constitution as it may facilitate or retard their designs, without regarding the merits of the great question." In a letter to Madison, quoted in a communication to Washington, February 3, 1788, it is stated that " the leaders (in Massachusetts) of this party (Anti-Federalist) are Mr. Widgery, Mr. Thompson, and Mr. Nasson, from the province of Maine, Dr. Taylor, from Worcester County, and Mr. Bishop, from the neighborhood of Rhode Island." This town, then, was Anti-Federal, and one of the five towns leading the opposition.

The objections of Major Nasson can be best understood from his speeches, which have been published in the printed reports of the proceedings of the convention. The section relating to the apportionment of representatives and direct taxes was under consideration when " Mr. Nasson remarked on the statement of the honorable Mr. King (Hon. Rufus King, of Newburyport), by saying that the honorable gentleman should have gone further, and shown us the other side of the question. It is a good rule that works both ways—and the gentleman should also have told us that three of our infants in the cradle are to be rated as high as five of the working negroes of Virginia. Mr. N. adverted to a statement of Mr. King, who had said, that five negro children of S. Carolina were equally rateable as three governors of New England, and wished the honorable gentleman had considered this question upon the other side—as it would then appear that this state will pay as great a tax for three children in the cradle as any of the southern states will for five hearty working negro men. He hoped while we were making a new government, we should make it better than the old one; for if we had made a bad bargain before, as had been hinted, it was a reason why we should make a better one now." In another speech, again discussing the matter of taxation, Major Nasson further treated of the slavery question as follows : " On this footing, the poor pay as much as the rich. And in this way is laid that five slaves shall be rated no more than three children. Let gentlemen consider this—a farmer takes three small orphans, on charity, to bring up—they are bound to him—when they arrive at twenty-one years of age, he gives each of them a couple of suits of clothes, a cow, and two or three young cattle—we are rated as much for these as a farmer in Virginia is for five slaves, whom he holds for life—they and their posterity—the male and the she ones too."

The president of the convention, Governor Hancock, had submitted a proposition that certain alterations and amendments should be made to the Constitution. That was conciliatory, and had a favorable influence upon some delegates, who assented to the Constitution, when they saw that some objectionable features of it would be removed by the adoption of the proposed amendments. After others had discussed the proposition of the Governor, Major Nasson made his chief effort of the proceedings, in which he regarded the Constitution as "so pregnant with danger," and occasionally rose to heights like this : "Oh Liberty, thou greatest good, thou fairest property! with thee I wish to live, with thee I wish to die! Pardon me if I drop a tear on the peril to which she is exposed. I cannot, sir, see the brightest of jewels tarnished! a jewel worth ten thousand worlds! And shall we part with it so soon? Oh, No."

Major Nasson's grounds of objection to the Constitution, as stated in his speech (which did not deal with the propositions of Governor Hancock), were the dangers of a central government with a sovereign power, vested in Congress, as making for the " annihilation of the state governments ;" of biennial elections of Congressmen ; of apportionment and taxation according to population, as being unequal ; of the equality of large and small states in the national Senate ; of the terms for which Senators were to be chosen, as being too long to trust any body of men with power ; of the exercise of the right conferred upon Congress to change the time and manner of holding elections, as putting " it in the power of a few artful and designing men to get themselves elected at their pleasure ;" and of the menace to the people's rights in maintaining a standing army and in suspending the writ of *habeas corpus* under certain conditions. Major Nasson laid especial stress upon the maintenance of a standing army, " that bane of republican governments," recurring to the Boston Massacre to illustrate his argument, and in stentorian tones he exclaimed : " Sir, had I a voice like Jove, I would proclaim it throughout the world, and had I an arm like Jove, I would hurl from the globe those villains that would dare attempt to establish in our country a standing army."

Nasson did not escape severe criticism for the stand taken, nor was he free from the charge that this appeal to the convention was not his own production. David Sewall, afterwards writing to Mr. Thatcher, said of it : " Who fabricated Mr. N. last Speech I am uncertain — one thing I am satisfied of, he never made it himself not that I conceive it an Elegant one."

Notwithstanding the speeches and exertions of the Anti-Federalists, — they were, undoubtedly, as sincere in their opposition as the

Federalists were in their support — the Constitution was ratified by a small majority, one hundred and eighty-seven yeas to one hundred and sixty-eight nays, Major Nasson, of course, being recorded among the latter. The situation was gracefully accepted, and the opposition manfully ranged themselves on the side of the majority in support of the new form of government. On the 7th of February, the day on which the convention adjourned, Nasson, " in a short address, intimated his determination to support the Constitution, and to exert. himself to influence his constituents to do the same." That we believe they did, and this town has ever been faithful to the obligations imposed upon it by the fundamental law of our country. A few weeks later, Major Nasson wrote to Mr. Thatcher, saying : " If their is any Pleasuer in Beaing in the Minority on Such Greate Questions I have it first in Contemplating that I have done my duty and in Receiving the thanks of my fellow Citizens through the Countery when I Arrived att the County of York I Received in General the Thanks of all I Mett, while our Friend Bar'el (for Such I yet Esteem him) was much Abused how far the Town will Carry their Resentment I Cannot Say I Strove as much as in me Lay to keep down the Sperite of the people and I hope that they will not hurt his person or his property. . . . . . I hope that we Shall Continue Peacable and Try this New Constitution and allso hope I Shall be Agreeably Supprised by finding it to turn out for the Best. . . . . My Pollitical day is Just at an end for the Town of Sanford is so poor I cannot Recomend it to them to Send any Member (to the General Court) Next Year." Nasson further writes, however, that there was talk of sending him to the General Court, but he was doubtful about accepting the honor, because " I feel the want of a proper Education."

Party feeling ran high in the early days of the republic, particularly during the administration of John Adams, extending as it did to the most remote frontier towns and plantations. To increase the revenue to meet the expenses incurred by preparations for the threatened war with France, stamp duties were imposed on certain documents, and a land tax, the first direct tax, was levied ; and in consequence of the impending war, the Alien and Sedition laws were passed. To all these acts of the Federalists there was strong opposition. In January, 1799, Captain David Bean, Stephen Gowen, Captain Sheldon Hobbs, James Gare, Joseph Shaw, Zebulon Beal, and Moses Witham were chosen a committee from Sanford to petition Congress and the General Court in hope of securing relief from the obnoxious laws. The petition, while setting forth the loyalty of the people of

Sanford to the government, and their obedience to the Constitution and laws, strongly expressed the belief that the stamp tax worked injustice to the poor; condemned the Sedition act as an abridgment of freedom of speech and the liberty of the press, and the Alien law, as destructive of "that great and inestimable jewel, trial by juries;" and protested against the manner of assessing and collecting the direct tax. "Secure to us," the petition concluded, "our liberties that we have exposed our lives to obtain, and take our money, nay our estates, for what is money or estate without liberty to use it as we think will be best. We praying for your happiness and the happiness of this country are we wishing to be dutifully children." That petition was of little avail, but the effects of the laws in question, and kindred acts, were to change the political complexion of the town from Federal, in 1798, to Republican, three to one, in 1799, and throughout the country in 1800 were disastrous to the Federalists.

American commerce suffered severely from the wars in Europe, between Great Britain and France, in the early part of the century. The Embargo act, passed as a retaliatory measure against Great Britain in 1807, forbade the departure of any vessel from the United States for a foreign port. The people of New England especially writhed and groaned under the exactions of that law, which by a reversal of the letters, was dubbed the "O grab me" act. In 1808, on petition of James Chadbourn and others, a town meeting was called, which voted to petition to President Jefferson to suspend the several acts of Congress laying the Embargo. The selectmen, Ezra Thompson, Elisha Allen, and Rufus Bennett, were designated a committee to draft the petition. Their prayer, respectful in tone, as was fitting, represented that the town's chief industry, the lumber business, had been so injured by the Embargo as to leave the people in great distress; and asked, in case of the inability of the executive to suspend the law, that a special session of Congress be called to take action. To this petition, Jefferson replied at length, in the only state paper ever transmitted direct by a President of the United States to the citizens of Sanford. The original document, which descended from the chairman of the committee to his daughter, Miss Joanna Thompson, who presented it to the writer, reads as follows:

"To the inhabitants of the town of Sanford in legal town meeting assembled: Your representation and request were received on the 8th instant, and have been considered with the attention due to every expression of the sentiments and feelings of so respectable a body of my fellow citizens. No person has seen with more concern than myself, the inconveniences brought on our country in general by the circumstances of the times in which we happen to live ; times to which the history of nations presents no parallel. For years we have been looking as spectators on our brethren of Europe, afflicted by all those evils which necessarily follow an abandonment of the moral rules which bind men and nations together ; connected with them in friendship and commerce we have happily so far kept aloof from their calamitous conflicts, by a steady observance of justice towards all, by much forbearance, and multiplied sacrifices. At length, however, all regard to the rights of others having been thrown aside, the belligerent Powers have beset the highway of commercial intercourse with Edicts which taken together expose our commerce and mariners, under almost every destination, a prey to their fleets and armies. Each party indeed would admit our commerce with themselves with the view of associating us in their war against the other. But we have wished war with neither. Under these circumstances were passed the laws of which you complain, by those delegated to exercise the powers of legislation for you, with every sympathy of a common interest in exercising them faithfully. In reviewing these measures, therefore, we should advert to the difficulties out of which a choice was of necessity to be made. To have submitted our rightful commerce to prohibitions and tributary exactions from others would have been to surrender our independence. To resist them by arms was war, without consulting the state of things or the choice of the nation. The alternative preferred by the Legislature of suspending a commerce placed under such unexampled difficulties, besides saving to our citizens their property, and our mariners to their country, has the peculiar advantage of giving time to the belligerent nations to revise a conduct so contrary to their interests as it is to our rights.

" ' In the event of such peace or suspension of hostilities between the belligerent Powers of Europe, or of such change in their measures affecting neutral commerce as may render that of the U. S. sufficiently safe in the judgment of the President,' he is authorized to suspend the Embargo. But no peace or suspension of hostilities, no change of measures affecting neutral commerce, is known to have taken place. The Orders of England, and the Decrees of France and Spain, existing at the date of these laws, are still unrepealed, as far as we know. In Spain, indeed, a contest for the government appears to have arisen ; but of its course or prospects we have no information on which prudence would undertake a hasty change in

D. M. FRYE.

our policy, even were the Authority of the Executive competent to such a decision.

" You desire that, in this defeat of power, Congress may be specially convened. It is unnecessary to examine the evidence or the character of the facts which are supposed to dictate such a call; because you will be sensible, on an attention to dates, that the legal period of their meeting is as early as, in this extensive country, they could be fully convened by a special call.

" I should with great willingness, have executed the wishes of the Inhabitants of Sanford had peace, or a repeal of the obnoxious Edicts, or other changes, produced the case in which alone the laws have given me that authority; and so many motives of justice and interest lead to such changes, that we ought continually to expect them. But while these edicts remain, the Legislature alone can prescribe the course to be pursued.

" TH: JEFFERSON."

" Sep. 10, 1808.

Although the reply of the President was couched in language as respectful and free from party feeling as that of the petition, it was not satisfactory to the petitioners, who could not accept the reasoning of the executive. His refusal to accede to their wishes aroused an unusual bitterness of feeling, and increased their animosity against the administration. Strong language was heard everywhere against the " cursed Jacobins." Another town meeting was called, on request of a number of the inhabitants, in January, 1809, at which a committee was chosen to draft an address to the Legislature, asking aid, and to prepare resolutions. The address and resolutions, which in time were accepted by the town, denounced the Embargo acts as "unnecessary, unequal, unjust, oppressive, and tyrannical," but they did not succeed in accomplishing the purpose sought. The Non-Intercourse act in 1809 took the place of the Embargo, and the series of events followed which resulted in the War of 1812.

The question of the separation of the District of Maine from Massachusetts, thus bringing about the formation of a new state, began to be agitated as early as 1784. In the following year a convention of the three counties then comprising the District, York, Cumberland and Lincoln, was called to meet in Falmouth (Portland), to act on the proposal. This convention, meeting several times in 1785 and 1786, proved " a conspicuous failure," for after adjourning from time to time, it finally dissolved with only three delegates in attendance. Meanwhile, however, a list of grievances had been given to the pub-

12

lic, which caused the selectmen of Sanford to call a town meeting to take action on the matter of sending a delegate. At first it was voted not to be represented, but at a second meeting, Daniel Gile was chosen delegate to Portland, and Nathaniel Conant, Samuel Nasson, and Eleazar Chadbourn a committee to give him directions. The tenor of these directions is not disclosed, but subsequent votes show that the town was nearly a unit in opposing separation.

It was not until 1791 that another movement was made. Then the Senators and Representatives of the District sent out an address in favor of separation, to which the town responded in May, 1792, by a vote of two for and one hundred and two against. This decided majority is attributed to the influence of a convention held at the North meeting-house in Sanford, May 1. Sixteen towns and plantations were represented by thirty-one delegates. Ichabod Goodwin was president and John Storer clerk. The reasons advanced for separation were : New Hampshire intervenes ; the population is more than that of Rhode Island, Delaware, Georgia, Vermont, or Kentucky ; distance from seat of government, unnecessary travel, and papers of Supreme Judicial Court at Boston ; District pays taxes to the support of a government where no part of the same taxes is spent, operating as a foreign tribute ; the willingness of Massachusetts to allow the District to separate. On the other hand, the reasons against separation were : The District is within seventy or eighty miles of Boston ; not to be bettered by separation ; it would be an " uncertain piece of business ;" may be obliged to go to Penobscot (capital) ; the eastern counties are poor, and have petitioned the General Court for an abatement of taxes. This convention voted against separation, thirteen nays to three yeas, as follows : Yeas, Biddeford, Buxton, Waterborough ; nays, York, Kittery, Wells, Berwick, Arundel, Sanford, Pepperrellborough, Lebanon, Shapleigh, Parsonsfield, Coxhall, Limington, Newfield. In twenty-one towns, the following week, the vote in York County stood overwhelmingly against separation.

Sanford took no part in the convention in Portland in 1794. When the question was again agitated, in 1797, the vote was unanimously against separation at a town meeting at which thirty-five were present. Ten years later the subject was again brought up, and Sanford spoke much as before, giving four for separation and one hundred and fifty-one votes against it. The population of the District so increased that the opinion prevailed it had ability enough to take care of itself, and was worthy to bear the dignity of a state. In 1816, the General Court having received many petitions in favor of separation, ordered the towns and plantations in the District of Maine to vote on the question in May, with the result that there was a majority of about four thousand in favor. The vote of the town was forty for separation and fifty against it. A bill was reported in the legislature for the creation of Maine as a separate state, but with the proviso that towns should again vote on the question in September and at the same time choose delegates to a convention to be held at Brunswick, where, if the majority in favor of separation was as five to four, they were to form a Constitution. A marked change is noticed in the vote in Sanford, one hundred and eighteen votes for, fifty-six against separation. Elisha Allen and Ezra Thompson were chosen delegates. The convention met at Brunswick as appointed, and while the majority of votes for separation were not as five to four, the juggling of figures by the advocates of the measure made it so appear, with the result that the "Brunswick Arithmetic" was known in political circles for years thereafter. The General Court took summary action, dissolving and thereby rebuking the convention.

The subject of separation continued to be discussed, and the party in favor grew stronger year by year. It assumed the phase of a political question, favored by the Democrats and opposed by the Federalists. Some of the opponents of the measure proposed the annexation of York County, in part, at least, to New Hampshire. But the opposition was of no avail. A bill was passed in the legislature June 19, 1819, calling for a vote on July 26, separation to prevail if there should be a majority of fifteen hundred. The majority was about ten thousand. Sanford's vote stood ninety-seven for and sixty-nine against.

Elisha Allen and Timothy Shaw were chosen as the town's delegates to the convention for the formation of a state Constitution which met in Portland, October 11-30. A committee of fifteen, to give the delegates instruction was provided, but the vote authorizing such a committee was rescinded at the same town meeting. At the convention, Colonel Allen was on the committee of nine to propose a name and title for the new state. The committee reported "Commonwealth of Maine." It was moved to substitute "State" for "Commonwealth," which was seconded by Colonel Allen, and carried. When the article in regard to the militia was under consideration, and the question arose whether minors should vote for company officers, Colonel Allen spoke of the difficulty of discriminating between those of age and minors. Both of the delegates recorded their

votes, with twenty-eight others, against the adoption of the Constitution, and refused to affix their signatures to it when engrossed, for
which they were given a vote of thanks by the town on the grounds
of the manifestation of "their integrity and patriotism." It is
thought that the provision in regard to the apportionment of Representatives was one objectionable feature to the Sanford delegates,
and perhaps that not requiring a religious qualification for holding
office was another. December 6, the town voted on the ratification
of the Constitution, giving only ten votes for, and eighty-five against.
Maine was admitted as a state of the Union on March 15, 1820.

The question of removing the courts seems to have been frequently
agitated. The early shire-town, York, was at the southern extremity
of the county, and the other, Biddeford, near the eastern extremity.
In 1773 the town authorized a committee to petition the General
Court that the courts held at Biddeford "may be Removed to the
Town of Wells, as it Near the Centor of the County." In 1790,
Joshua Gooding and twenty-seven others petitioned for the removal
of the courts from York and Biddeford to Waterborough. The last
named was made a shire-town in 1790, where the Courts of Common
Pleas and Sessions were held until removed to Alfred in 1806.

The town voted in November, 1796, ten for, three against, removing
the courts from York to Sanford ; and the year following, only three
voted against removing the Superior Court from York. At the annual meeting, April 3, 1797, it was "Voted the Delegates from this
town viz—Samuel Nasson Esq Dr Elezer Chadbourn and Capt Shell-
don Hobbs be desiered to Use there Influence that the Sd Court be
Removed to Sanford or the next Adjeacant Place."

In 1801 the question of removing the courts to Alfred came up,
and the town petitioned to the General Court to remove the Supreme
Court from Kennebunk (Wells) to Alfred. In 1802 the question
again came up. The year following a jail lot was selected at Alfred,
and in 1806 "the next Adjeacant Place" became a shire-town. The
vote for a fire-proof building for the county records in 1814 was: Alfred one hundred and sixty-six; Wells, thirty-nine ; and Kennebunk,
four. In 1859 the town voted against the removal of the courts or
any term of court from Alfred.

CHAPTER XV.

Post-Roads — Horseback Mail Carriers — Stage Routes — Complete
List of Postmasters — Locations of Offices.

IN May, 1775, the first regular post-office in Maine was established
in Kennebunk (Wells).[1] The first post-road was established in
1792, by Congress, to whom power is given by the Constitution. The
road extended from Wiscasset, Maine, to Savannah, Ga., and, lying
along the seaboard, passed through Portland, Saco, Wells and York.
Mail matter for Sanford came to Kennebunk (Wells), and was
brought thence by teamsters, and distributed, or left at the grocery
store. As late as 1805, letters were sent that way ; for April 1,
among the letters remaining in the Kennebunk post-office, as adver-
tised, were two for John Powers, Junior, and Daniel Wadlin (Wadlia), of Sanford.

By the act approved February 25, 1795, a post-road from Dover,
N. H., through Berwick to Waterborough court house, was established, and the year following a post-office in Sanford, of which Colonel Caleb Emery was appointed postmaster.

Another post-road was established June 1, 1810, from Portland
through Gorham, Buxton, Limerick, Limington, Cornish, Parsonsfield,
Newfield, Shapleigh, Lebanon, Berwick, Sanford, Alfred, Waterborough, and Phillipsburg (Hollis), to Buxton ; and April 20, 1818,
still another from Alfred by Sanford and Lebanon to Shapleigh. Another, June 15, 1832, began at Great Falls, N. H., and passed
through Lebanon, Sanford, Emery's Mills in Shapleigh, Acton Corner, and Newfield, by the post-offices called by those names, and
through the west part of Parsonsfield to the post-office in Effingham,
N. H. It is interesting to notice that these routes began at centres
of commerce or manufacturing, or business, at a time when they began to develop. One route strikes us today as being exceedingly
circuitous. In 1839, all railroads were made post-roads. From them
shorter routes have gradually been established.

---

[1] Bourne's " History of Wells and Kennebunk."

At first the mail was carried in saddle-bags on horseback. The first wagon for the accommodation of passengers from Boston to Portland left Motley's tavern, with the mail, Saturday morning, and reached Portland in six days (Thursday evening). In 1809, the mail from Portland, by the circuitous route mentioned, left at eleven in the forenoon Monday, and arrived at Doughty's Falls (Dowty's), by six o'clock Wednesday evening; returning at six in the morning Thursday, arrived in Portland by seven o'clock Monday evening.

After 1813, the stage started daily, Sundays excepted, at seven in the morning, from Hale's or Wild's tavern, Ann Street, Boston, for Portsmouth and Portland. Jefferds's tavern, Kennebunk, was its stopping-place. To meet this stage once a week in 1820, the mail was delivered at Kennebunk from Alfred, Sanford, Lebanon, Shapleigh, Newfield, Parsonsfield, and Cornish, on Saturday, and returned to Alfred the same day (evening), on the same route. In 1824, the mail reached Sanford Corner, Sunday morning, and was eagerly looked for by those shut out from the world beyond their home. One man, Rev. Mr. Marsh, "remembered the Sabbath day to keep it holy," and never called for his mail until Monday morning.

"Old Tucker," as the mail carrier, James D. Tucker, was familiarly called, performed his duties with remarkable fidelity. Beginning with October, 1811, he served the people regularly through summer's heat and winter's cold, always as punctual as the weather and roads would allow. Two hundred and thirty miles a week, year in and year out, was his customary ride on horseback. That he might not be incapacitated for his duties, his diet was spare and his only drink a glass of home-made beer or a draught of cold water. Speaking to the writer of the olden times, Joshua Hobbs remarked: "The mail was carried on horseback in saddle-bags by Tucker. I can see him now, horse with head right down." At one time, Nathan Lord carried the mail.

In 1825, Joseph Clark left Alfred on Sunday and Thursday mornings at eight o'clock, and passed through Sanford and Emery's Mills in Shapleigh, thence to Lebanon, Sanford, and back to Alfred by three o'clock in the afternoon, same day. In his advertisement of January 20, 1825 (in the Columbian Star), he says that "he will carry passengers when convenient, who wish to go on his route, for a reasonable compensation." His was probably the first wagon used in town for carrying the mail. In 1826, a stage left Portland at eight o'clock in the morning Mondays, Wednesdays, and Fridays, passed through Sanford, and reached Dover, N. H., at five o'clock in the afternoon. It returned on alternate days. It brought the mail twice a week.

The writer's first recollections of the mails are of their being brought from the North Berwick depot, about one o'clock every week-day, by Stackpole, George or Joe, driver. His coach ran to Spring-vale, Alfred, Waterborough, and Limerick. Mondays, Wednesdays, and Fridays, at eight o'clock he returned, leaving Alfred at seven o'clock, and on alternate days between one and two starting from Limerick in the morning. At a later period, the route was extended to Cornish. Charles Roberts of Alfred was then proprietor. Keay's stage also ran from Great Falls, through Sanford, Shapleigh, Acton, Newfield, and Parsonsfield, to Effingham, and returned on alternate days. When the route was established from Wells instead of North Berwick, it extended to Shapleigh, possibly to Newfield, and Jona-than Ross became mail-carrier.

The first post-office was established in 1796, at what is now South Sanford, but eight years later removed to the Corner ; the second at Springvale, in 1832 ; and the third at South Sanford in 1854. The following persons have held commissions as postmasters :

Sanford.—Caleb Emery, July 1, 1796 ; Thomas Keeler, December 31, 1804 ; Ebenezer Linscott, November 10, 1806 ; Stephen Gowen, January 18, 1816 ; Elisha Allen, December 13, 1817 ; John W. Bod-well, December 8, 1820 ; Elisha Allen, April 20, 1821 ; Timothy Shaw, February 27, 1830 ; Francis A. Allen, November 19, 1831 ; Timothy Shaw, August 6, 1833 ; John W. Bodwell, July 13, 1841 ; Timothy Shaw, January 31, 1846 ; John H. Kimball, May 3, 1849 ; Increase S. Kimball, December 20, 1849 ; James H. Hubbard, May 31, 1852 ; Salter Emery, December 2, 1852 ; Timothy Shaw, April 14, 1853 ; William H. Miller, September 3, 1861 ; Increase S. Kim-ball, May 8, 1865 ; Miriam W. Emery (deputy, 1876), January, 1885 ; Lebbeus Butler, December, 1885 ; George H. Fogg, October 29, 1887 ; Samuel O. Nicholls, May 28, 1889 ; Howard E. Perkins, March 29, 1894 ; Newton H. Fogg, May 4, 1898.

Springvale.—John Storer, December 8, 1832 ; Calvin R. Hubbard, July 29, 1833 ; Nathan D. George, May 27, 1835 ; John T. Paine, June 15, 1836 ; Tristram Gilman, April 4, 1849 ; Samuel Lord, April 11, 1853 ; James H. Hurd, August 7, 1861 ; George A. Rollins, December 23, 1862 ; Howard Frost, January 26, 1864 ; Amos W. Low, June 19, 1885 ; Willis E. Sanborn, September 9, 1889 ; Elmer E. Harris, January 15, 1895 ; George H. Roberts, February 14, 1899.

South Sanford.—Joseph H. Moulton, October 6, 1854 ; George

Clark, Junior, January 8, 1862; Joseph H. Moulton, December 17, 1862; Mrs. Hannah Dorr, May 8, 1893.

Colonel Emery kept the post-office in his store, nearly opposite his old house. Thomas Keeler's office was in a small store at the Corner, near the site of the Deacon Frost store. Dr. Linscott moved the office to his house, now occupied by Charles O. Emery, and Stephen Gowen discommoded the people somewhat by having the office at his house across the river, where Edgar J. Wentworth now lives. General Allen, John W. Bodwell and probably Francis A. Allen, kept it in Allen's store. In 1820, Allen having been chosen presidential elector, resigned, and Bodwell, a clerk in his store, just rising twenty, was appointed in his stead, but having performed his duty as an elector, Allen was again commissioned. General Shaw transferred the office to his store at the upper end of the village, but General Bodwell kept it in the Morrill store, on the site of which Daniel G. Clark's house now stands. When General Shaw again received the appointment, he occupied a small office built for that purpose, in the corner of his houselot, where Estes's drug store stands. A change of administration carried the office to Kimball's store on the corner above, where the Kimballs and Hubbard kept it, until it was removed, for reasons not political, to the Emery store at the lower corner, when Salter Emery was appointed postmaster. General Shaw again slowly distributed the mail in his post-office until William H. Miller changed the location to the Shaw store above. From there it was moved to the Kimball store on the site of Porrell's store, where it remained till the building was burned in April, 1866. Then it was located in the Shaw building, next in a small building on the corner of Daniel G. Clark's houselot, from there moved to Hobbs's store, next to S. B. Emery's store, and from there to the corner of School and Washington Streets. The building was soon after moved down School Street, where the office remained till Gowen's block was built on the corner of School and Washington Streets, when it was moved to that structure, where it remained till the building was partially destroyed by fire in 1899. For a few months it occupied a location near the old Nasson cemetery on Main Street, until it went into the fine new block on Central Square on the last day of September, 1900.

At Springvale, Hubbard kept the office in Moses Butler's store and Butler was clerk. The people objected to going to a place where liquor was sold for their mail, and succeeded in securing the appointment of Nathan D. George as postmaster. The office was in his shoe shop. Paine kept it in the building in which his office was, and

Gilman in his drug store. Samuel Lord kept it in the corner store. During Frost's postmastership, a new building was erected just below the Lebanon road, which has been occupied since 1878.

The pay of the early postmasters was small. In 1822–23 General Allen received about nine dollars and fifty-two cents per annum. John W. Bodwell's compensation in 1841 was fifty-six dollars and twenty-four cents, and John T. Paine's for one year, thirty-seven dollars and eighty-two cents. Letter postage was considerable in the first part of the century, ten cents being the charge in 1816 from Sanford to Portland.

Sanford and Springvale for some years have had presidential post-offices; that at South Sanford is a fourth-class office.

CHAPTER XVI.

TAVERNS AND TRADERS.

Wayside Inns of the Olden Time — List of Early Innholders — Louis Philippe's Visit to Colonel Caleb Emery's Hostelry — Licensed Retailers Prior to 1800.

WAYSIDE inns were a feature of life in the frontier settlements. The dispensing of good cheer to man and beast was evidently deemed of greater necessity than the providing of facilities for general trade, if we are to judge by the records, the first innholder being licensed in 1749, and the earliest retailer in 1763. Following is a list of the first men licensed to keep public house in the community :

John Stanyan, 1749–50, 1755–56, 1758, 1760–73. He probably kept tavern nearly twenty-five years, though licensed only about twenty. His inn stood near the site of John Fletcher's house at South Sanford.

Ephraim Low, 1769–71, 1773–75, 1777, 1778–84. His house stood where Bert Goodrich's house now stands. In 1773, Amos W. Goodwin logged above Sanford, and lodged in Low's tavern, which was then plastered. It is believed that the old part of the late John Lord's house on the site was the tavern.

Jonathan Johnson, 1769–75, 1777–81, and Mary and Jonathan Johnson, 1782. The Johnson tavern was at South Sanford, in the house where the late Abiel H. Johnson resided for many years, now owned and occupied by his son Chase Johnson.

Ebenezer Hall, 1779–84, 1791–92. His house was the first inn in what is now Alfred. It was about a mile above the village. In 1794, he was a licensed innholder in the " District of Alfred."

Caleb Emery, 1782–86. He built a large two-story house at South Sanford, the second, if not the first, of its kind in town. He was "principal" when Johnson was licensed in 1781, and his son William in 1787.

William Emery, 1787–88, 1791–95. It is presumed that he took his father's business, and occupied the same tavern.

William Frost, 1785, 1791-1807. His house was at what is now Springvale. About 1848, Dennis Hatch bought it, or part of it, and constructed part of a house from it.

Obadiah Low, 1791. Presumably at his father's old stand.

James Heard, 1785, 1791, 1793-96.

Jesse Colcord, 1794-96, 1803-05. He was living just below the old meeting-house at South Sanford in 1804.

Samuel Nasson. There is a tradition that he kept a tavern at the Corner, and that his widow continued the business several years after his death. No record of license is found Mrs. Nasson boarded Elisha Allen.

In the fall of 1797, Louis Philippe, King of the French, then in exile, passed through Sanford on his journey from Portsmouth to Portland. He was accompanied by his two brothers, the Duke de Montpensier and the Count de Beaujolais, and Talleyrand, afterward the noted French diplomatist. They travelled leisurely in a covered carriage, and remained, according to tradition, a day or two at Colonel Emery's tavern. The "old Colonel" and his wife received their royal guests with native hospitality, and seated them at a table loaded with good cheer. It is said that Louis Philippe, being a late riser, had breakfast served in his room in the morning. The King and his suite were much pleased with the pictures that hung upon the walls of the "spare room." They were probably the work of some French artist, who had designated them in the French language. Colonel Emery's tavern was a palatial residence for those days, and was widely known throughout this section. It was standing until a few years ago, being occupied by David Cram, and was finally torn down, much of the lumber being used to construct the houses of Mrs. David Cram (now standing on the spot), and of Christopher Cram.

Most of the early traders whose names have been handed down to posterity were licensed retailers. Some sold only intoxicating liquors, but the majority dealt in groceries, among which, it should be said, one of the leading articles was New England rum. The dates given, for the most part, designate the years for which the parties were licensed, although in some cases they were engaged in trade after the expiration of their licenses :

Daniel Coffin, 1763. In that year he bought of Naphtali Harmon forty acres of land lying along the Mousam. He probably traded in the Moulton neighborhood at South Sanford.

Ephraim Low, 1768, 1770. His store was at or near his residence, one mile below the Corner.

John White, 1768. He settled, about 1766, near what was later Conant's mill, Alfred, and appears to have been the earliest trader in that part of the town.

William Bennett, 1773-74. South Sanford.

Tobias Lord. There is a tradition that he traded at Moulton's mill, Mouse Lane, but whether before he was drafted during the Revolutionary War, we have no knowledge.

Samuel Nasson, 1778-1800. The time of the opening of the first store at Sanford Corner is fixed by his day book, which was begun September 29, 1778. The store stood opposite his dwelling-house, on the site of S. Benton Emery's house on Washington Street. There he traded more than twenty years, though he seems to have been licensed only eight years.

Caleb Emery, 1780-81, 1796-1805. His store stood near his tavern at South Sanford.

Joseph Leigh, 1781-87 (?). Leigh lived and traded in the house owned by Simon Stackpole. We know that he was licensed four years, and that complaint was made against him, in 1787, for not paying his excise.

Nathaniel Bennett, 1782-84. South Sanford.

William Parsons, 1783, 1792-93. He was a licensed retailer in the North Parish.

Joshua Taylor, 1784.

Thomas Gile, 1790-92 (Guild in 1790). North Parish.

Joshua Goodwin, 1791-93. He probably traded at Mouse Lane; was at Alfred, in 1796.

James Heard, 1792.

Jesse Colcord, 1792-93, 1799-1805. South Sanford.

William Frost, Junior, 1792-93, 1808-12. His store was south-east of his dwelling-house at Springvale. It was moved to the brow of the hill near Murray's stable, and was owned of late years by Sylvanus B. Hill.

John Knight, 1792-93. North Parish.

Joseph Carl, 1793-94.

Samuel Hill, 1794.

Robert Johnson, 1797-98. South Sanford.

George Frost, 1799.

Moses Chick, 1800.

The form of a license in the first years of the settlement was as follows :

———— ———— to be a Retailer, the said - ——— ————, principal,

became bound by way of recognizance to our Sovereign Lord the King in the penal sum of Ten Pounds, ———— ————— and ———— ————, sureties, in Five Pounds each, to be paid unto our said Sovereign Lord the King his heirs or successors on condition that the said ———— ———— is admitted a Retailer in said Town of ————, shall use, uphold, and keep good rule and order in his said house, and duly observe the laws relating to persons so licensed, and the said ———— ————, principal, entered into recognizance to his Majesty in the sum of Ten Pounds, ———— ————— and ———— ————, sureties, in Five Pounds each, on condition that the said ———— ———— shall duly and truly pay the duties of excise and observe the laws relating thereto.

CHAPTER XVII.

WAR OF 1812.

Feeling of the People — Failure of Crops Causes Filling of Sanford's Quota — Patriotic Ode Gives Lieutenant John Hanson His Commission — Names of Soldiers.

THE Embargo, as we have already stated, was followed by acts which resulted in the second war with Great Britain in 1812. A large and strong party, especially in New England, opposed this war, and placed obstacles in the way of carrying it on. The people of Sanford had protested against the Embargo with vehemence, but a small majority of voters for electors in 1812 showed their preference for the war candidate for President, and a much larger number declared themselves to be satisfied with the war party by casting their votes for the Republican candidates for Governor during the three years' war. And yet, it was with difficulty that the town's quota was filled. The late William Emery informed the writer that the government " could not have filled the ranks here, if the crops had not been cut off."

At a Fourth of July celebration in 1812, held in Stephen Gowen's orchard, an original patriotic ode was sung which is said to have won for its author a commission in the army. The ode revealed the spirit of the times, not only in its expression of patriotism, but also in the implication that Revolutionary soldiers, pensioned on account of wounds received in their service, were opposed to the war recently declared ; that there were civil discords and factions endangering the country from within ; and that some persons even preferred a civil war to one with another country. It is stated that John Hanson composed this ode, and because of it, received a commission, unsought, as Lieutenant in the regular army. It is certain that Madison commissioned him in 1813, to date from November 13, 1812. Lieutenant Hanson served in a rifle regiment. His first engagement was at York, April 27, 1813. He was afterward present at the attack of the British under General Drummond upon Fort Erie, September 17, 1814, of which one bastion was taken, so vigorous was the assault, but was recovered through the persistence and daring of our troops. Captain

Hanson (he received this title in 1807, in the militia), died August 12, 1842, aged sixty-one years.

In September, 1812, one hundred and seventy-four soldiers, or men liable for military service, were enrolled in Sanford.

The following Sanford men in addition to Lieutenant Hanson are known to have served in the war:

John Batchelder, blacksmith, twenty-three years of age, served in Colonel Lane's regiment, Thirty-Third United States Infantry, as corporal, and was discharged at Plattsburg, N. Y., May 5, 1814, having served the term of his enlistment. He married Betsey, daughter of Ezra and Abigail (Wilson) Thompson, and had two children, Justus and Mercy. He was lost at sea.

Stephen Bridges (in the Revolutionary War?), was a private in Captain Isaac Hodsdon's company, Colonel Lane's regiment. There is a tradition, however, that he could not pass muster on account of defective eyesight; whereupon he exclaimed with fervor: "Thank God, I can't see as well as some folks!"

Levi Chadbourn.

Nathan Goodwin, afterwards Captain in the Maine militia, was in Captain Goodnow's company, Thirty-Third Infantry.

John Gowen, Junior.

Isaac Hanson died in the service. He was in Captain Rufus McIntire's company, Third United States Light Artillery, which saw service on the western frontier and in Canada, from July, 1812, to June 15, 1815.

Samuel P. Hayward, died June 2, 1875, aged eighty-two years.

Nathaniel Hobbs.

Jotham Johnson, was at Kittery.

John Moore, musician, in Captain Peter Chadwick's company, Thirty-Fourth United States Infantry, April, 1813–1814. He was last seen at Sackett's Harbor, where he was left sick.

John Moore, Junior.

Japhet Morrison.

Hiram Murray, who enlisted from Shapleigh, but lived in Sanford nearly forty years, served at Kittery Point in the fall of 1814. He was the son of William Murray of Berwick, a Revolutionary soldier, and was born in Shapleigh, November 26, 1792. From March 9, 1878, he received a pension of eight dollars a month, and died at his daughter's home in Mansfield, Mass., May 28, 1886.

Samuel Nasson, died in the service. He was in Captain Rufus McIntire's company, Third United States Light Artillery, which saw service on the western frontier and in Canada, from July, 1812, to June 15, 1815.

John Plummer.

John Quint.

Nathaniel Quint, died May 16, 1831, aged forty-nine years.

William Tripp.

Obadiah True, a Revolutionary soldier.

Simeon Wallace.

Caleb Willard, never returned.

Jotham Willard.

Levi Willard, son of Evat, at Kittery Foreside.

Moses Witham, musician, in Captain Chadwick's company, Colonel Learned's regiment, April, 1813–1814. He was a fifer, and at his death left his fife to his daughter, Mrs. Hiram Witham. He was at Stony Creek, June 6, 1813, and at Plattsburg. September 11, 1814. He was the son of Jacob Witham, born about 1791, and died in Madrid, Maine, in 1874, aged eighty-three years.

Aaron Young, died in the service.

The compiler has also found, among the notes of the author, the following lists of names, unexplained, but undoubtedly a number of the soldiers there given were from Sanford :

Captain Isaac Hodson's company, Thirty-Third United States Infantry : Jeremiah Goodwin was paymaster ; Joseph Pattee, sergeant ; John Stanyal, private.

Captain Rufus McIntire's company, Third United States Light Artillery : Samuel S. Stacey, Benjamin Cheney, sergeants ; Abraham Crosby, Ezra Haskell, Corporals ; George Garey (?) artificer ; William Webber, Daniel Bridges (?), Ebenezer Clark, Daniel Garey, John Quint, Junior, Aaron Welch (?), and Daniel Welch (?) privates.

Roster of Captain Bartholomew Thompson's company, second regiment, First Brigade, Major Nowell, at Kittery, from October 1 to November 1, 1814 :

Captain — Bartholomew Thompson, Berwick.

Lieutenants — Alexander Worcester, Lebanon ; Ephraim Low, Sanford.

Ensign — Wentworth Butler, Berwick.

Sergeants — Elias Libby, Samuel Drew, Samuel Frost, Reuben Dennett, Thomas Abbot, John Abbot.

Musicians — Jacob Hamilton, Phineas Morrill.

Corporals — Alpheus Hanson, Temple Lord, Joseph Spinney, James Pray.

HON. ERNEST M. GOODALL.

Privates — J. R. Bragdon, Ebenezer Brackett, Joseph Boston, David Brackett, Gideon Brooks, Tilley Clement, George Carlisle, Samuel Chick, Thomas Chick, Oliver Cutts, Benjamin Chadbourn, Isaac Courson, Joel Emery, William Estes, William Fogg, Alexander Ferguson, John Fall, Benjamin Goodwin, John Goodwin, Thomas Grant, Nelson Hill, John Hooper, James Heart (Heard?), Meshach Horn, Samuel Hanscom, Mark Hart, Stephen Jellison, Hugh Kennison, Alpheus Kennard, Thomas Keay, Abednego Leathers, Jeremiah Low, John Linscott, William Linscott, John Libby, Nathaniel Low, Ivory Murry, Oliver Marrs, Joseph Muchmore, Adam Murry, Hiram Murry, Caleb Miller, Junior, Seth Maxwell, Peletiah Mason, Nathan Nason, David Nock, Mark Nowell, Hopkins Pierce, Stephen Pierce, Nahum Perkins, Jesse Perkins, Nathaniel Pike, John Penny, John Raitt, Alexander Raitt, John Roberts, William Randall, Thomas Roberts, Jacob Ricker, Richard Ricker, Joshua Rankin, Theodore Round, Theodore Ricker, Nathaniel Ricker, Levi Ricker, Enoch Remick, Hutchings Remington, Stephen Stackpole, Stephen Smith, Joseph Smith, Thomas H. Stanley, S. R. Spinney, Timothy Staples, Rook Stillings, Oliver Staples, William Staples, John Spinney, Hiram Snow, Absalom Stackpole, George Sherburn, Samuel Thurrell, John Thurrell, Oliver Thompson, Ezekiel Twombley, Obadiah Taylor, Jotham Taylor, Zacheus Trafton, Ivory Trafton, James Varney, Samuel Wilkinson, Clement Wooster, John Whitehouse, Enoch Wentworth, John Weymouth, Moses Welch, Richard Young.

13

CHAPTER XVIII.

EARLY YEARS OF THE CENTURY.

Growth of the Town — Business Prosperity — Houses — Sanford Corner — Springvale — Naming of the Village — Deering Neighborhood—South Sanford—Oak Hill—Shaw's Ridge and "Grammar Street " — Mount Hope — Innholders and Traders.

FOR several years prior to the Revolution, the town was quite prosperous, notwithstanding the poor condition in 1768. The valuation of 1771 gave the annual worth of the real estate one year with another as two hundred and four pounds, ten shillings. The lumber business was thriving, and farming and stock raising were quite successful. The Revolution put a stop to the lumber operations, and the people, not away in the army, had to turn their attention exclusively to farming. Every family felt compelled to raise its own food and clothe its own backs. After the Revolution, business took a fresh start. New impulse was given by the influx of population. Lumber of all kinds sold quickly, and at good prices. Ship timber was in demand. One Paul Shackford, of Arundel, built a small coasting vessel in Sanford, near Moulton's mill, and hauled it to Kennebunk Landing on the snow. Lumber was dull during the War of 1812, the Embargo having crushed out shipping and destroyed commerce. At Kennebunk, where the market price of lumber was fixed, good merchantable boards were worth only four dollars a thousand.

Before considering Sanford in the early days of the century, let us look back for a moment at the style of houses built in the beginnings of the settlement. Frame-houses, gradually supplanting log and block-houses, were erected, generally one story in height, with now and then a two-story dwelling. At the opening of the century, there were not more than ten or twelve two-story houses in town, and not one painted. The Nasson and Colonel Emery houses were the first of the former, and Ezekiel Gowen's, on the Mount Hope road, the first of the latter. The body of Mr. Gowen's house was painted

yellow, and the roof, Spanish brown. Master Gowen's house was
another of the early painted houses. His paint was red ochre, from
the Red brook on Hanson's ridge. He pounded and sifted the ochre,
and mixed it with fish oil and skim milk. It stood the test of time,
and some parts of it were quite bright in the writer's early years.

The Nasson house,[1] which stood until within a few years on the
brow of the hill, opposite S. Benton Emery's on Washington Street,
was known more than a century ago as the Brigadier Moulton house.
It was built by Jeremiah Moulton's grandfather, General Jotham
Moulton, of York, about a mile below the Corner, opposite George
Brearey's present residence, in 1740–41. After General Moulton's
death in 1777, it was moved to the "Iron Works lot," probably in
1778, for it was standing on its location of late years in 1779. It
was the largest house in town, and was called the "great house."
It took two or three days to move it, and it is said that when the
oxen hauling it were unhitched, they ran as if pleased to be freed
from restraint. In 1858, Mrs. Sophia Webster, a daughter of Major
Nasson, gave this account: The first house in this village was
hauled here from the hill just below John Lord's (Bert Goodrich's).
When hauled by Colonel Moulton, it was a one-story house, but soon
after another story was added. In those days, it was the fashion to
name houses, and the following couplet was used on that occasion :

> "Here's a new addition for the old foundation;
> May it be a blessing for the rising generation."

We have reason to believe that such a blessing it proved to be, for
Mr. Nasson had six children by a former wife, Mrs. Nasson had six
by her first husband, and they had four, making sixteen who were at
one time living under the same roof. In this house were held a number of the most important town meetings of the young days of Sanford.

The one-story dwellings were generally of the style known as the
" five room " houses. The front door was in the middle of the side
toward the road, though in some cases it was on the back side, and
frequently the house was built with reference to the slope of the site,.
not to the road. The chimney, with its huge fireplace and brick oven,.
was in the centre. On each side of the front entry was a large room,
back of which were two small bed rooms. Between them was the
kitchen. Sometimes a porch or back entry was built, adjoining the
kitchen. In the attic were two low, unfinished rooms, sometimes

[1] It was moved in 1894 from its original location to the rear, on the same lot.

separated only by the chimney and a board partition. Boards were put on with pins, not nails, as seen in David Bean's old house.

Such houses as (1875) Joel Moulton's, Abiel H. Johnson's, and the ell, or old part of John Lord's, were of the style built subsequently to the block-houses. Mr. Moulton thought his house, originally twenty by thirty-six feet, with only two rooms, was built by John Willard, not far from 1758. Mr. Johnson said, in 1875, that his house had been standing one hundred and ten years. At any rate, at one time during the Revolution, the quota of Sanford met there to start for the seat of war. Mrs. Lord told the writer that Amos Goodwin logged above Sanford in 1773, and lodged in the house. Ephraim Low then kept tavern there.

As late as 1797, a timber house was built on the farm afterward occupied by John Bean.

One Moore commenced building a house or store near Bert Goodrich's. After it was boarded, Moore died. The house was moved to Gowen farm, and was occupied for years by the Gowen family.

Frost Garey built a house in Jotham Moulton pasture, of late years Wentworth Davis's.

The Wadlia house was hauled to the Corner, and set on land of William Emery, by Thaddeus Littlefield, about 1845. It was afterwards owned by Deacon Stephen Dorman.

The old Linscott house at Mouse Lane fell many years ago, and another was raised on the other side of the river the same day.

When Parson Sweat came to town, he moved into one chamber in Ephraim Low's house, in which chamber were two windows of six panes each.

Stephen Gowen raised his house-frame, June 28, 1791. Six years later he raised his barn.

Jotham Wilson built a house up from the road, which was occupied by John T. Paine, and of late years by Asa Low. He also built on Main Street, where his widow lived for years. The next house above was built by a widow, Mrs. Batchelder, of Shapleigh. The Greenhalgh house was hauled there.

Sanford Corner.—The Nasson house was the first at the Corner, unless the Stackpole house across the river was standing when the Nasson house was moved. The Moulton house was built prior to 1797, the Chick house about 1800, the Eliot Frost house after 1803, and the Keeler house about the same time. In 1805 or 6, these houses were standing: Joshua Batchelder's, Nasson's, Moulton's, Keeler's, Frost's, Stimpson's, Chick's, and Dr. Linscott's. Mrs. Sophia Webster informed the writer in 1858 that she could remember when there were only three houses between her father's (Major Nasson's) and William Frost's. These were probably "Gansby" (Gatensby) Witham's, John Adams's, and Jonathan Adams's. One of the Adamses lived where Ira Witham lives. Two houses across the river were the only ones to be seen from the Nasson house, so thick were the woods all around.

In 1877, Deacon Joshua Hobbs, born February 8, 1805, gave the writer this account of the Corner : He came to Sanford in 1821, as clerk in the store of John Storer and Co. They traded in the Chadbourn house, where Obed Littlefield now lives. It was one story then. There were at that time Deacon Frost's house (General Shaw's), John Frost's store (moved to Springvale), the Eliot Frost house, John Hanson's (Dr. Weld's), Jonathan Clark's office and house (General Bodwell's), Joseph Webster's, Willard family in house above (Stimpson's), Dr. Linscott's (Storer house) ; back on the other side, Nathaniel Chadbourn's house on the corner (moved up), the Dr. Linscott house (occupied by George Heard) toward Lebanon, Samuel Chadbourn's house, Deacon Frost's barn and store, Deacon Moulton's house and small house below ; across the road, General Allen's house and store, the Nasson house, occupied by Thomas Nasson ; across the river, Joshua Batchelder's (Stackpole's), Stephen Gowen's, and James Gowen's, near the mill. There was a saw-mill at the upper falls, and a grist-mill at the lower falls. Joseph Webster was a carpenter, and John Hanson, blacksmith.

When Deacon Stephen Dorman came to Sanford in 1824, the following houses were standing : Elisha Allen's, on corner (burned in 1853), Jeremiah Moulton's, Jotham Wilson's (S. Benton Emery's), Nasson house, Deacon Frost's, Moses Morrill's, opposite the tin-shop (built by Eliot Frost), Captain John Hanson's (the Dr. Weld house, burned), Jonathan Clark's (opposite Miss Ellen M. Emery's), Dr. Dow's (in process of building), Joseph Webster's (above Clark's), Rev. Christopher Marsh's (Charles O. Emery's), Jotham Moulton's (burnt), John Storer's, Widow Linscott's (Storer house) ; across the river : "Colonel" Batchelder's (Stackpole house), Stephen Gowen's (Edgar Wentworth's), Webber house ; on "Hardscrabble :" Captain Wilkinson's, Solomon Thompson's, J. Wilkinson's, Flanders Hatch's, and one other ; below the Corner : Joshua Tebbets's, Jonathan Tebbets's, Amos W. Goodwin's (Bert Goodrich's) ; towards Lebanon : Gowen's house.

Springvale. — In 1770 a saw-mill was built on the province land

above the head-line of the town, which was known as the Province
mill. It was the first mill at Springvale. In 1787 Margaret Adams
owned and occupied a hut in the vicinity. The land lying between
the road running past her hut and the river was sold to William
Frost. Prior to 1790, Ichabod Spencer, Ephraim Getchell, John
Beatle, and Joseph Chaney lived across the river.

The early settlers in the north part of the town, beginning at the
Shapleigh line, on the main road, were: Aaron Jellison; ———
Cousens, on left of road below the bridge; Captain David Morrison.
The latter came into town about 1785. John Morrison lived in the
third house on the place. The first was a log-house. On the back
road ending at Morrison's Corner lived David Welch, first settler in
that section, his land being deeded in 1773; Ebenezer Morrison;
Ephraim Curtis, on hill near Morrison's mill; house near the grist-
mill, occupied by the miller. Below Morrison's Corner: Joshua
Goodwin, shoemaker and tanner; ——— Murray; Jasper Grant;
William Frost. John Thompson built a log-house on the cross road
about 1820.

In 1821, between Sanford Corner and the Shapleigh line, the houses
of the following persons were standing, in the order named: William
Gowen, Joseph Beatle, William Chapman, Jonathan Adams, William
Frost, Jasper Grant, Joshua Goodwin, John Frost, Thomas Shackley,
Captain David Morrison, Jotham Stevens, Aaron Jellison.

In 1827, the site of the village of Springvale was a tract of land
partly covered with wood, lying open to the public, and not fenced.
A school-house, the Frost house, and two or three other houses were
all the buildings there. William H. Frost, in 1883, gave the writer
the following account of the village: "Joseph Witham's, Ichabod
Frost's, and Henry Grant's houses were standing in 1827. Benjamin
Chaney lived where Isaac Reed afterward lived; Ichabod Spencer,
where Asa Low; Dodipher Ricker, near Darling H. Ross's, and a
Murray where Charles H. Frost's house stands. Ichabod Frost
bought land of Theodore Willard and Ephraim Getchell, and built a
mill the same year. The deed was to Frost and Jotham Wilson. They
sold one-half of the water power to the Manufacturing Company. The
Province mill stood where Butler and Fogg's shoe factory stands. It
fell on account of its age. Two mills have been burned on the site.
Frost built for Lewis, of Boston, the first saw-mill across the river."

The Province mill privilege was sold in 1828 to John Whitaker and
Co., who engaged in calico printing, erecting several buildings on the
brow of the hill and near the spring. Among those interested in the

Print Works was Thomas Greenhalgh, who had been in his native Lancashire an acceptable local preacher of the Methodist denomination, but, for two years after his arrival in America, before coming to Sanford, superintendent of the Tourlin Print Works in Dover, N. H. To him, William H. Frost told the writer, we are indebted for the beautiful name of the village. In the presence of villagers and English operatives, gathered near the cold, crystalline spring, Elder Greenhalgh, mounted on a box, offered prayer. Then answering the question, " What shall we call it?" he thus named the settlement: " Spring," pointing to the clear water at his feet, and with a gesture down the valley, " vale, Springvale."

It was not long before a number of the English residents petitioned to be naturalized, among whom were : John Whitaker, 1827 ; Thomas Clark, Matthew Hodgdon, James M. Gratrix, Robert Moon, 1828 ; Jonathan Chadwick, Edward Thompson, James McA. Teer, William Waddington, 1829 ; James Ashton, Thomas Greenhalgh, James Hamer, George Barnes, Henry Hampson, 1830.

Above Springvale, Ephraim Getchell, Enoch Lord, Joseph Chaney, Elias Littlefield, Solomon Littlefield, Abraham Morrison and John Bedell lived ; the first two on the Beaver Hill road, and the others on the other road. Chaney, Getchell, and Morrison married sisters of the two Littlefields.

Deering Neighborhood. — William Merrifield (March, 1776), Francis Pugsley (Captain Nathan Goodwin settled on the Pugsley place), Joseph Butler, Gideon Deering, Jethro Heard, William Deering, Edmund Goodwin, William, Samuel and Simeon Ricker, Abraham Carroll, Moses Butler, Moses Pray, and William Worster were among the early settlers. The Worsters, William, Samuel, and Fernald, were blacksmiths. Elder Robinson also lived in this neighborhood. Among the old-time school teachers were Abraham Carroll, Joseph Dam, John Hanson, Daniel Gowen, William B. Merrick, Tobias Emery, and Ivory M. Thompson.

South Sanford. — Within the memory of the late Miss Mary Ann Emery, the following lived at South Sanford, probably about 1810 : John Thompson, Jesse Thompson, Stephen Johnson, John Parsons, Thomas Parsons, Robert Tripp, Samuel and George Tripp, Caleb Emery, William Nasson, Jotham Johnson, Moses Tebbets, —— Stanley, —— Garey, John Powers, Joel Moulton, Moses Sweat, Josiah Paul (the last four beyond Powers's bridge).

Oak Hill. — Robert Allen was the first settler on Oak Hill. Solomon, his son, and Elijah, his brother, were early settlers there.

James Heard, born in Dover, N. H., moved from Beech ridge to
Oak Hill in 1783. His son, Jacob, and grandson, Jacob S., inherited
or purchased his estate, above the Allens. Daniel Getchell and Jabez
Perkins came from Wells, and took up land at the foot of the hill
below the Allens. Mrs. Martha (Patty) Johnson, eighty-three years
of age in 1878, said there were on the hill in her childhood, James
Heard, James Cole, Caleb Cole, Solomon Allen, James Allen, Jede-
diah Allen, and Andrew Allen. At the foot Joshua Brooks lived.
Toward Wells, James Davis, father and son, Jabez Perkins, and
Daniel Getchell.

Shaw's Ridge and "Grammar Street." — Three sons of Ephraim
Low, who settled below the Corner, took up farms on the ridge formerly known by their name, — David, Ephraim, Junior, and Obadiah. Their farms afterward came into the possession of Jeremiah,
Joseph, and Samuel Shaw, respectively, though Pelatiah Penney preceded Samuel Shaw in the occupancy of his. Ephraim Low, Junior,
was on the ridge in 1777. There was a Boston on the farm owned
by the late George W. Gowen, and Jeremiah Witham and Ezra
Thompson lived in the neighborhood the last part of the last century.
Jeremiah Witham owned three fifty acre lots, one for each of his
children, Stephen, Sarah, and Huldah (?). Going up, came Boston,
Samuel Shaw, Jeremiah Shaw, and Ephraim Low, Junior. Reuben
Wilkinson, at one time, lived below Daniel Garey's on the same side.
Others in the section were Naphtali Harmon, Nathan Powers, Will-
iam Powers and William Tripe.

Mount Hope. — Charles Annis, Joseph Hill, Jeremiah Wise and
Simon Tebbets were among the early settlers on Mount Hope, which
until 1806 was known as Annis's Hill.

The innholders in town in the early part of the century were : Jeremiah Moulton, 1800–02, at Sanford Corner; Pelatiah Ricker, 1806 ;
Elisha Allen, 1815, at the Corner; John Powers, Junior, 1819–33,
(except for about four years), at South Sanford, at the corner between the county and Alfred roads ; James B. Shapleigh, 1828–30,
1832–33, who built a hotel at the Corner, afterwards owned and occupied by Simon Tebbets ; Ichabod Frost, 1832–33, at Springvale.

The traders from 1801 until 1830, or thereabouts, comprised : William Emery, 1801, 1809–10, South Sanford ; William Stanley, 1801–
02 ; William Simpson, 1801–02, probably opposite Lebanon Street
at the Corner; Elisha Allen, 1802–31, traded in the store which he
built in 1802, on the corner just northwest of the site of Hosea Wil-

lard's house at the Corner. It was destroyed by fire, February 27, 1853 ; Job Winchell ; Jotham Stevens, 1802–10 ; Thomas Shackley, 1802–21, Morrison's Corner ; Samson Johnson ; Thomas Keeler, came from Wells in the summer of 1802, and began trade at South Sanford, in a small store probably occupied previously by the Bennetts. He then moved to the Corner, where according to tradition he traded in the Deacon Frost store until 1806 ; Eliot Frost, 1803–06, 1809–10, 1812–13, built the store which stood on the site of Daniel G. Clark's house at the Corner, and in 1845 removed to Springvale ; Jeremiah Moulton, 1803–05, Sanford Corner ; George Leighton, 1804 ; Robert Tripp, 1806–07, South Sanford ; Ichabod Lord, 1807–11 ; Currier and Brown, 1807 ; Henry T. and Caleb Emery, 1807, Caleb Emery, Third, 1808, Caleb Emery, Junior, 1809, and Caleb Emery, Fourth (?), at the Corner ; John Powers, Junior, and Otho Hamilton, 1808, South Sanford ; Joseph Webster, 1809–12, Stimpson store, Corner ; Ebenezer Nowell, 1809 ; John Frost, 1810 (?) ; John Colcord, regarding whom there is a tradition that he traded in the upper part of John Frost's house, a mile or more above Springvale ; John Hanson, 1810–12 ; Samuel S. Stacey, 1810 ; William Gowen, Junior, 1810 ; Jedediah Allen ; John S. Cram ; Jonathan Johnson, Junior ; Henry Hamilton ; ——— Moore, in a store in Bert Goodwin's garden ; Abner Hill, 1811–13 ; John Frost, Junior, 1811–15, and John Frost, Second, 1818, 1820–29, 1830–39 (?), in the store at the Corner, formerly occupied by Frank Broggi on the site of Garnsey's block, and burned May 1, 1892. Deacon Frost bought out the Emerys (Henry T. and Caleb), moved their store to the northwest side of the road to Alfred, and fitted it up for a tin-shop for Edwards and Hill. He then built a two-story store, in two weeks, and had his goods in. He was the first trader in town to give up the sale of intoxicating liquors. His son, George A., was with him the last three years of his trading ; John Powers, Junior, 1811–13, 1825–29, South Sanford ; Nathaniel Chadbourn, 1812–13, at the Corner, in the Chick house, or the house occupied by Obed Littlefield ; Henry Wadlia, 1813 ; Samuel Chadbourn, 1815, probably where Nathaniel Chadbourn traded ; Moses Morrill, 1816–20, at the Corner in the Eliot Frost store. There was a firm, Frost and Morrill, in 1818 ; Samuel Shackford, 1816 ; Thomas Shackford (Shackley ?), 1818 ; John Storer and Co., 1820, 1824–25, 1826–28, and John Storer, 1821–24, 1825–26, 1828–29. They traded three or four years in the Chadbourn house, then one story, and then built the large square store which stood on the opposite corner, on the site of Fred Porrell's. The building was burned in 1866 ;

Major John Frost, Third, 1821–25, in the store formerly occupied by Moses Morrill; Robert Fernald, 1822–30, first at Morrison's Corner, and afterwards at Springvale; Nancy Shackley, 1822–23, she being probably the widow of Thomas Shackley, who traded at Morrison's Corner; Jotham Storer, 1825, 1836, 1840, in the Deacon Frost store at the Corner. He traded at one time at Springvale, where James Butler had traded; Timothy Shaw, 1825–39, in the Stimpson store at the Corner; William Stanley, Junior, 1825–27; John Linscott, 1825–30, on Shaw's ridge; James Butler, 1826–31, 1832–33, 1840–41, at Springvale; William Hobbs, 1826–28; John Butler, 1828–30, 1832–33 (?), at Butler's Corner (?); John Hill, 1829–30; Micah Phillips; Roswell Phillips; Thomas Bennett; Rufus Hatch; John Cram; William B. Merrick; James Allen; John Hubbard; John Tobey; Japhet Hill; Stephen Young; Jacob Hodsdon; Skeele and Hobbs, 1829–30. They bought out John Storer and occupied the Storer store; Skeele or Emery succeeded Skeele and Hobbs, 1832 (?), and was in turn succeeded by John Skeele. The dates given, for the most part, designate the years the parties were licensed.

Early auctioneers were: Caleb Emery, Third, 1809–10; Ebenezer Linscott, 1811; Samuel S. Stacey, 1812; Ephraim Low, Junior, 1812; Abner Hill, 1814, 1816–17; William Butler, 1822; Ebenezer Nowell, 1825.

As early as 1816, Joseph Edwards had a tin-shop on the site of the Emery store. He removed to Lyman, and afterwards to Biddeford·

CHAPTER XIX.

MILITARY HISTORY.

The Village Train-band — Horrible Casualty at General Frost's Funeral — General Muster — List of Militia Officers — Florida War — Madawaska War.

WILLIAMSON informs us that in 1744 there were one hundred and fifty able-bodied or fencible men in Phillipstown, belonging to Colonel Pepperrell's regiment. While this is evidently a mistake as to figures, it is of interest as indicating the attention that was given from the start to the subject of citizen soldiery. The train-band existed in almost every town, and long after the necessity for the minute-man had passed away, the continuance of the militia served to foster the military spirit of the forefathers. As early as 1762, there is record of a Phillipstown company, of which Benjamin Harmon was Captain, Jonathan Johnson, Lieutenant, and Naphtali Harmon, Ensign. In 1776, besides the soldiers actively engaged in the warfare of the Revolution, there were in the ten towns of York County three militia regiments, in which Sanford was well represented. York, Sanford, Coxhall, Massabesec, and the First Parish of Wells constituted the First York regiment; Kittery, Berwick, and Lebanon the Second; and the rest of the county the Third. Prominent among the Sanford officers in the ninth, eleventh (matross, or artillery), and twelfth companies, were Captains Edward Harmon and Morgan Lewis, and Lieutenants Nathaniel Bennett, Samuel Willard, Junior, Ebenezer Hall, and Tobias Lord.

Details are lacking of the history of the town's militia, but we are enabled to give a few incidents.

When Washington died, the company in town paraded and, under the command of Major Samuel Nasson, marched, with arms reversed, down to Colonel Emery's tavern, and was treated, — a customary proceeding on occasions of either joy or sorrow.

Major General William Frost died December 23, 1821, and was buried with military honors two days later. His sorrel and white-faced horse, saddled and bridled, followed the remains to their last resting place. Some of the militia of Sanford, perhaps thirty or forty men, and a part of the Kennebunk Artillery, with one field-piece, a six pounder, were called out. The company of infantry was drilled to fire a volley over the grave. The field piece was on a small hill about twenty-five rods from the house, and, perhaps, as far from the grave, and was to be fired once a minute while the procession was passing. That would have given the gunner, Oliver Perkins, time to cool the gun by sponging, and to prevent any fire from remaining within. He was cautioned to sponge frequently, and could have done so by dipping his sponge in the snow that covered the ground. Neglecting to do this, he was warned not to allow his piece to get hot. " Oh, d—n her, she is not half hot enough yet," said he ; " I can fire four times without sponging." These are his words as given by an eye witness, but it is also said that he added, " and go to h—l the next." The gun became heated; the man at the vent drew his thumb away, while Perkins was paying in the charge ; a little fire from the wrapper of the former charge ignited the powder ; it exploded as Perkins stood at the mouth of the cannon. Both of his arms were blown off, the right near the elbow, the left near the wrist. He was thrown ten feet, perhaps, and fell sticking the stubs of his arms into the snow. Rising to his feet before anyone reached him, he cried out, " God have mercy on my soul! " Terribly frightened, he thought he could not live an hour. Enoch Stanley took his place at the gun, and the salute went on. Perkins lived, however, and had iron hooks attached to the stumps of his arms, by means of which he could help himself, and even do some kinds of work. He was pensioned by the state, at the rate of eight dollars a month, payable semi-annually from December 25, 1821, in consequence of having lost both arms and one eye while in the service of the state. In 1827 and 1837, fifty dollars in addition to his regular pension were allowed him.

For much of the time between 1800 and 1830, perhaps 1843, general muster, as the annual " training " was called, was held at the Corner. Perhaps the place was selected because it was central and easy of access, or afforded a better parade ground than any other place within the limits of the brigade, or because the General in command resided in town. Generals Frost, Allen, and Shaw were at different times in command. Muster was generally held in the field below the old mill road, now thickly covered with dwelling-houses. One muster, at least, was held in the field back of Jotham Moulton's house, afterwards owned by Hon. I. S. Kimball, and destroyed by fire. The last " training " in Sanford was in May, 1843, but in November of that year the Sanford company went to Brackett's ridge, in Acton, and " trained " and that was the last general muster. The company, however, participated in a regimental muster at South Berwick a few days after the one at Acton.

The writer, from his recollections of the muster in May, 1843, was inclined to think that the event was the great holiday of the year, before which the Fourth of July and Thanksgiving were cast into the shade. Men and boys were on the ground early, that they might have the full enjoyment of the day. Women and girls also came from the neighboring towns that they might see the " troopers," hear the music, and enjoy the festivities of the occasion. Tents were pitched and booths set up near the training field, where gingerbread, buns, apples, cider, and liquor could be bought. These were always well patronized during the day, and after the muster, were cleaned out by the soldiers, who thoughtfully remembered their families left at home. Horse jockeys, gamblers and pugilists would come long distances to find victims. Many returned home cheated, many intoxicated, some with bruised faces, and all, with few exceptions, with less money in their pockets than they brought. The officers, in the habiliments of war, with cocked hats and waving plumes, were inspired with an unwonted dignity, which showed itself in the pomp and display of marching on parade.

The boys greatly enjoyed the day, and were sorely disappointed if they were debarred from attending muster. One clear day, preceding the muster, a boy looking forward with intense interest and much fear that the next day would be stormy, remarked to a companion : " I shouldn't dread dying one day sooner, if today was general muster." At another time, John and Caleb were going to muster, when Sam, John's younger brother, determined to accompany them. To prevent trouble, as Sam was too young to go, the father sent John, under pretext, to a neighbor's to borrow some tools. John and Caleb started, knowing that they were to reach the muster-field, while Sam remained at home, awaiting their return. The morning hours dragged slowly by. About ten o'clock, Sam asked his mother where John was. " Why, gone to muster," was her answer. " Oh, Lord, I'm dead, I'm dead !" cried Sam, with a wail of agony, and throwing himself down upon the floor, he kicked until nearly exhausted.

But musters for boys' pleasure and men's glory finally had to be given up. The law of March 22, 1844, requiring the enrollment of all able-bodied white male citizens between eighteen and forty-five years of age, with few exemptions, who were to perform no active duty except for the choice of officers, or in case of an emergency, amounted to an abandonment of the old military system of the state, and ended the annual general muster.

Five persons attained the rank of General in the militia. Their names, with those of other officers who served from Sanford, appear below :

Major-Generals — William Frost, 1817–21, Sixth division ; Ebenezer Ricker, 1856.

Brigadier-Generals — Elisha Allen, 1822–25, First brigade, First division ; John W. Bodwell, 1826–31 ; Timothy Shaw, 1838–46.

Colonels — Caleb Emery, Fourth regiment, First brigade, Sixth division, 1788. The companies of Sanford, Lebanon, Shapleigh, Waterborough, and Coxhall constituted his command ; William Frost, by brevet, 1816, Third regiment ; Elisha Allen, 1818 ; Timothy Shaw, 1828–38 ; Nehemiah Butler, 1838–43.

Lieutenant-Colonels — William Frost, 1799 ; Ebenezer Nowell, 1817–19 ; Timothy Shaw, 1826–28 ; Nehemiah Butler, 1838.

Majors — Caleb Emery, prior to 1785 ; Samuel Nasson, prior to 1786 ; William Frost, 1794 ; Elisha Allen, 1812–13 ; Timothy Shaw, 1822–26 ; Nehemiah Butler, 1836–38.

Brigade-Majors — John W. Bodwell, 1825–26, aid to Brigadier-General ; Francis A. Allen, 1826–34, aid to Brigadier-General and inspector ; Samuel M. Shaw, 1841–44 ; Samuel Tompson, 1844–51.

Adjutants — Daniel Webber, 1790 ; Jonathan Burrows, 1794 ; Elisha Allen, 1808 ; Ephraim Low, Junior, 1818–26 ; Timothy Shaw, Junior, 1838–46.

Aids-de-Camp — John Frost, Third, 1817–21 ; Nicholas E. Paine, 1839 ; Samuel M. Shaw, 1839–41 ; Samuel Tompson, 1841–44.

Quartermasters —William Frost, 1790 ; Elisha Allen, 1807 ; Ebenezer Nowell, 1808 ; Henry T. Emery, 1808 ; John W. Bodwell, 1821–22 ; Francis A. Allen, 1822–24 ; James B. Shapleigh, 1830–37.

Brigade Quartermasters — John W. Bodwell, 1822–24 ; Francis A. Allen, 1825–26 ; John T. Paine, 1827–37 (Shapleigh) ; Samuel B. Emery, 1839–1846.

Division Quartermaster — Samuel Lord, 1856–57.

Surgeons — Abiel Hall, 1796 (Alfred) ; Usher Hall, 1814 ; Caleb Emery, 1817 (Eliot).

Surgeons' Mates — Charles Powers, 1807 ; Caleb Emery, 1810 (Eliot) ; Usher Parsons, 1812 ; Ebenezer Linscott, 1813 ; George Weld, 1828–30, 1836–37 (Lebanon) ; Silas B. Wedgewood, 1839–42.

Paymasters — William Frost, Junior, 1811–1821 ; Ichabod Frost, 1821–40 ; Samuel S. Stacey, 1847–49 (United States Army).

Chaplains — Moses Sweat, 1807–14 ; Gideon Cook, 1821–28.

Captains —Samuel Nasson, 1777 (matross company) ; Enoch Hale, 1788; Ebenezer Hall, 1788 ; John S. Cram, 1792 ; David Morrison, 1792 ; Samuel Cluff, 1792 ; Ephraim Grant, 1799 ; Mark Prime, 1800 ; Caleb Emery, Junior, 1806 ; John Hanson, 1807 ; Ebenezer Nowell, 1808 ; John Powers, Junior, 1810 ; Aaron Jellison, 1812–17 ; Stephen Willard, 1814, 1822 ; Timothy Shaw, 1817–22 ; Nathan Goodwin, 1817–25 ; Thomas S. Emery, 1822–24 ; William Wilkinson, 1822–27 ; Abner Hill, 1823–25 (cavalry) ; Benjamin Sweat, 1824–27 ; Daniel P. Shaw, 1825 ; Naphtali Chadbourn, 1827 (refused to accept commission) ; Jeremiah Moulton, Junior, 1827–30 ; Enoch Frost, 1827 ; Moses Goodwin ; Nathaniel Hobbs, 1829 (cavalry) ; Theodore Tripp, 1830 ; Ira Hurd, 1832–33 ; Nathaniel Bennett, Third, 1833 ; Nehemiah Butler, 1835–36 ; Zebulon Durrell, 1836 ; Joshua Littlefield, 1836–39 ; Samuel Jackson, 1838 ; Nahum Bennett, 1839 ; Josiah Paine. 1841 ; Otis R. Libby, 1842 ; Charles Butler, 1842–43.

First Lieutenants — James Heard, 1788 ; William Parsons, 1788 ; William Gray, 1792 ; Ephraim Grant, 1792 ; Benjamin Trafton, 1792 ; Rufus Bennett, 1797 ; Samuel Shaw, 1800–07 ; John Powers, Junior, 1806 ; Theodore Emery, 1807–11 ; Robert Johnson, 1810–12 ; Ephraim Low, Junior, 1811 ; Samuel S. Stacey, 1812–15 ; Nathaniel Bennett, 1812–15 ; Abner Hill, 1813 (cavalry) ; Joshua Hanson, 1815–26 ; Ebenezer Garey, 1815–21 ; William Wilkinson, 1818–22 ; Thomas S. Emery, 1821–22 ; Benjamin Sweat, 1822–24 ; William Jacobs, 1822–27 ; Jeremiah Moulton, Junior, 1824–27 ; Solomon Frost, 1826 ; John Linscott, 1826 (refused to accept commission) ; Phineas T. Witham, 1826 (or 27) ; Theodore Tripp, 1827–30 ; Jonathan Tebbetts, 1828 ; Ira Hurd, 1830 ; John T. Storer ; Nathaniel Bennett, Third, 1830 ; Nehemiah Butler, 1833 ; Horace Bennett, 1833 ; Levi Barnes, 1835 ; Jackson W. Quint, 1836 ; Abiel H. Johnson, 1839 ; Charles Butler, 1840 ; Thaddeus Littlefield, 1840 ; Albert Day, 1840 (cavalry) ; John Lord, 1840 (cavalry) ; Joseph Littlefield, 1842 ; Samuel Thompson, Second, 1843.

Ensigns, or Second Lieutenants — John S. Cram, 1788 ; Samuel Cluff, 1788 ; William Johnson, 1792 ; William Ricker, 1792 ; Joseph Parsons, 1792 ; James Garey, Junior, 1800 ; Phinehas Calcut, 1802 ; Homer Sweat, 1806–12 ; Jeremiah Wise, Junior, 1807–13 ; Joshua Hanson, Junior, 1812 ; Moses Lord, 1812–15 ; Thomas A. Smith, 1812 ; Samuel Nowell, 1813–21 ; Wentworth Quint, 1815 (refused to be qualified) ; Thomas S. Emery, 1815–21 ; Benjamin Chaney, 1816–

23 ; Samuel S. Stacey, 1817–21 (Fifth United States Infantry) ; Israel Lassell, Junior, 1821 ; Elisha Sweat ; William Jacobs, 1821–22 ; Benjamin Sweat, 1821–22 ; Jeremiah Moulton, Junior, 1822–24 ; Adrial Thompson, 1822 (refused to accept commission) ; William C. Linscott, 1823 ; Daniel P. Shaw, 1823 ; Theodore Tripp, 1824–27 ; Solomon Frost, 1826 ; James Butler, 1826–30 ; Ira Hurd, 1827 ; Jonathan Tebbetts, Second, 1828 ; Joshua Littlefield, 1834 ; James Tebbetts, 1835 ; Nahum Bennett, 1836 ; Joseph W. Chaney, 1836 ; Zebulon Durrell, 1836 ; Jonas Littlefield, 1839 ; Otis R. Libby, 1840 ; Joseph Littlefield, 1841 ; Samuel Thompson, Junior (Second), 1842 ; Stephen Goodwin, 1842 ; Samuel Gowen, 1843.

For convenience, in connection with the military history, mention of Sanford's participation in two minor wars is here recorded.

The Florida War (1835–42) caused but little excitement in Maine. A few enlisted in the regular army, of whom the names of only two are learned. Justus Batchelder, son of John, of the War of 1812, born October 15, 1817, enlisted in August, 1839, for five years, and was accidentally shot near Fort King, Florida, March 27, 1840. Jacob Hamilton, enlisted in Portsmouth, N. H., served in Florida, and was killed. He married Dorcas, daughter of William Deering.

The Madawaska War, so-called, of 1839, created great excitement throughout the state. Some lumbermen from New Brunswick entered the territory in dispute between Maine and the British government, on the northeastern frontier, and began to cut and carry off the best timber. The land agent, Rufus McIntire, of Parsonsfield, with Sheriff Strickland of Penobscot County, went thither with a posse of two hundred men to protect the property and drive off the trespassers. One night the agent, with a small company, was seized by the trespassers, and carried to Woodstock, and thence to Fredericton, where they were imprisoned. The militia, one thousand men, were ordered out, the legislature made a large appropriation to prosecute a war, and the Governor ordered a draft of ten thousand men from the militia, to be held in readiness for service. Early in March, General Scott and staff arrived on the scene of action, and Congress even went so far as to pass a bill endorsing the proceedings in Maine. Though several hundred volunteers were hurried down to the Aroostook, their services were of little use, only as they, by their presence, had much influence in bringing about peaceful negotiations, which were soon arranged between Governor Fairfield and the Governor of New Brunswick, aided by General Scott. General Shaw went to the front, accompanied by a number of drafted men from his brigade. Their names we have not learned.

CHAPTER XX.

First Mill at South Sanford — Second, on the Chadbourn Privilege
— Cane's, Willard's, Moulton's, and the Province Mills — The
Iron Works — Morrison's Mills and Others — Springvale Print
Works — Woollen Mills — Cotton Manufacturing at Springvale
— Shoe Factories.

AFTER the first mill in Phillipstown had been erected at what is
now South Sanford, by Dr. David Bennett and others, as already
described in Chapter III, it was probably several years before the
second mill was built. There is a tradition that the mill lot known
for years as the Chadbourn privilege (the present site of the Mousam
River mills, so-called), was offered to the person who would build a
mill thereon, and that James Chadbourn, accepting the offer, built
the first mill there. We have not learned when it was built, but
know that it was standing in 1754, for on the 14th day of March, in
that year, John Chadbourn sold to Samuel Fernald, of Kittery, one
twenty-fourth of the mill, being the upper mill on the Mousam River.
It was adjoining Thomas Hobbs's. In 1761, John Chadbourn, and
Mary, his wife, sold to Captain James Littlefield, one-fourth of the
mill privilege. Four years later, a writ of possession was granted
to Jeremiah Moulton, who had brought a law suit against Gideon
Warren and Gabriel Hamilton, of Berwick, Joseph Killgore, Benjamin Killgore, John Chadbourn, and Ephraim Low, of Phillipstown,
and James Littlefield of Wells, for one acre of land and mill thereon,
northwest of number twenty. The land had been occupied within
twenty years. From this it would appear that the mill builders had
encroached upon the land of Moulton, and were ejected by a writ
issued by a competent court. In 1766, John Chadbourn sold to
James Littlefield one-fourth of the mill privilege, with transportation
and exportation to and from the said mill on the twentieth lot. When
Jeremiah Moulton died, in 1777, he owned one-half of the mill, appraised at twenty pounds. The mill was burned November 24, 1817.

14   (209)

It was then rebuilt, and was run for many years by Elijah Witham. The mill was known as the Chadbourn mill, and the branch upon which it stood was the " west way," evidently misconceived by the people at a later day, who applied the term " waste way " to the eastern water course, as if the surplus water was carried off by it, or " wasted."

Cane's Mill, probably the third in town, stood about ten rods above Willard's bridge. It was built about 1756, by James Littlefield, of Wells, John Hamilton, of Berwick, and Samuel and Joshua Cane, of Phillipstown. The dam caused the water to overflow lands of Benjamin and Naphtali Harmon, and a suit arose out of it in 1760. The mill was burned in 1764, the fire being supposed to have been set by an incendiary. Naphtali Harmon and others were sued for trespass, for setting fire to the mill, but were acquitted. Nearly a hundred years afterward, a part of the timber of the dam was hauled to Kennebunk, and sold for ship timber. Joel E. and Stephen H. Moulton made a horse cart of some of the oak timber remaining, which did them service for years.

Willard's mill was built between 1755 and 1761, probably by Thomas Hobbs, Junior, of Berwick, and John Stanyan, Joseph Killgore, and Samuel Willard of Phillipstown. In 1755, Stanyan sold to Willard, then of York, one-half of lot number one, with mill privilege. The mill to be built was to be held in equal parts by the two parties. Two years later, Stanyan sold to Thomas Hobbs, Junior, of Berwick, millwright, one-fourth of the mill privilege, with one-fourth part of three acres of land on both sides of the Mousam. In 1761, Joseph Killgore, Junior, sold to Joseph Simpson, Junior, one-sixteenth part of the mill, privilege, etc. This part was purchased by Stanyan in 1767. Meanwhile, Hobbs sold one-eighth of a double saw-mill and one-eighth of the mill privilege, to Willard, and an equal share of the south side of the mill, with one-sixteenth part of the stream, etc., to John Stanyan. The saw-mill was at the upper falls, and in 1785 was known as Emery's mill, Colonel Emery having come into possession of the same, or a large part of it. Adjacent and below was the grist-mill, standing in 1783, and known as Willard and Stanyan's grist-mill. This is the earliest mention we have found of this mill. The saw-mill was for many years known as Willard's mill. Otis R. Willard, Christopher Cram, and the heirs of Walter Cram are the present owners.

Subsequently to 1766, Charles and John White, Thomas Kimball, Seth Peabody, Benjamin Tripe, and one Ellenwood, of Wells, erected a double saw-mill in the eastern part of the town, which was owned for years by Nathaniel Conant, and known as Conant's mill. It was the first erected in what is now Alfred. The second, according to Parsons, was at the extreme south end of the town, and was formerly owned by John Parsons.

The Province mill at Springvale was built in 1770. It was erected by John Stanyan, Simon Hobbs, Samuel Moody, and Thomas Morrill, as appears from the following:

" This indenture Witnesseth that John Stanyan Simon Hobbs and Samuell Moody of Sanford in the County of York and Thomas Morrill of Berwick in the above s^d county have Settled all accounts for a Mill above Sanford on the Province Land and the s^d John Stanyan owns Eight Days in twenty and four Days or one-third Part Simon Hobbs owns Seven Days in twenty-four Days which is his Part of sd mill and Samuell Moody owns one Eight Part which is three Days in twenty four Days Which is his Part of sd mill and Thomas Morrill above sd owns Six Days in twenty four Days which is his Part of the above sd mill and Likewise the above sd owners all being Pressant this day and Settled all the accounts for sd Mill and balenced the Same by ajusting all our accounts.

" as Witness our hands and seals this 30 days of January 1771 in the Eleventh year of the Reign of King Georg the third AD 1771.

	THOMAS MORRILL	[seal]
	SIMON HOBBS	[seal]
	SAMUELL MOODY	[seal]
	JOHN STANYAN	[seal]

" Signed and sealed in Presents of us
" JOSEPH LEWIS
" THOMAS CHASE."

The document also contained a memorandum that Moody should begin his "turn in the above sd Mill" on January 31, 1771, Morrill on February 4, Stanyan on February 11, and Hobbs on February 20. It was further " Agreed towards fixing the Mill at three Shillings four Pence pr day and accompts to be settled every six months by us the Subscribers." In 1794, William Frost owned three-eighths of the privilege. One old mill fell on account of age, and two mills were burnt on the site.

In 1772, the Iron Works were built at the upper falls at the Corner. Stephen Gowen made this memorandum in 1837:

" A memorandum on oners and works on the falls in mousom River

so caled in Sanford, Maine : in the year 1771 Jotham Moulton moulten, Joseph Persons of York and Some others began to bild a dam
on Said falls and in 1772 it was finished and a bilding set up for the
manufacturing of iron. After the deth of moulten it fell into the
hands of the folowing owners, Moulten the first No. 1, S. Nason No.
2, Allen No. 3, do Allen No. 4, Pray, No. 5, Cuts No. 6 and 1835 in
to the hands of a factory company.   7th it is now under morged for
$6500.   1837.   I worked on the dam when firs bilt.

" STEPHEN GOWEN."

These works stood several years, and gave the name, Iron Works
lot, to Moulton's four hundred acre lot along the river above the
settlers' lots.   The ore used was obtained in town or in Shapleigh ;
the iron manufactured was used, in part, at home, and sold, in part,
in York, Wakefield, and elsewhere.   The ore passed through what
is known as the "bloomary process," giving a very good quality of
iron at a reasonably low price.   Slag was found in 1836, when the
dam was rebuilt.   Joshua Hanson and Joshua Batchelder were
'bloomers."   In 1777, General Moulton owned one-half of the
Iron Works.   Whether they existed as late as 1800, we have no
knowledge, but are of the opinion that they did not.

Moulton's grist-mill was built about the same time as the Iron
Works, on the northeastern side of the river at the second falls at
the Corner.   One-half of it, valued at one hundred pounds, was
owned by General Moulton at the time of his death.   In 1782, it
came into the hands of his widow, then the wife of Major Samuel
Nasson, as a part of her dower.   In 1800, Nasson and others erected
a saw-mill near the site of the Iron Works.

In 1781, there were seven "distill houses, mills, etc.," valued at
eighty shillings apiece.   These were Moulton's, owned by Samuel
Nasson, and leased by Tobias Lord, of Kennebunk, and Benjamin
Estes in 1781–82 ; Willard's saw-mill, and probably Willard and
Stanyan's grist-mill ; Chadbourn's saw-mill ; Nasson's grist-mill ; the
Province mill ; and Conant's mill.   We presume there were no "dis-
till houses," for we have never heard of any in town.

When the great freshet occurred in 1785, there were nine mills
damaged :   Estes's grist-mill, Swett's saw-mill, Nassou's grist-mill,
Chadbourn's saw-mill, Moody's saw-mill, Emery's, Moulton's, the
Province mill, and Bennett's.   According to the valuation of 1786,
there were thirteen and one-quarter grist- and saw-mills, and one
other mill, in the town.   If Parsons is correct in his statement that

Swett's mill, half a mile southeast of Conant's, was the fifth mill in
the North Parish, then five or six of these were in that parish, of
which all except Conant's were built between 1781 and 1785, — that
at the extreme south end of the town, Moody's, near " the Gore,"
York's above Moody's, and Swett's, and possibly, Conant's grist-
mill. The " other mill " was probably the fulling-mill built by Major
Nasson, and at a later day owned by Jeremiah Moulton and Elisha
Allen. It was on the southwest side of the river at the second falls
at the Corner, and was standing in the writer's boyhood.

Not far from 1780, David Morrison came into town, and settled
a mile above Springvale. Several years later he built a saw-mill
some forty rods below the old bridge. The dam was thrown across
the narrow channel between two ledges ; one abutment rested on a
ledge on the northeast side, a portion of the timber of which could
be seen not so many years ago. Soon after, he erected a grist-mill
about one hundred rods below, following the river down. The mill-
stones came from York woods, were got out by Morrison, and were
lying in a pasture on the mill privilege when the writer visited the
spot. Two negroes, named Cæsar and Sharp, hauled the crank from
Wells, on the snow crust, making the distance, seventeen miles, in
good time. Prior to 1791, Morrison built some iron works. Pieces
of slag and ore are found in the river bed. The ore was obtained
from the mines in Shapleigh and Newfield, and in the vicinity of
the bloomary. The rocks in the neighborhood show the presence
of iron, especially near Frost's brook, below Morrison's Corner. In
1791, Morrison deeded one-eighth of his iron works on " the Gore "
on Mousam River to Joshua Hanson, " bloomer." Subsequent owners of the grist-mill were Elisha Allen, Harriet Allen, and Increase
S. Kimball ; of the saw-mill and privilege, Joshua Hanson, John
Colcord, William Stanley, E. and M. Goodwin, Ansel Gerrish, J.
Ricker and A. Lord, Ebenezer Ricker and Whitefield Lord, Ebenezer
Ricker, who built a new mill in 1856, Hemingway and Co., Hemingway and Lord, Jordan and Allen, Ebenezer and Freeman Jordan.

At one time four privileges on the Great Works River were utilized : Hobbs's, Gowen's, Bennett's, and Johnson's. Hobbs's grist-
mill, standing in 1798, was on the upper course, on land afterwards
owned by Sheldon and Stephen Hobbs. The mill was sold to Joseph
Quint and torn down ; the stones were purchased and used by James
O. Clark in his mill at the Corner. Farther down the Gowens owned
a grist-mill, which was standing as late as 1845. A mile southeast
of this, on the old county road over Mount Hope to Lebanon, the

Bennetts had built a mill before 1785. Some years later, Daniel Chadbourn, Levi Chadbourn, and Nathaniel Quint had a tannery on the privilege. At the end of the tannery, a shingle-mill was first built, and then a grist-mill. A threshing machine was subsequently put in by Nathaniel Bennett, Daniel Chadbourn, Francis Chadbourn, William Stanley, and Robert Johnson. The mill came into the possession of Johnson, then of Johnson and Simon Tebbets, and finally of Tebbets alone. It was changed into a saw-mill.

A wooden dam was thrown across the stream between Sanford and Berwick, by William Johnson, about 1790. A grist-mill, running one set of stones, was erected on the Sanford side, and a saw-mill, with a single saw, on the opposite side. The latter tumbled down; the former was taken down in 1865, by Jotham Johnson.

According to plans of Sanford and of the District of Alfred, in 1794, there were the following mills : On the Mousam : Iron Works, saw-mill and grist-mill, at Morrison's ; saw-mill, at Springvale ; saw-mill and grist-mill, and fulling-mill, at Sanford ; saw-mill (Chadbourn's) ; saw-mill, at Willard's ; saw-mill, above confluence of western branch and eastern ; grist-mill, below, and saw-mill still below. On the Great Works : Bennett's saw-mill ; Johnson's saw and grist-mill. In Alfred : Saw-mill and grist-mill, Conant's : saw-mill, near junction of the eastern and middle branches ; saw-mill, near the Waterborough line ; three saw-mills and one grist-mill on the middle branch ; saw-mill in lower part of the town, presumably the last one on the Mousam, mentioned above.

At one time a mill called Jellison's mill stood near the Shapleigh line. There was an Eastman's grist-mill in the southeast or east part of the town, but whether one already mentioned in the vicinity of Mouse Lane we cannot say. We do not know what mill was Deacon Joshua Goodwin's, or Day's, nor can we tell how many of those referred to by Parsons were built before Alfred became a separate town. There were Nowell's, on the middle branch, Knight's, north of Shaker Hill, Ricker's, near Knight's, Sayward's, and Littlefield's, near the bridge ; also, the Shakers', Littlefield's, Estes's, Moulton's, and Burleigh's grist-mills, the last near " the Gore," the two preceding at Mouse Lane. We do know, however, that Estes's grist-mill was standing in 1785 (it may have been the mill built by Estes in 1783, for Samuel Nasson), and conclude that some of the others were built earlier, unless Parsons has made a mistake in the order of time. We are much in doubt in regard to that one-third of a mill mentioned in the valuation of 1786.

In Stephen Gowen's old account book, Jonathan Low is charged, August, 1788, with " 600 foot of White Oak Plank at my mill." From this we infer his ownership of a mill at that date. His son Walter informed the writer, however, that Stephen Gowen built a dam across the river, about one mile above the Corner, in 1815, and completed a grist-mill, running one set of stones. About three years later, Stephen, James, and Walter Gowen erected a saw-mill below and adjoining, of which each owned a third. Dr. George Weld bought James Gowen's right. Either Gowen owned a mill elsewhere, or a saw-mill antedated the grist mill. The capacity of this mill was such that eight or ten bushels of corn could be ground per day.

Few of the grist-mills of this date, about 1820, had more than one run of stones, and some of them no bolting-machines. Whenever there was a bolter, it went by hand, and was turned, like a grindstone, with a crank. The meal or flour to be bolted was taken from the trough, carried up a short flight of stairs, and put into the hopper of the bolter. The owner of the grist did the bolting. It was a tedious task for the poor boy, upon whom the duty of going to mill fell, to turn the crank slowly, and hear the thump, thump of the old machine. Going to mill might have been poetry in comparison with the prosaic duties of the farm, but there was no music in turning a bolting-machine of rude construction, an hour at a time. The saw-mills of that date were cumbersome and slow; one thousand feet of boards per day were as high as they would average. If for any reason a grist-mill should fail, the people were somewhat discommoded, and were obliged to resort to pounding their corn to meal. This was coarse food, but it sufficed until they could get better. After the grist-mill at the Corner was burned in 1809, there was no mill near, and several families had recourse to Gatnsby Witham's samp-mortar, in which they pounded corn. The mortar was a hollow log, raised about breast high, with a pestle attached to a sweep, like a well sweep. " Aunt Polly " Witham, deceased, often stated that she was among those who used to exercise themselves at the samp-mortar.

In January, 1805, Joanna and Thomas Nasson sold to Charles Dennett and Thomas Frost, of Salisbury, Mass., a privilege for a carding-mill and a trip hammer, between the Iron Works, and grist-mill, for the purpose of plating scythes.

Not far from 1805, " old Shepherd " built a dam across the brook which empties the water of the Fishing Pond into Great Works Brook, erected a small shop, and manufactured nails.

In 1810, there were one hundred and sixty looms in town, and 29,369 yards of cloth were manufactured.

The Province mill privilege was sold by Ichabod Frost, Betsey Frost, widow, and Henry Grant to George Holt and John Oldham, of Dover, N. H., for two hundred and thirty-two dollars, February 5, 1828. The grantees, in turn, conveyed their purchase to John Whitaker and Co., of Sanford, June 17, Whitaker's joint partners being Matthew Hodgdon, Edward Thompson, George Holt, and John Oldham. On the 10th of December, the company, comprising in addition to the above, Thomas Clark, Thomas Greenhalgh, John Ramsbotham and Thomas Read, quitclaimed their property to Luke Whitney for eight thousand dollars, and took a bond from him for the return of said property after Whitaker and his associates had obtained an act of incorporation under the name of Springvale Print Works. Meanwhile and subsequently several buildings were erected for the purpose of manufacturing prints. Four dwelling-houses, a factory store, a dry shed, and a print-house were built on the brow of the hill, and near the road, and a dye-house and bleachery, and several other buildings, under the hill. The company failed, and in 1831 Caleb Duxbury, as superintendent, was running the works for the assignees of Avered and Goddard (?). There were then twenty blocking tables upon which cloth was printed by hand, and two printing machines. Cloth at first had been brought from Dover, but at this time it came from Boston to be printed. About 1835, calico printing was revived under the management of Eleazar D. Chamberlain, Samuel Dunster, of Dover, and Abraham Folsom, of Boston. Cloth came from Dover and Providence, from the former at the rate of one hundred thousand yards per month. After about three years another failure was made, and the business passed into the hands of the Franklin Manufacturing Company. The accounts of the changes which have been received are conflicting, so we cannot speak with certainty in regard to them. One statement is that Joshua Hanson, Nathaniel Hobbs, Enoch Lord, William Chadbourn, Ephraim Getchell, John Bedell, Samuel Littlefield, Moses Heard, Thomas Hobbs, and Wentworth Quint (?) were owners in 1838. It appears, however, that Danforth White, John Montelius and William Montelius had charge of the works, with Reuben S. Denney, Abial Lewis, and William G. Lewis, as capitalists, to furnish the means of carrying on the business. It also appears that John Paul, George Livsey, and George Hargraves, calico printers, constituted the firm of John Paul and Co., in 1844, and that later Livsey had severed his connection with the firm. The Lewises came into possession of all the property; it lay idle for some time; the buildings were destroyed, in part, by incendiarism; then the property changed hands again, coming into the possession of the Springvale Manufacturing Company, John and Stephen Merrill, George Nasson, George Rollins, and Irving Butler.

In 1835, Hutchinson, Sawyer and Co. bought the upper privilege at the Corner. They put up a woollen mill on the eastern side of the river, and began the manufacture of cassimeres. In a year or two, the mill was burnt, and another built. The firm had dissolved prior to August 27, 1839. The property passed into the hands of a Mr. Cutts. About 1840, William Miller, who had been engaged in the manufacture of woollens at Emery's Mills, hired the mill and commenced operations. Later he purchased the mill and continued the manufacture of flannels until 1867, when he sold to Thomas Goodall, a full account of whose resulting enterprises will be given in a subsequent chapter. During the Civil War Mr. Miller made woollens for army use.

About the same time with Hutchinson, Sawyer and Co., Timothy Shaw, Nicholas E. Paine, and Samuel M. Shaw began to occupy the second falls at the Corner, where the grist-mill stood. They erected a main factory, a dye-house, a store-house, a boarding-house, all two stories high, and other necessary buildings, all of which with machinery, personal and real estate of the firm, Shaw, Paine and Co., was valued in 1831 at $35,493.49. One mill was burned and rebuilt. The company failed about 1840, and the privilege was idle about fifteen years.

At the upper falls at Springvale, Ichabod Frost had a saw-mill standing on the southwest side of the river, in 1838. Isaiah Shackley began to run it for him that year, and continued in his employ some two years. With it there was a grist-mill, run by Solomon Frost. After Ichabod Frost had sold the privilege to the Sanford Manufacturing Company about 1841, the mill was moved down to the site of the Province mill, and years later burnt. A mill was moved from Emery's Mills to the latter site.

In 1841 the Sanford Manufacturing Company was organized to build a cotton factory at Springvale. At the first meeting Isaac Hayden was chosen chairman, Theodore Willard, clerk, Amos H. Boyd, treasurer, and Ichabod Frost, agent to superintend the building of the bridge, the dam, and the digging and laying of the foundation for the mill. The nearest depots of supplies were

Kennebunkport, whither freight came by water, and Dover, whither it came by the railroad, completed to that point only. The prices for cartage may be seen in a vote of the company, passed at the house of Ichabod Frost, January 13, 1842 : "Voted to give Caleb S. Emery, for one year from time mill is put into operation, thirteen and three-fourths cents per hundred pounds each way to and and from Kennebunk Port, and sixteen cents each way to and from Dover Railroad." The associate company was changed to a corporate body in 1842 by an act of the legislature, which authorized Isaac Hayden, Ichabod Frost, Theodore Willard, Caleb S. Emery, Amos H. Boyd, Benjamin F. Hodgdon, Andrew Cooper, Daniel Ward, Stephen Ward, Danforth White, John Montelius, Junior, Samuel V. Loring, Amos Getchell, David Fall, Daniel Chaney, Charles Allen, and Francis Allen, their associates and successors, to engage in the manufacture of cotton, wool, iron, and steel at Springvale, and to hold real and personal estate not to exceed $50,000 in value. Isaac Hayden was president, Samuel V. Loring, clerk, and Ichabod Frost, Danforth White, Benjamin F. Hodgdon, Theodore Willard, Samuel V. Loring and Andrew Cooper, directors. The machinery from the Belknap mill, Dover, was mostly in by May, 1842, and the first card started. The first loom, however, was not started until August, when Benjamin F. Hodgdon began to weave the first yard of cloth. It is a matter of regret to state that at this time the company was laboring under a heavy load of indebtedness. A severe blow came in the great freshet of 1843, by which the concern met with considerable loss, and in August of that year the mill was considered as unsafe, and greatly exposed to serious injury from freshet or other casualty.

Such men as John Fairbanks, Benjamin E. Bates, of Boston, Colonel Alexander DeWitt, afterward member of Congress, of Franklin, Mass., Mason and Co., and Dewey and Bourne, of Worcester, were at times stockholders. Among the agents, mention may be made of Isaac Hayden (afterwards agent of the "duck" mill, Lawrence), General Amos H. Boyd, Samuel Houghton, and William B. Boyd. Houghton and Waterman A. Fisher bought three hundred and seventy-six shares of Boyd and DeWitt for $37,600. Under the management of Fisher, president, John T. Paine, Caleb S. Emery, Theodore Willard, and Houghton, agent, treasurer, and superintendent, as directors, the company manufactured for a short time print cloths, and a few three-fourths sheetings. Houghton sold ten shares to William B. Boyd, Fisher sold to Dickenson, and about 1850, Fitch, Hodgdon and Co., with Austin G. Fitch as agent, leased the property for five years. They made a new kind of figured goods, Scotch plaids, ging-hams, nankeens, and other fancy goods. Of this firm, only Hodgdon was a practical manufacturer. After four years the property passed into the hands of Tufts, Everett and Co., Boston, and was managed by a Mr. Hewitt, agent. From 1857 it was idle a year, and was then run until the Civil War. Hodgdon acted as agent for a time, and was succeeded by Oliver Boyd. He died in March, 1862. His son, W. W. Boyd, afterward a Baptist clergyman, had an oversight of the property during the war, a part of the time, at least, though the mill was not in operation.

In 1865, J. H. and L. M. Smith, and A. D. Shattuck, of Grafton, Mass., and E. W. Holbrook, of New York, purchased of the Spring-vale Manufacturing Company (Springvale had superseded Sanford years before) their property, and continued the manufacture of cot-tons, mostly print cloths, and mosquito nettings, under the name of the Grafton Mills. Shattuck acted alternately as agent and treasurer. In 1873, Holbrook purchased the interest of the Smiths, Shattuck having sold out previously. According to the general statutes of Maine, the Springvale Mills were organized in 1873, with a capital of $100,000. The owners were Edwin W. Holbrook, Clarence D. Newell, Charles W. Force, Edgar F. Grout, all of New York, Aaron Holbrook, of Lexington, Mass., George K. Gibbs, of Sanford, and Joseph W. Hall, of Boston. All except Grout and Hall were direc-tors, of whom E. W. Holbrook was president, and Gibbs treasurer. They began business, January 1, 1874, under the superintendency of Mr. Gibbs, running eight thousand spindles, and employing one hun-dred and fifty hands, in the manufacture of sheetings. In 1883 the company was obliged to suspend operations.

In June, 1891, the Springvale Cotton Mills Company was incor-porated under the laws of Maine, with William D. Wheelwright as president and J. O. Bloss, treasurer, with offices in New York. The company manufactured cottons, satteens, and twilled goods. Joel B. Ricker was agent. In 1899 the company sold its plant to the Goodall Alpaca Company, and went south, locating in Fort Valley, Georgia, where it is operated under $100,000 capital.

In 1844, Abiel H. Moulton built a foundry with a furnace twenty feet wide and seven and a half feet high. Three horizontal bellows, blown by one horse, were used. At one blast twenty-five hundred pounds could be taken out. Four or five men were employed, manu-facturing plows, cultivators, sled shoes, and castings for repairing stoves, and machinery. The foundry was carried on by Mr. Moulton

until 1855. In March, 1857, Jotham K. Moulton purchased and
continued the business a few years.

In 1854, Hayden, Wilcox and Co., rebuilt the lower dam at the
Corner, and put machinery into the Shaw, Paine and Co. factory for
the purpose of weaving seamless bags. This mill was known during
the three years' continuance of this business as Victory Mill. In
1857 the mill was destroyed by fire.

About 1847, Daniel Clark bought the saw-mill and upper privilege
at the Corner, and some three years later built a grist-mill on the
ledge between the two dams. About 1860, he gave this property to
his youngest son, James O. Clark. In June, 1862, the grist-mill was
destroyed by fire, and the following spring the saw-mill, with flour-
mill connected, was also burned. Clark bought the Victory Mills
privilege, and erected a flour-mill, which he continued to run until
Thomas Goodall began to improve it.

One Paul first made brick near his house on "Hardscrabble."
Flanders Hatch and Daniel L. Littlefield also made brick near the
Hay Brook, the latter for eight or ten years from 1829 making from
50,000 to 100,000 brick. Thomas Goodall has also occupied their
yard. Aaron Witham and Charles and John Chapman had a yard
near the Hay Brook.

About 1871, Jordan and Allen began to make shooks at the Morrison Iron Works privilege.

In the fall of 1876, Lyman H. Shackley erected a steam grist-mill
at Springvale depot, close beside the railroad track. In the summer
of 1878, L. H. Shackley and Co. bought the Low privilege, half a
mile below Springvale, and built a substantial stone dam. During the
fall they erected a grist-mill on the east side of the river.

In the spring of 1883, Winslow L. and Orin A. Moulton erected
a wood-working and saw-mill, near Willard's bridge, for which the
power was steam. This mill was afterwards burnt.

Knight and Warren, corn packers, about 1881, erected a factory
near Springvale depot, where they canned corn for several seasons.
In 1886, Joseph Knight put up 180,000 cans of corn.

In the fall of 1839, Captain Joshua Littlefield began to work at
shoemaking at the Corner, and continued at it during the winters
for more than forty years, a part of the time on Main Street, and later
on Lebanon Street. R. W. Thurston occupied a small shop near his
house on Main Street for something like half a century.

Between 1850 and 1857, small shops were built in different parts
of the town, and a large number of people were engaged in making

shoes for Lynn and Danvers firms.   Luther Paul, John Merrill, David
L. Tebbetts, the Bennetts, at South Sanford, George W. Gowen and
the Bodwells at the Corner were engaged therein.   In 1861, Oliver
C. Dorr began shoemaking at South Sanford, doing pegged work.
Emery and Lord, Amos W. Lord, and William H. Miller were in the
shoe business shortly after the Civil War.

In 1864, Sylvester Cummings built a shoe manufactory on the
west side of the river at Springvale, just below the upper bridge, at
a cost of about $10,000, which was successfully run by Cummings
and Co., superintended by P. E. Cummings, partner and superintendent.   They moved all their machinery from Worcester, and made
ladies' shoes, about eight cases a day, employing one hundred and
fifty hands, and doing $50,000 worth of business annually.   They
used machinery, although the work outside, sewing, stitching, and
binding, was done by hand.   In 1872, they removed to South Berwick.

In 1870, Butler and Fogg built a shop on the Province mill privilege, western side of the river, at a cost of $10,000.   The firm was
subsequently Fogg and Vinal, Irving A. Butler and Co., Butler,
Clark and Davenport, and finally Butler and Clark.   Butler and Merrill, and Butler and Stiles also carried on shoe manufacturing at
Springvale.

The A. and E. Mudge Shoe Company, Danvers and East Rochester, moved to Springvale in 1889, $10,000 having been raised by the
citizens for the purpose.   A large shop, five stories in height, and
accommodating five hundred hands, was erected.   This factory is
now occupied by the Shaw-Goding Shoe Company, of which John
D. Fogg is manager.

William A. Usher is engaged in the manufacture of shoes in a shop
on Bridge Street.

The Springvale Shoe Shop Company is a corporation organized by
the citizens to purchase the Shaw-Goding shop, for the purpose of
transferring it or leasing it to some firm to induce them to locate in
Springvale.   The company purchased the shop and made a contract to
sell it to the Shaw-Goding Company.   The officers of the Springvale
Shoe Shop Company are : President, George W. Hanson ; treasurer,
W. E. Sanborn ; clerk, Frank H. Dexter ; collector, James H. Makin ;
directors, George W. Hanson, Edmund E. Goodwin, Dr. I. C. Sawyer, Charles A. Bodwell, Samuel D. Hanson.

The Springvale Woollen Company carries on the manufacture of
woollens in the former shoe factory of Butler and Clark.   It employs

thirty-six hands, and the output is six hundred yards a day. The officers are : President, C. M. Abbott; treasurer, Charles W. Low ; clerk, F. H. Skofield ; directors, George W. Hanson, Charles W. Low, Fred Smith, C. M. Abbott, F. H. Skofield.   Willis A. Fogg is manager.

Fred S. Sherburne has a mill at Sanford in which he manufactures sashes, blinds, doors and general building materials.   He formerly operated a grist-mill.

At Springvale, W. H. Nason and Co. own and operate a grist-mill near the depot.

CHAPTER XXI.

THE POOR.

Privations of the Pioneers — Protest Against Taxation, 1768 —
Warning Out of Town — Scarcity of Food — Votes Relative to
the Poor — Disposal by Vendue — Town-Farm Established.

THE early settlers endured the hardships incident to pioneer life.
The new soil yielded slowly to the advances of man. Scarcity
of provisions and scantiness of clothing were the common fortune of
many, perhaps most, of the actual settlers. Into their dwellings,
poverty like an armed man stalked, less dreaded than the Indian lurk-
ing in the forest, but scarcely more merciful. The descent of the one
upon the frontier, the tenacious hold of the other upon an unfortunate
victim, were enough to appall the stoutest heart, and to deter the
man of weak spirit from subjecting himself to the dangers and privations of the wilderness. Sometimes poverty at home drove men into
the forests, where, expecting little, suffering much, they obtained
more than their expectations.

The pioneers of Sanford were distant from the market, had small
facilities for intercourse with the neighboring towns, had but little
ready money, and frequently found themselves in straitened circumstances. At times, they needed help from their neighbors; occasionally, when some severe calamity had befallen them, they received
assistance from the province, as was the case in 1761, when the plantation was distressed by reason of the small-pox. The taxes of individuals having suffered losses were sometimes abated, and the town
itself was more than once in so poor a condition that it called for assistance or an abatement of taxes from the commonwealth. The condition of the town only three months after its incorporation may best
be understood in the words of the selectmen in a petition to the General Court:

"To his Excellency Francis Barnard Esqr Governer & Commander in Chief in and over the Province of the Massachusetts Bay &c:

To the Honourable his Majesty's Council and the Honorable House of Representatives in General Court assembled May 1768

"The Petition of Benjamin Harmon Naptali Harmon and John Stanyan Selectmen of the Town of Sanford in the County of York in behalf of said Towns Humbly shews

"That said Town was Incorporated into a Town the present year, and that the assessors have Taken the valuation as by Law Directed according to the best of there understanding That there is a considerable number of Polls contained in the list of valuation of People latly come in said Town from the Province of N Hampshire in very Poor Circomstances and as your Petitioners apprehend there stay will be very short as they have no Lands of there own, and that most of the Inhabitants of said Town are very Poor and unable to support themselves, That they are destitute of a minister and School Master, which by Law they are now obliged to be Provided with nor have they any meeting House in said Town. That the Town is now obliged to Clear & make new Roads through the Town leading to other new Towns beyond them, the Lands in General but very Ordinary they never had any help from the Proprietors to enable them to support the Gospel or makeing Roads in said Town and the settlers but Small Tracts of Lands for settlements Tho the Township is Eight miles Square Your Petitioners apprehend that a Province Tax Even a Pool Tax at this Time would Greatly Distress the Inhabitants of s^d Town Wherefore your Petitioners Humbly prays your Excellency and Honours that you will not Lay any Province Tax on said Town the present year on the Polls and Estates—That they may be enabled to settle the Gospel which they are now engaging in and Your Petititioners as in Duty Bound shall ever pray—

" Benja Harmon
Naptali Harmon
John Stanyan "

This was indeed a deplorable condition, out of which the town came, not by sudden and rapid strides, but by a slow and gradual process, the natural result of toil, economy, privation. The Revolutionary War was a serious drawback in that it was constantly drawing from the material wealth of the town, and took away men who would otherwise have been engaged in tilling the soil and improving the lands. Following it, however, was an accession of sturdy men, who developed the resources of the heretofore unoccupied territory and added much to the wealth of the community.

GEORGE B. GOODALL.

The poorer classes from the neighboring state, referred to in the petition of the selectmen, had secured a foothold prior to the incorporation, and, in case they came to want, would be dependent upon the town for their support. New-comers could be, and frequently were, prevented from gaining a residence; for, availing themselves of the provisions of the law, or rather, performing the duty enjoined by the law, the selectmen warned such persons, male or female, to depart from the town. Thus warned they were not compelled to leave; but the formal warning was only a legal precaution necessary to avoid the support of any comers that might become public charges. In that case, the towns whence they came or where they had previously resided were held responsible for their support. The warning-out of Elder Tingley, in our possession, reads as follows:

" York fs Sanford June ye 28 : 1771

" Paletiah Tingle Wereas you have come into this Towne Withoute Leav of the Towne This is to warne you forthwith to Departe out of this Towne forthwith for Wee Disowne you for an inhabitant

" SAMUEL WILLARD } Select
JOHN STANYAN } men
WILLIAM BENNET }

" Sanford June yᵉ 28 : 1771   Mr Edward Stanle Constable you are Requiered to warne the above said Paletiah Tingle to Depart forthwith or expect to be Dealt With as the Law Directs.

" Saⁿ = WILLARD } Select
JOHN STANYAN } men "
WILLIAM BENNET }

[Return on back of warrant.]

" Sanford July yᵉ 13 : 1771   1 have Warned the Within Named Paletiah Tinale to Depart out of this Towne.

" EDWARD STANLEE Constable"

Martha *alias* Patt Chick, a single woman, and Widow Susanna Davis were warned out in 1772. It would appear from the records that the town would have been the gainer, could the residence of the last-named, by any process of law, have been established elsewhere.

Two or three incidents of the last century will serve not only as an illustration of the condition of things, but also as a revelation of the character of the early inhabitants.

At one time, not long after the beginning of the Revolution, there

15

was a great scarcity of bread-stuff. Very little corn and grain had
been raised the year before, but out of this enough had been saved
and sowed by some farmers, to ensure that year's harvest, if it prospered. One June morning, Mrs. Thompson, wife of Deacon Thompson, announced to her family that the bread just eaten for breakfast
had been made of her last bit of meal. Deacon Thompson then
made a little speech to his children, telling them that there was not
any corn or grain that he could buy, and they would all have to do
without bread until bread-stuff grew again ; that they could live very
well on such things as they had, and that they must do it cheerfully,
and have no complaining about it — no murmur must be heard in the
house. When he had impressed it on their minds, he and the boys
went out to their hoeing. At noon, little Patty (born March, 1772)
went to call them to dinner. " What have we got for dinner ? " asked
one of the boys. " Bread and things," she answered. " Bread ! that's
a story ! " said he, " we can't have bread ! " " Yes, we have ; come
and see," said she, running back to the house. The boys ran with
her, and were rejoiced to find a heaping plate of bread on the table.
When Deacon Thompson came in, he looked at the bread, and turned
around and wept like a child. His son Ezra, then a boy of about
fourteen years of age, thought within himself, " Why, what a foolish
man father is, to be so cheerful about doing without bread, and now
to cry when we have some ! I should think it is the last thing to cry
about ! " It seems that a miller living a mile or two away, wishing
some peas or beans that Deacon Thompson had, had ground some of
his saved " toll," and sent to exchange. Before that had gone, there
was corn to be bought, a vessel having brought some to Wells, which
supplied the people until the earlier crops were gathered.

At another time, corn was very scarce, and a poor family, consisting of husband, wife, and three children, had nothing in their house
to eat. One morning he started on foot for Quampegan, to see if his
father could possibly furnish him with some corn, as he had nothing
with which to buy. During the day she sat with a nursing child and
spun two double skeins of yarn, with only cold water to put into her
mouth until her husband's return at night. He returned as destitute
as he went away, for his father could not help him. The next day
he walked to Coxhall, to her father's where he obtained half a bushel
of corn.

A bride from " below," about to move into town to the cabin prepared for her future home, tied up all her marriage portion in a yard-
square handkerchief, and made the journey on horseback behind her

husband. A pail of water served her as a looking-glass for a number of years. During the short days of winter, he felled and trimmed trees, which, by the light of a camp-fire in the evenings, she helped saw with a crosscut-saw into shingle-butts. When he had split these into thin pieces, and, with a drawing-knife, shaved on a shave-horse enough for a load, he would draw them to Wells on a hand-sled, and exchange for such necessaries as he could not raise.

During the Revolutionary War, the families of some soldiers were in need of assistance, but the only recorded action of the town regarding it is a vote of September 6, 1779 : " Vot^d the method that the Town has agreed upon to Suply the solgers families is by Superscription."

In 1781, the town " Voted to help the widow Powers which is now distract^d out of the town stock," and the next year "to chuse a Committe^e to Draw up Petion to send to the general court for to see wyther they abate any part of our taxes or Delay the Execution for a longer time."

Overseers of the poor were first chosen in 1785, subsequently to which special votes were frequently passed, relative to the care of the poor.

March 9, 1789. " Vot^d to abate mr Moses Tebbets taxes so long as he has and will have the two children of his son Jonathan Lord."

April 4, 1791. " Vot^d that John Adams agrees to take his Mother and Sister for twenty Six dolers only the Town finds Cloth for Shiffs and for a bed tow & linnen as so long as they live in Propertion to the above Sum and his town County & Satete tax abat^d so long as they live."

July 25, 1791. " Voted the Selectmen Purchase a Cow and let Mr. John Stanyan have the use of her he keeping and to remain the Towns property and to be taken from him at the towns pleasure."

May 13, 1793. " Vot^d that the Selectmen are to deal with the poor as the Law provides."

March 9, 1801. " Voted to give Jona. Adams 50 cts. per week for supporting his mother in victuals and clothes ;"   April 5, 1802. " Voted the selectmen to put Mrs. Adams out to Best advantage the year ensuing."

April 5, 1802. " Voted the selectmen take Care of hartwell Best, way they can."

In 1803, " Old Mrs. Adams " was to be kept for ninety-one cents per week, and widow Mary Johnson was vendued to Captain Mark Prime for sixty-seven cents per week, the doctor's bill in both cases excepted.

In February, 1819, arrangements were made for bringing a Day family from Augusta, and a man was to be sent for that purpose. " Voted to set it up to vendue to see who would go as above cheapest and that if the town should accept of the person who bid lowest. Joseph Shaw offered to go as above for twenty-two dollars $22.00. And if the family should come the selectmen are to allow the said Shaw a reasonable bill for the support on the road: but the said Shaw is to conduct in the most prudent manner viz. to purchase bread and beef sufficient for their support: but not to have pay at tavern prices."

May 3, 1819. " Voted the selectmen be directed to prosecute Levi Bracket for fetching ——— ——— a pauper into the town unlawfully."

March 4, 1820. " Voted that the overseers of the poor of Sanford be directed to prosecute Joshua Emery, of South Berwick, for bringing ——— ——— into this town and leaving her here."

April 4, 1825   "Voted to vendue the Poor. The condition is they are to be fed & clothed & to be returned at the year's end as well as when received: but the town is to pay doctor's bills and nursing should they be sick."

Various persons were thereupon " struck off " to a number of citizens for sums ranging from one cent to one dollar per week.

In 1838, the poor were bid off by John Garey for four hundred and eighty-nine dollars, and in 1840 by William L. Emery for five hundred dollars. In 1842, the town voted to dispose of the poor singly, by auction, but after disposing of two persons the vote was reconsidered, and the care of the poor was left with the selectmen, who were to act in the " manner most proper for best interests of the town."

From time to time, objections were raised against the prevailing custom of venduing the unfortunate poor in open town meeting. It cost too much, and the poor could be supported in a cheaper manner. The aged and infirm in comfortable quarters with families whom they liked were too often moved, because the town could save a few dollars by making a change, little or no consideration for the feelings of the poor being exercised. The contracting parties were not always reliable and responsible. Sometimes complaints were made of the treatment received at the hands of the keepers of the poor, though such cases, were, fortunately, of rare occurrence. At length, public sentiment or public interests demanded a change. Accordingly, at the annual meeting, April 1, 1850, the selectmen were authorized to purchase a town farm, at a cost of twenty-five hundred dollars or less. On the 22d of that month, however, they were authorized to use their own discretion in the purchase, but it must be made within three weeks. Stock and farming implements were to be bought, and some one put in charge of the farm, and the poor to be moved thereto, from the several places at which they had been kept. The farm and buildings of Timothy Ham, on Hanson's Ridge, were purchased, and Mr. Ham engaged to take charge for one year. Since the establishment of the farm, the wisdom of having a permanent abode for the indigent has been apparent. Whether through misfortune or improvidence or intemperance the inmates of that home have become chargeable to the town, they have generally been treated with the feeling and consideration due to humanity, and received the sympathy which Christian communities bestow upon the unfortunate and suffering. In sickness, they have been well cared for: in death, they have received a decent burial.

The town report of 1900 shows the pauper expenses for the preceding year to have been slightly in excess of two thousand dollars.

CHAPTER XXII.

THE TEMPERANCE MOVEMENT.

Common Use of Intoxicants in the Early Days — Meeting-Houses Raised with Rum — First Restrictive Action of the Town — Decided Stand of Rev. Mr. Marsh — Granting of Licenses — Early Temperance Workers and Organizations — Incendiarism at Springvale — The Prohibitory Law.

THE sale and use of intoxicating liquors were prevalent in the early days of the plantation. The custom of using such liquors, which nearly every one followed, did not have the appearance of a moral wrong, and could not be so regarded as long as there was no higher standard with which to compare. Its evil effects were experienced, bitterly, too, at times, and yet, they were recognized only as the results of a necessity. No words of condemnation were uttered, no voice of warning was heard, and it was many years before the people were aroused from their lethargy.

For nearly eighty years licenses were granted almost every year, to both innholders and retailers. The number varied, but the maximum was reached in 1810, when eleven licenses were issued to retailers. The same number was granted in 1829 and in 1832 : in the former year, nine to retailers, and two, to innholders ; in the latter, eight, to retailers, and three, to innholders. After 1842, licenses to sell spirituous liquors for mechanical and medicinal purposes only were granted. Since 1857, licenses have not been granted.

Rum was formerly used upon all occasions. That it was deemed necessary when meeting-houses were raised is evident from the following votes, from the records of the two parishes :

(North Parish.) "April 6, 1784. The inhabitants of this parish met, pursuant to adjournment, and passed the following vote : Voted, To purchase two barrels of rum, one barrel of pork, four bushels of beans, ten gallons of molasses, ten pounds of coffee, and twenty-eight pounds of sugar, to raise the meeting-house. Voted, That Nathaniel Conant was desired to procure said articles."

(230)

(South Parish.) April 14, 1788. "Voted, To procure and order for Mr. Cram, to provide 1 berrell ½ of N E Rum, 2 quintals ½ of fish and 10 Gallons of Molasses, and hogsfat if he can get it," to be paid out of the meeting-house tax.

When these meeting-houses were ready for occupancy, and the formal dedicatory services had been performed, the event was celebrated, in private, over the social glass, by those engaging in the services. The ministers occupying the pulpits even wrote and delivered their sermons under the "inspiration," i. e., exhilaration, of rum. Whenever they made pastoral calls, the decanter was set before them, of the contents of which they were expected to partake, especially where they were, for the first time, visitors of their parishioners. The teacher took rum as part of his daily rations; the farmer and the wood-cutter carried it with them into their fields and woods; the teamster needed it to protect him from the heat or cold, as the case might be; the mourner found consolation in the cup; wedding-guests were stimulated by it. On all occasions, huskings, raisings, dances, trainings, musters, spirituous liquors were alike needed. Some of the best men of their times sold intoxicants, and had as customers their equals in rank and character. Their account-books were filled with charges for rum and toddy. We do not wonder that the town, from 1800 to 1825, was scourged with intemperance. It was a necessary and legitimate result of the custom that prevailed among all classes and supported for that period an average of seven retailers and tavern keepers. As the population was from fourteen hundred to twenty-one hundred, the average was one rum-seller to every two hundred or three hundred inhabitants.

The first recorded action of the town, tending to restrict the sale of intoxicating liquors, was in 1803, April 4: "Voted, the Selectmen Not to give any the Shopkeepers or Tavern-keepers any Apprebtion if they Sel any Licker to any of the Inhabitants of this Town on the Lord's day, Only in Case of Nesesity that Excepted."

May 5, 1817. "Voted to raise a committee of three to order no tents within forty rods of the Baptist Meeting House on the days of the Association in June next, and that they be directed to prosecute any offender who shall not comply." The object of such a vote of the town was that the meeting might be less disturbed by the quarrelling, fighting, and confusion which prevailed among those congregating in the vicinity of liquor dealers. That this was the case we have abundant evidence. When Thomas Keeler was elected representative in 1806, his seat was contested. One of the allegations of his opponents was, that Keeler after the election gave public invitation to all the voters to go to any or all of the public houses or stores in Alfred, or to his own house in Sanford, to receive such refreshments as they should want; that there was the appearance of riot and drunkenness at Keeler's store, with fighting and quarrelling. That such an allegation should be made, when intoxicating liquors were in general use, and that the vote of 1803 should be passed, give us strong reason for the assertion that the people had fallen on troublous times, owing to the unrestricted sale and excessive use of spirituous liquors. We have heard from eye-witnesses and from others who had listened to their reports, that drinking, carousing, horse-racing, gambling, and fighting constituted the pastime of Saturday afternoons, when, from all parts of the town, large numbers assembled at the Corner, to enjoy their usual weekly holiday. Says one, a native whose memory ran back more than sixty years: "In my younger days there were four stores at the Corner, and all of them rum-shops. There was then an immense sight of liquor sold, and an immense sight of fighting and quarrelling and business enough to support two lawyers."

In 1823, an attempt was made to prevent the sale of spirituous liquors near the Congregational meeting-house, on the 8th of September (annual state election), but a motion to complain of every person who should sell such liquors, except in houses, within sixty rods of the meeting-house was negatived. The spring meeting, April 5, 1824, was a stormy meeting, the effect, one would naturally infer, of the free use of intoxicating drinks. Much business had been transacted, but, at length, there was so much confusion that it was impossible to proceed. Then the following votes were passed: "35th. Voted the throng-men be seated. 36th. Voted the aisle be cleared. 37th. Voted that the doors be closed, and no person enter." (This was subsequently reconsidered.) "46th. Voted the town agent be directed not to suffer any ardent spirits sold within one mile of the meeting-house." Though no time is mentioned, we presume that the intention was to restrict the sale on town-meeting days.

Moral reform is of slow progress. At times it scarcely seems to make any advance, and yet, like the glacier, its onward movement is irresistible. This general truth has an illustration in the temperance reform. It was near the close of the last century that the clergy began to make active efforts against intemperance. It was subsequent to 1790 that Parson Sweat preached a sermon on temperance. We conclude that it could not have been very radical, and obnoxious to his hearers, for the innovation did not, so far as we know, cause any disaffection. That would have been the case, in all probability, had the preacher borne down severely on the failings of his hearers, or denied them the right to use intoxicating liquors as they pleased.

In 1813, the Massachusetts Society for the Suppression of Intemperance was formed, and in February, 1826, the American Society for the Promotion of Temperance was organized in Boston. Though total abstinence had been advocated in 1820, the latter society and its auxiliaries did not oppose the use of wine, cider, or malt liquors. The only general requirements were total abstinence from distilled spirits, except when prescribed for medicine, and moderation in the use of other drinks less intoxicating. In 1827, Rev. Christopher Marsh delivered a sermon on total abstinence, which was at that time in advance of the principles disseminated by temperance societies throughout the state. It bore good fruit, though of small quantity, and in after years its influence was long felt. Rev. Mr. Marsh was always consistent, and commanded the attention and respect of those who differed with him on the temperance question. What was a duty for his hearer to perform, was equally a duty for him to obey, though sometimes his conscientious obedience of the call of duty brought him into unpleasant opposition to his ministerial brethren, for whose age and experience he had great respect. It was the invariable custom when Rev. Mr. Marsh came into town, to have spirituous liquors at the meetings of the York County Association of Congregational Ministers, which were furnished by the clergyman entertaining the Association. Rev. Mr. Marsh and another young minister, members of the Association, discussed the custom, and agreed not to furnish the usual entertainment, when their turns came to have the Association meet with them. At length it met in Sanford. The usual exegetical exercises were performed. The discussions may not have been animated, but we cannot conceive why a deep spirituality may not have pervaded every soul, though the exercises were conducted with less *spirit* than similar exercises on previous occasions had been conducted. There was much surprise because spirituous liquors were not offered. The host did not feel that any apology was necessary nor was any made. This lack of Christian courtesy, so called, this breach of ministerial etiquette, drew forth sharp and severe criticism from outside busybodies as well as from clerical guests, but the young minister, having followed his honest convictions, had no compunctions of conscience to disturb him.

It is evident that public opinion was advancing. The treasurer and selectmen refused to attend a meeting, February 16, 1829, to license persons to sell liquors. One retailer, convinced of the wrong of selling intoxicating liquors, gave up the business, sacrificing trade and gain. On the 14th of September, the town "Voted the select-men shall be authorized to license retailers, innholders, and victualers to sell spirituous liquors to be drunk in their stores, etc.," and in the following two years, a similar vote was passed. In 1832, several of those licensed by the proper authorities did not call for their licenses, or some of the retailers did not receive licenses. On the 1st of April, 1833, therefore, it was "Voted the treasurer of said town call upon every innholder and retailer of spirituous liquor in said town who have sold spirits since the second Tuesday of September last, and request them to take their license and pay for the same, and upon refusal to enter a complaint before the grand jury at the next court of Common Pleas."

At the annual meeting, April 6, 1835, the question in regard to granting licenses for the retail of ardent spirits came up. The first vote stood one hundred and three " for," one hundred and five " against." The vote was doubted, and the house polled. A second time the vote was doubted, and the voters polled in the highway. The meeting was immediately dissolved; but a vote reconsidering the one dissolving the meeting was declared in the affirmative. The tem-perance party was in the majority, and yet several persons were li-censed. One of the selectmen, however, refused to sign any licenses.

There are several reasons why a change of sentiment was effected. Rev. Elisha Bacon was an efficient worker in this cause. Soon after his settlement he made war on rum-drinking, whether in his church or out of it, and held temperance meetings in school-houses in various parts of the town, at which he read Beecher's sermons on intemperance. In 1832, the Congregational Church became a temperance society, and most of its members signed the pledge. Many moderate drinkers became strictly temperance men, and many hard drink-ers became temperate, though constantly struggling against the habits of years. Agents employed by the American Society for the Promotion of Temperance were actively engaged in discussing the great moral question of the day. An address delivered in town before the first temperance association in York County, January 7, 1835, by George W. Wells, may have aroused the people. His subject was " The Cause of Temperance is the Cause of Liberty."

Who were active workers in town? Let one of the number name some of them. " Rum was rampant there (Springvale) at that time

(1834–6). I felt called upon to give battle and there were some noble men who were with me in the work. Among them Mr. Skeele at the Corner, Dr. J. Smith, and Caleb Emery, a noble young man, who was right and fearless on all the moral questions of the day . . . . . . ' Mr. Dustin (agent of the Print Works) was an active temperance man, and so was Elder Julian, who was pastor of the F. W. Baptist Church. Elder Cook, of the other part of the town, did not come up well on temperance."[1]

In 1836, John Skeele, William Emery, and others formed a Total Abstinence Society, among the first, if not the first, of its kind in the state. Albert Day and Alfred H. Emery circulated the pledge among the scholars, and obtained several signatures. When the Washingtonian movement took place, Hawkins, Bartimeus, of Boston, and Parkinson of Wells, were among the public speakers that advocated temperance in Sanford.

In 1840, the Baptist Church adopted a temperance pledge, and in 1843 the Baptist Church at Springvale took a decided stand in favor of total abstinence. Intemperance caused much trouble in all the churches, and gave frequent occasion for discipline. At one time, a member of the Congregational Church was disciplined for drunkenness. One of the deacons or prominent church members suggested that, if he must drink, he had better drink at home, where his fault would not be publicly known. Not long after, another member got intoxicated, and was summoned before the church. He acknowledged the charge against him, but, in defence, pleaded that he had followed the advice given to his erring brother, and got drunk at home, not at the Corner.

In 1844, two persons were licensed to sell spirituous liquors for medicinal purposes only, in accordance with a vote of April 1: " Voted and directed the selectmen, treasurer, and town clerk to license two individuals in said town to sell spirituous liquors for all necessary purposes, and that they prosecute all persons who sell spirituous liquors without a license." The license law in force was violated, and fines were imposed upon the violators. The town, on the 7th of April, 1845, " Voted and authorized the selectmen to appropriate the several fines imposed for the violation of the ' License Law' to the support of the poor in said town."

Licenses were not granted from 1844 to 1850, though some in 1846 desired to have an agent or two agents appointed to sell spirituous liquors for medicinal and mechanical purposes only. Their desire in

[1] Elder Nathan K. George.

the form of a petition is expressed in an article in the warrant for the annual meeting, April 6, 1846.

"Art. 31. To see if they (the town) will grant the petition of Ichabod Frost and seven others, as follows: 1st. To see if they will vote to instruct the selectmen, town clerk, and treasurer to license one or two persons to sell intoxicating liquors and that to[o] for medicinal and mechanical purposes only. 2d. To see if such person or persons shall have [a] stipulated compensation for such services, and, if so, what, and how to be paid, and see if the town will furnish the liquors and receive the profits. 3d. To see if the town will elect an agent or committee whose duty it shall be to prosecute all violations of the license law with the advice and consent of the selectmen."

This petition was not granted.

York Division, No. 111, Sons of Temperance, was instituted at Springvale, March 8, 1848. Samuel Lord was Worthy Patriarch, Albert Day, Worthy Associate, and Daniel E. Lucy, Recording Scribe.

Union Section, No. 13, Cadets of Temperance, was organized November 24, 1848. This organization was composed of boys over fourteen years of age.

Star in the East Union, No. 26, Daughter of Temperance, was instituted April 26, 1849. It numbered twenty-eight members. They ceased to meet about the last of March, 1851.

In the spring of 1850, Albert Day Encampment, No. 1, Cadets of Temperance, was formed. It was named in honor of its chief patron, an efficient worker in the cause of temperance.

All of these organizations did good service in their day, helping to suppress the sale and use of intoxicating liquors.

In 1850, Tristram Gilman and John W. Bodwell were licensed to sell liquors in less quantity than twenty-eight gallons for medicinal and mechanical purposes. During the five years in which licenses were not granted, intoxicating liquors were quite freely sold. There were three or four open bars. In fact, a hotel without a bar was an anomaly. One had been opened, however, in 1814, and continued a year. It was done at the solicitation of the temperance people, by Deacon John Webster, a thorough-going Washingtonian.

It was during those years that so much trouble arose at Springvale, resulting in lawsuits and incendiarism. Rum-sellers were prosecuted, and in turn, became complainants against violators of law, who had been foremost in prosecuting them. Robert Moon sold rum in defiance of the law. Conviction did not always follow prosecution. One night the heads of his liquor casks were knocked in, and his liquors spilled upon the cellar bottom. Dennis Hatch intimated that, if his sledge-hammer could speak, it might reveal the secret of the destruction of the liquors. Counter prosecutions resulted in compromise. Hatch's blacksmith shop was fired, its posts were cut or sawed nearly off, and the building otherwise damaged. This was done in retaliation, or because his enemies were afraid that a fire from his shop might sweep the village away. Several incendiary fires occurred during those troublous times, most of which were attributed to the minions of rum-sellers. It is said that several buildings at the Print Works were burned on account of the prosecutions of liquor-sellers.

At one time Clement Parker, Junior, burned Albert Day in effigy, near Mrs. Wilson's house. "Glory to God," said old "Father" Greenhalgh, as he laid his hand upon Day's head soon after the affair, "there are better men than you that have been burned at the stake."

When right and wrong come into conflict, such scenes are the natural results, especially when radical opinion, ill-timed remark, and bitter denunciation are the weapons of contending parties. Whatever weight may have been attached to the arguments for or against a licensed rum-traffic, the temperance party presented one fact that was effective against its adversary ; namely, the town had lost heavily by the use of intoxicating liquors. Said a well-known temperance man, more than fifty years ago, "More than seventy-five per cent of these farms has run through the rum-tap." He was accused of making a false statement, and uttering a libel upon the town. He replied to his accuser that his statement was true, and he could prove it. Beginning at one section of the town, and taking the farms one after another, he found that seventy-five out of a hundred had been exchanged by their owners on account of the losses incurred by intemperance.

After the "Maine Law" of 1851 was passed, there was manifestly a design to bring the law into disrepute, and make it unpopular, even among its supporters. At the annual meeting, April 5, 1852, the town "Voted and instructed the selectmen not to appoint an agent to sell spirituous or intoxicating liquors for medicinal or mechanical purposes. Voted that the selectmen be and are hereby authorized to prosecute all violations of the liquor law." This was at the request of George Nowell and seven others. Whether the last vote was obeyed to the letter, we know not, but we have evidence in a subsequent vote of the town that the people were willing for the violators of the law to bear the burden of the fines imposed upon them when the law was enforced. That vote was the indefinite postponement of an article in the warrant for a town-meeting, March 13, 1854 : "To see if the town will vote to remit the fines against Clement Parker, Jr., George Wilkinson, Zebulon Nason, Joseph Morrison, Timothy Shaw, and others, for violation of the Maine liquor law."

There was a reaction throughout the state in 1855, and the legislature chosen that year enacted a license law. John W. Bodwell was licensed to sell intoxicating liquors from July 23, 1856 to May 1, 1857. His was the last license granted in town.

The town voted June 7, 1858, in relation to " An act to restrain and regulate the sale of intoxicating liquors, and to prohibit and suppress drinking houses and tippling shops," approved April 7, 1856, and in relation to " An act for the suppression of drinking houses and tippling shops," approved March 25, 1858. The result was, for the " License Law " of 1856, two votes ; for the " Prohibitory Law" of 1858, eighty-five votes. On the 12th of March, 1866, the eighth article in the warrant was postponed indefinitely : "To see if the town will raise or appropriate a sum of money for the selectmen to purchase spirituous liquors for the town, to be sold by an agent to be appointed by the selectmen." Upon " An act additional to and amendatory of chapter thirty-three of the laws of eighteen hundred fifty-eight for the suppression of drinking houses and tippling shops," the vote of June 3, 1867, was " Yes," eleven, " No," six.

Prior to the formation of the present Good Templars' Lodges in the town, the following were organized in the years specified : Springvale Lodge, 1868 ; Riverside, 1880 ; Amethyst (South Sanford),1883. Organizations of Juvenile Templars, which include Rising Sun Temple, Sanford Temple, and Dawn of Hope Temple, have existed during the past twenty years.

Torsey Lodge, No. 16, Independent Order of Good Templars, was organized December 2, 1881, with over forty charter members. Its first Chief Templar was Frank J. Nutter, with Rev. Henry J. Stone as Chaplain. The membership is now one hundred and three, and the present officers are as follows : C. T., Edward H. Emery ; V. T., Abbie Ford ; Secretary, Gertrude Wilcox ; Assistant Secretary, Inez Merrill ; F. S., Villa Chadborne ; T., George L. Stackpole ; Chaplain, Orrin Pillsbury ; M., Ralph W. Jones ; D. M., Ida Downes ; G., Evaline Quint ; S., Adam Dehaven ; P. C. T., Don A. Wright ; Superintendent Juvenile Temple, John P. Bowley ; L. D., W. O. Emery.

Beacon Light Lodge of Good Templars was instituted January 18, 1888, by Mr. and Mrs. J. T. Mason of Biddeford. Fifty persons received the initiatory work. Rev. F. G. Davis was the first Chief Templar. The present officers are: C. T., Charles E. Gould; V. T., E. S. Grogan; Secretary, Bessie A. Smyth; Assistant Secretary, Mrs. H. M. Smyth; F. S., Frank H. Dexter; T., Emma S. Hanson; Chaplain, Mrs. E. S. Grogan; M., Elmer B. Ferguson; D. M., Mattie B. Hinkley; G., Harry Howes; S., Ralph E. Yeaton; P. C. T., Wilbert N. Goodwin.

A Sanford Corner branch of the Woman's Christian Temperance Union was organized September 21, 1892, with more than forty members. Mrs. E. P. Allen, wife of Rev. E. P. Allen, was the first President. The present officers are: President, Miss Ellen M. Emery; Vice Presidents, Mrs. Nathaniel Bennett and Mrs. Samuel Poindexter; Recording and Corresponding Secretary, Miss Mary L. Trafton; Treasurer, Mrs. Frank Albee. The present membership is about twenty.

The Springvale W. C. T. U. was organized in January, 1892. The present membership is thirty, and the officers are as follows: President, Mrs. Mary H. Roberts; Vice Presidents, Mrs. Lydia Frost and Mrs. Sarah Pierce; Recording and Corresponding Secretary, Mrs. Hattie Goodwin; Treasurer, Mrs. Flora Walters.

CHAPTER XXIII.

SURPLUS REVENUE.

A Gift From the National Government — Perplexity as to Disposition of Sanford's Share — Final Payment to Heads of Families.

DURING Jackson's administration the United States government passed an act authorizing the distribution of the surplus revenue then in its treasury, amounting to nearly forty million dollars, among the states, provided they would stand ready to refund the same on demand. The proportion of Maine in this distribution was $955,838.25. The legislature passed an act to deposit this amount with the towns of the state, in proportion to their population, upon the conditions prescribed by the national government.

January 28, 1837, the town voted that John T. Paine, Representative, be instructed by the town clerk to vote that the surplus revenue be divided among the several towns in the state. April 3, 1837, it was voted that this town will receive its proportion of money which is or may be deposited with this state by the United States, in pursuance of an act to regulate the deposit of the public money on the condition specified in the act of this state, entitled "An Act providing for the disposition and repayment of the public money apportioned to the State of Maine on deposit by the Government of the United States." John Frost, Second, was appointed agent to receive said proportion, and authorized to give receipt therefor.

At a second meeting two weeks later, the town voted "to loan the public money apportioned to this town on deposit from the state of Maine to any person in this town in sums not exceeding three hundred dollars nor less than twenty-five dollars to any one person or corporation on he or they producing two good sureties for the repayment of the same on demand and interest at 6 per cent." It was also voted "that the interest on the money deposited as aforesaid shall be used to pay the poll tax of the inhabitants of this town — and every person who is taxed for property and not for a poll and resides within the town of Sanford are to receive the amount of a poll tax to be deducted from his or her tax on their property, and after appropriating a sufficient sum of the interest of said money for the aforesaid purpose, then, if any remain, it is to be used toward defraying the expenses of the poor of said town."

A feeling of jealousy sprang up, because some thought that every individual was entitled to a share of the money, and accordingly at a meeting, June 3, the foregoing votes were reconsidered, and it was " voted to loan this town's proportion of the public money to each individual of the town in equal proportions."

Trouble arose. The selectmen refused to call a town meeting. Upon the application of ten freeholders, William C. Allen, of Alfred, one of the justices of the peace of Maine, directed Joshua Hanson, constable, to call a meeting to be held on the 24th of June, 1837, for the purpose of seeing whether the town would direct the treasurer to collect the two instalments of surplus revenue received by the town and loaned, of those to whom loaned, and to receive the other two instalments, and to loan it to individual heads of families, taking their notes therefor. The second article in the warrant was : " To see if the town will direct the Treasurer of said town to collect the two instalments of the surplus revenue received by said town, and loaned, of the several persons to whom loaned, to receive the two remaining instalments from the State Treasurer when due, and to loan the whole to individual heads of families, each his or her proportion according to the census of said town ; to see if the Treasurer shall be directed to take notes of the several individual heads of families as security for said money, to pay him or his successor in office the amount each is entitled to receive and promising to pay the same on demand whenever the Treasurer of the town shall be called upon to pay the same into the treasury of this state by direction of the government of the United States, and that said notes shall be deemed good and sufficient security, and the Treasurer of said town shall be authorized to purchase a book of blank note-forms for the above purpose, the said notes to be the property of said town and sufficient to indemnify said Treasurer from the liabilities from failures on the part of heads of families."

Only one of the selectmen, Jotham Welch, was present. The meeting was called to order by the clerk, and duly organized, and the following resolution passed :

" Resolved, that the Treasurer of said town be directed to proceed according to the second article in said warrant, in the collection of the surplus revenue, to loan the same in manner as is therein speci-

16

fied, that he be authorized to purchase a book of blank note-forms for the purpose, and that he be indemnified as is therein specified."

The doings of this meeting were confirmed September 11, when it was " voted that the agent who was appointed to receive the surplus revenue be directed to receive the third instalment and pay the same over to the treasurer of said town, and that the treasurer be directed to loan the same to heads of families according to a resolve passed June 24, 1837." This vote was subsequently reconsidered.

There was something wrong in the account of the treasurer, or unsatisfactory in his report at the annual meeting in 1838, and the selectmen were appointed as a committee to settle with Thomas Hobbs, late treasurer, relative to his receiving, loaning, dividing and paying out the surplus revenue, and to report a statement of facts at the next town meeting. They made their report June 16, when it was voted that the treasurer be desired to call upon the late treasurer, Thomas Hobbs, for fifty-five dollars and ten cents, it being the sum that he paid of the surplus revenue to heads of families for persons that were not taken in said families by the selectmen in the census taken by them in the spring of 1837; and, if Hobbs refused to refund that amount, the treasurer was directed to prosecute him.

On the day last mentioned the town voted (this vote seems to have been final), " that the present treasurer pay out the residue of the surplus revenue to heads of families according to the number in each family, as taken by the selectmen in 1837; and if it should be the case that certain persons were living in Sanford on the first day of March, 1837, and were omitted and not taken by the selectmen, then in that case the present treasurer is to pay them in the same proportion as he pays those that were taken in said census."

The reason for this change in the disposal of a gift may be attributed to the fact that each voter and his dependents received a small portion of the money. It should be noticed that the legislature of 1838 (?) passed an act authorizing the different towns to distribute this fund among the inhabitants *per capita*. It seems to have been an unwise thing to do, but, at this late day, it will not change the fact to suggest what advantages might have accrued to the town, if it had appropriated the money for the foundation of some permanent institution.

CHAPTER XXIV.

BUSINESS.

List of Traders and Merchants, Beginning with 1830 — Innholders and Hotel Keepers from 1835 to 1870 — Residents of Sanford Corner Fifty Years Ago.

TAKING up the list of traders where we left off, about 1830, we find the following:

Theodore Willard and Co., 1829–30, Theodore Willard, 1831–33, 1835–38; where they traded at first we do not know, but in or about 1834, Willard built a store on the southeast corner of Main Street and the county road. Francis A. Allen, 1831–33; presumably in the Allen store at the Corner; in 1832, Francis A. Allen and Co. was the firm name, Emilus Allen being the company. Jethro Heard, 1831–33. Ira Tebbets, 1832–35; he built a small store on what was known as the "heater piece." Moses Butler, 1832–33, and Moses Butler, Junior, 1835, at Springvale. Joshua Hobbs and Co. traded in the store which John Storer built at Springvale about 1830, until they sold out to Hobbs and Conant (William G., of Alfred), about 1838. Amos F. Howard and Co. bought out Hobbs and Conant, Hobbs leaving town in 1841; Nathan O. Kendall was Howard's partner. William Emery, Junior, and Co.; about 1834, Mr. Emery built a store at Springvale, on the corner opposite Theodore Willard's store, where, with his son Caleb, he traded three years. In 1837, Caleb S. Emery bought out Caleb Emery, and continued the business with his uncle William three or four years. Samuel Jackson, 1837–38, was a licensed retailer, in a store subsequently occupied by James Tebbets, and then removed to become an ell of William Miller's factory; it finally was burnt in part and torn down. Samuel Tripp and James H. Clark, under the firm name of Tripp and Clark, occupied the Storer store a short time from 1837. George Weld, 1839–41, 1842, 1845, George Weld and Co., 1843, Weld and Tripp (?); Dr. Weld was a licensed retailer, 1839–41; we have the impression that he and Samuel Tripp succeeded Tripp and Clark, and afterward moved to the Allen store, where Dr. Weld traded during the Clay campaign in 1844 and subsequently. Eliot Tebbets, 1839, was licensed as a retailer and traded in the Allen store. George Miller, 1839–41, kept a groggery at Springvale, near the site of the store built by Ichabod Frost, corner of Main and Lebanon Streets. Other licensed retailers of this period were the following: Hugh Ashton, Springvale, 1840; Josiah Paul, 1840; Robert Moon, 1840; Benjamin Melvin, and James Tebbets, at the Corner; Andrew Allen, Oak Hill; Ivory Johnson and Daniel Maddox, South Sanford: James Boston, Zebulon Nason, William M. Roach, and Ezra D. Manahan, Springvale; and William Burnham, Manius Moore, and John Littlefield.

In the fall of 1840, Stephen Hatch succeeded Jotham Storer in the Deacon Frost store at the Corner, where he continued until 1848. Frost and Storer (George A. and Horace P.), 1841–43 (1); George A. Frost and Co. (Amariah Frost), 1843–46 (2); George A. Frost, 1847–52, 1869–74 (3); George A. and Charles H. Frost, 1852–1869 (4); Charles H. Frost (5); this firm (1) began trade in the Storer store at Springvale, then (2) continued in the same location until George A. had built a store above on the opposite side of the street, when they moved into it about 1845. For five years George A. (3) was alone, when his brother Charles H. formed a copartnership with him. In 1870 Charles H. (5) returned from Portland and set up in the dry and fancy goods business, in the store built by Albert J. Smith, just above the Emery store.

In 1834, Samuel B., William L., and Caleb S. Emery opened a tinshop at South Sanford, near the old Colonel Emery house. In 1837 the firm dissolved, the shop was moved to the Corner, and enlarged, and Samuel B. and William L. continued the business five years. Salter Emery, Christopher H. Bennett, and Albert Day, under the firm name of Bennett, Emery and Day, carried on the buisness one year, and in 1843 William L. Emery and Bennett entered into a five years' partnership. Upon its dissolution in 1848 Mr. Emery took in as partner Nahum Thompson, and continued the manufacture of ware and sale of stoves three years. All of these, with one exception, had been tin peddlers. From 1851 until 1866 Mr. Emery was alone, but he then took in his son Prescott as a partner in the firm of William L. Emery and Son, which firm name continued some years after the death of the senior member in 1876. In 1875–6 the old shop was moved back, and a two-story front erected on the street. All was burnt July 1, 1878. In the shop on the site of the old one Prescott Emery continued the business until his death in 1898, since which time it has been conducted by George W. Huff.

The following firms occupied the Emery store at Springvale; William Emery, Junior, and Co. (Samuel B. Emery), 1842–44; Emery and Lord (Samuel B. and Samuel), 1844–46; Samuel Lord and Co. (P. M. Frost), 1846–48; Lord and Frost (Samuel and Amariah), 1849; Lord and Co. (Samuel and Charles O.), 1852; Hersom and Reed; Edwin Reed. The Factory Company carried on a store in the Willard building about 1841, with C. S. Emery as agent. John W. Bodwell traded in the Morrill store at the Corner, 1841–45. Caleb S. Emery, 1842–46, began trade in his store, constructed from a blacksmith shop, and afterward raised one story, above the Emery store. In 1846, his brother, John F., became his partner, and later, Otis R. Chadbourn. They went out of business in 1850. John H. Shapleigh and Amos F. Howard, were in business in the Willard store at Springvale, about 1843, for a few years. Timothy Shaw, Junior, Tripp, and Shaw, 1844–45, and Samuel Tripp, 1845, occupied the Stimpson store at the Corner. During the presidential campaign of 1844, a Polk and Dallas flag floated over their store, while at the lower end of the village, a Clay and Frelinghuysen flag waved over Dr. Weld's store. Kendall and Merrill (N. O. and John), and Merrill and Hubbard (John and A. P.), occupied the Wilson store at Springvale. John Merrill and Co. (Stephen Merrill), Stephen Merrill, alone, Merrill and Ricker, and Ricker and Hersom occupied the Willard store at Springvale.

Albert Day opened a tin-shop at Springvale in 1844. Soon after, he took his brother, John W. Day, into copartnership, and later Abram D. Hubbard and Luther W. Godding. In 1849, Stephen Hatch bought out John W. Day. Albert Day left in 1850, and Mr. Hatch remained a year or two later. Their shop was just above the Lebanon road, on the west side of Main Street.

Druggists prior to 1850 were Reuben W. Hill, who occupied the Fernald store after it was moved upon Ichabod Frost's land, and Tristram Gilman, who kept in the Shapleigh store. Gilman was succeeded by John Merrill and John Merrill and Co.

Between 1846 and 1853, John H. Kimball, Kimball and Hubbard, and James H. Hubbard traded in the Storer store. "Dry Goods, Groceries, Farming Implements, and Hardware" was the long sign, on cloth that attracted the writer's eye when a boy. David Cram built a small store above his house at South Sanford, and traded in it. Samuel B. Emery built a store on the corner of the present Main and Washington Streets at the Corner, in 1846, and traded there some twenty-five years. His partners were Salter and Moses W. Emery, and the firm names were as follows: Samuel B. Emery,

1846; Salter Emery and Co., 1849; S. and M. W. Emery; M. W. Emery and Co., 1857; S. B. Emery and Co., 1861; S. B. Emery and Son, 1862; M. W. Emery and Co., 1871; M. W. and S. B. Emery, 1872. S. Benton Emery was in trade with Moses W. when Nowell and Bennett bought out the business, to be succeeded by Warren and Mason, and by Kimball Brothers and Co., in 1876. Samuel Thompson succeeded Dr. Weld in the Allen store. Christopher H. Bennett succeeded Stephen Hatch (1848), in the Deacon Frost store, and after two or three years moved into the Allen store, where he was later burnt out. Then he had charge of the Protective Union store, and was in company a short time with Jonas K. Dorman. He built a two-story store below the old Nasson Cemetery, where he continued in trade until he sold out in 1871. Elisha A. Bodwell traded at the Corner in the Stimpson store, 1850-53. Amariah Frost was in business at Springvale in 1850. Clement Parker, Junior, had a confectionery store below George A. Frost's, prior to 1850. Fitch, Hodgdon and Co. occupied the C. S. Emery store three or four years (1851-54?). Joseph H. Moulton traded at South Sanford. George H. Day and Co. succeeded Kimball and Hubbard, or Hubbard.

About 1851, James M. Clough engaged in the tin business in the old factory store, where he remained for about forty years, alone, or with his son-in-law, William Smyth. About the same time, George Willard occupied a small shop on the Lebanon road.

John Dennett, about 1856, built a store on the site of the Wilson store, removed, which he occupied until 1890. Moses B. Greenhalgh opened a dry goods store on the corner of Main Street and the Lebanon road, Springvale, and was burnt out in 1857. Monroe Cook's shoe store adjoining Greenhalgh's was burnt at the same time, and John W. Frost's store was torn down to prevent the spread of the fire. Jonas K. Dorman was trading in the Storer store when it was destroyed by fire in 1866. Benjamin F. Hanson and Co. (Hosea Willard and Daniel G. Clark), bought out Christopher H. Bennett in 1871, and carried on business four years, when they sold out. Rev. Sumner Estes opened his apothecary store at the Corner in 1873. William H. Hobbs occupied a small store below the tin-shop at the Corner. Nowell and Libby began business in 1876, in the "Blue Store." I. B. Stiles opened a store at Springvale in 1865, and was succeeded by Stiles Brothers in 1890. The Sovereigns of Industry occupied a store in Nason's building at Springvale in 1876, and were bought out by J. A. Lord, 1878.

The Deacon Frost store, on the site of Garusey's Block of the present day, was unoccupied for some time after Christopher H. Bennett left it. In 1866, Moses W. Emery and Amos W. Lord engaged in the manufacture of shoes therein, and Emery continued the business with W. H. Miller and others. In 1873, S. Benton Emery began the manufacture of mattresses in this building, soon after opening his furniture store, which he removed to Washington Street in 1889.

Among those engaged in sale-work at Springvale have been : John Merrill and Co. ; Isaac Brackett, removed to the Corner in 1876 ; Stiles and Hersom (I. B. and J. G.), bought out Isaac Brackett at the Corner in 1877, burnt out July 1, 1878, removed to Springvale, and dissolved, 1879, Stiles carrying on the business alone ; R. A. Kempton and Co. ; Weeks and Cheney ; Lougee and Fenderson, 1878, Frank Lougee selling out his interest to James Allen in 1880, and the business being continued under the name Fenderson and Allen ; E. and E. E. Goodwin, 1877, succeeded by E. E. and J. W. Goodwin, manufacturers of clothing.

Early tanners were : Stephen Dorman, 1825–37, 1843–50 ; James Heard, 1825 ; Jeremiah Moulton, 1810–60.

James B. Shapleigh carried on the business of harness making, 1826–38, at first in a shop at the Corner, on Lebanon Street, near Obed Littlefield's house, and afterward in a shop which he built above his hotel. From 1834, he was at Springvale, just above the factory store. One Wetherby had a harness shop at Springvale, 1846–47 (?).

Otis Keay was a harness maker in the Samuel Chadbourn house about 1830. Jacob Littlefield was a hatter in the same house afterward. He was in town, 1832–43. Dresser and Bean made pegs in the Deacon Frost store. Samuel B. Low was a cabinet maker.

In 1847, Edwin A. Moulton commenced the carriage business at his father's at the Corner. A year later he bought out Alfred Littlefield, at Springvale, and continued the business in a shop owned by Samuel B. Low, near the Theodore Willard store. In 1850, he removed to the Lebanon road and carried on the carriage and coffin work. A blacksmith shop was attached to the wood work shop. In 1852, his shop, carriages, stock and tools were burned. He returned to the Low shop, and there remained until 1856, when he sold out to Francis H. Butler and removed to Shapleigh.

In 1857–58, Jacob Baird carried on the box business in the Jackson house near the Chadbourn mill.

Innholders and hotel keepers between 1835 and 1870 were : Timothy

Shaw, 1835-39, at Sanford Corner where Frank Gowen now resides, and after the date last mentioned he continued the business some thirty years, though there might have been an interruption prior to 1852; Abraham Coffin, 1837-38, at Springvale. Coffin and Allen built the upper hotel, afterwards known as the Burbank Hotel; Hugh Ashton, 1840, at Springvale; Deacon John Webster, November, 1841, to December, 1842, a temperance hotel at Springvale; Nathan O. Kendall; P. W. Downing, 1844, at Springvale; Samuel F. Nasson, who, about 1845, remodelled the Hobbs store, and opened a public house, which at one time was known as the Mousam River House; George Nasson; Noah M. Phillips; John Hubbard; Stephen Henderson; James M. Burbank, who moved into town in 1846, taking charge of the upper hotel, which he carried on for several years; Dr. William Gage, Stephen Otis, and William A. Rollins, who ran the Burbank House. Fiually George Nasson bought it, and closed it; Clement Parker, Junior; Samuel D. Tebbets, 1866, who built a hotel on the corner of Main and Lebanon streets, and occupied it several years.

In a series of historical reminiscences, contributed to the Sanford Tribune in the spring of 1900, George E. Allen wrote as follows of the Sanford Corner of fifty years ago:

"Fifty years ago the following named people, together with their families, lived within a radius of three-fourths of a mile of Central square: The house now occupied by Charles H. Tebbets was occupied by Stephen Hatch and Hannah Hussey; Fred Goodall's by Samuel Tompson; Miss Ellen M. Emery's by her father, Deacon W. L. Emery; Charles F. Tebbets's by Allen H. Bodwell; Obed Littlefield's by his father, Captain Joshua Littlefield, on Lebanon Street; C. O. Emery's by his father, William Emery; Bradley Cook's by Deacon Stephen Dorman; Moses Rankin's by Rev. Gideon Cook; John D. Whitehead's by Enoch Stanley; Fred Porrell's by Robert Newman; Preston C. Lord's by John Batchelder; Henry Nason's by Deacon John Frost; Abe Young's by John Storer; Mrs. Nancy Smith's by Jonathan Smith; J. K. Dorman's by Nahum Littlefield; Freeman Watson's by Hon. I. S. Kimball; Mrs. R. W. Thurston's by same family; Dr. Burnham's by Joseph Webster; on the site of Moses Wentworth's lived General John W. Bodwell and Daniel Clark; George H. Nowell's by John S. Philpot; on the site of Watson's fish market, Dr. George Weld; Samuel Mitchell's by Rev. Jacob C. Goss; Frank Gowen's by General Timothy Shaw; Hosea Willard's by Harriet Allen; George Emery's by Christopher Bennett; on the site of

Smith's block, Dennis Hatch; site of Sanford meat market, Harriet Butler; Leavitt's new block, Emilus Allen; on site of Bodwell's block, Salter Emery; Dr. Blagden's by Samuel B. Emery; George Bemis's by William Miller; Simeon Stackpole's by his father, Edmund Stackpole; Edgar Wentworth's by Walter Gowen; George Pilling's by William Webber; Miss Amanda Hatch's by Elijah Witham and Nathau Hatch; Mrs. Daniel Gowen's by Hannah Emery; the house adjoining Mrs. Gowen's, with the brick basement, by Stephen Wilkinson and Peletiah Witham; on site of Worsted Company's boiler house, Samuel Shackford; Joseph Burroughs's by Jeremiah Moulton; George A. Moulton's by his father, Deacon George Moulton; Dr. Bernier's by Joel Maddox; George Thompson's by his father, Adrial Thompson; Wilson place on the hill by Nathaniel Chadbourn; Nelson Bennett's by Samuel Jackson; house opposite fair ground, by Mrs. Jonathan Storer."

CHAPTER XXV.

THE MEXICAN WAR.

Seaman George W. Bean Sees Active Service — Company of Volunteers Raised — Captain Goodwin Hoodwinked, but Comes Out Ahead.

SANFORD furnished one man for active service in the Mexican War. There were many others that volunteered, three of whom were line officers, but they were not called from the state.

George W. Bean shipped as a landsman on the steam frigate "Mississippi," carrying eight guns, Commodore Henry A. Adams, and was afterward rated as an ordinary seaman. The frigate left Charlestown, Mass., in June, 1845, for Pensacola, and sailed thence, after hostilities had commenced, to the gulf near Vera Cruz. Bean went up some of the rivers in small steamers and row-boats on expeditions, and was at the bombardment of Vera Cruz in March, 1847. He was in actual service in the gulf till 1849. He had his ankle and heel crushed by a fall from the fore-peak, fifty-five feet, for which he received a pension of four dollars a month. Bean was a great-grandson of Captain David Bean, an early settler, and was born January 22, 1821.

Nahum Russell, born in Sanford, enlisted from Kennebunk.

Moses Goodwin, Junior, of Shapleigh, and William Emery, Junior, of Sanford, raised two companies for the Maine Volunteers. On the 27th of July, 1846, Goodwin's company (C) consisted of seventy-seven men from Sanford, Shapleigh, and Lebanon. On August 7, Goodwin was chosen Captain, and Charles E. Weld and Samuel S. Thing of Springvale, Lieutenants. At a grand meeting at the Springvale House, speeches were made by John T. Paine, Major F. A. Wood, Lebanon, Timothy Shaw, Asa Low, and others. All present were ready and willing to serve their country.

On the 12th of December, Captain Emery's company (A) consisted of ninety men in York County. Ezekiel K. Lord, Lebanon, and Charles Carpenter, Hollis, were Lieutenants.

Let one of Captain Goodwin's Lieutenants (Charles E. Weld) tell the story of the company: "Early in the year 1846, the state of Maine was authorized by the general government to raise one regiment of volunteers for service in the Mexican War. As soon as this was understood, Mr. Moses Goodwin, Junior, of Shapleigh, made application to our state authorities for leave to raise a company for the regiment. So zealous was he in the matter that he at once proceeded to enlist men without waiting for proper authority. He was very successful in securing names to his informal enlistment papers, and soon secured the requisite number to form a company. His headquarters were in Springvale, and nearly all the young men of suitable age in the vicinity were thus informally enlisted. The informality of the whole matter was well understood, and few were unwilling to show their patriotism at so cheap a rate, believing that Mr. G. would not receive authority to raise a company, and that, if he should, their present action would not bind them. Without waiting for the tardy action of the state officials, he called his company together for the choice of officers, on which occasion the men feasted at the hotel at Mr. Goodwin's expense, very much to their satisfaction, regarding the whole thing as a farce, and that they were bound to nothing except to the good things furnished by Captain Goodwin.

"At length Mr. Goodwin's warrant to raise a company with the requisite enlistment papers arrived, but this, with the advice of a few friends, was kept a profound secret, until such time as it might be disclosed with effect. His first move after receipt of his papers, was to call his company together with the understanding that Captain Goodwin with his usual liberality would furnish a supper at J. M. Burbank's hotel, Springvale, for the whole company. Every one responded promptly to the call, and when all were seated at the table expecting the good things to come, the regular enlistment papers with pens and ink were quietly passed from hand to hand. The larger number present signed willingly. Some objected that it was taking an unfair advantage of them, but signed, seemingly ashamed to do otherwise under the circumstances. A few only refused to enlist regularly, and at the close of the day nearly the required number was obtained, and the deficiency was speedily made up. Soon after this, the company was duly organized under the state authority. The officers first elected informally, refusing to serve, with the exception of Captain Goodwin, others were of course elected in their places. This was the third company for the before named regiment organized in the state and was known as Company C.

"The one hundred and sixty-seven dollars and thirty-six cents which you name as having been paid to Captain Goodwin was no doubt to repay him the expenses incurred as before stated, and other expenses in raising the company. I have no recollection of the nine dollars said to have been paid to me, but it was probably for assistance rendered Captain Goodwin in getting up the company. The three dollars was paid me and every other enlisted man of the company as a gratuity, *for our patriotism*, I suppose. On the day of the regular organization of the company, Captain Goodwin, as usual, ordered supper at his own expense, at Mr. Burbank's hotel. At the organization, Mr. Thing and myself having been elected Lieutenants believed it but fair that we should assume a portion of the expense of the supper, and Mr. Burbank joined with us by reducing his bill one-fourth. We then had no expectation that the state would repay any portion of the expense. Captain Goodwin was elected to the next legislature, and during the session succeeded in getting all expenses incurred repaid, including expenses of the final supper. I would only add further that Company C was never called into active service."

Between June 12 and August 7, Goodwin was engaged forty-two days enlisting volunteers, for which he received one dollar a day. He paid James M. Burbank at two times thirty-six dollars, fifteen and twenty-one, Charles E. Weld, twelve dollars, nine and three, and Samuel S. Thing seven dollars. His bill for one hundred and sixty-seven dollars and thirty-six cents was allowed by the legislature, but ten dollars for a band on the 17th of June were not allowed.

Captain Goodwin was undoubtedly hoodwinked, but in the end came out not the second best.

CHAPTER XXVI.

LAW AND MEDICINE.

Doubt as to the First Practicing Attorney — Laymen Display Their Legal Gifts—Colonel Caleb Emery's Opinion — John Holmes— The Case of Henry Hamilton — Famous Lawsuits — The First Physicians.

SANFORD seems to have been an attractive field for members of the legal profession. We notice, especially, that a large number of lawyers settled in town between 1820 and 1850. Several reasons may be assigned for such an influx, conspicuous among which were the prospective growth of the town as soon as the water power of the Mousam began to be utilized in the manufacture of prints, cottons, and woollens; the reputation enjoyed by several of the early counsellors as instructors in legal knowledge; and the numerous cases growing out of disputed land titles, petty quarrels of a personal nature, and the sale and use of intoxicating liquors, for the successful prosecution or defence of which, legal advice and service were in constant demand.

Caleb Emery, father of Colonel Caleb Emery, is the first lawyer of Sanford of whom we find mention, and it is by no means certain that he ever followed the practice of his profession in town. He was a native and long a resident of Kittery. Our only evidence to show that he practiced in Sanford appears in a Maine Register of 1770, in which his name is mentioned as an attorney in this town. We are well aware that Williamson refers to him as a resident of Sanford, subsequent to his residence in York, but he is undoubtedly in error, evidently having confounded Caleb Emery, Senior, with Colonel Caleb, his son. It is possible that Mr. Emery moved into town soon after its incorporation, and was in practice here when the Register of 1770 was published, and of that fact Mr. Williamson may have been cognizant. If Mr. Emery resided in town, it is highly probable

(253)

that he removed within a year or two, and did not spend the last years of his life here. For, according to the author already referred to, there were six practicing attorneys in Maine in 1768, and five in 1780, of whom Caleb Emery, of York, was one. Caleb Emery was born October 17, 1710, the son of Daniel and Margaret (Gowen) Emery, of Kittery, and younger brother of Noah Emery, the earliest resident lawyer in Maine. He was a tanner by trade, though farming was his chief and favorite occupation. A man of plain manners, and a peaceful citizen, he discouraged litigation among his neighbors, even after he had entered the legal profession. He read law with his brother, Noah, and, in 1750, was admitted to the bar of the Common Pleas. He seems to have succeeded his brother in practice in Kittery and York, was King's Attorney in 1761, and, during the Revolution, retired from the law to engage in agricultural pursuits. Mr. Emery was successful in practice, had the confidence of his fellow citizens, and was noted for his integrity. His daughter, Jane, married Simon Frost, Junior, and had a daughter, Jane, who became the wife of William Nasson, of Sanford, and mother of Elders William H., Nathaniel F., and Samuel S. Nasson. Her son, Henry Frost, was for many years a minister of the Christian denomination. Mrs. Jane Frost, having become a widow, married Peaslee Morrill, grandfather of Hon. Anson P. and Hon. Lot M. Morrill, both of whom filled the gubernatorial chair of Maine.

For forty years, no lawyer settled in town. Counsel was sought in neighboring towns, when needed, though several leading men acted as such in cases where common sense, not technical law, was required. Major Nasson and Captain John Hanson were frequently employed, but it is uncertain whether " old Master " Hamilton ever served as counsel, although he made some pretension to legal learning. Colonel Emery had some knowledge of law, and for more than thirty years, performed the duties of a justice of the peace. It is worthy of note that his decisions were scarcely ever reversed by a higher court. At one time, Captain Hanson appeared as counsel in a case brought before the " old Colonel " (pronounced " cunn'l "). In his plea in behalf of his client, he quoted Judge Holt's opinion in a similar case, and from it argued, of course, that judgment should be rendered in his favor. We infer the decision from the reply of the justice : " I care nothing about Judge Holt's opinion, or the devil's ; I have an opinion of my own !"

A few cases only, and those of more recent date, have come to our knowledge, of the people being at once counsel, judge, and executive, when the law had been violated, or humanity and decency outraged. Some of the older inhabitants of a few years ago had distinct recollections of the effective work, in one direction and another, of "Captain Joe's company." Happily, however, the calmer judgment of the people generally prevailed, and satisfaction was obtained by the usual recourse to law.

While Alfred was yet a district, John Holmes, in 1799, engaged in practice there. Ambitious, politic, witty, argumentative, ready of speech, he gained a great reputation in his contests with such advocates as Cyrus King, Prentiss Mellen, Nicholas Emery, Dudley Hubbard, and Joseph Bartlett, who then adorned the York County bar, and thereby was trained and disciplined to become a skilful pleader.[1] Representing the town and the district two terms at the General Court, in 1802 and 1803, he won for himself distinction as an able speaker, and rendered efficient service as a legislator. The town had the benefit of his legal knowledge as well as of his legislation, for he was often called to plead her cause and to defend her people.

Grove Catlin, Junior, was the first regular practitioner of authentic record in what is now Sanford. He opened his office in 1812, and remained in town about three years.

In April, 1797, the town " Voted Whereas it is Notorious Henry Hambelton doath and hath been the means of Stirring up Many and friviolous lawsuits, Voted, that the Town Disapprove of his Proceeding, and do not think that he aught to be impaneled on any jury Therefore Voted that the Selectmen be directed to withdraw his Name from the Jury Box." In April, 1801, Hamilton having sued the town clerk, Stephen Hobbs, for giving a copy of a part of the town records and attesting to the same, it was voted to restore his name to the jury list. The wording of this vote took a very apologetic tone, as will be seen by the following extract from the records : " Whereas at a Meeting of Some of the Inhabitants of Sanford Held April 17, 1797, on very Short notice in the abstance of Said Hamilton Some malevolent Persons Procured a Vote to Be passed Intimating that He had been the means of Stirring up many and frivolous Lawsuits the town now manifest their total Disapprobation Thereof the number of Persons at this meeting Being Eighty Voted that the town Clerk serve Said Hamilton With a true attested Coppy of the Proceeding of this meeting Examined and approved By the Selectmen. Voted the above accepted and the town to Pay Hamilton's Cost of

[1] Parsons's "History of Alfred."

prosecuting and this to Be a final End of all former Proceeding Respecting the said matter the Cost above mentioned to Be Left to the
Selectmen."

Among the famous lawsuits of the early days of the township were
the following :

James Chadbourn, Junior, *vs.* Noah Emery, executor of the will of
Tobias Leighton, April, 1750. Verdict for plaintiff, one hundred and
four pounds, sixteen shillings and costs, amounting to nearly two
pounds more.

In 1760, Benjamin and Naphtali Harmon petitioned the Court of
Sessions that a jury be summoned to assess damages done to their
land by overflow. Fifteen acres belonging to each, and seven acres
additional to Naphtali were overflowed. The mill and dam were
built on or about 1756, by James Littlefield, Wells, Samuel Cane,
Phillipstown, John Hambleton, Berwick, and Joshua Cane, deceased,
Phillipstown. When the suits came to trial, Benjamin Harmon did
not appear, and his case was dismissed. A jury having viewed the
land, awarded Naphtali thirty shillings a year from 1760.

Daniel Hubbard sued the town of Sanford, in 1789, because one
of his steers " slumped" through Jellison's bridge, a pole bridge, and
broke his leg. Verdict for defendant.

In 1806, the town voted unanimously to " prosecute villain or villains who took the body of James Hartwell from his grave," and the
next year Sheldon Hobbs was agent to York term of court to prosecute. Peter Whittemore and Caleb Emery were indicted for digging
up the body of Hartwell, proved guilty, and fined ten dollars each,
and costs, May, 1807.

Aaron Gowen *vs.* Rufus Bennett, Ephraim Low, Junior, and James
Garey, Junior. The case was brought before Benjamin Warren at
his house in Waterborough, March 7, 1812, and judgment rendered
in plaintiff's favor for one dollar and ninety cents, and costs of suit.
This was a case of trespass, in that the defendants took from plaintiff, January 30, 1812, five hundred feet of pine boards. The case
was appealed to the Court of Common Pleas, where the following year judgments were given for the defendants. The latter were
assessors in 1810, and in levying the tax, assessed the plaintiff forty-
eight cents. As Gowen refused to pay, the boards were sold to pay
the tax. A similar case was that of Solomon Welch *vs.* the Assessors. Here a steer had been sold. Two dollars and fifty cents, and
costs, were awarded, but on appeal the case went against the plaintiff.

LOUIS B. GOODALL.

In 1820, two suits were brought against Levi Brackett and Joshua Emery, for bringing a pauper into town. Neither party appeared in the first case. In the Circuit Court, the case went against Emery, and in April, 1821, he appealed to the Supreme Judicial Court, where he recovered the costs of the suit, amounting to something like sixty-four dollars.

In 1844, Jeremiah Goodwin moved to Great Falls just before the first of April or May, assessors' day. His tax assessed was not paid, and on the 9th of September, the town voted not to abate the tax, but the constable was to collect it immediately. Having paid his tax, Goodwin brought suit against the town and secured judgment. An appeal was taken, and during 1845, $1350 was raised to prosecute the suit. Judgment was ultimately against the town.

At various times the state prosecuted the town in consequence of roads being out of repair. Fines were imposed, the money to be expended in repairing the roads in question.

The disposition of cases of crime was for years under the trial justice system. In 1897, however, the Sanford Municipal Court was established, of which George W. Hanson was appointed Judge, and George E. Allen, Recorder. This Court also has jurisdiction over minor civil causes.

Among those who obtained deeds of land from the proprietors in 1739 were Dr. David Bennett and Dr. Alexander Bulman, of York. They were physicians of good repute, and had a large practice, extending into adjoining towns. It is reasonable to suppose that they — the one interested in the erection of the first saw-mill within the limits of the town, the other in the improvement of the settlers' lots, — made frequent visits to the new plantation, of a professional, no less than of a business nature. For many years after their deaths in 1743 or 45, urgent calls for a doctor were answered by physicians from Wells, Berwick and York, while less serious cases were intrusted to experienced nurses. In 1745, Hannah Chadbourn nursed a sick soldier on the eastern frontier, and John Stanyan lodged and nursed another soldier, for whom a doctor was twice called. Dr. Gideon Frost, of Wells (Kennebunk), took charge of the patients in a hospital, established in the northeast part of the town, when the small-pox prevailed about 1780. Dr. Abiel Hall, Senior, then recently settled, having been inoculated for that disease, was one of his patients. Prior to 1796, the services of Dr. John Gates, of Wells, were sought by the people of Sanford. We may infer that Major Samuel Nasson, for years regarded as lawyer and doctor of

17

the South Parish, and even designated by the title "Doctor," was somewhat acquainted with the nature and use of medicine, and in cases of sickness was often consulted. The first resident physician, however, was Dr. Hall, mentioned above.

Sketches of the lawyers and physicians of Sanford will be found in the biographical section of this work.

CHAPTER XXVII.

ROADS.

Early County Roads — Highway Surveyors — The First Town High-
way — County Road to Fryeburg of 1783 — Bitter and Stubborn
Controversy Over a Highway From 1804 to 1810 — List of
Roads and Dates of Acceptance.

AFTER the " mast-ways," as we have already seen, the first roads
in the township were the proprietors' roads between the ranges.
The county road from Gorhamtown to Newichawannock (Berwick),
passing through Phillipstown, laid out in 1774, and three other county
roads, laid out in 1751, have previously been described. Although
in March, 1769, " Nathan¹ Bennet (was) Survey^r of High Ways in
the Town, and Simeon Coffin Survey^r for that part of the Township
called Massabeseck," it was not until March, 1770, that the first town
road was accepted. On that occasion the vote was : " Vot^d by the
town to Receive the Road on Moses Tibotse's Land and Walter Pow-
erse's Land for a Town Road."

In 1773 the residents of Massabesec desired accommodation, as
voiced by the following petition :

" To the Honourable Select-Men of Sanford :

" Where as we the Freholders and inhabitants of that Part of the
aforesaid Sanford cauled Massebesick do Stand in nead of a Publick
road or Highway from Thomas Williamss to Walthar Powarss & we
do Hearby beg your Honours would take it into Consideration & Lay
us out a road or Highway where youre Honours shal think most Con-
venant for the People of the Town and others that may wont to Pase
therein.

" N : B : We the Subscribers that do own Land where said road
is Expected to be Laid out Do here by Promise to freely Give the
Same for the benefit of a Publick road or highway for Ever. two
rods wides

" Daniel Gile	Eben^r Hall
" Daniel Coffin	Arch^d Smith
" Thomas Williams	Moses Stevens
" And^w Burley	Jeremiah Eastman

" Dated Sanford 21th May 1773 "

(259)

The following year, the town voted to accept this new highway as laid out by the selectmen, two rods wide, beginning at Thomas Williams's, and running to Walter Powers's. In March of 1774, the Hay Brook and Thompson bridge road was accepted, as follows:

" A Return of a rode Laid out on the Esten Side of Mousem river begining at a pine Stump on the northwest Side of the rode to the haei brook oppset of the widow Powrses hous and from thence acrost the lots of mr Linsets to a yalo oak tree spoted on Mr Joel moltens lot and from thence acrost sd moltens to the Esterd of his houel to Moses Pettes Lot and from thence acrost sd pettes to the westward of sd pettes hous to a white pine tree spoted in the Croch of the Path and from thence as the Path Goes round by Bostons Cosey and so to the Bridg on sd Mousam River at Phincses thompsons shop and from thence to sd thompsons Line between Edward harmon and sd thompson and from thence on the South Side of sd line out to the Contry Rode Free from all cost to the town."

The annual town meeting of March 14, 1775, was adjourned to May 22. There was an article in the warrant, " To see where the town will swop there Road that gowes to Berwick with John Thompson," but the action thereon is not recorded.

The Mouse Lane road as laid out was accepted at the meeting of May 22 : " A Return of a Road Laid out by the Selectmen of Sanford. Beginning at the Estren branch of mousam river by Joshua Goodwins and from thence to Linscot mill so called the Convenernt way that may be and from thence to Aaron Days as the Road now Gowes and from thence to wells Line as the Road now Gowes." Also the following road : " Begining at the western line of James burks land at a white oak Tree mark^d I : B from thence to John Emmons house and from thence to m^r Benjamin Stephens mill as the Road now gows and from thence to m^r William Leabathy barn as the road now gows and from thence to wells Corner furthemore begining at Kennebunk River and keeping the line Between m^r Elisha Smith and Elisha Littlefield land as far as s^d Littlefield land gows and from thence to Joseph Taylor and from thence to Caleb Kimbal and from thence as the road now runs to a pitch pine tree spotted on three sides and then to a white burch mark^d on three sides and then folling the spotted trees till it comes to the Road."

In 1776, the town, though hard pressed by the demands of the Revolutionary War, raised one hundred pounds to " mend the highways." The men employed were to be paid four shillings a day, and three for their oxen.

On the 16th of May, 1777, the following return of a road from the Corner to Low's ridge was made : " A Return of a Road except'd by the Town, laid out by us the Selectmen beginuing at the Country Road at the S. E. Corner of Joshua Chadbourn Lot, and from thence as sd Lot runs as far as the Cart path and from thence as the road now gows to the Iron Works, and from thence on the N. E. Side of Mousam River in the Convenent place that may to Joshua Batclor land and from thence as sd road is fenst to William Tripe land and from thence as sd road is now fenst to William Gowen land and from thence as the road is fenst to John Waterhouse land and from thence in the Convenentes place to the undivided land, and from thence to Ephraim Low Junr in the conveenents place that may be found."

March 16, 1779, the town " Vot^d the Selectmen are to Settle the road that is in Despute betwick Thomas William and Daniel Scribner."

On the 24th of May, 1779, the town voted to accept a new highway leading from the Corner to Hanson's ridge : " Beginning at the road that now leads to the Iron Works near the house formerly call'd Brig^{er} Jotham Moulton now deceas, at the corner of the field that the s^d house now stands in, and from thence to Eleaz^r Chadbourn as the road now gows and from thence to Joshua Hanson near as the road now gows and from thence to Reuben Hussey near as the road now gows, and from thence Extends to the Town line as the road now gows." This was a two-rod road.

In May, 1780, the selectmen laid out a road two rods wide beginning at the Great Works brook on the land of Ezekiel Gowen, and thence in a general northeasterly direction to a road already laid out. A new road on John Thompson's land towards Berwick was accepted May 25, 1780. Satisfaction for the same was to be made to the said Thompson. " Voted that John Thompson shall have all our Right and title to that Road on the South-East Side of Said thompsons Land untill Such time as any Dispute may arise concerning s^d. Road as far as a Committee shall say the same shall Pay."

In 1781, the town voted and allowed the petitioners a road from Mr. Conant's to Linscott's mill, so called, and another laid out by the selectmen, beginning at the Great Works Brook near Stephen Weymouth's, and from thence to Eleazar Chadbourn's, and so out to the county road.

April 7, 1783. " Excepted roads laid out beginning at Coxhall line running near Coffin's mill so called."

June 16, 1783. James Garey and Eleazar Chadbourn, selectmen,

made this return : " Agreeable to request of Capt David Bane and
others we Poseded and laid out a roade : begining at the Corner of
Edmund Welch field and running as the Spot^d trees gow by lands of
David Bane & Solomon welch to lands of Ezekiel Gowns and from
thence as the Spot^d trees gows by s^d gowen land and s^d Solomon land
to the Great Works brook so call^d tow a road which was laid out by
the Selectmen of said town."

In 1783, John Frost, Ichabod Goodwin, Samuel Leighton, Joseph
Farnham, and Nathaniel Bennett, appointed by the Court of General
Sessions, laid out a county road four rods wide from Ephraim Low's,
Sanford, to Major Osgood's, Fryeburg. Their report is dated at Berwick, October 8, 1783. About thirty courses were in Sanford. It
appears that some years before, Colonel Joseph Frye had taken the
first steps for a road by felling the trees the whole distance, fifty-
four miles, as appears by the following extract from his petition :

"However your petitioner used means which revived the courage
of his associates to abide by him in a third trial; pitched upon a
time when he would go (with two men only) to look out the way and
accordingly went; and through much difficulty found a passage
through the wilderness which he thought might possibly answer and
made report thereof to his associates, who thereupon went with him,
cleared, bridged and causewayed the same where it wanted (except
Great and Little Ossipee Rivers) then measured the road and found
that from the town then called Phillipstown (which was the place of
their departure) to Fryeburg was fifty-four miles. Cost with two
other attempts to lay out a road more than £400."

May 9, 1784. " Vot^d and except^d the road from the Bridge at the
foot of Massebeseck pond so called out to the main road."

March 8, 1785. Roads laid out June 1, 1784, were accepted :
" Begining at the house formaly own^d by Mr Saml Friend and from
thence to Cockhall line near Mr John Kilham, also from Mr Humphrey Whitton to Mr Saml Cluff and thence to Mr James Barrous."

In 1786, a road from Mr. Robbert's to Mr. Bean's was laid out.

March 13, 1786. " Voted to have road laid out from Jonathan
Johnson to John Willard & from their over to Sweet Bridg so call."

May 8, 1786. " Vot^d the Town agreed to except Mr. John Thompson road be exchange for that Gow to Berwick all his right and
title."

In September, 1786, Samuel Nasson and Caleb Emery laid out a
road from James Chadbourn's house to the Shapleigh line.

March 12, 1787. " Voted that the selectmen shall lay out a high way from John Saywards to Joel Allen and from thence to Benjamin Trafton Provis[d] that they give their lands."

March 19, 1787. A road two rods wide was laid out, beginning at Sweet's bridge, so called, across the Hay Brook, to John Gowen's house, thence to Josiah Norton's house, past John Pugsley's house to the end of John Gray's field, thence to Daniel Gray's house, and from thence "as the road now goes to the road laid out from Joshua Goodwin's to Linscott's mill" (Mouse Lane). Also, beginning at John Willard's rye field and running across Samuel Willard's lot to Willard's mill.

May 7, 1787. "Voted the selectmen are to lay out a road agreeable to the Petitions that was handed in this begining to Nathan Powers so running up to Ephraim Low Jr if in case the people give there lands."

April 7, 1788. "Voted that the Selectmen are chosen to view the road that gows through Daniel Wadley land and lay it out in a more convenient place, if it tis agreeable to the Inhabitants where the road is wanting."

May 7, 1788, it was voted to empower the selectmen to lay out a new highway from Jeremiah Wise's to the county road, and "to Prize all the Damages;" also one from Waterborough line down to the main road, and then from Moody mill "down lead into the same road in the most convenient Place." These roads were accepted June 2. The selectmen's return of this road over Mount Hope is endorsed on the back: "A Return of a road from Annefs to Bennet Mill." Damages to the amount of twenty pounds were assessed to Jonathan Tebbets, Edward Stanlee, Ephraim Low, Nath. Bennet, and William Bennet.

May 23, 1788, the selectmen laid out a road two rods wide from Ebenezer and Samuel Roberts's land to Henry Smith's and Archibald Smith, Junior's land. Damages were awarded to Ebenezer Hall and Henry Smith.

March 9, 1789. A road was laid out through Captain Ebenezer Hall's land.

April 6, 1789. "Voted that the selectmen are to lay a road from Trip to Ithamar Littlefield Jun[r] so to Well line. Voted that selectmen are to gow & view a rourd that is lay[d] through Mr. Daniel Wadley land & see where they can commoad the inhabitants Better." (He is to give the land.) "Voted that the Selectmen are view a road from Ephraim Low Jun[r] down to Wil Trip and so down to Besick road to commodate the Inhabitants."

May 4, 1789.   A road was laid out for Samuel Robberts.

In 1789, Gideon Hatch, Joshua Hanson, Joseph Carll, Jonathan Low, James Chadbourn, Joshua Bane, Moses Plumer, Solomon Allen, Jonathan Witham, Robert Ford, Sheldon Hobbs, Joseph Quint, Thomas Abbot, Stephen Hobbs, Nelson Hill, Reuben Hussey, David (or Daniel) Quint, Nathan Hatch, Caleb Hanson, Frost Gary, Zebulon Beall, and John Quint, owners in the " Six Hundred Acre Lot," petitioned for a road from the main road leading from Eleazar Chadbourn's over Deering's ridge, beginning where the road " is now used which leads to Hobbses Mill." This road, from the Red brook to the Hobbs neighborhood, was laid out two rods wide in March, 1791.

May 9, 1791, it was voted that the selectmen lay out a new highway from Ephraim Low, Junior's, to John Trafton's, and also from said Low's to Ezra Thompson's and thence to the Hay Brook; also, a highway from the " old Province mill " to John Beetle's.

August 8, 1791.   " Accepted road down by Mr. Daniel Gile." This road ran from William Worster's land to Deering's.

March 12, 1792.   " Vot^d to Chues a Committee to go View and Examining and See where there is any Prospeck for a road from a meeting (house) in the South Parish over towards the fishing pond so call^d so to Come out in Berwick road."

May 7, 1792, a road was accepted from the Province mill through land of Ichabod Spencer, Ephraim Getchell, Javish Jenkins and James Perree, and from the latter's " to the road lately laid out the same course two rods wide ;" also, a road starting at the same point, and running to the house of John Beadle, and from thence " to the head of the town on the same course, two rods wide." Other roads were accepted on the same date. Two had been laid out April 28, one from the house of Ephraim Low, Junior, via Samuel Shaw's, William Tripp's, and Nathan Powers's, to the old "Proprietors' road," and the other from the " Proprietors' road," " from the corner of the lot called the mill lot," by land of Samuel Shaw and Timothy Baston, to the house of Ephraim Low, Junior. The record is, " Accepted May 7, 1792, provided they give their land." The second of these roads is marked as if accepted in preference to the other. Another road accepted on May 7 was one starting from a town road laid out the same day at a point between the houses of Ephraim Low, Junior, and Joseph Shaw, by the land of James Gerry, Third, to a rocky ledge, and thence to a town way laid out near the house of John Trafton, this road to be two rods wide.

During 1792, Thomas Williams and Daniel Gile objected to Captain Daniel Scribner's being set off from Waterborough to Sanford, because, as they alleged, Scribner wished to get more power that he might force a road through their lands, to their injury.

In August, 1791, Simon Frye, Ichabod Goodwin, Joshua B. Osgood, Jonathan Kinsman, and John Low laid out a county road from Sanford through Waterborough, three rods wide. In Sanford it extended from the county road where the old pound formerly stood, near Moses Tebbets's, to the Waterborough town line. This road was accepted in August, 1792.

A county road leading to Wells was laid out August 29, 1792. It ran from the county road near Colonel Emery's to Wells line, three miles, two hundred and ninety rods.

November 13, 1792, John Frost, John Hill, Ichabod Goodwin, Andrew Burley, and John Low laid out a county road from Garland's mill bridge on the Salmon Falls, Lebanon, to Sanford. This road was to be three rods wide in Sanford.

May 1, 1793. A road was laid out from the county road to Captain Bane's.

In October, 1794, a road was laid out from Elisha Allen's, Wells, to the foot of Oak Hill, passing through lands of Andrew and Ephraim Allen. This road to be three rods wide.

November 3, 1794. A town road was laid out and accepted, running from Mount Hope to the county road near the Baptist meetinghouse.

November 20, 1795. Nathan Hatch and ten others petitioned to have a road laid out across Hatch's land, and a portion of the road laid out in 1791 discontinued.

A road laid out from the county road near Charles Annis's, and running to Rook Stillings's, was laid out in June, 1795, and accepted March 14, 1796.

Another road accepted March 14, 1796, was laid out November 26, 1795, from Sheldon Hobbs's house to Nathan Hatch's.

In May, 1796, a petition was addressed by George Chapman and twelve others "To the Gentlemen Selectmen of Sanford," setting forth that " meny of the freeholders and inhabitents of said Sanford suffer By being shet up and no Publick rode to Pas in and sum of us the subscribers are so shet up that we cannot git to or from our Houses with out Climing over our neighbours fences and crosing Their fields and Pasters and have ben for biden to cros Them." Therefore, the petitioners prayed for a town way from the road crossing the Muddy brook to one crossing the Mousam River, near the

Province Mill. In accordance with this petition, Ezra Thompson and Eleazar Chadbourn, selectmen, laid out a road June 24, 1797, which was accepted April 2, 1798. It ran from a point near Ichabod Spencer's and the Province mill to the road leading from Samuel Nasson's to Alfred.

Three roads laid out in 1798 were accepted May 6, 1799. They were two rods wide. One began in the middle of the Hay Brook bridge, near Jedediah Jelison's, and ran over Linscott's mill bridge to Moulton's mill bridge on the line between Sanford and Alfred; the second began at the place before mentioned and led by Joshua Goodwin's to the branch bridge; and the third ran from William Heard's to Joseph Moors's.

April 4, 1801. A road was accepted from Mount Hope to the Berwick line.

November 22, 1802. Objection to road near Bauneg Beg Hills, crossing the county road at Allen's Marsh brook.

May, 1803. Road from William Heard's through Jeremiah Wise's land discontinued, on petition of Mark Prime and twelve others.

A road laid out in 1802, from Berwick to the road leading to Wells, at the branch, was accepted in April, 1803.

In 1804, Jedediah Allen was chosen agent to petition the General Sessions to take up the county road laid out along the northern side of Bauneg Beg Hills and leading to Wells, or so much thereof as is on the easterly side of Sugar brook, so called.

June 18, 1804. Voted to accept a road laid out between Timothy Gowen's land and Joseph Shaw's, leading to Alfred, on condition that the District of Alfred meet said road at the town line, and that the parties give the land for said road; also, to accept a town road laid out from the Province mill, leading to James Garey, Junior's.

These roads and most of the others in town were laid out and accepted with little opposition, but when the new county road from Alfred by the Province mill to Eliot Frost's on Mount Hope was proposed, it was bitterly and stubbornly opposed. This was a subject of controversy for several years. At a session of the Court of Sessions held in August, 1803, at Waterborough, Joseph Wilkinson and forty-seven others petitioned that a way be laid out beginning at the dwelling house of Charles Annis, and leading by the Baptist meeting-house, to the dwelling house of the Widow Joanna Nasson, thence in the most convenient route to Alfred meeting-house. John Storer, John Low, and Joseph Savage were appointed to view the place mentioned and any other places near it, and consider the expediency of laying out such highway, and to report as soon as might be. They reported October 14, 1803 :

"Pursuant to the foregoing order of court, we the subscribers have viewed the ground in the different places for a county road, and are of opinion that the road leading from Charles Annis's to the Widow Nasson's, which is now a town road, may be shortened from Ezekiel Gowen's on a straight line to Jeremiah Moulton's dwelling house leaving the Baptist meeting-house on the left; and from the Widow Nasson's to Ephraim Low's and Joseph Shaw's dwelling-houses is a town road from thence through the ' Wilderness ' about one mile across several lots to the town road in Alfred, where Joseph Gerry lived, thence in said road to Alfred meeting-house, which route might accommodate several individuals to have a town road, but not the community at large. To accommodate the community at large, it is our opinion that a county or town road beginning at Mr. Eliot Frost and Mr. Prime's land by the road leading from Shapleigh and across Prime's lot to the line between Daniel Bean and Timothy Langton to the road leading from Shapleigh, thence to and through Colonel Frost's land to the Province mill, so called, the whole being the distance of about three miles, thence in a town road to Enoch Lord's, thence partly through James Gerry, Junior's land to John Trafton's, thence in a town road by Deacon Gerry's to Alfred meeting-house ; which we suppose may greatly accommodate the community, and a number of the inhabitants much better than the first mentioned road, although both places is pretty rough and rocky.

" All which is humbly submitted,

JOHN STORER,
JOHN LOW."

The road was laid out June 25, 1804, by Ezra Thompson, surveyor. At a town meeting held in June, objections were made to the acceptance of this highway, and Jedediah Allen was chosen agent to prevent acceptance of the same.

Andrew Rogers and Benjamin Warren were added to the committee. They awarded damages and made their report August 23, 1804. During that month several petitions (of Joseph Prime and thirty-nine others, Solomon Thompson and forty-seven others, mostly in Sanford, and Robert Tripe and seventy-four others, in Sanford and Alfred) were handed in, opposing the county road on the ground that it would be a costly road to make, and injurious to persons on whose land it is. If intended to accommodate the Lebanon people, the ground of the old county road is much better, and the distance by Jesse Colcord's only two hundred and sixty rods further. If, to accommodate Shapleigh, etc., there is a town way from the Province mill to answer that purpose; also, that the town road from Charles Annis's by widow Nasson's to Alfred, though very crooked, is much shorter than the new road.

April 1, 1805. Voted to petition the Court of Sessions for a committee to view the county road from Eliot Frost's to Alfred.

Joseph Prime and forty-five others, and Dominicus Lord and sixty-eight others signed petitions for the discontinuance of the county road. The committee asked for was not granted, and the petitioners had leave to withdraw.

May 6, 1805. Voted to give leave to the selectmen to lay out a town road from Hanson's ridge to the Province mill on condition that they give the same for said land as the court committee gave, and that William Frost, Esquire, sign an obligation to take up the county road laid out through the northerly part of the town of Sanford.

June 17, 1805. Another meeting, to petition the General Court of Sessions for a committee to view the county road and discontinue it.

April 7, 1806. Voted not to accept return of road from Solomon Welch's to county road to Lebanon. In 1807 the opposition to the county road continued. Ezra Thompson was appointed an agent to make plans of the old and new roads.

During 1806 a road had been laid out from near Sugar brook to the county road near Colonel Emery's, a road four rods wide.

In 1808 the selectmen were directed to lay out a road near Moses Goodwin's to the county road leading from Kennebunk to Shapleigh, to strike said road near Captain David Morrison's. This road was accepted May 2, two rods wide. During 1808 a road from Doughty's Falls to Lyman through the lower part of the town was opposed.

In April, 1808, the selectmen petitioned that the county road might be discontinued. This was not granted, and the town was allowed, at the September term, until December to make it passable as a winter road, and two years to make it passable in the summer season.

May 2, 1808. Voted not to lay out a town way from William Frost's to Daniel Bean's until after the next adjourned meeting. Later in the same year it was voted that the selectmen lay out the road from William Frost's to Bean's house, provided the holders of land will take what the former county committee appraised it at; and at still a later meeting, it was voted that the selectmen be directed not to lay out the road from William Frost's to Daniel Bean's till after the Court of General Sessions at York, and if Colonel Frost advocate the former county road laid out from Alfred to Lebanon, or near Eliot Frost's, the selectmen are not to lay it out at all. Voted to have county road from Eliot Frost's to Alfred meeting-house discontinued.

September 5, 1808, two roads were laid out, one beginning at the Alfred meeting-house, and running past the Widow Lewis's, the Haleys', Nathaniel and Richard, Junior, to the Sanford line, thence to the middle of the county road at Sanford Corner, thence past the Baptist meeting-house and Solomon Welch's house, to the middle of the road opposite Eliot Frost's house, said road to be three rods wide. From the Hay Brook to the top of the ridge this road was to be new, or a deviation from the old road; from the meeting-house to near Ezekiel Gowen's, new; and from near Solomon Welch's to near Butler's, new. The second road was to begin at the above described highway near Ephraim Low's, running thence to the county road. Damages in Sanford, two hundred and eighty-three dollars. Accepted with this alteration: To begin at Lebanon line and keep the old county road to the corner near Eliot Frost's, then northerly in the town road till it intersects the county road leading to Colonel William Frost's. The county road laid out from near the Province mill to James Garey's was discontinued September, 1808. Two years were allowed for building.

September 26, 1808. Raised money to build county roads from Mrs. Nasson's to Alfred, and from Province mill to intersect said road.

October 10, 1809. Voted to open the county road from Abner Hill's to Solomon Welch's. (Reconsidered.)

During this year Ezra Thompson was chosen to make a plan of the town with the roads therein. It was also voted to lay out a town way from near Colonel William Frost's to Hanson's ridge, near where laid out by the county committee in 1804; also, one from Eliot Frost's to Mrs. Nasson's as laid out in 1808 by the county committtee.

1810. Voted to open road from Eliot Frost's to Hanson's ridge.

Several interested parties, Joseph Shaw and ten others, were dissatisfied with the damages awarded for the county road, and in 1809 petitioned for an increase. A jury was summoned, and gave damages of three hundred and eighteen dollars in Sanford. A number of alterations were made in the road about this time.

In 1812 the town road from the new county road near Isaac Chapman's corner to the county road near Muddy brook was discontinued. A road from John Libbey's to the Lebanon line, laid out in 1811, was accepted April 7, 1812.

October 11, 1813. A town way was laid out from Linscott's mill to the road leading to Ithamar Littlefield's house. Also, a road from Linscott's mill to the Kennebunk line.

June 25, 1814. Road from Oak Hill to near Branch bridge accepted.

Article two in the town meeting warrant of July, 1816, was as follows: "To see if the town will support Mr. Moses Witham, Junior, surveyor of the tenth highway district in said town, in removing the fences and all other obstructions thrown across or in any way incumber so much of the town road in said highway district as was laid upon the land of Mr. Joseph Shaw, and indemnify said surveyor against any prosecution which may incur thereon, or otherwise provide a road for the convenience of said district, and the other inhabitants of said town." At the meeting it was "Voted the selectmen be directed to lay out a road through Joseph Shaw's land to accommodate the inhabitants and to report at the next meeting. Mr. Shaw agrees to give the land, but the town will not agree by the passing this vote to lose their title to the road where it was laid out and said Shaw agrees to pay the expense of laying out said road." When the alteration was made, the old road, or part of it, was discontinued. July 29, the town accepted the alteration of the town way running from the old proprietors' road near Ezra Thompson's to and through Joseph Shaw's land.

December 20, 1817. Voted that the said agent (Dr. Linscott) inspect the road between Jelison's bridge, and the line between Sanford and Shapleigh, and to pursue any measure that shall be lawful for the removing (of) every incumbrance from said road, whether logs, boards, or whatever the incumbrance may be. At the same meeting a town way from the Hay Brook Hill to the Corner was accepted, two rods wide, and the old "Brick road" from Josiah Paul's to Hay Brook road was discontinued.

April, 1818. County road accepted from road to Little River Falls to county road.

May 3, 1819. Road two rods wide laid out from Shapleigh line near Benjamin Webber's, to road leading by David Welch's.

1819. Voted not to discontinue way from Enoch Lord's to John Garey's; also not to accept one from Willard's mill to George Tripp's.

September, 1819. Road from Bauneg Beg to Sanford accepted.

In September, 1820, Mehitabel Wise petitioned that the road laid out from Lebanon might be altered so as to pass before her house, which was done a year later.

Some parties feeling aggrieved petitioned to have the road through Tebbets's land altered. This was done, and the new road · accepted in May, 1822.

In 1822, the proprietors' road led from the road running to Colonel Emery's from Willard's mill to the brook near George Tripp's.

April, 1822. Road from Joshua Danielson's, Lyman, to Jonathan Hamilton's, Berwick, passing through Sanford, four roads wide, was accepted.

April, 1823. Road two roads wide, laid out in December, 1822, from Moses Pray's to Robert Carroll's, was accepted.

September 11, 1826. Voted to discontinue that part of the town road commencing at the road leading from Andrew Allen's to Wells, and ending where it intersects the county road leading from Moulton's mill to Oak Hill.

April 2, 1827. Road from Moulton's mill to Oak Hill opened.

June 16, 1827. Road from Samuel Worster's to Lebanon line discontinued.

April 9, 1830. A two-rod road, starting at Shapleigh town line, was accepted from Beatle's house to the Province mill road; also a second road, starting from the northwest side of the Province mill road and running to the Shapleigh town line.

September 13, 1830. Road from Reuben Chick's to Aaron Worster's accepted.

In 1828 or 29 a road laid out on Mount Hope was not accepted. In 1830 a committee laid out a road three rods wide, which was accepted in May, 1832.

May, 1833. Road from Emery's mills to Lebanon laid out. Road from North Berwick to Alfred straightened.

1834. Road from Alfred through Shapleigh to Springvale laid out.

September 14, 1835. A three-rod road was accepted from the county road to T. K. Bennett's, the land to be given, provided the old road be discontinued between the Congregational meeting-house and point of intersection. This was done.

May, 1840. Petition that road through the south part of the town from Hollis be opened. Road built, but the town appealed to the Supreme Judicial Court in 1841.

November 9, 1840. Road leading from Moulton's mill to Oak Hill ordered opened.

1841. Road from Thompson's bridge out near Joshua Tebbets's laid out.

April 12, 1841. Two-rod road accepted from John Beatle's house, Springvale, to Elias Littlefield's.

May, 1842. Road from Alfred line to Berwick laid out.

1842. Road from Wells line, three rods wide, to county road from Lyman to Oak Hill.

November 13, 1843. Road from Captain Moses Goodwin's, Lebanon town line, to Moses Pray's.

May, 1844. Road from Dowty's Falls to Waterborough.

1844. Road from Springvale to Sanford Corner straightened.

May, 1845. A road from North Berwick to Wells was laid out. The road had been used before, but had sometimes been fenced by land owners.

1845. Fifty-four rods through land of Ira Heard, bought of Samuel B. Emery, discontinued.

April 6, 1846. Town road from Oliver Frost's to Charles Emery's discontinued.

July 11, 1846. Road one rod and a half in width was accepted, from the Deering school-house to Samuel Worster's blacksmith shop, on county road leading from Emery's Mills to Lebanon.

October, 1846. Road from Sanford Corner to South Sanford was straightened and made three rods wide. Road from the Corner to Samuel Merrill's was laid out, and road from Samuel Merrill, Junior's, to the North Berwick line was ordered opened and made.

September 13, 1847. Road from Jesse Furbish's to Samuel F. and Francis Allen's accepted. This road was discontinued the following spring.

April 29, 1848. The warrant called for action in regard to county road from near Joshua Littlefield's house to Great Works River. Article passed.

In the fall of 1848 a road was contemplated from Sanford Corner to Thompson's bridge and Willard's mill to Wells Depot. Ichabod Frost was chosen agent to petition the county commissioners to discontinue the road from Sanford Corner to Samuel Merrill's, and to appeal to a higher court if necessary. Later the road asked for was duly laid out and accepted. The road laid out by the county commissioners in 1841, to Allen's Marsh brook, was discontinued; also part of one laid out in 1844, from Great Works stream to old road leading over Oak Hill. A road from Hay Brook Hill to Mouse Lane was laid out, three rods wide.

HON. THOMAS GOODALL.

In 1849, roads from Sanford to Great Falls (following the old road in North Berwick), and from Springvale to Sanford Corner were laid out.

1850. Road laid out in 1849, from Emery's Mills to Little River Falls, accepted. April 1, three roads located below Sanford Corner, towards North Berwick, and below Oak Hill, to be built; from Jesse Furbish's to Oak Hill accepted. April 22, old road from Thompson's bridge to John Lord's discontinued.

April 7, 1851. Road located on petition of George Chadbourn and others (Mouse Lane?).

October 25, 1852. A town road two rods wide was laid out from Springvale (county road), across land of Springvale Manufacturing Company, to Amos Getchell's. In 1853 the town refused to accept the foregoing, and the county commissioners laid out a town way, practically on the same layout.

1854. Road laid out in 1853 from Nahum Perkins's to Thomas Hobbs's accepted.

September 10, 1855. Road accepted from the Springvale Manufacturing Company's cotton factory to the Province mill.

In 1856 the road to Lebanon was straightened.

In 1857 the road from Joel E. and Stephen Moulton's to ———— Moulton's was laid out.

March 10, 1862. Road laid out in December, 1861, accepted, from Joseph Perkins's to Thomas Hobbs's, three rods wide. The old road which this one superseded was discontinued the following year.

February 21, 1870. School Street, Sanford Corner, as laid out June 26, 1869, was accepted, to be two rods and nineteen links in width.

November 30, 1870. Road laid out to the depot, November 15, not accepted. This road was to start near William Webber's, and be three rods wide.

Hon. Thomas Goodall and thirty-one others presented to the selectmen, December 1, 1870, a petition praying that a town way might be laid out, beginning at the bridge over the Mousam River near Goodall's mill, and ending at the Portland and Rochester Railroad, in Springvale. This road the selectmen refused to lay out, and at the March town meeting following, two resolves were adopted : " First, that the town is opposed to the location of the town way or road in Sanford on the petition of Thomas Goodall and others as prayed for in said petition ; Second, That the town has no objections. to the location of a town road leading from the road (leading from

18

Sanford Corner to the Brick school-house, so called), commencing near the house where Mr. Bedell formerly lived to or near the bridge at the foot of the Brick school-house hill, so called." The Brick school-house road on petition of Asa Low and others, was accordingly accepted on June 17, by a vote of one hundred and thirteen to fifty-one, and an attempt at a special town meeting held ten days later to discontinue this road was defeated. This highway was three rods in width. Meanwhile the petitioners for the Goodall road, as it came to be called, had, at the April session of the county commissioners, prayed that honorable body to lay out and order said road to be built. The commissioners met in Sanford, August 3, 1871, and proceeded to view the route set forth in the petition. Afterwards a hearing was given at the town-house to all interested. Having adjourned to meet at the county commissioners' office at Alfred, August 18, to hear the arguments of counsel, the commissioners decided that the prayer of the petitioners ought to be granted. Accordingly, on the 27th day of September, they laid out and located the said town way, the road to be three rods wide. Land damages, amounting to three hundred and thirty-five dollars, were awarded to David Goodwin, William Webber, William H. Conant, William Hanson, and Samuel D. Tebbets, and the town was to pay sixty-six dollars costs. At the March town meeting in 1872 the town voted to appeal from the county commissioners' decision to the Supreme Judicial Court, before which the case came in May, 1873. The town's exceptions were overruled, and costs of three hundred and ten dollars were charged to the town. William H. Conant was not satisfied with his damages of fifty dollars awarded by the county commissioners, and on his petition, a special committee allowed him one hundred and seventy-five dollars.

March 10, 1873, it was voted to authorize the selectmen "to open and build the road the present year" as laid out by the county commissioners, beginning at the depot at Springvale, and extending across to the road leading by the house of Enoch F. Lord, and that the amount of money to be raised therefor should be discretionary with the selectmen.

On September 18, 1875, after several futile attempts to have the Goodall road discontinued, the matter was finally settled by the passage of the following votes: "Voted to instruct the selectmen to build and open the road laid out by the county commissioners in the town of Sanford, and known as the Goodall road, as soon as practicable. Voted to raise the sum of twenty-five hundred dollars by taxation to build the Goodall road, so called, and to pay the land damages."

In 1871 a road from the Sanford line to town road leading to David Fall's was laid out, and completed in 1872.

In 1872, road from the depot to Alfred was laid out three rods wide.

1874. Road leading from the house of Jesse Furbish over Oak Hill laid out and accepted.

March 13, 1876. Road to Porter Hobbs's accepted (discontinued November 7, 1876) ; road from Province mill bridge by the house of J. G. Wilkinson to the Shapleigh town line widened and straightened.

March 16, 1878. "Voted that the sum of one thousand dollars be appropriated out of the money raised this year to repair the highways and bridges in town, the said sum to be equally divided between the two villages, and three special surveyors to be appointed in each village to superintend the expenditures on the improvements called for by this article ; and they be authorized to make the improvements as soon as the condition of the soil will permit." Sewers and culverts were to be constructed to drain water from the streets of the two villages. The following were the surveyors appointed : Asa Low, William A. Ricker, John Merrill, Edward K. Bennett, Thomas Goodall, and Hosea Willard.

March 10, 1879. Road laid out on Benjamin Beal's petition accepted.

March, 1880. Voted to discontinue road from John Morrison's to Jordan's mill, and parts of road above Springvale past the house of Samuel Morrison, and old road between the houses of Charles Butler and Elisha Goodwin.

Miscellaneous matters pertaining to early roads and bridges :

1800. Thompson bridge built (rebuilt?).

1801. The county road from Sanford to Shapleigh repaired.

1803. County road from Berwick line below Oak Hill to Alfred line at the Hay Brook out of repair, and the town fined. Eleazar Chadbourn agent to go to Alfred to have the fine remitted.

1803. Ezra Thompson agent to go to Waterborough to have road from William Johnson's mill to Wells discontinued.

1804. Voted that the town direct that the inhabitants living on the main road leading from Shapleigh to Wells keep their cattle from troubling teamsters travelling on said road. Sheldon Hobbs came forward and protested against the proceedings of this meeting.

In 1819 and 1820 $2,000 was appropriated each year for highways.

1824.   Voted to build a causeway over Allen's Marsh brook, to be built by laying a tier of logs a foot through in the bottom and brushed over and sanded sufficiently to make it permanent, with a water-way four feet wide, to the acceptance of the selectmen.   Robert Johnson bid off the work for twenty-four dollars and fifty cents.

1830.   Powers's bridge rebuilt.

In 1852 there were thirty-seven highways ; in 1858, thirty-eight ; in 1863, thirty-seven.

CHAPTER XXVIII.

THE CIVIL WAR.

Beginnings of the Abolition Movement — Anti-Slavery Societies — Outbreak of the War — Captain John Hemingway Raises a Company for the Eighth Maine — Bounties for Soldiers and Aid for Soldiers' Families Voted by the Town — Sanford's Company in the Twenty-Seventh Maine — Four Brothers Enlist — The Roll of Honor.

BEFORE proceeding to the history of the town during the dark days of the Civil War, let us consider the beginnings of the Abolition movement in Sanford some twenty years prior to the opening of that bloody conflict. Quite a difference of opinion on the subject of slavery existed among the voters. A few thought slavery right and proper. A larger number thought it wrong, but said that the people of the free states had nothing to do with it in the slave states. Some good people said we ought to pray for the poor slave, and leave the rest with God. Others said we ought to pray certainly, but vote as we pray. These men accepted the Abolition doctrine, and espoused its cause. There were five only. We can count on the fingers of a single hand the number of the original members in Sanford. Their names are Elder Theodore Stevens, Deacons Stephen Dorman and William L. Emery, and the brothers Charles and Francis Allen. They believed that anti-slavery principles were Christian principles, and in advocating them that they were exemplifying their Christian faith and doctrine. It required no little moral courage at that time to take a pronounced stand upon the question, yet those five men boldly proclaimed their views, and exerted their influence in opposition to negro slavery. They endured reproach and contumely; they were taunted and stigmatized as the "Long Heel" party. Elder Stevens was outspoken on the subject in his pulpit, and was obnoxious to quite a number of his church. He told them that he should preach Abolitionism, bread and butter, or no bread and butter. His principles could not be bought for money, or his voice silenced. A clergyman preaching a Fast Day sermon in the Congregational meet ing-house at the Corner, gave such offence, on account of his Aboli- tion views expressed, that some of his hearers left the house in dis- gust and in a very noisy manner. Others declared that they would not pay Abolitionists for preaching at all. A leading Democrat once met Deacon Emery, and denounced him as a mischief maker, and a disorganizer, called him a " Long Heel " in derision, and jeeringly questioned, " What do you expect to accomplish?" Having faith in the cause which he believed to be right, the deacon simply answered, " Wait a while, and you will see." His prophecy was fulfilled, and each of those five men rejoiced that his efforts, small and feeble though they might have appeared, had not been in vain. The great, grand object was accomplished in their day, and their eyes beheld the glory of their work. The brothers Allen suffered some loss of property through the malicious mischief of their opponents. Yet they were not turned from their righteous purpose, nor willing to sell their birthright of manhood for a mess of pottage.

In July, 1843, a mass meeting was called at Alfred, to consult in regard to nominating a list of county officers. About sixty attended, and nominated officers, and pledged themselves to use all honorable means to bring out a good vote at the September meeting. Six men from Sanford attended : Charles and Francis Allen, Ivory Brooks (?), Stephen Dorman, William L. Emery, and John Parsons. Elder Ste- vens was selected by the Abolitionists as their candidate to represent the classed towns, Sanford and Lebanon, in the state legislature. He declined the nomination, and Deacon Dorman was nominated. No choice was effected, as a majority was necessary. until the last of December, when by the combined Abolition and Whig vote Deacon Dorman was successful, receiving in Sanford one hundred and thirty- five of the two hundred and ninety-four votes cast. He was thus the first Abolitionist elected to any public office in the County of York. In the legislature, only two others of his party were in the house, namely, Henry K. Baker, of Hallowell, and Lyndon Oak, of Exeter ; and one in the senate, Dr. Ezekiel Holmes, of Winthrop. In 1844, the Abolition presidential electors had seventeen votes, and James Appleton twenty-three for Governor. For the latter office, in 1845, Samuel Fessenden had thirty-two votes, and in 1848, sixty-seven votes. The Abolitionists, or Free Soilers, cast thirty-one votes for Van Buren the year last named. Albert Day had sixty-one votes for County Treasurer, and Samuel V. Loring one hundred and thirty- three for Clerk of the Courts. In 1845, Theodore Stevens received thirty votes for Congressman, and twenty-five at the next election. The party in Sanford, as all over the country, was merged into the Republican party in 1856, and gave its influence and vote in favor of the great principle for which it was founded. In its transition it was a constituent part of the Free Soil Democratic party, which supported John P. Hale and George W. Julian for President and Vice President in 1852, and of the Know Nothings of 1854.

April 7, 1854, some of the women of Springvale formed a woman's anti-slavery society, which was afterward called the Daughters of Freedom. Among its first members were Mrs. W. H. Waldron, Mrs. Nancy Reed, and Mrs. Eliza D. Willard. It numbered at one time about eighty members, and continued until November 13, 1855, when free soil took another form. The Sons of Freedom were formed some time in the spring or summer. Both societies, Sons and Daughters, held their meetings separately, but sometimes jointly for the sake of union of action.

The Nathanites were made up of both political parties, of men only, mostly of the Sons of Freedom, and were organized as a secret society about 1854. The first members were Henry Gloucester (colored), George A. Willard, Lyman Littlefield, William P. Rankins, Dennis Hatch, and nine others. The paraphernalia, consisting in part of an exceedingly gorgeous regalia, and the property of the order were owned by Gloucester, who seems to have been chief. He failed, and the property was attached by his creditors. It was receipted for by a few of the members, paid for according to appraisal, and not permitted to be sold by a public auction. The society did not remain long in existence.

Though Sanford was not strongly in favor of prosecuting the memorable war which began in the spring of 1861, yet before the struggle was ended, it had sent its quota into the field. The feeling which existed in town during the first year of hostilities, is evidenced by the action at a town meeting held on May 14, called " to see if the town will vote to make proper provision for the support of the families of any persons having their residence in said town, who may enlist into the service of the United States, during their absence from the state, and whose families may stand in need of assistance, by virtue of an act passed by the legislature of this state and approved by the Governor thereof, April 25, 1861, and, if they so vote, to see what sum of money they will raise for that purpose." The record of the meeting assembled upon that warrant is brief : " First, chose moderator. Second, dissolved the meeting." Another meeting was called for a like purpose one week later, when a motion that the town provide for families of the soldiers, was decided in the negative.

In the fall, however, the patriotism of the citizens manifested itself. John Hemingway received a commission as Captain of Company F, Eighth Maine Volunteer Infantry, and opened a recruiting station in the interests of that company, in which a goodly number of the young men of Sanford enlisted. Alonzo E. Kimball, of Biddeford, was First Lieutenant, and John H. Roberts, of Alfred, Second Lieutenant. The regiment was composed of companies organized in all parts of the state. Company F's contingent from Sanford included Corporals Edmund G. Murray, Frederick A. Henderson, William J. Reed, and Benjamin Ricker, and Privates Norris E. Bancroft, George W. Brackett, John M. Brackett, James W. Butler, John S. Carter, Simeon B. Coffin, Thomas W. Frost, John B. Goodwin, George Hubbard, Francis Hurd, Henry A. Hurd, John Jacobs, Alonzo Littlefield, William A. Moore, Ebenezer Ricker, Thomas B. Seavey, William W. Wentworth, and William F. Willard. The regiment was organized September 7, 1861, at Augusta, the place of general rendezvous, and left the state on September 10, under command of Colonel Lee Strickland, of Livermore. "No finer body of men has entered the service from this state," says Whitman and True's "Maine In The War For The Union," from which we have drawn our facts. The regiment proceeded first to Hempstead, Long Island, and after a few weeks in Washington and Annapolis, took part in the Port Royal expedition, landing at Hilton Head on November 9. In May following the command participated in the bombardment and capture of Fort Pulaski, S. C., in which several batteries were successfully operated by soldiers of the Eighth. From that time until the spring of 1864, the regiment did guard duty at Hilton Head and Beaufort, S. C., and at Jacksonville, Fla., during which time there was much sickness and death. Three hundred recruits joined the regiment in the fall of 1862, including Samuel Allen, Seth H. Colby, Elias L. Goodwin, Jonathan Hamilton, Moses Hemingway, William P. Rankins, Warren Thompson, Ira M. Welch, Stephen F. Welch, and Andrew J. Wentworth, of Sanford. During the summer of 1863, Companies F, I, and K were detached for provost guard duty at Hilton Head, where Captain William M. McArthur of Company I, of Limington, was Provost Marshal. "During the month of June Lieutenant Lord of Company F was detached to engineer and cut a road through a dense and swampy forest on Hilton Head Island, where many of the men contracted a swamp fever which proved fatal in many cases." Captain Hemingway had been commissioned Major in March, 1862, and in April of 1863 was promoted to be Lieutenant Colonel of the regiment, serving until February, 1864. Early in 1864 the following Sanford recruits joined the command: Edward L. Boyd, John Duncan, Edward Eldridge, Edwin W. Gould, and William H. Harmon. Corporal E. G. Murray became First Lieutenant in the latter part of the year, and later a Captain.

The Eighth moved on Petersburg and Richmond in April, 1864, and distinguished itself in action. "Of the regiment, both officers and men, it may be said that in bravery and efficiency they have been excelled by few regiments, if any, in the service." They saw hard fighting at Drury's Bluff, Wier Bottom Church (where Private Colby was killed), Cold Harbor (where Corporal Reed was killed), Fair Oaks, Hatcher's Run, and Appomattox. Principal Musician Willard was killed before Petersburg on July 31. After the surrender of Lee the regiment went to Richmond, where it camped until August, being stationed later at Manchester and Fortress Monroe. The men were mustered out January 18, 1866, and returned to Maine on the 25th of that month.

By the spring of 1862 public sentiment in Sanford in regard to encouraging enlistment had undergone a radical change. At the town meeting held in April, it was voted, under provision of the legislative enactment of the month previous, to raise the sum of three hundred dollars to aid the families of volunteers. During the summer following, as an additional inducement, it was decided to offer bounties to all who should enlist. On the petition of Samuel B. Emery and sixteen others, a meeting was held July 22, at which this vote was passed: "Voted, that the selectmen be authorized to pay each volunteer that enlists in this town when he shall be mustered into the United States service, one hundred dollars out of the town treasury." This vote was reaffirmed early in August, in a slightly amended form, when it was provided that the bounty should be paid to "each volunteer who shall legally enlist for the quota of this town," and at the same meeting the treasurer was authorized to borrow $2,400 "on the credit of said town of Sanford," for the payment of bounties. The meeting was called on petition of John Lord and eleven others. It was followed by a meeting on August 25, William F. Hanson and others being the petitioners, when the bounty was for a third time fixed at one hundred dollars for nine months' men, and the following votes were passed:

"Voted to pay A. W. Dam the sum of $3,300 to procure fifteen volunteers to serve under the President's call for 300,000 volunteers for three years' service in the United States army, and in that same proportion for a larger number, if necessary, to fill this town's quota, when they are mustered into the service of the United States, and that sum to include this town's bounty in full for said men. Voted to chose a committee of twenty-three persons to hire money to pay the sums on the votes passed this day to pay volunteers for this town's quota when mustered into the service of the United States, and that said committee be empowered to pledge the credit of the town for the payment thereof, payable in one year and interest, and that John Storer, John Merrill, George A. Frost, Nathaniel F. Heard, Charles Butler, Increase S. Kimball, Stephen Hatch, Benjamin F. Hanson, Simon Tebbets, Porter Willard, Otis R. Willard, John Lord, David Pray, Samuel B. Emery, Jonathan Tebbets, Samuel D. Tebbets, Irving A. Butler, George Bennett, Calvin Bennett, Oliver F. Dennett, Robert Carroll, Jacob P. Allen, and John H. Shaw be that committee. Voted that the treasurer of this town be authorized to endorse the notes given for said sums of money borrowed by said committee, as town treasurer. Voted to authorize the treasurer of said town to hire any or all of the said sums of money by giving the treasurer's notes of the town alone to those who will accept of them without the signatures of the committee. Voted to choose a committee of five persons to procure enlistments for the 300,000 nine months' men, to fill up this town's quota, and that five dollars be paid to each of the committee for each man enlisted by them when they are mustered into the service of the United States, and that the committee to borrow money or the treasurer be authorized to hire the same. Voted that John L. Huston, Lorenzo Dow, William H. Miller, John Lord, and Benjamin Beal, Junior, be that committee. Voted to instruct the town treasurer to go with the volunteers to the place where they are mustered into the service of the United States, and see that they are mustered in for this town, and pay them their bounty, and that he be paid for his time and expense while doing the same. Voted that George A. Frost be a committee to see if the volunteers sent heretofore from this town are credited to this town's quota. Voted that each one of the committee to procure enlistments for the nine months' men have ten dollars extra paid to them if they will volunteer and place their own names at the head of the enlistment papers."

At an adjourned meeting, August 28, reports of the committees to hire money and procure enlistments were made, and Jesse Giles was added to the committee to procure enlistments for the nine months' service. On September 5, Increase S. Kimball, Benjamin F. Hanson, and Moses W. Emery were chosen a committee " to take one of the papers prepared by the committee to hire money to pay volunteers, and signed by about eighty-five inhabitants of said town of Sanford, and go to the North Berwick Bank and hire upon that and the town note given by the treasurer of the town as such, five thousand dollars to pay volunteers their bounty ;" and it was also voted " that the same committee take the other prepared and signed as aforesaid, and when needed hire upon that and the note aforesaid the money necessary to finish paying all the sums voted by the town for volunteer bounties and expenses connected therewith." At the same meeting the bounty for nine months' men was increased to one hundred and fifty dollars, and A. W. Dam was added to the committee to procure enlistments.

It was at this time that the Twenty-Seventh Maine Infantry, to be composed of nine months' men, was being organized, almost exclusively in York County. Of Company E, of which John M. Getchell, of Wells, was Captain, Sanford furnished a large share. William H. Miller, of Sanford, was First Lieutenant. The men generally volunteered in order to prevent a draft. We quote from a private letter of date of September 10, 1862 : " Yesterday morning at nine o'clock, the time set to draft, the quota of the company in this part of the town was full, excepting four or five. Mr. Miller suggested they put off the draft until eleven or twelve o'clock. It was put off until eleven, and the quota was filled by volunteers. It was the same with the company at Springvale. It was pretty hard work, but they got their number at last, and no draft. There was great excitement here all the forenoon ; many trembling hearts until we heard the glad news, ' No draft.' " Those who volunteered from Sanford at this time were : Sergeant George W. Thompson ; Corporals Jesse Giles, William B. Gowen, and Ivory Johnson ; and Privates Jedediah Allen, William A. Allen, Philip Banfield, Joseph W. Bartlett, Luther H. Butler, Willis H. Butler (afterwards First Lieutenant, Ninth Infantry), William Chapman, George E. Currier, Benjamin N. Day, George W. Edwards, William R. Emery, Hugh A. Frost, George W. Gerrish, Freeman B. Hill, Christopher Hussey, Charles Jacobs, John W. Jellison, Edward P. Johnson, John T. Johnson, John W. Lord, James G. Perkins, Trafton Phillips, Joseph P. Richardson, Joseph Ridley, Seth M. Sylvester, Adriel Thompson, Junior, Josiah Welch, and

Stephen Wilkinson.   Reuben O. Littlefield, Frank E. Needham, and
Herman Stevens joined the company in October.

The regiment rendezvoused at Portland, going into camp on the
10th of September, and being mustered into the service on the 30th.
Rufus P. Tapley of Saco was Colonel.   On the 11th of October, the
Sanford "boys" came home for a short furlough, and on the 20th
the regiment left the state for Washington.   It was sent into camp
at Arlington Heights, on General Robert E. Lee's estate, where it
engaged in picket duty and in labor on the unfinished works in the
vicinity. . December 12 it went to Hunting Creek on picket duty.
About this time the guerrilla, Mosby, was on his raids, and the winter of 1862–63 was passed by the Twenty-Seventh at Chantilly, near
Fairfax Court House, in guarding against such attacks.   The regiment returned to Arlington Heights in June, joining the Army of the
Potomac, which was then moving to meet Lee, who was advancing to
invade Pennsylvania.   The term of service of the Twenty-Seventh
was about to expire, but the men were appealed to by the President
and Secretary of War to remain for a short time and assist in the
defence of Washington.   Volunteers from the regiment, officers and
men, to the number of three hundred and fifteen, did remain, and were
on duty until after the decisive battle of Gettysburg had been fought.
On the 4th day of July the regiment marched into Washington, and
taking cars for home, arrived in Portland on the 6th.   These men
who had stayed by when danger threatened the capital were tendered
receptions by the citizens generally all along the route, and were
given a most notable demonstration in Portland.   "There were
thanks and blessings in every eye, and welcome on every hand," says
Whitman and True's work.   "It may be doubted if any army has
ever seen better material than that which composed the nine months'
regiments from this state, and the Twenty-Seventh had its share of
it."   The regiment was mustered out July 17, 1863, after serving ten
months and seventeen days.   Later on medals were awarded the officers and men by the war department for remaining beyond the expiration of their term.

In November, 1862, the town decided to pay drafted men for nine
months' service the same bounty as volunteers, and it was voted to
communicate with the Adjutant General, "and have the town given
full credit for the men sent and paid, which is twenty-five."   From
the other records, it would appear as if there were an error in the
number.

Further votes of the town making provision for soldiers and soldiers' families are of interest. In July, 1863, the town voted two hundred and seventy-five dollars for each man drafted and accepted to pay exemption, which sum was raised to three hundred dollars a few days later. " Voted and chose a committee of six persons, consisting of Hampden Fairfield, Samuel B. Emery, William C. Weymouth, Charles F. Moulton, Samuel Lord, and Henry W. Bodwell (all Democrats) to hire money upon the credit of the town and pay it out to the drafted men as voted to each man." One thousand dollars was raised to aid the families of volunteers. The following fall, George A. Frost was chosen a committee to visit Augusta to arrange, if possible, for a reduction in the town's quota. At the same time it was voted to pay A. W. Dam $15,600 to fill the quota of forty men for the town, " or in that ratio, if the quota should be reduced to a less number." It was also voted to hire money to pay the bounties, and Benjamin F. Hanson and Asa Low were chosen a committee to borrow the money of banks in Portland. It appears to have been necessary to raise considerable of the money needed by individual loans in town, and it was voted " to exempt those who loan money to the town from taxation for that money for one year."

Early in 1864, after the President had called for 500,000 men, Hampden Fairfield and George A. Frost were chosen a committee to arrange for filling the quota of the town. It was voted to raise $3,233 for bounties for drafted men, $9,200 for the payment of notes, and $1,000 to aid the families of volunteers, if needed. In the summer a committee which had been appointed to see that the town was given proper credit for its quota, reported that three names of men who had enlisted in the navy had been found, and properly credited, thus "reducing the quota with the overplus of six before had from thirty-six to twenty-seven." George A. Frost was at this time chosen agent to fill the quota, either by recruiting men or finding substitutes. A little later it was voted to raise two hundred dollars for one year's, three hundred for two years', and four hundred for three years' service of each volunteer, drafted man, or substitute. In September, $2,000 additional was raised to pay bounties. November 8, Hampden Fairfield and George A. Frost were engaged to procure thirty men at three hundred dollars each to fill the next call for troops, and it was voted to raise $9,000 on town notes to pay the bounties.

January 23, 1865, it was voted to pay the enrolled men who have or may put in substitutes for three years, or who volunteer and are mustered in on the town's quota, four hundred dollars each. The sum of $12,000 was raised to pay the same, town notes for one year to be given. In March the town decided to raise $3,500 to pay notes given in 1863; $9,000 to pay bounties on the call before the last; $10,000 to pay bounties under the last call; and $1,000 to aid the families of volunteers.

Four years later, A. W. Dam was chosen a committee to receive state bonds of one hundred dollars each, as equalization of bounty.

A list in the possession of the author indicates that sixty-six men were drafted from Sanford during the war. In 1863, eighteen conscripts were accepted.

A list of Sanford men who served in the Civil War is as follows, the regiment being from Maine in each case, unless otherwise stated:

ALLEN, GEORGE H. November 29, 1864. Navy.

ALLEN, JEDEDIAH. Single, twenty-seven years. Company E, Twenty-Seventh Infantry. Private, September 30, 1862 to July 17, 1863.

ALLEN, ORRIN. Single, eighteen years. Company K, Fourteenth Infantry. Private, January (July?) 16, 1862.

ALLEN, SAMUEL. Single, nineteen years. Company F, Eighth Infantry. Private, August 20, 1862. A. E. hospital nurse, November, 1864. Discharged, June 5, 1865.

ALLEN, WILLIAM A. Company E, Twenty-Seventh Infantry. September 30, 1862.

AULD, WILLIAM M. October 15, 1862.

BAKER, GRANVILLE M. Single, twenty-eight years. Company D, Twentieth Infantry. Private, August 30, 1862. Hospital nurse, 1862. Assistant Surgeon, April 5, 1863. Mustered out, June 4, 1865.

BALZ (BALTZ), JOHN. Married, thirty years. Company B, First Infantry, January 2, 1865. Company mustered out, July 25, 1865.

BANCROFT, NORRIS E. Single, eighteen years. Company F, Eighth Infantry. Private, September 7, 1861. Sick at Beaufort, November, 1862. Re-enlisted, February 29, 1864. Corporal, June 12, 1865. Company mustered out, January 18, 1866.

BANFIELD, PHILIP. Single, twenty-eight years. Company E, Twenty-Seventh Infantry. Private, September 30, 1862, to July 17, 1863.

BARTLETT, JOSEPH W. Single, eighteen years. Company E, Twenty-Seventh Infantry. Private, September 30, 1862, to July 17, 1863. Re-enlisted, March 3, 1864; Corporal Company A, Thirty-Second Infantry. Wounded June 18, 1864. Sergeant, Company A, Thirty-First Infantry, December, 1864. Mustered out, July 5, 1865.

BEARNS, WILLIAM. September 16, 1864.

BEAUCHAMP, EDWARD. Company A, Ninth Infantry. September 15, 1864.

BEDELL, IRVING A. New Hampshire Infantry. September 18, 1862.

BEDELL, IVORY. Seventh New Hampshire Infantry.

BENNETT, EDWARD. Single, eighteen years. Company F, Thirty-Second Infantry. April 5, 1864. Transferred to Company F, Thirty-First Infantry, December 1, 1864. Company mustered out, July 15, 1865.

BENNETT, FRANK. Son of T. K. Bennett. Drafted in Boston. Killed, 1864.

BLAIR, ALEXANDER. March 4, 1865.

BOSTON, JAMES. Fourteenth New Hampshire Infantry.

BOYD, EDWARD L. Single, twenty-five years. Company F, Eighth Infantry. Private, April 12, 1864, to June 12, 1865. Wounded, June 18, 1864. Discharged for disability.

BRACKETT, GEORGE W. Single, twenty years. Company F, Eighth Infantry. Private, September 7, 1861. Sick at Beaufort, November, 1862. Discharged at expiration of service, 1864.

BRACKETT, JOHN M. (W?). Single, twenty-two years. Company F, Eighth Infantry. Private, October 5, 1861. Sick at Hilton Head, S. C., December, 1861. Discharged for disability, June 21, 1862.

BRIANT, CHARLES H. Company F, Thirtieth Infantry. January 4, 1864.

BUTLER, JAMES W. Single, twenty-four years. Company F, Eighth Infantry. Private, September 7, 1861. Discharged for disability, 1861.

BUTLER, LUTHER H. Single, twenty years. Company I, First Cavalry. Private, October 31, 1861. Private, Company E, Twenty-Seventh Infantry, September 30, 1862. Saw later service and was mustered out, August 1, 1865.

BUTLER, WILLIS H. Single, twenty-three years. Private, Company E, Twenty-Seventh Infantry, September 30, 1862. Private, Company K, Ninth Infantry, September, 1864. Second Lieutenant, September, 1864. First Lieutenant, Company B, Ninth Infantry, January 4, 1865.

CAMPBELL (CAMPWELL), GEORGE. Navy, December 13, 1864.

CARROLL, JOHN W. Thirteenth Massachusetts Infantry. Died in Boston, October 2, 1893, aged fifty years.

CARTER, JOHN S. Single, thirty-eight years. Company F, Eighth

Infantry. Private, September 7, 1861. Discharged for disability, 1861. Died, September 3, 1882, aged fifty-nine years, seven months. CHADBOURN, HENRY.

CHAPMAN, WILLIAM. Single, nineteen years. Company E, Twenty-Seventh Infantry. Private, September 30, 1862, to July 17, 1863. CLANCY (CHANCY), JOHN. Seventeenth United States Infantry. November 29, 1864.

CLARK, GEORGE, JUNIOR. Married, twenty-five years. Company F, Thirty-Second Infantry. April 4, 1864. Transferred to Company F, Thirty-First Infantry, December 1, 1864. Discharged, December 2, 1864, by order of General Dix.

COBB, DR. STEPHEN M. Born in Gorham, Maine; in Sanford, November, 1852, to June, 1856, Surgeon, Thirty-Fifth Iowa Infantry, September, 1862 to August, 1865. Muscatine, Iowa.

COFFIN, SIMEON B. Single, nineteen years. Company F, Eighth Infantry. Private, September 7, 1861. Corporal, July 1, 1863. Re-enlisted February 29, 1864. Died of wounds, August 13, 1864.

COLBY, SETH H. Married, twenty-two years. Company F (K?), Eighth Infantry. Private, August 25, 1862. Killed at Bottom's Church, May 20, 1864.

CRAM, EDWIN J. Son of John and Deborah Cram. Third Assistant Engineer on United States Steamer " R. R. Cuyler." Died, April 14, 1882, aged forty years.

CRAM, WALTER. Navy, October 5, 1863. Landsman. On the " Niagara " and " Hartford." August 5, 1864, at Mobile Bay. Discharged in Philadelphia, November 5, 1864. Nurse at Pensacola Naval Hospital.

CURRIER, GEORGE E. Single, eighteen years. Company E, Twenty-Seventh Infantry. Private, October 5, 1862, to July 17, 1863.

DAVIS, DAVID. Navy, 1863.

DAY, BENJAMIN N. Single, twenty-one years. Company E, Twenty-Seventh Infantry. Private, September 30, 1862, to July 17, 1863.

DAY, LEONARD. Served in a Massachusetts regiment.

DAY, ORRIN. Served from Massachusetts.

DAY, SAMUEL. Served from Massachusetts.

DENNEY, JOHN. Navy. January 19, 1865.

DOBLE, HIRAM H. Company F, Thirtieth Infantry. January 4, 1864.

DORMAN, GEORGE H. Single, eighteen years. Company K, Fourteenth Infantry. Private, January (July?) 16, 1862. Discharged for disability, January 27, 1863.

DORMAN, STEPHEN G. Second Lieutenant, Thirty-Second Infantry. Wounded in leg and face, 1864. Died, October 26, 1898.

Dow, CHARLES H. C. Twenty years. Company B, Second (Twentieth ?) Massachusetts Infantry, May 25, 1861 to May 28, 1864.

DOWNS, JOSEPH W. Company D, Thirtieth Infantry, January 26, 1864.

DUNCAN, JOHN. Company F, Eighth Infantry, February 29, 1864.

EDWARDS, GEORGE W. Single, twenty years. Company E, Twenty-Seventh Infantry. Private, September 30, 1862, to July 17, 1863.

ELDRIDGE, EDWARD. Company F, Eighth Infantry. February 29, 1864.

EMERY, CYRUS C. Sergeant, Troop C, Second Massachusetts Cavalry, December 8, 1862. Second Lieutenant, July 27, 1863. First Lieutenant, Fifth Massachusetts Cavalry, January 13, 1864 ; Captain, January 18, 1864; Major, May 30, 1865. Discharged, December, 1865.

EMERY, EDWIN. Company F, Seventeenth Infantry. Private, September 10, 1863; Sergeant, November 1, 1863; Color Sergeant, April 27, 1864; wounded, Spottsylvania, May 12, 1864; Second Lieutenant, June 28, 1864. Mustered out, June 4, 1865.

EMERY, WILLIAM H. Born May 11, 1848. Served four months in Company D, Forty-Second Massachusetts Infantry, in 1864.

EMERY, WILLIAM R. Company E, Twenty-Seventh Infantry. September 30, 1862.

ENGLISH, HENRY. Served in the navy from Massachusetts.

EVANS, FRANK. September 17, 1864.

FARNHAM, STEPHEN. Served from New Hampshire.

FERNALD, HORATIO P. Company F, Seventh Infantry. January 6, 1864.

FOOT, EBENEZER. Served in the navy (?).

FOSTER, CHARLES E. Company I, Twentieth Infantry. December 1, 1863.

FROST, HIRAM. Single, twenty years. Company E, Ninth Infantry. Private, September 22, 1861, to September 27, 1864.

FROST, HUGH A. (H.?) Single, twenty-four years. Company E, Twenty-Seventh Infantry. Private, September 30, 1862, to July 18, 1863. Battery E, Second Massachusetts Heavy Artillery. Died, August 18, 1865.

FROST, THOMAS W. Single, twenty-one years. Company F, Eighth Infantry. Private, September 7, 1861. Sick at Beaufort, November,

19

1862. Discharged for disability, January 25, 1863. Died, February 20, 1863.

GAREY, CALEB E.

GAREY, CYRUS M.

GAREY, MOSES E.

GERRISH, GEORGE W. Single, twenty years. Company E, Twenty-Seventh Infantry. Private, September 30, 1862 to July 18, 1863.

GETCHELL, EDWIN S. Served from Massachusetts.

GILES, JESSE. Married, twenty-eight years. Company E, Twenty-Seventh Infantry. Corporal, September 30, 1862, to July 17, 1863.

GILES, JOHN. Seventeenth Regulars.

GILES, WILLIAM D. Seventeenth Regulars. Died, June 23, 1867, aged thirty-two years.

GOODWIN, ALVIN. Single, eighteen years. Company H, Third Infantry. Private, August 9, 1862. Wounded at Fredericksburg. Discharged, 1863.

GOODWIN, DAVID S. Navy.

GOODWIN, EDMUND F. Born January 1, 1844. Battery G, Second Massachusetts Heavy Artillery, August 19, 1863.

GOODWIN, ELIAS L. Single, thirty-four years. Company A, Eighth Infantry. Private, September 2, 1862. Wounded, June 18, 1864. Discharged, June 12, 1865. Died, April 27, 1883, aged fifty-five years.

GOODWIN, ELISHA J. Served from New Hampshire.

GOODWIN, JOHN B. Single, twenty-one years. Company F, Eighth Infantry. Private, September 7, 1861. Sick at Hilton Head, December, 1861. Discharged for disability, May 27, 1863. Re-enlisted, December 18, 1863 (64?). Died at Hampton, Va., January 10, 1866.

GOODWIN, JOHN H. Served from New Hampshire.

GOULD, EDWIN W. Company F, Eighth Infantry. February 29, 1864.

GOWEN, EMILUS S. Navy (?).

GOWEN, FRANK A. Seventeenth Regulars. July 20, 1864.

GOWEN, OREN A. Navy (?).

GOWEN, WILLIAM B. Single, twenty-seven years. Company E, Twenty-Seventh Infantry. Corporal, September 30, 1862, to July 17, 1863.

GOWEN, WILLIAM J. Single, twenty-six years. Company H, Second Infantry. Private, September 29, 1864, to August 29, 1865.

GREEN, WILLIAM. April 13, 1865.

HAM (HANS), JAMES D. Company H, Thirtieth Infantry. January 19, 1865.

HAMILTON, ALVAH M. Died, August 25, 1870, aged twenty-eight.

HAMILTON, GEORGE. Died, November 16, 1873, aged twenty-eight.

HAMILTON, JONATHAN. Single, forty-one years. Company A, Eighth Infantry. Private, September 2, 1862. Died of disease, March 3, 1865, Point of Rocks, Va. A carpenter by trade.

HAMILTON, RICHARD W. Battery G, First Heavy Artillery. January 6, 1864.

HANSON, WILLIAM M. Navy. February 9, 1865.

HARMON, WILLIAM H. Company F, Eighth Infantry. February 29, 1864.

HATCH, FRANKLIN N. Single, sixteen years. Company A, Fifth Infantry. Private, September 22, 1861. Discharged for disability, July, 1862.

HATCH, DR. GEORGE W. 1862. Assistant and surgeon in charge, hospital, Washington. 1863–1865, medical officer, navy. At Mobile Bay, August 5, 1864.

HEMINGWAY, JOHN. Married, forty-three years. . Company F, Eighth Infantry. Captain, September 7, 1861. Major, May 18, 1862. Lieutenant Colonel, December 1, 1863. Resigned, on account of disability, February 16, 1864.

HEMINGWAY, MOSES. Single, eighteen years. Company F, Eighth Infantry. Private, September 2, 1862. Discharged, September 10, 1863. Re-enlisted, March 21, 1865, Company K, Twelfth Infantry. Discharged March 23, 1866.

HENDERSON, FREDERICK A. Married. Twenty-six years. Company F, Eighth Infantry. Corporal, September 7, 1861. Sergeant, September 1, 1862. Detached service in Maine, November, 1863. Discharged, June 18, 1864. February 7, 1865, Hancock's Corps.

HERSOM, DR. NAHUM A. Single, twenty-seven years. Twentieth Infantry. Assistant Surgeon, August 9, 1862. Surgeon Seventeenth Infantry, April 11, 1863. Mustered out, June 4, 1865. .

HERSOM, STEPHEN M.

HILL, FREEMAN B. Single, forty-four years. Company E, Twenty-Seventh Infantry. Private, September 30, 1862, to July 17, 1863.

HILL, JOSEPH. Served from Massachusetts.

HILL, REUBEN. Single, forty-one years. Company I, Third Infantry. Private, August 9, 1862. Transferred to Company D, Seventeenth Infantry. Wounded. Discharged, June 1, 1865. Died in West Newfield, December 29, 1893.

HILLER, CHARLES. Died, September 4, 1868, aged twenty-eight.

HOBBS, JOHN H. Served from New Hampshire.

HODGDON, JAMES M. Thirteenth New Hampshire Infantry. Sergeant, September 18, 1862. Second Lieutenant.

HOUSTON, ITHAMAR. First Infantry (?).

HOUSTON, JOHN L. (S.?) Son of James and Sylvina (Hussey) Houston. Born September 28, 1834. Company I, First Infantry. Enlisted Westbrook. Died, August 26, 1868.

HUBBARD, GEORGE. Eighth Infantry. Died in the service.

HUBBARD, THOMAS. Navy (?).

HUNT, LEVI. Company F, Thirtieth Infantry. January 9, 1864.

HURD, FRANCIS. Single, twenty-two years. Company F, Eighth Infantry. Private, September 7, 1861. Corporal, November 1, 1862. Died of wounds, June 1, 1864.

HURD, HENRY A. Single, eighteen years. Company F, Eighth Infantry. Private, September 7, 1861. Re-enlisted, February 29, 1864. Corporal and Sergeant. Missing, October 27, 1864.

HURD, LUTHER J. Born, January 11, 1842. Company H, Sixteenth Infantry. Private, August 14, 1862. Shot through the arm.

HUSSEY, CHRISTOPHER. Married, twenty-four years. Company E, Twenty-Seventh Infantry. Private, September 30, 1862, to July 17, 1863.

INGERSOLL, ARTHUR S. Troop M, Second Cavalry. January 2, 1865.

JACOBS, CHARLES. Married, forty-three years. Company E, Twenty-Seventh Infantry. Private, September 30, 1862, to July 17, 1863.

JACOBS, JOHN. Married, thirty-eight years. Company F, Eighth Infantry. Private, September 7, 1861. Discharged, June 21, 1862.

JAMESON, W. H.

JELLISON, GEORGE C. Married, nineteen years. Private, Company K, Ninth Infantry. September 20, 1864, to June 30, 1865.

JELLISON, JOHN W. Single, eighteen years. Company E, Twenty-Seventh Infantry. Private, September 30, 1862, to July 17, 1863. Re-enlisted, September 20, 1864. Corporal, Company K, Ninth Infantry. Discharged for disability, May 24, 1865.

JELLISON, JOSEPH R. Twenty-two years. Second Massachusetts Infantry. May 25, 1861. Died, November 12, 1862.

JELLISON, NORRIS F. Sergeant, Eleventh Ohio Battery. October 27, 1861.

JENNISON, WILLIAM H. Company B, Twentieth Infantry. October 29, 1862.

JOHNSON, EDWARD P. Single, twenty years. Company E, Twenty-Seventh Infantry. Private, September 30, 1862 to July 17, 1863.

JOHNSON, HARVEY B. Single, nineteen years. Private, Company D, Eleventh Infantry. August 25, 1864, to February 2, 1866.

JOHNSON, IVORY. Married, forty-four years. Company E, Twenty-Seventh Infantry. Corporal, September 30, 1862. Company mustered out, July 17, 1863.

JOHNSON, JOHN T. Single, twenty years. Company E, Twenty-Seventh Infantry. Private, September 30, 1862. Died, December 26, 1862.

JOHNSON, ROBERT.

JOHNSON, SAMUEL F. Served from New Hampshire.

JONES, EZRA E. L. Single, eighteen years. Troop L, First Cavalry. Private, November 30, 1863. Sick, November, 1864. Mustered out, August 1, 1865.

JONES, ORIN E. Served from New Hampshire.

JONES, RUFUS L. Single, twenty years. Troop L, First Cavalry. Private, December 18, 1863, to December, 1864.

JONES, RUFUS. Served from New Hampshire.

KAMES, JOHN. Company D, First Vermont Infantry. January 1, 1864. Re-enlisted.

KENNISTON, ELEAZAR B. January 25, 1864.

KENNISTON, WILLIAM R. Battery E, First Heavy Artillery. December 22, 1863.

KNOX, SUMNER. Company D, Twentieth Infantry. August 29, 1862.

LEACH, FRANK. January 31, 1865.

LEIGHTON, WARREN C. Company D, Twentieth Infantry, August 25, 1862.

LITTLEFIELD, ALONZO. Single, nineteen years. Company F, Eighth Infantry. Private, September 7, 1861. Died at Hilton Head, July 6, 1863.

LITTLEFIELD, ELIAS. Single, forty-one years. Company K, Fourteenth Infantry. Private, December 17, 1861. Died at Carrolton, La., October 31, 1862.

LITTLEFIELD, ORLANDO.

LITTLEFIELD, REUBEN O. Single, eighteen years. Company E, Twenty-Seventh Infantry. Private, October 5, 1862, to July 17, 1863. Re-enlisted, Troop I, First Cavalry, September 27, 1864. Discharged, May 25, 1865.

LORD, ALBION A. Thirteenth New Hampshire Infantry. Corporal, September 18, 1862. Wounded, September 29, 1864.

LORD, CHARLES O. Single, eighteen years. Company F, Thirty-First Infantry. April 5, 1864 to January 30, 1865.

LORD, HIRAM. Served from Massachusetts.

LORD, JOHN, SECOND.

LORD, JOHN W. Company E, Twenty-Seventh Infantry. September 30, 1862.

LORD, STEPHEN. Seventh Massachusetts Infantry.

LYONS, CHARLES. Company H, Thirtieth Infantry. January 6, 1864.

MAHONEY, CHARLES. August 26, 1864.

MAHONEY, PATRICK. September 5, 1864.

MARSH, ASBURY C. Major, Second Missouri Infantry, 1862. Provost Marshal. Died, January 22, 1887.

MEDCALF, GEORGE. Company F, Thirtieth Infantry. January 4, 1864.

MERRICK, STEPHEN W. Single, nineteen years. Troop I, First Cavalry. Private, October 31, 1861, to November 25, 1864. Died, October 6, 1865.

MERROW, ARVENDEN. Single, eighteen years. Company A, Twentieth Infantry. Private, August 29, 1862. Discharged for disability, January 2, 1863.

MESSER, ALVIN A. Company G, First Vermont Infantry. December 14, 1863.

MILLER, GEORGE W. Navy (?).

MILLER, WILLIAM G. Navy.

MILLER, WILLIAM H. Single, twenty-seven years. Company E, Twenty-Seventh Infantry. First Lieutenant, September 30, 1862, to December 16, 1862.

MILLETT (MILLER?), JARED F. Company B, Twentieth Infantry. October 29, 1862.

MILLETT, JOHN B. Invalid Corps. December 1, 1863.

MILLIKEN, GEORGE W. Company F, Thirtieth Infantry. January 4, 1864.

MOORE, WILLIAM A. Single, twenty-seven years. Company F, Eighth Infantry. Private, September 7, 1861. Re-enlisted, February 29, 1864. Subsequent records are contradictory. One states, died, March 8, 1864; another, missing, October 27, 1864.

MOTT, PERKINS F. Second New Hampshire Infantry. Navy (?).

MURRAY, EDMUND G. Married, twenty-five years. Company F, Eighth Infantry. Corporal, September 7, 1861. Re-enlisted, February 29, 1864. First Sergeant, May 1, 1864. First Lieutenant, October 3, 1864. Captain. Provost Marshal, Richmond, Va., for nearly a year. Mustered out, January 18, 1866.

MURRAY, JONATHAN C. Company H, Thirtieth Infantry. January 6, 1865.

MURRAY, SIMON. Fourteenth Massachusetts Infantry.

NASON, HENRY. Battery C, First Rhode Island Artillery. Wounded near Robertson's Tavern, Va., November 30, 1863. Died December 23, 1863, aged thirty-seven years.

NEEDHAM, FRANK E. Company E, Twenty-Seventh Infantry. October 15, 1862.

NEWELL, IRA A. Single, twenty-eight years. Company C, Twenty-Ninth Infantry. Private, November 13, 1863. Absent sick, December, 1864. Company mustered out, June 21, 1866.

NUTTER, ALBERT. Navy (?).

OTIS, CHARLES H. C. Thirteenth New Hampshire Infantry. September 18, 1862.

PAIGE, SMITH C. Thirteenth New Hampshire Infantry. September 18, 1862. Invalid Corps, December 13, 1863.

PARRY, RICHARD. November 21, 1864.

PARSONS, ALONZO Z. (Y.?) Company B, Twentieth Infantry. October 29, 1862.

PAUL, LEVI H. Served from Massachusetts.

PERKINS, JAMES G. Son of James and Experience Perkins. Born September 15, 1840. Single. Company E, Twenty-Seventh Infantry. Private, September 30, 1862. Absent sick, December, 1862. Mustered out, July 17, 1863.

PERKINS, THOMAS B. Company F, Seventeenth Infantry. September 30, 1863.

PHILLIPS, TRAFTON. Married, forty-two years. Company E, Twenty-Seventh Infantry. Private, September 30, 1862. Absent sick, December, 1862. Mustered out, July 17, 1863.

PIERCE, IVORY M. Served from Massachusetts.

PILLSBURY, EMERSON. Single, nineteen years. Company H, Third Infantry. Private, August 9, 1862. Prisoner, May 2, 1863. Transferred to Company G, Seventeenth Infantry, 1864. Mustered out, June 4, 1865.

POLLARD, DAVID O. Battery G, First Heavy Artillery, December 16, 1863.

POPOLI, PIERRE. April 4, 1865.

POTTER, WILLIAM. Single, twenty-three years. Company H, Eleventh Infantry. Private, December 22, 1864. Detached service, November, 1865. Company mustered out, February 2, 1866. (Name given on Dr. Dam's list as Potter Williams.)

POWERS, SAMUEL H. Battery G, First Heavy Artillery. December 16, 1863.

QUINT, JOSEPH. Served from New Hampshire.

RANKINS, WILLIAM P. Married, forty-four years. Company F, Eighth Infantry. Private, August 25, 1862. Detailed as regimental tailor, 1863. Missing in action, May 16, 1864. Died in Andersonville prison.

REED, WILLIAM J. Single, twenty-five years. Company F, Eighth Infantry. Corporal, September 7, 1861. Sergeant, July 1, 1863. Killed in action near Petersburg, Va., June 18, 1864.

RICHARDSON, JOSEPH P. Company E, Twenty-Seventh Infantry. September 30, 1862.

RICKER, A. A.

RICKER, BENJAMIN. Married, forty-four years. Company F, Eighth Infantry. Corporal, September 7, 1861. Color bearer, 1863. Re-enlisted, February 29, 1864. Sick at Fortress Monroe, November, 1864. Discharged January 2, 1865.

RICKER, EBENEZER. Single, twenty-one years. Company F, Eighth Infantry. Private, September 7, 1861. Wounded, June 18, 1864, In hospital, November, 1864.

RICKER, ELI R. Married, forty-four years. Company B, Fourteenth Infantry. Private, December 30, 1861. Transferred to Company K, 1862. Discharged, May, 1862.

RICKER, GEORGE. Single, nineteen years. Company K, Thirty-Second Infantry. May 6, 1864. Died at Annapolis, Md., October 30, 1864.

RIDLEY, JOSEPH. Single, nineteen years. Company E, Twenty-Seventh Infantry. Private, September 30, 1862. Absent, December, 1862. Mustered out July 17, 1863.

ROBERTS, JOHN H. Second Lieutenant (?).

ROGERS, EZRA P.

ROWE, CHARLES M. Company H, Thirtieth Infantry. January 6, 1865.

RYAN, PETER. January 10, 1865.

SCOTT, JOHN. December 1, 1864. Navy.

SEAVEY, ASA W. Single, eighteen years. Troop I, First Cavalry. Private, November 30, 1863. Absent sick, November, 1864. Mustered out, August 1, 1865.

SEAVEY, SAMUEL. Single, twenty years. Company K, Fourteenth Infantry. Private, December 28, 1861. Died, December 14, 1862.

SEAVEY, THOMAS B. Single, twenty-five years. Company F, Eighth

Infantry. Private, September 7, 1861. Fourth New Hampshire Infantry.

SEWELL, CHARLES W. Company D, Thirtieth Infantry. January 26, 1864.

SHACKLEY, LEWIS.

SKILLIN, SUMNER L. Company D, Twentieth Infantry. August 25, 1862.

SKILLIN, THOMAS J. (A.?) Company D, Twentieth Infantry. August 25, 1862.

SMITH, ARTHUR W.

SMITH, CHARLES. Single, twenty-two years. Co. H, Fifteenth Infantry. March 23, 1865.

SMITH, HENRY (A). Navy (?). December 17, 1864.

SMITH, WILLIAM H. Single, twenty-two years. Company G, Fifteenth Infantry. January 25, 1865.

SPAULDING, RANDALL H. Company B, Twentieth Infantry. October 29, 1862.

SPENSER, JOHN. Served from Massachusetts.

SPOONER, ASA. First Heavy Artillery.

STEVENS, HERMAN. Company E, Twenty-Seventh Infantry. October 15, 1862.

STROUT, HENRY A.

STUBBS, FREDERICK A. Company C, Thirtieth Infantry. January 12, 1864.

SUTTEN, CHARLES H. Colored. September 27, 1864.

SWETT, HENRY A. Company D, Twentieth Infantry. August 25, 1862.

SYLVESTER, SETH M. Married, twenty-seven years. Company E, Twenty-Seventh Infantry. Private, September 30, 1862. Killed by accidental discharge of musket, May 28, 1863.

THOMPSON, ADRIEL, JUNIOR. Single, twenty-one years. Company E, Twenty-Seventh Infantry. Private, September 30, 1862. In hospital, December 1, 1862. Mustered out, July 17, 1863. Re-enlisted, Company F, Thirty-Second Infantry, April 5, 1864.

THOMPSON, GEORGE. Served from Massachusetts.

THOMPSON, GEORGE W. Single, twenty-six years. Company E, Twenty-Seventh Infantry. Sergeant, September 30, 1862, to July 17, 1863.

THOMPSON, JOHN. Born, November 22, 1844. Served from Massachusetts.

THOMPSON, JOSEPH. Born, September 2, 1846. Served from Massachusetts.

THOMPSON, MOSES. Born, March 1, 1834. Served from Massachusetts.

THOMPSON, WARREN. Born, January 17, 1836. Married. Company A, Eighth Infantry. Private, September 2, 1862. In hospital, Hilton Head, November, 1863. Eighteenth Corps Hospital. November, 1864. Discharged, June 12, 1865.

John, Joseph, Moses and Warren Thompson were brothers, sons of Ebenezer and Rachel Thompson. The three serving from Massachusetts enlisted from Danvers.

TODD, FRANCIS. December 7, 1864. Navy.

TRAFTON, DR. CLARK C. Born in Alfred, April 9, 1831. In Sanford, 1858–60. Surgeon Thirty-Second Infantry, 1864. Died in Washington of malarial fever, August 11, 1864.

TRAFTON, EDWIN (EDWARD) T. Married, nineteen years. Private, Company K, Ninth Infantry. September 20, 1864, to October 19, 1864. Died of disease.

VANDERLINDEN, CHARLES. December 2, 1864.

WAKEFIELD, GEORGE. Served from Massachusetts.

WATSON, CHARLES. Single, eighteen years. Company K, Seventh Infantry. Private, November 25, 1862. Wounded and missing, May 4, 1863.

WATSON, DR. DAVID. Born, November 6, 1836, Limerick. In Sanford, 1861–63. Assistant Surgeon, United States Steamer "Onward." Resigned, July 3, 1865.

WEAVERLEY, JOHN. August 19, 1864.

WELCH, IRA M. Born, February 28, 1844. Company B, Eighth Infantry. Lost a limb at Bermuda Hundred, May 20, 1864. Died, October 24, 1871.

WELCH, JOSIAH. Company E, Twenty-Seventh Infantry. September 30, 1862.

WELCH, STEPHEN E. Married, twenty-six years. Company K, Tenth Infantry. Private, July 18, 1862. Transferred to Company A, 1863 ; to Company G, Twenty-Ninth Infantry, 1864. Absent sick, December, 1864. Discharged, May 31, 1865.

WELCH, STEPHEN F. Married, forty-three years. Company A, Eighth Infantry. Private, September 2, 1862. Wounded, June 18, 1864. Absent, November, 1864. Discharged, April 27, 1865.

WENTWORTH, ANDREW J. Eighth Infantry. September 2, 1862. Transferred to the regular army.

WENTWORTH, JOSEPH W. Third Infantry. August 26, 1862.

WENTWORTH, THOMAS S. Thirteenth New Hampshire Infantry, September 18, 1862. Wounded severely May 16, and September 29, 1864.

WENTWORTH, WILLIAM W. Married, twenty-six years. Company F, Eighth Infantry. Private, September 7, 1861. Hospital nurse, November, 1863. Re-enlisted, February 29, 1864. Discharged for disability, August 28, 1865.

WENTWORTH, JACOB. Company C, First Vermont Infantry. December 14, 1863. Re-enlisted.

WHITEKNOCH, GEORGE W. Single, nineteen years. Company G, First Infantry (Cavalry?). Private, December 20, 1864. Discharged, June 5, 1865.

WHITTEN, JAMES G. Served from Massachusetts.

WILBUR, D. W. Company B, Thirty-First Infantry, March 8, 1864.

WILKINSON, CHARLES. Single, eighteen years. Company B, Fourteenth Infantry. Private, December 30, 1861. Transferred to Company K, 1862. Re-enlisted, January 1, 1864.

WILKINSON, GEORGE H. Company F, Thirtieth Infantry. January 4, 1864.

WILKINSON, STEPHEN. Married, forty-four years. Company E, Twenty-seventh Infantry. Private, September 30, 1862.

WILLARD, HENRY C. Tenth New Hampshire Infantry. Corporal, September 18, 1862. Wounded, June 1, 1864.

WILLARD, WILLIAM F. Single, nineteen years. Company F, Eighth Infantry. Private, September 7, 1861. Principal Musician, July 1, 1863. Re-enlisted, February 29, 1864. Killed before Petersburg, July 31, 1864.

WILLIAMS, JOHN H. January 25, 1864.

WITHAM, ALVAH C. Single, thirty-six years. Company K, Thirty-Second Infantry. May 6, 1864. Wounded, June 3, 1864. Transferred to Company K, Thirty-First Infantry, December 1, 1864. Killed in the service.

WITHAM, OTIS. Born, December 22, 1819. Company G, Thirtieth Infantry. January 1, 1864.

WITHAM, PHINEHAS C. Company K, Tenth Infantry. August 26, 1862.

YOUNG, MOSES C. Company H, Thirtieth Infantry. January 6, 1865.

The above list contains two hundred and sixty names. Sanford was credited by the state for one hundred and forty-seven soldiers, but there were one hundred and sixty in the army, and fifteen in the navy.

CHAPTER XXIX.

THE GOODALL ENTERPRISES.

Thomas Goodall Comes to Sanford, 1867 — Starts the Manufacture
of Carriage Robes and Kersey Blankets — The Sanford Mills —
Mousam River Mills — Goodall Brothers' Mills — Consolidation,
1885 — Goodall Worsted Mills — Maine Alpaca Company —
Sanford Light and Water Company — Electric Roads Established — Sanford Power Company — The Great Dam.

TO give, in detail, the history of the Goodall enterprises, would
require a volume of well filled pages, devoted absolutely to
nothing else. This chapter will therefore be confined to the most important features of these enterprises, affecting the growth of Sanford.

It is acknowledged that Goodall enterprise has been chiefly instrumental in transforming the Sanford of yesterday, into the thriving
industrial centre of today. The actual conversion of this rustic,
farming village, composed of thirty dwellings and a corner grocery,
into the important commercial and manufacturing Sanford of the
present, had its beginning in the summer of 1867, when Thomas
Goodall, born in Dewsbury, County of Yorkshire, England, September 1, 1823, came here from Troy, N. H., where he had previously
been engaged in the production of horse blankets and blankets for
the army and navy, and purchased from William Miller and James
O. Clark, the flannel factory of the former and grist-mill and saw-
mill of the latter, together with the entire water privilege of the
Mousam, controlled by them at this point, paying for the same, the
sum of $15,500. Mr. Goodall began immediately the enlargement
of the property, and early in the following year, had two sets of
cards and ten looms in motion, the entire plant, at that time, giving
employment to fifty operatives, in the production of carriage robes
and Kersey blankets. These carriage robes were the very first of
the kind to be manufactured in the United States. Mr. Goodall,
while sojourning in England, had been engaged in exporting carriage
robes to this country, and it was this experience that induced him to
come here and undertake their production.

The products of his plant finding a ready market, with an ever increasing demand, further enlargements became necessary for the accommodation of constantly augmented manufacturing facilities, until, at the present time, The Sanford Mills have a capital of $750-000, turn out an annual product valued at $1,000,000, and provide employment for seven hundred and fifty operatives, many of whom own their own homes.

In 1873, Lucius C. Chase of Boston, and Louis B., George B., and Ernest M. Goodall, sons of Thomas Goodall, together with Amos Garnsey, Junior, formed a co-partnership and during the following year, 1874, began the manufacture of plain and fancy blankets in newly erected factories known as the Mousam River Mills, and occupying the site of an old saw-mill once operated by Elijah Witham. The business was conducted under the firm name of Goodall and Garnsey. Ere long these factories were consuming two thousand five hundred pounds of wool daily. On the morning of Thanksgiving day, November 24, 1892, the larger of the factories constituting the plant, was entirely destroyed by fire, entailing a loss of $120,000. Strange as it may seem, this disastrous conflagration was caused, undoubtedly, by ice that had collected beneath the waterwheel gates, which becoming loosened by the action of the water, allowed a sufficient quantity to set one of the waterwheels in motion, to escape. Once the wheel was in motion, the automatic regulator would raise the gate until the highest rate of speed had been attained. A heavy leather belt being driven rapidly over a wooden pulley that remained stationary because connected with a waterwheel that had not thawed out, created sufficient friction to set fire to the factory.

On October 1, 1881, George B., Louis B., and Ernest M. Goodall organized the firm of Goodall Brothers and began the manufacture of mohair car and furniture plushes, and of mohair carriage robes, the very first of each of these fabrics to be produced on this side of the Atlantic. Their venture in this new field proved eminently successful, and on April 4, 1885, the plush business of Goodall Brothers and the blanket business of Goodall and Garnsey at the Mousam River Mills, were consolidated with the Sanford Mills, founded by Thomas Goodall.

The present officers of the Sanford Mills Company are: E. M. Goodall, President; Frank Hopewell, of Boston, Treasurer; L. B. Goodall, Clerk; E. M. Goodall, George B. Goodall, and Louis B. Goodall, of Sanford, and John Hopewell and Frank Hopewell of Boston, Directors.

On October 19, 1889, the Goodall Worsted Company was organized with a capital of $30,000, with the following officers : George B. Goodall, President ; Louis B. Goodall, Treasurer ; William Batchelder, Junior, Clerk ; E. M. Goodall, L. B. Goodall, George B. Goodall and H. Hodgson, Directors. The growth of this branch of the Goodall enterprises has been phenomenal, as is amply evidenced by the fact that its present authorized capital is $350,000.

Taking a just pride in the township of their adoption and determined that it should not longer linger in darkness, the Goodalls interested themselves in the organization of the Sanford Light and Water Company.

During all these years of progress, the raw material and manufactured products of the Goodall industries, as well as all fuel and mercantile supplies for business houses of all kinds, were conveyed to and from the railway station at Springvale by heavy truck teams, the expense keeping pace with the ever increasing capacity of the plants and the growth of the town. With a view to reducing this expense, and rendering an actual necessity a possible source of profit, the Goodalls turned their attention to electric railroading, organizing and operating the Mousam River Railway, the first car traversing the rails between Sanford and Springvale in March, 1893.

In 1897, the Goodalls were instrumental in organizing the Sanford and Cape Porpoise Railway, which has been in operation since the summer of 1899.

In 1897, the Sanford Power Company was organized and has been dispensing power since February 20, 1899.

On October 3, 1899, the Maine Alpaca Company was organized, and has been in successful operation since the spring of 1900.

These industries constitute the chief features of the Goodall enterprises.

The reader will appreciate the magnitude of the present plant operated by the Sanford Mills Company by the following brief description :

Mill Number One is devoted to the carding, spinning and weaving of carriage robes and velours. This factory, now forty feet wide and one hundred and sixty-five feet long, three stories including basement, with two-story ell, forty by seventy-five feet, was, previous to the first enlargement, the Miller flannel factory in its entirety. When Mr. Goodall began operations in 1868, after remodelling to some extent, the main structure was forty feet wide and sixty-five feet long. It constitutes the actual nucleus of all the Goodall enterprises.

A portion of Mill Number Two, which occupies the site of Clark's old grist-mill of the early sixties, was used for many years for the printing department in connection with the manufacture of carriage robes and furniture plushes, but in the winter of 1888-89, a commodious structure was erected on the westerly side of the Mousam, connected with Mills Numbers Two and Three by grade and overhead bridges, and here the color making, chemical, block cutting, printing, steaming, washing, fibre fixing, pile raising and drying departments are now concentrated under one roof. At the southerly end of this structure and adjoining it, is a brick building containing a battery of thirteen boilers, their furnaces consuming thirty tons of coal every twenty-four hours, and sending their dense volume of smoke into the tallest chimney in the state of Maine, an attractive piece of architecture, measuring fourteen feet square at its base, reaching skyward one hundred and fifty-seven feet, with a diameter of eight feet, and a circumference of twenty-four feet at its apex. The carriage robe and velour finishing departments now occupy the first and second floors of Mill Number Two, while the third floor is devoted to the drying and storing of unprinted fabrics. This factory is a three-story structure with basement, one hundred and forty-five by forty feet, with an ell forty feet square.

Mill Number Three is a three-story building, fifty by one hundred and twenty feet. The ground floor is devoted to the storage of raw material; the second contains the blending department, while the third is provided with plush stretching machinery and appliances for the drying of printed and unprinted fabrics. Parallel with Mill Three and connected with Mill Two by an overhead bridge, is an immense building for the storage of raw material on the ground floor, and finished carriage robes and blankets on the second and third floors. This structure also contains the packing and shipping departments, from which the products of the factories are distributed all over the United States and Canada.

Mill Number Four is the monster of the entire aggregation of factories and occupies a position directly across the Mousam, looking in an easterly direction from Mill Two. It is three stories high, and the dimensions of the main structure are fifty by two hundred and seventy feet, while the dyeing department, with which it is connected, occupies a one story ell, forty by one hundred and twenty feet. In Mill Four are the fulling and pile or nap raising machines on the ground floor, also the mohair warping department, while the second and third floors give space to the mohair spinning departments.

Mill Number Five, connected with Mill Four, by a covered bridge, is a weaving shed with monitor roofs of glass, constructed with especial attention to ample lighting, and contains a veritable forest of plush looms. The main structure is one hundred by two hundred and fifty feet. In the northerly end of this building are the mohair combing and preparing machines, exceedingly interesting pieces of mechanism, while the basement below is devoted to the mohair scouring department. Mill Five also gives space to the drying, cropping, embossing, steaming, packing and shipping departments, in connection with the manufacture of car and furniture plushes. In close proximity to Mill Five is a two-story structure containing a store room for raw material and the wool sorting department.

Of Mills Number Six and Seven, formerly known as the Mousam River Mills, the larger of the two main structures is fifty by one hundred and seventy feet, and the other, forty by one hundred and twenty feet. In the last mentioned, the raw material undergoes the initial process toward conversion into blankets. In the larger factory, the carding, spinning, weaving, dyeing and finishing departments are concentrated.

In a building located just south of Mill Five, a skilled tinsmith and his assistants manufacture the long wire knives used for loop cutting in the plush looms, and attend to the repairing of the long tin cylinders used in the mohair spinning frames. Scattered about the factory yard, which includes many acres, in locations convenient to the factories with which their contents are identified, are innumerable storehouses, containing raw material valued at hundreds of thousands of dollars. The plant operates its own saw mills for the manufacture of shipping cases, and for the turning out of lumber for building and all other purposes. A large corps of skilled machinists and wood workers are constantly employed in splendidly equipped shops. There are also blacksmith shops where the music of the anvil is seldom hushed.

Every factory is provided with the sprinkler system for protection from fire, the same being connected with huge reservoirs, each with a capacity of 50,000 gallons. In addition to this, the Sanford Mills have a thoroughly equipped fire department, including an Amoskeag steamer, hose trucks, and combination hook and ladder apparatus, all manned by trained fire fighters. In a brick structure, located at a considerable distance from any other building in order that it may not become a prey to the flames in the event of a conflagration, is an automatic force pump, operated by steam, with a capacity of twelve

HON. BENJAMIN F. HANSON.

hundred gallons of water per minute. The giving way of a single fusible plug, all of which are governed by temperature, in any part of the sprinkler system, suffices to set this pump in motion. The opening of a hydrant will operate in the same manner, and should it be necessary, in case of a stubborn blaze, to augment the service of the village water system, one of the finest in Maine, the opening of a single valve, connecting the two systems, is the only requisite.

The Goodall Worsted Mills.—Nothing like the rapid but permanent growth of the plant of the Goodall Worsted Company has ever been witnessed in this section of the country, and it is extremely doubtful if its parallel can be found elsewhere. Established in 1889, operations were begun in a two-story structure, fifty-three by one hundred and fifty-three feet. Since that time an addition of thirty-five feet has been made to the main factory, while other additions include a machine shop eighteen by one hundred and five feet; twisting room thirty-seven by fifty-five feet; engine room thirty-two by fifty feet; scouring department, forty-seven by one hundred feet; together with ample and well appointed offices. The building now occupied by the cloth dyeing and finishing departments was erected in 1893, taking the place of a similar structure destroyed by fire on January 18th of that year, and entailing a loss of $100,000, while fully one hundred operatives were thrown out of employment. This new building is eighty-nine by one hundred and thirty-seven feet, and two stories high. A yarn dyeing house, twenty-seven by one hundred and two feet, was erected in 1892. To this structure, additions twenty-seven by fifty-two and thirty-eight by fifty feet have since been made. The so-called "Hill Mill" was erected in 1890–91 and after being twice enlarged in 1892, is now forty-two feet wide, five stories high and two hundred and thirteen feet long. A building, erected in 1896 for the accommodation of the increasing demands on the weaving department, with an addition made in 1899, is now fifty-four feet wide, two hundred and forty eight feet long and three stories high. The boiler house is sixty-seven by ninety-seven feet, the drug building sixteen by sixty-six feet, piping shop, fifteen by thirty feet, while the new fire-proof warehouse is fifty by ninety-five feet. In addition to the buildings mentioned above, there are numerous smaller structures, giving to this plant that has been in operation less than a dozen years, a total of twenty structures erected at different periods in its brief history.

But perhaps a better comprehension of its enormous growth and capacity will be gleaned from the statement that the value of its

20

annual production of worsted and mohair yarns and worsted and mohair dress goods and men's wear, is $1,500,000; that 750,000 pounds of yarn are consumed by the weaving department annually in the production of 1,200,000 yards of dress goods and men's wear, while 984,000 pounds of worsted and mohair yarns are annually shipped to other fabric manufacturers, and employment provided for eight hundred and fifty operatives. It may also be added that this corporation is almost constantly employing other New England factories in commission weaving and spinning in order to supply the demand for its product.

When running at their fullest capacity, the mills of Sanford consume more mohair than all other mills in the United States combined.

Sanford Light and Water Company. — The Sanford Light and Water Company was organized December 29, 1886, with a capital of $2,000, increased from time to time until its present capital is $25,000. The present officers are: E. M. Goodall, President; George H. Nowell, Treasurer; E. E. Hussey, Clerk. The undertaking has been a success from the beginning. The water supplied is of the purest, and the source unfailing, while Sanford's street and residential lighting will compare favorably with that of any of the smaller towns in New England where arc and incandescent systems are in vogue. The electric plant of the Sanford Light and Water Company was leased to the Mousam River Railway in 1899, and is now installed in the power house of the railway. A stand-pipe with a capacity of 500,000 gallons was erected in 1899. The present pumping station, located just across the highway from the power plant, was erected in 1898.

The Maine Alpaca Company. — The Maine Alpaca Company was organized October 3, 1899, with a capital of $300,000, and the following 'officers: George B. Goodall, President; Louis B. Goodall, Treasurer; William Batchelder, Junior, Clerk; E. M. Goodall, L. B. Goodall, G. B. Goodall, J. Hollinrake and H. Hodgson, Directors. This plant is located at Springvale, occupying the factories formerly operated by the Springvale Cotton Company. The products are mohair and alpaca linings. The mill gives employment to one hundred and forty operatives.

The Sanford Power Company. — The Sanford Power Company was organized in 1897 with a capital of $100,000 and the following board of officers: E. M. Goodall, President; Frank Hopewell, Vice President; George B. Goodall, Clerk and Treasurer. It began supplying power to the Sanford factories on February 20, 1899. The electric generating plant is located at the Old Falls of the Mousam and the structure containing the three monster turbines, an exciter and three powerful generators, one double current and two alternators, is a model of attractive neatness in modern architectural design, finished in faced brick and chiseled granite, while surmounting an eminence overlooking the river are the homes of the workmen, supplied with hot and cold water, electric heat, baths, electric lights and telephonic communication with Sanford and the world in general.

The great dam, planned and constructed under the personal supervision of Hon E. M. Goodall, is a solid mass of masonry, sixteen to twenty feet high, and stretching like a Chinese wall, across the river, two hundred and thirty-five feet from border to border, and capable of resisting the floods of a thousand years. It is, in its immensity and in the thoroughness of its construction, a marvel of modern engineering skill. From this dam, a tube of steel nine feet in diameter and four hundred and fifty feet in length, serves as a means of communication between the confined volume of water and the turbines in the power station, giving a head of sixty-three feet and developing two thousand five hundred horse power. Of this, one thousand five hundred horse power is necessary for the operation of the factories at Sanford, while the balance is utilized according to the demands of traffic by the electric railways.

From the power station, seven miles of wire transmit an alternating current of 10,000 volts to the transformers in a brick structure at Sanford, where the voltage is decreased to four hundred and forty. Ordinarily, five hundred volts is sufficient to operate the two electric railway systems.

During the year 1899, the Sanford Mills acquired, by purchase, the water privilege at Emery's Mills, formerly owned and controlled by the Springvale Cotton Mills, and replaced the old dam by one of solid stone and cement, not using a piece of wood in the entire structure.

CHAPTER XXX.

BANKS.

Mousam River and Sanford Banks, 1854–1861—Sanford National Bank — Loan and Building Associations.

FEELING that the business interests of the community demanded a banking institution in the town, a number of influential citizens, sometime in 1853, set to work to secure a charter for the purpose. Their endeavors resulted in the incorporation by act of the Legislature of the Mousam River Bank of Sanford, on March 22, 1854. The corporators were twenty-three in number and the capital stock was $50,000, divided into shares of fifty dollars each. The bank began business August 16, 1854, and its career from almost the start appears to have been attended by misfortune. Judge Shepley, on application of the bank commissioners, issued a writ of injunction against the bank, September 22, 1854. The difficulty, however, was adjusted, and the bank continued business for a year or two. We find the following in the report of the bank commissioners for 1857 :

"The condition of this (the Sanford) bank was such on the 11th day of November last, that, on application of the bank commissioners to Judge Goodenow for an injunction, it was granted, and at the hearing before him the 12th of November, it appeared that the circulation was $27,498. The amount due depositors was $2,545.94. Total, $30,043.94. The resources of the bank consisted of specie in bank, $4.07 ; Suffolk Bank, $3,000 ; loan, $76,665.45. Of the debts due, about $40,000 were considered very doubtful, if not bad ; the residue is considered available. The Judge, on motion of the bank, continued the injunction in a modified form, to December 23, at which time the bank had reduced its liabilities, exclusive of capital stock, to $19,029.91, and a further continuance was granted to the 2nd of February. Its officers confidently believe they shall be able to redeem all its bills. Oliver Hill has been elected president in place of Samuel Tompson, resigned."

(308)

On April 9, 1857, the name of the bank had been changed to Sanford Bank, and by an enactment of the same day, the president, directors, and company had been authorized to increase the capital stock, by adding thereto the sum of $25,000, to be paid in gold or silver, on or before the 1st of October following, to be divided in shares at fifty dollars each. The commissioners' report of December 1, 1859, showed that the injunction had been removed, that the deficiency in the capital stock, amounting to about $37,000, had been subscribed and paid in, and that all matters had been satisfactorily arranged for a resumption of business, which occurred during 1860. The affairs of the bank ran along smoothly for about a year, when the commissioners again stepped in, and in May, 1861, secured an injunction from Judge Goodenow, at Alfred. Receivers were appointed, and as it was deemed impracticable to continue the bank, its affairs were wound up and its existence terminated.

The Sanford National Bank was organized in March, 1896, and was opened for business on July 27 of that year. Its capital stock is $50,000. The officers are : Louis B. Goodall, President; George H. Nowell, Vice President; M. A. Hewett, Cashier; L. B. Goodall, George H. Nowell, Fred J. Allen, E. E. Goodwin, and Harmon G. Allen, Directors. At the time of its last report the bank had the largest deposit of any bank in York County, $416,093.12. That report was as follows :

Resources : United States treasury government bonds, $15,000 ; United States treasury reserve, $750 ; premium, $1,882.50 ; notes discounted, $354,015.72 ; Boston banks, $53,335.82 ; Portland banks, $54,476.97 ; stocks and bonds, $6,940 ; expense account, $861 ; revenue stamps, $106.03 ; real estate, furniture and fixtures, $7,337.-59 ; cash, $29,262.26 ; $523,967.89.

Liabilities : Capital stock, $50,000 ; profit and loss, $15,139.76 ; circulation, $15,000 ; surplus, $10,000 ; individual accounts, $416,-093.12 ; interest, $1,340.28 ; discount, $6,347.88 ; exchange, $46.85 ; certified deposits, $10,000 ; $523,967.89.

The Sanford Loan and Building Association was organized March 17, 1890, and began business on the 2nd of April following. Its accumulated capital November 1, 1900, was $71,324.19, and its loans on the same date, $78,657.37. The officers are : William Kernon, President; Frank L. Senior, Vice President; George H. Nowell, Treasurer; Frank Wilson, Secretary, who, together with Samuel Littlefield, Orrin Roberts, Charles O. Emery, Second, Fred J. Allen, Albert W. Hunt, John Howgate, Ben Ramsden and Jerry

A. Low, form the Board of Directors. Orville V. Libby, Daniel T. Hill, and Charles D. Clark constitute the security committee, and John Nutter and William E. Nutter are the auditors.

The association has been very successful from its organization, always paying good dividends. It has enabled a number to own houses by small weekly payments, who probably otherwise would still be paying rent. Since its inception the association has had but two presidents, John H. Neal, M.D., and William Kernon; two treasurers, Samuel Littlefield and George H. Nowell; and two secretaries, Fred A. Springer and Frank Wilson.

The Springvale Loan and Building Association was organized as a branch of the Granite State Provident Association of Manchester, N. H., July 25, 1893. The officers were: E. E. Goodwin, President; Harley O. Witham, Vice President; S. F. Felker, Secretary; Leroy Haley, Treasurer. The association was discontinued about two years ago.

CHAPTER XXXI.

RAILROADS.

Project of 1850 a Failure — The Portland and Rochester Road —
Town Refuses to Invest in Stock — The Mousam River and
Sanford and Cape Porpoise Railway Companies.

ABOUT 1850, the York and Cumberland Railroad Company made
surveys of several routes through the town, for a road from
Portland and Great Falls (Somersworth), N. H. Bauneg Beg and
Mount Hope were the great obstacles in the way, preventing a comparatively straight road through the town. That year or the next,
ground was broken with appropriate ceremonies west of Springvale,
and for several months the work of excavating, filling in, and grad-
ing was quite rapidly carried on. Money was not advanced in payment for stock subscribed, sub-contractors failed to meet their obligations, and work was suspended. Not only stockholders, but others
interested in the project were losers by this unfavorable beginning.

For nearly twenty years nothing more was done on the road, west of
the Saco River. At length, after various vicissitudes, the company
reorganized, or a new company, under the name of the Portland and
Rochester Railroad Company, completed the road to Rochester, which
was made the western terminus. The road was finished in running
order, rough, in 1870–71, and on Monday, December 5, 1870, the
first passenger cars, two trains daily, were run between Portland and
Springvale. Before this, however, and while the road was under
construction west of the Mousam, a car ran from Saco River to the
Mousam, with an engine in one end. This dummy used to stop at
any and every road crossing to leave or take on passengers, and was
the subject of much jesting. The bridge over the Mousam was tested
December 7, 1870, with an engine, tender, and two cars, with forty
tons of iron rails thereon.

Before the work was begun, a large majority of the voters thought
it advisable to give the company material encouragement by subscrib-
ing liberally for its stock. Accordingly, at the annual town meeting,
April 6, 1868, Moses W. Emery offered the following:

"That the selectmen of the town be and hereby are authorized and directed to take and subscribe $20,000 to the stock of the Portland and Rochester Railroad, Provided, that the amount is not to be paid until the road is completed to and into the town of Sanford, and suitable passenger and freight depots erected."

The vote was, yeas, two hundred and twenty-four; nays, one hundred and forty-seven. This being less than the required two-thirds, the proposition fell through. The advocates of the measure were not daunted, but attempted to weary the minority by calling meetings, hoping that more than two-thirds at some' meeting would favor loans ing the credit of the town to the company. April 13, the town voted not to subscribe $19,900 (yeas, two hundred and eighty-four; nays, one hundred and eighty-six), if the road is completed to the main road between Emery's Mills and Wells Depot. April 14, the proposition to subscribe $15,000 was lost. The meeting of April 25 was adjourned to the 27th. On that day, Asa Low's motion to subscribe $20,000 contained two provisos : "That ten or more citizens or responsible parties should give bonds to take and pay for said stock at fifty cents on the dollar of its cost ; and that if $10,000 were received from the state as equalization of bounties, the bonds thus received should be used instead of bonds to be issued." This was lost, two yeas, one hundred and eighty-two nays.

Between May 25 and June 4, nine different meetings were held, at each of which the vote was unanimously against taking any stock in the road. To prevent the calling of such frequent meetings, it was voted, on June 4, on motion of Charles F. Moulton, that for all future special town meetings, until otherwise directed, the warrant must he posted at least three months before the day named for the meeting.

The railroad matter thereupon rested until May 31, 1869, when a motion to transfer the bonds that may be received on account of the equalization of the war debt, to the Portland and Rochester Railroad was negatived, one hundred and seventy-two yeas to one hundred and forty-six nays. A month later, June 29, it was voted to exchange the state bonds due the town of Sanford for stock in the railroad, a vote which was reconsidered and rescinded the following February, thereby finally disposing of the matter which had so long disturbed the community.

The telegraph along this road was completed to Springvale from Portland, December 19, 1870.

In the spring of 1871, a platform car just unloaded and standing on the rails, at the foot of Deering Pond, a mile west of Springvale, but detached from the engine and other cars, was discovered by the work-men to be sinking. The rails bent downward, and all went down to-gether. The car could not be found the next day, nor was it ever seen afterward. The depression was soon filled with stone and gravel, and in a week or two, the engine and cars ran back.

In due time the Portland and Rochester road was absorbed by the Boston and Maine system. In 1880, a railroad from Springvale to the Corner was proposed, and a survey of the routes suggested was made in December of that year, but the project went no farther.

The Mousam River Electric Railway Company, already mentioned as one of the Goodall enterprises, was organized July 18, 1892, and began carrying passengers and transporting freight in March of 1893. The authorized capital of the company is $200,000. This road was among the very first in New England to inaugurate the trans-portation of freight by means of electrical power, and to adopt the electric system of heating. The present officers are: E. M. Good-all, President; L. B. Goodall, Clerk and Treasurer. By means of this road the villages of Sanford and Springvale have been brought into closer commercial and social relationship, while the cost of freight and passenger transportation has been very materially reduced.

The Sanford and Cape Porpoise Railway Company was organized in 1897, and began operations on August 1st of 1899. Its capital is $250,000, and the existing official board is composed of E. M. Goodall, President; Frank Hopewell, Vice President; L. B. Good-all, Clerk and Treasurer. This railway is one of the most modern in the country in the matter of equipment, and its road-bed one of the finest in New England. The entire length of the road from ter-minal to terminal, including sidings, is twenty-five miles. Like the Mousam River Railway, the Sanford and Cape Porpoise transports both passengers and freight. Its southern terminus at Cape Porpoise is one of the most exclusive and picturesque spots on the Atlantic seaboard, and with the advent of railway facilities, is rapidly growing in popularity as a summer resort. Under government appropriation, a vast amount of work is being accomplished with a view to improv-ing the harbor so that connection may be made with freight and pas-senger vessels to be operated by a new corporation in which Goodall enterprise is again displayed, and for which charter rights have al-ready been granted.

The route followed by the Sanford and Cape Porpoise line to which the Mousam River road has been leased, is from Sanford proper, through South Sanford, Lyman, West Kennebunk, Kennebunk Vil-

lage, to connection with the New Atlantic Shore Line which the
Goodalls have been instrumental in constructing as far as Kennebunkport, and will extend to a junction with the Portsmouth, Kittery
and York Electric Railway at Ogunquit, thence to the southern ter-
minal at Cape Porpoise.

At the Old Falls of the Mousam, seven miles south of Sanford, and
from which the power to operate this road, as well as the Mousam
River road, is derived, pleasure grounds have been arranged, supplied
with an open air theatre and dancing pavilions, the forests surrounding this section forming a beautiful natural park system. Already
this spot rivals the beaches as a picnic and outing rendezvous during
the summer months, and when contemplated improvements are completed, it will become one of the most attractive pleasure grounds in
New England.

At West Kennebunk, connection is effected with trains to and
from Portland and Boston, over the Eastern division of the Boston
and Maine Railroad, while at Kennebunk Village, a loop runs through
Storer Street to Main ; the main line continuing along Fletcher Street
to a junction with the loop line, and thence by the way of Summer
Street to the Western Division station of the Boston and Maine Railroad, where connection is made with that division and with the Kennebunkport branch of the Boston and Maine. The trip through Kennebunk Landing, and to the Cape, or over the intersecting line of the
Atlantic Shore road to Kennebunkport, is full of interest, revealing
as it does, odd examples of ancient and modern architecture, and new
beauties of nature, glimpses of forest primeval, stretches of seashore
with shifting sands, cosy summer retreats, and the broad expanse of
old ocean, at every turn of the wheels.

CHAPTER XXXII.

FIRE HISTORY.

Record of Fires from 1754 — The Big Conflagration of 1878 — Fire
Department — Water Supply — Electric Alarm System.

FIRES were a source of dread to the settlers of the frontier towns
With no adequate means at hand of fighting the flames, and
generally with no suitable water supply convenient, the work of
months would be wiped out almost in a twinkling. For years the
"bucket brigade" was the only source of protection against the devouring element, and as can be inferred from the records that follow,
its efforts were only too often of no avail. Sanford was for many
years without a fire department or engines, and suffered much, but
with the increased growth and responsibilities of the last two decades,
the town has placed herself in the front rank in this as well as in all
other matters pertaining to the public weal.

No details are given us of the first fire in the settlement, which
took place on settler's lot number ten, occupied by the pioneer clergyman of Phillipstown. Mention of it, however, is found in the proprietors' records.

A chronological list, without pretensions to completeness, of the
more important fires in Sanford, is herewith presented :

1754. (Probably.) Rev. Samuel Chandler's house was burnt. On
November 22 of that year, the proprietors voted, " That Rev. Mr.
Samuel Chandler be indulged with one year more to complete the
settlement of his lot according to condition of his deed, in consideration of house he built having been consumed with fire."

1764. October 29. Cane's saw-mill, South Sanford, with two
thousand feet of boards and one thousand feet of plank, was destroyed by an incendiary. Loss, one hundred and fifty pounds. John
Powers went out in the evening for water, and, seeing a light like
the flash of a gun, discovered the mill all afire.

1784 or 1785. Josiah Norton, Mouse Lane, lost his house, probably by fire. The town voted, March 8, 1785, to give him the rates
against him, on account of his losing his house.

1805. March (?). Jonathan Tebbets, Junior, lost his house. It was two-story, built by Samuel Colley, and occupied by Abraham Crosby. It stood near Bert Goodrich's.

1809. August 31. A grist-mill, at the Corner, on the site of Number Two mill, was burnt.

1817. November 24. The Chadbourn mill at the Corner was destroyed by fire.

1821. October. About ten o'clock one evening a fire caught in the ell of John Paul's house, Mount Hope road, and entirely consumed the house. Theodosia Paul, then a baby in the cradle was almost forgotten, and Josiah Paul narrowly escaped being burned to death.

A school-house on Shaw's ridge, near the Madison Shaw place, was burnt before 1822.

1826. Spring. Willard's saw-mill, South Sanford.

1837. December 11. A school-house at Springvale.

1838. Hutchinson, Sawyer and Co's factory at the Corner.

183-. Shaw, Paine and Co's factory at the Corner.

184-. Dennis Hatch's blacksmith shop at the Corner.

1843. August. Thatcher Jones's barn, at Mouse Lane, was struck by lightning, and consumed with hay and tools.

1847. April 30. School-house in district number twelve, was burned by an incendiary.

184-. The Baptist meeting-house was set on fire under the porch, but the fire was extinguished without much damage.

1848. June 15. The old meeting-house at South Sanford was destroyed by incendiarism about nine o'clock in the evening.

1849. February 19. The ell of William Miller's factory at the Corner. The fire caught in the picker one afternoon, but was stayed by pulling down the ell. By the timely exertions of the people, the main building was saved. Loss, $500; covered by insurance. The fire occurred on an intensely cold afternoon.

1851. August 2. Dennis Hatch's blacksmith shop was entirely destroyed by fire about three o'clock in the morning. A store contiguous, occupied as a shoemaker's shop, and a shed belonging to James M. Burbank, were burnt; also, a small store. Loss, $800.

1851. September 4. John Shaw's barn, Shaw's Ridge, was struck by lightning and consumed. Mr. Shaw and his son Daniel, were in the barn, but escaped uninjured. They attempted to stay the flames in the hay, but to no purpose.

1851. September 30. About midnight, a two-story house, unoc-

cupied, owned by Mr. Goodwin of Lawrence, was burned at Spring.
vale.

185–. Harriet Allen's house, with ell and store. The fire caught
in the store, occupied by C. H. Bennett, and totally consumed his
stock. Most of Mrs. Allen's furniture was saved.

185–. Ivory Clark's barn at South Sanford.

185–. A meeting-house at Mouse Lane. Incendiary.

185–. A school-house at Oak Hill.

185–. Joshua Littlefield's shoe-shop at the Corner caught fire
around the chimney, and was destroyed.

1852. Edwin A. Moultou's carriage-manufactory, with carriages,
stock, and tools, at Springvale, was burnt. Loss, $1,000 ; insurance,
$844.

1852. January 19. George A. Willard's tin-shop, Springvale.

1853. February 22. Nearly all of the Print Works at Springvale
was destroyed by an incendiary. The dry-house and another building were likewise destroyed at a later day.

1854(?). William Gowen's house, standing at the forks of the
road on Mount Hope, was burnt January 18, 1854, says one of his
daughters. (The writer thinks that the fire occurred as late as 1856
or 7 ; as January, 1857, came in on Thursday, the 18th was Sunday,
and the house was burnt on Sunday.) The fire is supposed to have
caught from turpentine on mantel-piece behind the stove and over
the fire-place, in both of which there had been fires the evening previous. It was discovered about two o'clock Sunday morning, during
a heavy snow-storm. Everything was lost. No insurance. Loss,
$500.

1855. August 15 (?). John Nowell's house, Mount Hope, was
burnt about ten o'clock at night. It caught in the shed, probably
from ashes containing fire. It was discovered by one of his daughters, who heard what seemed to her to be rain falling, and got up
a second time, to see the flames bursting out through the shed. A
part of the furniture was saved. Loss, $1,500 to $2,000.

1856. April 14. William Gowen lost his house and barn by fire,
between two and three o'clock in the afternoon. Cause, a defective
chimney. Loss, $600. This house was on " Hardscrabble."

1857. June 20. A fire occurred on the corner of Main and Lebanon streets, on Sunday morning, burning out Moses B. Greenhalgh's
dry-goods store, Monroe Cook's shoe-store, and Sanborn's saddler's
shop. The fire caught in Cook's store, and is supposed to have been
the work of an incendiary. Dr. Dam's office was in one of the build-

ings. Greenhalgh estimated his loss at $2,500. John W. Frost's store was torn down to prevent the spread of the fire. William Emery, James M. Burbank, and Nathaniel Hobbs were appointed a committee to investigate and report whether the town was liable to pay Mr. Frost for store damaged.

1857. December 27. The Victory Mills was burnt Sunday morning. It had been idle several months, but a man had been employed to look after the machinery, and so it is questionable whether the fire was the result of carelessness or incendiarism.

1859 or 1860. An unoccupied house, formerly the Kendall store, owned by William H. Frost, and standing on the street back of the Baptist meeting-house, at Springvale, was burnt. Loss, $600; insurance, $400.

1862. June 30. About half-past eleven o'clock in the evening, the grist-mill at the Corner, James O. Clark's, was discovered to be on fire, and was completely destroyed. Probably caught from overheated machinery. Insured for $750.

1863. Spring. James O. Clark's saw-mill caught fire from a stove, and was entirely consumed.

1864 or 1865. A dwelling-house owned and occupied by Jacob Ellis on the Hartwell place, South Sanford, was burnt.

1865. December. Sometime during the week before the 23d, a fire was discovered in the barn of William Gowen, on "Grammar Street," which destroyed it, together with hay, one cow, two heifers, and fifteen hens. Loss, $250 to $300; insurance, $50. It was Mr. Gowen's second loss by fire. Origin, unknown.

1866. April 14. Saturday night. Increase S. Kimball's store at the Corner was burnt. It was occupied by Jonas K. Dorman, merchant, I. S. Kimball, lawyer, and the post-office. It was a total loss, though Mr. Dorman had his goods partially insured.

1867. September 27. The Parker Gowell house near the Lebanon line was burned.

1869. August 25. Monsieur R. Merrifield's buildings were burnt. They consisted of house, two barns, and shed. Hay, farming utensils, and household furniture were consumed. Loss, $2,500 to $3,000. Insured $1,500 in a worthless company. The barn, evidently set on fire, was all aflame when discovered between two and three o'clock in the morning.

We have knowledge of the following fires, of which the dates are not known : Moulton's mill, Mouse Lane; Estes's mill, Mouse Lane;

Moses S. Moulton's house, South Sanford; the pest house, near Chapman's brook; the Province mill, Springvale, burned twice, once by an incendiary; Dr. A. W. Dam's office, Springvale; William H. Brown's buildings, Deering neighborhood; and the Trafton Phillips house at the " Branch," occupied by Simon Bennett.

1871. April. Christopher Shackford's house, occupied by Simon Bennett, was burned on Fast Day.

1871. October. Mrs. Theodore Willard's house, shed, and barn, at Springvale, were burnt. Loss, $3,000. Insured $1,400.

1873. June 17. A fire caught in the ell of Nahum Littlefield's house at the Corner, and burnt his house and barn, and Increase S. Kimball's house. It broke out about three o'clock in the afternoon, during a high wind, which, fortunately, changed, thus preventing a more serious conflagration. Mr. Kimball's furniture and the greater part of Mr. Littlefield's and Mr. Dorman's were saved. Loss, $4,000; insurance, $2,600. This fire led to the organization of a fire company of forty-five men.

1875. Stephen Lord's barn in the Deering neighborhood.

1876. February 24. About nine o'clock Thursday evening, Dr. Brooks's house caught fire in the attic, probably from a defective or overheated chimney, which had been on fire during the afternoon, and was wholly consumed, though his furniture was saved. A small building, occupied by D. D. Ricker, just south, was torn down. Insured.

1877. March 8, Thursday. Garnsey and Goodall's picker caught fire. Part of the roof of the storehouse was also burnt.

1877. October 10. Wednesday night. A house occupied by George Goodwin, near the Deering meeting-house, was burnt. Furniture mostly saved. Insured.

1877. October 17. A fire caught in the front entry clothes-press of a house occupied by Harry Downing, near Jordan's mill and burnt into a chamber, but was soon extinguished.

1878. February 5. Emery and Bodwell's bakery at the Corner caught fire in the attic. The damage, all inside, was slight. In March, the bakery was again on fire.

1878. March 16. The house, shed, and barn, owned by Mrs. Theodosia (Paul) Moulton, or by her son, were wholly consumed. The house stood on the site of the Paul house burnt in 1821.

1878. March 26. Frank Beal's house, corner of Mill and Paine streets, Springvale, together with furniture and clothing, was burnt. The fire caught from a stove-pipe passing through a closet. Mr.

Crooker, living in the house saved most of his furniture, however. Insurance, $800 on the house, but nothing on Beal's furniture.

1878. July 1. The most disastrous conflagration that had ever been witnessed in Sanford occurred on Monday afternoon and evening. The fire caught in the northerly end of Nowell's block, occupied by Nowell and Libby, merchants, Stiles and Hersom, manufacturers of clothing, and J. Charnley, shoemaker, which, owing to the intense dryness of the building and the lack of fire apparatus, was in one vast flame in a few minutes. From this the fire spread in both directions, to Prescott Emery's store and tin-shop above, and to the bakery of Emery, Bodwell and Co. below. Then William Miller's house adjoining the tin-shop caught fire, and an attempt was made to blow it up with gunpowder to stay the flames but without success. Then the two churches, the Congregational on the north, and the Baptist on the south, fell a prey to the devouring element. The steeple of the former was the first to take fire, and the flames rapidly worked downward. Amid the fire and smoke and heat, the bell kept ringing the fire-alarm until the rope burnt off and came down. Meanwhile Prescott Emery's stable and the ice-houses in rear of the store and bakery had been destroyed, and a small dwelling-house owned by Thomas Goodall and occupied by John Clayton had been torn down in part to prevent the further spread of the fire northward. Fortunately, the wind changed. But the doors of the Weld barn on the opposite side of the street were opened, and the sparks set that on fire and it was burnt, with the house adjoining. Thus thirteen buildings were consumed — two churches, two stores, three dwellings, three barns, one bakery, and two ice-houses. Loss, $20,000 to $25,000; insurance, $11,400. Prescott Emery lost $6,000, insured, $3,200; William Miller's loss, $1,500; insurance, $1,000; Stiles and Hersom's loss, $3,000 to $4,000, insurance, $2,700; Nowell and Libby had $1,500 insurance on their stock, and Samuel Nowell, $3,000 on his block and bake-shop; the Knights of Pythias, whose hall was in Nowell's block, had $500 insurance on their furniture. The Sanford Mills had $15,000 worth of goods stored in the Congregational vestry, all of which were saved except $1,500 worth of camel's hair and $1,500 worth of goods. Increase S. Kimball's house and barn valued at $2,500, and Emery, Bodwell and Co's stock, valued at $4,000, were not insured, neither were the meeting-houses and their organs. The engine did good work after it got under way, and it was a fortunate thing that the hose of the Sanford Mills reached to the top of the hill.

1878. October 15. The Charles Emery house on Oak street,

HON. I. S. KIMBALL.

Springvale, near the railroad crossing, was damaged to the amount of $200. Covered by insurance. Cause, lamp upsetting.

1878. December 19. H. Downing's house, formerly owned by C. E. Butler, was destroyed by fire, caused by a defective chimney. Furniture saved. House insured.

1878. December 22 or 23. The double house of Stephen H. and Joel E. Moulton, and the barn of the latter were burnt at South Sanford. The fire caught in Joel's barn. Stephen's barn was saved by tearing down a shed. Part of the furniture was saved. Insurance on house, $1,600.

1879. January 22. The picker-room of the Mousam River Mills suffered slightly from fire.

1879. May. The roof of the new Congregational meeting-house caught fire from pot used while tinning. There was a high wind, and the fire was discovered just in time to prevent a repetition of the conflagration of the preceding summer.

1879. June 6. The Moon house was struck by lightning and burnt to the ground. It was owned by the Portland and Rochester Railroad Company, and occupied by Charles Ogden. The fire consumed $600 worth of rags, upon which there was an insurance of $300.

1879. August 31. William B. Emery's house, South Sanford, was burnt. The lower part was cleared of furniture. Insured $650.

1879. During the summer, a barn owned by James and John Allen, at Oak Hill, was burned.

1879. November 14. Charles Merrill's barn, farming tools, and several tons of hay were burnt by an incendiary, in the Deering neighborhood. No insurance.

1879. December 23. Edmund Goodwin's shop, with a pung and set of carpenter's tools, was destroyed by fire. Loss estimated at $200, without insurance.

1881. January 21. There was a slight fire in the machine shop of the Mousam River Mills.

1881. March 21. The dry-house of the Mousam River Mills was slightly damaged by fire.

1881. July 12. About eleven o'clock Tuesday night, the stable and house of Mrs. Stephen A. Hersom and Mrs. Smith, Springvale, were burnt. Loss, $2,500; insurance, $2,000. The house and store of Moses Dennett, the store of George A. Frost, and the stock of I. B. Stiles were damaged by the fire, but were fully insured.

1881. November 23. The Gowen house on the Lebanon road,

21

near the Corner, owned by Simon Tebbets, and occupied by Mrs. Eunice Joy, was wholly destroyed by fire. Cause, unknown, but supposed to have caught from the fireplace during her absence.

1881. December 14. The dry-house connected with S. Benton Emery's furniture store at the Corner, was burnt.

1882. September 19. The Mousam Mills dry-room was damaged about $100 by fire.

1882. December 29. The studding between the walls of Miss E. J. Andrews's millinery store, Springvale, caught fire from a defective chimney, doing but little damage.

1882. During the fall, a dwelling-house at Mouse Lane, owned by Isaiah Linscott, and occupied until the day of the fire at nine o'clock in the evening, was burned. Probably incendiary.

1883. May 26. During a high wind, fire caught on the roof of Joseph H. Moulton's house, South Sanford, but owing to the coolness of Mrs. Moulton was extinguished with a few buckets of water.

1883. July 29. A house and barn containing a cow and a pig, belonging to Fairfield Butler, were burnt.

1883. October 3. By the explosion of a lamp in Hill and Gowen's market at the Corner, a window-casing was set on fire, but was extinguished with but little damage.

1883. October 4. Emery and Batchelder's stable floor caught fire from the hot coals of a stove put into the stable the night before. Discovered in the morning.

1883. November 28. The dwelling-house of James Wilson, well known as the Nathaniel Chadbourn house, was totally destroyed by fire. Cause, a defective chimney.

1884. October 31. An employe at the Mousam River Mills weave room filled a lighted kerosene lamp, with the old result. An alarm was rung, but fortunately the fire was smothered with blankets, and the services of the fire department were not required.

1884. November 5. About eleven o'clock at night the blacksmith shop of Samuel R. Day, on Water Street, Springvale, was discovered to be a mass of flames. All efforts to extinguish the fire proved unavailing, and the shop and its contents were totally destroyed. A high wind prevailed. The fire was the work of an incendiary.

1885. October 27. Moulton Brothers' saw-mill was burned. Loss, $2,500; no insurance. Cause, unknown.

1886. December 31. A fire caused by a defective flue broke out in the Hovey Low house near the Freewill Baptist Church, in the tenement occupied by Frank N. Butler, who lost considerable furniture.

1887. April 16. Shortly before midnight a fire was discovered in the old bowling alley just below Hotel Hanson. The dwelling-house, stable, and carriage-house adjoining were burned to the ground. Total loss, nearly $5,000. The house, owned by Mrs. David Welch, of Beverly, was only partially insured. William Merrill and Charles Ricker, occupants, lost considerable furniture. Captain Murray was also a loser by the destruction of the carriage-house. C. L. Bodwell lost billiard tables and other furniture.

1887. April 22. Fred Sargent's house was entirely consumed by fire between twelve and one o'clock in the morning.

1887. September 10. About two o'clock in the morning the store-house of Joseph Knight's corn factory, near the station, was discovered to be on fire. The flames had then obtained complete sway, and the building and its contents, empty cans and most of the corn packed during the season, were totally destroyed. Loss, $6,000; insurance, $3,000.

1887. September 20. A barn owned by Howard Frost, on Paine Street, was completely destroyed.

1887. October 23. The house of Atwood Allen caught fire from a defective chimney, and was completely destroyed. Loss, $1,000; insurance, $650.

1888. July 6. S. B. Emery's dry-house was burned. A high wind prevailed, but owing to the extra precautions against fire, the flames were extinguished. Loss about $500. No insurance.

1888. August 10. The picker room of the Mousam River mill was damaged by fire about $75.

1888. December 13. Sanborn's shook shop was burned to the ground.

1889. January 9. A fire caught near the boiler in Wingate's drug store. The damage by fire was confined to one partition, though the apartments of Messrs. Twombly and Mr. Boocock were damaged by smoke and water.

1889. September 18. A two-story building belonging to the Nasson heirs in Springvale, occupied by Andrew Hilton, fruit-dealer, and by Miss Lord as a tenement, was discovered on fire in the basement at two o'clock in the morning, but the flames were extinguished with small damage. The fire was evidently an incendiary, as the building was saturated with kerosene.

1890. January 29. The mixing mill of the Mousam River Mills was gutted by fire. Loss $3,000. No insurance. It caught from the picker.

1890. May 5. Joshua Littlefield's buildings took fire from a defective chimney and burned to the ground. No insurance.

1890. August 2. Three houses on Mill Street, Springvale, were destroyed by fire. They belonged to the Springvale Cotton Mills, the heirs of Samuel Willard, and D. C. Ingraham. Loss, $5,000, covered in part by insurance. The fire caught from matches, with which some boys were playing in a shed adjoining the block.

1890. August 5. Fogg's shoe factory caught fire, from a cigar stub carelessly thrown away by some employe, as it is supposed, and it grew to be quite a blaze before it was extinguished.

1890. November 17. A barn on Main Street near the railroad, owned by Thomas Makin, and occupied by Frank Fellows, was set on fire about six o'clock in the morning by an overturned lantern, and consumed. The house adjoining was partially destroyed.

1891. April 9. The new steam mill of the Hutchins Brothers was burned between nine and eleven o'clock in the evening. Total loss; insured.

1891. May 6. The sheds attached to the Arcade Block, Springvale, were burned, and the block damaged. The Advocate office, B. P. Hamilton's harness store, and Hamilton Brothers' barber shop were thoroughly drenched. "The condition of a printing office after such a visitation can be better imagined than described," says the Advocate.

1891. September 27. Simon Littlefield's barn, together with some live stock therein, was burned by an incendiary.

1892. May 1. Sunday evening, Frank Broggi's store (the old Deacon Frost store), R. A. Kempton's building and stable, Smith's photograph gallery, and Haigh's restaurant, occupied by C. F. Tebbets, were burned, and other buildings slightly damaged. Loss estimated at $7,700; insurance, about $4,500. The Broggi store was owned by Hon. I. S. Kimball.

1892. June 12. E. K. Bennett's building, occupied by the American Express Company, W. S. Lord, harness maker, and Miss Cook, dressmaker, was damaged.

1892. November 24. Thanksgiving morning, at half past nine o'clock, Mill Number Six was burned. It was fifty feet wide and one hundred and fifty feet long, and contained the carding, weaving and dyeing departments of the blanket manufactory. The origin of the fire was the friction of a large belt over a wooden wheel. Total loss estimated at $120,000, including $40,000 on stock in the process of manufacture, and $80,000 on building and machinery; insured for

$70,000. The mill was built in 1874. By its destruction one hundred and twenty-five persons were thrown out of employment.

1893. January 18. For the second time within two months the mills at Sanford Corner were visited by fire. Wednesday morning, between two and three o'clock, the dyeing and finishing mill of the Goodall Worsted Company, and a dwelling near by were burned. The loss was estimated at $100,000, covered by insurance. It was a bitter cold morning, and the firemen had a severe fight to save the boiler-house, which furnished power for the rest of the corporation. A week after this fire, the balance-wheel of the Sanford Mill Company's engine in Mill Number One burst, and pieces were hurled through the air. One fragment, weighing one hundred and thirty-five pounds, was sent as far as the junction of Allen and Washington Streets. Another piece, of one hundred and seventeen pounds, passed through the side of the mixing mill, and up through the floors. Strange to say, no one was injured.

1893. July 25. Shortly before midnight, the laundry of Roberts and Co., situated near Butler and Clark's shoe factory at Springvale, was burnt. Loss about $1,700; partially insured.

1893. September 19. Frank Broggi's fruit store was set on fire on the outside, but was fortunately discovered in time to prevent serious damage.

1894. January 17. Jeremiah Moulton's house, on Pleasant Street, was completely destroyed, about two o'clock in the morning. Insurance, $1,100. The Pillsbury brothers' house near by was badly damaged.

1894. February 3. Nahum Day's barn at East Sanford, with four oxen, four cows, thirty-five sheep, and thirty-five tons of hay, was totally destroyed. Cause, unknown. Loss, $1,500.

1894. June 26. Between twelve and one o'clock Tuesday morning the box mill near the railroad bridge over the Mousam was burned. It was occupied for about two years by the Springvale Wood and Paper Box Company, but for about the same length of time was unoccupied. The fire was undoubtedly of incendiary origin. The building was owned by the Sanford Loan and Building Association. Insurance, $1,000.

1894. July 21. Houses on Cross and Emery Streets were damaged by lightning.

1894. December 11. The Joe Bean house, Mount Hope, owned by Herbert Welch was burned. It was undergoing repairs, and the fire is supposed to have caught from an overheated stove.

1895. January 23. The house of George Jacobs of South Sanford was destroyed by fire between one and three o'clock in the morning. Mr. Jacobs and his family had a narrow escape, the former's hands, face, and feet being badly burned and terribly blistered.

1895. February 16. A barn containing a horse, a pig, and five tons of hay, owned by John E. Greenwood was burned.

1895. April 22. The ell of James Phillips's house at South Sanford caught fire, and was badly damaged, but the house was saved by the timely assistance of a fishing party from Springvale.

1895. July 24. The two-story house and barn owned by Charles B. Jacobs of South Sanford were burned. The property was set afire by children playing with matches in the barn.

1896. January 14. Amos Lord's house burned.

1896. January 22. Abby Taylor's house burned.

1896. January 25. Destruction of Frank Bean's house by fire.

1896. February 25. William Wilson's picture frame shop was burned.

1896. March 19. Porell's store was partially destroyed by fire.

1897. February 10. John Brierly's blacksmith shop was gutted by fire.

1897. October 3. Frank Bodwell's house at Springvale burned.

1899. February 9. Otis R. Willard's two-tenement block burned.

1899. May 12. Mrs. Adriel Thompson's house burned.

1899. July 20. Two-tenement block owned by the Sanford Mills burned.

1899. September 29. The post-office block was burned at two o'clock in the morning, causing a total loss of $16,000. The building was owned and occupied on the ground floor by Leavitt and Co., dry goods and grocery dealers. The fire started from some cause unknown, and at one time the firemen thought they had it under control, but the flames broke out again, and before they were subdued the loss was practically total. Leavitt and Co's loss was $10,000 on stock and about $5,000 on the building. The post-office did not contain a large quantity of mail and the loss to the government was not heavy. The offices of the Loan and Building Association were on the upper floors and most of their property was burned. The building and contents were insured.

1900. September 25. Charles Bedell's house at Springvale was burnt.

1900. October 17. Johnson Brothers' laundry burnt.

From the records it appears, although there was an engine in town at an earlier date, that in May, 1887, an engine, two Babcock extinguishers, and eight hundred feet of hose were purchased. E. F. Davenport was chairman of the fire apparatus committee.

In April 1887, a company was formed to be attached to Deluge Fire Engine No. 1, and officers were elected as follows: Foreman, F. A. Goodall; Assistant Foreman, Elmer D. Bennett; Clerk and Treasurer, C. E. Twombly; Foreman of Suction Hose, Augustus Houle; Foreman of Leading Hose, Nathaniel Bennett.

Prior to May 20, 1887, the Dirigo Fire Company was organized at Springvale, with E. F. Davenport, Foreman; F. O. Goodwin and R. G. Mansell, Assistants; B. P. Hamilton, Clerk; and Eben Libby, Treasurer.

Sanford village at present enjoys fire protection from two well organized companies, the Sanford Mills Company, of which Eugene Gerry is Foreman, and the Alert Hose Company, with A. E. Garnsey as Foreman. The former has its engine house at the mills, and is equipped with a powerful steam fire engine, hose carriages, ladder truck, and an abundant supply of hose. The Alert's machine is a hand engine, and they also have a hose wagon, with plenty of hose, and a ladder truck. The engine house is on Nasson Street. At Springvale is the Dirigo Fire Company, Fred Shackley, Foreman, fully equipped with hand engine and other apparatus, which is kept at the engine house on Bridge Street. The fire wardens for 1900 are: For Springvale, H. B. Rowe, A. J. Fernald, Alvah Garvin; for Sanford, Orrin Roberts, Samuel Littlefield, C. O. Emery, Second.

At the Corner the water supply comes from a spring near the power station of the Mousam River Railroad, which is pumped into the stand pipe situated on Chadbourn's Hill, east of the village. The pipe is forty feet in diameter, and sixty feet in height, giving a pressure in the village of about sixty pounds. There are hydrants at nearly all the street corners, and the system can be instantly connected with the service at the mills.

Springvale is supplied by two water companies, the Springvale Aqueduct Company, and the Butler Spring Water Company. The former had its beginnings in the summer of 1876, when Samuel D. Tebbets, John A. Dennett, Moses Dennett, and Stephen M. Hersom formed themselves into a company, and laid a pipe from Littlefield's pond, a mile and a quarter north of Springvale, and east of the Mousam, down to and through the river, and up to Main Street, thus bringing water of an excellent quality into the village. The Springvale Aqueduct Company was incorporated in 1878, and the enterprise has always proved a success. In September, 1890, the company laid a six-inch iron main from Littlefield's pond. C. H. Pierce is President of the corporation at the present time. The Butler Spring Water Company was organized April 17, 1889, with a capital of $25,000. Irving A. Butler was elected president, and has since held that office. This company takes water from the spring which gave the village its name. The water from both sources of supply is of remarkable purity.

The Gamewell electric fire alarm system has been installed in both villages during the past year. There are thirteen signal boxes in Sanford and eight in Springvale. The Sanford alarm is connected with a large steam gong or whistle at the mills, and Springvale's with the factory bell.

Mention may appropriately be made here of attempts other than the foregoing, to secure a water supply in the town. During the first part of the century there was no water fit for drinking purposes nearer than half a mile from the Baptist meeting-house, and in 1811 or 12 the society decided to help Deacon Eleazar Chadbourn build an aqueduct to his house on the west (?) side of the Hobbs road several rods from the church. The principal men of the church and society who helped were Gideon and William Deering, Thomas and William Worster, Stephen and Sheldon Hobbs, Daniel Bean, and Zebulon Beal. Many others gave work and timber. The water was brought in bored logs, from a spring on a hill, on the right hand side of the Hobbs road. It was on Deacon Chadbourn's land, and the water came into his porch, where it was drawn from a wooden faucet. It was also carried to his barnyard. Over the log at the spring, a pewter platter pierced full of holes was fastened to prevent dirt from going into the log. All that went to the Baptist meeting were at liberty to go to Deacon Chadbourn's on Sunday to get water to drink.

An iron tank, six feet in diameter, was sunk during 1886 under the band stand, and connected with the Sanford Mills force pump, by a four-inch pipe, and with several hydrants on the street, to be used in case of fire. The cost was paid by contributions.

In 1887 a company was formed to furnish Sanford Corner with water, from the " cold spring " in Charles O. Emery's field, west of the village. An analysis of the water showed that it was entirely free from organic matter, and of remarkable purity.

In 1888 a reservoir was built in W. H. Nason's pasture.

CHAPTER XXXIII.

MEMORABLE OCCURRENCES.

Freshets on the Mousam River — Natural Phenomena — Extremes of Weather —Heavy Snow-Storms — Epidemics of Small-Pox and Other Diseases — Violent Deaths.

FRESHETS along the Mousam River have done great damage from time to time, especially to the bridges. Bourne says: " October 21, 1755, a great freshet, surpassing any which had been known before or since, carried away every mill on the Mousam River. The water rose to the height of eleven feet."

In October, 1785, another great freshet occurred. Four days, from the 20th to the 23d, it rained, but " two days and nights it rained without cessation, as powerfully as was ever known." It swept away mills and dams and bridges, and did much damage to the roads and fences. At a town meeting, April 3, 1786, it was " voted to choose a committee to estimate the damage was done by the freshet last October," and Caleb Emery, Samuel Nasson, and Henry Smith were chosen for that purpose. They brought in a report fixing the total damage at nine hundred and forty-two pounds. Their report concludes :

" This being the Best information we can get and we after Consideration Cannot but think it is full low Considering how much the people Suffered in Delayes on account of the Bridges being Gone Could not go to Market."

The General Court was petitioned to grant relief to those towns along the Saco and the Mousam, which suffered most from this extraordinary freshet, and the prayer of the petitioners was granted by abating the taxes of seven towns. Those of Sanford were abated sixty pounds.

In 1793, Morrison's bridge was carried away. May 13. " Vot^d that the Selectmen are to direct^d to Give David morrison Some help out of other Destricts to Build a Bridge that was carried away by the freshet."

Another freshet occurred in 1814, and still another in May, 1843. The factory at Springvale sustained quite a loss, and was so damaged as to be considered unsafe. At the Corner the water spread over the whole surface above the bridges, and was about a foot deep upon and between the two bridges. The force with which the water flowed may be estimated from the fact that a huge rock supposed to weigh three tons was carried down the stream some fifty feet.

On the 14th of April, 1857, Willard's bridge and four or five others were carried away, and likewise the corporation blacksmith shop at Springvale.

The water rose so high on April 19, 1870, that it carried away all of the bridge at the Province mill, and most of the upper bridge.

In 1876, the dam of Number Three mill at the Corner was swept away, and the water flowed over the dam of the Springvale mills for the whole length, something never before known, filling the lower rooms to the depth of ten or twelve inches.

April 19, 1895, the Mousam rose to the same height it did in 1870.

1896. March 1. The greatest freshet on the Mousam that Sanford had seen since 1843 occurred on Sunday. At the foot of Washington Street the water ran over the dam to the depth of three feet, and at one time it was about up to the railroad bridge. The lower floors of some of the buildings of the Sanford Mills Company were flooded, and machinery ruined, doing several hundred dollars' worth of damage. The electric power house was crippled for several days. Numerous bridges were carried away or badly damaged. At Springvale, Charles H. C. Otis was drowned during the freshet. The monetary damage was figured at $5,000.

1900. February 12-13. Owing to a heavy rain, the Mousam River was flooded to a point within three inches of the high water mark of the freshet of 1896. Some bridges were carried away.

Natural Phenomena.—In 1761, droughts prevailed in this part of the state, and again in 1765, when aid was asked of the state by some towns.

1803. October 9. The snow fell to the depth of two feet, and drifted badly. The wind was so heavy that it uprooted first-growth trees and threw them across the roads. Teams at the Landing were delayed on the road and almost frozen. Some did not reach home till the storm was over. The people were entirely unprepared for it; their barns were full of unhusked corn, so they could not put up their cattle, and the poor creatures blinded and almost frozen rushed to the woods for shelter.[1]

Miss Carrie Hatch.

1806. June 6. There was a total eclipse of the sun, causing no little consternation. Mrs. Edmund Stackpole told the writer that she remembered the eclipse, having had to come home from school to her dinner, when it was so dark as to frighten her very much. The morning was bright and sunny, but after the eclipse came on, the stars appeared, and the birds ceased singing till it passed.

1806. In October, a terrific snow-storm occurred. The weather for some days previous to the 9th, when it began, was warm. Cattle, sheep, and hogs were in the pastures or woods. Corn was standing in the fields, and potatoes remained in the ground. Nobody was prepared for such an event. Many teams were hauling lumber to Berwick or Kennebunk. One man, a Mr. Ford, from the vicinity of Bauneg Beg, was barefooted, while driving his team to Quampegan Landing. The storm began at noon of the 9th, with thunder, lightning, and rain. Toward night a northeast wind blew with great violence, and snow fell to the depth of eighteen inches. The storm extended over New England, many vessels along the coast were damaged, and much timber was blown down in the forests. After the storm the weather was warm, the snow melted in the fields, though it remained in the woods till spring, and the farmers harvested their crops in good order. (The writer thinks this and the 1803 storm may be the same.)

1812. The summer was very cold. Frost killed the corn and potatoes. Corn brought two dollars and a half per bushel and pork twenty cents a pound.

1813. December 22. Remarkably clear atmosphere. A fire at Portsmouth lighted up the southwest horizon so that small objects could be picked up in the road at the Corner.

1815. May 18. (Some papers say Friday, May 19). It snowed five or six inches, and the snow lay on the ground till the next morning. The apple trees were in full bloom, people were planting their corn, and it had been a forward spring.

1816. This was a cold year, but there were sudden changes from cold to hot. It snowed in June, the season was dry, and there was frost every month of the year. There was not corn enough for seed the next year raised in town. The price of corn for consumption was two dollars a bushel, and of hay, thirty dollars a ton. Though cattle and sheep were reduced one-half, those wintered were nearly starved before spring. In June, spots appeared on the sun, and in July one very large spot. Some attributed the cold to the sun-spots, cutting off part of the heat.

1823. July 23. An earthquake was felt in this section.

1826. The spring and summer were dry. Towns suffered on account of grasshoppers. They moved in swarms, and consumed such grass as had leaves and the heads of herds-grass. When corn silked they ate the silk, and down into the ears, even. So numerous were they that the sun was obscured by clouds of them, like a fog. A storm drove them seaward, and large windrows of them were washed up on the coast. In their course they seemed to follow the Salmon Falls River.

1839. July 13. A hail storm of considerable severity passed over the town. Several fields of corn were damaged, and more than a hundred panes of glass broken.

The winter of 1843 was very cold, except January. The cold weather set in the latter part of November, 1842. From twelve to fifteen feet of snow fell. On the 20th of April, the snow was deep and solid ; there was very good sleighing, with little bare ground. Two days later wagons were used.

An earthquake occurred on August 25, 1846.

The winter of 1846-7 was one of excellent sleighing and sledding. It began December 11, 1846, and lasted till April 1, 1847, with just snow enough to keep the ground well covered, and without a single day during the winter that a team could not work. From April 14 to 16 it was very cold. Water froze four inches in thickness, in tubs, and Mousam pond froze over. On the 19th of April, 1847, six inches of snow fell, and less than seven months later the first snow of the following season occurred. By eight o'clock Sunday morning, November 14 (?), three or four inches covered the ground.

1869. Friday, October 22. Earthquake felt.

1876-77. Snow, six feet, seven inches ; two feet less than in 1875-76.

1878. Tuesday, January 8. Thirty-one degrees below zero.

1880. Tuesday, March 29. Earthquake shock.

1881. July 10. One hundred and three degrees in the shade.

1881. Tuesday, September 6. The celebrated " yellow day."

1883. January 26. Twenty degrees below zero.

1883. November 12. Monday night, a heavy wind blew down chimneys, telegraph poles, trees, and Mr. Goodall's windmill, and broke glass to some extent.

1885. November 25 and 26. Fourteen inches of snow fell.

1886. On the 2nd and 6th of January, plowing was done by two different persons. By way of contrast, less than a week later, the thermometer dropped to the following figures : January 11th, fourteen degrees below zero ; 12th, twenty below ; and 13th, thirty below.

1888. The mercury fell seventy-one degrees during the twenty-four hours beginning at five o'clock in the morning of February 15.

1888. March 12. Twenty-six inches of snow fell during the blizzard.

1889. February 23. Sunday. The coldest day of the season, the mercury registering twenty-two degrees at seven o'clock in the morning.

1889. April 20. A hail-storm passed over Sanford, doing several hundred dollars damage. Hail-stones as large as hens' eggs fell, and a great many windows were broken. The glass roof of Hon. Thomas Goodall's conservatory was ruined. One hail-stone was an inch and three-fourths in diameter. It seems to have been central below Washington Street.

1889. June 15. The lightning struck the tower of the Baptist Church, tearing the shingles from all the corners of the upper part. It then passed down one corner of the tower, entered the church above the gallery, passed down the electric light wire, and utterly demolished the cluster of lamps near the door. It apparently passed off by the steam piping. Comparatively little damage was done. Several in the village (Corner) received shocks more or less severe.

1890. January 22. The fall of a very brilliant meteor was observed Wednesday evening. It fell about nine o'clock, and the whole western heavens were ablaze with light.

1890. August 19. A heavy rain and wind storm blew down, in part, R. A. Kempton's barn near Lebanon, injuring an ox so that it was necessary to kill the animal.

1894. April 11. Twelve inches of snow fell.

1894. September 2. " Yellow Sunday," similar to the " yellow day" of September 6, 1881.

1898. January 31. A blizzard prevailed in this section, and Sanford was cut off from the outside world for a day or two. Steam and electric car service was entirely stopped, and business generally was suspended. The heavy wind piled the snow up in drifts from two to fourteen feet deep. The storm was the worst for twenty-five years.

1898. November 26. Sanford did not suffer as much from the awful blizzard which caused the loss of the steamer City of Portland, as from some previous storms. The drifts were so deep in the outskirts, however, as to prevent the people there from reaching the villages for several days. The wind played considerable havoc, but caused no extensive damage.

Small-Pox and Other Epidemics. — There is a tradition that the small-pox, brought from Mast-bridge camp by a man named Johnson, raged in town about 1760. Several died, of whom two were buried in the pasture belonging to the heirs of William L. Emery, and others back of the Silas Moulton pasture. In this as in several other instances, tradition accords in part with the facts in the case. In 1761, Phillipstown was visited by a contagious and mortal distemper of the small-pox, so that a committee, consisting of Foxwell C. Cutts, Benjamin Chadbourn, and Capt. John Lord, was appointed by the Court of General Sessions, to furnish the inhabitants with physicians, nurses, and the necessaries of life. The distemper was brought among the said inhabitants by soldiers employed by the government in the expedition for the reduction of Canada. The names of the soldiers who brought it were Joseph Stanley, Edward Whitehouse, and John Whitehouse, who enlisted in March, 1760, in the above-named expedition, and returned in December of that year. Soon after they took or had the small-pox and died. The disease seems to have spread all over the colony, and a large number of towns were reimbursed for money paid out for nurses, medical attendance, etc. . At this time, Dorcas Goodridge was employed as a nurse, twenty-three days, at four shillings per day. Dr. Sayer served as physician, and Foxwell C. Cutts furnished twenty-six pounds of beef and pork at four pence per pound, in January.

The following petition was acted upon by the General Court:

" To his Excellency Francis Barnard Esq'' Captain General & Governour in Cheif in & over His Majesty's Province of the Massachusetts Bay &c The Honourable his Majesty's Council and House of Representatives for said Province in General Court Convened ye 25th Day of March 1761

" The Petition of Benjamin Harmon of Phillipstown in behalf of the Heirs & Orphans of Edward Whitehouse enlisted into his Majesty's Service Some Time in the Month of March last in Capt. Simon Jefferds's Company & Continued in the Service till he Return'd home which was Some time in Decem'' last & immediately after his Return home was taken sick with the small-pox of which he died & his Expences in the Time of his Sickness was Eight pounds Sixteen shillings & Nine pence according to the account herewith Exhibited wherefore your Petitioner humbly prays that the said Account May be allowed or as much as your Excellency & Honours in your Great Goodness shall think fit & your Petitioner as in Duty bound shall ever pray

BENJAMIN HARMON."

" The Com^{tee} Report Six pounds fifteen Shillings nine pence In full to be paid Doct^r Sayer for ye use of the Use of ye Peti^r

" W LAWRANCE p order"

Similar petitions for the heirs of Joseph Stanley and John Whitehouse were presented, and seven pounds, fifteen shillings, four pence, and six pounds eight shillings, respectively, of eleven pounds, twelve shillings, four pence, and nine pounds, thirteen shillings, asked, were granted.

In 17—, the throat distemper prevailed. Mrs. Linscott, of Mouse Lane, told Mrs. David Clark, mother of Abner Clark, that she lost several children by it, and that her nearest neighbors to call upon for assistance were John Stanyan's family.

The spotted-fever, or plague, as it was called, was prevalent in 1814–15. Parson Sweat records the deaths of sixteen persons, all young with one exception, between November 14 and March 11. Theodore Linscott lost three children in November, the 24th, 25th and 29th, and Joseph Paul, four in February, one on the 17th, the others on the 18th. The number of deaths is not known. The severity of the disease and the fatality of the distemper threw consternation among the people, and caused the stoutest heart to tremble. For months they rehearsed the sad and sickening details, and even more than three score years later the impressions of that season were fresh in the minds of a few of the older people. This account furnished by Rev. Nathaniel F. Nason, though incorrect as to time, may convey an idea of the character of the disease. " In 1813, the spotted-fever or plague, as it was called, went through Sanford. Seven of our family had it. Samuel was sick but a few days. He died. Fourteen days before he was buried he helped to carry three children from one family to the grave. They were put in one grave. My sister Mary was sick. She lived till June, 1814, then died. There were not well people enough to care for the sick. The fever ran thirty-six days. I had it. I was taken sick in January. I lost my reason. Miss Sarah Emery, Mr. Moses Garey's wife, made my grave clothes. I came to my senses in April. My arms, neck, and legs were sore with fly blisters. I had a large number of boils on my neck, under each ear, over one eye, on one thumb, on both legs. My teeth turned black, my under jaw was twisted, one tooth did not cover the other. Many died who did not suffer one hundredth part that I did. So fatal was the disease, many died in a few hours. Blood-letting was fatal, none that were bled lived."

The small-pox broke out in the spring of 1846, in the hotel kept by James M. Burbank, at Springvale. It spread quite rapidly, and a large number of cases of small-pox and varioloid was reported. Dr. Brooks says there were fifty or sixty cases, though that seems to be an exaggeration. A hospital was established in the Beatle (Bedell) house, near the Chapman brook, and several patients were carried there for treatment. In the majority of cases, however, the sick were cared for at their own homes. Nurses who had had the small-pox were employed, and every thing that could be done was done for the afflicted, though through fear and excitement some things may not have been well done. Only one case proved fatal, that of Betsey, the eleven-year-old daughter of Deacon William L. Emery. The town took stringent precautions to prevent the spread of the disease and to exterminate the same.

It was at this time that a company of young men at the Corner built a fence across the road above John Storer's, and surmounted it with a red flag bearing this inscription, " Small-pox, don't come." It did not keep travel away, for the next day, Sunday, the people as was their custom, rode down to church, turning out into the field to get around the fence. Nor did it prevent the small-pox from coming, for one of the young men was shortly after taken down with the disease.

In 1860, there were some ten or twelve cases of the small-pox, and on subsequent occasions there was a great scare when the disease prevailed. Although vaccination has counteracted this disease, and lessened the liability of the people thereto, and physicians have a better knowledge of it and the proper treatment thereof, a single case cannot occur without creating the greatest excitement, and giving rise to as wild and unfounded reports as those which were circulated in 1846. This statement can be substantiated by those who remember the exaggerated stories that were afloat when a single case occurred on School Street, in 1872. A wise precaution, however, is commended. Such was observed in 1885, during the prevalence of the small-pox in Montreal, when the selectmen provided " for the free vaccination with the cow-pox, of all the inhabitants over two years of age," by employing Drs. Durgin and Brooks to attend to this duty.

In 1861 and 62, the diphtheria raged to an alarming extent. This was a new disease, or an old epidemic, perhaps the throat-distemper, under a new name, and baffled at first the skill of the best physicians. The number of fatal cases was small.

No more severe bereavement have we to record than that which sadly afflicted the family of Mr. and Mrs. Joseph Shaw, of Shaw's ridge, in the winter of 1883–84. They had seven children, one son and six daughters, bright, attractive, intelligent, lovely, — a family to attract attention in any community. Five of the daughters and the babe of the oldest, Mrs. O. V. Libby, were taken away within two weeks, by that terrible disease, malignant diphtheria.

During six weeks between January and March, 1887, more than forty cases of pneumonia were reported in the town. Diphtheria was prevalent, with a number of fatal cases, in the fall.

During the winter of 1889–90, la grippe raged all over the country, its first appearance. The secretary of the local board of health estimated that there were more than two hundred cases in Sanford. The schools were closed by the advice of physicians.

Violent Deaths.—A few of the violent deaths occurring in town are here mentioned. Probably the first drowning in the settlement was prior to the Revolution, when George and Joshua Chadbourn, sons of Joshua Chadbourn, were drowned in the Mousam River, near Chadbourn's mill. When found they were locked in each other's arms.

1846. March 9. Isaiah Gowen and Aaron Jellison were killed by the caving-in of a frozen sand-bank, near Gowen's mill. They with others were repairing the dam, and had dug into the bank on the east side of the mill road, leaving a thick frozen crust hanging over them. Their attempts to break it off had failed. Suddenly it gave way, late in the afternoon, and fell upon Gowen and Jellison as they were shovelling. They were extricated about half an hour after the accident. Gowen was dead, and Jellison, dreadfully mangled, lived an hour and a half.

1857. May 16. George W. Hewes, aged twenty-six years, was drowned in the Mousam River, at Springvale. He and William J. Reed were out rowing, when they began to rock the boat. At length they were capsized, and Hewes drowned. Reed reached the shore with difficulty.

1861–65. Davis Estes, Junior, was killed on the street, in Boston, some time during the Civil War, while arresting a desperado. He was on duty as a special policeman. His burial took place in Sanford.

1869. November 28. Nathaniel C. Lord, son of William and Huldah (Getchell) Lord, was killed in Peabody, Mass. Frank D. Bowers and James E. Ricker were convicted of manslaughter, and given a life sentence for the crime, although they were pardoned after serving fifteen years.

22

1875. November 20. Stillman A. Bodwell, son of Mrs. Eliza Bodwell, was drowned near the Corner. He and several other boys were skating on a small pond at the "parsonage," when the ice broke and plunged five of them into the water. Stillman went to the rescue of his older brother, William, caught him by the hand, and was drawn in and under the ice. He remained in the water some three-quarters of an hour, and when found was standing on his feet under the ice. All efforts to resuscitate him were in vain.

1893. January 6. John Derom (De Coreau) was killed on the Mousam River Railway. A gang of workmen were pushing a flat car over the bridge, when the engineer of the old engine Rochester saw a signal for assistance, and drove his engine toward the men. Not expecting it, they jumped for their lives, and all escaped except Derom, who was caught by the engine and killed.

1895. January 29. Daniel O'Connell, about twenty-five years of age, in trying to board the noon passenger train for Portland, after it left the station, fell under the cars, injuring him about the head, and crushing his right leg below the knee. At nine o'clock he submitted to amputation, but survived only two hours.

1896. March 1. Through the great freshet on the Mousam River, Charles H. C. Otis, aged fifty, boss carpenter at the Springvale cotton mills, lost his life. Early in the morning a crew of men were at work at the mills endeavoring to lessen the danger to the property. About half past eight o'clock the water had risen so high, and was still rising, that an attempt was made to pull the flush boards off the dam. In trying to fasten a hook to the board, Mr. Otis was swept over the dam to the rocks beneath, the water carrying him about twenty-five feet, landing him on a small ledge. While lying there a rope was thrown him from the shore, but his strength was not equal to the task of tying it around his body. Thereupon, William Galloway, foreman in the card room at the mills, after attaching a rope to his body, managed to wade through the rushing water and reach Mr. Otis, whom he grasped by the hand, and both started for shore. When within seven or eight feet of land the force of the water swept both men off their feet, Mr. Galloway's handclasp was broken, and Mr. Otis was carried under the water, the other being saved only by the rope around his body. All this occurred in less than fifteen minutes, and in sight of several hundred people who thronged the bridge and banks of the river. Mr. Otis was a veteran of the Civil War.

1896. September 2. Willie Rankin of Sanford was killed in a bicycle race at Lewiston.

1898. July 30. Mrs. Lillian Swett was burned to death at Spring-vale while attempting to kindle a fire with kerosene oil. The house was partially destroyed.

One of lightning's most curious freaks, though not fatal, occurred during a terrific tempest at midnight August 11, 1845. The two-story house of Captain Stephen Willard was struck upon one chimney, the fluid separating on reaching the roof. The lightning smashed a large chest at the head of Captain Willard's bed, then passed to the left arm of the Captain, burning him, and stripping off his night clothing, and that of one child. Thence it passed from Mrs. Willard's feet towards her head, severely lacerating her lower limbs. One daughter in the room above was badly burned, and two injured in their hearing. The room was shattered into splinters.

CHAPTER XXXIV.

THE FRATERNAL ORDERS.

Free Masons — Odd Fellows — Knights of Pythias — Grand Army — Golden Cross — Red Men — Other Secret Societies.

SANFORD is abundantly supplied with lodges of the mystic orders. All of the leading secret societies are represented, in some instances with organizations both at Sanford and Springvale, and the officers report the condition of the various fraternities as flourishing. The oldest of them all is Preble Lodge, No. 143, A. F. and A. M., which was organized in 1867, and worked under dispensation until May, 1868, when a charter was granted by the Grand Lodge. May 29, 1876, Preble Lodge was reorganized, and took on a new lease of life, under Moses W. Emery as Worshipful Master. The officers for 1900 are : W. M., Fred Hodgson ; S. W., Edmund F. Low ; J. W., C. W. Blagden ; Secretary, Joseph Leckenby ; Treasurer, George H. Nowell ; S. D., W. T. Beck ; J. D., C. S. Holmes.

Springvale Lodge, No. 190, A. F. and A. M., was organized under dispensation June 23, 1885, and was constituted by the Grand Lodge of Maine, June 17, 1886, with William Dart as Worshipful Master. The following officers have served during the past year : W. M., W. F. Ferguson ; S. W., George H. Drew ; J. W., William J. Gowen ; Secretary, William H. Wood.

Another Masonic organization is the White Rose Chapter, No. 54, of the Royal Arch degree. The officers include : High Priest, Frank H. Dexter ; King, Samuel Jaggar ; Scribe, William T. Black ; Secretary, Calvert Longbottom.

Ruth Chapter, No. 14, Order of the Eastern Star, is a Springvale lodge. The officers are : Worthy Matron, Annie E. Moulton ; Worthy Patron, Joseph P. Moulton ; Secretary, Frank H. Dexter ; Treasurer, Nettie Shackley.

Friendship Lodge, No. 69, I. O. O. F., was instituted March 13, 1872, with nine charter members. The first Noble Grand was George E. Allen. At present H. O. Witham is Noble Grand, and John A. Dennett, Secretary.

Ruhamah Rebekah Lodge, No. 53, I. O. O. F., was organized at Springvale. The officers are : N. G., Lucy M. Garvin; V. G., Fannie A. Clark ; F. S., Clara Elwell ; R. S., Ella H. Smith.

Riverside Lodge, No. 12, Knights of Pythias, dates back to 1875, having been instituted February 10 of that year with twelve charter members. Gilbert G. Littlefield was the first Chancellor Commander. The present officers are as follows : C. C., Guy B. Stover ; V. C., Harry E. Whicher ; Pre., Alberto I. Gerry ; K. of R. and S., Charles O. Emery, Second ; M. of F., George E. Allen.

Mousam River Lodge, No. 72, Knights of Pythias, holds its meetings in Pythian Hall, Kempton's Block, Springvale. George Goodwin is the Chancellor Commander, and Joseph P. Moulton, K. of R. and S.

Arbutus Assembly, No. 43, Pythian Sisterhood, was instituted at Sanford May 5, 1900, with fifty charter members. The officers are : C. C., Winifred Hill ; V. C., Nellie Dart ; P., Sadie Ford ; K. of R. and S , Violet McCrellis ; M. of F., Mrs. A. M. Dart.

William F. Willard Post, No. 75, G. A. R., was organized and mustered March 22, 1883. W. H. Rodgers was the first Commander. The present officers include : Commander, W. H. Rodgers ; Adjutant, G. H. Roberts ; Quartermaster, S. Stokes. This is a Springvale organization.

At Sanford the Civil War veterans are mustered in William Reed Post, No. 164, G. A. R. The officers are : Commander, John M. Hayes ; Senior Vice Commander, Noah Gerrish ; Junior Vice Commander, Moses Twombly ; Adjutant, Frank Engel.

Each Grand Army Post has its associated Woman's Relief Corps. Of Willard Corps, No. 52, Springvale, Mattie S. Ferguson is President, and Louisa Getchell, Secretary. Of Reed Corps, No. 53, of Sanford, Lilla Ricker is President, Elizabeth Dyer, Vice President, and Bessie Shepard, Secretary.

Brown Camp, No. 44, Sons of Veterans, is also an auxiliary to the G. A. R. Frank McCann is Captain, Jesse Tarbox, Lieutenant, and B. F. Dyer, Secretary.

Springvale Commandery, No. 197, United Order of the Golden Cross, was organized May 24, 1882. E. E. Goodwin was the first Noble Commander. The present officers are : N. C., Hattie E. Cooper ; V. N. C., Isadore A. Horne ; P., Lizzie E. Jenness ; K. of R., Frank H. Dexter ; F. K. of R., Herbert Smith ; Treasurer, Mrs. Herbert Smith.

Sanford Commandery, No. 341, United Order of the Golden Cross, was instituted April 13, 1888, with sixteen charter members. George R. Bowley is N. C., and E. K. Allen, K. of R.

Pioneer Lodge No. 150, Order of the Sons of St. George, of Sanford, was instituted March 1, 1884, with sixteen charter members. Charles H. Ogden was the first President. The officers for 1900 include : Thomas Kaye, President; John Hargraves, Vice President; Samuel Needham, Secretary.

Victoria Lodge, No. 15, Daughters of St. George, is also a Sanford organization. It was instituted November 26, 1895. The officers are : President, Miss M. Pickles ; Vice President, Mrs. S. Taylor; Recording Secretary, Miss S. Denby; Financial Secretary, Mrs. S. Nutter; Treasurer, Miss M. Ramsden.

T. F. Boylen Lodge, No. 15, New England Order of Protection, was instituted at Springvale, December 20, 1887, with thirty-five charter members, by T. F. Boylen of Boston. The first Warden was B. P. Hamilton. At present the officers are : Warden, Charles W. Belden ; Secretary, Leroy A. Wentworth ; Financial Secretary, Cora A. Graves ; Treasurer, E. E. Goodwin.

Thomas Goodall Lodge, No. 51, Ancient Order of United Workmen, was instituted September 14, 1889, with twenty-two charter members. This Lodge was named for Hon. Thomas Goodall, whose likeness appears on the seal. William Kernon was the first presiding officer. At present Herbert J. Hope is Master Workman, and Robert Halford Secretary.

Sagamore Tribe, No. 33, Improved Order of Red Men, was organized at Sanford June 29, 1894. The present officers are as follows : Prophet, Eugene M. Hewett; Sachem, Charles Hooper; Senior Sagamore, Fred Jagger; Junior Sagamore, Robert Halford; Chief of Records, Frank McCann.

Fluellin Tribe, No. 49, Improved Order of Red Men, was organized at Springvale, July 17, 1900. The name was selected to commemorate the original Indian proprietor of the lands of the town of Sanford. The officers are : Prophet, Rev. E. M. Trafton ; Sachem, W. H. Wood; Senior Sagamore, W. H. Folsom ; Junior Sagamore, E. A. Hanson; Chief of Records, F. A. Clark.

The officers of Garfield Lodge, No. 416, L. O. I., are as follows : Master, W. O. Nute; Deputy Master, George Harding ; Recording Secretary, Henry Neal; Financial Secretary, Freeman Brierly ; Treasurer, Abraham Young.

Loyal Sanford Lodge, I. O. O. F., Manchester Unity, has the following board of officers : N. G., Arthur Wilcock; V. G., Alfred

Parker; P. S., Arthur F. Engel; C. S., Charles Whidden; Treasurer, Harry Johnson; Auditor, John W. Thompson.

Washington Council, No. 9, Junior Order of United American Mechanics, meets in Knights of Pythias Hall, Springvale. Its officers are Councillor, Arthur C. Goodwin; Secretary, W. H. W. Bartlett; Treasurer, E. E. Goodwin; Financial Secretary, C. L. Hayes.

The Order of Knights of Maccabees is represented by Mousam Lake Tent, No. 5. Walter Ashworth is Secretary.

Of Mercier Court, No. 822, Catholic Order of Foresters, William George Milne is Secretary.

Pride of the Juniors Council, No. 20, Daughters of Liberty, was instituted at Springvale, in May, 1900. The officers are: C., Nellie M. Horne; A. C., Geneva Hanson; V. C., Mrs. H. J. Sanborn; R. S., Frank H. Dexter; T., Jeanette Shackley.

Two camps of the Modern Woodmen of America were organized in town during 1900. Springvale Camp, No. 7995, was first in the field, being instituted May 1, with a charter membership of twenty-seven. The officers are: V. C., Joseph P. Moulton; W. A., John F. Peabody; C., William H. Wood; B., Charles E. Adams; E. M., Harry Dorsey.

Sanford Camp, No. 8238, of the same order, was instituted June 13, with thirty-seven charter petitioners. The officers are: V. C., Benjamin Jepson; W. A., F. L. Brown; C., Charles Whidden; B., B. F. Albee; E., R. W. Jones.

The lodges of Good Templars have already been mentioned in the chapter on Temperance.

Among the lodges which have been organized in town in the past, but which have passed out of existence are the following: Prospect Rebekah Lodge, No. 14, organized February 14, 1877; Springvale Encampment, No. 26, P. M., I. O. O. F., organized October 16, 1877; Nazarite Legion, organized February 22, 1883; Warren Camp, No. 44, Sons of Veterans, organized July 23, 1886; Martha Washington Lodge, Knights and Ladies of Honor, organized January 5, 1886; and Columbia Assembly, No. 18, Pythian Sisterhood.

CHAPTER XXXV.

CEMETERIES AND GRAVEYARDS.

Family Burial Places — The Nasson Burying Ground — Removal of Bodies — Riverside Cemetery, Springvale — Oakdale Cemetery, Sanford.

EVERYBODY travelling through the western part of Maine must have noticed the numerous graveyards along the roads, in the fields and pastures, and adjoining the churches. We can trace the practice of burying the dead in churchyards back to our English ancestors, but the peculiar custom of having family burial grounds instead of a town cemetery can only be explained as arising from the conditions and circumstances in which the early settlers found themselves, remote from their neighbors, and in scattered and sparsely settled communities. The family burial place was established where it was easy of access, and the old usage was followed in many towns until within a comparatively few years, when modern demands resulted in the laying out of public cemeteries.

One of the oldest burying grounds in town was the Nasson graveyard at Sanford Corner, located at the corner of Main and Roberts Streets. The first person interred there was Peter, eldest son of Major Samuel Nasson, who died December 15, 1784, aged eighteen years, eight months. His grave was marked by a rough, unhewn stone, bearing the inscription, " P. N., Di^d Dec 1785." This is an error, as the family record shows that he died a year earlier. Beside him was buried his sister, Susannah Colcord, and by her side, Mrs. Joanna Nasson, wife of Major Samuel. Others of the family were also buried there, and in May of 1900, this cemetery contained fifty-six known graves. In that month, however, the bodies were removed to other localities, owing to the need of the lot for a public building site. The necessity for such a lot had been apparent for some time, and Hon. E. M. Goodall, after consulting other prominent men of the town concerning the matter, generously offered to defray all the expenses of removing the bodies and monumental fixtures of the cemetery, providing the owners would deed the land to the town to be used as the site of a public building, to which the owners readily agreed. The work of exhumation was duly performed, a large majority of the bodies being transferred to Oakdale cemetery, although several were sent to distant points. The lot has a frontage of eighty feet on Main and one hundred and twenty-seven feet on Roberts Street. The opposite sides measure eighty and one hundred and thirty-seven feet respectively.

On the 30th of September, 1854, Asa Low, John Merrill, James M. Burbank, and thirteen others purchased six acres of land at the confluence of the Mousam and a brook entering the pond above the upper dam at Springvale, and laid it out for a cemetery. Albert J. Smith was the first president of the company. The first interment to be made there was of the body of Dr. William Gage, a prominent Baptist, and a Thomsonian practitioner of medicine. He was buried by the Masonic order in the fall of 1854. In 1868 the Springvale Cemetery Company added two acres to the lot, and seven acres more in 1882, at which time the company was reorganized. The cemetery is now known as Riverside.

For the past twenty years or more, there has been a cemetery on Main Street, about half a mile below the main part of Sanford village, which was generally known as the town cemetery. This is still used, although many families have removed the bodies buried there to Oakdale cemetery, on Berwick Street. This fine burial ground was laid out by the Oakdale Cemetery Association, organized in 1893. We quote from a circular issued by the association: "The cemetery has a frontage on the Berwick road of about a thousand feet, marked by a substantial iron fence, through which there are three entrances guarded by large double gates of iron for the use of carriages, and single gates for foot passengers. The first entrance is located in a little dell between two small hills wooded by beautiful oak groves—a delightful spot. Further on and similarly located is the main entrance, opposite which, and facing it, is the receiving vault, a substantial structure of stone and brick with heavy oak doors, the whole of modern design and built upon the most approved principles. The grounds are diversified by hills and dales, wooded to a proper extent by groves of oak and pine, with a liberal scattering of maple, ash and elm. Running directly across, and just in the rear of the plotted land, as shown in the plan, is the Great Works Brook, which by the construction of a dam can be readily converted into an artificial pond, there being excellent natural facilities. The land near the first entrance is reserved for a park, and other plots throughout the grounds will be set aside for ornamental purposes. The soil is a sandy loam with hardpan subsoil, very free from stones, and never caves in excavating. There are at present some twenty-five acres in the cemetery, and additions can be made at any time should it become necessary, so that there never will come a time when Oakdale will not be the principal burial ground in this section. With its little hills and dales, its miniature plains and plateaus, its stream of sparkling water, its groves of soughing pines, majestic oaks and stately elms, its location, and many other desirable advantages, the question arises, ' Can a more suitable spot for a cemetery be found?' ' One desirable feature in connection with this cemetery is the record kept by the clerk of all interments, with name, age, time of burial, number of lot, and other essential particulars. The superintendent has a plan of every lot, on which is shown the exact location of any grave, a matter of importance for the future, as well as for the present.

CHAPTER XXXVI.

LATTER DAY SCHOOLS.

Establishment of Free High School, 1874 — The School Discontinued and Finally Re-Established — List of Principals — New Building at the Corner, 1888 — The Present School System — Expenditures — Complete List of Members of the School Committee.

A GREAT advance in the line of improvement of the educational system of the town was the establishment of a free High School. The legislature of 1873 passed a law which conferred upon every town in the state the right to establish and maintain a free High School; a law by which the state was to pay one-half the actual cost of instruction in any school established in accordance with the provisions of said law, on condition that it be continued ten weeks, and that the appropriation and expenditure therefor on the part of the town be exclusive of the amount required by law to be expended for common school purposes. An article looking towards the establishment of such a High School was inserted in the warrant for a special town meeting, June 21, 1873, but was not acted upon.

At the annual town meeting the following spring, however, it was "Voted, that the town of Sanford establish a free High School of two terms a year of at least ten weeks each term, the first term to commence in the town-house at Springvale, some time in the month of August next, and the second term to commence at Sanford Corner, at Goodall's Hall, if it can be obtained for such purpose; or if said hall cannot be obtained, then some other suitable place at Sanford Corner. And the town does hereby raise the sum of six hundred dollars for maintaining said High School and providing equipments for the same, providing school districts Nos. 1 and 2 shall warm the building, when said school shall be kept in their respective districts."

In accordance with this vote, seats, desks, and blackboards, costing about two hundred and fifty dollars, were placed in the town hall,

(347)

and S. C. Page engaged to teach the first term. The school began August 17, 1874, and continued twelve weeks. There were fifty-two students in attendance, and an average of forty-five. The second term, under the same instructor, began in the school-house at the Corner, February 22, 1875, and continued ten weeks. A larger number of pupils entered, and the classification was not so good. Ellen M. Emery assisted in instruction a portion of each day.

In 1875 the town voted to raise four hundred dollars to continue the school. The same principal had charge, and was assisted during the first term by Phoebe Bodwell, and the second by Maria L. Witham. Eighty-three scholars were enrolled during the second term. Each term was of twelve weeks' duration.

Three hundred and fifty dollars were appropriated for the school in 1876. Daniel L. Lane, Junior, assisted by his older pupils, taught the fall term at Springvale, and E. N. Mitchell, of Newfield, a graduate of Harvard, assisted by Ellen M. Emery, taught the spring term at Sanford.

At the annual town meeting in 1877, the article in the warrant relating to the High School was indefinitely postponed. A petition, signed by nearly twenty voters, asking that a meeting be called to reconsider the vote, was subsequently presented to the selectmen, who, however, declined to call a meeting. The matter came before the town in July, but with a result similar to that of the previous spring. It was a noticeable fact that those without children, and those outside of the villages, whom it would greatly benefit, were alike opposed to the continuance of the High School. There is much truth in the remark of one of the scholars of that day: "It does not make much difference to District Number One whether they have a High School or not; but it does make a great deal of difference whether the smaller districts outside have it or not." That the districts outside of the two villages, in a great degree, availed themselves of the opportunities with which they were favored, is shown by the report of the fourth term. The number of scholars then in attendance was eighty-one, of whom seven were from the first district, forty-seven from the second, four from the fifth, two from the sixth, one from the eighth, eight from the tenth, six from the eleventh, four from the sixteenth and two from the seventeenth.

The town was fortunate in the teachers employed in that school. They were competent instructors, and labored with much zeal and interest for its advancement, proficiency, and thoroughness. An indirect advantage, worthy of mention, was the influence upon the other schools, exerted from the beginning. Rev. Edward P. Roberts, a member of the school committee, said at the end of the first year: "I can see that the High School has already infused new life into all the other schools in town."

Another advance was suggested in 1876, when it was proposed to abolish the district system. The time for so radical a change had not come, however, and the people, accustomed to have a voice in their little democracies, were unwilling to give up the control of the schools wholly into the hands of others. They could not endure the thought of losing their long cherished privilege, for they virtually selected their teachers.

In the spring of 1881, the town voted " to instruct the selectmen to see that all children between the ages of six years and seventeen years of age attend school according to law."

It was not until 1887 that the free High School question found a permanent and satisfactory solution. At the annual town meeting that spring an effort was made to pass an appropriation of two hundred and fifty dollars to maintain a High School, in order to secure a like amount offered by the state. The appropriation was refused, and it appeared as if the town were to continue without a High School, until a thorough agitation was started, and finally Hon. E. M. Goodall generously agreed to furnish the sum required. This public spirited act was productive of a beneficial and healthy result, for, after Mr. Goodall had contributed the money for one year, the voters arose to meet the educational demands of a modern and rapidly growing community, and have supported two High Schools ever since.

The school at Sanford opened in December, 1887, with A. W. Langley as principal. He was succeeded in 1888 by Samuel Perry. The spring term of 1889 was conducted by Miss Mason, while E. C. Cook had charge during the fall and winter terms following. J. Herbert Maxwell was principal in the spring term of 1890, and was closely followed by O. Howard Perkins, now a Universalist clergyman at New Bedford, Mass. During the five years in which Mr. Perkins was at the head of the school he met with great success as a teacher, and won the lifelong esteem of his pupils and associates. Frank C. Thompson, of Lewiston, succeeded him in 1895, serving as principal for two years. In 1897 Frank O. Small, of Oldtown, was chosen, but his stay was brief, as he decided to study law, and resigned in March, 1898. Since that time Harry E. Bryant has filled the position to good acceptance.

Feeling the need of a new school building at Sanford Corner, the town made appropriation therefor, and a handsome and commodious structure was erected in 1888 at a cost of about $15,000. The former school-house, built twenty years before, was sold to S. B. Emery, who moved it to Washington Street, and converted it into the furniture store now occupied by him; and the new building was erected on the site of the old, on School Street, at the junction of Mousam Street. In it are located the High and common schools to the number of ten, including all the grades from the first to the highest. The High School principal has entire charge. The building is heated with steam, and is furnished with electric bells and many other conveniences.

The principals of the Springvale High School, within the same period, have been: Samuel E. Berry, 1888; A. M. Richardson, 1889; W. B. Moore, 1890–91; F. P. Knight, 1892–95; Rev. F. G. Davis, 1896–1900, thirteen terms; and Frank C. Thompson, the present incumbent. Mr. Thompson has previously taught the Sanford school.

In the main, it can be said that the principals of the High Schools, from the first, have been earnest, zealous, and faithful teachers, who have awakened the minds of their pupils, inspired them with a love of learning, and created enthusiasm among them in behalf of broad and liberal education.

The school-house at Springvale is the one erected in 1855, mentioned on page 154. About eight years ago, a two-story wing was added, and the building now contains six rooms.

The two High Schools maintain a praiseworthy standard of excellence. Three four-year courses of study of three terms a year, are offered: English, or scientific; classical; and business. The first is designed to prepare pupils for the higher technical and scientific schools. The classical instruction is such as to furnish complete preparation for the entrance examinations of the leading colleges. The business course, while affording thorough training in English and scientific studies, offers in addition instruction in commercial arithmetic and book-keeping. Special students are also accepted in the two schools, but they are not awarded diplomas. Honorary parts for graduation are assigned, according to rank, in the following order: Valedictory, salutatory, history, prophecy.

District Number One is at Springvale. Beside the High School, there are also the grammar, first and second intermediate, and first, second and third primary. At Sanford, District Number Two, there are, in addition to the High School, first and second grammar, first and second intermediate, and first, second, third, and fourth primary. The outlying districts are well housed, and during the past year, the school buildings have been named, in honor of distinguished men, as follows : District Number One, Lincoln ; Two, Longfellow ; Three, Hawthorne ; Four, Edison ; Five, Holmes ; Six, Grant ; Eight, Whittier ; Nine, Emerson ; Ten, Jefferson ; Eleven, Washington ; Thirteen, Webster ; Sixteen, Bryant ; Seventeen, Franklin.

In 1899 Myron E. Bennett was appointed Superintendent of Schools, the office then being filled by act of the school board. In the present year, when it was deemed desirable to make the position an elective office, and to fix a salary for the same, Mr. Bennett was the unanimous choice of both political parties at the annual town meeting. During his incumbency he has made several improvements in the school system, among them the introduction of teachers of music for all schools in Districts One and Two, and the establishment of a night school, of which Mr. Bennett himself is the teacher.

The last school census showed a total of 2072 scholars, an increase of more than one hundred over the previous year. The annual appropriation for schools is : Common schools, $5,000 ; High School, $1,900 ; Superintendent's salary, $1,000 ; books, $500 ; insurance, $350 ; total, $8,750. The town draws over $5,000 from the state as its share of the so-called " mill tax," and also the High School aid, hence, the total expenditures are about $14,000. The figures are in telling contrast to the appropriations of earlier times. We quote the sums raised for school purposes in other years : 1826, $732.80 : 1850, $1,000 ; 1856, $1,500 ; 1865, $2,000 ; 1870, $2,500 ; 1871, $3,000 ; 1874, $2,400 ; 1876, $2,000 ; 1881, $2,200.

A complete list of the members of the school committees who have served the town is appended. It will be noticed that for several years a Supervisor of Schools was chosen instead of a committee of three. At the present time, one member of the committee is elected each year. In 1835, the town voted that the committee be paid a reasonable compensation, which, in 1836, was fixed at fifty cents per day. In 1837, no pay was allowed, and the year following they were requested and required to perform their duties as the law required. In 1842, a reasonable compensation was voted. In passing, we may notice the fact that three young men were elected as committee in

1843, one of whom was only nineteen years of age, and the others were but a few years more than their majority. The list:

1797.

The Selectmen,
Caleb Emery,
Jeremiah Wise,
William Frost,
Joshua Getchell,
Moses Sweat.

1798.

Moses Sweat,
William Frost,
Eliot Frost,
Francis Pugsley,
Nathaniel Bennett.

1799.

Moses Sweat,
Ezra Thompson.

1801.

Moses Sweat,
Sheldon Hobbs,
Joseph Shaw.

1812.

Moses Sweat,
Eleazar Chadbourn,
Ezra Thompson.

1821.

Moses Sweat,
Ezra Thompson,
William Gowen, Jr.

1822.

Moses Sweat,
Ezra Thompson,
William Gowen, Jr.

1823.

George Heard,
William Gowen, Jr.,
Ezra Thompson.

1824.

Gideon Cook,
Christopher Marsh,
Ezra Thompson.

1825.

Ezra Thompson,
John Shaw,
William Gowen, Jr.
John Shaw refused to
  serve, and Daniel
  Gowen was chosen
  in his place.

1826.

Ezra Thompson,
William Gowen, Jr.,,
Daniel Gowen,
George Chadbourn, in
  place of William
  Gowen, Jr., excused.

1827.

Christopher Marsh,
Timothy Shaw,
Daniel Gowen.

1828.

Timothy Shaw,
Daniel Gowen,
Jonathan Clark.

1829.

Elisha Bacon,
John Hanson,
Daniel Gowen.

1830.

Elisha Bacon,
Timothy Shaw,
William L. Walker.

1831.

William L. Walker,
Elisha Bacon,
John Frost, 2d.

1832.

Elisha Bacon,
William L. Walker,
John Frost, 2d.

1833.

Elisha Bacon,
John Skeele,
Nicholas E. Paine.

1834.

George Heard,
Nicholas E. Paine,
Gideon Cook.

1835.

Nicholas E. Paine,
John Skeele,
John Shaw.

1836.

Nicholas E. Paine,
John Shaw,
Calvin R. Hubbard.

1837.

John T. Paine,
John Frost, 2d,
John Storer.

1838.

John T. Paine,
Nicholas E. Paine,
Daniel P. Shaw.

1839.

John Shaw,
George Heard,
Daniel P. Shaw.

1840.

George Heard,
Nicholas E. Paine,
Daniel P. Shaw.

1841.

John T. Paine,
John Shaw,
John L. Allen.

1842.

George W. Bourne,
John Shaw,

HON. SUMNER I. KIMBALL.

1842.

Charles E. Weld,
Daniel P. Shaw, to fill
vacancy created by
the removal of
George W. Bourne,
prior to December 3.

1843.

Moses M. Butler,
William Gowen,
James Chadbourn, Jr.

1844.

Jacob C. Goss,
Mark F. Wentworth,
John L. Allen, .
May 29, Charles E.
Weld, in place of
Mark F. Wentworth,
left town.

1845.

Jacob C. Goss,
John Boyd,
Ivory Brooks.

1846.

John Boyd,
Ivory Brooks,
Samuel S. Thing,
September 11, William
Emery, 3d, in place
of John Boyd, re-
moved.

1847.

Ivory Brooks,
Timothy Shaw,
William Gowen.

1848.

Samuel S. Thing,
Asa Low,
Elias Libbey.

1849.

Asa Low,
Samuel S. Thing,
Elias Libbey.

23

1850.

Austin Robbins,
C. B. Mills,
Clement Parker.

1851.

C. B. Mills, 3 years,
Austin Robbins, 2
years,
Clement Parker, 1
year.

1852.

Albert Cole, 3 years,
Clement Parker, 2
years,
Austin Robbins, 1
year,
November 15, Asa Low
in place of Austin
Robbins, removed;
William H. Waldron,
in place of Albert
Cole, removed.

1853.

Stephen M. Cobb, 3
years,
Nicholas Branch, 2
years,
Clement Parker, 1
year,
September 24, Asa
Low, in place of
Nicholas Branch,
not accepting.

1854.

Asa Low, 3 years,
Stephen M. Cobb, 2
years,
Alvah W. Dam, 1 year.

1855.

Alvah W. Dam,
Asa Low,
Stephen M. Cobb.

1856.

Stephen M. Cobb,
Alvah W. Dam,
Asa Low.

1857.

Asa Low, 3 years,
John W. Bodwell, 2
years,
Alvah W. Dam, 1 year.

1858.

Gershom Ricker,
Asa Low,
John W. Bodwell.

1859.

Clark C. Trafton,
Gershom Ricker,
Asa Low.

1860.

Asa Low,
Clark C. Trafton,
Gershom Ricker.

1861.

Evat Willard,
Asa Low,
Clark C. Trafton.

1862.

Hampden Fairfield,
Evat Willard,
Asa Low.

1863.

Asa Low,
Hampden Fairfield,
Evat Willard.

1864.

Evat Willard,
Asa Low,
Hampden Fairfield.

1865.

William W. Boyd, 3
years,
Charles O. Emery, 2
years,
Asa Low, 1 year.

1866.

Alvah W. Dam, 3 years,
Charles E. Lord, 2
years,
Charles O. Emery, 1
year.

1867.

Charles O. Emery,
Alvah W. Dam,
Charles E. Lord.

1868.

Charles E. Lord,
Charles O. Emery,
Alvah W. Dam.

1869.

Asa Low,   *
Charles E. Lord,
Charles O. Emery.

1870.

Hosea S. Merrifield, 3
years,
Asa Low, 2 years,
George B. Ilsley, 1
year.

1871.

George B. Ilsley,
Hosea S. Merrifield,
Asa Low.

1872.

Asa Low,
George B. Ilsley,
Hosea S. Merrifield.

1873.

Howard Frost,
Asa Low,
George B. Ilsley.

1874.

Edward P. Roberts,
Howard Frost,
Asa Low.

1875.

Asa Low,
Edward P. Roberts,
Howard Frost.

1876.

Howard Frost, 3 years,
Asa Low, 2 years,
John H. Mugridge, 1
year.

1877.

Charles O. Emery,
Howard Frost,
Asa Low.

1878.

A. S. Bird,
Charles O. Emery,
Howard Frost.

1879.

Howard Frost,
A. S. Bird,
Charles O. Emery.

SUPERVISORS.

1880.

Asa Low.

1881.

Asa Low.

1882.

Charles O. Emery.

1883.

Frank L. Durgin.

1884.

Frank L. Durgin.

1885.

Edward C. Frost.

1886.

Edward J. Hatch.

1887.   .

William J. Maybury.

SCHOOL COMMITTEE.

1888.

F. G. Davis,
Nahum P. Allen,
George W. Trafton.

1889.

Nahum P. Allen,
George W. Trafton,
F. G. Davis.

1890.

Amos W. Low,
Edward H. Emery,
Nahum P. Allen.

1891.

William J. Maybury.

1892.

Mrs. Ella M. Little-
field.

1893.

Edward H. Emery,
George A. Goodwin.

1894.

George A. Goodwin,
Frank H. Dexter,
John J. Merrill.

1895.

Mrs. Ella M. Little-
field.

1896.

Frank H. Dexter,
Nahum P. Allen.

1897.

Fred J. Allen,
W. E. Sanborn.

1898.

E. L. Thompson,
Edward H. Emery,
Mrs. Ella M. Little-
field.

1899.

George W. Hanson.

1900.

Mrs. J. D. Weymouth.

CHAPTER XXXVII.

MUNICIPAL MATTERS.

Town-Houses — Panic at Town Meeting, 1897 — Pounds — Population — Sanford the Second Largest Town in Maine, 1900 — Valuation and Polls — Lists of Town Officers — Representatives — Other Officers — Votes for President and Governor.

TOWN meetings were held, at first, in various places, but after the meeting-houses were built, in them for the most part. On the 4th of April, 1820, when the article in the warrant relative to holding the annual town meeting in the Baptist Church was acted upon, it was voted, " that the town-meeting shall be held at the Congregational Meeting-House." In 1839, the parish voted to allow the town to have the old meeting-house to hold town meetings in. The next year Thomas Hobbs offered a lot of land below the Corner for a town-house. At the annual meeting in 1848, it was voted to build a town-house, and Nehemiah Butler and Horace Bennett were added to the selectmen as a committee for that purpose. They were to act under the following instructions : That they select a suitable lot as near Sanford Corner as can be obtained, and cause a town-house to be built thereon by the lowest bidder on or before the first day of September next. Four hundred dollars were raised for the purpose. A lot was purchased adjoining Christopher H. Bennett's house-lot, and the town building erected, David Cram furnishing the frame. The first meeting held therein was the annual meeting for the election of state and county officers, September 11, 1848. The last meeting in the old meeting-house was April 3. In the meantime that old dilapidated structure of nearly sixty years was destroyed by fire.

March 9, 1868, land of Mr. Emery, adjoining the town-house, was accepted, to be fenced with stone posts and slats. In March and August warrants, 1870, articles were inserted in reference to building a new town-house, but they were " passed."

Four votes were passed August 3, 1872, by which alterations were to be made. By two of them, the Sanford Dramatic Club was permitted to make an addition of thirty feet in length to the town-house

and to put in such partitions as it needs, at its own expense; and to
have free use of the house for entertainments. The town on its
part was to put on another story of suitable height for a hall; and
chose Increase S. Kimball, Hosea Willard, and Moses W. Emery as
a committee to superintend the alterations. Another meeting was
called on the 12th, but the active member of the committee anticipat-
ing objections, or a rescinding of the votes, had put the house in a
condition unfit for use, thereby setting the majority against the proposed alterations, so that when the voters met in a house roofless and
with walls defaced, they were ready to vote anything to show their
disapprobation. Accordingly, the four votes passed August 3 were
" rescinded, abrogated, revoked and annulled," two hundred twenty-
five to fifty-one, and the town voted to sell " all the right, title, and
interest the town has in the town-house and lot on which said house
stands," to instruct the selectmen not to draw any orders to pay bills
contracted by the pretended committee chosen August 3, on the
ground that the town meeting of that date was illegal and void, and
" to build a new town-house, and that the same be located on the
main road leading from the corner of the roads at Springvale to the
post-office at Sanford Corner, at such place as the building committee
hereinafter named may designate." William Russell, Asa Low, Moses
H. Libby, A. W. Dam, and Howard Frost were chosen as that committee with full powers.

Owing to a defect in the notification, another meeting was called at
the Calvinistic Baptist vestry at Springvale, August 23. It adjourned
to meet immediately after at the front steps of the church, where votes
of like tenor as those of August 12 were passed. " Voted that the
town does hereby authorize a suit to be commenced against the persons that have torn down and injured their town-house." All persons
were forbidden doing any work on the town-house, and all legal con-
tracts were rescinded, abrogated, and annulled, on the ground that
the town meeting, claiming said contract, was illegal and void, and
of no binding effect on the town. Another meeting, called August 31,
to rescind the votes passed on the 23d, was adjourned without date.

The selectmen refused to issue a warrant for another meeting, but
Simon Tebbets, trial justice, issued one for a meeting, December 12,
to rescind the votes of August 23, and to take action with reference
to paying for the house altered at the Corner. This meeting was adjourned without date.

The town-house was located at Springvale, between the points
designated in town meeting, August 12. The final vote in regard
thereto was passed March 10, 1873. " Voted that each and all votes

passed at a town-meeting of the legal voters of this town, in town-
meeting assembled at the vestry of the Calvin Baptist Meeting-House
in the village of Springvale in the town of Sanford, on Friday the
twenty-third day of August, A. D. 1872, be and the same are hereby legalized, confirmed, and made valid and binding on this town in
as full and ample a manner as if the same had been originally passed
at this meeting," one hundred and fifty one to sixty-seven.

But this was not the final action of the town. Its agent, Asa Low,
brought a suit against Orren G. Jones and George W. Thompson for
trespass, which was entered at the September term of the Supreme
Judicial Court, 1872. At the January term, 1873, Jones entered a
suit against Sanford for money due him from the town for additions
and alterations of the town-house. The town lost both cases, and
judgment was rendered in Jones's favor for $2,625. By the sale of
the town-house at the Corner, $1,008 was received. The cost of the
new building, lot, fencing, etc., was $4,754. The old structure at
first became Goodall's Hall, and was later converted into a theatre
or opera house. It was torn down in 1900.

On the 27th of March, 1897, a panic, caused by the giving way of
the floor, interrupted a town meeting which was being held in the
Springvale town-house, and several citizens were bruised, while Captain Edmund G. Murray had two ribs broken. The hall was packed
at the time, and a stringer broke, owing to the heavy weight put upon
it. As a consequence, an area of about twenty square feet of floor
gave way. Between sixty and seventy-five men were precipitated
through the opening, most of them landing in the soft earth about
five feet below.

The early settlers were obliged to protect themselves against the
depredations of domestic animals. Fences were few, and much land
was lying in common. Swine, especially, made sad havoc of grass
plots and growing crops. According to an act of 1693, swine were
to be yoked from April to October 15, and ringed all the year. It
depended upon the vote of the towns whether they should go at large.
The town took action in regard to the matter several years as appears
from such votes as these : March 22, 1769, " Voted that Hogs go
at large except they do mischief ; " March 21, 1770, " Voted that
Hoggs shall goe at large with yoking and ringing untill they Do mischief." The latest vote noticed was in 1809, when it was " voted
that Hogs may run at large the present year, provided they are yoked
and Rung according to law."

Prior to 1774, there seems to have been occasion for impounded
cattle ; for, at the annual town meeting in March it was voted to

build two pounds, one in each part of the town, for the accommodation of the inhabitants. The record for March 21, 1774, thus reads : " Voted one to (be) Built at the mouth of the new road moses Tibbets engaged to give the Land and near his House and he to be Pound Keeper and the other to be Built in that Part of the Township called massabeseck where the Selectmen see fit and the Persons Imployed to do the Labour on these Ponds to have Three Shillings p^r Day."

The first pound stood at the corner of the road at South Sanford laid out in 1770 across the river to Powers's. The second was thus located May 19 : " Voted that moses Stevens Give a Peace of Land for a Pound by the Road East of his Barn for that Part of the Township called Massabeseck." Stevens lived above what is now Alfred Corner, on the road on the southwest side of Shaker Pond. Fifteen years later, the town voted to have two pounds, one in each parish, but nothing was done toward building the same for two years. Then it was decided that they should be built near each meeting-house in each parish.

One would hardly suppose that any advantage could come from the location of a pound, and yet there was, at one time, much local jealousy manifested in discussing the question, " Where shall the new pound be built ? " We surmise that there was also considerable society feeling, from the fact that the sites proposed were in the vicinity of the two meeting-houses. After two previous ineffectual attempts to have stone pounds, the first, forty feet in diameter, the second, thirty-six feet square, on Wadlia's land near the Baptist meeting-house, on the 4th of April, 1820, the town voted to erect a pound in the same place where it formerly stood. Everything in regard to it was done in a truly democratic spirit; for it was not left with a committee or the selectmen, but in open town meeting decided what the enclosure should be and how built. The draft having been presented by the town, it was accepted. Thomas S. Emery bid off the same for twenty-four dollars, and Nathaniel Bennett became his surety. That the work was well done we infer, from the length of time during which the pound at South Sanford was used. The troubles arising from impounding cattle and the bad blood stirred up need not be mentioned.

According to Williamson, there were about nine thousand souls in the Province of Maine in 1735. Of these there were, by estimation, five hundred in the plantations and new townships, Brunswick, Topsham, Harpswell, Towwoh, Narraganset, Numbers One and Seven, New Marblehead, and Phillipstown. As the last named had been laid out but a short time, and the proprietors had not sold any of their lands, it is unlikely that there were any settlers. In 1744, according to the same authority, there were in the two eastern provinces, Maine and Sagadahock, two thousand eight hundred and fifty-five able-bodied or fencible men, of whom one hundred and fifty were in Phillipstown, and belonged to Colonel Pepperrell's regiment. This cannot be possible, for it was only five years after the coming of the first recorded settlers, and it is not likely that more than twenty families had moved into the plantation. From two petitions of 1752 and 1756, we learn that there were more than twenty families and upwards of one hundred souls in 1752, and about thirty families and upwards of one hundred and fifty souls in 1756. The estimated population in 1764 was one hundred and fifty. In 1771, there were eighty-nine ratable and nine non-ratable polls. In 1777, when the census of the town was taken, according to an act of December 9, 1776, the number of male inhabitants at home and abroad, sixteen years old and upwards, was found to be one hundred and fifty-eight; Quakers, eight; Indian, one; and "Molatoe," one. Total, one hundred and sixty-eight. In 1779, there were one hundred and eighty-five polls; in 1781, two hundred and nine; in 1785, one (two?) hundred and sixty-two; in 1789, two hundred and thirty-five in the South Parish; and in 1794, four hundred and ten polls. A list of voters, March 1, 1805, contains one hundred and eighty-one names. Alfred, set off as a separate district in 1794, had a population of nine hundred and six in 1800.

According to the first census in 1790, the population was eighteen hundred and two. The following table gives the population of the town by decades, with the percentage of gain or loss every ten years:

YEAR.	POPULATION.	GAIN OR LOSS, PER CENT.	YEAR.	POPULATION.	GAIN OR LOSS, PER CENT.
1790	1802		1850	2330	4.34
1800	1374	31.74*l*	1860	2221	4.67*l*
1810	1492	8.58	1870	2397	7.92
1820	1831	22.72	1880	2734	14.05
1830	2327	27.08	1890	4201	53.65
1840	2233	4.03*l*	1900	6078	44.68

Distribution by sex from 1800 to 1860 inclusive was as follows:

	1800	1810	1820	1830	1840	1850	1860
Males	681	727	896	1185	1112	1152	1098
Females	682	765	935	1142	1121	1178	1123

Miscellaneous census statistics of various years : Not taxed, 1800, eleven; colored, one male, 1840, one female, 1860 ; natives, 1870, twenty-two hundred and twenty-four; foreign born, 1870, one hundred and seventy-three ; aged between ninety and one hundred years, 1830, one man and two women; ditto, 1840, one woman; pensioners, 1840, six men and three women ; there were in 1840, one thousand and fifty-two scholars, twelve persons over twenty years of age not able to read or write, and seven insane persons and idiots.

It will be seen that from 1790 to 1830 there was gradual increase in population, and then for thirty years a very slight decrease. In 1870 the increase had been only seventy during the forty years previous. The opening of the water power at Springvale prior to 1830 accounts for the gain at that time, and the impetus given to manufacturing just after the Civil War, when Hon. Thomas Goodall began to improve the mill privileges at the Corner, caused the increase between 1860 and 1870, which has been enormously augmented during the past three decades. From 1870 to 1900 the gain in population has been 3681, or about one hundred and fifty-four per cent. The census returns of 1900 make a most gratifying showing for Sanford as compared with other places in the state. Sanford is thereby given a place of honor as the second largest town in Maine, Brunswick alone outranking her; and of the twenty cities, Sanford exceeds seven in population, as follows : Belfast, Brewer, Eastport, Ellsworth, Gardiner, Hallowell, and Oldtown. Given fifty more people, and Sanford would outstrip Saco. Her relative rank among the cities and towns of the state is fifteenth. Small wonder then that a proposition looking toward the granting of a city charter by the legislature of 1901 has been under consideration.

The following table gives the town's valuation and the number of polls by decades for the past eighty years :

Year.	Valuation.	Polls.
1821.	$102,950.	372.
1831.	$108,759.	360.
1841.	$321,314.	336.
1850.	$334,654.	423.
1860.	$447,061.	526.
1870.	$560,542.	526.
1880.	$654,303.	599.
1890.	$1,173,883.	840.
1900.	$2,288,954.	1550.

The amount raised by town appropriations in 1900 was $25,450; total tax, $36,695.35. Rate of taxation, 1900, fourteen dollars on one thousand; poll tax, three dollars per capita.

The principal town officers from the time of incorporation to the present have been:

Town Clerks — 1768, records lost; Samuel Willard, 1769; John Stanyan, 1770–73; Joel Moulton, 1774–79, 1781–96; Caleb Emery, 1780; Samuel Nasson, 1796–98, 1800; Stephen Hobbs, 1799, 1800–03; Sheldon Hobbs, "protempory clerk," September 2, 1800; Thomas Keeler, 1804–07; Ezra Thompson, chosen November 9, 1807, to fill vacancy; Elisha Allen, 1808–09, 1811–29; Ebenezer Linscott, 1810; Timothy Shaw, 1830–38; Timothy Shaw, Junior, 1839–41; Samuel Tripp, 1842–45; Charles O. Lord, 1846–49, 1850–52; Caleb S. Emery, 1850; Stephen Merrill, 1853–55; Asa Low, 1856–58; Salter Emery, 1859–60; Moses W. Emery, 1861–65; John A. Dennett, 1866–82, 1884, 1887, 1890–91; Howard J. Frost, 1883; Willis A. Fogg, 1885–86, 1888–1889; Charles O. Emery, Second, 1892–93; Charles B. Allbee, 1894 to the present time.

Treasurers — James Gare, 1775; Joel Moulton, 1776–77, 1779–80; Selectmen, 1782–88, 1791; Samuel Nasson, 1789; William Parsons, 1792; Henry Smith, 1793; William Frost, 1794–1803 (the selectmen acted as treasurers to receive and collect all moneys due the town prior to the division); Stephen Gowen, 1804–06, 1810–15, 1820; Ezra Thompson, 1807–09; Stephen Hobbs, 1816–18, 1821–25; John Frost, Second, 1819, 1828; William Hobbs, 1826–27; Timothy Shaw, 1829; Elisha Allen, 1830; Francis A. Allen, 1831; Nathaniel Hobbs, 1832–36; Thomas Hobbs, 1837; Daniel P. Shaw, 1838–49 (no record of election in 1844); Nehemiah Butler, 1850–53; Jonathan Tebbets, 1854–55; Joseph Butler, 1856–57; Samuel D. Tebbets, 1858–59, 1864–65; Simon Tebbets, 1860, 1869; Albert J. Smith, 1861, 1863, 1874–75 (Mr. Smith was elected at the March meeting, in 1863, but declined to do all the business connected with the offices of treasurer, collector, and constable, for twenty-five dollars, the amount which he bid); Moses W. Emery, 1862; William Emery, 1863 (having agreed to do the business, which Mr. Smith declined to do, for eighty-eight dollars, he was elected, April 18); Samuel B. Emery, 1866–68; Jonas C. Littlefield, 1870–72; Charles Butler, 1873; Charles O. Emery, 1876–82; Benjamin F. Hanson,

1883–86, 1888–89 ; Lewis Butler, 1887 ; Orville V. Libby, 1890–93 ;
Willis A. Fogg, 1894 to the present time.

Selectmen, Assessors, and Overseers of the Poor.

1768.

Benjamin Harmon,
Naphtali Harmon,
John Stanyan.

1769.

Jonathan Johnson,
William Bennet,
Samuel Willard.

1770.

Jonathan Johnson,
Samuel Willard,
William Bennet.

1771.

Samuel Willard,
William Bennet,
John Stanyan.

1772.

Jonathan Johnson,
William Bennet,
Daniel Gile.

1773.

Daniel Gile,
James Geary (Gare),
William Bennet.

1774.

Daniel Gile,
Morgan Lewis,
James Gare.

1775.

James Gare,
Daniel Gile,
Morgan Lewis.

1776.

James Gare,
Morgan Lewis,
Daniel Gile.

1777.

James Gare,
Morgan Lewis,
Joel Moulton.

1778.

Daniel Gile,
Morgan Lewis,
Phinehas Thompson.

1779.

Morgan Lewis,
Walter Powers,
Joel Moulton.

1780.

Caleb Emery,
Nathaniel Bennett,
Ebenezer Hall.

1781.

James Gare,
Morgan Lewis,
Eleazar Chadbourn.

1782.

William Person,
James Gare,
Eleazar Chadbourn.

1783.

James Gare,
William Person,
Eleazar Chadbourn.

1784.

William Person,
Eleazar Chadbourn,
Joel Moulton.

1785.

Caleb Emery,
Eleazar Chadbourn,
Henry Smith.

(Overseers of the
Poor first elected this
year).

1786.

Caleb Emery,
Henry Smith,
Samuel Nasson.

1787.

Henry Smith,
Eleazar Chadbourn,
Joshua Goodwin,
Samuel Nasson, to fill
vacancy.

1788.

Samuel Nasson,
Eleazar Chadbourn,
Henry Smith.

1789.

Samuel Nasson,
Eleazar Chadbourn,
William Parson.

1790.

Samuel Nasson,
Joel Moulton,
Henry Smith.

1791.

Caleb Emery,
William Parson,
Henry Smith.

1792.

Samuel Nasson,
Henry Smith,
Sheldon Hobbs.

1793.

Henry Smith,
Samuel Nasson,
Sheldon Hobbs.

1794.

Samuel Nasson,
Sheldon Hobbs,
Ezra Thompson.

1795.

Sheldon Hobbs,
Ezra Thompson,
Eleazar Chadbourn.

1796.

Samuel Nasson,
Sheldon Hobbs,
Ezra Thompson.

1797.

Samuel Nasson,
Eleazar Chadbourn,
Ezra Thompson.

1798.

Samuel Nasson,
Eleazar Chadbourn,
Ezra Thompson.

1799.

Samuel Shaw,
Stephen Gowen,
Sheldon Hobbs.

1800.

Samuel Nasson,
Sheldon Hobbs,
Ezra Thompson,
August 13, Zebulon
Beal, in place of
Samuel Nasson, deceased.

1801.

Ezra Thompson,
Caleb Emery,
Eleazar Chadbourn.

1802.

Ezra Thompson,
Eleazar Chadbourn,
Jedediah Allen.

1803.

Eleazar Chadbourn,
Ezra Thompson,
Jedediah Allen.

1804.

Jedediah Allen,
Samuel Shaw,
Ezra Thompson.

1805.

Samuel Shaw,
Thomas Keeler,
Jedediah Allen.

1806.

Thomas Keeler,
Samuel Shaw,
Rufus Bennett.

1807.

Thomas Keeler,
Samuel Shaw,
Rufus Bennett,
Elisha Allen, to fill
vacancy caused by
the removal of
Thomas Keeler.

1808.

Elisha Allen,
Ezra Thompson,
Rufus Bennett.

1809.

Ezra Thompson,
Rufus Bennett,
Elisha Allen.

1810.

Rufus Bennett,
Sheldon Hobbs,
Elijah Allen.

1811.

Sheldon Hobbs,
Rufus Bennett,
Elijah Allen.

1812.

Sheldon Hobbs,
Rufus Bennett,
Elijah Allen.

1813.

Sheldon Hobbs,
Rufus Bennett,
Timothy Shaw.

1814.

Sheldon Hobbs,
Thomas Shackley,
Elisha Allen.

1815.

Sheldon Hobbs,
Timothy Shaw,
John Libbey.

1816.

Sheldon Hobbs,
Timothy Shaw,
Enoch Lord.

1817.

Sheldon Hobbs,
Timothy Shaw,
Enoch Lord.

1818.

Timothy Shaw,
Enoch Lord,
John Frost, 2d.

1819.

Timothy Shaw,
John Frost, 2d,
Enoch Lord.

1820.

Timothy Shaw,
Sheldon Hobbs,
Ezra Thompson.

1821.

Timothy Shaw,
Sheldon Hobbs,
Ezra Thompson.

1822.

Sheldon Hobbs,
Timothy Shaw,
John Frost, 3d.

1823.

Sheldon Hobbs,
Timothy Shaw,
John Frost, 3d.

1824.

Sheldon Hobbs,
Timothy Shaw,
John Frost, 3d,
John Powers, in place
of John Frost, 3d,
declined.

1825.

Timothy Shaw,
John Powers,
Sheldon Hobbs.

1826.

Sheldon Hobbs,
Timothy Shaw,
John Powers.

1827.

John Powers,
Timothy Shaw,
Nathan Goodwin.

1828.

John Powers,
Daniel Gowen,
John Frost, 2d.

1829.

John Powers,
Daniel Gowen,
Timothy Shaw.

1830.

John Powers,
Timothy Shaw,
Daniel P. Shaw.

1831.

Timothy Shaw,
Daniel P. Shaw,
John Powers.

1832.

Timothy Shaw,
Daniel P. Shaw,
John Powers.

1833.

Timothy Shaw,
Daniel P. Shaw,
John Powers.

1834.

Timothy Shaw,
Daniel P. Shaw,
William B. Merrick.

1835.

Timothy Shaw,
Daniel P. Shaw,
William B. Merrick.

1836.

Timothy Shaw,
Daniel P. Shaw,
Jotham Welch.

1837.

Jotham Welch,
Daniel P. Shaw,
John Storer.

1838:

Timothy Shaw,
Daniel P. Shaw,
Jotham Welch.

1839.

Daniel P. Shaw,
Theodore Tripp,
Nehemiah Butler.

1840.

Nehemiah Butler,
Jotham Welch,
Timothy Shaw.

1841.

Nehemiah Butler,
Jotham Welch,
Timothy Shaw.

1842.

Amos F. Howard,
Enoch Frost,
Stephen Willard.

1843.

Amos F. Howard,
Enoch Frost,
John Shaw.

1844.

Samuel B. Emery,
Thomas J. Allen,
Nathaniel Hobbs.

1845.

Nathaniel Hobbs,
Samuel B. Emery,
John Merrill.

1846.

Enoch Frost,
John Shaw,
Horace Bennett.

1847.

Samuel B. Emery,
Enoch Frost,
John Carroll.

1848.

Samuel B. Emery,
Enoch Frost,
John Carroll.

1849.

Samuel B. Emery,
John Carroll,
Jonathan Tebbets.

1850.

Theodore Willard,
Daniel Cheney,
Christopher Shack-
ford.

1851.

Theodore Willard,
Daniel Cheney,
Christopher Shackford.

1852.

Theodore Willard,
Albert J. Smith,
Theodore Tripp.

1853.

James M. Burbank,
Stephen Willard,
Nehemiah Butler.

1854.

James M. Burbank,
Nehemiah Butler,
Horace Bennett.

1855.

James M. Burbank,
Nehemiah Butler,
Horace Bennett.

1856.

James M. Burbank,
Horace Bennett,
Nathaniel Chadbourn,
   Jr.

1857.

James M. Burbank,
Horace Bennett,
Nathaniel Chadbourn,
   Jr.

1858.

James M. Burbank,
Horace Bennett,
Nathaniel Chadbourn,
   Jr.

1859.

Jonas C. Littlefield,
Albert J. Smith,
Gershom Ricker.

1860.

Jonas C. Littlefield,
John Carroll,
Nehemiah Butler.

1861.

Asa Low,
Moses H. Libby,
George Bennett.

1862.

Asa Low,
Moses H. Libby,
George Bennett.

1863.

Asa Low,
Moses H. Libby,
George Bennett.

1864.

Asa Low,
Moses H. Libby,
George Bennett.

1865.

Asa Low,
Moses Jellison,
Jesse Furbish.

1866.

Asa Low,
Moses Jellison,
Jesse Furbish.

1867.

Irving A. Butler,
Daniel G. Clark,
George Jacobs.

1868.

Alvah W. Dam,
Daniel G. Clark,
George Jacobs.

1869.

Alvah W. Dam,
William Russell,
Lewis Butler.

1870.

Lewis Butler,
William Russell,
Hosea Willard.

1871.

Alvah W. Dam,
Lewis Butler,
William Russell.

1872.

Alvah W. Dam,
Walter Cram,
John B. Libby.

1873.

Alvah W. Dam,
Lewis Butler,
Enoch F. Lord.

1874.

Alvah W. Dam,
Enoch F. Lord,
Lewis Butler.

1875.

Alvah W. Dam,
Lewis Butler,
Enoch F. Lord.

1876.

Alvah W. Dam,
Enoch F. Lord,
Lewis Butler.

1877.

Alvah W. Dam,
George W. Gowen,
Walter Cram,
July 14, Asa Low, in
   place of Alvah W.
   Dam, deceased.

1878.

George W. Gowen,
Walter Cram,
Darling H. Ross.

1879.

Darling H. Ross,
Ernest M. Goodall,
Ivory C. Allen.

1880.

Enoch F. Lord,
Ernest M. Goodall,
Moses Jellison.

1881.

Enoch F. Lord,
Moses Jellison,
James L. Tripp.

1882.

Ernest M. Goodall,
James B. Clark,
Jeremiah G. Wilkinson.

1883.

George Bennett,
Elihu Parsons,
Francis Chadbourn.

1884.

George Bennett,
Jeremiah G. Wilkinson,
Charles O. Emery, 2d.

1885.

George Bennett,
John Merrill, 2d,
Charles O. Emery, 2d.

1886.

John Merrill, 2d,
Moses B. Twombly,
George Bennett.

1887.

Isaiah B. Stiles,
Moses B. Twombly,
William H. Nason.

1888.

Benjamin Beal,
George Bennett,
Winslow L. Moulton,
Bennett resigned November 17, and Frank Wilson was chosen to succeed him.

1889.

Edmund G. Murray,
Frank Wilson,
Winslow L. Moulton.

1890.

Enoch F. Lord,
Charles O. Emery, 2d,
N. Y. Morrill.

1891.

Edmund G. Murray,
Elmer E. Harris,
Moses H. Libby, Jr.

1892.

Frank Wilson,
Horace T. Bennett,
Charles F. Derby.

1893.

George W. Hanson,
Leroy Haley,
Moses H. Libby, Jr.

1894.

George W. Hanson,
Hiram B. Rowe,
Jerry A. Low.

1895.

George W. Hanson,
Hiram B. Rowe,
Jerry A. Low.

1896.

George W. Hanson,
Hiram B. Rowe,
William H. Nason.

1897.

George W. Hanson,
William H. Nason,
Leroy A. Wentworth.

1898.

George W. Hanson,
William H. Nason,
James H. Makin.

1899.

George W. Hanson,
William H. Nason,
James H. Makin.

1900.

George W. Hanson,
Ernest M. Goodall,
Elmer E. Harris.

Deer Reeves, or Deer Informers.

1769.

Michael Brawn.

1771.

Robert Miller.

1772.

William Bennett,
Thomas Williams.

1773.

Thomas Russel.

1775.

Michael Brawn.

1776.

Daniel Gile,
John Stanyan.

1777.

Jonathan Adams.

1778.

John Stanyan.

1779.

Jonathan Johnson.

1780.

Samuel Merrill.

1781.	1786.	1797.
Naphtali Harmon.	Samuel Willard.	David Bean.
1784.	1794.	1798.
Samuel Willard.	John Stanyan.	David Bean.
1785.		
John Stanyan.		

One or two men were chosen annually, whose duty it was to inform if any one molested the deer at certain times during the year, and to assist in punishing offenders.

At the town meetings in the spring of 1900 the following officers were elected : Moderator, Joseph Hollinrake; Town Clerk, Charles B. Allbee; Selectmen, Assessors, and Overseers of the Poor, George W. Hanson, Ernest M. Goodall, Elmer E. Harris; Treasurer, Willis A. Fogg; Town Agent, James M. Ricker; Auditor, William H. Wood; Superintendent of Schools, Myron E. Bennett; School Committee, Mrs. J. D. Weymouth; Road Commissioners, Elmer E. Wentworth, Winfield Moulton; Constables, Charles H. Tebbets, J. W. Brierly, Frank S. Beal, C. F. Miles; Truant Officers, Minor H. Spinney, Walter C. Remick.

REPRESENTATIVES TO THE LEGISLATURE.

To the General Court — 1785, Captain Caleb Emery; 1786, Major Caleb Emery; 1787, Major Samuel Nasson; 1788, Major Samuel Nasson; 1802, John Holmes, Alfred (Sanford classed with the District of Alfred); 1803, John Holmes, Alfred; 1806, Nathaniel Conant, Junior, Alfred, Thomas Keeler, Sanford; 1807, Nathaniel Conant, Junior, Alfred, Thomas Keeler, Sanford; 1810, Sheldon Hobbs; 1811,Sheldon Hobbs; 1812,Elisha Allen and Sheldon Hobbs; 1813, Elisha Allen and Sheldon Hobbs; 1814, Elisha Allen; 1815, Sheldon Hobbs; 1819, Elisha Allen.

To the Legislature of Maine after the Separation — 1820, Elisha Allen; 1821, Elisha Allen; 1822, John Frost, Second; 1826, John Powers; 1827, Timothy Shaw; 1828, Timothy Shaw; 1829, John Powers; 1830, John Powers; 1831, John Powers; 1832, Timothy Shaw; 1833, Timothy Shaw; 1834, Timothy Shaw; 1835, John Powers; 1836, Timothy Shaw; 1837, John T. Paine; 1838, John T. Paine; 1839, John T. Paine; 1840, John T. Paine; 1841, John T. Paine; 1842, Nehemiah Butler.

At this time the number of Representatives was reduced to one hundred and fifty-one, and Sanford and Lebanon were classed together, the first Representative being from Sanford, the second from Lebanon, and so on.

1844, Stephen Dorman; 1845, Alpheus Staples (elected May 19, but his name does not appear on the pay-roll for 1845); 1846, Samuel Tripp; 1848, Nathaniel Hobbs; 1850, Ichabod Frost; 1851, Rev. Oren B. Cheney; 1852, Rev. Oren B. Cheney (held over); 1853, Charles O. Lord; 1855, Nehemiah Butler; 1857, Lyman Butler; 1859, Ebenezer L. Hobbs; 1861, Increase S. Kimball; 1863, Benjamin F. Hanson; 1865, Charles H. Frost; 1867, Samuel Nowell; 1869, Edward K. Bennett; 1871, Simon Tebbets; 1873, William P. True; 1875, William F. Hanson; 1877, Hosea Willard; 1879, Jeremiah Moulton, Second; 1880, Isaac Hanson (Stephen D. Lord, "counted in," took his seat in the "bogus" legislature, of which H. Carleton Cheever of Springvale was assistant clerk); 1881–82, Ernest M. Goodall; 1885–86, Benjamin Beal; 1889–90, George H. Nowell.

In 1892 a new apportionment of legislative districts was made, under which Sanford was no longer a classed town with Lebanon, but chose its own Representative at each election.

1893–94, Orville V. Libby; 1895–96, Charles F. Moulton; 1897–98, Willis E. Sanborn; 1899–1900, William Kernon; 1901–02, Fred J. Allen.

In 1806, when Thomas Keeler was elected a member of the House of Representatives, objections to his taking his seat were made by John Sayward and others. It is alleged that Ebenezer Sayward, innholder, of Alfred, furnished voters with victuals and drink, and that Keeler paid the bill; that Keeler made a similar agreement with Paul Webber; that the meeting was tumultuous and disorderly, and conducted with an unusual and unpardonable degree of spirit and acrimony, probably as a result of hard drinking; that Keeler gave a public invitation after the election to the voters to go to any or all of the public houses or stores in Alfred, or to his own house in Sanford to receive such refreshments as they should want, and that he and his colleague, Nathaniel Conant, Junior, paid more than fifty dollars (some were furnished with refreshments at Keeler's house and store); that there was the appearance of a riot and much drunkenness, fighting and quarreling at his store; and that Keeler was a deputy postmaster, and had no assistant in that office. The decision rendered, however, was that Keeler was duly elected, and nothing appeared to prevent him from holding his seat.

In 1813–14 the election of Sanford was controverted, but no report or action of the House was taken thereon.

In 1836 there was an exceedingly long-drawn-out contest over the election of a Representative. On the first ballot, the vote stood as follows : John T. Paine, eighty votes ; Jotham Welch, sixty-two ; John Powers, one hundred and ten ; Daniel P. Shaw, twenty-two ; John Frost, Second, one. There was no choice. Nicholas E. Paine was substituted for John T. Paine. Three more ballots were taken, without a choice, and the meeting adjourned for one week. As no election then resulted, the meeting was further adjourned from week to week, for four weeks, when, finally, on the thirty-third ballot, on the sixth election day, a choice was made. John T. Paine, John Powers, and Daniel P. Shaw were the principal candidates, after the first meeting, the last named controlling the election. The final ballot stood : Paine, one hundred and seventy-nine votes ; Powers, one hundred and sixty-eight ; Shaw, seven ; scattering, two. The following year, three ballots were required to elect. John T. Paine was again the successful candidate.

OTHER OFFICERS.

Senators—General Timothy Shaw, 1839 – 40 ; Benjamin F. Hanson, 1874 – 76 ; Ernest M. Goodall, 1883 – 84 ; Charles H. Frost, 1889 – 90.

Councillors—Dr. Caleb Emery, 1829 (born in Sanford) ; Elisha Allen, 1830 ; Increase S. Kimball, 1841 (residing in Lebanon) ; Ichabod Frost, 1857 ; George A. Frost, 1861 – 62 ; Ernest M. Goodall, 1885 – 86.

Deputy Sheriffs—Caleb Emery, 1784 – 86 ; William Emery, 1788 – 1810 ; Jedediah Allen, 1812 – 15, 1817 – 19 ; Abner Hill, 1813, 1815 – 19 ; John Powers, Junior, 1816 – 19 ; Moses Lord, 1820 – 24 ; William Emery, Junior, 1825 – 30, 1838 ; Ebenezer Garey, 1827 – 28 ; James B. Shapleigh, 1828 – 29, 1831 – 33, 1838 ; Ebenezer Nowell, 1830, 1838 ; Emilus Allen, 1832 – 34 ; William B. Merrick, 1835 ; Samuel B. Emery, 1834 – 37, 1839 ; Nathaniel Bennett, Third, 1838 ; Nathaniel Hobbs ; Caleb S. Emery, 1840–41 ; John Shaw, 1840 – 41 ; Ivory Johnson, 1841 ; Samuel Lord, 1842, 1846, 1850, 1863 ; Timothy Shaw, Junior, 1842 ; Daniel L. Littlefield, 1845 – 48 ; John Lord, 1848 ; John Hemingway, 1854 ; Simon Tebbets, 1854, 1857 ; George Nowell, 1856 ; Albert J. Smith, 1857 ; Charles O. Lord, 1859 ;

24

John W. Bodwell, 1859; Samuel D. Tebbets, 1860, 1865, 1867, 1879; Samuel Nowell, 1861; James M. Nowell, 1869; Edmund G. Murray, 1871–99; Charles Oscar Emery, 1879–81; William A. Allen, 1881–88; Frank N. Butler, 1885–88; Thomas Reid, 1889–95; Newell T. Fogg, 1895–1900 (elected Sheriff); Hiram B. Rowe, 1900–01; Thomas T. Rankin, deputy sheriff and keeper of Alfred jail, 1901.

"*Goal*" *Keepers*—Nathaniel Bennett, Third, 1843; William Emery; Ebenezer Nowell.

Coroners — Henry Hamilton, 1777–85; Ezra Thompson, 1803–19; Samuel Moulton, 1807–19; Stephen Gowen, 1811; Ebenezer Nowell, 1818–19, 1822–33, 1836, 1840, 1842; Ephraim Low, Junior, 1820–25; Stephen Hobbs, 1822–25; Moses Lord, 1822–24; Ebenezer Garey, 1828–31; John Hanson, 1829–33, 1836; William Emery, Junior, 1829–31, 1840, 1842; William Butler, 1833–36; James B. Shapleigh, 1833–34; Samuel B. Emery, 1836, 1840; Nathaniel Bennett, 1840, 1842; Samuel Nowell, 1871–1882; Charles F. Moulton, 1893 to the present time.

VOTES FOR PRESIDENT.

1788. Two electors were chosen by the legislature immediately. Of the candidates (two names on each ballot) voted for in each district, the General Court chose one of the two receiving the highest number of votes, as elector for that district. For candidates, David Sewell and Joseph Noys (Noyes), Federalists, received in Sanford, nine votes; William Widgery and Samuel Nasson, Anti-Federalists, twenty-three votes. In the Maine district, Daniel Sewell received two hundred and thirty-one votes and Daniel Cony, two hundred and thirteen. The former was chosen, and voted for George Washington.

1792. For electors, York County, Edward Cutts, 16 votes; Cumberland, Peleg Wadsworth, 16; Lincoln, Hancock, and Washington, Nathaniel Twing, 16, John R. Smith, one. Nathaniel Wells, Peleg Wadsworth, and Daniel Cony were chosen, and voted for George Washington.

1796. Nathaniel Wells, Federalist, 10 votes; John Adams, Federalist, was elected.

1800. Federal electors chosen by the legislature.

1804. James Sullivan and seventeen others (Suffolk district not mentioned in the records), Republicans, 101 votes; John Coffin

Jones and fifteen others, Federalists, 8 ; John Lord, Berwick, Federalist, 6 ; Reverend Moses Sweat, Sanford, Federalist, 2. Thomas Jefferson, Republican, was elected. Charles C. Pinckney was the Federalist candidate.

1808. Federal electors chosen by the legislature.

1812. York County, John Woodman, Cumberland, Theodore Mussey, Oxford, Henry Rust, Republicans, or Democrats, 115 votes ; York County, Nathaniel Goodwin, Cumberland, Samuel Parris, Oxford, Lothrop Lewis, Federalists, 109. James Madison, Republican, or Democrat, was elected. DeWitt Clinton was the Federalist candidate.

1816. Federal electors chosen by the legislature.

1820. . At large, Joshua Wingate, Junior, William Moody, Republicans or Democrats, 76 and 73 votes respectively ; First District, Elisha Allen, Republican, or Democrat, 74 votes. Colonel (afterward General) Allen received 793 of the 861 votes cast in the district. James Monroe, Republican, or Democrat, was elected.

1824. At large, Thomas Fillebrown, James Campbell, and York District, Nathaniel Hobbs, National Republicans, 83 votes ; at large, William Chadwick, Peleg Tallman, and York District, John McDonald, Democrats, or Democratic Republicans,' 18, 18, and 19 respectively. John Quincy Adams, National Republican, was elected. Andrew Jackson was the Democrat, or Democratic Republican candidate.

1828. John Quincy Adams, National Republican, 114 ; Andrew Jackson, Democrat, or Democratic Republican, 4.

1832. Andrew Jackson, Democrat, 205 ; Henry Clay, National Republican, or Whig, 143.

1836. Martin Van Buren, Democrat, 123 ; William H. Harrison, Whig, 66.

1840. William Henry Harrison, Whig, 172 ; Martin Van Buren, Democrat, 254.

1844. James K. Polk, Democrat, 230 ; Henry Clay, Whig, 144 ; James G. Birney, Abolitionist, 17.

1848. Lewis Cass, Democrat, 227 ; Zachary Taylor, Whig, 152 ; Martin Van Buren, Free-Soiler, Abolitionist or Whig (?), one. (Tristram Gilman and eight others had one vote each.)

1852. Franklin Pierce, Democrat, 222 ; Winfield Scott, Whig, 182 : John P. Hale, Free-Soiler, 40.

1856. John C. Fremont, Republican, 257 ; James Buchanan, Democrat, 215 ; Millard Fillmore, Whig, 9.

1860. Abraham Lincoln, Republican, 222 ; Stephen A. Douglas,

Northern Democrat, 163; John C. Breckenridge, Southern Democrat, 15; John Bell, Union, 6.

1864. Abraham Lincoln, Republican, 218; George B. McClellan, Democrat, 265.

1868. Ulysses S. Grant, Republican, 240; Horatio Seymour, Democrat, 194.

1872. Ulysses S. Grant, Republican, 210; Horace Greeley, Democrat and Liberal, 100.

1876. Rutherford B. Hayes, Republican, 224; Samuel J. Tilden, Democrat, 270.

1880. James A. Garfield, Republican, 253; Winfield S. Hancock, Democrat, 338; James B. Weaver, Greenback, one.

1884. James G. Blaine, Republican, 315; Grover Cleveland, Democrat, 267; Benjamin F. Butler, Greenback, 12; John P. St. John, Prohibitionist, 10.

1888. Benjamin Harrison, Republican, 425; Grover Cleveland, Democrat, 295; Clinton B. Fisk, Prohibitionist, 9; Alson J. Streeter, Union Labor, 14.

1892. Benjamin Harrison, Republican, 488; Grover Cleveland, Democrat, 398; John Bidwell, Prohibitionist, 31; James B. Weaver, People's Party, 26.

1896. William McKinley, Republican, 662; William J. Bryan, Democrat, 176; John M. Palmer, National Democrat, 7; Joshua Levering, Prohibitionist, 14; William J. Bryan, People's Party, 8.

1900. William McKinley, Republican, 775; William J. Bryan, Democrat, 256; John G. Woolley, Prohibitionist, 37; Eugene V. Debs, Democrat Socialist, 5.

The Presidential campaign of 1840, known as the "log cabin and hard cider campaign," was very exciting everywhere. The Sanford delegation to a convention at Kennebunk went with a large log cabin built upon wheels and drawn by oxen. The old men rode in it, having a barrel of hard cider to drink. Its walls were hung with coon skins. Sanford gave Van Buren a large majority, but the state went for Harrison.

During the "Know Nothing" agitation, a subordinate council of the organization, located at Springvale, though ultimately extending throughout the town, was instituted August 3, 1854, by Charles E. Weld. It was composed of William Gage, Loammi K. Moulton, and sixteen others. This council ran till it numbered, August 10, 1855, ninety-seven members. It finally went mostly into the Republican party.

VOTES FOR GOVERNOR.

1780.	John Hancock,	14
1781.	John Hancock,	13
	John Savage,	1
1782.	John Hancock,	14
1784.	John Hancock,	17
1785.	Thomas Cushing,	19
	James Bowdoin,	0
1786.	Benjamin Lincoln,	16
	James Bowdoin,	2
1787.	John Hancock,	60
1788.	John Hancock,	24
	Elbridge Gerry,	21
	James Bowdoin,	3
1789.	John Hancock,	74
1790.	John Hancock,	51
	James Bowdoin,	5
1791.	John Hancock,	63
1792.	John Hancock,	58
1794.	William Cushing,	53
	Samuel Adams,	43
	Theodore Lyman,	3
1795.	Samuel Adams,	26
	Theodore Lyman,	11
1796.	Samuel Adams,	14
	Increase Sumner,	15
	Samuel Nassou,	1
1797.	James Sullivan,	29
	Increase Sumner,	21
	Samuel Nasson,	1
1798.	Increase Sumner,	26
	James Sullivan,	17
	Theodore Lyman,	4
1799.	Increase Sumner,	15
	William Heath,	48
	Theodore Lyman,	1
1800.	Caleb Strong,	23
	Elbridge Gerry,	14
	Oliver Keating,	2
1801.	Caleb Strong,	16
	Elbridge Gerry,	31
1802.	Elbridge Gerry,	44
	Caleb Strong,	25
1803.	Elbridge Gerry,	59
	Caleb Strong,	25
1804.	James Sullivan,	124
	Caleb Strong,	10

1805.	James Sullivan,	131
	Caleb Strong,	15
1806.	James Sullivan,	140
	Caleb Strong,	18
1807.	James Sullivan,	149
	Caleb Strong,	22
	Benjamin Austin,	4
1808.	James Sullivan,	110
	Christopher Gore,	38
	Benjamin Austin,	2
1809.	Levi Lincoln,	95
	Christopher Gore,	87
	Joseph B. Varnum,	1
	David Cobb,	1
	Nahum Morrill,	1
1810.	Christopher Gore,	73
	Elbridge Gerry,	107
1811.	Elbridge Gerry,	109
	Christopher Gore,	75
	William Gray,	2
1812.	Elbridge Gerry,	154
	Caleb Strong,	53
1813.	Caleb Strong,	99
	Joseph B. Varnum,	144
1814.	Caleb Strong,	98
	Samuel Dexter,	138
1815.	Caleb Strong,	79
	Samuel Dexter,	136
1816.	Samuel Dexter,	145
	John Brooks,	76
1817.	John Brooks,	60
	Henry Dearborn,	108
1818.	John Brooks,	61
	Benjamin W. Crown-ingshield,	97
1819.	John Brooks,	60
	Benjamin W. Crown-ingshield,	73

After Separation.

1820.	William King, Rep.,	164
	Ezekiel Whitman,	9
	John Holmes,	1
	Samuel Merrill,	1
1821.	Albion K. Parris, Rep.,	30

1821.	Joshua Wingate, Jr.,	
	Rep.,	14
	Ezekiel Whitman,Fed.,	69
	William D. William-	
	son,	10
	Benjamin Ames,	1
	Samuel Merrill,	3
1822.	Albion K. Parris,Rep.,	59
	Ezekiel Whitman,Fed.,	83
1823.	Albion K. Parris,Rep.,	148
	Ezekiel Whitman,Fed.,	3
	Ephraim Low, Jr.,	1
	John W. Bodwell,	1
	Thomas Nasson,	1
	Reuben Chick,	1
1824.	Albion K. Parris,Rep.,	122
1825.	Albion K. Parris,Rep.,	63
1826.	Enoch Lincoln, Rep.,	131
1827.	Enoch Lincoln, Rep.,	83
	John Holmes,	1
	Thomas Merrill,	1
1828.	Enoch Lincoln, Rep.,	140
	John Powers,	1
1829.	Jonathan G. Hunton,	
	Nat. Rep.,	181
	Samuel E. Smith,	
	Dem. Rep.,	126
	Joseph Dane,	1
1830.	Jonathan G. Hunton,	
	Nat. Rep.,	193
	Samuel E. Smith,	
	Dem. Rep.,	174
	Timothy Shaw,	1
1831.	Samuel E. Smith,	
	Dem. Rep.,	183
	Daniel Goodenow,	
	Nat. Rep.,	140
1832.	Samuel E. Smith,	
	Dem. Rep.,	212
	Daniel Goodenow,	
	Nat. Rep.,	116
1833.	Samuel E. Smith,	
	Dis. Dem.,	156
	Daniel Goodenow,	
	Whig,	80
	Robert P. Dunlap,	
	Dem.,	1
	Joseph Dane,	1

1834.	Robert P. Dunlap,	
	Dem.,	150
	Peleg Sprague, Whig,	145
	Samuel E. Smith,	
	Dis. Dem.,	2
1835.	Robert P. Dunlap,	
	Dem.,	144
	William King, Whig,	59
1836.	Robert P. Dunlap,	
	Dem.,	157
	Edward Kent, Whig,	91
1837.	Gorham Parks, Dem.,	174
	Edward Kent, Whig,	118
1838.	John Fairfield, Dem.,	257
	Edward Kent, Whig,	181
1839.	John Fairfield, Dem.,	212
	Edward Kent, Whig,	126
1840.	John Fairfield, Dem.,	236
	Edward Kent, Whig,	165
1841.	John Fairfield, Dem.,	244
	Edward Kent, Whig,	130
	Daniel Goodenow,	1
	Jeremiah Curtis,	1
1842.	John Fairfield, Dem.,	221
	Edward Robinson,	
	Whig,	105
1843.	Hugh J. Anderson,	
	Dem.,	203
	Edward Robinson,	
	Whig,	79
	James Appleton, Lib.,	49
1844.	Hugh J. Anderson,	
	Dem.,	245
	Edward Robinson,	
	Whig,	160
	James Appleton, Lib.,	23
1845.	Hugh J. Anderson,	
	Dem.,	187
	Freeman H. Morse,	
	Whig,	107
	Samuel Fessenden,	
	Lib.,	32
1846.	David Bronson,Whig,	156
	John W. Dana, Dem.,	147
	Samuel Fessenden,	
	Lib.,	26
	Reuel Williams,	2
1847.	John W. Dana, Dem.,	176

1847.	David Bronson, Whig,	106
	Samuel Fessenden,	
	Lib.,	36
1848.	John W. Dana, Dem.,	207
	Elijah L. Hamlin,	
	Whig,	110
	Samuel Fessenden,	
	Lib.,	67
1849.	John Hubbard, Dem.,	223
	Elijah L. Hamlin,	
	Whig,	156
	George F. Talbot, F. S.,	44
1850.	John Hubbard, Dem.,	196
	William G. Crosby,	
	Whig,	174
	George F. Talbot, F. S.,	28
1851.	No election. The Gov-	
	ernor of 1850 held	
	over.	
1852.	Anson G. Chandler,	
	A. M. L.,	232
	William G. Crosby,	
	Whig,	132
	John Hubbard, Dem.,	88
	Ezekiel Holmes, F. S.,	8
1853.	Albert Pillsbury, Dem.,	204
	William G. Crosby,	
	Whig,	102
	Ezekiel Holmes, F. S.,	47
	Anson P. Morrill, M. L.,	21
1854.	Albion K. Parris,	
	Dem.,	134
	Anson P. Morrill, M.	
	L. and K. N.,	135
	Shepard Cary, Opp.	
	Dem.,	95
	Isaac Reed, Whig,	21
1855.	Samuel Wells, Dem.,	275
	Anson P. Morrill,	
	Rep.,	190
	Isaac Reed, Whig,	15
1856.	Samuel Wells, Dem.,	295
	Hannibal Hamlin,	
	Rep.,	234
	George F. Patten,	
	Whig,	2
1857.	Manasseh H. Smith,	
	Dem.,	214

1857.	Lot M. Morrill, Rep.,	221
	Robert Thompson,	1
	Edward Kent,	2
1858.	Manasseh H. Smith,	
	Dem.,	299
	Lot M. Morrill, Rep.,	205
1859.	Lot M. Morrill, Rep.,	200
	Manasseh H. Smith,	
	Dem.,	253
	Simon Tebbets,	2
1860.	Israel Washburn, Jr.,	
	Rep.,	232
	Ephraim K. Smart,	
	Dem.,	273
	Phinehas Barnes,	
	Whig,	2
1861.	John W. Dana, Dem.,	217
	Israel Washburn, Jr.,	
	Rep.,	229
	Charles D. Jameson,	
	War Dem.,	23
1862.	Bion Bradbury, Dem.,	240
	Abner Coburn. Rep.,	202
	Charles D. Jameson,	
	War Dem.,	2
1863.	Bion Bradbury, Dem.,	273
	Samuel Cony, Rep.,	230
	I, Esq.,	1
1864.	Joseph Howard, Dem.,	267
	Samuel Cony, Rep.,	210
1865.	Joseph Howard, Dem.,	226
	Samuel Cony, Rep.,	192
1866.	Eben F. Pillsbury,	
	Dem.,	251
	Joshua L. Chamber-	
	lain, Rep.,	230
	Pelatiah Witham,	11
1867.	Eben F. Pillsbury,	
	Dem.,	271
	Joshua L. Chamber-	
	lain, Rep.,	202
	Pelatiah Witham,	3
1868.	Eben F. Pillsbury,	
	Dem.,	283
	Joshua L. Chamber-	
	lain, Rep.,	253
	Pelatiah Witham,	1
1869.	Franklin Smith, Dem.,	189

1869. Joshua L. Chamber-
lain, Rep., 179
Nathan G. Hichborn,
Tem., 20
Lot M. Morrill, 1
1870. Chas. W.'Roberts, Dem., 185
Sidney Perham, Rep., 187
1871. Chas. P. Kimball, Dem., 201
Sidney Perham, Rep., 202
1872. Charles P. Kimball,
Dem., 259
Sidney Perham, Rep., 241
Charles O'Connor, 2
1873. Nelson Dingley, Jr.,
Rep., 171
Joseph Titcomb, Dem., 164
1874. Joseph Titcomb, Dem., 186
Nelson Dingley, Jr.,
Rep., 181
1875. Charles W. Roberts,
Dem., 211
Selden Connor, Rep., 161
1876. John C. Talbot, Dem., 322
Selden Connor, Rep., 260
1877. Joseph H. Williams,
Dem., 273
Selden Connor, Rep., 187
1878. Alonzo Garcelon, Dem., 172
Joseph L. Smith, Nat.
G. B., 148
Selden Connor, Rep., 145
1879. Daniel F. Davis, Rep., 199
Joseph L. Smith, Nat.
G. B., 192
Alonzo Garcelon, Dem., 141
Bion Bradbury,Dem., 5
1880. Harris M. Plaisted, Fus., 339
Daniel F. Davis, Rep., 245
1882. Harris M. Plaisted, Fus., 320
Frederick Robie, Rep., 297
1884. Frederick Robie, Rep., 337
John B. Redman, Dem., 313
Hosea B. Eaton, G. B., 2
William T. Eustis, Pro., 1
1886. Joseph R. Bodwell,
Rep., 356
Clark S. Edwards,
Dem., 324

1886. Aaron B. Clark, Pro., 6
1888. Edwin C. Burleigh,
Rep., 489
William L. Putnam,
Dem., 334
Volney B. Cushing,
Pro., 6
William H. Simmons,
Lab., 19
1890. Edwin C. Burleigh,
Rep., 389
William P. Thompson,
Dem., 316
Aaron B. Clark, Pro., 15
Isaac C. Clark, Lab., 13
1892. Henry B. Cleaves, Rep., 466
Charles F. Johnson,
Dem., 412
Timothy B. Hussey,
Pro., 32
Luther C. Bateman,
Peo., 7
E. F. Knowlton, Un.
Lab., 2
1894. Henry B. Cleaves,
Rep., 506
Charles F. Johnson,
Dem., 225
Ira G. Hersey, Pro., 18
Luther C. Bateman,
Peo., 39
1896. Llewellyn Powers, Rep., 626
Melvin P. Frank, Dem., 194
A. S. Ladd, Pro., 29
Luther C. Bateman,
Peo., 6
William H. Clifford,
Nat. Dem., 3
1898. Llewellyn Powers, Rep., 542
Samuel L. Lord, Dem., 251
A. S. Ladd, Pro., 39
Robert Gerry, Peo., 4
Erastus Lermond. Nat.
Dem., 2
1900. John F. Hill, Rep., 831
Samuel L. Lord, Dem., 249
Grant Rogers, Pro., 23
N. W. Lermond. Soc., 1

CHAPTER XXXVIII.

ODDS AND ENDS OF HISTORY.

The Press — Public Library — Opera House — Public Observances, the Centennial Fourth, and Other Occasions — Some " First Things " — Longevity — Large Families — Musical Organizations — A Trout-Breeding Experiment — Christian Civic League and Other Organizations — War With Spain — The Filipino Insurrection.

FOR the past quarter of a century the town of Sanford has had a weekly newspaper, and for most of the time two. The Springvale Reporter was the first to be issued. In November, 1875, H. Carlton Cheever, having sold out his office at Danvers, Mass., visited Springvale to look over the ground, and locate, if advisable. This latter he concluded to do, and by the first week in December had part of his material on hand ready for work. His first office was in the Frank Butler building, corner of Main and Bridge Streets. Mr. Cheever's first compositor was Mrs. Jesse Giles, who had worked many years in the Argus office, Portland. In press work he had the assistance of Thomas Slater, who had learned the trade more than fifty years before, in Manchester, England. The first number of the Reporter was printed Saturday, January 1, 1876, at about nine o'clock in the evening, and its appearance was the occasion of considerable excitement on the part of the people of Springvale (who crowded in to see the thing done), and of a great deal of labor and anxiety on the part of the publisher. The venture, however, proved a success. For one year from March 1, 1879, Cheever and Noyes were the proprietors. Mr. Cheever then assumed sole charge again, and continued till May 15, 1880, when he removed from Sanford.

On the 19th of June, 1880, D. M. Frye and E. Lord, under the firm name of D. M. Frye and Co., started the York County Advocate at Springvale. This paper passed into the hands of Mr. Frye, January 6, 1881, and in December following was purchased by Frank H. Dexter, who still continues its publication, having changed its name to the Springvale Advocate, September 29, 1882. Mr. Dexter issues a wide awake, readable, newsy sheet, in which local happenings and those of the surrounding towns are chronicled with care. The editor being a prominent temperance worker, the Advocate is a staunch supporter of the temperance cause, as well as of everything else that makes for the good of the community.

The first paper at Sanford Corner was the Sanford News, of which Rev. Henry J. Stone began the publication July 3, 1880. It was printed at W. A. Allen's printing office. Rev. Mr. Stone, although pastor of the Congregational Church at the time, had been previously engaged in the printing business, which he had always found congenial, even fascinating, and his active, untiring spirit led him to assume editorial duties in addition to those of his pastorate. The paper was continued until October 27, 1883, shortly before Mr. Stone severed his connection with the Sanford church, the name having been changed to the Sanford Weekly News after April 23, 1881.

The Sanford Herald was printed by T. P. James from October 1, 1884, to October, 1885.

November 8, 1888, James H. and Frank A. Goodall started the Sanford Siftings, of which the former was announced as publisher, and the latter, who had been, and is at the present time, although removed from Sanford, correspondent for papers in Boston and other large cities, as editor. After one year, Siftings retired from the field, but on March 5, 1892, the Messrs. Goodall made their second venture with the Sanford Weekly Ledger. The publication of the Ledger was continued until October 31, 1895.

Since December 19, 1895, Sanford village has been represented in the journalistic world by the Sanford Weekly Tribune. This paper was established by Mr. and Mrs. George W. Huff, who carried it on successfully for over three years. In the spring of 1899, Mr. Huff retired, to take charge of another line of business which demanded all his time, and on May 1 of that year the Tribune was sold to Fred B. Averill, the present editor and publisher. Soon after taking control, Mr. Averill issued a special edition, illustrated with half-tone pictures of well known citizens and buildings in the village. The Tribune has taken as its motto, " A Live Paper in a Live Town," and Mr. Averill has lived up to it. The paper is now issued in attractive eight-page form, and its columns bear evidence of the enterprise and ability of its editor.

The N. E. O. P. Journal, organ of the New England Order of Protection, was published at Springvale by D. M. Frye from October, 1889, to 1894.

The Star, a monthly paper devoted to the interests of the Christian Endeavor movement, was published by Fred B. Averill for two years from December, 1895.

The Sanford Directory was issued by D. M. Frye in December, 1893. It contains a historical sketch of Sanford by Edwin Emery.

Sanford has had a free public library, open to all residents of the town, since June 1, 1900. The story of the organization and growth of the library is best told in the following extract from the Sanford Tribune of May 18 of this year:

" For the past twenty years or more a few public spirited citizens have been agitating the question of a free library for the town, but no definite action was taken until about five years ago, when the Woman's Literary Club, organized for the purpose of collecting books to be given to a public library at some future date, commenced by purchasing an edition of Chambers' Encyclopædia. Other books were added from time to time as fast as the Club's means would permit, until, in 1898, when the library became a fact, quite a respectable collection had been made. Meanwhile the ladies had not been alone in the field. Several young men had been continually agitating the question, among them being Messrs. Bentley Aveyard and Edward H. Emery, through whose persistent efforts the public were compelled to keep the matter in mind. Superintendent E. E. Hussey of the Sanford Mills, was among the first to become interested and other prominent men, including Mr. Thomas Goodall, took the matter in hand. June 18, 1898, the Sanford Library Association was organized with eighty members and the following officers chosen : Thomas Goodall, President ; Fred J. Allen, Vice President ; William Batchelder, Junior, Clerk ; E. E. Hussey, Treasurer ; Fred J. Allen, George H. Nowell, Moses Wentworth, Thomas Goodall, William Batchelder, Junior, Trustees. The Woman's Literary Club donated their collection, and it was decided to open a library at once, to be run for an indefinite period on a membership basis, each member to pay two dollars per year for use of the books, and non-members to pay five cents per week if they desired library privileges. Bentley Aveyard was chosen librarian, which position he has held ever since. At that time about thirteen hundred dollars had been pledged for support of the library. Of this amount the Sanford Mills subscribed five hundred dollars and the Goodall Worsted Company two hundred and fifty dollars, the remainder being given in smaller sums by individuals. Mr. Goodall offered free use of the rooms on the ground floor of the building on School street where the library is now located, and about six hundred volumes were purchased with the money subscribed. The library was first opened to the public December 31, 1898. At the beginning of the second year the membership fee was reduced to one dollar. The librarian's report for the year ending April 30, 1900, showed that one hundred and seventy-one volumes had been added during the year, one hundred and fifteen by purchase, and fifty-six by gift. Some twenty public documents and pamphlets have also been donated. The reading room was opened to the public for free use February 1, 1899, and has been extensively patronized. The library now numbers nine hundred and fifty volumes."

There was a library in existence — the Social library — in 1819, for the town voted not to give Hubbard's "History of New England" to it, on May 3 of that year.

After its period of service as a public building was ended, the old town-house at Sanford Corner was purchased by Hon. Thomas Goodall, who added another story to it, and converted it into a public hall. It was called Goodall's Hall for many years, and on numerous occasions served as a place for public worship. About a dozen years ago it was converted into a theatre, or opera house, and was fitted with opera chairs, stage appliances and all the equipments of a modern playhouse. Many travelling companies have appeared there. During the past summer the building was torn down, on account of its being adjudged unsafe, and at this writing, a new theatre is being erected on the east side of School Street. It is to have a seating capacity of about a thousand people, and will embrace all the conveniences of modern theatre construction, the plans having been drawn by S. Tobey, architect, of Boston. The theatre is being built by the Sanford Mills, and is owned and controlled by that corporation.

The seventy-first anniversary of our national independence was observed at Springvale, Monday, July 5, 1847, with a celebration somewhat elaborate for those days. A salute of twenty-seven guns was fired at sunrise. At half-past ten o'clock a procession formed on Maple Street, and headed by the Saco Brass Band, moved to Picnic Grove, under the direction of John T. Paine, assisted by four marshals. This procession consisted of the president of the day, orator, and reader of the Declaration of Independence, committee of arrangements, ladies of the village and vicinity, strangers and citizens. At the grove the exercises comprised : Music by the band ; reading of the Declaration of Independence ; salute of thirteen guns, and "Hail Columbia" by the band ; oration. After the exercises, the procession reformed and proceeded through Maple, Prince,

Bridge, and Water Streets to Market Square, where refreshments
were served. The "Hydrosquabntic Dragoons" made their second
annual appearance in full uniform at seven in the morning and half
past five in the afternoon, under the direction of Corporal Snooks,
Commander-in-chief, who "conducted his forces through the principal streets, lanes, courts, and avenues of the large and flourishing
village of Springvale."

The Fourth of July, 1876, the nation's one hundredth birthday,
was celebrated in Sanford, in common with other places, with special
exercises, including an historical address. We quote from the
Springvale Reporter, an account of the day's observance in Sanford :
" The Centennial Fourth is now past, and the forms and actions of
its observance have passed into history, to be studied and reviewed
by the generations who are to control and give shape to the destiny
of the great American nation through its second century of existence.
In Springvale the only recognition of the day was the ringing of the
bells at sunrise and the hoisting of the nation's ensign by several of
our patriotic citizens. At Sanford the day was ushered in by the
usual noisy demonstrations of Young America and the national salute
at sunrise. Next on the programme were the Horribles, over one
hundred in number, under the command of Fred Kimball personating
the Indian chief, Wahwa, a celebrated sachem of the tribe occupying the territory embracing what is now Sanford, mounted upon the
spirited coal-black steed, St. Lawrence, Junior. All sorts of funny
ideas were represented with good effect. The 'Centennial Thoughts'
by Lew Ginger were full of happy hits, and were received by the
listening crowd with frequent bursts of applause. The song, entitled
' One Hundred Years Ago,' written, composed, and sung with great
success by Mr. Ginger, needs no comment from us. At eleven
o'clock, L. B. Goodall, president of the day, took the stand, accompanied by Edwin Emery, Esq., who being formally introduced, proceeded to give an historical sketch of the town from its first settlement
until 1800. After the address the Declaration of Independence was
read by I. S. Kimball, Esq. The celebration was closed by a fine
display of fireworks in front of Mr. Goodall's residence, which was
gaily illuminated with numerous Chinese lanterns, which were also
displayed by Kimball Brothers and Company. There was a large
gathering of people from the adjoining towns and the scene was one
not soon to be forgotten by all who witnessed it. The music for the
day was furnished by the Sanford Cornet Band." The committee of
arrangements comprised W. A. Allen, L. B. Goodall, and C. C.
Littlefield.

Memorial services on the death of President Garfield were held on Sunday, September 25, 1881, in the Freewill Baptist Church, Springvale, Friendship Lodge, I. O. O. F., being present. The church was draped in mourning. The services were conducted by Rev. Mr. Blaisdell, assisted by Rev. Mr. Osborn. At the Corner on Monday, the 26th, the day of the funeral, business was generally suspended, and the mills and stores were draped in mourning. In the square, a beautiful monument, with the name, "James A. Garfield," inscribed on the four sides, was erected. Services held in the Congregational Church included a sermon by Rev. Mr. Stone and an address by Rev. Mr. Blaisdell.

Memorial Day had been informally observed prior to 1883, but the first stated ceremonies occurred in that year. At ten o'clock in the morning, squads of Grand Army members decorated the graves of deceased soldiers and sailors. At eleven o'clock the Limerick Band gave a concert, and a procession was formed, made up of William F. Willard Post, G. A. R., Knights of Pythias, Encampment of Odd Fellows, temperance organizations, and school children. The parade moved through Springvale, starting from the town-house, and proceeding to the school-house yard, where an oration was delivered by Rev. T. C. Russell, after which the line of march was taken up for the cemetery, where Post services were held. The parade then returned to Main Street Square and was dismissed.

On August 9, 1885, memorial services for General Grant were observed by William F. Willard Post, G. A. R. Services in the morning were held in the Congregational Church at Sanford, Rev. Mr. Cook preaching. The church was appropriately draped. In the afternoon, services were held at the Freewill Baptist Church, Springvale, which was festooned with black and white. Addresses were given by Rev. R. D. Frost, Rev. C. P. Bennett, and Rev. George A. Tewksbury of Cambridge, Mass., and the Sanford Cadet Band and the Springvale Male Quartette participated.

March 1, 1891, the Sherman Porter memorial service was held in the Baptist Church, Springvale. Willard Post, G. A. R., and Willard Relief Corps attended. The pulpit was draped with the American flag. The house was filled with an attentive audience. Rev. George S. Chase delivered the address.

Columbus Day exercises were held by the public schools of Sanford at the Opera House on Friday evening, October 21, 1892. There were appropriate tableaux, recitations, and music, and addresses by George Goodwin, Rev. C. C. Speare, Edward H. Emery, and Dr. J. H. Neal.

The first carriage in town is said to have been owned by Dr. Ebenezer Linscott, who began to practice in Sanford not far from 1800. Timothy Gowen purchased it, and made it over into a wagon. According to tradition it was painted yellow. Mrs. Nicholas E. Paine probably owned the first pianoforte, John Storer, the second, and Rev. Mr. Goss, the third.

The national game of base-ball was introduced in 1861.

The first steamboat, " Elfin " was launched May 15, 1877. She was twenty-five feet in length, and could carry ten or fifteen passengers. Her owners were Goodall Brothers, and William A. Allen, Sanford, J. Hopewell, Jr., and Edwin Ham, Boston, and E. A. Noyes, Portland.

Louis B. Goodall introduced the bicycle in April, 1879.

The telephone was first used in May, 1883, when the office of the Sanford and Mousam River Mills, about a quarter of a mile apart, were connected by Holcomb's acoustic telephone. The long distance telephone service was instituted May 1, 1894.

The first electric light machine in town was set in motion at William A. Allen's printing-office, October 5, 1886. It was attached to six arc lights. On November 27 of the same year, I. B. Stiles lighted his store by electricity in the presence of four hundred people.

The first automobile in town was purchased by Hon. E. M. Goodall in June, 1900.

Five centenarians have died in Sanford : Susannah Davis, November 25, 1835, aged one hundred and four years ; Patience Plummer, January 17, 1840, aged one hundred years, eleven months and twenty-seven days ; Moses Tebbets, August 25, 1825, aged one hundred and one years, five months and thirteen days ; Eleanor Worster, widow of William, November 24, 1852, aged one hundred years and six months ; and Nancy Paul Welch, March 17, 1893, in her one hundred and first year.

Nonogenarians who have died in Sanford, or having long been residents of Sanford, have died elsewhere, are as follows, given alphabetically : Ephraim Allen, died November 14, 1868, aged ninety-one years ; Lydia (Mrs. Ephraim) Allen, October 28, 1878, ninety-one ; Solomon Allen, December 19, 1826, ninety-eight ; Hannah Bean, July 11, 1823, ninety-three ; Joseph Bedell, December 31, 1851, ninety ; Asenath (Mrs. George) Chadbourn, January 15, 1892, ninety-two years, one month, fourteen days ; Abner Clark, September 16, 1882, ninety-two years, nine months, eight days ; Mary (Mrs. William) Deering, July 13, 1859, ninety-three ; Mrs. Lavinia Dodge, March 10, 1891, ninety-four years, nine days ; Eliot Frost, January

30, 1840, ninety-two years, nine months, four days; Hannah (Morrill) (Mrs. John) Frost, October 1, 1884, ninety-four; Abigail (Mrs. Timothy) Gowen, January 11, 1878, ninety-six years, four months, twenty-five days; Hepzabeth Gowen, February 15, 1897, ninety-two years, ten months; Stephen Gowen, March 14, 1846, ninety-two years, eight months, twenty-five days; Walter Gowen, July 18, 1887, ninety-two; Mrs. Hannah Haines, March 27, 1890, ninety-eight; Betsey (Mrs. Nahum) Hersom, October 25, 1893, ninety years, five months; Jane Hough, June 26, 1899, ninety-one years, five months, five days; Scholastique Houle, February 28, 1899, ninety-seven; James Hurd, June 16, 1837, ninety-one years, four months; Sarah (Mrs. Abijah) Hussey, November 28, 1877, ninety-two years, eight months, twenty-five days; Jane Jackson, March 4, 1855, ninety-one; Margaret Johnson, March 30, 1831, ninety-one years, nine months; Sarah Johnson, 1862 (?), ninety-five; Betsey Leavitt, August, 1858, ninety; Ithamar Littlefield, December 24, 1837, ninety-three years, eight months, twenty-seven days; Louisa Lord, July 11, 1899, ninety-two years, eight months, five days; Betsey Moore, November 19, 1877, ninety-one years, five months; Hannah (Mrs. Jeremiah) Moulton, November 25, 1869, ninety-one; Hiram Murray, May 28, 1886, ninety-three years, six months, two days; Margaret (Mrs. Michael) O'Connor, November 1, 1894, about ninety years; Mary (Mrs. John) Paine, May 15, 1861, ninety-two years, two months, ten days; Mrs. Lucy Parsons, October 21, 1871, ninety-two years, seven months, nine days; Mrs. Experience Perkins, October 4, 1889, ninety-two years, five months; Mary H. Perkins, April 11, 1895, ninety years, eight months, sixteen days; Moses Plummer, April 1, 1850, ninety-three years, six months; John Quint, June 24, 1856, ninety-five or ninety-six years; Gideon Ross, June 25, 1887, ninety years, three months; Keziah Smith, June 25, 1819, ninety-nine; Joseph Smyth, March 27, 1876, ninety-seven years, two months, twenty-eight days; Fannie (Mrs. Enoch) Stanley, March 26, 1876, ninety; John Stanyan, November 18, 1794, ninety-three; Mary (widow of Captain Jonathan) Tebbets, April 26, 1893, ninety-seven; Tirzah (Mrs. Simon) Tebbets, September 19, 1863, ninety-four; Priscilla Thompson, May 24, 1793, ninety; George Tripp, October 22, 1859, within a few days of completing his ninetieth year; Samuel Willard, December 12, 1792, ninety; Aaron Witham, July 14, 1841, ninety-one years, two months, ten days; Jerusha (Mrs. Joseph) Witham, June 23, 1883, ninety years, one month, eleven days.

John Paul had eighteen children by three wives; six by each. The oldest was born near the close of the Revolutionary War; the young-est, some thirty years after. One of the oldest, John, of Wakefield, N. H., was shipwrecked near New Orleans about 1812, and with several others walked home from there, being about nine months on the way.

Henry Hatch and Ennice his wife had a family of sixteen children, including two pairs of twins, in about twenty years. The oldest was born in 1802.

William and Huldah Lord, of Beaver Hill, were the parents of sixteen children.

Eugene C. and Marilla F. (Davis) Perkins are the parents of fourteen children, all but one of whom are living. The eldest, Howard E., was born July 5, 1869.

In January, 1868, triplets, two boys and a girl, were born to Mr. and Mrs. Samuel Slater.

William N. and George T., sons of Noah and Joanna (Nasson) Phillips, were born October 22 and 25, 1857, respectively. The former died August 20, 1858.

The original Sanford Band, known as the Moulton Band, or "Cast Iron Band," was organized in the fall of 1844, and continued two or three years. David 'Cram was leader, and the players were as follows: David Cram, Calvin Bennett, Joseph Cram, and Lewis Moulton, B-flat post-horns; John Parsons, trombone; Joel E. Moulton and Rufus Bennett, B-flat bugles; Abiel H. and John H. Moulton, ophicleides; Ivory Clark, trumpet; Stephen H. Moulton, bass drum; Henry Whitten, tenor drum. Orin Day joined some time afterward.

The second band, the Sanford Cornet Band, was organized September 14, 1860, with twenty-two men, twenty of whom are given here: David Cram, first B-flat cornet, leader; Rufus Bennett, first E-flat cornet; John B. Bodwell, second E-flat cornet; Moses H. Libby, second B-flat cornet; William Bennett, third B-flat cornet; Walter Cram, first E-flat alto; Edward K. Bennett, second E-flat alto; John B. Libby, baritone; Stephen Ford, Third, B-flat tenor; Lebbeus Butler, first B-flat bass; Daniel G. Clark, second B-flat bass; Christopher H. Cram, first E-flat bass; George Bennett, second E-flat bass; John Merrill, Second, third E-flat bass; Thaddeus L. Tebbets, fourth E-flat bass; Calvin Bennett, fourth B-flat cornet; Otis R. Libby, third E-flat alto; Joshua M. Roberts, bass drum; Edmund Johnson, tenor drum; David B. Tebbets, cymbals.

The South Sanford Brass Band was organized May 9, 1866. It

25

was largely composed of Moultons, the following representatives of that family being members : Stephen H., Joel E., John H., Lewis, Joseph H., Jotham K., Elisha B., and Charles P. The other members were Edward P. and James C. Johnson, Herbert Lunny, Wesley W. Frost, and David Cram.

The Springvale Philharmonic Club was organized March 1, 1876, with the following officers : H. C. Cheever, President; John Pound, Vice President; Clara Crooker, Secretary; Asa Low, Treasurer; H. C. Keen, H. C. Cheever, J. W. Lowe, Executive Committee ; H. C. Keen, Director.

Weeman and Low's Quadrille Band was organized in 1876. John Weeman, A. W. Low, Albert Crooker, and Thomas Banks were members.

Under the leadership of Nathaniel Bennett the Mechanics Cornet Band was organized April 10, 1878. George F. Kimball was Second Leader, E. E. Hussey, Clerk, and F. A. Garnsey, Treasurer. The original members were : E. E. Hussey, first E-flat cornet ; George F. Kimball, second E-flat cornet; C. F. Gerry, third E-flat cornet ; James Thompson, first B-flat cornet ; Moses H. Libby, Junior, second B-flat cornet ; J. B. Clark, solo alto trombone ; Almon Garnsey, second alto horn ; Charles Clark, first tenor trombone ; Nathaniel Bennett, second tenor horn ; O. V. Libby, B-flat bass ; F. A. Garnsey, first E-flat tuba ; George E. Allen, second E-flat tuba ; Edward Gerry, bass drum ; Nelson Bennett, snare drum. The following joined after the band was organized : E. S. Wright, first alto horn ; Edward Gowen, cymbals ; Thomas Sykes, clarinet. This organization disbanded in 1883.

Sanford's present musical organizations include the Springvale Brass Band, Frank Shackley, leader ; Sanford Drum Corps, H. Wiggins, manager ; and Smith and Gerry's Orchestra, Sanford, William Smith, conductor.

The old liberty-pole that stood so many years near the Allen store was raised in 1838.

Hon. E. M. Goodall and Charles A. Bodwell built a trout-breeding house in 1879, at the Birch Log brook, and hatched out about 50,-000 trout. In the spring following, 100,000 fry were purchased. As the trout grew, it was thought the water supply would be insufficient, so a tile pipe was laid to the river. In July the water became so warm that the fish died by thousands. What remained were placed in the "Muck Hole" brook, but the experiment was finally abandoned, as the trout were fished out by boys at night, and it was felt that the results would give no adequate return for the efforts made.

A skeleton was unearthed, August 7, 1880, in front of George Nason's house, when the Springvale Aqueduct Company was laying its pipes. It was supposed to be of some one buried in an old graveyard.

In 1885, John Buzzell, of Mount Hope, raised cotton from seed picked at New Orleans by George B. Goodall.

A Christian Civic League, known as the Sanford Auxiliary to the Maine State Christian Civic League was organized April 23, 1899, in the Baptist Church at Sanford, with Edward H. Emery as President. The League holds public meetings, upholds those officers who discharge their duties faithfully, and takes an active part in town elections. There are eighty-two members. The present officers are: President, Edward H. Emery; Vice Presidents, Frank H. Dexter, Rev. Sumner Estes; Secretary and Treasurer, John P. Bowley; Executive Board, George H. Nowell, William H. Whitcomb, Clarence Goodwin, and W. F. Ferguson.

The Social Club has comfortable quarters in Gowen's Block on School Street. Thomas Howe is President, and John Hargraves, Secretary.

The Sanford Cycle Club is a flourishing organization, located in Bodwell's Block on Washington Street. Samuel Mitchell is President and Will Leavitt, Secretary.

One of the popular organizations of Springvale is Springvale Grange, No. 310, of which the officers are as follows: Worthy Master, Joseph P. Moulton; Overseer, Daniel L. Ellis; Lecturer, George W. Hanson; Steward, Anson M. Butler; Assistant Steward, J. Wesley Joy; Chaplain, Mrs. G. W. Hanson; Treasurer, Henry C. Welch; Secretary, Annie E. Moulton; Gate Keeper, Harry B. Goodwin; Pomona, Mrs. C. L. Libby; Ceres, Lena A. Welch; Flora, Mrs. H. C. Welch; Lady Assistant Steward, Mildred R. Welch.

The Sanford Agricultural and Mechanical Association built Oak Grove Park, Springvale, and conducted agricultural fairs thereon for a number of years. The Association has dissolved, and the park was sold. Mousam River Park, Sanford, was conducted by the Sanford Fair and Trotting Association, which, although in a state of inactivity, is still in existence.

Sanford sent several men to the front in the War with Spain in 1898, and the resulting hostilities in the Philippine Islands. Abraham Lincoln Frost, son of the late Howard Frost of Springvale, was in the south when the Spanish War began, and enlisting in the Vicksburg

Southerns, of Vicksburg, Miss., at the first call for volunteers, became a private in First Mississippi Infantry. He was in camp at Chickamauga for several weeks, when he was transferred to the Signal Corps, and attached to the First Army Corps, under General Brooke. Going with his command to Porto Rico, he was in the entire campaign on that island, and was present at the surrender of San Juan. Afterwards he was assigned to service at various cities on the island. Mr. Frost died from cerebral congestion at Mayaguez, on February 9, 1899. His remains were brought home, and buried in the family lot at Springvale. He was in his thirty-sixth year, having been born October 14, 1863.

Hugh H. Thompson, an employe of the Goodall Worsted Company, enlisted in the army in November, 1899, and was assigned to the Fourth Cavalry. Being sent to the Philippines, he was promoted to corporal of Troop I. Under General Lawton he saw considerable active service. He died of disease on the Island of Luzon, May 14, 1900. The remains were brought to Sanford, and given a soldier's burial, a squad of militia from Company G, Biddeford, participating. Mr. Thompson's age was twenty-seven years, nine months. He left a widow and one son.

John S. Goodrich, son of Sewall Goodrich, enlisted in Company D, Twenty-Sixth United States Volunteers, and saw active service in the Philippines.

Fred Ashworth, son of Henry Ashworth, was with the Fifth Artillery at Pekin at the time of the capture of the Chinese capital by the allies during the summer of 1900.

During the British-Boer War in South Africa, in 1900, the English sympathizers in Sanford raised nearly $1,000 for the Mafeking relief fund, which brought to Joseph Hollinrake, treasurer of the committee in charge, a cordial letter of thanks from Lady Georgiana Curzon:

"My Dear Sir: I have just received your letter of June 6, and I write at once to re-echo the thanks which I have already begged Messrs. Baring Bros. to convey to you and your committee. I am deeply touched at this generous assistance from the British Americans of Sanford, and I trust you will assure them of my gratitude, and that you will also tell them that my sister, Lady Sarah Wilson, and the mayor of Mafeking, have both cabled to me expressions of sincere thanks from the townspeople. I am quite sure the efforts you and your community have made will be amply repaid by the knowledge of the assistance you have rendered to that gallant little town of Mafeking, and that this material form of acknowledging their loyalty must please them as much as your liberality compensates them for their losses. It is indeed sincerely to be hoped that ere long peace will reign throughout South Africa, and I heartily reciprocate your hopeful expressions, that with the rule of the queen over that distressed country, the South Africans may derive all the benefits of good government to be found in every other British colony, and which are so thoroughly appreciated by them.

"I remain, yours faithfully,

"GEORGIANA CURZON."

The upper story of the Church of St. Ignatius, Martyr, being finished, the church edifice was formally opened to the public on Christmas Day, 1900, when masses were celebrated by Rev. John J. McGinnis, and his assistant, Rev. George J. Pettit.

BIOGRAPHIES AND GENEALOGIES.

BIOGRAPHIES AND GENEALOGIES.

Robert Allen was the first settler on Oak Hill. In 1743 he purchased one hundred acres of land near Bauneg Beg Pond for thirty-five pounds, and settled thereon in 1745/6, coming from Kittery or Berwick. He was the son of Francis and Hannah Allen, of Kittery, was born July 24, 1710, and died before the third Tuesday of June, 1763. Elijah Allen, his brother, was born March 12, 1719/20. September 26, 1763, Solomon Allen, administrator of the estate of Robert Allen (and probably his son), sold to Elijah Allen, Kittery, yeoman, lands of said Robert. Solomon Allen had a few years previously purchased thirty acres at Oak Hill of Jacob Perkins, and twenty-four acres of Robert Allen. From these Allens the numerous Allen family of the south part of the town descended.

Allen, George, *Descendants of.* The Allen family that included General Elisha Allen, his sons, Francis A., Horace O., and Emilus, and his grandsons, Stillman B., Hon. Frank A., William A., George E., and Rev. Henry E., trace their genealogical line back as follows :

1. George Allen, b. 1568 in Braintree, Essex County, England ; d. April, 1648, in Sandwich, Mass. Came to America (Saugus, Mass.) in 1635. In 1637 he with several others, purchased of the Indians the township of Sandwich on Cape Cod and settled there. He was a Puritan ; a member of the Baptist Church ; a "Freeman" and the first town officer of Sandwich. In his will he appoints his wife, Catherine, executrix, and mentions Matthew, Henry, Samuel, William and "least five children."

2. Samuel Allen, b. about 1597 in Braintree, England. Came to America seven years before his father, arriving in 1628. His first wife, Ann, died September 29, 1641. Second wife was Margaret Lamb. He settled in Braintree, Mass., and died there in 1671. His will is preserved in Suffolk County Probate office. Children by first wife : Samuel, b. 1632 ; Mary, b. 1634 ; James, b. 1636 ; Sarah, b. 1639 ; and by second wife : Joseph, b. 1650.

3. James Allen, b. 1636, d. 1714 ; m. Elizabeth Perkins. Children : Ebenezer, and seven other sons.

4. Ebenezer Allen, b. 1671, d. 1724 ; m. Rebecca Gould. Children : James, and four other sons.
5. James Allen, b. 1716, d. 1786 ; m. Abigail Pease. Children : Eleazer, and two other sons.
6. Eleazer Allen, b. about 1742, d. August 29, 1782. As an "impressed seaman" he was on board the British battleship " Royal, George," Commander Kempenfelt, when she capsized in Spithead harbor, and sank with nearly all on board, August 29, 1782. He married Mary Sherman of Bridgewater, and settled in Rochester, Mass., where their children were born : Zephaniah, Jesse, Elisha, Mary, Elizabeth, Lydia and Lois.
7. Elisha Allen, b. November 7, 1775, d. in Sanford, August 8, 1831 ; m. Harriet Matilda, daughter of Samuel Nasson (see Nasson genealogy), in 1804.

GENERAL ELISHA[7] ALLEN (Eleazer,[6] James,[5] Ebenezer,[4] James,[3] Samuel,[2] George[1]) came from a family whose motto was " Un yield ing Perseverance." Of this his life was an exemplification. He was born in Rochester, Mass., November 7, 1775. After his father's death, which occurred when he was seven years of age, Elisha's mother married a Gilbert, and removed to Brookfield, and he went to New Braintree, Mass., to live with a man named Pepper. Upon the death of Mr. Pepper's son John, whom the boy liked very much, young Allen ran away, because he could not agree with Mr. Pepper. While working in a paper-mill in Dorchester, not long after, his brother, Captain Jesse, persuaded him to leave and go to sea. He sailed from Boston to New York for freight, but while delayed there, the young sailor grew sick of a seaman's life, as its hardships began to be realized, told the captain that he had seen as much sea as he wished, and refused to go with him, notwithstanding the persuasive words of his brother. He thereupon returned to his work at Dorchester. Jesse sailed from New York as soon as his vessel was loaded. The brothers never met again, for the vessel was never heard of after her departure. From Dorchester young Allen went to Saccarappa, Maine, and, after working a short time on a canal, opened a store. Not long after, he removed to Readfield, and formed a copartnership with another man. While engaged in trade, he discovered that his partner was in the habit of carrying goods from the store to his home without charging them. Telling him that partnership was no ship for him, Mr. Allen proposed a dissolution, and bought him out. From Readfield, he went to Boston in 1801, and opened a store in or near what was called " Hatters' Square." One year sufficed, and he again turned his footsteps toward the east.

Early in 1802, Mr. Allen came into town on foot, and lodged at Ezra Thompson's. During their evening conversation, he revealed the object of his eastern journey, whereupon his host recommended the Corner as a promising field for a trader. William Stimpson was then trading in a store at the upper end of the village. Allen's objection, that there was one trader at the Corner, was met with the reply that a new man could get most of the trade. Mr. Allen listened with interest, gave the matter due consideration, visited the Corner on the following day, and concluded that it was a desirable location for him. He immediately began to trade near the site of the little cobbler's shop near Mrs. R. W. Thurston's residence on Main Street, and was licensed as a retailer in April, 1802. Stimpson, licensed in 1801 and 1802, does not appear among the retailers after that. According to General Allen's memoranda, his store, built in 1802, cost two hundred and twenty-nine dollars and sixteen cents. It was a one-story wooden building, with a large fireproof brick vault at the southeast end. It stood on the corner in what is now Hosea Willard's yard. In 1804, he erected a two-story, flat-roofed dwelling house, southeast of his store, and connected therewith by a long, narrow ell. The buildings were burned February 27, 1853. One item in his memoranda may be of interest: "8 poplars @ 20, $1.60." These stood nearly fifty years, and were the only ones at the Corner.

During his residence of nearly thirty years in Sanford, General Allen was engaged in trade, was prominent in town affairs, and held various offices, both civil and military. He was town clerk twenty-one years, selectman four years, treasurer two years, Representative to the General Court four years, and also to the first Legislature of Maine, delegate to the convention that framed the Constitution of Maine, Presidential Elector, councillor, and postmaster. He was a justice of the peace ten years, and of the peace and quorum eleven years, and appointed to qualify civil officers four years. In the militia he was Quartermaster, Adjutant, Major, Colonel and Brigadier General. He was postmaster in 1820, when he became a candidate for Presidential Elector. That he might be eligible, he resigned his office, though his successor was not commissioned until after the election. After Monroe had taken his seat in 1821, Colonel Allen was reappointed. He received seven hundred and ninety-three of the eight hundred and sixty-one votes cast in the first district. It was indeed an "era of good feeling." In 1800, when at Readfield, he boarded with a Mr. Mitchell, one of whose daughters was the wife

of Jonathan G. Hunton, a young lawyer.   By a strange coincidence,
that young lawyer and the young merchant met in the council of the
state in 1830, the former as Governor, the latter as a member of the
Governor's council.

Just before the War of 1812, in company with Captain Hugh Mc-
Cullough, of Kennebunk, General Allen built a ship called the
"Sabine." He was the first owner of ships in Sanford. We have,
in a memorandum of money, May 14, 1803, a little evidence of his
trade at that time. He then had in bills, $506 ; dollars, $629 ;
change, fourteen dollars ; "four oz."(?) eleven dollars ; cents,
seven dollars and fifty cents ; gold, eight dollars and fifty cents ;
total, $1176.

General Allen married Harriet Matilda, daughter of Major Samuel and Joanna Nasson, April 8, 1804. They had six children :
Harriet M., born October 19, 1804, married Jonathan Clark, and
died December 16, 1831 ; Julia A., born September 23, 1806, married John W. Bodwell, and died April 20, 1875 ; Francis A., born
June 27, 1808, married Rowena C. Paine, and died December 4,
1834 ; Horace O., born March 16, 1810, married Elizabeth Derby,
and died May 30, 1837 ; Emilus, born June 19, 1811, married Sarah
Hanson, and died December 23, 1855 ; Maria Louise, born May 6,
1818, died April 15, 1825. Francis A. was the father of Mrs. Frank
Gowen, and the late Mrs. Louise Frances, wife of Major General
Schuyler Hamilton of New York. She married, first, Hon. James
M. Cavanaugh, a prominent lawyer and member of Congress, who
died October 30, 1879. Mrs. Hamilton died in New York, March 31,
1898, and was buried in Sanford. She was much admired by her
friends and acquaintances as an exceedingly brilliant woman.

General Allen died August 8, 1831. His widow died May 13, 1872,
aged eighty-nine years, six months, thirteen days.

Hon. Mark Dennett, of Kittery, who was a member of the first
Legislature of Maine with General Allen, said of him : "He took
a deep interest in legislative affairs, and sometimes took part in discussion with great caution, being rather diffident because his education had not been so good as he desired. He was an honorable and,
I think, an honest gentleman." His last surviving child, Mrs. Bodwell, thus wrote of her father : "My father was one of the kindest
fathers that ever children had. They all loved him very dearly. He
could never do too much for them,—I revere his memory,—was a
noble-hearted man, was rather quick-tempered, but was always ready
to make the 'amende.' He despised meanness in any shape whatever."

HORACE OCTAVIUS[8] ALLEN (*Elisha,*[7] *Eleazer,*[6] *James,*[5] *Ebenezer,*[4] *James,*[3] *Samuel,*[2] *George*[1]) was born in Sanford, March 16, 1810, and died in Sanford, May 30, 1837. He prepared for college at Gorham Seminary, and entered Bowdoin in 1823, when thirteen years old, graduating in 1827. He studied law in the office of John Holmes at Alfred, married Elizabeth Derby of Lyman, and lived in Waterborough until 1831, when he moved back to Sanford into the old Nasson homestead situated on the top of Nasson Hill. This "oldest house in the town" is still standing. He practiced his profession here during the rest of his lifetime. Children: Stillman Boyd, born September 8, 1830, died June 9, 1891; Frank Augustus, born January 29, 1835; Rufus Derby, born March 8, 1837, died November 23, 1867. Mrs. Allen is still living, making her home in Cambridge, Mass. Her ancestry is as follows:

1. John Derby arrived in Marblehead previous to 1679. He moved to Ipswich, where he died about 1688.

2. John Derby, son of John (1), b. October 8, 1681, d. March 7, 1753; m. Deborah Conant of Beverly (a descendant of Roger Conant). Moved from Ipswich to Concord, Mass., where some of their descendants are now living on the old homestead farm.

3. Ebenezer Derby, son of John (2), b. December 7, 1712. Moved to Kittery, Maine, in 1767, with his sons Samuel and Silas.

4. Silas Derby, son of Ebenezer (3), b. in Concord, Mass., April 20, 1745; m. Sarah Norwood of York.

5. Rufus Derby, son of Silas (4), b. in York, April 22, 1778; m. Sarah Bragdon in 1798, and moved to Lyman, Me., in 1800, where he died December 29, 1859. Children: Mary, b. November 11, 1798; Rufus, b. November 5, 1800; Hannah, b. December 25, 1803; Sally, b. November 19, 1806; Olive, b. September 13, 1809; Elizabeth, b. March 28, 1812; Silas, b. January 31, 1815; Lucy, b. April 24, 1818; Eunice, b. April 26, 1821.

6. Elizabeth Derby married Horace O. Allen of Sanford.

EMILUS[8] ALLEN (*Elisha,*[7] *Eleazer,*[6] *James,*[5] *Ebenezer,*[4] *James,*[3] *Samuel,*[2] *George*[1]) was born in Sanford, June 19, 1811. He was educated in the town schools and Gorham Academy. At the age of eighteen he went to sea and made several voyages to the West Indies. After leaving seafaring life he returned to Sanford and learned the mason's trade with the late Adrial Thompson. March 3, 1832, he was united in marriage to Sarah Hanson. They had six children: Octavius, born December 21, 1832; Lucy A., born March 19, 1836; William A., born October 12, 1842; George E., born July 13, 1846; Henry E., born September 8, 1851, and one who died in infancy. Mr. Allen served as a Deputy Sheriff for several years. The remainder of his life he spent in working at his trade. He was an omnivorous reader and was considered one of the best informed persons in town in general history. He died December 23, 1855.

STILLMAN BOYD[9] ALLEN (*Horace O.*,[8] *Elisha*,[7] *Eleazer*,[6] *James*,[5] *Ebenezer*,[4] *James*,[3] *Samuel*,[2] *George*[1]) was born in Waterborough, Maine, September 8, 1830. On him, his mother's first born, devolved, after the death of his father, the duties of father, brother, and son. His natural force of character was thus early developed. As a mere lad, he was a clerk in the store of Samuel B. Emery. At the age of eighteen he shipped for Liverpool and New Orleans as a sailor. On his return voyage, while scarcely recovered from an attack of malarial fever, his vessel was totally wrecked, and he was washed ashore, more dead than alive, on the sands of Cape Cod. Abandoning the sea he obtained a responsible position in the Kittery navy yard. Mr. Allen secured his early education in the village and private schools in Sanford and Springvale, and later attended the Kennebunk, Alfred, and North Yarmouth Academies. He taught school in Kittery in 1849–50–51. Reading law with Judge Daniel Goodenow, of Alfred, and Hon. William H. Y. Hackett, of Portsmouth, N. H., he was admitted to the bar of York County, September Term, Supreme Judicial Court, 1853. He immediately began to practice at Kittery Foreside, where he remained until May, 1861, when he removed to Boston and opened an office at No. 20 Court Street (now Young's Hotel building), and at once commenced the practice of his profession. Two years later Hon. John D. Long (then a young lawyer, now Secretary of the Navy), entered his office as clerk on a salary of ten dollars per week. Mr. Long's ability was quickly appreciated by Mr. Allen, and his salary was rapidly increased until it reached $3000 per annum, and finally resulted in an equal partnership which continued until Mr. Long was elected Governor of Massachusetts. For many years, and until the time of his death, June 9, 1891, Mr. Allen was senior member of the law firm of Allen, Long and Hemenway, Secretary Long, after his retirement from Congressional life, resuming his former relations in the firm. The third partner was Alfred Hemenway.

Mr. Allen took a prominent place in the courts about 1868, and for more than a score of years was one of the most successful jury advocates at the Suffolk bar. No man, probably, ever secured such a succession of large verdicts in actions of tort as he. His reputation was such in that respect that his docket was always full and he was largely retained as senior counsel in the trial of cases by other attorneys. Among the verdicts obtained by him was one of $39,500, in 1879, against the old Eastern Railroad Company for personal injuries suffered by Dr. Charles W. Hackett. Another was a verdict of $28,000 against the Boston and Maine Railroad, on behalf of a boy, injured in Springfield, and he obtained a great many verdicts ranging from $10,000 to $20,000. Mr. Allen had a natural taste for practical business, and also for mechanics, both of which gifts gave him special facilities in comprehending and explaining the details of intricate cases and making them plain to the jury. His great forte was his persuasiveness, his happy power of illustration, and a knowledge of human nature and sympathy with the common experience of men which enabled him to come closer than any other advocate to the hearts and common sense of a jury. He was, besides, a man of great intellectual power. He was very ready as a speaker on the platform, and was always attractive in debate. Of a kindly, sympathetic and generous nature, he never forgot an old friend, and especially those who befriended him in the early days of his life. People came to him for friendly counsel, and young men were constantly being aided by him. For thirty years he was a prominent and active member of the Berkeley Street Congregational Church in Boston, devoting much of his time to the work of the Sunday School. He was the largest financial contributor to that church and society during his connection with it.

Early in life Mr. Allen served on the school committee in Kittery. In 1876 and 1877 he represented the city of Boston in the Massachusetts Legislature, serving the first year upon the judiciary committee. The following year he was chairman of the committee on probate and chancery. In 1877 he conducted an examination made by the Legislature into alleged abuses existing in the State Reform School at Westborough, which resulted in an entire change in the management of that institution. In December, 1889, he was elected a member of the Boston school committee. He was deeply interested in this work and devoted all the time to it his declining health would permit. The very last active duty of his busy life was attending a meeting of the school committee on a cold stormy evening in January, 1891. A severe cold which he contracted that evening resulted in confining him to a sick room, from which he was only released by death the following June.

September 8, 1854, Mr. Allen married Harriet S., daughter of Joseph and Mary Seaward, of Kittery, by whom he had two children,

Willis Boyd Allen, born July 9, 1855, and Marion Boyd Allen, born October 23, 1862. His widow and children reside in Boston. His son is the well known and successful writer, author of "The Pine Cone Stories," "The Lion City of Africa," "Navy Blue," "Cleared for Action," and other attractive books for the young.

HON. FRANK AUGUSTUS[9] ALLEN (*Horace O.*,[8] *Elisha*,[7] *Eleazer*,[6] *James*,[5] *Ebenezer*,[4] *James*,[3] *Samuel*,[2] *George*[1]) was born in Sanford, January 29, 1835. When he was two years of age, his father died, leaving the care of three small boys to their mother. She was a most faithful mother, and in addition to instruction in the public school and neighboring academy, they received excellent home training. Frank attended school at the Corner until sixteen years of age, and completed his schooling with one year at the academy at Alfred. He was then employed one year in the mill, beginning in William Miller's woollen factory, and continuing at Limerick, Alfred and Biddeford. At eighteen years of age he began his mercantile life as a clerk in Portland, and there remained three years. Having attained his majority, he engaged in business for himself, at Saccarappa one year, with Augustus G. Paine, under the firm name of Allen and Paine. Removing to Portsmouth, N. H., they commenced the sale of woollens and the manufacture of ladies' cloaks, which they prosecuted with energy and business tact. After three years in Portsmouth and three years in Boston, they removed to New York. During these six years, their sales amounted to many million dollars, and during their seven years in New York their sales were enormous. Mr. Allen's brother, Rufus D., had charge of one department of their extensive business in New York. At one time the firm employed six hundred persons, and one hundred sewing machines.

After fourteen years of active business life, Mr. Allen retired. One year of inactivity was spent before he embarked in another enterprise. He and other York County men formed a copartnership in Boston in 1867, under the firm name of the Oriental Tea Company, and for years this company has carried on a large business in teas and coffees at 87 and 89 Court Street, Boston. He moved his family to Cambridge, Mass., in 1870, and has resided there since that time.

In 1874 Mr. Allen was elected a member of the common council of Cambridge, and was re-elected the following year. and became president of that body. In December, 1876, he was elected mayor by a majority of 654 votes over his opponent. During his membership in

COLONEL EBENEZER NOWELL.

the common council Mr. Allen had been a leader in the investigation of the hack and cigar scandals, and the examination of the books in the office of the water registrar, whereby glaring abuses and irregularities were discovered. His determined stand that the business of the treasury department should be conducted on strictly business principles made him the natural head of the reform movement in 1876, and his administration resulted in practical and gratifying reform in the management of the city's affairs. In a speech made at the time of his election, Mr. Allen said: "1 shall come to the office under no pledge or obligation to any individual or party, but under the most solemn obligations to my fellow citizens to do all in my power to promote their welfare. In this work I shall ask, and I am sure I shall receive, the co-operation of you all, of those whose choice I am not, as well as of those whose choice I am. My ambition will not be to have held the high office to which you have elected me, but to have merited the confidence to which I owe it. But gentlemen, speech making is not my forte. I prefer to be judged by what I do, rather than what I say." These remarks received the editorial endorsement of the Congregationalist in the following terms: "These are sentiments and language which would do honor to anybody. They deserve to be published abroad in the political world, as profitable for doctrine, reproof, correction, and instruction in righteousness." Mr. Allen, as mayor, exemplied his platform. He placed the system of keeping the accounts of the city upon a substantial basis, and accomplished reforms at City Hall of great and permanent benefit to the tax payers. "The city owes him a debt of everlasting gratitude which it will never repay," we quote from an editorial in a Cambridge paper of the time. At the conclusion of his term of office, Mr. Allen declined a re-election. He was a member of the Cambridge water board from 1894 to 1899, and has been a member of the board of sinking fund commissioners from 1878 until the present time. Mr. Allen has been a member of the Prospect Street Congregational Church since his residence in Cambridge.

In January, 1858, he was married to Annie G. Scribner of Gorham, Maine, by whom he had three children: Annie E., born September 4, 1858; Georgie, born January 23, 1860, died in infancy; Herbert M., born February 22, 1865. His wife Annie died March 2, 1865, and April 3, 1866, he was married to Elizabeth M. Scribner.

WILLIAM A.[9] ALLEN (*Emilus*,[8] *Elisha*,[7] *Eleazer*,[6] *James*,[5] *Ebenezer*,[4] *James*,[3] *Samuel*,[2] *George*[1]) was born in Sanford, October 12,

26

1842. He received his education in the public schools of Sanford. At an early age he displayed a natural tendency towards mechanics. In the summer of 1861 he took sole charge of the steam engine in Littlefield Brothers' saw-mill in York. For some time thereafter he was engaged as an engineer in different localities. August 29, 1862, he enlisted as a private in Company E, Twenty-Seventh Maine Volunteers, which was attached to the Army of the Potomac under Generals Hooker and Meade. He was discharged July 17, 1863. After the close of the war he was engaged as foreman of the stitching room of a large shoe manufactory in Marlborough, Mass. After Hon. Thomas Goodall located in Sanford, Mr. Allen was employed as a general mechanic, where he remained until failing health caused him to resign his position. He was for a short time employed as overseer of the stitching room of Butler and Fogg's shoe manufactory in Springvale. Upon recovering his health he was engaged by the Sanford Mills Company as master mechanic, which position he held for fourteen years, when his health again failed, and he was compelled to resign his position. For the next six years he had sole charge of the large building on Huntington Avenue, Boston, owned by the Massachusetts Charitable Mechanics Association. In 1895 Mr. Allen became master mechanic of the Goodall Worsted Company, which position he held for three years. Since that time he has resided in Belmont, Mass.

In public affairs Mr. Allen has been quite prominent, having served as Deputy Sheriff for eight years and for three years as tax collector. He was the founder of Allen's tag manufacturing business and sold out to James H. Goodall. He is a member of the G. A. R., and the Masonic fraternity.

Mr. Allen was united in marriage, December 6, 1863, with Louisa Bennett, of Alfred. Carrie, the only child of this union, is the wife of William J. Kammler of Boston.

GEORGE E.[9] ALLEN (*Emilus*,[8] *Elisha*,[7] *Eleazer*,[6] *James*,[5] *Ebenezer*,[4] *James*,[3] *Samuel*,[2] *George*[1]) was born in Sanford, July 13, 1846. He received his education in the town schools. At the age of sixteen years he learned the shoemaker's trade, which occupation he followed till 1872, when he entered the employ of the Sanford Mills Company. In 1876 he learned the business of printing carriage robes, which he has followed until the present time. In 1887 Mr. Allen was appointed a Trial Justice by Governor Bodwell, and was reappointed in 1894 by Governor Cleaves. In 1897 the Sanford Municipal Court was established, and George W. Hanson, Esquire, appointed Judge, and Mr. Allen was appointed Recorder. Mr. Allen served as Auditor of Sanford two years. In 1887, he was appointed a member of the Board of Health and was elected Secretary, which position he has held ever since, and since 1896 has been the executive officer of the board.

Mr. Allen is deeply interested in the history of his native town, and has contributed a number of articles on the subject to the press.

He is quite prominent as a secret society man, being a charter member of Preble Lodge, No. 143, F. and A. M., under its restoration, and for six years its Worshipful Master. He is also a charter member of Friendship Lodge, No. 69, I. O. O. F., and was its first Noble Grand. A charter member of Riverside Lodge, No. 12, Knights of Pythias, he has filled every office in the lodge and was for three years District Deputy of the First Pythian District. Mr. Allen was a charter member of Harmony Council, No. 10, Jr. O. U. A. M. ; also a member of Torsey Lodge, I. O. G. T., and was District Templar of York District Lodge one year and Lodge Deputy of the local lodge for eight years.

Mr. Allen married Hannah M. Carpenter, August 22, 1865, and they have two sons, Frank L., and Edward E., who reside in Sanford.

Dr. John Larrabee Allen, son of John and Mary (Larrabee) Allen, was born in Cornish, April 26, 1814. He fitted for college at Alfred and Limerick ; studied medicine with Dr. Stephen C. Brewster, of Buxton ; and graduated at the Maine Medical School, Brunswick, in 1836. Soon after his graduation, he settled in Springvale, where he enjoyed a large and successful practice until the fall of 1852, when he removed to Saco. There he became one of the best known physicians in this section. During the Civil War he offered his services to Governor Washburn, and was ordered to Fairfax Seminary Hospital, near Alexandria, Va., in September, 1862, where he rendered valuable service. He was United States examining surgeon for pensions for nearly twenty years. He died September 4, 1897, at Saco. Dr. Allen married Mehitable B., youngest daughter of Theodore and Anne (Harmon) Elwell, of Buxton. They had eight children : Lucinda R., Marianna, Amelia, Francesca B., Georgianna B., and a son and two daughters (triplets) who died in infancy, unnamed.

Fred John Allen, son of John and Caroline P. (Hill) Allen, was born in Alfred, July 27, 1865. He lived on a farm until he was nineteen years of age, and attended the Alfred High School. Graduating from Nichols Latin School, Lewiston, in 1886, he entered Bowdoin College, from which he graduated in 1890. After studying law, Mr. Allen was admitted to the bar, at Alfred, in May of 1893. The following August, he opened an office in Sanford, and has been located here ever since, meeting with much success. In September, 1900, he was elected Representative to the Legislature by a large plurality. Mr. Allen has made his way by pluck and perseverance, as instanced by the fact that he was dependent largely upon his own resources in defraying college expenses, which he met by teaching school and working in summer hotels. He was married, June 8, 1892, at Alfred, to Ida S. Leavitt, and has two sons.

ELDER PAUL S. ADAMS supplied the pulpit of the Sanford Baptist Church for a time in 1838, and was ordained September 19 of that year. He was subsequently pastor of Baptist churches in Brunswick, from January 3, 1841, to 1843, South Reading, Newburyport, and Georgetown, Mass., leaving the last named town in 1851, Newport, N. H., and Brattleboro, Vt. He was born in North Berwick, May 5, 1812. In 1843, he married Susan, daughter of Dr. Ebenezer and Olive (Chadbourn) Linscott, born in 1821. They had seven children. In 1861, when the Civil War broke out, Elder Adams was an ardent patriot, and on one occasion exhibited his love of country in a very practical way. In a blacksmith's shop, he knocked down with his fist, a man who dared to give utterance to treasonable sentiments.

CHARLES B. ALLBEE, who is now serving his seventh term as town clerk of Sanford, was born in Somerset County May 31, 1865, being a son of Benjamin G. and Lois C. Allbee. He received his education in the public schools and at Anson academy. He began his business career at the age of fifteen, joining with his brother, Benjamin F. Allbee, in the clothing business at Milton Mills. After remaining there a number of years he came to Sanford and opened a tailoring and clothing establishment, which he conducted independently until 1891, when he received his brother Benjamin in partnership. Since that time the business has been managed under the firm name of Allbee Brothers. Mr. Allbee also acts as manager of the Sanford exchange of the New England Telephone and Telegraph Company.

In 1894 he was elected town clerk, to which office he has been re-elected annually ever since. In politics he is a Republican. Mr. Allbee is prominent in fraternal organizations, being a member of Preble Lodge of Masons, and White Rose Royal Arch Chapter; a past noble grand of Miltonia Lodge of Odd Fellows, Milton Mills ; a member of Riverside Lodge, Knights of Pythias, and of Sagamore Tribe Independent Order of Red Men.

On May 30, 1892, Mr. Allbee was united in marriage with Elizabeth H. Emery, daughter of the late B. Frank Emery of Sanford.

BELLE ASHTON is the first woman lawyer of York County, and the second in the state of Maine. She was born in Wetmore, Kansas, the daughter of Thomas G. and Mary (Kernon) Ashton, Mrs. Ashton being the sister of William Kernon of this town. The mother dying when Miss Ashton was a child, the latter was obliged, from the age of eleven years, to depend upon her own resources, and she acquired a shorthand training by attending a night school while working days to secure the necessary funds to pay her school expenses. Coming to Sanford in 1893, she secured employment in the office of the Goodall Worsted Company. In 1894 she accepted a situation as stenographer in the office of Fred J. Allen, where she began the study of law in her spare moments. Completing her course, she was examined at the term of the York County Supreme Court in Alfred last June, and was admitted to the bar. On the day of her admission she was complimented by the presiding judge and by the members of the bar assembled for her high rank in both written and oral examination.

GEORGE ASHWORTH, son of John R. and Alice Ashworth, was born in Newchurch, near Manchester, England, June 23, 1856. He received his early schooling in his native town, and at the age of fifteen was apprenticed to learn the carpet printer's trade. At the close of his apprenticeship of seven years he worked as a journeyman operative for a time, coming to the United States in 1881. For three years he was employed in a number of places, and in 1884 came to Sanford to enter the printing department of the Sanford Mills, where he has since continued. Mr. Ashworth resides upon a large farm, which affords him ample opportunity to indulge his taste for gardening and fruit culture. While in England he had always devoted much leisure time to gardening, and had won many prizes at agricultural fairs ; and since his residence in Sanford he has been very successful as a large grower of fruit and vegetables, and a stock and poultry breeder. Mr. Ashworth married, March 9, 1874, Elizabeth A. Clark, a native of Lancashire, England, daughter of Henry and Ann Clark. They have six children. Mr. Ashworth was practically the founder of the Sons of St. George of Sanford.

FRED B. AVERILL, editor and publisher of the Sanford Tribune, is a descendant of one of the oldest families in the Pine Tree State. His grandparents, John and Mary (Moulton) Averill, lived at the old homestead in York, where their son Joseph B., father of the subject of this sketch, was born. Joseph B. Averill learned the blacksmith trade in his father's shop, remaining there until the time of his marriage. His wife, Luella Frances, was a daughter of Tracy P. and Ellen (Wallingford) Wales, of Beverly, Mass. Captain Tracy P. Wales, for many years commander of a trans-Atlantic steamer, was a native of Beverly. He died in Liverpool, England. Mrs. Wales was a native of Lebanon, Maine. Joseph B. Averill settled in Great Falls (now Somersworth) and there his elder son, Fred B., was born May 31, 1872. A few years later Mr. Averill purchased a blacksmith shop in Dover, N. H., moving with his family to that city, where Fred B. attended the public schools until about thirteen years of age. Mrs. Averill died in 1883.

At the age of thirteen young Averill commenced to earn his own living by working in a Portsmouth grocery store, giving up his situation there to come to Sanford in the fall of 1887, where he worked for about one year in the plush department of the Sanford Mills. During the five years following he attended the New Hampshire Conference Seminary at Tilton, and the Maine Wesleyan Seminary at Kent's Hill; working his way by teaching school and in various other pursuits, such as giving public entertainments with phonograph, lecturing, etc. He owned the first improved Edison phonograph ever exhibited in Eastern Maine, and for a time the business proved quite profitable. In 1893 he determined to enter the printing business, and in November of that year purchased a small outfit, including an eight by twelve job press. With such a knowledge of the business as could be acquired from studying trade journals and close application to his work, Mr. Averill soon had all he could do; in ten months he found his quarters in the basement of A. E. Garnsey's store on School Street altogether inadequate, as was the original outfit, for his business requirements. In September, 1894, he increased his type outfit to more than double its original size, and purchased a larger press, moving the plant to E. K. Bennett's building on Washington Street, where the Sanford National Bank now stands. In 1896, the business, now known as the Averill Steam Print, had grown to such proportions that another move was necessary, and Mr. Averill leased the entire building at the rear of Garnsey's new block on Main Street, where he remained until November 12, 1898. On that date he purchased the land and building on Washington Street known as the Goodall Tag Works, of Newell T. Fogg, selling agent for James H. Goodall. It was in this building that the printing and shipping tag industry had been founded years before by William A. Allen. Since its purchase by Mr. Averill it has been known as the Averill Press, and is the only job printing establishment in Sanford, and one of the largest in York County.

In December, 1895, Mr. Averill entered the field of journalism by issuing the first number of the Star, a monthly paper devoted to the interests of the Christian Endeavor Societies in this section; continuing the publication for two years, during which period he enlarged it twice, and then sold it to a Boston publishing house. May 1, 1899, he purchased the Sanford Tribune of its founder, George W. Huff. Since that date the paper has been enlarged to eight pages and its circulation is rapidly increasing in Sanford and surrounding towns.

Mr. Averill held the office of town auditor for two years. He is a member of Sagamore Tribe, Improved Order of Red Men; Riverside Lodge, Knights of Pythias; Friendship Lodge, Independent Order of Odd Fellows, and has been identified with the Junior Order of United American Mechanics, having held the trusted position of state treasurer in that organization.

Mr. Averill was united in marriage with Ida M. Lord, September 19, 1894. Mrs. Averill is a granddaughter of the late John D. Cook, who is remembered by some of the older residents as one of the founders of the Republican party in York County.

Rev. Elisha Bacon was born in Freeport, Maine, June 17, 1799. Having lost his father when four years of age, he was brought up by Deacon John Webster, and, in youth, apprenticed to a shoemaker and tanner. Afterwards he prepared for college at Gorham Academy, and graduated at Bowdoin College in 1825. Among his classmates were Longfellow, Hawthorne, John S. C. Abbott, and George B. Cheever, distinguished in literature, and Cilley, Bradbury, and Sawtelle, men of note in political life. After graduation he engaged in teaching a short time on Cape Cod. Mr. Bacon read theology with Rev. P. Fish, of Mashpee, Mass., and was employed for a few months, by the Maine Missionary Society. He supplied the church at Shapleigh part of a year. On the 6th of May, 1829, he was ordained pastor of the Congregational Church of Sanford, and at his own request was dismissed September 10, 1834. He removed to Eliot, and was there installed January 2, 1836. Prior to his dismission, June 1, 1840, he had removed to Centreville, in Barnstable, Mass., and was during that year invited to become pastor of the Congregational Church in that village. He did not accept the pastorate, though he continued to preach to the church seventeen years, until a throat trouble compelled him to give up preaching. He then opened a family boarding school at Centreville, which he taught until the Monday before his death. He died just as the bells were ringing for meeting, Sunday afternoon, January 11, 1863.

Rev. Mr. Bacon married Emeline W. Basset, of Hyannis, Mass., January 10, 1828. They had five children : Mary B., who married Captain J. C. Case, and now resides in Springfield, Mass. ; George B., died in New Orleans ; Sarah L., died in infancy ; Sarah L , who married Captain H. A. Bearce ; and Elisha W., lost at sea. Mrs. Bacon died in New Bedford, Mass., March 20, 1887.

Mr. Bacon was a preacher of fair abilities, and a ready speaker. He seldom preached doctrinal sermons, but dwelt on themes of a practical nature, and insisted upon a godly life as the best evidence of true religion in the heart. His sermons were written, his evening discourses, extemporaneous. Genial, social, sympathetic, he was beloved by all who knew him ; and his influence, especially among the young, was deeply felt. He was a considerate pastor, always ready to minister to the wants of the feeblest of his flock, especially in their afflictions by sickness or death. He was of medium height, quick, active, and strong physically. He suffered from a spinal difficulty, though not to such a degree as to incapacitate him from work. A firm temperance man, even to avoiding the use of tea and coffee, he was the happy instrument of saving a number of young men from ruin. His pastorates were eminently successful, and his death was " a loss to the church and the world."

CAPTAIN DAVID BEAN, son of Captain Joseph Bean, of York, was born about 1723. His father was in the Provincial service for many years, as an Indian interpreter (his Indian captivity fitting him admirably for that duty), lost an arm in the service, was pensioned, and received a grant of land from Massachusetts, in 1734, for his four children, then in their nonage. In 1755, the three surviving sons, John, James, and David, gentlemen, then of St. Georges, petitioned the General Court for a survey and lay-out of their father's grant. This was done, and in course of time the lands came into the possession of Captain David. This grant contained four hundred acres, and lay southwest of what is now Sanford Corner. For many years Captain Bean was engaged in navigation in the eastern part of the state, thus acquiring his title. His descendants claimed that he, for services rendered to the Province, or for a nominal price, received a deed of that territory now embracing the city of Ellsworth and its environs, and that they have a claim thereupon. Returning from the east to York, he removed to town about 1780, and settled upon the Bean grant. He came up from York alone, and camped out, boarding at David Bennett's. He was engaged in clearing a portion of his land, and preparing it for occupancy. The wild beasts of the forest howled around his camp. One night in particular, he had reason for fear. In a temporary camp, without gun, by accident left at William Bennett's, he heard crossing the brook near his camp, with much noise, what he supposed to be a catamount. He was not molested, however, and, of course, could tell only by the tracks of the beast that it must have been a powerful animal. He built the frame or timber house (we used to call it a log-house) occupied by his son John Bean, some fifty years ago. He was one of the original members of the Congregational Church, and was its first and only elder. He died March 15, 1800, in the seventy-eighth year of his age. One of his great-grandsons, George W. Bean, served in the navy during the Mexican War.

Rev. Isaiah M. Bedell, son of Deacon John and Polly Bedell, was born in Sanford, July 11, 1820. He indulged in the Christian hope during a revival at Springvale, in the spring of 1831. He prepared for college at North Parsonsfield Academy, and studied for the ministry at Whitestown, N. Y. At his ordination in Buxton, Maine, February 19, 1851, Elder Gorham P. Ramsay, formerly pastor of the Freewill Baptist Church, preached the sermon. Rev. Mr. Bedell filled pastorates or preached at Buxton, Woolwich, Farmington, and Topsham, Maine, Meredith, Gilmanton, and Strafford, N. H., and Lynn, Mass. He married June 1, 1846, Ellen E. Roberts, of Lyman.

Bennett Family. Although Dr. David Bennett, of York, was an original grantee of four of the settlers' lots (on one of which he built the first " proper house " in Sanford), and erected, in company with others, the first mill in town in 1739, there is no evidence to show that he was a settler or ever a resident of Sanford. In March, 1803, Edward Standley, aged seventy-five years, made a deposition, in which he stated that in 1743, Dr. Bennett's house, which stood on settler's lot number twenty-seven, was occupied by Samuel Staple.

In 1797, Ephraim Low, aged seventy-eight, also made a deposition, stating that Dr. Bennett owned lots twenty-six, twenty-seven and twenty-eight; that he (Low) fenced said lots about fifty-five years before (1742); that, about that time, Dr. Bennett built the first proper house in Sanford, and that he put Samuel Staple, one Howard's family, and others into it. Susannah Hatch, aged seventy-six in 1797, made a similar deposition in regard to the ownership and occupancy of the lots. These depositions would tend to confirm the belief that Dr. Bennett was not a settler of the town, although active in promoting the settlement. His wife was named Alice, and their children were William, Hannah, David, Nathaniel, and John. After Dr. Bennett's death, which occurred probably in 1745, his widow married Joseph Simpson, Junior. She gave her lands in Sanford, in part before her death, and in part by will, to her sons William and Nathaniel. In 1790, William sold one-half of lot twenty-seven to William Bennett, Junior. Nathaniel Bennett was a Lientenant in the Revolutionary War (see page 73). His son Joseph, born February 11, 1786, died in August, 1846, married Abigail Batchelder, born April 4, 1792, died in December, 1875, and after having four sons, born in Sanford, moved to Hiram, March, 1824, and to Denmark, December, 1825.

EDWARD K. BENNETT, son of Nathaniel and Abigail (Hanson) Bennett, was born at South Sanford, November 2, 1837. He was left fatherless at the age of three years. When he was seven years old he went to live with Jotham Moulton, with whom he remained one year. About a year later he went to live on Dr. Bennett's farm, where he received two dollars a month for the work he was able to do. He remained six months, and then began to work regularly each summer on the farm of Calvin Bennett, until he reached his fourteenth year. His wages, meanwhile, had increased from five dollars a month to nine. He decided to learn a trade, and for this purpose entered the shoemaker's shop of Eben Hobbs, at the end of the year receiving thirty dollars and a set of shoemaker's tools. For twenty years he was engaged in shoemaking, at one period employing sixteen workmen. He afterward moved to Sanford Corner and bought an interest in an express business, continuing this work for many years. He also was a successful dealer in coal. In 1869 he was sent as Representative to the Legislature from the classed towns, Sanford and Lebanon. Mr. Bennett married Calista, daughter of Stephen Willard, of South Sanford. They have two sons: Willard H., proprietor of Hotel Sanford; and Myron E., superintendent of Sanford's public schools.

MYRON E. BENNETT, son of Edward K. and Calista (Willard) Bennett, was born in this town December 2, 1876. He attended the schools in Sanford until 1893, when he entered the Maine Wesleyan Seminary at Kent's Hill, from which he graduated with honors in 1896, and completed a post-graduate course at that institution in 1897. Returning to Sanford, he became his father's successor as agent of the American Express Company, which position he retained until the spring of 1900, when he resigned.

In 1899 Mr. Bennett was appointed superintendent of schools, that office then being filled by act of the school board. In the present year, when it was deemed practicable to make the position of superintendent of schools an elective office and to fix a salary for the same, Mr. Bennett was nominated by the Republicans as their candidate for the new position. His nomination was endorsed by the Democrats, and he thus became the first salaried superintendent of schools in Sanford by unanimous choice of the town. Since entering upon the duties of his office he has made several improvements in the school system, and introduced a number of innovations, with great success. He is a member of the Maine School Masters' Club, the School Improvement League of Maine, and of Riverside Lodge, Knights of Pythias.

DR. CHARLES W. BLAGDEN, only child of Eli N. and Hannah (Eldridge) Blagden, was born in Blue Hill, July 18, 1867. His grandfather, Charles W. Blagden, fought in the American army in the War of 1812, and his father did his full duty as a soldier in the Civil War. Dr. Blagden was left an orphan at the age of seventeen, dependent upon his own resources, but he overcame all obstacles and secured a medical training. He had been educated in the common schools of Blue Hill and at the Coburn Classical Institute, Waterville; and after attending the Medical School of Maine, at Brunswick, he further pursued his studies at the College of Physicians and Surgeons, Baltimore, from which he received the degree of M. D. He has been settled in the practice of his profession in Sanford several years. Dr. Blagden was married May 16, 1894, to Edith V. Maxwell of Baltimore.

GENERAL JOHN W. BODWELL came into town in his minority, and entered the employ of General Elisha Allen, as clerk in his store. He was the son of John and Sally Bodwell, of Shapleigh, now Acton, where he was born September 2, 1800. As a young man he was smart and capable, and gained the confidence of his employer. In 1820, when General Allen, then Colonel, resigned the office of postmaster to serve as a Presidential elector, young Bodwell, then only twenty years of age, was appointed to fill the vacancy. He served until April, 1821, when General Allen, having performed his duty as an elector, was reappointed. Prior to 1825 General Bodwell removed to Kennebunk, and engaged in trade, but returned to Sanford in a few years, and resided in the Clark house until his death.

He was successively Quartermaster, Brigade Quartermaster, Major and Aide to the Brigadier General, and at the age of twenty-six, Brigadier General in the militia. He was postmaster from 1841 to 1846, and served two years on the school committee.

He married November 10, 1823, Julia A., daughter of General Allen, and had four sons : Elisha A., born January 10, 1826, died May 12, 1827 ; Elisha A., born May 2, 1829, married a Miss Robinson, and died August 13, 1853 ; Henry W. G., born December 31, 1834, married Elizabeth Tebbets, and Almira Richardson, and died August 9, 1873 ; William H. G., born December 31, 1834, married Eliza Bennett, and died July 20, 1866. General Bodwell died April 28, 1861, and his widow, April 20, 1875. A remarkable coincidence in the hour of their deaths is noticed. Elisha A., Second, died at five o'clock, in the morning ; Henry W., at twenty-two minutes past five in the morning ; William H. and General Bodwell, each at five in the morning.

General Bodwell was a natural mechanic, and occasionally engaged in cabinet work. Whatever came from his hands was well done. He carried on gardening and farming on a small scale, and was interested in fruit-raising. Garden sauce and apples were specialties. His orchard extending southeast from Nasson's Hill was the best cultivated in town, and his hand-picked gilly-flowers, " sheep-noses," " goose-eggs," Baldwins, greenings and russets were the best fruit that the market afforded. In his field and orchard, he was neat, orderly, and methodical as elsewhere. As an illustration of his methodical manner, we may instance his manner of planting corn and potatoes, in straight rows in perfect squares, so that whichever way seen they appeared to be almost mathematically straight. It was frequently remarked that, if a six-inch cannon ball should be shot at a row lengthwise, it would cut down every stalk of corn growing in that row. He was one of the first, if not the first, to cultivate to-matoes for table use. When first cultivated, they were a curiosity and an ornament.

CHARLES A. BODWELL, son of William H. and Eliza (Bennett) Bodwell, was born in Sanford, September 4, 1857. He received a pub-lic school education, and afterwards entered the employ of the San-ford Mills as block printer. For a number of years he was also a dealer in real estate. At present Mr. Bodwell is superintendent of the Mousam River Railway, the Sanford and Cape Porpoise Rail-way, and also of the Sanford Light and Water Company, besides which he finds time to carry on the coal business. He married, Au-gust 21, 1878, Annette S., daughter of Moses H. Libby, and has three children : Stillman A., Lillian, and Vernon C.

WILLIAM J. BODWELL, son of William H. and Eliza (Bennett) Bodwell, was born in Sanford, February 19, 1864. Since the age of ten years he has been connected with the Sanford Mills in various capacities, and is at present superintendent of the printing depart-ment. He is also a dealer in ice, and a partner in the granite firm of Bodwell Brothers. Mr. Bodwell married, April 21, 1886, Emma, daughter of George Haigh. They have three children : Edward L., Donald R., and Nellie M.

JOHN B. BODWELL, son of Colonel Horace Bodwell, of Acton, was born in that town, October 5, 1838. He received his education in the common schools of Acton, at Limerick, and Alfred, and New Hampton and Gilmanton, N. H. ; read law with Hon. I. S. Kimball ; was admitted to the bar in 1862 ; practiced at Union Village, N. H., 1863-64, and at Sanford and Acton, 1864-77 ; and in the latter year, removed to Logan, Kansas. Subsequently he was located in Georgia and Florida. He married, July 11, 1862, Charlotte S., daughter of Samuel B. Emery, who died in Logan, April 9, 1882, leaving one daughter, Argie.

REV. WILLIAM WILLARD BOYD, D.D., was the son of Oliver Boyd, who was agent of the Springvale Manufacturing Company. Experi-encing religion at an early age, he joined the Congregational Church where he was living, but, years later, having changed his views in regard to baptism, he joined the Baptist Church at Springvale. He attended public and private schools in town, and after his father's death in 1862, had the oversight of the works and property of the Springvale Manufacturing Company. Naturally fluent in speech, and ready in discussion, he began to exhort in meeting, with much acceptance, and in April, 1864, to preach. He labored with much zeal and earnestness with the Springvale Baptist Church until the summer of 1866, when he went to Boston to prepare for college. Entering Harvard University in 1867, he was graduated in 1871. During his college course, he was class orator, Sophomore year, and in 1869 took a Boylston prize of sixty dollars for excellence in elocution. His high scholarship is evidenced by his assignment to a part on the Commencement platform. He was in Germany the first year after graduation, and, for a time, proctor at Harvard. After a short theological course, Mr. Boyd was ordained as pastor of the Baptist Church in Charlestown, Mass., April 28, 1873, on which occasion Rev. George B. Ilsley and Deacon F. A. Butler were delegates from the Springvale church. In May, 1877, Mr. Boyd became pastor of the Second Baptist Church in St. Louis, where he now preaches. In 1878 Shurtleff College, Upper Alton, Ills., conferred the degree of Doctor of Divinity upon him. He has held the offices of trustee of several seminaries and colleges, curator and counsellor, and has written and published various works. He married Cora Dunham, June 2, 1880.

DR. FRED AUGUSTUS BRAGDON has been engaged in the practice of medicine in Springvale since 1891. The son of George and Amanda (Sawyer) Bragdon, he was born in Limington, October 24, 1858, and was educated in the public schools of his native town. In 1883 he graduated from the Medical School of Maine, at Brunswick. During a portion of his medical course he had taught school, from 1877 to 1882. After graduation he commenced practice in Shapleigh, and meanwhile took two post-graduate courses in New York, in 1886 and 1891. Dr. Bragdon married, November 22, 1884, Nellie, daughter of Aaron Welch of Shapleigh, and they have four children, Blanche A., Lena B., Florence E., and Fred Ray.

DR. IVORY BROOKS, son of Samuel Brooks, a farmer of Waterborough, was born in that town, June 13, 1816. He lived on a farm during his youth, and worked out at six dollars per month, to which kind of work he demurred, and sought other employment. His early education was limited to town schools, and one term each at Alfred and Strafford, N. H., Academies, and evening schools at Great Falls

(Somersworth), N. H. He read medicine with Dr. Charles F. Elliot, of Great Falls, from 1840 to 1844, during which time he attended four full courses at the Maine Medical School, Brunswick, from which he graduated in 1844. While yet a student, he was commissioned surgeon's mate of the Second Regiment of New Hampshire militia. By hard work, prior to 1840, by teaching day and evening schools, and practicing dentistry during his medical studies, with rigid economy, he was able to pay nearly all his expenses during his four years' course. On June 24, 1844, he entered upon his profession at Springvale, and there continued in practice until his death, April 24, 1892. He served on the school committee for several years, and was prominent in the organization of societies for benevolent and reformatory objects. During the first twenty-five years of his practice, he devoted his leisure hours to dentistry. Dr. Brooks was twice married. His first wife was Betsey A. Littlefield, and his second, Hannah C. Hill. The latter died February 12, 1876.

HARRY E. BRYANT, principal of the Sanford High School, was born in Saco, October 26, 1872. He enjoyed all the facilities offered by his native city for obtaining an education, graduating from Thornton Academy in 1890. He immediately entered Bowdoin College, from which he graduated with honors in the class of 1894. While in college he was a member of the Delta Upsilon fraternity, and one of its most active supporters. After graduation, Mr. Bryant began teaching at Abbott, Maine, and has since been constantly engaged in his chosen profession, filling a number of exacting positions with great credit. He has been principal in Sanford since March, 1898, during which time his success has been marked. Full of zeal and enthusiasm, he has given his school a high rank.

HON. JAMES M. BURBANK, seventh son of Samuel Burbank, was born in Newfield, Maine, December 30, 1811. He was a merchant in Waterborough, and represented that town in the Legislature in 1845. In 1846, he removed to Springvale, and opened a hotel. He was a prominent Democratic politician, and was frequently selected by his party for office. He was moderator of the annual town meeting several years, chairman of the board of selectmen six years, sheriff of York County, 1863–65, after his removal to Saco one of the selectmen of that town, and, after its incorporation as a city, marshal, and in 1868, state senator. He married Phœbe Hill, of Waterborough, November 1, 1835, and had several children. His

oldest child, an only son, a young man of much promise, died at
Springvale about 1854. Mr. Burbank died in Saco, April 26, 1875.

BUTLER FAMILY. Shortly after the Revolutionary War, LIEUTEN-
ANT THOMAS BUTLER came from Berwick and settled on Mount Hope,
where he lived for a quarter of a century. He was the fourth child
of Captain Moses and Mercy (Wentworth) Butler, and grandson of
Thomas and Elizabeth Butler, early settlers of Berwick. His father
saw service at Louisburg. Thomas was baptized in Berwick, May
27, 1733. He was living in South Berwick in 1773, and signed a
petition opposed to certain "laws of the British Parliament for raising a revenue tax in North America." In 1775 he was First Lieutenant in Captain Ebenezer Sullivan's company, Colonel James
Scammans's regiment, and served three months at Cambridge. He
married, March 10, 1757, Bridget Gerrish, and they had twelve children, as follows : Mrs. Elizabeth Chadwick, Mrs. Sally Libbey, Mary,
married Isaac Gerrish, Junior, Mrs. Mercy Stone, Mrs. Susan Edgerly,
Mrs. Eunice Hatch, Mrs. Bridget Hurd, Mrs. Hannah Sawyer, William (drowned), Thomas, married Olive Abbott, Nathaniel, William,
married Lois Littlefield. Lieutenant Butler died August 24, 1809,
and his widow September 18, 1813.

NATHANIEL[4] BUTLER (*Thomas,*[3] *Moses,*[2] *Thomas*[1]) was born in
Berwick, July 5, 1762, and died in Sanford, November 25, 1841. During the Revolution, in 1775, he served as private in the Continental
army, a part of the time as waiter to his father, Lieutenant Thomas
Butler. Mr. Butler was a trader in general merchandise, and filled the
office of selectman for several years. He married Tabitha Joy, born
April 25, 1769, died September 13, 1852, and they had ten children, as
follows : Moses, b. April 21, 1791, d. October 9, 1806 ; Nathaniel,
b. March 24, 1794, d. December 11, 1872, m. Joan Keay ; Mehitable,
b. October 3, 1796, d. September 16, 1870, m. Elias Libbey ; Bridget,
b. January 7, 1799, d. June 18, 1826, m. Hawley Keay ; Nehemiah,
b. April 14, 1801, d. April 8, 1877 ; Susan, b. April 4, 1803, m.
Ebenezer Libbey ; John, b. August 1, 1805, d. September 7, 1806 ;
Mary, b. June 30, 1807, m. Ivory Libbey ; Tabitha, b. December
19, 1810, d. April 24, 1865, m. Sheldon Beal ; Moses, b. June 10,
1814, d. September 12, 1853, m. Philena Johnson.

COLONEL NEHEMIAH[5] BUTLER (*Nathaniel,*[4] *Thomas,*[3] *Moses,*[2]
Thomas[1]), fifth child of Nathaniel and Tabitha (Joy) Butler, was

born April 14, 1801, on his father's farm at Mount Hope, where he lived until the time of his marriage. While he was a mere youth, his father gave him fifty acres of land, to which he added from time to time. He cut and carted logs to mill, and framed and finished a house for himself, into which he moved in the fall of 1825. Descended from a line of soldiers, the military had an early attraction for him, and for ten years he took an active part in the affairs of the militia.. July 22, 1833, he was commissioned First Lieutenant of the Sixth company, Third regiment of infantry, First brigade, First division. Two years later, August 7, 1835, he was promoted to a Captaincy in the same regiment, which was followed by his elevation to be a Major, September 17, 1836. He was commissioned Lieutenant Colonel, June 21, 1838, and in quick succession, on October 4 of that year, was promoted to Colonel commanding the Third regiment. This position he held for nearly five years, resigning April 21, 1843, and was given an honorable discharge. The chapeau, epaulets, sword, belt, stirrups and spurs which were used by Colonel Butler in his militia service are now in possession of his grandson, Dr. Nehemiah Butler Ford.

Colonel Butler served the town as selectman, 1839–41, 1853–55, and 1860. He was town treasurer in 1850, and treasurer and collector, 1851–53. He was also the town's Representative to the Legislature for two terms, in 1842 and 1855.

Colonel Butler was one of the foremost men in town during his lifetime, and at his death was mourned by the whole community. He possessed a character of sterling integrity, was always just and true, and his townsmen considered his word as good as his bond at any time. He was singularly clear in his estimates of men, and his judgment in public affairs was invariably reliable. In his family he was a loving husband and father, and in return he enjoyed the affection and respect of those with whom he came into daily contact, to an unusual degree. A large family of children, trained under his watchful care, have profited by his worthy example, and gone forth to become active and honorable workers in the world. In short Colonel Nehemiah Butler was a typical, staunch hearted gentleman of the old school. That he enjoyed the confidence of his fellow townsmen to an unusual degree, is shown by the record already presented.

In 1824 he married Affa, daughter of John Libbey, born March 15, 1803, died April 6, 1843. They had eight children, as follows : Lewis, b. December 15, 1824, d. September 23, 1893 ; Adah, b. November 10, 1826 ; Dennis, b. August 21, 1828 ; d. October 26,

27

1858; Emily Augusta, b. November 9, 1830; Lavinia, b. August 8, 1833; Draxcy, b. October 26, 1835; Nathaniel, b. March 30, 1838, d. October 26, 1858; Lebbeus, b. February 3, 1841, d. September 30, 1887. Colonel Butler married, second, in April, 1844, Rhoda, widow of William Chadbourne, and sister of his first wife, born July 22, 1813. Their children were: Affa, b. May 15, 1845, m. June 17, 1863, Ivory Hill Ford, b. June, 1844; Rosilla, b. November 22, 1847, d. January 10, 1851; Rosilla, b. December 15, 1851. Sketches of Colonel Butler's children are given below.

LEWIS[6] BUTLER (*Nehemiah,*[5] *Nathaniel,*[4] *Thomas,*[3] *Moses,*[2] *Thomas*[1]) served as selectman of Sanford seven terms, 1869–71, and 1873–76. He was in the teaming business in Boston for many years, in the firm of Butler and Littlefield. Mr. Butler married, September 5, 1855, Hannah Jane, daughter of Jonathan and Mary Tebbets, of Sanford, and they had one child, who died in infancy.

ADAH BUTLER[6] LIBBEY (*Nehemiah,*[5] *Nathaniel,*[4] *Thomas,*[3] *Moses,*[2] *Thomas*[1]) married, March 8, 1851, John Butler Libbey. Children: Emma Rosina, b. March 11, 1856, m. Orlando Staples; Eben H., b. June 1, 1860, m. —— Ridley; Charles I., b. August 11, 1862; m. Myra Belle Ford; John Haven, b. October 25, 1864; Parepa Rosa, b. August 26, 1867; Lewis Butler, b. June 8, 1869.

DENNIS[6] BUTLER (*Nehemiah,*[5] *Nathaniel,*[4] *Thomas,*[3] *Moses.*[2] *Thomas*[1]) removed from Sanford to Boston and became superintendent of the Bowman Oil Works, a manufactory of rosin oil, located on Swett Street, on what was called Pine Island, Roxbury. His brother Nathaniel also worked there. Both met their death at the same time by suffocation, and their remains were buried in Sanford. Dennis Butler married, February 22, 1856, Frances Fidelia Guptill, and their children, born in Boston, were Arthur Dennis, b. December 7, 1857, and Nathaniel, b. June 8, 1859. Arthur Dennis married, August 20, 1879, Melvinia E. Nason, who was shot through the heart in her house in East Boston, September 2, 1884, by a marine who was firing from the Charlestown navy yard at a boy who was stealing junk.

EMILY AUGUSTA BUTLER[6] PRAY (*Nehemiah,*[5] *Nathaniel,*[4] *Thomas,*[3] *Moses,*[2] *Thomas*[1]), married, May 30, 1857, George Washington Pray (born July 15, 1834). Children: Alice J., b. August 10, 1858, d. April 15, 1881, m. Charles Libbey; Charles A., b. November 17,

1861; George Fred, b. May 30, 1868, d. July 1, 1868; Eva Louise, b. August 22, 1870, d. May 10, 1871; George William, b. April 12, 1873.

DRAXCY BUTLER [6] FORD (*Nehemiah*,[5] *Nathaniel*,[4] *Thomas*,[3] *Moses*,[2] *Thomas*[1]) married, February 22, 1856, Horace Martin Ford (born October 7, 1831, died February 9, 1900). Children: Myra Affa, b. May 26, 1857, d. September 4, 1858; Nehemiah Butler, b. October 2, 1863. The latter graduated at Bowdoin College in 1885, and Boston University School of Medicine, M.D., in 1888, and is now a physician in Owasco, N. Y. He married, September 9, 1891, Eleanor Soule Myer.

LEBBEUS[6] BUTLER (*Nehemiah*,[5] *Nathaniel*,[4] *Thomas*,[3] *Moses*,[2] *Thomas*[1]) was postmaster at Sanford Corner from December, 1885, to the time of his death in Boulder, Col., September 20, 1887. He married, November 29, 1866, Olive Orinda Ford, born October 26, 1846. Children: Harvey Ashton, b. April 3, 1872; Aubrey Osmond, b. March 23, 1874, m. Maude Leila Hobbs, February 20, 1895.

ROSILLA[6] BUTLER (*Nehemiah*,[5] *Nathaniel*,[4] *Thomas*,[3] *Moses*,[2] *Thomas*[1]) removed to Boston in 1867, and in 1873 established a fine hairdressing and manicuring business at 131 Tremont Street, which she continues to carry on with great success.

ICHABOD BUTLER, son of Ichabod and Abigail (Wentworth) Butler, was born in Berwick, now South Berwick, June 13, 1793 (June 30, 1791, according to the Wentworth Genealogy). He read law with Hon. John Holmes, of Alfred, and was practicing in town in 1821, having been admitted to the bar as a practitioner at the Common Pleas. At the April term, 1824, he was admitted to practice at the Supreme Judicial Court. In 1823, he married Mrs. Mary (Wise) Morrill, daughter of Daniel Wise, of Wells (Kennebunk), and widow of Moses Morrill. They had two sons, Edward Heyman, died in infancy, and Moses Morrill, a prominent lawyer of Portland. After living at the Corner some time, Ichabod Butler built a house near the Thompson bridge, so called, and thus gave it another name, Butler's bridge. He lived at the Corner the last part of his life, and died there March 28, 1833 (March 11, according to the Wentworth Genealogy).

HON. MOSES MORRILL BUTLER, son of Ichabod and Mary (Wise) (Morrill) Butler, was born in Sanford, March 8, 1824, and died of paralysis in Portland, October 21, 1879. He prepared for college at Alfred, Gorham, and North Yarmouth Academies, and graduated at Bowdoin College, in 1845, with the highest honors of his class. During his collegiate course, he taught school in his own district at the Corner, and immediately after graduation, a school at Springvale, at the same time pursuing his professional studies. He read law with Hon. Edward E. Bourne, of Kennebunk, and completed his legal course with Hon. Samuel Wells, of Portland, subsequently one of the judges of the Supreme Court of Maine, and Governor in 1856. Mr. Butler was admitted to the bar of Cumberland County, November 9, 1847, and immediately took the office in Portland vacated by the elevation of his instructor, Mr. Wells, to the bench. He soon after took the office and business of Hon. Augustine Haines, and subsequently formed a law partnership with Hon. William Pitt Fessenden, United States Senator, and at a later period with James D. and Francis Fessenden, his sons. In December, 1875, he formed a copartnership with his nephew, Hon. Charles F. Libby, which continued until his death.

Mr. Butler married Olive M., daughter of John Storer, May 1, 1850. Mrs. Butler and two of his three children, a son and a daughter, survived him.

Mr. Butler was county attorney from 1859 to 1865, Representative in 1859, and Representative-elect at the time of his death. He was mayor of Portland, 1877–79, two terms, during which time his services in the interest of the city were efficient, and will long be remembered. One anecdote will illustrate his strict integrity in the discharge of his official duties. Among the items of a bill presented to him for approval was one for cigars. The bill was respectfully returned with this endorsement thereon : " The city never smokes."

We well remember his stern appearance in the school-room, and the severity of his government. But it was such as the make-up of an ungraded village school demanded that the pupils might not feel that they could rule or bully the youthful teacher, who had been brought up in the community in which he taught. His studious life and untiring industry in the home of his maiden aunt, his quiet dignity and reserve, his manly deportment, are not forgotten by those with whom he then came in contact. In 1843, before he reached his majority, he was chosen a member of the school committee, and did his duties well in that capacity. One of his old pupils, Stillman B. Allen, once said of him, " He was the smartest man that Sanford has ever produced."

On the 5th of February, 1880, at a session of the Supreme Court in Portland, Judge Symonds presiding, the Cumberland Bar Association took action with reference to Mr. Butler's decease. Hon. Bion Bradbury, president, addressed the Court, and James D. Fessenden offered a series of resolutions, which were adopted, prefacing them with a few fitting remarks. A eulogy was delivered by Hon. Nathan Webb, to which Judge Symonds replied. The latter's estimate of Mr. Butler was : " He was a man of experienced and disciplined sagacity, a wise counsellor, prudent in the management of affairs, cool and adroit in doubt and strife. No motive of personal ease or comfort, nor indolence, nor carelessness, ever held him from fidelity to the trusts committed to him. His work was faithfully done."

GROVE CATLIN, JUNIOR, the first lawyer to settle in town, was born in Litchfield, Conn., May 29, 1787. He was an elder brother of Hon. Julius Catlin, Lieutenant Governor of Connecticut in 1858–60. In 1806, at the age of nineteen, he entered the celebrated Litchfield Law School. It was there that young Catlin made the acquaintance of John C. Calhoun, with whom he was on terms of intimacy. It was his pleasure, in after years, when Calhoun had become one of our foremost statesmen, to relate incidents of their student life, referring especially to the fact that they were both experts in fencing, and often parried foils in the manly exercise. When and where Catlin was admitted to the bar, we know not. About 1812, he came to Sanford, and opened an office in Deacon Moulton's house. He had considerable practice, though not enough to encourage a long residence in town ; and not far from 1815 he sold out to Arthur McArthur and removed to Waterborough Corner. There, in addition to his legal business, he did some copying for lawyers at Alfred, and taught school near his home. He was a popular and successful teacher. It was his custom to bolt the door of his office, and to pass out and enter through the window. In 1832, he moved his office to the Centre, and the year following left town. A day or two before his departure, meeting several of his associates in a store, he remarked that he was going to do something that the devil never did. Surprised at the strange remark, they eagerly asked what that was. " I am going to leave town," was his answer.

From Waterborough he went to Harrison or Bridgton, in 1833, and later took up his residence at Livermore Falls. There and on a farm in Jay, he lived and practiced some thirty-five years, when he removed to Keene, N. H. In 1870 he went to live with his children in Fitchburg, Mass., and there died February 21, 1873. Six years before, at the age of eighty, he had been converted while attending a Methodist camp-meeting.

Mr. Catlin married Theodosia Wakefield, born in Kennebunkport in 1800, by whom he had several children, of whom the oldest, Albert G., was United States Consul at Prince Edward's Island in 1859. Mrs. Catlin died at Keene, July 2, 1868.

Mr. Catlin's abilities were such as to have placed him in the front rank in his profession. His form and bearing attracted attention, even among strangers. " He was one of the handsomest and most fascinating men I ever saw," wrote Dr. James H. Peirce, one of his old-time acquaintances in Waterborough. He was gifted with uncommon powers of anecdote and repartee, and was quick, apt and witty. His law arguments were usually logical and to the point, and he was especially skilful in the examination of witnesses. Somewhat irritable withal, he would chafe when overruled in a trial. Illustrative of this, we have this story from one of his contemporaries at Livermore Falls: " I had brought an action before a justice of the peace, and at the trial Catlin was on the defence. The court had ruled in my favor on every contested point. At length he became so irritated that he got up, took his hat, and as he was passing out of the door, turned around and said, 'D—n such a court, to be ruled by that calf's head of a lawyer!' and went home, leaving his client to look out for himself."

HON. JAMES M. CAVANAUGH was born in Springfield, Mass., July 4, 1823. In 1854, he was a lawyer in Minnesota, and a member of Congress. Seven years later, he was a member of the Constitutional convention of Colorado. In 1866, he was in Montana, and was a delegate from that territory to Congress, 1867–71. He married Louisa F., daughter of Francis A. Allen, and though not residing here, spent a part of his time in town, especially near the end of his life. He died in Colorado, October 30, 1879. His remains were interred in the Nasson cemetery at the Corner. The following was inscribed on his monument: " Learned, eloquent and brilliant, he made fortunes in his profession, and in the warmth of his great heart, poured them out in benefactions to those who came in need of his aid."

CHADBOURN FAMILY. John Chadbourn, an early settler, and one of the owners of Chadbourn's mill, the second mill in town, was a son of James Chadbourn, of Kittery. He was born March 23, 1716, and died April 5, 1789. He married Mary Spinney, born 1722, died January 10, 1789. They had four children, Eleazar; (Rev.) John, born March 24, 1752 ; James, born February 4, 1758 (see page 74) ; and Polly, who married a Grant. Deacon Eleazar Chadbourn, who was a prominent man in town in the time of the Revolution, serving as selectman, was the father of seven children, among them Olive, wife of Dr. Ebenezer Linscott, and Elder John Chadbourn, Second. The latter was born May 10, 1778, was pastor of Baptist churches in Shapleigh and at Mouse Lane, Sanford, and died in Hiram in 1860. He had nine children. One of his grandchildren, Rev. George S. Chadbourn, was a prominent clergyman of the Methodist denomination.

ELDER JOHN CHADBOURN, son of John and Mary (Spinney) Chadbourn, was born in Sanford, March 24, 1752. Having experienced religion, he united with the Baptist Church, became a leading member, and was "proved" as a deacon, June 5, 1788. Between 1788 and 1790, he moved to Cornish, and undoubtedly preached there. He was one of a committee to set off the Fryeburg and Bridgton branch as a church by itself, in October, 1790, and in November "received approbation to improve his gift in public." When the church at Cornish (then Francisborough) became a separate organization, he was one of its original members, though not a member of the branch church. In the fall of 1797, subsequently to October 7, he was ordained. During a portion of the following year, he preached in Lebanon, and baptized several persons, who were admitted to the Lebanon branch of the Sanford church. "He was among the first Baptist ministers to preach in Buxton. In 1802, he withdrew from the pastorate of the church in Cornish, and became the pastor of the church in Limington."[1] Prior to his ordination, however, it is probable that he removed to Bethel, for one of his children was born in that town in 1795.

Elder Chadbourn married Elizabeth Grant in Berwick, October 27, 1774, and had nine children : In Sanford, Daniel, born October 3, 1775 ; Elcy, born November 29, 1777; Polly, born August 2, 1780 ; James, born January 12, 1783 ; Sarah, born June 29, 1785; Eliza, born January 1, 1788 ; in Cornish, John, born July 21, 1790 ; Benjamin, born January 19, 1793 ; in Bethel, Hannah, born October 1, 1795.

In 1806, while on a visit to his eldest daughter, Elcy, who married

_____
[1] Millet's "History of the Maine Baptists."

Samuel Sherburne, and lived in Prospect, Maine, he purchased a tract of land in Collegetown, now Dixmont. In April of the same year, his sons, Daniel and John, left their father's house in Harrison, Maine, for the distant purchase, arriving there on the 16th of that month. The father and youngest daughter, Hannah, joined them in the fall, and on February 10, 1807, the other members of the family reached the settlement. Elder Chadbourn was a millwright by trade, and a good mechanic otherwise, so that his hands found busy work in the new town. With the aid of his sons above mentioned, he built the first grist-mill erected in the town of Dixmont. They did all the work themselves, including the iron-work, and preparing the stones for grinding grain. In 1810, largely as a result of his labors, a church was organized at Dixmont, to which he preached, and of which he was pastor at various times, until his death. In 1807–08 he was a missionary in Etna and Carmel, and was instrumental in establishing a church at the latter place. He died in Dixmont, February 25, 1831, aged nearly seventy-nine years, universally loved and respected. His wife died May 23, 1837, at the age of eighty-five.

Elder Chadbourn was a self-made, self-educated man, of good natural ability, and strong mental power. His hospitality was proverbial. The poor found in him a warm, sympathizing friend. He was more liberal in his views than many of his contemporaries. As one of the early pioneer ministers of his denomination, he travelled long distances, preaching the Word, as he understood it, visiting the sick and administering words of hope and consolation, his only reward being the consciousness of having done his duty.

His grandson, Hon. S. J. Chadbourne, former Secretary of State of Maine, kindly furnished many of the foregoing particulars.

GEORGE CHADBOURN, seventh child of James and Deborah (Harmon) Chadbourn, was born February 21, 1797, and died April 20, 1878. He married, June 18, 1820, Asenath, daughter of Stephen and Betsey Hobbs, born December 1, 1799, died January 15, 1892. Two of their sons, James, and William H., went to Wilmington, N. C., and became prominent and successful citizens. WILLIAM H. CHADBOURN was born February 18, 1841, on "Grammar Street." He prepared for college in the Boston public schools, and graduated from Harvard University in 1862. He was for a while in business in Memphis, Tenn., before locating in North Carolina.

REUBEN W. CHADBOURN, second son of Nathaniel (born 1788,

died 1863) and Ruth (Hill) Chadbourn, was born in Sanford, October 18, 1819. He worked on his father's farm in his boyhood, and was educated at the public schools in town and the academies at Alfred, Yarmouth, and Gorham. From 1841 to 1846, young Chadbourn was engaged in teaching in Virginia, later returning to Maine. From 1847 to 1849, he was employed as a clerk in a store in Great Falls. In 1849 he went to Columbus, Wis. At first, he engaged in making land entries for immigrants, and otherwise aided them in securing homes. He gradually worked into money lending, and in 1855 secured the incorporation of a bank. Thereafter, for nearly forty years, he continued in the banking business, becoming very wealthy, and was reputed to be a millionaire. When he began business in Columbus, he had a capital of one thousand dollars, the savings of seven years. He died in 1894. In 1866, Mr. Chadbourn married Catherine, daughter of T. C. Atwater, a native of Catskill, N. Y., and had one son, Frederick A., who succeeded his father in the banking business. Perhaps mention should have been made of the fact that Mr. Chadbourn came near losing his life when a youth, in this way: He, with other boys was in Skeele and Emery's store at the Corner, when Edwin Skeele took up a gun, pointed it at Chadbourn, and, by accident, discharged its contents into his face and neck.

Reuben W. Chadbourn had four brothers: William, older than himself, who died in Bangor when about twenty-five years of age, and Nathaniel, Junior, Henry, and Smith W., who followed Reuben West. Nathaniel settled in Blue Earth City, Minn., where he still resides; Henry in Minneapolis, where he died about a year ago; and Smith W., who was in business at Columbus with Reuben, and died suddenly in 1890.

REV. ANDREW L. CHASE, present pastor of the Congregational Church, was born November 28, 1859, in Atkinson, Maine. His parents were Andrew J. and Lois K. Chase. He graduated at Bucksport Seminary in 1883, pursued three years of his college course at Boston University and the fourth at Harvard, receiving his degree from the latter in 1890, and graduated from the Theological School of Boston University. Although reared and educated a Methodist, he became a Congregationalist, and was ordained to the Congregational ministry February 10, 1891, at Montrose, Col. Later he filled pastorates in Maine, at Foxcroft, Eliot and York, and was installed at Sanford, January 31, 1900. Mr. Chase married,

December 12, 1893, Martha L., daughter of George O. Durgin of Portland.

JONATHAN CLARK was a native of Berwick. He was admitted to the York County bar, at York, in May, 1814, and soon after entered upon practice in Shapleigh, whence he removed to Sanford. He was in town in April, 1815, and remained about fifteen or eighteen years, when he removed to South Berwick, where he died April 27, 1836. He married, March 4, 1822, Harriet M., eldest daughter of General Elisha Allen, and had two children, Augustus O., and Louisa. The former resides in Portland, and the latter died in Boston, some years ago. Mrs. Clark died December 16, 1831.

REV. JAMES EDWARD COCHRANE, present pastor of the Springvale Baptist Church, was born in Monmouth, Maine, July 4, 1854. He is a graduate of the Coburn Classical Institute, 1876, of Colby College, Waterville, 1880, and of Rochester Theological Seminary, Rochester, N. Y., 1883. He was missionary in Moulmein, Burma, 1886–88, and has been chaplain of the Second Regiment Infantry, of the National Guard of the State of Maine, since November, 1893. His pastorate at Springvale dates from November 1, 1899.

JOHN COLCORD was the son of John and Susannah (Nasson) Colcord, and grandson of Major Samuel Nasson and his first wife, Mary Shores. He was born April 18, 1793. Young Colcord was left an orphan when very young, and at the age of about twenty, ran away to sea. He shipped on a whaleship for a five years' voyage to the Pacific Ocean. Colcord was taken sick, and when the vessel touched at the Sandwich Islands for wood and water, he was left on shore to recover his health. "He had a hammer and a few other tools with which he built a crude forge and went into the blacksmith business. His principal trade was making idols for the natives, who were pagans. The deities he manufactured represented dogs, horses, dragons, etc., and were so superior in design, quality and durability to the native product that he was soon doing a thriving business. In a few years he had prospered wonderfully. He built a large house for the accommodation of the whalers that called there to obtain supplies, etc. Other settlers came, and soon there was a flourishing colony, of which Colcord was the master spirit." He married a native woman, by whom he had four sons and one daughter, John, Jesse, David, Phineas and Susannah. Soon after his wife died a vessel arrived at the islands having on board a sick sailor who went to Colcord's house to stop. In the course of conversation each man learned that the other came from Sanford, the newcomer being Otis Thompson, son of "Master" Thompson, Colcord's old school teacher. Colcord had been gone twenty years, and was supposed to be dead. He subsequently returned to Sanford, and married his cousin, Clara Webster, whom he took back to the islands, but as she did not like the country, he again came to the United States, and the pair settled in Woburn.[1]

ELDER GIDEON COOK, in later life familiarly known as "Father" Cook, preached more years in town than any other minister with the exception of Rev. Moses Sweat. At four different times, three at the First Baptist Church, and once at Mount Hope, he was engaged, covering a period of nineteen years. He was the son of Joseph and Sarah Cook, and was born in Eastham, on Cape Cod, November 5, 1787. In early life, he went to Fairfield, Maine, where he indulged a hope in Christ, and made a public profession of religion. May 20, 1808, he was baptized by Elder Henry Kendall, then an itinerant preacher. He began to preach in 1810, and not long after was ordained in Dixmont, where he succeeded Elder John Chadbourn, about 1812, and officiated until 1815.

He first came to York County as messenger from the Lincoln Association to the New Hampshire Association, with which the Baptist churches in the southwestern part of Maine were then connected. Having preached in town and been called to settle, he removed from Dixmont, and on December 27, 1815, was installed as pastor of the First Baptist Church. On July 2, 1825, he was dismissed. He began his labors with the Kennebunkport village church two weeks earlier, June 19, and closed them May 29, 1828. Soon after, he became pastor of the Baptist Church in Effingham, N. H.

In March, 1832, he returned to Sanford. On the 7th of April, 1838, he was dismissed, and on the 15th entered upon his work with the church at Cape Neddock, in York. Three years later, he was chosen pastor of the new church formed on Mount Hope, where he labored until dismissed at his own request, November 26, 1842. One year at Kennebunk, three years at Cape Neddock, a second time, and two at Great Hill, South Berwick, preceded his removal, in 1849, to Kennebunk, which was his home the remainder of his life, except two years, April, 1858—April, 1860, during which he officiated as pastor again in Sanford. From the time when he

---

[1] George E. Allen in Sanford Tribune.

settled in Kennebunk until near the close of his life, he preached there and in neighboring towns. During his ministry he baptized nearly six hundred persons.

In 1824, Elder Cook was elected clerk of the York Association, in which capacity he served several years, and subsequently, in that of moderator. His name appears in every copy of the Minutes from 1815 until his death, and it is said that he was present at every meeting of the Association during that time, with one exception, and then he was detained only by severe illness. He was active in the formation of the York Baptist Missionary Society, organized in 1824, at his house, of which a prime object was to supply the destitute at home with the preaching of the Gospel.

Elder Cook was twice married. His first wife, whom he married in 1811, was Mary Atwood, by whom he had ten children. Five of them survived him. His wife died in 1850, and in 1851 he married Hannah Lyttlefield, of Lyman, who outlived him. His death occurred December 27, 1869, the fifty-fourth anniversary of his installation as pastor.

In his series of reminiscences in the Sanford Tribune, during 1900, George E. Allen writes as follows of Elder Cook: "My earliest recollections are associated with the pastorate of Gideon Cook. He was a large man of commanding presence, and a fluent speaker, and always preached without a manuscript, according to the custom of the primitive Baptists. He was very sarcastic, as many of his church members had reason to know, for he frequently preached a whole sermon aimed directly at some unfortunate brother or sister. At one time they were holding union services at the Baptist Church and Elder Cook was called upon to make some remarks. On the front seat sat a gentleman between whom and the Elder there was no love lost, and this gentleman had said he would never hear Elder Cook speak nor pray if he could help it. As soon as the Elder arose this gentleman seized his hat and started for the door. As quick as a flash the Elder said, 'The wicked flee when no man pursueth.' He then proceeded with his remarks as though nothing had happened. At another time he had been away on an extended vacation, and his pulpit was supplied during his absence by a theological student from Newton, Mass. The young man was quite a brilliant speaker, very sociable, and completely captivated his congregation. When the Elder returned he heard nothing but praise for the young man who had officiated for him so acceptably during his absence. This was too much for the Elder, and the next Sabbath morning he took for his text, Galatians iii, 1, 'O foolish Galatians, who hath bewitched you?' and then proceeded to score the congregation for running after 'strange gods, etc.' At another time he was called to an adjoining town to officiate at the funeral of a woman in whose family there had been trouble which resulted in a separation from her husband, but through the intervention of friends they were again united. The Elder's theme on this occasion was the afflictions of Job, and after reciting his many troubles, he exclaimed, 'And last of all his wife left him,' and then the poor man wished he had never been born.''

Illustrative of another phase of his nature is the following, told by the late Miss Joanna Thompson: One Sunday, when Elder Cook had preached without "clearing up" his subject very well, and opportunity was given for the brethren to speak, as was the custom, Deacon Nathan Powers arose and proceeded to finish the "clearing up" and application of the subject, to the edification of all listeners. When they came out of church, Elder Cook happened to come near "Aunt Debby" Chadbourn, who touched his arm and said, "Don't you ever feel ashamed when Deacon Powers speaks after you?'' The Elder did not resent the remark, and answered, "I don't pretend to measure arms with Brother Powers.''

A few hours previous to his death, his brother, also a preacher, approached his bedside, and inquired, "Do you think you are dying, Gideon?'' The reply, sharp and quick, came, "Don't know—can't tell—never died yet!''

DR. ALVAH WARD DAM was born in Newfield, Maine, May 23, 1818. His youth was passed on his father's farm, and at the age of sixteen he left home, and worked for the next nine years in the cotton factories at Great Falls, Dover, and Manchester. He married Sophia W. Jones, of Lebanon, March 15, 1843, and moved to Parkman, Maine, where he settled on a farm. While engaged in farming, he turned his attention to the study of medicine, and in 1850, removed to Springvale, to practice his chosen profession. He was an ardent politician of the Democratic party, and took great interest in town affairs. He was a member of the school committee for several years, and for some time chairman of the board of selectmen. Dr. Dam died of consumption, June 29, 1877, leaving a widow, one son, three daughters, and an adopted daughter to mourn his loss. The son, DR. ALVAH M. DAM, was born February 19, 1851; graduated from the medical department of the University of New York City, February 20, 1873; and subsequently located at Suncook, N. H., and afterwards in Boston, where he at present resides.

Rev. Frank G. Davis, pastor of the Springvale Baptist Church from October, 1883, to October, 1889, and principal of the Springvale High School from 1896 to 1900, was educated at Lawrence Academy, in Massachusetts, and the Bridgewater (Mass.) Normal School, and was graduated, with honor, from the Newton Theological Institution. He resigned his pastorate in Springvale owing to the condition of his health, and between 1889 and 1896 taught in Jackson College, Jackson, Miss.

Dr. Albert Day, son of Nahum and Persis Day, was born in Wells, October 15, 1821. His father died when he was thirteen, leaving him an orphan, and he started out for himself. At fifteen he was apprenticed to Samuel B. and William L. Emery, to learn the tinman's trade, and for several years made his home in their families. It was during this time that he began his temperance work. When he could scarcely write his name legibly he signed the pledge, and at the age of eighteen became recording secretary of the first total abstinence society in Maine. After one year's business at the Corner in the firm of Bennett, Emery and Day, he opened a shop at Springvale, having various partners. During this time he was a warm advocate of temperance. In 1850 he removed to Lowell, and in 1852 to Boston. While in the Legislature in 1856, he introduced measures as to the practicability of establishing an asylum for inebriates who cared to reform. In 1857, he became superintendent of the Washingtonian Home in Boston, an institution established for the purpose of reforming inebriates, and filled that position for many years, although there was an interim in which he was superintendent of a like institution at Binghamton, N. Y. (1868–71), and at Greenwood, where he had a private home, 1871–75. In 1862, he entered the medical department of Harvard University, graduating in 1866 with honor, though having the care of a growing family and the charge of a large institution. The subject of his thesis at graduation was "Methomania," which in 1867 he published in book form. In this work he proved inebriety " a disease to be treated, and not a diabolism to be exorcised."

Dr. Day married Martha, daughter of Jeremiah and Hannah Moulton, April 23, 1841. They had four children : Ellen Persis, born April 15, 1842, died in May, 1842 ; Albert Augustus, born November 28, 1844, married Adelaide S. Cate, April 19, 1866, now in business in Boston ; Cora Maranda, born March 26, 1847, married General Charles L. Young, of Ohio, January 18, 1871 ; Lilla Alberta, born in Lowell, January 22, 1853. Dr. Day died at Melrose Highlands, Mass., April 26, 1894.

JOHN A. DENNETT, a retired merchant of Springvale, son of Moses and Hannah (Fernald) Dennett, was born in Sanford, August 10, 1826. His education was obtained in the common schools of the town, at Alfred Academy, Great Falls High School, and at a commercial college in Boston. He taught school before entering upon a business life. Mr. Dennett was town clerk of Sanford from 1866 to 1883, and as such transcribed the early records of the town. He is a Democrat in politics. He married, first, Henrietta A. Dennett, by whom he had one son, John A., Junior; and second, Mrs. Elmira L. Guptill, daughter of Rufus Allen, of Cornish.

FRANK H. DEXTER was born in Malden, Mass., February 2, 1856, and was one of a large family early bereft of a father's care. When he was four years old he was placed by his mother in the care of a family in Maine, where he remained until he was seventeen years of age, and during this period he experienced in the bitterest degree the feelings of a fatherless boy dependent upon those who had no sympathy with any ambition or desire beyond the present gratification of appetite. When he was seventeen years old he left all his old connections, and with nothing except the shabby suit of clothes which he wore, and his two hands with which to work, he struck out for himself. Improving every opportunity for study while working on a farm, he fitted himself for a school teacher, and followed this occupation until he procured a position on the Portland Globe, where he worked three years and rose to the chair of associate editor, and then accepted a position on the Springvale Advocate, which he afterwards purchased and of which he has been editor and proprietor for twenty years. At one time he was the editor and publisher of the Maine Good Templar.

He was early associated with church and Sunday School work, and has always been an active temperance worker, for he held the liquor traffic responsible for the misfortunes of his childhood. He has been grand chief templar of the grand lodge of Maine Good Templars, is a member of the international supreme lodge, and is the present deputy right worthy grand templar for Maine. He served three years as grand commander of the grand commandery of Maine, United Order of the Golden Cross, at present occupies the chair of past grand commander, and is a member of the supreme commandery.

He was elected state vice councillor of the State Council of Maine, Junior Order of United American Mechanics, at the state council session held at Springvale in September, 1898, state councillor at the session at Phillips in September, 1899, and was chosen by the state board of officers to attend the national council at the Philadelphia session this year, filling a vacancy in the national representatives. He was for two years superintendent of schools of Sanford, and served on the school board for several years.

DEACON STEPHEN DORMAN, son of Thomas and Mary (Miller) Dorman, was born in Kennebunkport, April 27, 1800, and died in Sanford, September 17, 1884. He received moral and religious instruction from a pious father, mother, and grandmother, but very little advantage from the public schools. At the age of sixteen he began to serve an apprenticeship with Edward Pearson, tanner, of Kennebunk, and during his five years' apprenticeship received only fourteen weeks' schooling. As soon as he attained his majority, he began business for himself at Wakefield, N. H., where he hired a tannery. He continued there four years, and then removed to Sanford, built a tannery, and began business. Owing to reverses, in 1837 he removed to Bloomfield, Maine, but returned in 1843, repurchased his old stand, and carried on tanning until 1850.

He united with the Congregational Church, upon profession, July 5, 1825, was chosen deacon, July, 1831, rechosen in 1853, and served until 1884. He was fond of singing, and sang in choirs at Kennebunk, Wakefield, and Sanford, until seventy-three years of age. Deacon Dorman was one of the original Abolitionists of the town, and by a coalition of Whigs and Abolitionists, was elected to the Legislature in 1844. He was the first Abolitionist elected to any public office in York County, and one of four members of that party sent to the Legislature that year. From 1847 to 1862, he was a justice of the peace, and a trial justice, 1862–69.

He married, January 17, 1822, Mary, daughter of Nathaniel and Olive Buzzell, of Wells, and had nine children: Betsey L., born December 15, 1822, married Christopher H. Bennett; Harriet N., born July 19, 1825, married Stephen Ladow, of Los Angeles, Cal.; Stephen, born December 17, 1827, died January 28, 1833; Mary A., born November 2, 1829, married Thomas Alexander, of Los Angeles, Cal., and died September 26, 1881; Jonas K., born April 22, 1832, married Sarah Haley, of Sebago, Maine, and Betsey A. Littlefield; Stephen G., born March 31, 1835, married Abbie Gooch, of Kennebunkport, died October 26, 1898; Hannah F., born November 8, 1837, married Henry Sutherland, of Biddeford; Caroline A., born February 6, 1841, married James Riley, of Los Angeles, Cal.;

GENERAL EBENEZER RICKER.

George H., born July 26, 1844, and married a California lady. All of these except Betsey L., born in Wakefield, and Hannah F. and Caroline A., born in Bloomfield, were born in Sanford. Two sons, Stephen G. and George H., served in the army during the Civil War. When seventy-seven years of age, Deacon Dorman could say that he had seen seven generations. He well remembered his great grandmother, and had lived to see a great grandchild. His wife died October 21, 1882; they had lived together sixty years and nine months.

Deacon Dorman was a great and good reader, and his retentive memory was of much service to him. The Bible was his storehouse of doctrine, and furnished him with religious belief. He was well posted in the church history of the county and state, and his constant reading of the newspapers of the day gave him familiarity with the political history of the country and with foreign affairs. He was a strong Calvinist, and could express his religious belief with force and clearness. He bore his prolonged last illness with fortitude and Christian resignation, calmly waiting his summons to depart.

Dr. John Dow was born in Kensington, N. H., August 23, 1796; studied medicine with his uncle, Dr. Jabez Dow, of Dover, N. H., and came into town early in the twenties. There is a tradition that he arrived in Sanford on the day of Dr. Ebenezer Linscott's funeral, in December, 1821, and, an opening presenting itself to the young physician, he decided to locate.[1] There is evidence that he was in town July 29, 1822. Dr. Dow practiced in Sanford until 1834, when he removed to Pittston, Maine. After remaining there twenty-five years, in 1859 he removed to Boston, and in 1870 to Chelsea, Mass., where he died March 19, 1871. Dr. Dow married, in 1824, Mary, daughter of Nahum Morrill, of Wells, and had six children, four sons and two daughters, born in Sanford, and two sons and one daughter in Pittston.

Emery Family. The Emery family of Sanford is descended from Anthony Emery, second son of John and Agnes Emery, who was born in Romsey, Hants, England, and came to America with his brother John, in 1635, in the ship " James." They settled in Newbury (Newburyport), Mass., Anthony afterwards removing to Dover, N. H., and later to Kittery, where in 1660, he was fined and disfranchised for entertaining Quakers. He removed to Portsmouth, R. I.,

---

[1] Deacon Stephen Dorman.

28

where he probably died. The dates of his birth and death are unknown.

COLONEL CALEB[5] EMERY (*Caleb*,[4] *Daniel*,[3] *James*,[2] *Anthony*[1]), pioneer settler of the name in Sanford, son of Caleb Emery, tanner and lawyer, of Kittery, was born in the latter town, April 6, 1741. He obtained a limited education, and learned the double trade of tanner and shoemaker. After serving in the French and Indian War (see page 42), he married, in 1764, Elizabeth, daughter of Hon. James Gowen, of Kittery, in whose company he had served in the Lake George expedition. There is a tradition in the family, that owing to parental objections, he eloped with the young lady, who made her escape from her father's house by a window, and rode away with Caleb to be married. They resided in Berwick for several years, and in 1773 removed to Sanford, Colonel Emery having purchased the Kilgore lot, so called. He at once established a tannery, and in connection therewith carried on shoemaking. To these he shortly added another branch of business, the manufacture of potash. The site of his pottery was just above Willard's bridge, on the right bank of the river. In 1780, he engaged in trade, and, in 1782, opened a public house and was a licensed innholder, continuing as such for more than twenty years. When he first lived in town, he occupied a small house near his tannery, but about 1780, built a two-story house on the county road from Wells to Shapleigh, on the present site of David Cram's house. There he kept tavern, and across the road opened his store. Besides the several industries mentioned, he engaged in milling and lumber operations. He was owner, in part, of saw- and grist-mills near Willard's bridge which were generally known as Emery's. By purchase he added to his original estate, so that in 1789, he was the second land-owner in town, and at one time was the possessor of a thousand acres of land in the south part of the town, much of it covered with a heavy growth of pine. His lumbering operations returned him a handsome income. He and his son William were two of the grantees of the town of Porter, Maine, each of whom received one-fifteenth, and Colonel Emery erected, in 1793, the first grist-mill in that town.

During the fifty-two years of his life in town, Colonel Emery held various offices, which he filled faithfully and efficiently. He was town clerk one year, selectman five years, first Representative at the General Court, in 1785, and re-elected in 1786, deputy sheriff three years, a justice of the peace thirty-four years, and first postmaster of the town. He took an active part in town affairs during the Revolution, serving on committees to procure soldiers, and devising means to fill the town's quota. In 1777 he took part, as a soldier, in the expedition to Rhode Island (see pages 60–61), and was a member of the Committee of Safety one year. He was a Captain in the militia as early as 1785, Major in 1786, and Colonel in 1788.

In physique, Colonel Emery was straight, well-built, somewhat portly, and about five feet ten inches in height. His eyes were blue, and his complexion light. Though handsome when a young man, his face became somewhat disfigured by a polypus, which enlarged his nose, and gave him a superabundance of that characteristic organ. It was frequently said that he found it necessary to turn his nose one side when eating.

Although he had but a limited education, he possessed remarkable business qualifications and much practical wisdom. Positive in his opinions, and bold in expressing them, he was a strong partisan in politics. A Federalist of the radical type, he denounced the administration of Jefferson as calculated to do irreparable mischief. In 1809 he was chairman of a committee on resolutions against the Embargo, in every one of which denunciatory resolutions can be read extracts from the "Old Colonel's" philippics, condemning in harsh and bitter tones the high-handed outrages against liberty, which the administration seemed to him to be committing. Over against an austerity of manner, stood a noble trait, kindness to the children and to the poor. Those who came to him in need went away well supplied. His fruitful orchard, set out on that memorable dark day of 1780, furnished him with a bountiful supply of apples. These, a great luxury in those days, carried in his capacious pockets or saddlebags, he distributed among the children wherever he went.

In religious belief, Colonel Emery was a Freewill Baptist, although he was one of the original members of the Congregational Church, and its first deacon. Becoming offended, he left the church and joined the Baptist society. He was a great reader of the Bible, and knew it well. He and his wife were wont to sit in the entry in warm weather and "talk Scripture."

He was thrice married. His first wife, Elizabeth Gowen, was born September 15, 1743, and died August 17, 1799. They had two children : William, born March 23, 1765, and Elizabeth (Betsey, as she was called), born October 21, 1771, died December 6, 1829. This daughter married Jesse Colcord, retailer and innholder in Sanford, subsequently of Porter, Maine, and had five sons and six daughters. Colonel Emery married, second, February 21, 1802, Eliz-

abeth, daughter of Simon and Elizabeth (Bean) Emery, who died
February 26, 1812. His third wife, whom he married in November,
1812, was Mrs. Hannah Gould, of Kennebunkport. She survived him.
Colonel Emery died March 4, 1825, at the age of eighty-four.

Colonel Emery was of humble birth, of indigent youth, of influential
manhood, of venerable old age ; endowed with good common sense,
remarkable business capacity, keen discernment, rare judgment; aus-
tere in manner, unpolished, ofttimes severe in speech, yet of large
heart and generous impulses ; a man of honor and integrity, though
shrewd and exacting; of Christian faith, but sometimes wanting in
Christian charity; a man, indeed, of many faults, of redeeming
virtues more.

WILLIAM[6] EMERY (*Caleb*,[5] *Caleb*,[4] *Daniel*,[3] *James*,[2] *Anthony*[1]), son
of the preceding, born March 23, 1765, died March 2, 1848, aged
eighty-three years. He kept tavern at South Sanford. He was a
deputy sheriff for twenty-two years, and was familiarly known as the
" Old Deputy." He married, December 3, 1786, Mary (born March
8, 1761, died May 2, 1842), daughter of Captain Titus Salter, of
Portsmouth, N. H. Their children were : Caleb, b. June 17, 1787 ;
Thomas S., b. May 13, 1789 ; William, b. April 10, 1791 ; John S.,
b. June 11, 1793 ; Elizabeth B.. b. August 1, 1795, m. Henry Hamilton, Junior, d. April 2, 1818 ; Mary Ann, b. November 3, 1797, d.
August 29, 1882 ; Hannah B., b. September 16, 1799, m. Nahum M.
Thompson and had four children, of whom John W. and Caleb E.
are stock raisers in Kansas ; Sarah, b. December 10, 1801, m. Moses
Garey and had six children ; Abigail, b. March 31, 1804, d. October
1, 1825 ; Samuel B., b. August 29, 1806.

DR. CALEB[7] EMERY (*William*,[6] *Caleb*,[5] *Caleb*,[4] *Daniel*,[3] *James*,[2]
Anthony[1]) was born in Sanford, June 17, 1787, and died suddenly of
heart disease at Eliot, February 16, 1831. He was educated at Phillips Academy, Exeter, N H., and studied medicine with the Drs.
Abiel Hall, father and son, of Sanford. After completing his medical studies, he removed to Eliot, where he engaged in practice. He
was a Captain of militia at nineteen ; and was a member of the Governor's Council in 1830. He married, October 14, 1813, Mary Ann,
daughter of Rev. Samuel Chandler, of Eliot, who, with six children,
survived him.

THOMAS S.[7] EMERY (*William*,[6] *Caleb*,[5] *Caleb*,[4] *Daniel*,[3] *James*,[2]
Anthony[1]) was born in Sanford, May 13, 1789, and died October 24,
1838 He married, first, Betsey. daughter of Noah and Elizabeth

(Gould) Emery; second, Hannah, daughter of Samuel, Junior, and Sarah (Clough-Dudley) Willard. Children, born in Sanford, except the first: William L., b. August 22, 1808; Caleb S., b. December 25, 1809, m. Caroline, daughter of Dr. Ebenezer and Olive (Chadbourn) Linscott, and had eight children, d. in Boston, April 23, 1879; Shem, b. March 3, 1812, m. Judith Junkins, d. in North Berwick, November 18, 1882; Mary Elizabeth, b. August 8, 1814, d. August 22, 1814; Mary E., b. April 7, 1816, m. Lyman P. Crown; Salter, b. August 23, 1818; John Frost, b. November 5, 1820, m. Nancy B. Churchill, and had five children, of whom Lieutenant Howard Emery, United States Revenue Cutter Service, alone survives; Henry, b. December 4,1822, m. Harriet Berry, d. May 5, 1860; Cyrus K., b. October 9, 1824, d. March 22, 1826; Susan A., b. June 13, 1827, d. July 26, 1832; by second marriage, Cyrus, b. June 3, 1830; Sarah C., b. April 12, 1832, m. Robert Evans, and had nine children; Cynthia A., b. December 19, 1834, m. Edwin L. Morse.

WILLIAM[7] EMERY (*William,*[6] *Caleb,*[5] *Caleb,*[4] *Daniel,*[3] *James,*[2] *Anthony* [1]) was born in Sanford, April 10, 1791, and died in Sanford November 23, 1877, aged eighty-six years. His only advantages for education were those of the common school at South Sanford and the fireside, and he made the most of his opportunities. When a mere lad, he made up his mind to follow the sea. At the age of seventeen he began the study of navigation that he might become an expert and skilful seaman. After failing to secure a berth from a sea captain at Portsmouth, he applied at Kennebunkport and was more successful, shipping as a green hand for a voyage to the West Indies. He made several voyages as a common sailor, then became first mate of a vessel, and was offered the position of master, when the Embargo detained him on the land, and changed all his plans and prospects for life. At this juncture, he received from his grandfather, Colonel Caleb Emery, a valuable farm in South Sanford, on which he lived several years, an industrious and successful farmer. He found leisure, during this time, for reading and for various kinds of incidental business, such as surveying land, settling estates, and in one instance, teaching school at Oak Hill. In preparation for the latter task he attended the school at South Sanford, taught by John Shaw, where he recited in classes with his oldest son.

About 1828, he removed to Sanford Corner, and there engaged in mercantile business; first, with Deacon John Frost, as silent partner, then with John Skeele, and finally at Springvale, in the firm of

William Emery, Junior, and Co., his son Caleb being the Company until 1836, and his brother, Samuel B., subsequently. He was a deputy
sheriff for a number of years, and town treasurer in 1863. An
active member of the Congregational Church, he, together with
Deacon Frost, John Storer, and Timothy Shaw, built the church at
the Corner in 1831.

In politics Mr. Emery was a Whig, and later a Republican.
Though not an office-holder, he took a deep interest and an active
part in the affairs of the town. He was long-headed, skilful in plan-
ning, and efficient in executing. His business capacity was of a high
order. In early life he made extensive real estate investments which
realized large returns. His opinions on all subjects were sound,
clear, and decided. He was exceedingly well informed, and an able
disputant in debate.

Mr. Emery was married four times. His first wife, whom he mar-
ried in 1812, was Elizabeth, daughter of Moses and Elizabeth (Par-
sons) Emery, of Berwick. They had eight children: Caleb, b.
March 18, 1813; William, b. March 3, 1815, d. February 28, 1821;
Mary A., b. January 7, 1817, d. April 28, 1821; Elizabeth, b. February 3, 1819, m. Timothy Shaw, Junior, d. August 11, 1899; Mary
A., b. April 5, 1821, m. Samuel Tompson, d. December 1, 1873;
William, b. March 15, 1823; Titus Salter, b. March 3, 1825, m.
Annie Witmer, manufacturer of bar-iron and nails, Philadelphia, d.
April 20, 1894; Martha G., b. May 27, 1827, m. Jeremiah Goodwin,
d. Great Falls, N. H., August 29, 1855. Mrs. Emery died August
29, 1827. He married, second, November 17, 1829, Abigail, daughter
of Jeremiah and Martha (Friend) Moulton, of Sanford, who died
May 8, 1834. They had two children: Dr. George, b. April 24,
1831, d. April 1, 1853, graduate of Philadelphia College of Medicine,
1852; Helen B., b. August 1, 1833, d. March 3, 1834. September
22, 1836, Mr. Emery married Mary J. Hill, of Limerick (died February 11, 1861), and they had three sons: Edward H., b. July 9,
1837, m. Mary A. Piatt, d. in Wetmore, Kan., January, 1898;
Charles Oscar, b. November 15, 1838; Howard, b. July 9, 1845, d.
July 15, 1869. Mr. Emery was united in marriage a fourth time,
October 20, 1861, with Mrs. Sarah A., widow of Isaiah Gowen, who
survived him ten years.

JOHN S.[7] EMERY (*William*,[6] *Caleb*,[5] *Caleb*,[4] *Daniel*,[3] *James*,[2] *Anthony* [1]) was born in Sanford, June 11, 1793, and died in Lowell,
December 21, 1846. He married Anna M. Ramsdell, of Parsons-

field, and had fourteen children, among them William Bowles Emery, of South Sanford, and Mrs. Melissa Marden Blanchard, of Ionia, Fla. William B. Emery married Abigail (Hanson) Bennett, and had three children, William P. Emery, of Lynn, b. March 12, 1849; Florence M. (deceased), wife of Bradford S. Bennett; and Charles Octavius Emery, b. August 1, 1853.

SAMUEL B.[7] EMERY (*William*,[6] *Caleb*,[5] *Caleb*,[4] *Daniel*,[3] *James*,[2] *Anthony*[1]) was born in Sanford, August 29, 1806. He received a common school education. After peddling tinware a few years, he formed a copartnership with his nephew, William L. Emery, for the purpose of carrying on the tin and stove business. After several years' successful partnership, he sold out, and associating himself with his older brother William, in general mercantile business at Springvale, and later with Samuel Lord, carried on trade until 1846. That year he erected a store at the Corner, in which he traded with various partners until 1869.

Mr. Emery was deputy sheriff for several years, and sheriff by appointment in 1856. He served the town on the board of selectmen five years, and was treasurer three years, discharging his duties with efficiency, zeal and fidelity. During the Civil War he rendered especially valuable service to the town. He was an ardent Democrat, and as such was several times a candidate for county offices. He was jealous of the reputation of his party, and resented any remarks against it as he would any against his own character. He was generous, and many a poor man owed him a debt of gratitude, because he had relieved suffering and given timely assistance. Mr. Emery died September 25, 1880, aged seventy-four years.

February 27, 1832, he married Alice (born June 3, 1803, died January 17, 1879), daughter of Moses and Rachel (Carroll) Pray of Sanford. They had five children: Harriet A., b. November 1, 1832, resides in Washington; Benjamin F., b. June 16, 1834, m. Angusta A. Tebbets, had five children (of whom only Mrs. Charles B. Allbee and Mrs. Fred Hodgdon survive), d. May 28, 1882; Moses W., b. April 1, 1836; Charlotte S., b. July 25, 1838, m. John B. Bodwell, d. April 9, 1882; and Samuel Benton, b. October 15, 1848.

DEACON WILLIAM LEIGH[8] EMERY (*Thomas S.*,[7] *William*,[6] *Caleb*,[5] *Caleb*,[4] *Daniel*,[3] *James*,[2] *Anthony*[1]), eldest son of Thomas S. and Betsey (Emery) Emery, was born in Kittery, August 22, 1808, and died in Sanford, October 2, 1876. He married, March 10, 1834, Mary E. (born October 31, 1810, died April 12, 1885), daughter of

Ezekiel and Betsey (Worcester) Prescott, of Acton. With his uncle, Samuel B. Emery, he began housekeeping in the old Colonel Emery house at South Sanford, and that year, 1834, in company with Samuel B. and Caleb S. Emery he opened a tinshop near by. In 1837, the firm dissolved, the shop was moved to the Corner, and Deacon Emery, with different partners, carried on the business until the time of his death. He served as deacon of the Congregational Church for thirty-five years, was one of the first Abolitionists in town, was an ardent temperance advocate, and was always to be found upon the side of the right. His sudden death was much lamented.

His children were: Betsey, b. March 26, 1835, d. May 25, 1846; Edwin, b. September 4, 1836, d. September 28, 1895; Elmira, b. November 22, 1837; Frances A., b. April 15, 1839, d. January 29, 1862; George P., b. December 21, 1840, d. December 25, 1840; George Albert, b. December 21, 1841, d. in Boston, November 21, 1890; Ellen M., b. July 24, 1843; Prescott, b. February 4, 1845, d. November 14, 1898; infant, b. 1847, lived one day; Willis Tappan, b. September 14, 1848.

Elmira married John Colbath, of Lebanon, and has one son living, William L. E. Colbath.

George A. married Susan Ellen Leavitt of York. He was in business in Boston for a number of years. Three children survive him: Minnie Laura, who married Charles E. Moore and resides in Norwood, R. I.; Fred Albert, designer, Roxbury Carpet Company, Boston, member Boston common council, 1899–1900, married Ada E. Stichel, who died February 3, 1897; and Arthur Willis, now in the concrete and asphalt business in Canada.

Willis T. married Mary Elizabeth Nute, and has two daughters, Amy Ethel and Marion Mabel. Mr. Emery is in business in Boston, where he has resided for many years.

SALTER[8] EMERY (*Thomas S.*,[7] *William*,[6] *Caleb*,[5] *Caleb*,[4] *Daniel*,[3] *James*[2], *Anthony*[1]), son of Thomas S. and Betsey (Emery) Emery, was born in Sanford, August 23, 1818, died in Melrose, Mass., April 29, 1894. He was a merchant in Sanford, and served as postmaster and town clerk; was a dealer in stoves and tin ware in Roxbury. He married Rebecca F. Kilham. One daughter survives, Susan A., who married Albert Nowell of Melrose, and has one child, Edith M.

CYRUS[8] EMERY (*Thomas S.*,[7] *William*,[6] *Caleb*,[5] *Caleb*,[4] *Daniel*,[3] *James*,[2] *Anthony*[1]), son of Thomas S. and Hannah (Willard) Emery, was born in Sanford, June 3, 1830. He has resided in Prophetstown,

Ill., since 1854, and is a merchant and farmer. He married, first, Caroline B. Trafton, of Shapleigh, and second, Martha A. Rose, of Limington. Mr. Emery has had eight children.

The eldest, Eva Lucinda, was born in Prophetstown, July 17, 1855, and married, July 13, 1882, Charles H. Dye, of Iowa. Both graduated at Oberlin in 1882. He is now a lawyer in Oregon City, Oregon. Mrs. Dye is a poetess, and is also author of "McLoughlin and Old Oregon," published in 1900, an historical work which has met with great success, having received lengthy and flattering reviews from newspapers and magazines all over the country, and has now gone into a third edition. She has also written "Stories of Oregon," in the Western series of readers, for use in the public schools. Mrs. Dye's sister, Cora Lilian, is a graduate in medicine and a practicing physician in Illinois.

CALEB[8] EMERY(*William,*[7] *William,*[6] *Caleb,*[5] *Caleb,*[4] *Daniel,*[3] *James,*[2] *Anthony*[1]), son of William and Elizabeth (Emery) Emery, was born in Sanford, March 18, 1813, and died in Charlestown, Mass., December 1, 1897. He graduated at Dartmouth College in 1842. Mr. Emery devoted the most of his long life to teaching, and was located at Westborough, Mass., Nashua and Derry, N. H. ; at Boston, where he was sub-master of the Latin School and also kept a private school ; and at Charlestown, where he was principal of the High School, 1848–50, 1863–85. He was a very successful teacher. It was a matter of especial pride with him that Phillips Brooks was one of his pupils. Mr. Emery married Marcia C. Choate of Derry, N. H., who, with one daughter, survives him.

WILLIAM[8] EMERY (*William,*[7] *William,*[6] *Caleb,*[5] *Caleb,*[4] *Daniel,*[3] *James,*[2] *Anthony*[1]), son of William and Elizabeth (Emery) Emery, was born in Sanford, March 15, 1823, and died in Alfred, August 31, 1889. After attending Alfred, North Yarmouth, and Phillips (Andover) Academies, he studied law with various preceptors, and at the Harvard Law School, and was admitted to the York County bar in May, 1847. From that time until August, 1848, he practiced in Biddeford ; then at Lebanon until 1871 ; and in Alfred to the time of his death. He held a number of town offices in both Lebanon and Alfred ; was Representative from Sanford and Lebanon in 1854 ; and in 1878 was elected county attorney by the Greenbackers and Democrats combined. In 1888 he was the Democratic nominee for Congress. Mr. Emery was a successful lawyer, and was kind-hearted

and benevolent, contributing liberally toward religious and charitable
objects. He married Harriet W. Fall, of Lebanon, who, with one
daughter, Mrs. John B. Donovan, survives him.

CHARLES OSCAR[8] EMERY (*William*,[7] *William*,[6] *Caleb*,[5] *Caleb*,[4] *Daniel*,[3] *James*,[2] *Anthony*[1]), son of William and Mary J. (Hill) Emery,
was born in Sanford, November 15, 1838. He has chiefly been engaged
in farming. Mr. Emery has held the offices of town treasurer, member of school committee, supervisor of schools, and deputy sheriff.
He married February 2, 1862, Abigail, daughter of Captain Nathaniel and Abigail M. (Hanson) Bennett, and has had five children, of
whom four survive : Edward H., George G., both of whom hold responsible positions with the Sanford Mills, William Oscar, and Nellie F.

MOSES W.[8] EMERY (*Samuel B.*,[7] *William*,[6] *Caleb*,[5] *Caleb*,[4] *Daniel*,[3] *James*,[2] *Anthony*[1]), son of Samuel B. and Alice (Pray) Emery,
was born in the old Colonel Caleb Emery house at South Sanford,
April 1, 1836. A year later his father moved with his family to
Sanford Corner. Moses was educated in the town schools and at the
academies at North Parsonsfield, Limerick and Limington. In 1858
he engaged in general merchandise business at Sanford Corner with
his father and Salter Emery under the firm name of M. W. Emery
and Co., and continued the same business with different partners until
1873. In 1866 he engaged in the manufacture of boots and shoes
with Amos W. Lord in the Frost store, located where Garnsey's
Block now stands, and continued in that business with Mr. Lord, W.
H. Miller, T. P. Collins and W. H. Hobbs as partners at different
times, until 1874. Mr. Emery married Miriam W., daughter of Hon.
Increase S. Kimball, September 28, 1858. Five children were born
to them, one of whom, Sumner Kimball Emery (born October 25,
1870), now survives.

In 1860 Mr. Emery was elected town clerk of Sanford, holding
that office until he declined re-election in 1866 ; in 1863 and again in
1868 he served as constable, collector of taxes and town treasurer.
In 1877 he was appointed trial justice. In 1881, on account of the
ill health of his son, Herbert L. Emery, he went with him to Logan,
Kan., remaining there until 1888. While there he formed a partnership with Thomas Dye and Herbert L., under the name of Dye, Emery and Co., and carried on an extensive and profitable business in
hardware, lumber and farm machinery. During most of the time he

resided in Logan he was township justice of the peace, was police judge two terms, a member of the city council one term, and in 1886 was mayor of the city. In 1888 he returned to Sanford to assist in the settlement of the estate of his wife's father, remaining there until February, 1890, when he located at Harriman, Tenn., where he has resided until the present time. In 1894 he was elected president of the board of aldermen of the city, which position he resigned in 1895 to accept the office of city engineer. In 1899 he was elected president of the water and light commissioners for the city, and as such has entire supervision of the extensive water plant that furnishes the whole city and manufacturing establishments with water, as well as the system of fire protection, and also the electric light plants for street lighting, and the incandescent system for business houses and dwellings.

In politics Mr. Emery is a Democrat. In local affairs he is liberal, often voting for those belonging to other parties, and in return has been elected to most of the offices he has held when the opposition politically was against him.

His son, Herbert Lawrence Emery, was born in Sanford, January 11, 1863, and died in Logan, Kan., July 25, 1898. At the time of his death he was a dealer in farm implements. He was prominent in the affairs of Logan, and was unanimously elected city judge a few months before his demise. He was twice married, and a widow and three children survive him.

SAMUEL BENTON[8] EMERY (*Samuel B.*,[7] *William*,[6] *Caleb*,[5] *Caleb*,[4] *Daniel*,[3] *James*,[2] *Anthony*[1]), youngest child of Samuel B. Emery, was born October 15, 1848, at the Emery homestead, Sanford, where he resided, with the exception of two or three years, until October, 1898, when on account of his wife's health, a residence was bought at Melrose, Mass. He attended school at Lebanon Academy and Maine State Seminary, Lewiston. At the age of eighteen he entered his father's store as clerk, and on January 1, following his nineteenth birthday, he formed a copartnership with his father under the firm name of S. B. Emery and Son, and continued the business with his father, until the latter's health failed, and for two years following with his brother M. W. Emery, when the business was sold to Nowell and Bennett. After several months spent at various occupations, he contracted with the Sanford Mills Company for the handling of their waste products and commenced the manufacture of mattresses for the trade. Being convinced that there was a demand for a furniture store in Sanford,

he added furniture to his business. The first lot received consisted
of about two car loads of common varieties. A well-known resident,
coming into the old Kimball building, where the business was located,
remarked to Mr. Emery, "You will never sell it, never sell it in the
world." However, the business prospered, and later on carpets,
crockery ware, wall papers and general house furnishings were added,
and about 1882, a further contract was made with the Sanford Mills
Company for the sale of their plush remnants and seconds. When
the citizens decided that a larger school building was needed and the
old one was to be sold, Mr. Emery saw his opportunity for a much
needed larger store, and buying the building moved the same to a
vacant lot on Washington Street and added largely to its length.
Again in 1898, still more room being needed, a further addition was
made, making the largest store building in Sanford. At the age of
twenty-one, Mr. Emery married Elizabeth F., daughter of Hon. I.
S. Kimball. There have been five children, two of whom died at an
early age. The two sons, Frank M., and Walter K., are associated
with their father in business. Mr. Emery has never taken an active
part in politics, often remarking that his father, an active politician,
only made enemies, that the successful politicians were few, and he
preferred to devote his energies in other directions. He has always
taken an active part in all enterprises of the town and at one time
was treasurer of no less than six different corporations and organizations. For several years Mr. Emery has had the honor of being
Sanford's largest individual tax payer, and in December, 1899, added
to his taxable property by purchasing the Springvale Cotton Mills
property and dwelling houses. His success can be attributed to
hard work, strict attention to business and honorable dealing.

EDWIN[9] EMERY (*William L.*,[8] *Thomas S.*,[7] *William*,[6] *Caleb*,[5] *Caleb*,[4]
Daniel,[3] *James*,[2] *Anthony*[1]), son of William L. and Mary E. (Prescott) Emery, was born in South Sanford, September 4, 1836, and
died in New Bedford, Mass., September 28, 1895. He received his
early education in the town schools, in which he was also a teacher
for several terms. Preparing for college at Limington and Lewiston
Falls Academies, he entered Bowdoin, where he was graduated in
1861, receiving the degree of Master of Arts three years later. He
was principal of High Schools at Gardiner and Belfast, Maine, Great
Falls, N. H., and Southbridge and Northbridge (Whitinsville), Mass.,
and in 1877 was appointed instructor of cadets in the United States
Revenue Marine Service, at New Bedford, being stationed on school-

ships " J. C. Dobbin " and " S. P. Chase." On these vessels young men were trained for positions as Third Lieutenants in the Revenue Cutter Service. After the system was abandoned, in 1890, Mr. Emery engaged in the insurance business.

He enlisted in Company F, Seventeenth Maine Infantry, September 6, 1863, was advanced to be a Sergeant and detailed as Color Sergeant, and participated in thirteen engagements in the Virginia campaign. At Spottsylvania Court House, on May 12, 1864, he was twice severely wounded, and a month later was promoted to be Second Lieutenant in Company A, for gallantry in action. He was mustered out June 4, 1865.

Mr. Emery had served as president of the Worcester County (Mass.) Teachers' Association, and as librarian of the Public Libraries in Great Falls, Southbridge, and Whitinsville. He was for years a member of the Congregational Church, and took an active part in church affairs in the various communities where he resided. A conscientious and consistent Christian, he enjoyed universal respect and esteem; his disposition was cordial, helpful and sympathetic. Of scholarly tastes, he devoted his leisure hours to historical and genealogical researches, and besides preparing the present work, he was one of the committee which compiled the Emery family genealogy, published in 1890. He was a member of the Old Colony Historical Society, of Massachusetts.

Mr. Emery married October 27, 1864, Louisa F., daughter of Samuel S. and Mary (Cook) Wing, of Brunswick, Maine. They had six children : William Morrell, b. October 2, 1866 ; Horace Frank, b. June 30, 1871, d. same day ; Fred Harold, b. March 4, 1873, d. July 11, 1873 ; Clarence Percy, b. July 28, 1874 ; Edwin Prescott, b. August 16, 1876 ; Mabel Louise, b. June 15, 1880, d. November 1, 1881. Mrs. Emery and the following children survive him :

William M., graduated Bowdoin College, 1889, A.M., 1892. Newspaper man, having been connected with the daily press of Lowell, Providence, and New Bedford, and now city editor of the Evening News, Fall River, Mass. Married, March 24, 1894, Margaret Calhoun Donaghy, of New Bedford. Member of the Old Colony Historical Society.

Rev. Clarence P., graduated Bangor Theological Seminary, 1899. Pastor, Congregational Church, Stowe, Vt. Married, September 19, 1899, Mabel Louise Bolton, of Bangor. They have one daughter, Rebecca.

Edwin P., graduated New Bedford High School, 1894. Insurance

business, New Bedford.   Married, November 8, 1897, Annie Louise
Ryder, of New Bedford.   They have one daughter, Idella.

Prescott[9] Emery (*William L.,*[8] *Thomas S.,*[7] *William,*[6] *Caleb,*[5]
Caleb,[4] *Daniel,*[3] *James,*[2] *Anthony*[1]), son of William L. and Mary E.
(Prescott) Emery, was born in Sanford, February 4, 1845, and died
November 14, 1898. With the exception of about a year, during the
Civil War, when he was located at Corry, Penn., and Boston, he had
always made his home in his native town. He was educated in the
Sanford public schools, the Gardiner High School, and Maine State
Seminary, Lewiston, now Bates College. From 1866 to the time of
his death he was in the tinware and stove business, in partnership
with his father until the latter's demise in 1876. Mr. Emery was thus
the longest established business man in town, a fact recognized in the
general closing of stores on the day of his funeral. He was one of
the best known men in this section of York County, having had for
many years a number of carts on the road, making regular trips to
towns not supplied by their local dealers. He married, first, June
16, 1871, Alma Olivia Cole, of Biddeford, who died October 16, 1872 ;
and second, April 15, 1878, Harriet L., daughter of John and Harriet (Wordsworth) Clayton, who survives him. Mr. Emery had one
daughter, Alta Olivia, who married George W. Huff, and resides in
Sanford.

Edward Henry[9] Emery (*Charles O.,*[8] *William,*[7] *William,*[6] *Caleb,*[5]
Caleb,[4] *Daniel,*[3] *James,*[2] *Anthony*[1]), son of Charles Oscar and Abigail (Bennett) Emery, was born in Sanford, August 22, 1864, and is
at present in the employ of the Sanford Mills. Under the second
Cleveland administration he was deputy United States marshal for
four years, and has been a member of the school board for eight
years. He has been an active member of the Congregational Church
since 1886, and is one of the deacons. A leader in the temperance
forces in his own town and county, he has held many high offices in
the Good Templars. He is also president of the Christian Civic
League. Mr. Emery married first, July 4, 1893, Lillie A., daughter
of Rev. Samuel Poindexter, who died December 3, 1895 ; and second,
April 9, 1898, Florence M. Watson. They have one child.

Major Cyrus Chadbourn[9] Emery (*Caleb S.,*[8] *Thomas S.,*[7] *Wil-
liam,*[6] *Caleb,*[5] *Caleb,*[4] *Daniel,*[3] *James,*[2] *Anthony*[1]), son of Caleb S. and
Caroline (Linscott) Emery, was born in Sanford, March 24, 1840 ;

died in Boston, February 15, 1896. In 1857 he enlisted in Company
F, Fifth United States Cavalry; promoted Corporal on account of
wounds and gallantry; discharged July 15, 1862; Sergeant and Second Lieutenant, Company C, Second Massachusetts Cavalry, 1862–3;
First Lieutenant, Captain and Major, Fifth Massachusetts Cavalry,
1864–5. He filled every grade from private to Captain in the National Lancers, Boston, a cavalry branch of the Massachusetts militia, from 1868 to 1874. Major Emery was an officer in the Boston
custom house from 1867 to 1896. He married Martha Bampton of
Roxbury, and had two children, Herbert Q. and Howard B.

CHARLES OCTAVIUS[9] EMERY (*William B.*,[8] *John S.*,[7] *William*,[6] *Caleb*[5], *Caleb*,[4] *Daniel*,[3] *James*,[2] *Anthony*[1]), son of William B. and Abigail M. Emery, was born in Sanford, August 1, 1853. He has served
as selectman several terms, as town clerk two years, and was a government clerk in the railway mail service from 1885 to 1889. He
married October 1, 1881, Nellie J. Moore.

REV. SUMNER ESTES was born in Bethel, Maine, June 11, 1827.
He received his preparatory education in the public schools and
Gould's Academy, of his native town, and at Hebron Academy. He
entered Waterville College (now Colby), in the class of 1854, but on
account of failing health, left at the end of the second year. Mr.
Estes experienced religion at the age of eleven years, and joined the
Baptist Church, of Bethel, by which, years later, he was licensed to
preach. In August, 1853, he was ordained in Canton, Maine, where
he remained three years. Subsequently he was pastor of Baptist
Churches in Sidney, Thomaston, Machias, Pembroke, Cherryfield,
and Lisbon Falls, before he came into town. He was pastor of the
First Baptist Church of Sanford, from 1871 to 1873. Since the latter year he has been in the business of druggist and apothecary, and
also, in company with his daughter, Eva M. Estes, has carried on the
millinery business. His son, Charles S., a graduate of Colby College,
is now principal of the Boys' High School, in Brooklyn, N. Y. Rev.
Mr. Estes married Sarah M. Holt, of Bethel.

HAMPDEN FAIRFIELD, attorney at law, now of Saco, was in town
from 1861 to 1864, and took a prominent part in town affairs during
the Civil War. His father, Hon. John Fairfield, was Governor of
Maine and a United States Senator. Hampden Fairfield was born in
Saco, December 8, 1835, graduated from Bowdoin in 1857, and was

admitted to the bar in 1860. After leaving Sanford he removed to Kennebunkport, and later to Alfred. From 1868 to 1871 he was clerk of courts for York County. Mr. Fairfield married, in 1859, Ellen K. Perkins of Kennebunk. They have had a large family of children.

WILLIS A. FOGG, son of Hubbard and Lois (Allen) Fogg, was born in Sanford, April 6, 1859. He was educated at West Lebanon Academy. After a short period of employment in Boston, he worked as clerk for E. and E. E. Goodwin, Springvale, until early in 1885, when he began business for himself, at the corner of Main and Bridge Streets. After a few years he disposed of this store to H. B. Rowe, and travelled for a Boston firm for a short time; then returning to Springvale, he erected the building known as Fogg block, on Bridge Street, where he opened a department store. A few years later, having again sold out his stock in trade, Mr. Fogg turned his attention to real estate matters, and in 1897 erected the Dirigo block, Springvale. He has been town clerk for three years and treasurer for seven years, and is at present town treasurer and tax collector. In September, 1895, Mr. Fogg married Clara, daughter of Charles H. Pierce, and they have two children, Louis and Philip.

NEWELL TRIPP FOGG, son of Hubbard and Lois (Allen) Fogg, was born in Sanford, July 1, 1864. At an early age he entered the employ of the Sanford Mills Company, but after a number of years resigned, and devoted himself to the real estate business, in which he has met with great success. In 1895 and 1896 he served the town as collector of taxes, and on January 1, 1895, was appointed a deputy sheriff, which position he filled with great credit, until his promotion, by the voters of York County, in 1900, to the responsible office of sheriff. Mr. Fogg was the nominee of the Republican party, and was elected by a flattering plurality.

NEWTON H. FOGG, twin brother of the preceding, was born in Sanford, July 1, 1864. At sixteen years of age he learned the block printing trade in the Sanford Mills, and remained with that company for twelve years. Since 1892 he has been extensively interested in real estate. Mr. Fogg was appointed postmaster at Sanford by President McKinley, May 4, 1898, and has proved a popular official.

GENERAL WILLIAM FROST. There have been two Frost families of prominence in the history of Sanford, at the head of one of which was Major General William Frost, son of William, of Berwick, who was born February 23, 1760, and died December 23, 1821. He had two brothers, John (father of Solomon), who lived above Springvale, and James. General Frost came to Sanford about 1785, built a house at Springvale, and had charge of the mill (Province?). He was an extensive owner of land, and, at one time, is said to have owned more than any other person in town. He always kept tavern while he lived in Sanford, was proprietor of a small store, and was interested in a number of lumber mills. General Frost took a prominent part in town affairs, being town treasurer for ten years, serving on the school committee, and frequently acting as moderator for town meetings. He was a justice of the peace from 1808 to the time of his death. His career in the militia covered over thirty years. May 6, 1790, he was commissioned by Governor Hancock as Quartermaster of the Fourth regiment, First brigade, Sixth division; was commissioned Major of the same regiment, May 5, 1794; was made Lieutenant Colonel in 1799; commissioned Colonel of the Third regiment, July 1, 1816; and on July 8, 1817, was commissioned Major General of the Sixth division by Governor John Brooks, serving until his death. He was buried under arms (see pages 203-4), and his remains now rest in the Springvale cemetery. General Frost married Betsey (born February 23, 1760, died 1828), daughter of General Ichabod Goodwin, of Berwick, and had four children : John; Mary, wife of John Powers; Elizabeth, wife of Dr. Hall of Alfred; and Ichabod.

It is a family tradition that when the General and his wife came to Sanford they brought with them a dog, which, after remaining a few days, returned to Berwick. In a short time the animal came again to the Sanford home, with a puppy, and after staying for several weeks, went back to Berwick for the second time, leaving the puppy behind. The older dog never returned to Sanford, but the puppy remained, and grew up to be a family pet. General Frost was a man of extremely large stature, and commanded the respect of all by his great physical and mental powers. On one occasion, while serving as moderator of a town meeting which was held in the church, he created considerable excitement by causing the men to be seated in the pews, with heads uncovered, and to remain perfectly orderly until recognized by the chair. The old Frost house, which he first erected, after having undergone many changes and modifications, is still standing on Main Street, Springvale.

29

Hon. Ichabod[2] Frost (*William*[1]), son of the preceding, was born July 2, 1798, and died August 8. 1866.   In the summer of 1816 he went to sea, sailing from New York on a voyage to Calcutta, and was gone three years.   Shortly after his return home, he married Theodate Hill (born February 6, 1809, died May 23, 1871), and soon moved to the old Frost place, where he kept tavern until about 1845. He was appointed Paymaster, with rank of Lieutenant, of the Third regiment, First brigade, First division, July 2, 1821, by Governor William O. Williamson, and honorably discharged February 29, 1840. He held many town offices, was elected to the Legislature in 1850, and was a member of Governor Hannibal Hamlin's Council.   Mr. Frost's children were as follows :

Maria A., born August 27, 1821 ; married Hon. Sanborn B. Carter, an attorney of Ossipee, N. H. ; died October 12, 1866.   Their children were Buel C., an attorney at Dover, N. H., now dead ; Henry, a merchant, and DeWitt, an attorney, both now living at Ossipee, N. H.

William H., born May 26, 1823, died 1892 ; married Lucy Campbell ; had one child, John, who died in Pennsylvania ; his second wife was Julia A. Clark, of Limington ; had two children, Charles O. and Elizabeth, both now living in Springvale.

John W., born May 16, 1827 ; married Louisa Talbot of Wells ; is now living at Alton, N. H.   They had three children, John Sumner, deceased, a graduate of Bowdoin, 1872 ; Howard J., a jeweller at Springvale, who married Emma Carpenter of Wolfboro, N. H., and has one son, George ; Wesley W., who married Augusta Ferguson of Berwick, deceased, and has four children living, as follows : W. E. Frost, who married Mary Getchell and has two children, Ermont and Augusta ; Sumner, of Boston ; and Ralph of Newfield, Maine.   John W. Frost's second wife was Martha Hubbard ; they had no children.

Jordan D., born June 23, 1829 ; married and lived in Newburyport, Mass. ; died September 19, 1895, leaving three children now living in Newburyport.

Susan E., born September 1, 1831, married Captain Joseph T. Nason and lived at Kennebunk ; died in August, 1893, leaving four children, including William H., a lawyer at Dover, N. H. ; Alvah, at Kennebunk ; and George F., of New York city.

Howard (see next page).

Edward P., born July 1, 1837 ; married Sarah Clark of Limington ;

has five children : Dr. E. C. Frost, a physician of Brockton, Mass. ; Maria, now living in Springvale ; Grace, married Leroy Haley, an attorney of Biddeford ; Antoinette, married Walter C. Remick, living in Springvale ; Sadie, married George Shaw, of Brockton, Mass., and lives there.

HOWARD³ FROST (*Ichabod*,² *William*¹), son of Hon. Ichabod and Theodate (Hill) Frost, was born in Springvale July 23, 1833. When a young man, he had a severe attack of rheumatism, which unfitted him for work. Much of his time was whiled away in reading, and after he had read everything that he could get hold of in his native village, he took up law as a diversion. He studied with his brother-in-law, Sanborn B. Carter, at Ossipee, N. H., a year and a half from 1857 ; with Asa Low ; at the Dane Law School, Harvard University, and with Moses Emery, of Saco. In January, 1860, he was admitted to the bar, and thereafter practiced at Springvale to the time of his death, September 7, 1898.

Mr. Frost was an ardent Republican, and served as postmaster of Springvale from 1864 to 1885, and also held a number of town offices. His administration of these various positions of trust was marked by efficiency and fidelity to duty.

Mr. Frost married Lydia F. Roles, of Ossipee, N. H., daughter of Azor and Roxanna (Wallace) Roles. Their children were : Abraham L., born October 14, 1863, died in Porto Rico, February 9, 1899 (see page 387) ; William I., born October 31, 1865, married Lillian G. Fuller, of Clinton, Mass., November 8, 1888, has three children, William H., Franklin Blaine, and Lillian G., now resides at Tiverton, R. I. ; Susan E. N., born April 21, 1868, now living at Springvale ; Howard (see below) ; Frank B., born March 2, 1873, now living at Springvale ; Fannie, who died at the age of eight years.

HOWARD⁴ FROST (*Howard*,³ *Ichabod*,² *William*¹), son of the preceding, was born in Springvale, March 21, 1871. After attending the public schools he was freight cashier for the Boston and Maine Railroad at Rochester, N. H., station agent at Gonic, N. H., and also station agent at Sharon Heights, Mass. He studied law with his father, at the Kent Law School, Chicago, and at Bloomington Law School, Bloomington, Ill. He was admitted to the bar at Springfield, Ill., in 1895, and to the Maine bar in February, 1899, since which time he has been practicing in Springvale.

FROST, REV. JOHN, *Descendants of.*   Rev. John Frost was an English Non-Conformist, whose son Edmund, with his wife, Thomasine, came from Ipswich, England, to New England in the ship "Great Hope" about 1635. Their children were John, Thomas, Samuel, Joseph, James, Mary, Ephraim, and Sarah. Edmund settled in Cambridge, was made freeman in 1636, was ruling elder in the church, and died July 12, 1672. Thomas, his second son, settled in Sudbury, Mass., and married Mary Goodridge, and had Thomas, John, Samuel, and Mary. Samuel Frost, Third, son of Thomas, resided in Framingham, married Elizabeth Rice, February 1, 1710, and was the father of Rev. Amariah Frost, who was his fifth child. Amariah was born in Framingham, October 4, 1720, graduated from Harvard College 1740, was ordained to the ministry at Mendon, December 24, 1743, and married Esther, daughter of Rev. Henry Messenger, of Wrentham, April 27, 1747. Rev. Mr. Frost died March 14, 1792, in the seventy-second year of his age and the forty-ninth year of his ministry over the East Precinct, Mendon, afterwards Milford. "Mr. Frost was reputed an excellent man, and one of the most popular preachers of his age, almost a half century a loved pastor with one church and society. He was extensively resorted to, as an instructor of young men fitting for college and the ministry." His second child, Rev. Amariah Frost, Junior, was born February 5, 1750, graduated from Harvard College 1770, married his cousin, Esther Messenger, daughter of John and Melatiah (Corbett) Messenger, born in Wrentham, March 25, 1759. Their children : Olive, died February 1, 1783 ; Clarinda, died September 23, 1784 ; Charlotte, died August 22, 1797 ; and Deacon John Frost, who settled in Sanford.

DEACON JOHN[7] FROST (*Amariah,*[6] *Amariah,*[5] *Samuel,*[4] *Thomas,*[3] *Edmund,*[2] *John*[1]) was born in Milford, Mass., February 20, 1787. At the age of fourteen years he removed with his father's family to Washington, D. C., where he resided some two years. For about the same length of time he was a clerk in Boston, and came to Wells, Maine, when about eighteen years of age. He came to Sanford in 1810, and for many years carried on a farm and general store, the latter being the building at the Corner formerly occupied by Frank Broggi, on the site of Garnsey's block. As a man of business, he was energetic, punctual, and upright. A successful merchant, he was one of the leading citizens of the town, and held various offices of public trust. He was eminently a friend of law and order, a lover of liberty and of his country. As a Christian and church member, he was most active, consistent, and useful. He was an influential member of the Congregational Church, serving it in the capacity of deacon for many years. Industry, faithfulness, stability, good sense, and integrity, were prominent features of his character, and during his last sickness, more than six years in length, and attended with great and constant bodily distress, his patience shone out with remarkable clearness. Spiritually, his end was peaceful and sweet. His death occurred September 2, 1851, at the age of sixty-four years.

Deacon Frost married, May 21, 1812, Hannah, daughter of Captain Nahum Morrill, of Wells. She died in Sanford, October 1, 1884, aged ninety-four years. Their children were : George Albert, died April 24, 1892 ; Sarah Esther, died April 28, 1884 ; Nahum Morrill, died March 19, 1826 ; Amariah, died June 13, 1886 ; John Willard, died September 26, 1837 ; Hannah, died April 30, 1898 ; Phineas Mitchell ; Charlotte, died June 2, 1894 ; Charles Henry ; Clarinda died April 3, 1893 ; Francis William.

Hon. George A.[8] Frost (*John*,[7] *Amariah*,[6] *Amariah*,[5] *Samuel*,[4] *Thomas*,[3] *Edmund*,[2] *John*[1]) was born in Sanford, April 2, 1813. He was educated in the common school and at Phillips Academy, Exeter, N. H. For the years 1836–37 he was partner with his father and afterwards he was in business with H. P. Storer, formerly of Portland. After the dissolution of that firm, he carried on a general merchandise trade at Springvale for thirty years. In politics he was first a Whig and afterwards a Republican. In 1861–62 he was a member of the Executive Council, and was a trustee of the Maine Insane Hospital for nine years, being a part of the time president of the board. He was interested in all local enterprises tending to the education of the rising generation and the prosperity of the people, and a promoter of religious and kindred interests. Always charitable and a friend of the poor, at his decease, which occurred April 24, 1892, he left a bequest of $2000 for the Maine Missionary Society, and $5000 to establish a free bed at the Maine General Hospital, Portland. Mr. Frost married, April 14, 1835, Mary, daughter of Moses Lord, of Sanford, who died December 22, 1881. They had one child, born in 1836, who survived only six years.

Hon. Charles H.[8] Frost (*John*,[7] *Amariah*,[6] *Amariah*,[5] *Samuel*,[4] *Thomas*,[3] *Edmund*,[2] *John*[1]) was born in Sanford, October 17, 1829. He was reared on the home farm, acquiring his education in the public schools and the High School of Sanford. He was twenty-two years of age when his father died, and up to that time had been chiefly occupied with farm work. He then engaged in a general merchandise business in Springvale with his brother, George A., the firm name being George A. Frost and Co. After they had conducted a successful trade for several years, the partnership was ended by Charles's acceptance of an appointment as inspector at the Portland custom house. He discharged the duties of this office for about a year and a half, when he resigned and returned to Springvale. Soon after, he opened a dry goods store, later adding a millinery department. He established a flourishing business, his store being one of the largest and most successful of the kind in this part of the county. Mr. Frost was married in 1858 to Abbie A. Wilson of Springvale, who died November 7, 1897.

A prominent member of the Republican party, he was elected in 1864 to represent the towns of Sanford and Lebanon in the Legislature, and served with credit to himself and his party. He was one of the Republicans who voted in 1865 for the amendment to the state Constitution abolishing slavery. In 1880 he was the United states census enumerator for the town of Sanford. August 9, 1888, at the York County Republican Convention, he was unanimously nominated for Senator, and on the 10th of September was elected by twelve hundred majority. Mr. Frost has been one of the leaders in local politics, his counsel being always wise and practical and his vote ever on the side of progress and public welfare. Mr. Frost is a member of Friendship Lodge, No. 69, Independent Order of Odd Fellows, of Springvale, in which he has been vice grand and noble grand.

September 1, 1900, after a successful business career of forty years, Mr. Frost sold out his business in Springvale, and purchased a home in Portland, whence he removed with his family, having married Miss Eva Harris of Brockton, Mass.

DANIEL M. FRYE, son of Edmund A. and Susan E. Frye, was born in Berwick, November 6, 1855. He was educated in the public schools of Berwick and Somersworth, N. H. He learned the builder's trade, but having a taste for newspaper work, moved to Springvale in 1880, and established the York County Advocate (now the Springvale Advocate), and later on, the Good Templars' Record. Mr. Frye became interested in the New England Order of Protection at its formation, and was the first grand secretary of Maine, continuing in that office until elected supreme secretary of the order in 1894 (which position he still holds), necessitating his removal to Massachusetts. He now resides in Somerville, and is a member of the board of aldermen of that city. In 1889, while at Springvale, he established the N. E. O. P. Journal, which he still publishes. Mr. Frye is a member of the Masonic order, and of the Knights of Pythias, being colonel and adjutant of the Massachusetts Brigade of the latter. His military experience was gained in the celebrated Cadet Association of Somersworth, of which he is president at the present time. Mr. Frye was married in 1882, to Addie T:, daughter of Porter and Ann M. Hobbs of Springvale, and has one daughter.

AMOS GARNSEY, JUNIOR, was born in Richmond, N. H., December 26, 1831, and died in Sanford, March 9, 1898. He was the son of Amos and Clarissa (Randall) Garnsey. At the age of thirty-five he came to Sanford, and from 1866 to the time of his death, was connected with the various Goodall manufacturing enterprises as a partner and stockholder, and was master mechanic of the Sanford Mills for many years. He accumulated a large property. He married June 15, 1854, Mary J. Martin, of Rochester, and had two children, Frederick A., deceased, and Almon E.

ALMON E. GARNSEY, younger son of the foregoing, was born in Richmond, N. H., March 11, 1863. When four years of age his parents moved to Sanford. He received his education in the schools of Sanford, and for some time afterward was employed as overseer in the Sanford Mills. He later attended the Parsons School for Watchmakers at La Port, Ind., and graduated in May, 1889. The same year he built a store on School Street, and at once commenced business as a jeweller and watchmaker. Shortly after a line of shoes was added, and business steadily increased, so that in 1896 he removed to Central Square, and occupied the new building known as Garnsey's Block which had just been erected by his father, and where he now has one of the finest stores in the state. In 1898 Mr. Garnsey received a diploma of graduation from the Spencer Optical School of New York city, and has since met with great success in this branch of his business. The family homestead on Main Street, surrounded by spacious lawns on every side, is one of the finest and most beautiful residences in the town.

REV. N. K. GEORGE was pastor of the Freewill Baptist Church at Springvale from 1858 to the spring of 1860. He was born in Wash-

ington, Vt., April 2, 1816. After leaving Springvale, he removed to
Franconia, N. H., where, on June 19, 1860, while hurrying homeward
on horseback for shelter from a shower, he was killed by lightning
near his own door.

REV. NATHAN D. GEORGE, at first a Universalist, afterwards a
Methodist, was in town from 1834 to 1836, during which time, as a
licensed local preacher, he ministered to the Methodists, who had
formed a class at Springvale (see page 138). During his stay he
was postmaster for one year, and kept the office in the shop where he
carried on his trade of shoemaking. Mr. George was born in Hampton Falls, N. H., June 24, 1808, and married Mary, daughter of Abner Hill. He rose to be a presiding elder in his denomination. He
was an able preacher and writer, and published several books, prominent among them being, " Universalism Not of the Bible."

THOMAS GOODALL, the originator of the horse-blanket and the
founder of the carriage-robe industry in this country, was born in the
town of Dewsbury, Yorkshire, England, September 1, 1823, being
the youngest son of George and Tabitha Goodall. He was but six
months old when his father died, and before he had attained the age
of three years he was left an orphan by the death of his widowed
mother. When quite young he entered a woollen manufacturing establishment, where he served an apprenticeship of eleven years. At
the age of seventeen he had acquired such a thorough knowledge of
the business in all its details that he was placed in charge of the establishment, buying all the wool and other supplies required for the
business and disposing of the product. When he became of age
which occurred on a Saturday, he worked until ten o'clock at night,
and then walked a distance of ten miles to a place called Castle Hill,
having but two English shillings, a sum equal to forty-eight cents in
American money, in his pocket. He has frequently remarked that
that was the very happiest day of his life. The very next week he
engaged in business on his own responsibility, meeting with a fair
degree of success. He came to this country in 1846, and after a
brief stay in Connecticut went to South Hadley, Mass., where he obtained a good position, which he afterward gave up to a needy coun-
tryman who located there with a large family in destitute circumstances. He then went to Rhode Island, where he remained for a
period of nearly two years.

Returning to South Hadley, Mr. Goodall married Ruth, the second daughter of Jerry Waterhouse, a leading manufacturer, the ceremony taking place on April 29, 1849. Mrs. Goodall was born in the town of Dudley, April 10, 1826. Shortly after his marriage Mr. Goodall removed to West Winchester, N. H., in the town of Ashuelot, where his first children, Louis Bertrand and George Benjamin (twins), were born September 23, 1851. Desiring to engage in business at this time, and there not being a factory in West Winchester suited to his requirements, he removed with his family in 1852 to Troy, N. H. There one son and two daughters were born, namely : Ernest Montrose, August 15, 1853 ; Ida May, August 15, 1858 ; and Lela Helen, January 23, 1864. Both daughters died at an early age.

In Troy Mr. Goodall first engaged in the manufacture of satinets and beavers, his goods finding a ready sale on account of their superior style and quality. One cold and windy day he observed a farmer endeavoring, with difficulty, to secure a blanket on the back of his horse, and he at once conceived the idea of producing horse-blankets, many bales of which he presented to Union soldiers. In 1865 he sold the plant to a syndicate of Keene, N. H., capitalists, by whom the business has since been conducted. Up to the date of the transfer Mr. Goodall was the only manufacturer of horse-blankets in this country.

Feeling the need of rest after twenty years of close application to business, he went with his family to England, resolved to take an extended vacation. But he could not content himself with an inactive life, as is evidenced by the fact that shortly after his arrival in his native country he began the exportation of lap-robes, largely manufactured there, for sale in the United States and in Canada. While engaged in this business he made numerous trips to this country. Convinced that the protective policy of the United States encouraged manufacturing of all kinds, he concluded to establish a plant for the production of the goods that he had been engaged in exporting from England. Accordingly, after having found a suitable location and secured by purchase the entire mill privileges, he removed with his family, in October of 1867, to Sanford, where he has ever since resided.

Many difficulties were experienced, and the English manufacturers, of whom he had formerly purchased, learning of his project, endeavored in every way imaginable to render him a prey to discouragement. He, however, surmounted all obstacles, and finally succeeded in driving nearly all of the foreign product from the American market. Seventeen years ago he resigned his position as president of the Sanford Mills, which had then been incorporated, and sought

rest and relaxation in retirement from business, his three sons, Louis,
George and Ernest, having proved themselves fully competent to look
after his interests and their own as well. He still, however, watches
the enterprise with the most jealous care, and renders material aid
by his advice as consulting member of the firm.

Though accounted one of the shrewdest and most successful of
business men, nature has endowed Mr. Goodall with one of the kind-
liest of dispositions; and to those whom he finds worthy and deserv-
ing of his charity he is ever ready to extend a helping hand. Few
have in a quiet way dispensed more charity; and the community in
which he lives, especially the poor in neighboring hospitals, have
reason to remember his liberality.

The handsome residence of Mr. Thomas Goodall, with its spacious
and tastefully laid out grounds and its conservatory of rare and
beautiful plants and flowers, is an ideally charming country seat, and
is counted among the most attractive in New England. Besides this
place he has a delightful summer villa on the sea wall at Old Orchard,
where he and Mrs. Goodall go each season; while the winters are
spent in Florida.

In politics Mr. Goodall is a Republican. He is naturally a man of
great influence in the community, for which he has done so much;
and he specially advocates all measures which tend toward the moral
and intellectual elevation of those about him. In reviewing his successful and honorable career in life, one feels how much may be accomplished by brains and energy. No doubt a loyal affection for and
recollection of the land over seas in which he was born and where
his first ambitions were aroused exists in his heart and mind; but,
notwithstanding this, he is an American to all intents and purposes,
and as a citizen of the United States he performs all of the duties
that an American would feel he must fulfil. Although the family
records show that seventy-seven years have elapsed since the date of
this gentleman's birth, he scarcely looks sixty, his agile step and
erect carriage betokening a sturdy constitution and sound physique.
The villagers all regard him as their friend and benefactor, and unite
in the sincere wish that his span of years may be lengthened to the
utmost. He has won for himself what is of more actual value than
the accumulation of goods and chattels, the honor and esteem of those
who know him, and has founded in this country a family that holds
an exceptionally high place in the land of his adoption.

Louis Bertrand Goodall, son of Thomas and Ruth Goodall, was
born in West Winchester (in Ashuelot), N. H., September 23, 1851.

He first attended the common school in Troy, N. H., to which place his parents had removed from Winchester in 1852. Then from the spring of 1862 until the spring of 1863 he was a pupil at a private school in Thompson, Conn. On leaving Thompson he entered the Vermont Episcopal Institute, a military school at Burlington, Vt., where he remained until August, 1866, when he was obliged to leave his studies in order to join his parents in England. While in England he received instruction at a private school, and returned with his parents to this country in 1867, when his father established the lap-robe business in Sanford. It was then his intention to fit himself for college, and with this end in view he attended Kimball Union Academy at Meriden, N. H., during the spring of 1870, when changes in his father's factories necessitated his return to Sanford, where he remained until the following winter, when he took a business course at Shaw's Commercial College in Portland.

On returning to Sanford he was installed as paymaster for the Sanford Mills, and later was promoted to the position of superintendent, which he filled very acceptably, displaying marked ability. In 1874, the blanket-mills were organized under the firm name of Goodall and Garnsey; and Louis B. Goodall was appointed treasurer and superintendent. On October 1, 1881, he entered into a copartnership with his two brothers, George B. and Ernest M., for the manufacture of car and furniture plushes, he accepting the treasurership. May 31, 1883, the factories in which the blankets are manufactured were incorporated as the Mousam River Mills, Mr. Goodall retaining the position of treasurer. July 1, 1884, the plush business was organized and incorporated under the name of Goodall Manufacturing Company, of which he was treasurer. When, on April 4, 1885, the Mousam River Mills were consolidated with the Sanford Mills, Mr. Goodall was placed in charge of the blanket department as superintendent. The plush business was absorbed by the Sanford Mills at the same time. In 1889 Louis B. Goodall associated himself with others in the organization of the Goodall Worsted Company (which has grown to six times its original capacity), accepting the office of treasurer, which position he still holds.

November 9, 1893, Mr. Goodall was elected clerk and treasurer of the Mousam River Railway Company. April 26, 1896, he was elected treasurer of the Harrison and North-Eastern Railroad, a coal railroad in Tennessee. For many years he has been associated with the Sanford Mills Company as one of the directors and clerk. April 7, 1896, he was again honored by being elected president of the Sanford

National Bank. He is also treasurer of the Sanford and Cape Porpoise Railway Company, the Atlantic Shore Line Railway Company, and treasurer of the Maine Alpaca Company. Is also a director in the Holyoke Plush Company, of Holyoke, Mass., and the Sanford Power Company.

Louis B. Goodall was united in marriage with Rose V. Goodwin, of Saco, July 21, 1877. Three children were the result of this union : Lela Helen, born in Portland, November 15, 1887 ; Mildred Vaughn, born in Sanford, June 25, 1891 ; and Thomas Milton, born in Sanford, August 31, 1893. The death of Mrs. Louis B. Goodall occurred in Sanford, April 15, 1894.

GEORGE BENJAMIN GOODALL, son of Thomas and Ruth Goodall, was born in the town of West Winchester (in Ashuelot), N. H., September 23, 1851. He first attended the common schools of the village of Troy, N. H., to which place his parents had removed in 1852. He next attended a private school in Thompson, Conn., for a period of one year from the spring of 1862 until the spring of 1863. He then entered the Vermont Episcopal Institute, a military school at Burlington, Vt., where he remained from 1863 to 1866, when he joined his parents in England. While in that country he was a pupil in a private school, and returned with his parents to this country in 1867.

Very early in life he displayed more than ordinary artistic ability. In later years his tastes in this direction especially fitted him to take charge of the coloring and designing departments of the carriage robe business in which his father engaged in 1867. This position he filled most acceptably for many years. He was the projector of the plush industry, and with his own hands placed the first warp in a rude wooden loom, and wove by hand the first piece of plush. As soon as he had demonstrated that mohair plush could be produced on a power loom, he entered into a copartnership with his two brothers, Louis B. and Ernest M., and the firm of Goodall Brothers was organized October 1, 1881, he taking upon his shoulders the management. The assistance of a first-class inventor of weaving mechanism was secured by the new firm, and the perfect-working wire motion plush loom, now in use in the factories, was the result. The company started with one loom, and now has one hundred and fifteen in operation. The struggle at the beginning was one that would have discouraged ninety-nine men out of a hundred. Days, weeks, and even months passed away before a piece of plush that could be termed perfect was produced ; but perseverance conquered, and the product of the company today will stand before the world on its merits. This branch of the business has been under the supervision of the projector from the start.

Mr. Goodall is an artist of recognized ability, and during the winter of 1872 was a pupil of Untemberger, the celebrated painter, at Brussels, in Belgium. All of the designs, colors, and shades pass under his personal inspection before being placed on the market.

He is president of the Goodall Worsted Company, a director in the Sanford Mills, and also in the Mousam River Railway Company, and Sanford and Cape Porpoise Railway Company, besides being the president of the Maine Alpaca Company, and treasurer of the Sanford Power Company, and director in the Holyoke Plush Company of Holyoke, Mass.

On October 28, 1872, he was united in marriage with Miss Henrietta D. Bennett, of Sanford. Miss Marion, their only child, was born in Sanford, May 24, 1876, and is a very accomplished young lady.

Hon. Ernest Montrose Goodall, the youngest son of Thomas and Ruth Goodall, was born in the picturesque village of Troy, N. H., on August 15, 1853. He attended school in his native village, Thompson, Conn., in Burlington, Vt., and in England during his parents' sojourn in that country from 1866 to 1867. On returning to this country he entered his father's factories, and after acquiring a thorough knowledge of the methods of manufacture, was appointed superintendent, having displayed marked executive ability. When his father retired from active business, he was promoted to the position of president of the Sanford Mills, which he has held since May 11, 1883. At the inception of the Sanford Light and Water Company in 1886 he was elected president, and on November 9, 1893, president of the Mousam River Railway Company.

In 1897, the Sanford and Cape Porpoise Railway Company was built and Mr. Goodall was chosen president. Afterwards the Atlantic Shore Line Railway Company was constructed, and he was elected president in 1898. He was made president of the Sanford Power Company, which was formed to furnish power by electricity to the mills in Sanford with the power house at the Old Falls. He is also president of the Cape Porpoise Land Company, the Holyoke Plush Company of Holyoke, Mass., and the Oakdale Cemetery Association; and is also a director in the Goodall Worsted Company and Maine Alpaca Company.

Mr. Goodall has served his town in numerous official capacities, being elected a member of the board of selectmen, March 10, 1879, and serving up to the spring of 1888. September 13, 1880, he was elected as Representative to the state Legislature, serving until September 11, 1882, when his constituency sent him to the state Capitol as a Senator. During the two years from January 1, 1885, until January, 1887, he was a member of Governor Robie's Council. At the expiration of his term of office he retired from political life (to reenter it as selectman the past year), and has since devoted his attention chiefly to the work of producing dividends for the stockholders of the Sanford Mills. He is a true sportsman in every sense of the word, and his friends are legion. He is the owner of a trim little yacht, the " Nemo," and finds much enjoyment in cruising about the rivers of Florida, having spent the last twelve winters in that part of the country.

EDMUND E. GOODWIN, of Springvale, was born in Shapleigh, June 9, 1852, the son of Hon. Edmund and Hannah P. (Webber) Goodwin. At the age of fifteen he began mercantile life as a clerk in a tobacco store in Brooklyn, N. Y., and later was a clerk in a number of dry goods establishments. In 1877 he entered into business with his father at Springvale, where he has since continued, and is now senior partner of the firm of E. E. and J. W. Goodwin, general merchants and manufacturers of clothing. Mr. Goodwin has been prominent in a number of corporations, and is at present a director in the Sanford National Bank. In 1872 he married Ellen R. Vance, of Brooklyn, by whom he had one daughter, Maud R. Mr. Goodwin married, second, Clara A. Johnson, by whom he had one daughter, Eva C. In politics he is a Democrat, and is a member of several of the secret orders.

GEORGE A. GOODWIN, son of Samuel and Sarah A. (Johnson) Goodwin, was born in North Berwick, December 15, 1862. He attended the Coburn Classical Institute, Waterville, and graduated from Bates College in 1885. After serving as principal of the academy at Blue Hill, he read law with Savage and Oakes, Auburn, was admitted to the bar in 1891, and opened an office in Springvale the same year. Mr. Goodwin has served as tax collector and member of the school committee. He married, October 16, 1893, Etta L., daughter of Nathaniel Gile, Waterborough.

REV. JACOB GOSS was stated supply of the Congregational pulpit from November, 1843, to November, 1846, when he was installed as pastor of the church, and remained until August 21, 1850. He was born in Henniker, N. H., in 1794, graduated at Dartmouth College in 1820, in the class with Rev. Christopher Marsh, was a home missionary in Georgia, preached in Topsham, Warren, Woolwich, and Wells, Maine, and Randolph, Vt., and died in Concord, N. H., April 21, 1860.

DR. R. S. GOVE, son of Almon and Jennie H. Gove, was born in Limington, April 2, 1870. He was educated at Limington Academy, and at the Maine Medical School, Brunswick, graduating from the latter in 1892. After practicing in Biddeford for about two years, he located in Sanford, where he has been since 1895. He married, in 1896, Suzelle E. Welch, of Biddeford.

WILLIAM GOWEN, JUNIOR, known as "Master" Gowen, was the son of Stephen and Molly (Powers) Gowen. In his boyhood he was so afflicted with asthma that he could do no hard manual labor, and therefore concluded to prepare himself to be a school master. He was educated in the public schools of Sanford, at Fryeburg (?) Academy, and at his own fireside. He was always a close student, even after reaching mature age. He began teaching in town not far from 1800, and continued for some thirty years, in winter (see page 150). Occasionally he taught evening school for business men to learn penmanship and book-keeping. In summer he carried on his farm and garden, having a fine garden for the times, with all kinds of vegetables and "garden-sauce" in their seasons. He had a good orchard of apple and plum trees. He built his own house, finished three rooms before his first marriage, and made nearly all of the furniture and household utensils used. His paint was red ochre, obtained from the Red brook. "Master" Gowen was never in more than comfortable circumstances, as he never received more than ten dollars a month for teaching, and could not carry on heavy farming.

He was a member of the school committee four years, and was re-elected in 1826, but was excused from serving.

"Master" Gowen was married three times: First, to Olive Witham, October, 1808; after her death in 1811, to her sister Mary, daughter of Jonathan and Lydia Witham; third, to Sarah H. Witham, cousin of the two preceding, who survived him nearly forty years. When his first and second wives died, he prepared their gravestones with his own hands, from flat stones, even to the cutting of the names. In person, he was of medium height, spare, light complexioned, with gray eyes, light hair and whiskers. He was a rigid moralist and a member of the Baptist Church. When the church was without a minister, he often conducted meetings on Sunday, reading a printed sermon.

(For other Gowens, see Revolutionary soldiers, pages 76–77.)

REV. THOMAS GREENHALGH, who gave to Springvale its name (see page 199) was a native of Clitheroe, England, where he was born in 1791. Early left an orphan, his youth was spent in poverty, and he did not learn to read until after his marriage, which occurred when he was twenty-one years old, at which time he was converted. He learned the alphabet from a Sunday School class of boys, to whom he gave religious instruction, and not long afterward, became a local preacher. Coming to America in the spring of 1826, he resided in Dover, N. H., for two years, and in May, 1828, removed to Sanford. He was a printer by trade, and was one of the members of the firm of John Whitaker and Co., that organized the Springvale Print Works. In 1832 he joined the Maine Conference of the Methodist Episcopal Church, having been engaged by the presiding elder to supply the charge at Saco. Even before that, in the fall of 1830, Elder Greenhalgh was recognized as a local preacher at Springvale, and the following year, assisted by several circuit preachers, conducted an extensive revival. He served the Maine Conference as an effective minister for nineteen years. About 1848, he took a house in Springvale, where his family lived for a few years, while he continued to preach in surrounding towns. He died in Hampden, June 23, 1866. Fourteen children survived him. " Father" Greenhalgh was deeply devoted to the cause to which he gave his life. It is narrated of him that he once left the printing business and a salary of $1200 a year, to preach for an annual salary of fifty dollars. He was a strong and fearless advocate of temperance. At one time in Saco, his life was threatened by a mob, for his bold denunciation of the liquor traffic, but he was rescued and taken home by John Fairfield, afterward Governor of Maine.

DR. ABIEL HALL, SENIOR, was the first resident physician in the town of Sanford. He was a son of Ebenezer and Dorcas (Abbott) Hall, of Concord, N. H., where he was born, in May, 1761. In 1777, when only sixteen years of age, he volunteered in Lieutenant Colonel Gerrish's regiment for the assistance of Ticonderoga, and subsequently served at Ticonderoga, in Captain Ebenezer Webster's

HON. CHARLES A. SHAW.

company, Colonel Stickney's regiment, General Stark's brigade. In 1780, he removed from Concord, settled in what is now Alfred, and there practiced medicine with much success until he was succeeded by his son, Dr. Abiel Hall, Junior. He married Mary, daughter of Benjamin Farnum, of Concord, and had seven children. Dr. Hall died October 13, 1829.

DR. ABIEL HALL, JUNIOR, the oldest son of the preceding, was born in Sanford (Alfred), September 6, 1787, and after pursuing a course of medicine with his father, began to practice in 1809, succeeding his father at the age of twenty-two years. He married Elizabeth, daughter of General William Frost, of Sanford, November 16, 1815. She died March 24, 1863, aged sixty-eight years and ten months. He died December 18, 1869, having been in practice sixty years. In 1823 he was chosen a deacon in the Congregational Church, and for the last twenty years of his life was one of its leading members.

HON. BENJAMIN F. HANSON, second son of Joshua and Philena (Hobbs) Hanson, was born in Sanford, July 31, 1818. He learned the blacksmith's trade of his father, and at the age of twenty left home to work at his trade. After spending several years at the quarries in Quincy, Mass., he went to Great Falls, N. H., where he followed his trade, and was also for some years engaged in the livery-stable business. It is stated that he, at the age of twenty-eight years, assisted by his brother George Marston, turned four hundred horse-shoes in eleven hours, a most remarkable amount of labor. He returned to Sanford in 1852, and devoted his attention to agricultural pursuits. From 1871 to 1875, in company with Daniel G. Clark and Hosea Willard, he traded at the Corner.

The fact that nine of the eleven children of Joshua Hanson attained their majority, and that six sons learned the blacksmith's trade, at which they were active and powerful workmen, shows that the family is one of strong and robust physical constitution. Resolution and firmness are delineated in their countenances, and physical endurance is indicated in their stalwart and muscular bodies. Benjamin F. had these family traits. His early education was limited to the instruction given in school district number twelve, but his practical knowledge, common sense, and vigorous intellect gave him a high standing among his fellow-citizens, and brought him into prominence as a leader in the affairs of the town and county. While residing at Great Falls, he was one of the selectmen of Somersworth. In 1863,

30

he represented Sanford and Lebanon in the Legislature, and served as Senator two terms, 1874 and 5. He was town treasurer for several years. Mr. Hanson was a member of the Republican party from its organization, and was for eight years on the Republican county committee.

His wife, whom he married February 21, 1840, was Mary E., daughter of Elias and Mehitable Libby. They had four sons: Luther L., born November 3, 1844, married M. Alice Rogers, of Freeport, Maine ; B. Frank, born December 12, 1848, married Fanny Thompson, of Shapleigh, and resides in Somersworth, where he has been mayor; Charles H., born March 3, 1858, graduated at Colby University, 1883, and is now a lawyer; and George William, born January 26, 1861. Mr. Hanson died February 15, 1891, and his widow, April 19, 1894.

GEORGE WILLIAM HANSON, son of Benjamin F. and Mary E. (Libby) Hanson, was born in Sanford, January 26, 1861. He attended the district school and prepared for college at the Coburn Classical Institute. In 1883 he graduated from Colby University. After graduation he took a two years' course in law under the direction of the Hon. W. F. Lunt of Portland. He then entered Boston University, where he completed the three years' course in one year. He graduated from the law school of that institution in 1886, standing fourth in a very large class. After practicing his profession in Boston for a short time he became a member of the editorial staff of the West Publishing Company of St. Paul, Minn., publishers of law reports. After a year's connection with the firm, he went to Sioux Falls, S. D., where he practiced law for three years. When his father died in 1891 Mr. Hanson returned to Maine and opened a law office in Sanford, where he has since remained.

In 1897 the Sanford Municipal Court was established by act of the Legislature, and as a result of a popular petition presented to the Governor and council Mr. Hanson was appointed Judge, which place he has filled ever since. Judge Hanson has been a member of the board of selectmen continuously since 1892, serving as chairman of the board for seven consecutive years. Although a staunch Republican in politics he has been honored by men of all parties, his name having appeared at the head of both tickets in the last four town elections. He is also serving his second year as a member of the school board.

In 1886 Judge Hanson married Maria H. Shaw, daughter of John

H. Shaw of this town. They have two daughters, Pauline and Mary, and a son, Benjamin S.

ELMER E. HARRIS, son of Enos and Louisa (Lord) Harris, was born in Springvale, March 21, 1862. He went to work at an early age, at first as clerk in a grocery store, and later as an employe of one of the village shoe factories, where he remained a number of years. He is at present in the grocery business. In 1891 he was elected on the board of selectmen, and was chosen chairman, and is again a member of the board, enjoying the distinction of being the only Democrat holding an elective office in town. During President Cleveland's second administration he served as postmaster at Springvale.

ELDER GEORGE HEARD was born in Berwick, now North Berwick, October 25, 1792. Fitting himself for a teacher by a course at South Berwick Academy, paid for from the proceeds of work on a farm, he began to teach at the age of sixteen. During his life he was the master of seventy-two different schools. He was the early classical teacher of the town, having studied Latin and Greek with Parson Sweat. When twenty-two years of age, he became a clerk for General Allen, and remained with him about two years. It is said that Allen was so pleased with Heard that he offered him $1200 a year for five years if he would continue with him, but he preferred to take a college course, and refused the tempting offer. He entered Dartmouth, but left at the end of six months, because Hebrew was not in the curriculum. Returning to North Berwick, he pursued the study of Hebrew under the tuition of Rev. Joseph Hilliard.

From 1821 to 1841 he resided in town, both at Sanford Corner and Springvale, during which time he served on the school committee. In 1841 he removed to Shapleigh, and resided for twenty years near Emery's Mills. In that year (although he had begun to preach a long time previously) he was ordained a Calvinistic Baptist minister. A Democrat in politics, he represented Shapleigh in the Legislature in 1844. He died in Lynn, Mass., in December, 1873.

Elder Heard was an excellent penman, a fact shown in the complete set kept by him of his written works. These show that he handled the pen of a ready writer, whether expressing himself in English or Latin, prose or poetry. It is related of him that he once demurred at paying his taxes, because they were too high, whereupon the assessors requested him to give, in writing, an inventory of his estate, real and personal. He returned the following:

" A shell of a house, a shattered barn,
Ten acres of terrell (?) comprise my farm ;
One orchard which haply six barrels may yield,
That covers a very good part of my field ;
One two-year-old, two yearlings compose my stock,
Quite meagre my apparel and scanty my flock."

It does not appear, however, whether the Elder's taxes were abated.

COLONEL JOHN HEMINGWAY was born in what is now Acton, October 16, 1818. As a boy and youth, he worked at farming, at the shoemaker's trade, and in a cotton mill at Great Falls, N. H., meanwhile gaining some schooling, and after serving on the selectmen and school committee of Acton, he moved to Springvale in 1851, and went into business with Clement Parker, Junior. From 1854 to 1856 he was a deputy sheriff. Later he went into the lumber business at Emery's Mills, and in 1860 was a selectman of Shapleigh and a county commissioner. That fall he removed to Springvale.

In 1861, after the battle of Bull Run, he enlisted a company, was commissioned a Captain, and joined the Eighth Maine. He served two and a half years, during which he was commissioned Major, and later Lieutenant Colonel of the regiment. He resigned February, 1864, having received an injury by reason of his horse falling with him in the night while making the grand rounds.

, Up to 1871, he was engaged in the shoe business and lumber business, when he engaged in farming in Charlton, Mass. Later he returned to Maine, and now resides at Emery's Mills.

DR. NAHUM ALVAH HERSOM was born in Lebanon, August 7, 1835, and died in Dublin, Ireland, while on a trip abroad in search of health, May 1, 1881. After attending Parsonsfield Seminary and Lebanon Academy he began the study of medicine in November, 1858, and graduated from the University of Pennsylvania, March 16, 1861. The following July he commenced practice in Sanford, remaining until he received a commission as Assistant Surgeon, Twentieth Maine Infantry, August 9, 1862. On the 3rd of March, 1863, he was promoted to Surgeon of the Seventeenth Maine, and about a year later took charge of the field hospital, Third division, Second army corps, where he remained until mustered out with his regiment, June 8, 1865. At the battle of Fredericksburg he was taken prisoner, but subsequently released. He was regarded as one of the most skilful of the younger surgeons of the army. After the war Dr. Hersom was in practice at Farmington, N. H., for two years, but was compelled to give up on account of ill health. For three years from December, 1869, he spent his summers in Springvale and his winters in the south, removing to Portland in November, 1872. There he enjoyed a successful practice until the time of his death. Dr. Hersom married S. Jane, daughter of Samuel and Sophia S. Lord, of Sanford, November 25, 1865, who survives him, with one daughter. After her husband's death, Mrs. Hersom pursued the study of medicine at the Woman's College of Pennsylvania, in Philadelphia, graduating in March, 1886, and has since been in practice in Portland.

CALVIN R. HUBBARD was the first lawyer at Springvale, moving into town from Shapleigh about 1832. Four years later he entered into partnership with Hon. John T. Paine. For two years he was postmaster, and died November 17, 1837, in his thirtieth year.

GEORGE W. HUFF, son of Laroy G. and Emma J. (Stone) Huff, was born in Biddeford in September, 1874. He was educated in the Cape Porpoise schools and at the Biddeford High School. After learning the printing business, he worked as job printer on the Biddeford Journal, Biddeford Times, and Old Orchard Sea Shell. Removing to Sanford, he conducted the Sanford Tribune from 1895 to 1899, and on the death of Prescott Emery in 1898, became his successor in the heating and plumbing business. Mr. Huff married, in June, 1894, Alta O., daughter of Prescott and Alma Olivia (Cole) Emery.

EDWARD E. HUSSEY, the popular and efficient superintendent of Department A of the Sanford Mills, was born in Charlestown, Mass., March 27, 1861, son of Burleigh S. and Lavinia T. (Miller) Hussey. His father was a native of Rochester, N. H. and his mother was a daughter of William Miller, of this town. Mr. Hussey's grandfather, Paul Hussey, was of Quaker parentage. Burleigh S. Hussey died in Charlestown, and Mrs. Hussey moved to Sanford when her son was twelve years of age. Edward E. Hussey began his education in the common schools of Charlestown, and completed his studies at the Sanford High School. At the age of sixteen he secured a subordinate position in the office of the Sanford Mills, where his superior business ability became so apparent to his employers that he was soon advanced to the position of bookkeeper and paymaster, being finally appointed to his present responsible position. He possesses to a high degree those sterling characteristics which are the principal elements in the make-up of a thoroughly capable business man, and his ability and integrity are both recognized and appreciated, as he is the representative of Hon. E. M. Goodall, in the absence of that gentleman. He is one of the directors of the Sanford Light and Water Company, which position he has held for fifteen years. He has been secretary and treasurer of the Maine Woollen Manufacturers' Club for the last six years, and when the Sanford Library Association was organized in 1898, he was chosen treasurer.

In 1882 Mr. Hussey married Abbie J., a daughter of William H. and Eliza Bodwell. Her father is no longer living; but her mother survives, and is a resident of this town.

In politics Mr. Hussey is a Republican; and, fraternally, he is connected with the Knights of Pythias. He has attained to an important and responsible position solely through his business ability, and is a typical representative of the self-made men of Sanford.

CAPTAIN SAMUEL JACKSON was born in Eaton, N. H., February 21, 1804, and died in Sanford, October 1, 1884. Before coming to town, in 1836, he lived in Lebanon. He was one of Sanford's early traders, and a Captain of militia in 1838. His wife was Abigail Nesbett, of South Berwick.

JOHNSON FAMILY. Jonathan Johnson, of York, husbandman, with his son, Jonathan, Junior, came to Phillipstown and took up lot number thirty-seven on May 1, 1739. The Johnsons served in the French and Indian Wars, and Jonathan, Junior, was a Lieutenant in the Phillipstown company of militia in 1762. He was an innholder at South Sanford for many years. Sampson and Stephen Johnson, members of this family, served in both the French and Indian and the Revolutionary Wars. Sampson was in town in 1796, and Stephen died November 12, 1790, aged forty-nine years. Jonathan Johnson, Junior, had three sons, Robert, Jotham, and William. The latter had a grist-mill on Great Works River. Robert was father of Ivory, Samuel, John, and Sally; Jotham, of Abiel H., whose son, James Chase Johnson, resides on the ancient homestead; and William of Rufus, William, Jotham, Robert, and Ira. John Johnson (1804–1854) of Lyon Hill, son of Robert, married Betsey Thompson, and had eight children, as follows: Bradford, of Dover, N. H.; George W., of Somersworth, N. H., born December 21, 1829; Olive J., of Sanford; Samuel F., of Dover, N. H.; Robert, deceased; John T., deceased; Hannah, deceased; and Emilus, of South Sanford. Three sons served in the Civil War: Samuel F., who enlisted three times from New Hampshire, and was wounded in the shoulder; Robert, who served in the Massachusetts Heavy Artillery; and John T., who died in the service, while in the Twenty-Seventh Maine. Hannah married Sumner Henry Needham, of Lawrence, Mass., a member of the Sixth Massachusetts Regiment, who was killed by the mob in Baltimore, April 19, 1861. So far as known, Chase Johnson is the only surviving descendant of any of the first settlers now residing on one of the forty original lots.

THOMAS KEELER was prominent in trade and politics nearly a century ago. It is supposed that he was a native of Pittsford, Vt. He was married in that state, and some of his children were born there. We find that he was licensed as a retailer in Wells, in 1802, April, and as such in Sanford the following August. He was town clerk three years and a half, selectman two and a half years, postmaster two years, and Representative to the General Court of Massachusetts two terms. At one election his seat was contested, but unsuccessfully. It is reported that, at another time, he carried a barrel of rum to town meeting, and offered to give it to the voters and serve the town as Representative for nothing, if they would elect him. But they would not. He removed to Alfred, where he was postmaster and Representative. Afterwards he removed to Kennebunk, where he built a schooner, became involved in debt, bought cattle and sold them in Brighton, and then ran away. He was afterwards heard of in Georgia, making shingles.

WILLIAM KERNON, superintendent of the block cutting department of the Sanford Mills, was born in Dublin, Ireland, and is the son of Charles and Ann (Sharp) Kernon. His education was obtained at an Episcopal church school in Manchester, England, and at thirteen he was an errand boy in Manchester. After being employed in the printing department of a felt factory in Leeds, and in business for himself, for a number of years, he came to this country in 1874, since which time he has been in the employ of the Sanford Mills. He is president of the Sanford Loan and Building Association, has been manager of the Opera House for a number of years, and served as Representative in 1898–99. Mr. Kernon married, in Leeds, Ann Beaumont. They had one child, a daughter, deceased.

HON. INCREASE SUMNER[7] KIMBALL (*Nathaniel,*[6] *Richard,*[5] *Ezra,*[4] *Ephraim,*[3] *Richard,*[2] *Richard*[1]), one of the most prominent and successful lawyers of his time, was born in North Berwick, August 30, 1800. He was a descendant of Richard Kimball, the common ancestor of the great majority of Kimballs in this country, a resident of the parish of Rattlesden, England, who, with his family, sailed for America in the ship "Elizabeth" in 1634. Landing at Boston, he took up his residence in Watertown, Mass., and two years later was invited to remove to Ipswich, where the community was in need of a competent wheelwright, there spending the remainder of his days. He was granted a house lot and other lands by the town. He died June 22, 1675. The subject of this sketch studied law with Hon. Edward E. Bourne and Hon. Joseph Dane, of Kennebunk (who had been a Member of Congress), and was admitted to the bar, Court of Common Pleas, in October, 1829, and Supreme Judicial Court, April, 1832. He entered upon his profession in Kennebunk, removed to Lebanon in 1831, and to Sanford in May, 1847, where he resided until the time of his death, July 26, 1888, enjoying a large and lucrative practice.

In 1837 and 38, Mr. Kimball represented Lebanon in the Legislature, was the youngest member of Governor Kent's Council in 1841, was Representative from Sanford and Lebanon in 1861, and county attorney 1864–67, three years. He held the office of postmaster in Lebanon, 1843–46, and was postmaster in Sanford from 1865 to 1885.

Mr. Kimball married, first, Miriam W., daughter of the Hon. John Bodwell, of Acton (born June 3, 1809, died April 10, 1866). They had the following children: John B., b. March 24, 1832, d. May 4, 1835; Sumner I., b. September 2, 1834; Miriam W., b. June 13, 1836, m. Moses W. Emery; Maria H., b. June 13, 1836, d. September 28, 1836; Helen M., b. August 30, 1839, d. December 9, 1854; Mary E., b. August 11, 1842, m. William H. Miller; Robert B., b. August 24, 1843, d. March 23, 1844; Sarah B., b. September 9, 1845, m. Rufus Cobb; and Elizabeth F., b. October 29, 1847, m. Samuel Benton Emery. All except the last were born in Lebanon. Mr. Kimball married, second, Eliza A., daughter of William Miller, who died April 29, 1872; and third, December 2, 1872, Mary A. Waterhouse.

In early life Mr. Kimball was a Whig, and later a staunch member of the Republican party. He was well versed in the technicalities of his profession, and was a logical, argumentative, and forceful speaker. A man of sound business judgment, as well as of legal skill, he invested largely in Sanford real estate which yielded him handsome returns.

HON. SUMNER INCREASE [8] KIMBALL (*Increase S.*,[7] *Nathaniel*,[6] *Richard*,[5] *Ezra*,[4] *Ephraim*,[3] *Richard*,[2] *Richard* [1]). Of all the names that have reflected honor upon the town of Sanford, none is so well known throughout the civilized world as that of the Hon. Sumner I. Kimball. For twenty-nine years he has occupied the post of chief of the United States Life-Saving Service, and wherever governments or individuals have organized kindred institutions his name is honored, and the great work he has established and raised to the foremost place among the nations has been carefully studied and lavishly commended.

While Mr. Kimball's early life was not passed among the practical affairs of the sea, he lived sufficiently near the coast to hear the good folk around the firesides on stormy nights repeat the common New England tales of wrathful gales and piteous wrecks, which, as the writer well remembers, struck so much of terror and yet of mysterious fascination into the hearts of the children, and always closed with the solemn ejaculation " God pity the poor sailors to-night !" In his later youth he was also witness to scenes around the ugly shores of Cape Cod, which were well calculated to intensify the earlier impressions ; so that from this point of view alone there was much fitness that circumstances should afterwards so happen as to place him at the head of a great organization having for its splendid object the rescue of life from the perils of the sea.

His mental and moral characteristics were well calculated to make him worthy of honors, and likely to receive them. His capacity for study and his clearness of intellect enabled him easily to enter Bowdoin College at the age of sixteen years. His earliest education was obtained in the public schools of Sanford, to which town his parents moved when he was twelve years of age from Lebanon, where he was born September 2, 1834. He attended afterwards, academies at Alfred and North Yarmouth, and the well known seminary at North Parsonsfield. In 1855 he graduated from Bowdoin, having taught school during his college course at Lebanon, Maine, and Orleans, on Cape Cod, at which latter place he came much in contact with coast life and those that followed the sea.

He was admitted to the York County Bar, then pre-eminent in the state for its great ability, in 1858, after three years' faithful study of the law in the office of his father, Hon. I. S. Kimball. For a short period thereafter he served as commission clerk at the State House in Augusta, and then located for the practice of his profession in North Berwick, representing that town and Berwick, in 1859, in the state Legislature, where, although he was the youngest member, he received the distinguished honor of a place on the committee on the judiciary. In 1860 he removed to Boston, and there practiced law until 1861, when the Civil War largely increased the public business in Washington, and he was offered a clerkship in the office of the second auditor of the treasury, which he accepted. In 1870 he had risen by successive promotions to the grade of chief clerk, and early in 1871 was invited by Secretary George S. Boutwell to become chief of the Revenue Cutter Service. The condition of this branch of the treasury department at that time was seriously demoralized by reason of political abuses and lax administration, and the object of Secretary Boutwell was to work out a reform through Mr. Kimball's well known integrity, inflexibility of will and executive ability. While the tender of this high position was duly esteemed by Mr. Kimball as a signal compliment, he realized the difficulties and dangers that would inevitably beset his path and possibly wreck his best endeavors, even to the ruin of his reputation, and he was not eager to accept. However, after making a full survey of the situation, charting, as it were, all the rocks and shoals and adverse currents that could be discovered, he concluded to take the helm, upon the assurance of Secretary Boutwell that the course laid out should be followed, and the chief be faithfully supported by him. Mr. Kimball was firm in his purposes, which he always took care to have founded upon exact justice, and Mr. Boutwell was uncompromising in his support. At the end of seven years (in 1878) Mr. Kimball gave up the place for his present position, and enjoyed the satisfaction and the credit, universally accorded him, of having raised the Revenue Cutter Service from a condition of disreputable inefficiency to one of very high repute.

Prior to this time the life-saving stations, few and poorly equipped, located solely upon the coasts of Long Island and New Jersey, had existed only as mere adjuncts of the Revenue Cutter Service, and when Mr. Kimball took charge in 1871 he found them in a deplorable condition of neglect and decay. As stated in one of the leading magazines of the country, " he at once began the seemingly hopeless task of converting the dirty, ruinous station houses and their lazy, disorderly keepers and crews, scattered along the coast, to the order, discipline and efficiency of forts and drilled soldiers, and the result proved that order and discipline, when evolved out of the worst materials, can grapple with and conquer even the sea."

The work grew under his hands to such proportions as to demand the entire attention and supervision of one man as chief or superintendent. Through his efforts a bill organizing the Life-Saving Service separate and distinct from the Revenue Cutter Service was reported in Congress, and became a law June 18, 1878. President Hayes at once appointed Mr. Kimball general superintendent of the new service, and the Senate instantly and unanimously confirmed the nomination. A remarkable feature of this promotion was the fact that it followed immediately upon the heels of a bitter attack made in Congress upon Mr. Kimball's administration, and was also conferred by the President without the slightest solicitation. Indeed, Mr. Kimball now holds in his possession a very notable petition for his appointment handed to him by his friends, which was never presented to the President. This paper bears the signatures of one hundred and twenty-one Representatives in Congress regardless of party affiliations, and among them are those of two men who afterwards became Presidents of United States, James A. Garfield and William McKinley; two, also, who became secretaries of the treasury, Charles Foster and John G. Carlisle; four who had been, or afterwards became speakers of the house, N. P. Banks, J. W. Keifer, Samuel J. Randall and Thomas B. Reed, as well as those of Benjamin F. Butler, Proctor Knott of Kentucky, and S. S. Cox of New York, Democratic leaders in the house; Eugene Hale, Heister Clymer of Pennsylvania, Gen. J. D. Cox of Ohio, William P. Frye, Omar D. Conger of Michigan, and many others almost equally well known, some of whom had been among Mr. Kimball's most formidable adversaries during the investigation which preceded his appointment. The result of that investigation is emphatically set forth in the following letter addressed to the President by the members of the committee who conducted the examination :

" HOUSE OF REPRESENTATIVES, June, 1878.
" To the President, Sir :
" We, the undersigned, have the honor to recommend that Mr. Sumner I. Kimball be appointed superintendent of the Life-Saving Service. In this connection, we desire to state that we constituted the sub-committee of the committee on commerce of the House of Representatives, to whom were referred the bills H. R. 1920 and H. R. 3462, together with various petitions, protests and memorials relating to the Life-Saving Service, and after a careful study of the whole subject, reported the bill H. R. 3988 to organize the service.

It is proper to add that the recent catastrophes at the wrecks of the

' Huron ' and ' Metropolis ' had somewhat prepossessed us against the present management of the service, and rather created a bias toward the proposition then advanced to transfer it to the navy. It was found, however, upon investigation that the disaster at the wreck of the 'Huron' took place before the time for the opening of the life-saving stations, as provided by law, the service being therefore not accountable for the loss of life upon that occasion. In the case of the ' Metropolis,' examination showed that the law had not provided the number of stations required for that coast, and that the assistance rendered by the life-saving crews was both heroic and considerable, and fully as efficient as the means provided by legislation allowed. The fact was also developed that Mr. Kimball in his successive annual reports as the officer in charge of the service had seriously urged the necessity of increasing the number of the stations in that section, and had in fact, predicted disaster as a consequence of their paucity, a prediction which the event verified. The calamity therefore, only afforded the committee evidence of his wisdom and foresight, and their further study of the subject showed that on all coasts where the means allowed him were at all adequate, his organization of the service, and its operation under his management, had yielded results without a parallel for beneficence in the annals of any life-saving institution in the world. It would indeed be difficult to conceive a more gratifying exhibit than the record of the seven years of the service previous to the present year gave to the committee. It also appeared that these important results had been accomplished with restricted means and under conditions which only the signal capacity of the general manager made other than adverse. The investigation of the committee left them, therefore, somewhat in the position of converts, and they became convinced that greater ability could hardly have been brought to the conduct of the Life-Saving Service than Mr. Kimball has shown. We therefore esteem it both a duty and a pleasure to urge his appointment as its general superintendent.

" We have the honor to be,

" Very respectfully,

" CHARLES B. ROBERTS.

" JAY A. HUBBELL."

" I concur in the foregoing in so far as it represents Mr. Kimball as a most efficient and valuable superintendent. I never regarded the loss of either the ' Huron ' or 'Metropolis' as in any way due to improper or unskilled administration of the Life-Saving Service. The true state of facts is very properly presented. My position as a member of the sub-committee gave me with my colleagues an excellent opportunity to learn and understand the efficiency of the superintendent of that important branch of the public service. I concur in the opinion that the retention of Mr. Kimball in his present capacity will be in the interest of that service and to its decided advantage.

"JOHN E. KENNA."

There can be no question that Mr. Kimball is entitled to the honor of conceiving and organizing the Life-Saving Service as it stands today. To quote again from an important public print: "The actual credit of this great national work of humanity is due to Sumner I. Kimball, who not only conceived the idea of the complete guarding of the coast, and prepared the bill for Congress, but has reorganized the entire system and carried it out successfully in all of its minute practical details." Hon. O. D. Conger, of Michigan, in a speech in the House of Representatives on June 4, 1878, declared that all the "splendor of glory that has been given to this branch of service is due, more than to any other executive officer, to that faithful laborer, the simple chief of a bureau, Mr. Kimball, in the treasury department. To him this country owes, more than to any and all other men, for the organization of the Revenue Cutter Service for life-saving purposes, and for the organization of these life-saving stations and making them efficient as they are today."

Referring directly to a proposition to transfer the Life-Saving Service to the supervision of the officers of the navy, Mr. Conger added :

"Sir, after this service in less than eight years, under the direction of a civilian, the little black-eyed man at the head of the revenue marine in the treasury, has won for himself such distinction, though without means, without proper appropriations, with stations scattered far along our dangerous coasts, I do not believe the American people or their representatives here will dare snatch from this service in the beginning of its career the credit it has acquired and give it to another."

On the same floor Hon. Samuel S. Cox of New York spoke eloquently of Mr. Kimball:

"He did what nobody else thought worth doing. He organized what we had. The officers who had preceded him for twenty years previously, might have done the same thing. This man, first of any, seized the unused opportunities. With skill, with patience, with perseverance, with energy that never faltered, with foresight that saw the end in the beginning, and judgment that discerned in small and scattered sources the amplest possibilities, he made the service what it is today. Hampered by legislative restrictions and slender appropriations, he has contrived to set barriers against the measureless destruction of the sea. With the aid of our funds and his subordinates —and with partisan preferences always in the way—he has lined our exposed beaches on seaboard and lake with improved stations. He has filled them with selected crews, the flower of the hardy beachmen ; he has stocked them with the best boats, wreck-ordnance and life-saving appliances of every kind that modern skill has been able to devise ; he has trained his heroic gangs with constant discipline, until, from simple fishermen, they have become soldiers of surf and storm and the defense of imperilled seafarers. He has by skill and patience far outdone my most sanguine expectations of 1870 ; for he has brought into existence that system of patrol which puts the American life-saving establishment in advance of any in the world ; that system by which, all night, from sunset until dawn, through all the months of tempest, no matter what the weather, those patrolmen and crews are watching along the coast from Maine to Florida. They form a cordon of marching sentinels to espy endangered vessels. They are ready always to summon relief and rescue. This system Superintendent Kimball has brought into unity out of incoherence, and where there was death he has made life."

In the Senate, on July 28, 1888, Senator Beck of Kentucky, well known as an uncompromising champion of economy, and a legislator of the sternest insistence upon what he believed to be right, used the following words :

" I can only add that if there is any branch of the public service that is carried on economically and carried on energetically, earning its money, and every dollar of it, it is the Life-Saving Service. Instead of being extravagant in this service, we have absolutely not gone to the point that common humanity requires us to go for fear that somebody would say that we are giving too much." ·

In the same debate Senator Sherman spoke as follows :

" I wish to say in connection with this service, that it has been so wisely and economically and carefully managed that one man, Mr. Kimball, has always had charge of it from the beginning to this hour ; and through every administration, in all the mutations of party life and the changes which have been made, he has been kept as a model officer. I do not believe that any administration would be courageous enough to remove him for any cause. Besides, there is no party politics in it in the slightest degree."

M. Emile Cacheux, secretary general of the fifth international congress of life-saving held at Toulon, France, in April, 1890, in his official report gracefully bears testimony in the following words to the world-wide pre-eminence of the Life Saving Service of the United States:

" Nearly all civilized nations have established life-saving stations along their coasts. The most complete service is, as shown by the documents which we have received, that of the United States, directed with so much devotion by General Superintendent Kimball. All along the coasts of the United States, life-saving stations have been established, manned by regular crews who are so paid as to allow them to devote themselves exclusively to the protection of mariners. The crews of the stations are drilled every day in launching the boats, in using the beach apparatus, or in resuscitating the apparently drowned; this is why the United States life-saving crews have such extraordinary skill and dexterity. In no nation of the old world is the life-saving service so well organized as in the United States. Nevertheless, Mr. Kimball is not yet satisfied."

Beyond question, the one great secret of Mr. Kimball's wonderful success in developing the Life-Saving Service has been his early and unwavering resolution to conduct it upon non-partisan lines. He realized at the outset that by this policy alone could it be made efficient, and he began at once to plead with Congress for the enactment of a law to place the service upon a non-political basis. In 1882 his efforts were rewarded by the passage of the following act of Congress, approved May 4, 1882: " Section Ten. The appointment of district superintendents, inspectors, and keepers and crews of life-saving stations shall be made solely with reference to their fitness, and without reference to their political or party affiliations." It is worthy to note that this law was the first of the kind ever enacted by Congress. Even this, however, did not fully protect the service from the assaults of politicians, and therefore, in 1896, upon the recommendation of Mr. Kimball, the President issued an executive order placing the life-saving establishment within the classified civil service. Its safeguards are now believed to be complete, and every lover of mankind rejoices that at last this sacred service of humanity is founded upon a basis where it may forever rest secure and command the respect and sup-

port of all men of all creeds and all parties, regardless of political
makeshifts or partisan quarrels.

The confidence reposed in Mr. Kimball during his incumbency by
the various secretaries of the treasury and Presidents of the United
States is shown by the frequency with which he has been designated
temporarily to perform the duties of other high officers during their
absence or disability.

On April 15, 1872, Mr. Kimball was appointed by President Grant
a member of the board of examiners for appointments and promotions in the treasury department under the rules promulgated on December 19, 1871. Looking back at the record of that first board of
more than a quarter of a century ago, one is decidedly impressed with
the excellence of its work, which may be confidently cited as unsur-
passed by any that has succeeded it.

As already stated, Mr. Kimball was appointed General Superintendent of the Life-Saving Service by President Hayes on the 18th
of June, 1878, and on that day the nomination was unanimously confirmed without reference to a committee, a most unusual honor.

On the 25th of February, 1889, he was appointed by President
Cleveland to the important diplomatic position of delegate on the
part of the United States to the international marine conference,
convened in Washington, and composed of leading representatives of
the principal maritime nations of the world. Before the committee on
life-saving systems and devices, of which he was chairman, he read
a paper entitled "Organization and Methods of the United States
Life-Saving Service," which commanded universal applause, and has,
at their request, been furnished in large numbers to foreign life-saving societies, mercantile associations and legislators.

On October 31, 1892, he was appointed by President Harrison
acting first comptroller of the treasury whenever the first comptroller
and his deputy should be absent, and on November 3, 1892, he received from the President a like designation as acting register of
the treasury, the duties of which office he performed for several
months.

On February 7, 1900, President McKinley appointed him acting
comptroller of the treasury to discharge the duties of the comptroller,
when necessary, which appointment he now holds.

On August 23, 1900, President McKinley apppointed him acting
solicitor of the treasury during the absence of the solicitor and assistant solicitor.

Thus it will be observed that seven times Mr. Kimball has been

JOHN STORER.

honored with appointments of great importance by Presidents of the United States.

In 1891 Bowdoin College conferred upon him the degree of Doctor of Science. Mr. Kimball is a member of the American Association for the Advancement of Science, of the National Geographic Society, of the Geological Society of Washington, and of other scientific bodies.

His lifework has been the creation and development of the present Life-Saving Service of the United States, an object worthy the ambition of the noblest mind. He has made it the best in the world, and such a monument of personal industry, wisdom and untiring fidelity as few men have ever been able to establish.

Mr. Kimball married Ellen Frothingham Fenno, daughter of Edward and Elizabeth Frothingham Fenno, of Augusta, Maine, October 12, 1858. Their only son, Edward Fenno Kimball, born November 17, 1859, married Ida Louise Packard, of New Bedford, Mass., and is now chief clerk of the office of the superintendent of the money order system, post-office department, Washington.

ORVILLE V. LIBBY, son of Moses H. and Martha (Moulton) Libby, was born in Sanford, March 21, 1851. After being educated in the public schools, and working for a time in Boston, he formed a mercantile partnership, in 1876, with George H. Nowell, under the firm name of Nowell and Libby, continuing to date. A Democrat in politics, he has served as Representative one term, and as town treasurer for four years. He married, first, in 1876, Susan A., daughter of Rufus and Elmira Bennett, who died in 1878; second, Abbie J., daughter of Joseph Shaw, who died January 1, 1884, leaving one daughter, now deceased; and third, November, 1890, Nellie, daughter of Charles C. Hamlin, of Bridgton, by whom he has had four children.

DR. EBENEZER LINSCOTT was the first resident physician in the South Parish, or Sanford. He was born in York, November 14, 1777, began to practice not far from 1800, and continued until his death, December 10, 1821. He built and occupied the house, afterward enlarged, now owned and occupied by Charles O. Emery, on Lebanon Street. He married, November 11, 1802, Olive, daughter of Deacon Eleazar Chadbourn, by whom he had six children. Mrs. Linscott died in Boston, December 15, 1862. One of their daughters, Caroline, married Caleb S. Emery, and another, Susan, Elder

31

Paul S. Adams. Dr. Linscott served as town clerk one year, and as postmaster ten years. He was an active member of the First Baptist Church. He owned the first carriage in town.

Asa Low, son of Jeremiah Low, was born in Shapleigh, September 24, 1817. He attended Alfred, Limerick, and Parsonsfield Academies, and taught school several years. For three years he pursued the study of law with Hon. John T. Paine at Springvale, and after a course at the Harvard law school, he was admitted to the bar of York County. He at once settled in Springvale, and continued in practice there until his death, June 13, 1899. For more than thirty years Mr. Low was on the school committee, was town clerk seven years, and chairman of the board of selectmen for several terms. In politics he was a staunch Democrat. He performed his public duties with fairness, earnestness, and fidelity, and as a member of the school committee was active and desirous of elevating the standard and increasing the efficiency of the schools. In 1849, he married Mary A., daughter of Amos Getchell (born April 15, 1824, died October 9, 1893), and had nine children, eight sons and a daughter, of whom Asa, Frank, Charles and Arthur Low survive. Another son, Amos W. Low, was postmaster at Springvale from 1885 to 1889, and died October 15, 1899.

Arthur McArthur, the second lawyer at Sanford, followed Grove Catlin, and was in town for a short time, probably only several months, settling here in 1822, shortly after his admission to the bar. Mr. Catlin's new home was so near that he retained his clients, and Mr. McArthur did not secure the practice he expected. Becoming discouraged, he jumped from the second story window of Captain John Hanson's, where he boarded, one night, and went away. Two or three years later he began to practice in his native town, Limington, where he was born, January 14, 1790, and died November 29, 1874. He was a graduate of Bowdoin in 1810. He married a daughter of Rev. William Miltimore, and had six children.

Rev. Christopher Marsh, second pastor of the Congregational Church, was born in Campton, N. H., August 4, 1794, and died in Sanford, June 30, 1859. He began the study of medicine, but, being converted at the age of twenty-one, he decided to enter the ministry, and attended Dartmouth College, graduating in 1820. After receiving private instruction in theology, he was ordained at Sanford, June

4, 1823, and was dismissed December 11, 1827. For the next thirty years he preached at Biddeford, and at West Roxbury and Jamaica Plain, Mass., and was secretary and agent of the Massachusetts Sabbath School Society. In 1858, he accepted an invitation to preach in Sanford, and was blessed with a revival. He had thought to settle over the church as pastor, but his health broke down, and he died through his labors. Mr. Marsh was twice married and left four children.

WILLIAM MILLER, born in England about 1802, came to America in 1822, and settled in Andover, Mass. In the fall of 1836 (?) he removed to Shapleigh, and engaged in manufacturing at Emery's Mills. Some three or four years later he hired of Captain Samuel K. Hutchinson the mill and privilege at the Corner, and began the manufacture of flannels. Afterwards he bought the property, and continued manufacturing until he sold out to Hon. Thomas Goodall, in 1867. During the Civil War he made woollens for army use. Mr. Miller was well informed, and by daily reading became well acquainted with the current topics of the time. He had well-defined opinions, and with facility could clearly and logically express them. He was a good and useful citizen. Mr. Miller's children were : Eliza A., who married Hon. Increase S. Kimball, and died April 29, 1872 ; Lavinia T., who married Burleigh S. Hussey ; William H., who married Mary E. Kimball ; and Ellen M. Mrs. Miller died November 22, 1867 ; Mr. Miller died March 12, 1884.

WILLIAM HENRY MILLER, son of the preceding, was born in Andover, Mass., January 20, 1834, and came to Sanford with his parents in 1839. From 1849 to 1851 he attended Limerick Academy, and between 1854 and 1857 visited California, where he had some mining experience, some of the western and southern states, and the eastern and northern parts of Maine. He read law in 1858–59 with Hon. I. S. Kimball, was admitted to the bar in April, 1859, and was in partnership with Mr. Kimball from 1859 to 1863. During 1862 he was a First Lieutenant in the Twenty-Seventh Maine. At one time he was engaged in the manufacture of flannels and blankets, in company with his father, and subsequently carried on the shoe business with Moses W. Emery. He was postmaster from 1861 to 1865. In 1868 he moved to Boston, where he continued in the practice of law until his death, April 22, 1896. He served on the Boston school committee. Mr. Miller married Mary E., daughter of Hon. I. S. Kimball, in 1859, and had two sons and a daughter.

MOSES MORRILL was prominently identified with the early development of the town. He carried on a store at the Corner for a number
of years. With Deacon Frost he built the store which formerly stood
on the site of Garnsey's Block. He married Mary Wise, of Wells,
in November, 1816. Mr. Morrill died about 1820, and his widow
married Ichabod Butler in 1823. Hannah Catherine Morrill was
born in Sanford, August 12, 1819.

DAVID MORRISON was the son of Daniel, and was born in Wells in
1745. He moved to Sanford about 1785 and built a grist-mill, saw-
mill, and iron works at the privilege one mile above Springvale. He
built the Iron Works prior to 1791, and the saw-mill prior to 1796.
His original purchase was one hundred and fifty acres on the Mousam
River. He had a son Joseph, and a grandson John. Mr. Morrison
died March 24, 1817, aged eighty-two years.

MOULTON FAMILY. Colonel Jeremiah Moulton, of York, from whom
many of the name in town are descended, was agent of the Phillipstown proprietors and an extensive land-owner (see pages 17–18).
His children were Thomas, Jotham, Jeremiah, Joel, Abigail, Hannah,
and Lucy. Jeremiah, Junior, of York, took up settlers' lots numbers
nine, twenty-one and twenty-two, November 18, 1742. At the time
of his death, in 1777, he owned two hundred and thirty-five acres of
land in Sanford, and half of Chadbourn's saw-mill, valued in all at
one hundred pounds, ten shillings. He had four sons, Jotham,
Thomas, Jeremiah and Joel. His son, Brigadier Jotham Moulton,
was born in York in 1740 (?), and June 10, 1765, married Joanna
Tilden, his cousin. He became an extensive owner of land in Sanford, owned a part of the Iron Works at the Corner, and helped build
the same. He built the first bridge across the river. He served with
honor in the Revolution, being chosen Brigadier in 1776 by the Provincial Congress. Brigadier Moulton died suddenly at York between
May 8 and 14, 1777, while at home on a furlough. He had made
arrangements to move to Sanford, and had built a large house at
South Sanford for a residence. This structure, afterwards moved to
the Corner, was known as the Nasson house; Brigadier Moulton's
widow married Major Samuel Nasson and occupied it. Brigadier
Moulton had six children: Jeremiah, b. March 7, 1766; George, b.
November 12, 1767; Jonathan, b. July 8, 1769; Jotham, b. January
15, 1771; Abigail Ruck, b. October 13, 1773, m. a Pillsbury; Rufus,
b. October 15, 1775.

JEREMIAH[4] MOULTON (*Jotham,[3] Jeremiah,[2] Jeremiah[1]*), eldest son of Brigadier General Jotham Moulton, was born in York, March 7, 1766, and came to Sanford when a boy. He was a farmer, and also manufactured cloth in a mill on the site of the present Sanford Mills as early as 1810. He became one of the town's most prominent citizens and largest land owners. He married Martha Friend, by whom he had seven children, Jotham, Rufus, Hannah, George, Nancy, Abigail, and Jeremiah. Mrs. Moulton died January 10, 1815, and on February 1, 1816, Mr. Moulton married her sister, Mrs. Hannah Friend Hobbs, by whom he had two children, Mary, who married a Hatch, and Martha, who married Dr. Albert Day. Mr. Moulton died February 2, 1849, and his wife Hannah died November 25, 1869, aged ninety-one years.

DR. JOTHAM[4] MOULTON (*Jotham,[3] Jeremiah,[2] Jeremiah[1]*), fourth son of Brigadier General Jotham Moulton, was born in York, January 15, 1771, and died in Bucksport, November 2, 1857. He came into town with his mother and step-father (Major Samuel Nasson) when he was about eight years of age. During his early manhood, he was sick with consumption, and apparently near the end of life. One night he dreamed that he went over to Mrs. Batchelder's house, across the river, and that she accompanied him out into the pasture to find a certain weed, which he had dreamed of seeing, and which would cure him. Seizing upon the dream as an omen of health and life, the invalid went next day to see Mrs. Batchelder, told his dream and together they sought the weed in the pasture. They found it, and gathered some. He carried it home, steeped it, and drank the extract,—and recovered his health. The weed was afterward known as "Jotham weed." [1] Young Moulton read medicine with Dr. Job Lyman, of York, and in 1795, with a little box of medicine, six inches square, journeyed eastward into the wilderness of Maine. He reached Buckstown (now Bucksport), where he settled, and continued in practice the remainder of his life. But few people dwelt along the river when he first located, so he went up and down the Penobscot in a birch canoe for many years, answering the calls of the sparsely settled country. He was a man of great integrity and benevolence, and a true Christian. He married Mary Farrar, of Hanover, N. H., October 16, 1802, and had four children, Lucy, George, Jotham Tilden, and Mary.

[1] Mrs. Theodate Moulton.

CAPTAIN JEREMIAH[4] MOULTON (*Joel,*[3] *Jeremiah,*[2] *Jeremiah*[1]), son of Joel and Eunice Moulton, was born December 9, 1786. About 1810 he established a tannery in Sanford, and carried on the business nearly fifty years. He served in the militia for eight years, rising to be Captain. He died May 5, 1860. Captain Moulton was twice married, his first wife being Patty Harmon, of York, and his second, Hannah, daughter of Rev. Moses Sweat. He had three children by the first wife, and eleven by the second. Of the latter, but two survive, only one of whom now resides in Sanford, Silas Moody Moulton ; he and his two sons, Moses Sweat Moulton and Benjamin Irving Moulton, are the only descendants of Parson Sweat in town at the present time.

CHARLES F. MOULTON, son of Jeremiah Moulton, was born in Sanford, February 23, 1836. In early life he was employed in the Quincy market, Boston, and after returning to his native town was in the employ of Willard Brothers at South Sanford for a number of years. In 1862, with George and Octavius Allen and George A. Moulton, he engaged in shoemaking in a shop on High Street, and subsequently worked for David Cummings, Springvale, and M. W. Emery and Co., Sanford, shoe manufacturers, for several years. In 1867 he entered the employ of the Sanford Mills, with which he is still connected, being the oldest employe of the corporation. Mr. Moulton has always taken an active part in town affairs, has served one term as Representative, and has filled the office of coroner for a number of years. He married, first, Lucy, daughter of Nathaniel and Abigail Bennett, by whom he had three children ; and second, Augusta, widow of B. Frank Emery, who died in 1896.

WINSLOW L. MOULTON, son of Lewis and Mehitable H. (Jones) Moulton, was born in Sanford, October 26, 1855. He received a common school education and at the age of twenty-six, associated with his brothers, James A. and Orrin, he erected a steam saw-mill in South Sanford and engaged in the manufacture and sale of lumber. Some time later James A. withdrew from the concern, leaving Winslow L. and Orrin the sole proprietors, and they have since continued to carry on the business under the firm name of Moulton Brothers. Mr. Moulton has served two years on the board of selectmen, and is at present road commissioner for the south district.

DR. BYRON M. MOULTON, of Springvale, was born in Sanford,

June 1, 1865; he is the son of Charles P. and Esther (Bourne) Moulton. He studied medicine under the tuition of Dr. Sawyer at Springvale (working in a drug store at the same time), and also at the College of Physicians and Surgeons, Baltimore, graduating in 1894. Since that time he has practiced at Springvale, and also carried on a drug store for several years. June 4, 1894, he married Olivia Woodburn, of Baltimore.

CAPTAIN EDMUND G. MURRAY, son of Horace and Lucy (Welch) Murray, was born in Shapleigh, March 5, 1835, but has been a resident of Springvale during the past forty-four years. His first employment was as a shoemaker. Later he engaged in the livery business, and for many years has been well known among the horsemen of the state. In 1861 he enlisted as Corporal in Sanford's company in the Eighth Maine Regiment. Shortly after his enlistment, he was promoted to the rank of First Sergeant, and for conspicuous bravery at the battle of Cold Harbor, was again promoted, being made First Lieutenant of Company F. At Petersburg he was twice wounded, and received his third promotion for gallantry in action, being made a Captain, with an offer of a commission in the regular army, but the latter he did not accept. After the capture of Richmond he was appointed Assistant Provost Marshal. He was mustered out January 18, 1866, having re-enlisted in the meantime. In 1870 Captain Murray was appointed a deputy sheriff, and served for twenty-eight years. He has also held various town offices. Captain Murray married, in 1855, Dorothy A. Quimby, of Newfield, and their only child, Etta, is the wife of Charles L. Bodwell, of Milton, N. H.

MAJOR SAMUEL NASSON (for so he spelled his name, although the form Nason is in use among his descendants), son of William and Mary (Fletcher) Nasson, was born in Portsmouth, N. H., February 1, 1744. His genealogical line ran back as follows:

1. Richard Nasson. Settled in the north part of Kittery, afterwards set off into Berwick, about 1647, died in the latter part of 1695. His will dated July 14, 1694, was probated March 15, 1696, and appointed his son Benjamin and his son-in-law Nicholas Follet executors.

2. Benjamin Nasson, third son of Richard, died in Berwick in 1714. His will was probated June 14, 1714, and mentions two sons, Benjamin, b. October 10, 1691, and William, b. July 18, 1695; also six daughters. His first wife was Martha Kenney, married June 30, 1687, and his second wife was Sarah ———.

3. William Nasson, born in Berwick, July 18, 1695, married Mary, daughter of Nicholas Fletcher. He was a "mariner" and resided in Portsmouth, N. H.   Probate records of Rockingham County, N. H., June 28, 1762, show that John Mackay was appointed guardian of Samuel Nasson, upwards of fourteen years of age, son of William Nasson, mariner, of Portsmouth, etc.

4. Samuel Nasson.

He was a trader in York when the Revolutionary War began, and served in the Continental army (see page 81). On September 29, 1778, he opened a store at Sanford Corner, and soon after, either in 1779 or 80, moved into town, took possession of the Brigadier Moulton estate, and carried on milling, trading and farming. He soon became prominent in town affairs, and for fifteen years was one of the foremost men in Sanford. He was one of the selectmen eleven years, town clerk three years, town treasurer one year, Representative to the General Court two years, a justice of the peace thirteen years, Major of the militia, delegate to the Massachusetts convention that ratified the Constitution of the United States (see Chapter XIV), a candidate for presidential elector in 1788, and also for councillor and senator several times, but failed of an election. He was one of the nine original members of the Congregational Church, and one of its first two deacons. It was at his house, probably, that the church was organized. While Major Nasson was an enterprising business man, he also exercised the functions of lawyer and doctor for the early inhabitants. His career in Sanford was such as to stand as a refutation of the malicious charge of enemies that he was not possessed of sufficient ability to write the speeches delivered by him at the Constitutional convention. For his position at the convention he was ranked among the Anti-Federalists, and with William Widgery, another leader of the party, received a large majority of the votes in town for candidate for presidential elector. Major Nasson died August 17, 1800, at Ballston Spa, N. Y., where he had gone for the benefit of his health.

He married, August 8, 1765, Mary Shores, of Stratham, who died in York, August 28, 1774. Their children were: Peter, b. April 15, 1766, d. December 15, 1784, served as a drummer boy in the Revolution; William, b. September 15, 1767, d. Monmouth, Maine, 1830; Susannah, b. November 6, 1768, m. Jesse Colcord; Samuel, a soldier in the War of 1812, but never returned, b. October 5, 1771; Gee Hodgkins, his twin brother, d. Dorchester, Mass , aged ninety; and Mary, b. September 15, 1773, m. Naphtali Harmon, d. Harrison,

Maine, 1848. The last-named was the mother of fourteen children, all of whom attained to manhood and womanhood. Major Nasson married, second, March 4, 1778, Joanna Tilden, widow of Brigadier Jotham Moulton, who at the time had six children, Jeremiah, George, Jonathan, Jotham, Abigail R., and Rufus. Major and Mrs. Nasson had four children: Thomas, b. June 6, 1779, father of Captain George Nasson and Mrs. Joanna Phillips; Harriet M., b. October 31, 1782, m. General Elisha Allen (see Allens); Joanna, b. February 15, 1785, m. Philip Hall, North Berwick; Sophia, b. May 20, 1787, m. Joseph Webster. It is reported that the sixteen children were at one time living under the same roof.

THE ELDERS NASSON. Three sons of William and Jane (Frost) Nasson, and grandsons of Major Samuel Nasson, William H., Nathaniel F., and Samuel S. Nasson, were clergymen. Elder William H. was born in 1804. In 1826 he left town and went to Monmouth, where his father died in 1830. He began preaching in 1831, and gave it up in 1836, only to resume in 1842, after he had lost a little boy by drowning. From that time until about a year before his death, which occurred March 28, 1877, he resided in a number of places in Maine, New Hampshire, and Massachusetts, engaged in the ministry of the Christian denomination. He travelled more than sixty thousand miles, and attended more than seven thousand meetings. Elder Nathaniel F. was born in 1808, and began to preach at the age of thirty-one, being prepared for the ministry by his wife, a former school teacher, who gave him instruction to supply the deficiencies in his education. He travelled through Eastern Maine, first as a Christian minister, and later as a Second Adventist. Elder Samuel S. was born in Sanford in 1818, and died in Bangor, July 3, 1865. He entered the ministry of the Christian denomination at the age of nineteen, filled several pastorates in Maine, and travelled considerably in the prosecution of his religious work.

WILLIAM HENRY NASON, son of James and Hannah (Welch) Nason, was born in Essex County, Mass., February 13, 1837. He attended the public schools of Alfred, where his early life was passed, and after his first marriage he removed to Shapleigh, where he resided for about thirteen years, being engaged in farming, lumbering and real estate operations. From September, 1862, to July, 1863, he served in Company I, Twenty-Seventh Maine Volunteers, employed in picket duty at Washington. In 1877 he came to Sanford and founded the firm of W. H. Nason and Co., which has since been engaged in the grain and lumber business. Mr. Nason is an extensive owner of real estate. He has served five years on the board of selectmen. Mr. Nason married, first, September 19, 1863, Sarah A. Wilson, by whom he had five children, three of whom survive; and second, February 13, 1879, Mrs. Lucy Edminster.

COLONEL EBENEZER NOWELL, son of John and Mary (Simpson) Nowell, was a native of York, where he was born April 17, 1780. With his brother John he removed to Sanford about 1800, both taking up their residence on a farm on Mount Hope, which their father had purchased for them of a Mr. Grant. On that farm they lived until their deaths. In 1808 he was commissioned Quartermaster of the militia, then Captain, and in 1817 Lieutenant Colonel. He was a justice of the peace several years, and coroner some twenty years. When he first moved into town he joined the Baptist Church, and in 1847 joined the Mount Hope Church. Colonel Nowell married February 24, 1803, Mary, oldest daughter of Joseph and Susannah (Whitcher) Hill, whose father was then a neighbor of the Nowells. They lived together fifty years and two days, when he died, February 26, 1853. Mrs. Nowell died March 25, 1874, at the age of eighty-nine years. They were the parents of twelve children, two of whom, the first and the fourth, died in infancy. Of the remaining ten, all were living in 1883, but only four now survive. The father's death was the first in the family for forty-four years, and the mother's, the second for over sixty-five years. The children who lived to manhood and womanhood were as follows:

George, married Sally A. Nowell, of Sanford; children, Mary Emily, Susan Jane, Edwin, Samuel, Olive A. Mary E. married Thomas Horne, Lebanon; children, Martha and Abby. Susan J. married Richard H. Goodwin, Lebanon; child, Charles, who married Mary Closson. Samuel married Lizzie Hamilton. Olive A. married William Hobbs; child, Leroy.

Oliver, married Mary A. Jaquith, Boston; children, Frank O., deceased, Josephine, Georgianna. The latter married David Horton, Somerville, has two children. Josephine is married, has no children.

Mary, married George W. Thompson, Somersworth, N. H.; child, Juliet, who married George Lougee. They had two children, Mary, who married Dr. Johnson, Philadelphia, and Edna, married Horace Morse, West Roxbury. After Mr. Lougee's death, Juliet married Frank Lord, West Roxbury.

Susan, married Amasa Wentworth, Somersworth, N. H.; children,

Laura A., Alonzo B., Eben Clinton. Laura married Major William Fowler of Elmira, N. Y., and now resides in Dedham, Mass. Though by profession a musician, she has always been identified with the newspaper fraternity as reporter, correspondent, and musical critic. She has had charge of the musical departments of Monticello Seminary, Ill., colleges in Lexington and Shelbyville, Ky., and Elmira College, N. Y. Descended of Revolutionary stock on her father's side, she organized Old South Chapter, Daughters of the American Revolution, Boston, of which she is regent. Alonzo B. Wentworth married Isabelle Goodwin, Somersworth; children, Gertrude, Marshall, Jere, Clinton, Frances, Katherine, Susan, Laura, Alonzo B. Eben C. was unmarried. He followed the sea, and was Captain of a ship, but lost his life in a railroad accident at the age of forty-three.

Phebe, married Captain Nicholas Varina, Newburyport, Mass.; children, Fannie A., George W., Edward E., Nicholas Benton. Fannie A. married, first, Daniel B. Knight, Boone, Ia.; children, Bertha E., Harold B.; married, second, E. J. Ingersoll, Des Moines, Ia. George W. married Elizabeth Cheever, Newburyport. Nicholas B. married Anna Bowlin, Newburyport; children, Theodate and Fred; resides in Aurora, Ill.

John A., married Frances Shaw, Boston; children, Mary, John Parker. Mary married John Faxon, and has three children.

Ebenezer S., married Abra D. Wentworth, Rollinsford; children, Jessie, Edward E., Annie, Mary, Lincoln. Jessie married Albert Morton; children, Albert and Howard. Edward E. married Dorothy Clark. Annie married Daniel Brackett.

Theodate, married John S. Haines, Somersworth; children, John N., Leonora, Theodate, Fred Sumner, Mary C. John N. married Tilda Page. Leonora married John W. Bates; children, Theodate and Leonora. Theodate Haines married Charles H. Gridley, Elmira, N. Y.; children, Haines, Frederick, and Gladys. Fred S. married Carrie Fatoute, Rochester, Minn., and has four sons. Mary C. married Rev. Sherrod Soule, Naugatuck, Conn.; children, Theodate and George.

Ann, unmarried; resides in Somersworth. She was for many years a teacher in the Boston schools, and an accountant in the Mercantile Savings Bank, Boston.

James M., married Evaline Nute, Somersworth; children, Maude and Georgianna. Maude married Edward Davis, Cambridge; child, Edward.

SAMUEL NOWELL, son of Samuel and Sally (Oates) Nowell, was
born in Sanford, July 10, 1825, and received a district school education and private instruction. He learned the trade of a carriage
builder at Somersworth, N. H., and carried on the business there for
some time. In 1851 he returned to Sanford, where he now conducts
a farm and carries on a carriage business. Mr. Nowell married, first,
April 18, 1841, Emily, daughter of Joshua Hanson, and had seven
children, of whom four survive, Mrs. Nelson Bennett, George H.,
Samuel J., and Charles H. Mrs. Nowell died August 24, 1892, and
Mr. Nowell married, May 24, 1894, Mrs. Mary Travis. Mr. Nowell
served as coroner for many years, and has been a deputy sheriff and
Representative.

GEORGE H. NOWELL, son of the preceding, was born in Sanford
August 30, 1850. For about thirty years he has been in business in
Sanford, since 1876 as member of the firm of Nowell and Libby. He
has served one term in the Legislature. Mr. Nowell has also been
treasurer of the Sanford Loan and Building Association, treasurer of
the Sanford Light and Water Company, and one of the directors of
the Sanford National Bank. He is likewise active in the fraternal
orders.

HON. NICHOLAS E. PAINE was one of the town's early lawyers. He
was born at Rye, N. H., November 23, 1809. Upon graduating from
Phillips Exeter Academy, he entered the legal profession, and in
1832 began practice in Sanford. While in town he was a member of
the school committee for six years, and also served on the staff of
Governor Fairfield. In 1842 he removed to Rochester, N. Y., where
he practiced law for more than a quarter of a century, moving to New
York city in 1868. During his residence in Rochester he was district
attorney of Monroe County, mayor of the city, president of the board
of education, and postmaster under President Buchanan. At the
time of his death he was president of the Dakotah Railroad Company,
and was prominently identified with numerous other enterprises. He
died March 23, 1887, full of years and honor, and his death was
mourned by very many friends throughout the state of New York.
Colonel Paine married, June 23, 1833, Abby M. Sprague, of South
Berwick. He left three children, Mrs. Wallace Darrow, Dr. Oakman
S. Paine, who was brevetted Lieutenant Colonel and Colonel for his
gallant service during the Civil War, and Colonel Willis S. Paine,
now the president of the Trust Company of New York and the

Merchants' Safe Deposit Company located in the metropolis, who was bank superintendent of the state of New York. The latter married recently Miss Virginia Crozier Brown at Fall River, Mass., the daughter of Eliphalet S. Brown of that city. General W. N. P. Darrow, a graduate of West Point, and now the chief of engineers upon the staff of the present Governor of Ohio, is a grandson of Colonel Paine.

Hon. JOHN TREAT PAINE, brother of the preceding, was born in Wakefield, N. H., August 20, 1800. Admitted to the Maine bar in 1826, he opened an office that spring at Emery's Mills, and soon had a large practice. In 1836, he moved to Springvale, and there remained until the fall of 1849, when he removed to Melrose, Mass. He represented Sanford in the Legislature for five terms, served as county attorney, and was postmaster of Springvale for thirteen years. He also served in the Legislature of Massachusetts. For many years he was one of the foremost members of the Boston bar. Mr. Paine married, September 2, 1827, Mary Eliza Rice, daughter of Jeremiah Goodwin, of Alfred. They had nine children. Their oldest son, John St. Clair, born August 12, 1828, graduated at Bowdoin College in 1849, and died in Florida, February 6, 1851. One daughter, Isabella Sewall, married Hon. Horatio G. Herrick, of Lawrence, formerly high sheriff of Essex County, Mass., and another daughter, Sarah Ann Penhallow, married Hon. Nathaniel Hobbs of North Berwick, who was Judge of Probate for York County for a number of years. Mr. Paine died June 21, 1865.

Rev. CLEMENT PARKER was born in Coventry, Conn., January 14, 1782, and died in Farmington, N. H., February 25, 1867. He began to preach, as a Methodist, as early as 1805. About 1808 he left the Methodist body, became a Congregationalist, and preached in various places in Vermont. Meanwhile he studied theology with Rev. Bancroft Fowler, of Windsor, Vt., and was licensed to preach. Between 1827 and 1829 he served two New Hampshire churches, and January 28 of the latter year was installed as pastor of the West Parish (Acton) of Shapleigh. In 1831 he went to Great Falls, in 1834 to the Second Church in York, and in 1838 a second time to Acton. November 9, 1847, he was installed pastor of the newly formed Congregational Church at South Sanford, to which he ministered until 1859, with the exception of one year when he was at Acton. He resided in South Sanford until 1866. His wife was Rachel Taylor, and his children were Dr. David T., of Farmington, N. H.; Clement,

Junior, formerly a candy manufacturer at Springvale; Dr. John S., of Lebanon; and several daughters. One of the latter married Joseph H. Moulton of South Sanford.

Dr. USHER PARSONS, son of William and Abigail Frost (Blunt) Parsons, was born in Sanford (Alfred), August 18, 1788, and died in Providence, R. I., December 19, 1868, in his eighty-first year. He attended school in winter, worked on his father's farm in summer, passed a year at Berwick Academy, and studied medicine with Dr. Abiel Hall, Senior. Then he placed himself under the tuition of Parson Sweat for eighteen months, to prepare for college, but finally resumed the study of medicine, and was licensed as a practitioner in 1812. Practicing a short time at Exeter and Dover, N. H., he obtained a commission as a Surgeon's Mate in the navy, later being promoted to Surgeon, and served with distinction through the entire War of 1812, winning for himself an enviable reputation at the battle of Lake Erie, and being highly commended therefor by Commodore Oliver H. Perry. Dr. Parsons continued in the navy until 1823, serving on the European station, and visiting many of the principal Continental cities. Meanwhile he had resumed his medical studies, received the degree of M.D. from Harvard in 1818, and subsequently held medical professorships in Dartmouth College, Brown University, and Jefferson Medical College, Philadelphia. In 1822, he took up his residence in Providence, where he lived nearly forty-seven years. He was active in founding the Rhode Island Hospital, and at its organization, gave one thousand dollars to it. He married Mary Jackson, daughter of Rev. Abiel Holmes, D.D., of Cambridge, Mass. She died June 14, 1825, leaving one son, Charles W. Parsons, M.D.

Dr. Parsons rose to a high rank in his profession. His practice was extensive, and he was prominent in the affairs of the American Medical Association. He was deeply interested in history and genealogy, and published several volumes on the genealogy of his ancestors. He wrote a series of addresses on the " Battle of Lake Erie," and among his numerous publications mention may be made of the " Sailor's Physician," " Boylston Prize Dissertations," and " Life of Sir William Pepperrell." He was a member of a large number of historical societies. Dr. Parsons was strongly attached to the home and friends of his boyhood and youth, and often revisited his native place. He left in manuscript a history of Alfred, which was published after his death in a small pamphlet. To it the writer is indebted for many facts relating to the history of the North Parish.

MAJOR NAHUM PERKINS was born in Sanford, April 25, 1787. When a young man he went to Topsham, Maine, where he resided until his death in 1865. He became prominent in business and political life in Topsham, and was chosen to the Legislature for four terms. He also served in the militia, whence his title. His father, Jabez Perkins, came to Sanford from Wells, and settled at the foot of Oak Hill. The elder Perkins was a man of strong physical powers, and is said, at the age of ninety-six, to have " cut, sharpened and carried out of the woods on his back, a hundred fence stakes in one day." Major Perkins's affection for his native town was shown in naming his two sons Sanford and Alfred.

HOWARD EUGENE PERKINS, eldest son of Eugene C. and Marilla F. (Davis) Perkins, was born in Sanford, July 5, 1869. His grandfather, Abner F. Perkins (1804–1876), was an early settler in the Oak Hill district, where he married Mary Allen. Howard E. was educated in the town and district schools, and for several years was in the employ of the Sanford Mills. In 1891 he went to Massachusetts, and learned telegraphy, and was in the employ of the Boston and Maine Railroad for two years. Later he was employed in the Western Union office in Sanford. From 1894 to 1898 he was postmaster. Afterwards he was connected with the Sanford Tribune, and is now in the insurance business. He is clerk of the York County grand jury.

DR. HOSEA POWERS was the first practicing physician at Springvale. He was the son of Deacon Nathan Powers, and was born in Sanford, March 28, 1808. His medical studies were pursued with Dr. Abiel Hall, of Alfred, and at the Maine Medical School, where he received the degree of M. D. in 1830. Dr. Powers practiced at Springvale for one year, and stricken on the threshold of life, died May 7, 1831, lamented by a large circle of friends.

ELDER ZEBADIAH RICHARDSON was the second pastor of the Baptist Church. He was born in Pelham, N. H., March 6, 1742/3, and died in Sanford, while on a visit to Ezra Thompson, in 1818. He served nine months in the Revolution, probably from New Hampshire. From October, 1786, to the summer of 1790, he ministered to the Baptists of Sanford, and for the remainder of his life preached at Fryeburg. Elder Richardson married, about 1762, Rebecca Snow, of Nottingham West, now Hudson, N. H., and they had nine children, of whom two were born in Sanford.

GENERAL EBENEZER RICKER was born in Shapleigh, now Acton, October 26, 1820. He was educated on his father's farm, in the public schools, and at the Wakefield (N. H.) Academy, and at the age of sixteen taught school in Ossipee, N. H., and later, in Acton. In 1837 he went to Boston, and a year after enlisted in the Second Regiment, United States Dragoons. Having served in the Seminole War in Florida, about a year and a half, he was discharged for disability arising from ill health, by order of the Secretary of War, on request of the Congressman from the first district, Hon. Nathan Clifford. In 1842, he married Mary A., daughter of Deacon Samuel Stacy, of Acton.

In 1854, General Ricker was elected to the Legislature, and in 1855 Captain of a cavalry company formed in Acton and Shapleigh. He was also appointed a justice of the peace. In 1856 he was elected Major General of the First division of the Maine militia, and the same year removed to Springvale. He built a mill at the old Iron Works privilege on the Mousam, which he occupied until March, 1866, when he removed to Spottsylvania County, Virginia. When that state was under military rule, he was appointed magistrate, and held that office until Virginia was re-admitted to the Union, when he was elected one of the supervisors of the county, and re-elected every term until he removed to Stafford County. General Ricker died at Fredericksburg, July 19, 1900. He is survived by two children, Prof. N. C. Ricker, and Miss Ella V. Ricker, of the Maryland State Normal School, Baltimore.

N. CLIFFORD RICKER, son of the preceding, was born July 24, 1843, in Acton. He attended school winters until nineteen, taught school in the Hooper district, 1861–62, and worked in Lord's piano case factory, Springvale, 1864 to 1867. That year he went to Illinois, and after working at carpentry and wagon making, entered the University of Illinois at Urbana, and graduated from the full architectural course in March, 1873. After six months of study and travel abroad, he became instructor in architecture at his alma mater in the fall of 1873, and has had charge of the department ever since. He has been dean of the College of Engineering since 1878. In 1900 he received the degree of Doctor of Architecture. Professor Ricker has written many volumes of text books and translations for use in his classes. He is a fellow of the American Institute of Architects.

SHERMAN A. RICKER was born in Lebanon in 1827, but removed

into town with his parents in 1829, and spent his boyhood and young
manhood on his father's farm. His parents were Ebenezer and Na-
omi (Sherman) Ricker. At one time he engaged in teaching, but
soon after the " California fever " broke out, he went to the land of
gold. He lived in the west and south till after the Civil War, when
he entered into business in New York. Selling out in 1872, he removed to Chicago, where he carried on the pork-packing business
eight years. In 1880, he went into the grain market, became one of
the largest operators, and was styled the " Corn King." The strain
was too great, and he broke down, and died at the Palmer House,
Chicago, August 27, 1882. At the time of his death he was estimated to be worth $1,250.000. His wife having died some six years
before, his only heirs were his brothers and sisters.

JAMES M. RICKER, town auditor, was born in Effingham, N. H.,
June 25, 1845, and came to Sanford nine years later. He learned
the shoemaker's trade, and later entered the employ of the Sanford
Mills, where he is now an overseer in the dyeing department. He also
carries on a large farm. Mr. Ricker married, first, Isadore Shackford,
and second, Lucy J. Hatch. He has two sons, Charles M. and
Ernest.

JOSEPH RIDLEY, son of Joseph and Phœbe (Getchell) Ridley, was
born in Sanford, December 3, 1842. His ancestors were early settlers of Alfred. During the Civil War he served in Company E,
Twenty-Seventh Maine Infantry. In 1872, he purchased his present
estate and engaged in general farming. January 2, 1870, he married
Mary, daughter of William K. and Abigail H. (Garey) Lord ; they
have had the following children : William T., John G., Lillian A.,
Mabel P., Mary E., and Joseph E.

GEORGE H. ROBERTS was born in Lyman in 1842, and was educated
at Alfred Academy. In his youth he taught thirty terms of school
in Maine and Massachusetts. During the Civil War he served in the
Twenty-Seventh Maine and Ninth Maine Regiments, as private, Sergeant, First Lieutenant, and Quartermaster. For meritorious service
in the field, he received from Congress a medal of honor. Mr. Roberts was baggage master at the railroad station in Springvale from
1880 to 1890, carried on a laundry for the next nine years, and in
February, 1899, was appointed postmaster at Springvale. He married, January 1, 1864, Mary, daughter of Colonel John Hemingway.

32

ORRIN ROBERTS, son of Thomas J. and Mahala (Cook) Roberts, was born in Lyman, September 3, 1847. At the age of fifteen he began to learn the trade of a blacksmith, which vocation he still follows, removing to Sanford in 1873. He is a director in the Sanford Loan and Building Association. Mr. Roberts married Abbie M. Cheney, of South Berwick, and has two children, Mrs. John Wright and Fred S. Roberts.

ELDER OTIS ROBINSON was one of the early pastors of the Baptist Church. He was born in Attleborough, Mass., January 7, 1764. At the age of fourteen he served in the Revolution, enlisting in a company of soldiers commanded by his father, Captain Enoch Robinson, and afterwards re-enlisted for three years, or to the end of the war. Twenty-six of his kindred, all bearing the name of Robinson, enlisted from Attleborough and its mother town, Rehoboth. At the close of the war he married Hannah Reed of his native town. A few years later he removed to Maine, living at Winthrop and Livermore. He was by trade a blacksmith. From June, 1798, to March, 1810, he was pastor of the Sanford Baptist Church, and from 1810 to the time of his death, March 1, 1835, pastor of the church in Salisbury, N. H. Elder Robinson was founder of the New Hampshire Association of Baptists.

WILLIS E. SANBORN was born in Baldwin, Maine, April 17, 1860, and at an early age became associated with his father, Ephraim Sanborn, who was actively engaged in several mills and various lumbering interests. When he came to Springvale in 1882, it was to take the management of the old Province mill opposite the Freewill Baptist Church. He is at present engaged in the real estate and insurance business. Mr. Sanborn is one of the promoters of the Bridgton & Harrison Electric Company, of Bridgton, Maine, of which he is president. He was postmaster of Springvale for five years, under the Harrison administration, and in 1897–98 represented the town in the Legislature. In 1888 Mr. Sanborn married Lizzie A., daughter of Joseph Shaw.

Rev. WALTER T. SARGENT was born in Methuen, Mass., February 3, 1809. He entered Waterville College (Colby) in 1834, but, owing to ill health, was unable to finish his course. Becoming a licensed preacher of the Baptist denomination in 1836, he labored in the following fields: Great Falls, N. H., 1836–37; Buxton, 1837–38;

Damariscotta, 1838 (where he was ordained) ; Nobleborough, one year ; Bowdoinham, one year; Mount Vernon, 1842–48 ; Acton, 1850–55 ; Sanford, 1855–57 ; and Greene and Freeport. He died in Freeport, May 13, 1886. His first wife was Mary L. Hayden, of Waterville. In June, 1841, he married Joan S. Quint, of Topsham, who died February 15, 1885. Of their several children, a daughter, Mary Ellen, married Hon. Andrew R. G. Smith, of Whitefield.

WILLIAM EDWARD SARGENT, son of the foregoing, was born in Sanford, May 23, 1856. He graduated from Bowdoin College in 1878. In April of that year he became principal of the Topsham High School, which position he held for two years, and then went to Freeport, where he was principal of the High School for five years. In 1885, he became principal of Hebron Academy, where he still remains, and for fifteen years has labored unceasingly in building up the institution, giving it a high rank among preparatory schools.

DR. IRA C. SAWYER was born in Hiram, Maine, March 2, 1840. He spent his childhood on a farm, and received his early education at Limington and Parsonsfield Academies. He taught school and studied medicine under Dr. Moses Sweat, Parsonsfield, four years. In 1863, he graduated from the medical department of Dartmouth College. Dr. Sawyer practiced at Naples, Maine, nineteen years, took a special course at Bellevue, New York, and has been located in Springvale since 1884. He married, first, Ellen Edes ; second, Georgia Page, and has had two children.

JAMES B. SHAPLEIGH, son of Samuel and Elizabeth B. Shapleigh, was born in Lebanon, February 20, 1805, and died in Somersworth, N. H., August 2, 1894. At the age of sixteen he began to serve a four years' apprenticeship at currying, tanning, and shoe making. In the winter of 1825–26 he came to Sanford, and commenced the business of shoe and harness making. He also kept tavern at the Corner. In 1828 he was appointed deputy sheriff, and held this position under several sheriffs, with his residence first at the Corner, and later at Springvale, until 1838. He was appointed coroner in 1832, and in 1838 jailer at Alfred. In 1840 he went to Boston, and entered the firm of Searle, Shapleigh and Co., ship chandlers and dealers in ship stores. After two years there, and a brief residence in Lowell, he established himself in Somersworth, where he passed the remainder of his life, engaged at different times in various business enterprises. During his residence in Somersworth, he served as coroner and deputy sheriff. He was deeply identified with the social, religious and business affairs of the community, and his death was a great loss. On September 20, 1827, he married Olive E., daughter of Joseph Lord, of Lebanon. They had three children, Elizabeth Bartlett, James Henry, and Marshall Thatcher. January 16, 1861, Mr. Shapleigh married Sarah A., daughter of Dr. Richard Russell, of Somersworth, who survives him. Their children were Richard Waldron and Fred Russell, both deceased. During the last years of his life Mr. Shapleigh wrote his recollections of early days, and together with his cousin, Waldron Shapleigh, he compiled a complete genealogy of the Shapleighs in America.

GENERAL TIMOTHY [3] SHAW (*Samuel*,[2] *Samuel*[1]), son of Samuel and Patience (Kingsbury) Shaw, was born in York, March 19, 1783. His father was a Revolutionary soldier (see page 83). He came to Sanford with his parents in 1788, and passed the remainder of his life in town. He was well educated, and was a teacher during his early manhood, and also a surveyor of lands. For a dozen years or more he was engaged in trade at Sanford Corner, and was also for a time interested in a manufacturing venture. He kept tavern from about 1835 to the time of his death, his hotel standing where Frank Gowen now resides. " There was a post in front of the house, on a projecting arm of which a sign creaked upon its rusty hinges as it swung to and fro in the passing breeze. The sign was inscribed, in gilt letters, ' Sanford Hotel. T. Shaw.' " [1] For much of the time between 1830 and 1861 he was postmaster at the Corner, having his office on the site of Estes's drug store. The building was afterward sold to the late Howard Frost, of Springvale, and occupied by him as a law office. General Shaw was identified with the Democratic party, and took an active part in local and state legislation. He was on the board of selectmen for twenty-five years, between 1813 and 1841, town clerk, nine years, on the school committee three years, Representative six years, and Senator for two years, 1839–40. For nearly thirty years, he was actively connected with the militia, being commissioned Captain in 1817, Major in 1822, Lieutenant Colonel in 1827, Colonel, 1828, and Brigadier General in 1838, serving until 1846. General Shaw married November 26, 1807, Lucy, daughter of Ephraim Low, Junior. She was born in Sanford, December 20, 1778, and died January 21, 1841, and, like her husband, was

[1] George E. Allen.

of Revolutionary ancestry (see pages 80–81). They had two children, Samuel Madison Shaw, born November 26, 1811, a resident of Alfred, and Timothy Shaw, Junior. General Shaw died August 20, 1870.

HON. TIMOTHY[4] SHAW, JUNIOR (*Timothy*,[3] *Samuel*,[2] *Samuel*[1]), son of the preceding, was born in Sanford, October 12, 1817. After spending his boyhood in school, he became, at the age of seventeen, clerk in his father's store, where he remained until 1838. The following year, with Samuel Tripp as partner, he went into trade for himself, and was afterwards a member of the firm of S. B. Emery and Co. From 1841 to 1845 he was deputy sheriff and crier of the court for York County. In 1845 he was appointed by the Governor as county commissioner to fill a vacancy, and was twice re-elected to the same office. From 1852 to 1857 he served as register of deeds, at Alfred, and from 1859 to 1861, as inspector of customs for the districts of Portland and Falmouth. In October, 1865, he removed to Biddeford to assume the duties of treasurer and bookkeeper of the Shaw and Clark Sewing Machine Company, which position he filled for several years. In 1875 he was elected an assessor of Biddeford, and was appointed to the office in 1879. During President Cleveland's first administration he was postmaster of Biddeford. His death, which occurred December 11, 1892, was deeply regretted. The Biddeford Standard referred to him as "our most eminent citizen," and said : " In his death our city meets with an irreparable loss."

Mr. Shaw married, June 14, 1837, Elizabeth, daughter of William Emery. They started from Sanford on their wedding journey in a two-wheeled chaise, with their wardrobes packed in a trunk suspended from the axle, and drove to Andover, Mass., the nearest railway station, to take the train. Mrs. Shaw died August 11, 1899, in her eighty-first year. Their children were : William G., b. August 3, 1839, d. September 30, 1857; Howard M., b. September 16, 1841, d. February 21, 1842; Lucy E., b. January 16, 1843, d. September 14, 1896 : Jeremiah G., of Biddeford, b. February 28, 1845 ; Marcia A., of Biddeford, b. January 4, 1852. Jeremiah G. married, November 14, 1878, Jennie P. Grant, of Philadelphia ; their children, Howard Grant (deceased), William Emery, and Ray Timothy. Marcia A. married, January 16, 1871, Orrin H. Staples, who died May 11, 1889, aged fifty years, four months; their children, Gracie May (deceased), Mary Elizabeth (deceased), Sidney Algernon, and Marcia Annie.

HON. CHARLES ALBERT[5] SHAW (*Samuel M.*,[4] *Timothy*,[3] *Samuel*,[2]
Samuel[1]), son of Samuel Madison and Susan H. (Lord) Shaw, and
a grandson of General Timothy Shaw, was born in Sanford, November 5, 1831. He was brought up on his father's farm, in that part
of the town known as Shaw's Ridge, where as a boy he attended the
district school, and after a term at a school in Springvale, then kept
by Moses M. Butler, Esq., and one or two terms at Alfred Academy,
he left home at the early age of fourteen to teach, afterwards fitting
for college under the tuition of Henry Holmes, Esq., a distinguished
scholar of that day, with whom he subsequently read law. In 1847,
his father having removed to Alfred, Mr. Shaw, in order to earn the
necessary means, and at the same time be conveniently located to
pursue his studies, served for a year as clerk in the store of Deacon
Nathan Kendall, in the village, and later as clerk in the store of
Silas Derby, Esq., who was also postmaster of the town, a position
which he left to accept a situation in connection with the management
of a newspaper in Boston ; but being a natural mechanic, and an inventor from earliest boyhood, none of these employments were congenial to him, and so he determined to avail himself of the first opportunity presenting itself to learn a mechanical trade. He therefore considered it fortunate when he soon after obtained a desirable
situation with a long established firm of skilful watchmakers and
jewellers with whom he served a regular apprenticeship.

Having finished his trade he started business in Biddeford in 1852,
as senior partner in the firm of Shaw and Clark, watchmakers and
jewellers, a partnership which was continued for fourteen years.
Their business, however, was early changed to that of manufacturers
of sewing machines, of which at that period they were among the
largest in the country, having at one time five factories in the United
States and Canada, and in their employ, directly and indirectly, over
six thousand men. They were also manufacturers of many other
articles of Mr. Shaw's invention, and nearly the largest advertisers
in the country. In the regular course of its business the firm became extensively interested in patents, more especially those relating
to sewing machines, cotton machinery, etc., and also involved, either
as plaintiff or defendant, in many of the most important and stubbornly contested patent suits ever fought in the United States courts.
Mr. Shaw had entire charge of his firm's interests in these suits, all
of which he won, displaying in their conduct such remarkable skill,
mechanical ability and knowledge of patent law as to establish for
himself a national reputation in that regard. Some of the inventions

formerly covered by these patents have proved to be of almost inestimable value to mankind, notably those relating to sewing machines and photography. Without the one relating to sewing machines every family sewing machine in the world, at the present day, would be absolutely worthless, while by means of that relating to photography, the time required for taking a perfect photograph has been reduced from minutes to the fraction of a second. It is due almost wholly to the financial aid and exertions of Mr. Shaw nearly half a century ago, that these two inventions were ever perfected and given to the world.

Mr. Shaw is a Democrat, both by inheritance and belief, and entered early into politics. After serving as councilman and alderman he was elected mayor of Biddeford in 1865, and re-elected in 1866. He also represented that city in the Legislature in 1865, where he at once became the leader of the minority and managed it with such tact, ability and fairness as to command the respect of the majority, thereby in many instances being able to control the balance of power, thus becoming an important factor in securing conservative legislation. He was twice his party's candidate for state treasurer, and was also commissioner from Maine to the World's Fair in Paris in 1867. In 1868 Mr. Shaw was his party's candidate for Congressman in the first Maine district, and although the party was in a hopeless minority, ran far ahead of his ticket and greatly reduced the majority of the opposing party. He was then offered, by President Johnson, the position of commissioner of patents, and also that of consul to Russia, both of which he declined.

In this campaign Mr. Shaw purchased the Maine Democrat, removed it from Saco to Biddeford, where he built and furnished a new printing office, greatly enlarged and improved the paper, and in less than one year more than quadrupled its circulation. It should be stated in this connection that at different times he has been the proprietor of five established and well-known newspapers, which, while under his management, were all successes, and which were finally disposed of by him at a large profit. While publishing the Democrat he started the Daily Evening Times, but soon discontinued its publication, becoming convinced that there was then no field for it. He was also the proprietor of The Western World, of New York, the first newspaper in America ever regularly printed in colors, but as it was a style that did not please him, that feature was abandoned, and forty years after has been adopted by many of the great daily and Sunday papers of the present day as if it were something new.

In 1872 Mr. Shaw moved from Biddeford to Boston, where he now resides, and opened an office as solicitor of patents and expert and counsellor in patent causes, for which he was most eminently fitted, and in which he built up the largest business of that kind, with perhaps one exception, in the country, but from which he retired several years ago. He is interested in a collateral loan and bank business, and is also a large owner of real estate both as an investor and for his private use.

For many years Mr. Shaw has been identified with the show business, but principally as an investor. He built and owned Shaw's Opera House, in Biddeford, and has been interested in theatres in Lowell and Providence. In 1888 he purchased and still owns a half interest in Austin and Stone's Museum and Theatre, a well known and popular Boston institution, established in 1883, and said to be the most successful family amusement resort in America, being visited every year by more than one million men, women and children. P. T. Barnum, the great showman, and Artemus Ward, the great American humorist, were for many years his intimate personal friends, and frequent visitors at his home. They both lectured extensively under his auspices, the famous lecture of Mr. Barnum, entitled " The Art of Money Making " and the equally famous one of Artemus, entitled " The Babes in the Wood" having been especially written for him. In addition to his other show business, Mr. Shaw is the owner of a large number of plays which he licenses to managers on royalty for use by travelling companies, the best known of these being the farce comedy entitled " Peck's Bad Boy," by Hon. George W. Peck, Ex-Governor of Wisconsin, now in its eighteenth year on the road. He is also the owner of all Mr. Peck's other plays.

Mr. Shaw studied medicine with a prominent physician before leaving Maine, and after moving to Boston completed his studies, being admitted to practice several years ago as a regular allopathic physician under the laws of Massachusetts.

In 1876, he was commissioner from Massachusetts to the Centennial Exhibition at Philadelphia, having been appointed at the earnest solicitation of a large number of inventors and manufacturers throughout the country. He is an Odd Fellow, a Mason of the thirty-second degree, and a member of a large number of other charitable and fraternal orders and associations. He is commissioner for all of the states, territories and British provinces, a notary public and justice of the peace.

Mr. Shaw's business engagements and enterprises have for many years been very extensive, so much so that even a brief outline of them would far exceed the limits of this sketch. He has now, however, substantially retired from all active business, and proposes so to continue.

In stature he is six feet in height, of good form, and weighs two hundred and twenty pounds. In habits he is strictly temperate, using neither liquor nor tobacco, has a strong constitution, capable of the greatest endurance, and is in robust health both in mind and body.

He was the oldest of five children, two sons and three daughters, all born in Sanford. His brother, George Green Shaw, died in Boston in 1878. His oldest sister, Susan Jane Shaw, married Otis T. Garey, and resides with her husband in Biddeford. His second oldest sister, Olive Lucy Shaw, is the widow of the late Usher A. Hall, of Alfred, where she now resides. His youngest sister, Harriet Butler Shaw, is unmarried and resides in Alfred.

Mr. Shaw was married in 1856 to Sophia L. Priest, of Biddeford, and has had one child, Otis Madison Shaw, born in 1857, who is unmarried, is a graduate of Bowdoin College and Boston University Law School, read law with Allen, Long and Hemenway (Stillman B. Allen and Secretary Long), and is now practicing law in Boston.

Mr. Shaw is pre-eminently a self-made man, whatever he has become or acquired having been solely by his own unaided exertions, his life presenting a striking illustration of what can be accomplished by the proper exercise of integrity, energy and perseverance. One of the most noted features of his character is his extreme benevolence, which is almost proverbial. Everything considered, his career may be set down as a very remarkable one.

JOHN SHAW was the son of Joseph and Betsey (Allen) Shaw, of York. They removed to Sanford and owned a farm on Low's ridge, afterwards Shaw's ridge. John was born in 1794. In early life he became a teacher, was long employed as such, and acquired the title, then common, "Master," by which he was well known. His abilities as a teacher commanded the highest praise from those qualified to judge. He was regarded as superior to the generality in town and county affairs, though he held but few offices. He served on the school committee five years, on the board of selectmen two years, and was one of the first auditors in town, chosen in 1840. A skilful surveyor, he was often employed in running and establishing roads and land boundaries. He was an exemplary man in all respects, and was a very useful man in the community, in giving advice to his less favored neighbors, in the settlement of estates, and in caring for the interests and welfare of minors and orphans.

Mr. Shaw married Abigail Smith, of York, born in 1795. They had seven children : Betsey, married I. B. Gerry ; Judith Ann, died in 1848 ; Joseph ; Laura Jane and Hannah, who were the first and second wives of Daniel E. Lucy, formerly a jeweller at Springvale ; Daniel, married Mary Dow ; and Sereno A. Mr. Shaw died in January, 1857, and his wife November 10, 1874.

JOHN SKEELE, son of John and Phœbe (Webster) Skeele, was born in Peacham, Vt., November 22, 1786, and died in Saco, May 2, 1853. He prepared for college in his very boyhood, and was admitted to Dartmouth when but thirteen years old. He was unable to enter upon his college course, however, and at once began teaching, having among his pupils one twenty-eight years of age. He taught in Wells (now Kennebunk), for fifteen years, and also at Kennebunkport. About 1829 he removed to Sanford and engaged in trade, at first with Joshua Hobbs, afterward with William Emery, and then alone. Upon his appointment as register of probate in 1838 (he served two years) he removed to Alfred. In 1845 he removed to Saco, and became cashier of the Saco and Biddeford Savings Institution, which position he held until age and ill health compelled him to resign. He had six children, one of whom, Rev. John Parker Skeele (1821–1881) was a graduate of Bowdoin College and a Congregational clergyman for thirty years.

JOHN STANYAN came into town about 1741. He built a timber house on the cross road near the range line, between the main road and Captain Willard's. He had one child. After the death of his first wife he married a daughter of Sampson Johnson. His was the only house in that vicinity for some time. Mr. Stanyan was an innholder as early as 1757. He made large purchases of land, built and owned mills, in part, and took a prominent part in the early history of the town. He was a town officer, and one of the original members of the Congregational church. We infer that he was not successful in business from the fact that he mortgaged his property, and that when he became aged the town purchased a cow for him, allowing him the use of it, but retaining ownership thereof. He died November 18, 1794, supposed to be about ninety-three years of age, and having resided more than fifty years in town.

REV. HENRY J. STONE was born in Wayland, Mass., May 14, 1843. His education was obtained in the public schools, and as a youth he was clerk in a fruit store in Boston, was in the grocery business in Malden, and for a short time in the dry-goods business. From 1868 to 1877 he carried on the printing business in Chelsea, Mass. He came to town in November, 1877, and began to preach for the two Congregational churches. He was instrumental in building the new meeting-house at the Corner, after the old one was burned in 1878. On December 25, 1879, he was ordained to the ministry. Mr. Stone remained in Sanford until 1884. During his residence in town he published the Sanford Weekly News. For the past sixteen years he has been preaching in various parts of Massachusetts.

JOHN STORER was a native of Wells, where he was born January 18, 1796. At an early age he secured employment as clerk in a store at Kennebunk. Benjamin Smith and Horace Porter, a wealthy firm of Kennebunk, who were engaged in shipping and other enterprises, having become acquainted with young Storer suggested to him that there was a good opportunity for business at Sanford, and if he would like to go there they would furnish the necessary capital. Mr. Storer soon visited Sanford and being well satisfied with the outlook, accepted this flattering offer and removed to Sanford, where he commenced business under the firm name of John Storer and Co. in 1820. The profits of the business were divided equally between him and his partners, the capital furnished by them being an offset for his services.

This business was conducted by him for several years, to the entire satisfaction of Smith and Porter, when Mr. Storer bought them out and continued the business on his own account until ill health compelled him to retire. He afterwards regained his health, and at two different times was associated in business with partners in Portland. He was a man of excellent business judgment, strict integrity and had a high sense of honor.

In politics he was a Whig and later a Republican, though not an active partisan. In 1837 he served as selectman and member of the school committee, and was postmaster at Springvale, 1832–33. He was a generous contributor to charitable and religious organizations. During the Civil War no other man in town had the Union cause more at heart. At the close of the war he offered to erect a monument in memory of the soldiers of Sanford who sacrificed their lives, but the town not complying with the conditions, the project fell

through. After the war Mr. Storer became much interested in the
work among the freedmen and contributed $10,000 in 1867 for the
purpose of founding a college for the education of the colored race
at Harper's Ferry. In his honor this institution was named Storer
College. He also contributed one thousand dollars for a library.
This school was opened on October 2, 1867. The work of this college has a glorious history and a more glorious promise for the elevation of the American colored race.

Soon after Mr. Storer moved to Sanford he married Meribah
Hobbs, who was born in Wells, January 17, 1797. Of this union
were born six children : Horace Porter, George (who died in infancy), Lewis (who died at the age of fourteen years), George L., Frederick, and Olive M., who married Hon. Moses M. Butler and removed to Portland, where she now resides. Horace Porter, George
L., and Frederick, all removed to Portland at an early age and for
several years were actively engaged in business there. Horace Porter died December 6, 1897, aged seventy-five years. Mr. Storer died
in Sanford on October 23, 1867. His wife died March 10, 1860.
Grief at her death and anxiety on account of the war completely
broke him down and shortened his life.

GEORGE L. STORER, son of the preceding, was born in Sanford,
and resided here until the age of eighteen. Going to Portland, he
was employed by his brother, Horace P., as clerk in the wholesale
dry goods business. March 4, 1857, he was admitted as a partner
in his brother's business under the firm name of H. P. and G. L.
Storer, and they continued together several years, when Horace P.
sold out his interest to Isaac M. Cutler, the firm name becoming
Storer and Cutler. A few years later Mr. Storer's brother Frederick
was admitted. Subsequently Mr. Cutler retired, and the firm became
G. L. Storer and Co. During all these changes the business was extensive and successful. In 1869 (the Storer brothers having disposed
of their interest), George L. went west and located at Madison, Wis.,
where he now resides.

FREDERICK STORER, brother of the preceding, went from Sanford
to Portland in 1848, and entered the dry goods business as clerk. At
the age of nineteen he formed a partnership with J. R. Corey, retail
dry goods dealer, and at the age of thirty entered the wholesale business with his brother, as above noted. Mr. Storer afterwards formed
the wholesale dry goods house of Locke, Meserve and Co. In 1866

he built the Pondicherry Woollen Mill at Bridgton, which he ran for several years. Mr. Storer married Annie E., daughter of Hon. N. S. Littlefield, who died in 1895. He resides in Portland.

CAPTAIN JONATHAN TEBBETS was born in 1795, and died suddenly of heart disease at his home on Mount Hope, September 5, 1880. He was a carpenter by trade. Captain Tebbets was prominent in the affairs of the Baptist Church at the Corner, and was active in the movement for the building of a new church edifice to replace the one destroyed by the great fire of 1878. He served the town on the board of selectmen. His widow, Mary, died April 26, 1893, aged ninety-seven years.

JAMES L. TIBBETTS was born in Sanford, August 30, 1824. His father, Eliot Tibbetts, served a seven years' apprenticeship as carder and clothier with General Elisha Allen, succeeding to his business in the carding and clothing mill, and also kept a general store. The son, James L., left Sanford in 1840, and for two years had charge of carding and spinning in a mill at East Wilton, Maine. In 1843 he went to Amesbury, Mass., and worked for the Salisbury Mills, now the Hamilton Woollen Company of that place, for forty-three years, nearly the entire time as an overseer. Since 1893 Mr. Tibbetts has been one of the assessors of Amesbury, and at the present time is chairman of the board. He is the senior member of the real estate firm of J. L. and F. O. Tibbetts, doing a large and successful business. During his life in Amesbury, he has been identified with the public interests, and is highly respected in the community. Mr. Tibbetts was a warm personal friend of the poet Whittier, and is the only survivor of the original thirteen Amesbury men, of whom Whittier was one, who voted the Abolition ticket in 1844, and were greeted with hoots and yells at the polls. In 1846 Mr. Tibbetts married Adeline Curtis, a native of Hebron, Maine, who still survives, together with their six sons and three daughters. He still retains a deep interest in his native town, as evidenced by his gifts to the Public Library.

EZRA THOMPSON was the oldest of the eight children of Phinehas (see page 84) and Martha (Willard) Thompson. He was born in Gorham, March 29, 1763, but came to Sanford when a babe with his parents, and spent the whole of his subsequent life here. His ancestors were of Scottish origin. On his father's farm at Thompson's, now Butler's bridge, Ezra grew up a farmer, a blacksmith, and a thinker. In 1781 his younger brother Samuel enlisted in the Revolutionary War, but so great were the anxiety and grief of the mother that Ezra resolved to take his brother's place. He served at Sudbury–Canada (Bethel), and came near losing his life by an accidental blow of an axe. Having been conveyed down the river in a boat, his party came to some rapids around which they felt unable to carry the weak and wounded soldier. Their only recourse was to leave him, with the hope of a possible chance to send for him. While young Thompson was viewing the fearful prospect of death by starvation or by the wild beasts, a Scotchman, "Kit" Chiffener by name, stepped forward, and saying "Thompson is too guid bluid to be left here !" placed him on his back, and carefully carried him to the desired place, three-quarters of a mile below.

When about twenty, Mr. Thompson attended "Master" Clark's school a short term, in which he learned, as he used to say, more than all he learned in other schools. For years he was a public school teacher, and that he was worthy the title of "Master" there is no doubt, for his old pupils were wont to speak very much in his praise. At the age of fifty-two, the father of ten children, farmer, blacksmith, teacher, and surveyor, he began the study of Latin and Greek under Parson Sweat.

For thirty-six consecutive years, 1794–1829, perhaps more, "Master" Thompson held some public office. He was selectman fourteen years, on the school committee eleven years, town treasurer three, coroner, seventeen, and justice of the peace seventeen, besides serving on many committees for the transaction of town business. He was one of the selectmen in 1808 when the town authorized them to petition President Jefferson for the removal of the Embargo, and in 1816, one of the delegates to the convention in Brunswick. In politics he was a Whig. Mr. Thompson united with the Baptist Church in 1798, and continued a strong pillar in church and society until his death.

In 1784 Mr. Thompson married Abigail, daughter of Moses Wilson. They had ten children : Caleb, b. 1785 ; Betsey, b. 1788, m. John Batchelder of Sanford ; Martha, b. 1790, m. Joshua Batchelder ; Lucy, b. 1793 ; Ezra, b. 1795 ; John, b. 1797 ; Isaac, b. 1799 ; Otis, b. 1800 ; Hannah, b. 1802 ; Abigail, b. 1806, m. Timothy Garey. In July, 1820, his first wife having died, Mr. Thompson married Joanna, daughter of David Clark of Sanford. They had four children : Samuel, b. 1821 ; Mary, b. 1823, m. George D. Palmer ; Clark, b. 1825 ; and Joanna, b. 1828, d. in Sanford several years ago. Mr. Thompson died November 8, 1835. Elder Cook preached his funeral sermon from the text, " He was a good man." From all that has come down to us, we can assert with all confidence that a truer word was never spoken.

DR. E. L. THOMPSON is a native of Kennebunk, and was born March 31, 1861. After graduating at the Biddeford High School in 1881, he studied medicine, graduating from the Medical School of Maine in 1887. He then practiced in Buxton, Durham, N. H., and Shapleigh until 1893, when he removed to Springvale, where he has since resided. He was elected to the school committee in 1898 for a term of three years. Dr. Thompson married December 31, 1889, Ella, daughter of James Paine of Buxton.

FRANK CLIFFORD THOMPSON was born in Lewiston, February 16, 1872. He graduated at Bates College in 1784, and has since devoted himself to teaching. He has been principal of the following schools : Grammar school, Head of Westport, Mass., 1894-95 ; Sanford High School, 1895-97 ; East Boothbay High, 1898 ; Lindsey High School, Shapleigh, 1898-1900 ; Springvale High, at the present time. Mr. Thompson married Leone Paul, a native of Sanford, August 30, 1897, and has two children.

SAMUEL TOMPSON was born in Standish, Maine, July 9, 1816. After reading law he was admitted to the bar in 1841, and practiced for twenty years in town, succeeding Hon. Nicholas E. Paine. In 1861 he removed to Boston, where he continued in practice. He married Mary Ann, daughter of William Emery, August 9, 1843. Their children were : Sarah M., born February 6, 1846 ; Edward W. E., born March 12, 1848 ; and Martha H., born January 12, 1858. Mrs. Tompson died in Brookline, Mass., December 1, 1873, and Mr. Tompson, April 12, 1893.

EDWARD W. E. TOMPSON, son of the preceding, was born in Sanford, March 12, 1848. He was educated in the schools of the town, at Brookline (Mass.) High School, and Harvard Law School. He was admitted to the Massachusetts bar in 1871, since which time he has practiced in Boston. He married Ruth H. Ward, of that city, and has three children.

SAMUEL TRIPP, son of George and Lois (Thompson) Tripp, was born at Lyon Hill, December 19, 1814. From 1831 to 1837 he worked in Great Falls, afterwards returning to Sanford, and commencing business in the Storer store with his wife's brother, James H. Clark. Subsequently, he was in company with Timothy Shaw, Junior, and Dr. George Weld. He was town clerk four years, Representative one year, and two years assistant clerk of the house. In 1848 he removed to Biddeford, where he lived, with the exception of a few years, until the time of his death, January 7, 1894, being connected with some of the cotton corporations. He was register of deeds from 1863 to 1873, and city clerk of Biddeford two years. He married a daughter of Ebenezer and Dorcas Clark, and had several children.

REV. WILLIAM TRIPP, son of William and Keziah (Thompson) Tripp, was born in Sanford, June 17, 1794. His father was a Revolutionary soldier (see page 85). He spent his boyhood and early life in his native town and in adjoining towns, at work upon his father's farm ("Grammar Street"), and in learning the shoemaker's trade, at which he worked more or less for years after he entered upon the work of the ministry. At the age of sixteen he was converted. First a Freewill Baptist, he later became a Methodist, and at twenty was an exhorter. During the War of 1812, he was a soldier, and received a pension for his service. In 1817, he bought a small farm in Bethel, and became a local preacher. Fourteen years later he sold out, and joined the Conference as a travelling elder. In 1836, he settled in Cambridge, Maine, as a local preacher, and in 1839 on a farm in Harmony. During his five years' residence there, he served one year in the Legislature. In 1844, he bought a farm in Ripley, Maine, where he spent the remainder of his days, working and preaching as he had in other places. In the summer of 1874, Rev. Mr. Tripp revisited his native town, and spent his eightieth birthday in the house where he was born. He preached several times during his visit. He died in Harmony, February 22, 1875.

Mr. Tripp's mode of travelling was that of a frontiersman. His covered wagon, sheltering his family and protecting his goods, was his home. His cow was fastened to the axle-tree. Hardship did not daunt him, but added zest to his itineracy. Mr. Tripp was one of earth's noblemen, much esteemed and respected for his consistent piety, and beloved for his attractive qualities, his social character, and his goodness of heart. Largely a self-educated man, his sermons possessed that originality of thought and expression which always engaged the closest attention of his listeners.

REV. WILLIAM TRIPP.

He was twice married. By his first wife, Lucy Tebbetts, of Wolfborough, N. H., whom he married January 3, 1814, he had three children. William, the oldest, at one time president of the Maine senate, became a lawyer, and removed to South Dakota. By his second wife, Naamah Bartlett, whom he married September 17, 1822, he had four sons and four daughters. His sons were Enoch B., now residing in Salt Lake City, Utah; Robert, a trader in Harmony; Paschal M., killed at the battle of Gettysburg; and Bartlett. The latter was born in Harmony, July 4, 1842, and is now a lawyer in Yankton, South Dakota. He has been chief justice of the territory of Dakota, was United States minister to Austria in President Cleveland's second administration, and in 1899 served as the United States representative on the Samoan joint commission.

Rev. Mr. Tripp's second wife, Naamah, the daughter of Enoch and Anna (Hall) Bartlett, was born in Bethel, October 13, 1798, and died in Ripley, October 9, 1875. Anna (Hall) Bartlett, daughter of John and Emma (York) Hall, was born April 28, 1768, in Standish, and died August 27, 1868, in Bethel. Emma (York) Hall was daughter of John and Sarah York, of Standish, and sister of Colonel John York.

JOSEPH WEBSTER was born in Hampstead, N. H., April 4, 1778, and died in Sanford, February 26, 1861. He was the son of Joseph Webster, and grandson of John Webster of Newbury, who was born about 1700, and moved to Hampstead. Joseph Webster married Hannah Page, March 24, 1802. She died in July, 1804, and he married, second, Sophia, daughter of Major Samuel Nasson, at Bucksport, Maine, in December, 1804. They afterwards settled in Sanford. Mrs. Webster died in Woburn, Mass., December 29, 1861. By his first wife he had one child, Mary Page, who married William Bell, of Lowell. Children by his second wife : Charles Sawyer ; Clara Tilden, married John N. Colcord ; Rev. Moses Pillsbury ; Joseph Albert ; Hannah Page ; Samuel Nasson ; George ; Harriet Sophia ; Sophia Joanna, married Abiathar M. Hall ; Louisa Jane, married Abram F. Morrell ; Ann Maria ; and Vienna Bell, married Cephas Turner. Rev. Moses P. Webster, who was born in Sanford, July 11, 1810, was a clergyman of the Methodist denomination in Maine and Massachusetts for thirty-three years.

DR. GEORGE WELD, son of Samuel and Sally (Hayden) Weld, was born in Randolph, Vt., September 8, 1796. He succeeded in acquir-

33

ing a common school education sufficient to enable him to find employment as a teacher during the winter months, in which employment he was successful. A few terms at an academy preceded the commencement of his medical studies. In 1820, he began to read medicine with Dr. Daniel Washburn, of Brookfield, Vt., afterwards attending three full courses and one private course at Dartmouth Medical College, and on December 5, 1823, he was approved and licensed as a practitioner by the laws of the New Hampshire Medical Society. Soon after he set out on horseback in search of a desirable location. Not knowing whither he was going, and without definite purpose in that regard, he directed his course eastward, and early in 1824 arrived at Legro's Corner, Lebanon, Maine. There he began to practice, and remained until 1827, when he removed to Little River Falls. In 1833, he was induced to remove to Great Falls, N. H., and for a time was copartner with Dr. Noah Martin, afterward Governor of New Hampshire, in the firm Martin and Weld, and later entered into copartnership with Dr. Oliver W. Austin. Being afflicted with asthma, he was obliged to leave Great Falls, and in November, 1834, he took up his residence in Sanford, where he practiced until his death, July 17, 1854. In 1839, he and Dr. Silas B. Wedgwood formed a copartnership under the firm name of Weld and Wedgwood, the former practicing at the Corner, the latter at Springvale. The firm dissolved in 1841. Dr. Weld served as Surgeon's Mate in the militia for several years.

During the last years of his life, owing to the asthma, he could not sleep except in a sitting posture, and could only visit patients by night in urgent cases, when he made his calls in an easy carriage, and in the agony of his own sufferings, bravely administered to the relief of others. He was a skilful surgeon, and was often called to perform difficult operations, in which he was generally successful. Eager in the pursuit of knowledge pertaining to his profession, he devoted much of his leisure to study, and by practice in dissection became unusually proficient in anatomy and surgery.

In addition to his practice, he engaged in trade (in the old Allen store, near Hosea Willard's present residence), carried on lumbering operations, and gave much attention to farming. He was fond of horses, and proud of the appearance of those which he drove. In his youth a stranger to fear, he often saved life by imperilling his own; in his manhood, courage, wit, and humor were his marked characteristics.

In 1828, Dr. Weld married Theodosia, daughter of Thomas M.

and Rebecca (Hasey) Wentworth, of Lebanon, born November 27, 1789, died April 15, 1862. One daughter, Rebecca H. Weld, now of Melrose, Mass., survives. Dr. Weld had a brother, Hon. Charles E. Weld, who practiced law in Sanford from 1842 to 1846, subsequently removing to Buxton.

ELMER E. WENTWORTH is a native of North Rochester, N. H. For some years he was in the hardware business, but in 1890 came to Springvale and purchased the livery and sale stable of Captain E. G. Murray. In 1899 he purchased the John Dennett and Stephen Goodwin farms in the Deering district, which have been united, and are now known as the Dennett stock farm. Mr. Wentworth has served the town as road surveyor, and is at present road commissioner for Springvale. He married Harriet B., daughter of James Alvah Lord.

MOSES WENTWORTH, son of Levi and Mary (Witham) Wentworth, was born in Milton, N. H., October 12, 1837. He began to earn his living at the age of eleven, although he was able to attend school until he was fifteen. In 1852 he was employed in a cotton mill in Somersworth, N. H., for a few months, and was subsequently en gaged in shoemaking at Milton, for fifteen years. Later he was proprietor of hotels in a number of places, and afterwards engaged in the undertaking business in North Berwick and Lynn. In 1892 he established an undertaker's business in Sanford. Mr. Wentworth married, first, in 1855, Emeline A. Frost, of Springvale, by whom he had two sons, Leroy A. and Barney M. He married, second, in 1877, Rena Hurd of North Berwick. While residing in North Berwick, Mr. Wentworth served as selectman and also Representative for one term. In politics he is a Republican.

SAMUEL WILLARD came into town from York in 1755, and settled near John Stanyan's. He built a grist-mill, and with others, a sawmill soon after (see page 210). He also helped build the Iron Works, at Sanford Corner, and likewise went up the river to Mousam Pond, and built a dam, the first one ever built there. He built the bridge called Willard's bridge, covered it with round timber, and made a toll-bridge of it. He had three sons and five daughters. The sons were Samuel, Junior, John, and Thomas (?) ; of the daughters, Martha married Phinehas Thompson ; Love married Moses Tebbets ; and Sarah married Naphtali (Samuel?) Harmon, and after his death, Elder Walter Powers.

SAMUEL WILLARD, JUNIOR, was twelve years old when his father moved to Sanford. He acquired considerable real estate, and had to pay for a part of his land twice in order to get a good title. His son Stephen came into possession of the property. He was a Lieutenant of militia at the time of the Revolution.

OTIS R. WILLARD, son of Captain Stephen and Lovica (Tripp) Willard, was born in Sauford, May 21, 1836. He has been engaged in the lumber business and farming on the home farm since reaching manhood. February 16, 1882, he married Lucy A. Burke, of Lyman, who died March 3, 1886.

WILLIAM F. WILLARD, for whom the Grand Army Post at Springvale is named, was born at Great Falls, N. H., October 1, 1842, the fourth son of Samuel Willard. He enlisted in Company F, Eighth Maine Volunteers, and was mustered into the United States service as a private, September 7, 1861. He served with the regiment in the Carolinas and Virginia. On the day following the battle before Petersburg, July 31, 1864, he went out to assist in bringing in the wounded, and was shot through the head, and died instantly. His remains were brought home and interred in the cemetery at Springvale.

FRANK WILSON, son of Dr. Timothy and Mary B. (Kimball) Wilson, was born in Orleans, Mass., September 1, 1849. His father (born in 1811, died July 18, 1887) was a native of Shapleigh, and graduated at the Maine Medical School in 1840. After a few months' residence at Sanford Corner, in 1848, he removed to Orleans. Frank Wilson was educated in the public schools of Orleans, and graduated from Harvard Law School in 1877. Coming to Sanford, he also read law with his uncle, Hon. Increase S. Kimball, and was admitted to the bar at the January term, 1878, in Saco. He has since been in practice in Sanford. Mr. Wilson served as register of probate for York County from 1885 to 1900. He served on the board of selectmen in 1888, 1889, and 1892; and has otherwise taken a prominent part in the affairs of the town. Mr. Wilson married, first, Abbie Hobbs, of Somersworth, N. H., November 17, 1880; and, second, in 1892, Alice Pike of Shapleigh. He has two children living.

AUSTIN A. WILSON, of Springvale, was born in Shapleigh, November 3, 1851, and was educated in the public schools of that town, where he lived until he was thirty-three years of age. In 1884 he became a member of the firm of W. H. Nason and Co., at Springvale, in which he still continues. He also owns a large farm in Shapleigh. Mr. Wilson married Annie L., daughter of Elijah Rowe, of Springvale, and has one son, Maynard R.

WILLIAM H. WOOD, town auditor, was born in Windham, December 12, 1872. He is a druggist, and has been in business for himself at Springvale since October, 1895. He is a member of many fraternal organizations. Mr. Wood married, December 25, 1895, Mary, daughter of Levi C. Weymouth, of Portland.

APPENDIX A.

WITCH STORIES.

In common with all ancient towns, early Sanford was not without its witch stories. During the latter part of the last century there lived in town an aged woman, " Granny " ————, who was known as a witch. Her most public action is thus handed down by tradition : When Elder Richardson baptized her son John, it was in the river not far from her house. A goodly company had assembled by the bank, and just as the elder and his candidate were walking into the water, " Granny " was seen coming at the top of her speed, dressed in white from top to toe ; and plunging through the crowd into the river,she came up to Elder Richardson, and exclaimed, "Here, Cæsar, take your piece !" and held out a shilling, or some other coin about that size, gesticulating fiercely for him to take it. He extended his hand, the shilling dropped into it, the hand, instead of closing upon it, tipped a little, and the piece slid into the water. " Granny " turned and ran back as fast as her wet clothes would allow, and the baptism went on, the clergyman keeping himself unruffled—outwardly. The evil spirit still had possession of her ; for, while in sight, she came to a long reach of sand, and dropping upon it, rolled the whole length of it, and then arose in her might and hastened across lots to her home. When one who had witnessed the baptism was going home, across lots too, the old " Granny " had her clothes washed and hung out to dry.

At one time, while Ezra Thompson was visiting his mother, who was ill, some one said : " Here comes ' Granny.' " " Don't let her come in," said Mrs. Thompson, " I'm afraid of her." Ezra stepped to the door just in season to keep her from entering. " Let me go in !" she exclaimed, vehemently, " I want to curse ' Mathy ' Thompson," as he closed the door behind him and stood on the step. " Oh ! no," said he, putting his hand on her shoulder, hard enough to keep her from rending the door. " I will go in," she persisted, struggling and springing toward the door. When she found that he was strong enough to keep her out, she said, " Well, I'll curse her here, before

(518)

I go." And there, turning and twisting herself into all conceivable contortions of the human body (for she was as lithe as a serpent), she cursed her "in her basket and her store, in her going-out and her coming-in," etc., repeating the curses for disobedience as recorded in the twenty-eighth chapter of Deuteronomy.

She had her better moods, however. Once when Martha Thompson's grandson John was at work near the river, in his cornfield, " Granny " came along. She stopped, and made neighborly inquiries as to what he was doing, for whom he was doing it, etc., and then blessed him " in his basket and his store," etc., going through with the blessings for obedience recorded in the same chapter.

After she was dead, they found her " witch-bridle," a string full of curious knots, so the story runs.

It may have been of " Granny " that the story was told, which the writer remember indistinctly, to have heard in his boyhood. One evening a man was returning home through a field, when a hog ran across his pathway. He attempted to drive it away but the animal persistently kept under his feet. With stones and sticks he drove it off, but not till he had beaten and bruised the hog considerably. The next day the reputed witch went about her house with head done up and body and limbs bruised and sore. The assumption was that the witch had turned into a swine, and run before the man to trouble or frighten him.

It might have been " Old Mother York " about whom the story was told ; the name of the alleged witch we do not remember. Who this old woman was, no one seems to know. Whence she came and whither she went remains a mystery. She was represented as " an ill-favored old hag, with no teeth save two great tushes, and with a beard on her chin which would shame a college sophomore's." She was the cause of all the misfortunes in town. " If a protracted drought or disastrous rains occurred ; if a child was still-born or a Saturday's baking went wrong, old Mother York was at her tricks again." She is reported to have lived in the Peacock or Garvin house, about a mile above Springvale, which house for years had the reputation of being haunted. Some years ago a number of sensational stories about it appeared in the newspapers, relating incidents that were apparently true, so that the credulous accepted them as real occurrences. One tenant of undoubted veracity affirmed that all the ghostly noises he ever heard were made by rats and mice. All the stories are as true, we think, as this statement, taken from one of the newspaper reports : " The house has been built upwards of sixty years, and was owned by Peleg Sanford, from whom the town of Sanford, of which Springvale is a village, derives its name."

The stories of the corn shelled in the attic when there was no corn there, of wood cut in the barn when the wood had been untouched, of chairs rocking in the sitting-room when no one was there, of the peddler who was murdered at " Old Mother York's," of the team drawn by four piebald horses, of the woman clothed in white, of the ghosts of the three murderers of the peddler, of the unearthly sights seen and sounds heard,—all may be summed up in one word—*humbug*.

APPENDIX B.

The late Miss Carrie Hatch furnished the author with the following account of early church-going:

"Grandmother Polly Witham said she could remember when the old Baptist meeting-house was finished, and of playing among the blocks and shavings. The names of some of the carpenters were Moses Chick, Nathaniel Harmon, and George Applebee. Before it was finished, a Dr. Barrett taught school in it. There was no fire, nor place to build one, yet when she was young, the house was full every Sunday, winter and summer, when there was a meeting. The people came from Deering's ridge, Mount Hope, Shaw's ridge, and other parts of the town. The elderly women carried tubical tin boxes pierced with holes on top, known as footstoves, which they filled with wood and coals at the houses nearest the meeting-house, and which served to keep their feet warm during the morning service. At noon they would replenish them at the neighbors.' Young people would have been ashamed to use a footstove. A few of the old people went to church in red sleighs, in winter, or on horseback, but the most of the congregation walked. Stephen Gowen had a chaise, and a few wagons called 'rattlers' were used in the summer. There was a place, called the 'shifting-place,' on the ridge road, where people put on their stockings and shoes when they came to meeting, and took them off when they went home. Many of the boys and girls were pleased to go barefooted, not because they were economically inclined, but because they were more comfortable. The people carried with them their lunch of Indian bannock and cheese, for they had nothing better in many families, and most of them were satisfied, if they had enough of that."

APPENDIX C.

LAWYERS AND PHYSICIANS.

Chronological lists of the lawyers and physicians who have practiced in the town are herewith presented:

Lawyers—Grove Catlin, Junior, Arthur McArthur, Jonathan Clark, Ichabod Butler, William L. Walker, Horace O. Allen, Calvin R. Hubbard, Nicholas E. Paine, John T. Paine, Samuel V. Loring, Samuel Tompson, Charles E. Weld, Asa Low, Samuel S. Thing, Increase S. Kimball, William H. Wiggin, William H. Miller, Howard Frost, Hampden Fairfield, John B. Bodwell, George Beacham, Leroy Haley, Frank Wilson, George W. Hanson, Fred J. Allen, Arthur F. Engel, Charles E. Engel, Belle Ashton, George A. Goodwin, John S. Derby, Fred A. Hobbs, Howard Frost.

Physicians—Abiel Hall, Senior, Ebenezer Linscott, John Dow, Hosea Powers, Jefferson Smith, George Weld, John L. Allen, Reuben Hill, Silas B. Wedgwood, William Gage, Mark F. Wentworth, Ivory Brooks, J. B. Manning, Charles H. Rowell, Timothy Wilson, Alvah Ward Dam, Stephen M. Cobb, Frank Turner, Clark C. Trafton, Chase Moulton, Nahum A. Hersom, David Watson, Noah Sanborn, Charles E. Gilpatrick, Benjamin Bussey, I. K. Bascom, William E. Pilsbury, J. T. G. Emery, F. J. Harmon, J. B. Wentworth, Arthur S. Bird, W. L. Simpson, H. B. Huntington, J. B. Andrews, Lorenzo Dow, William H. Milliken, Frank L. Durgin, J. V. St. Hilaire, E. C. Frost, William J. Maybury, W. L. Hough, W. L. Loudon, John H. Neal, F. Bernier, W. W. Frost, Charles W. Blagden, R. S. Gove, E. L. Burnham, J. W. Plaisted, G. H. Rand, F. A. Bragdon, B. M. Moulton, I. C. Sawyer, E. L. Thompson.

APPENDIX D.

Some of the town votes in matters not pertaining to any of the subjects that have been discussed in the body of this volume, are here recorded.

1776. Annual meeting, Tuesday, March 26, at the house of Nathaniel Conat (Conant). "Voted to Low John Stanyan his order that had against the town for writing Pertion to the General Court in the year 1773." July 8. "Met at the school-house. Voted Caleb Emery chosen Constable and sworn and have forty shillings for serving as his Turn for the year 1776." Thirty pounds were raised to defray town charges.

1777. Annual meeting, March 17, at the school-house. Daniel Gile was chosen constable, "but Andrew Burley to serve in his room." Thirty-three votes were cast for selectmen. At a later meeting this year, "Voted not to take any part of the Rats laid on the adjatient inhabitants. Voted to chuse a committee of three men to join the committee chosen by the adjatient inhabitants to Settle the Present Dispute of taxing them if sd committee cannot agree in settlement the sd committee together to chuse a Committee in sum other Town and Leave the matter to that Committee that they shall agree to chuse and this Committee so chosen Shall Settle this Dispute."

1778. March 17. "Vot was pass to alow Paul Chadburn & Benjn Warren fou shillings p^r day for numbering the male inhabitants in their Plantations." "Voted to allow the Treasurer five pence per pound negatived, and three pence allowed."

1779. September 6. "Voted and agreed upon to stand upon by the Regulation Bill till the first of October instant."

1780. May 25. A meeting was held in John Knight's barn to examine the several articles in the new form of government. September 4 the voters met at the school-house to vote for state officers. Fourteen votes were cast for John Hancock for governor.

1782. January 18. "Agreed upon and Vot^d to chuse two men

for agents. Vo^t Messrs Henry Hamilton & William Trip chosen for the above agents to take care of the two Lots of land approicat^d to the use and to help to maintain a minister in said town, and also the School lot belonging to sd town and are authorized to Prosecute to finall Judgment all and every Person or Persons that have or may make stripe or wast on any of sd lots and this town will stand by and defend any Lawfull Measures they Shall take to Recover Dammages from any Person that may or have commit^d trespass on any of sd Lots and this town give full Power to sd agents to settle with any Person or Persons that or have trespass on any of sd Lots. Agreed upon and Vot^d to chuse a Committ^e to Draw up Petion to send to the general court for to see wyther they abate any part of our taxes or Delay the Execution for a longer time." April 2 it was " Vot^d and considered those men that trespass^d on s^d Lots (i. e., the " minestreal" and school lots) and reduced there Vots to one-half of what the agent maid up with them for. Agreed upon and Vot^d what money those trepases pay shall go to the euse of a School. Agreed upon and Vot^d that the Selectmen be a Committee to take into the town Lotts cal^d the minestreall and School Lotts and Leace or improve it according to the best of their judgment for the Benefit of the town."

1783. March 10. " Voted the Selectmen to take an Invotary of the town." April 7. " Voted to allow the constables for the counterfeit money, and for them to take their oath before some justice and to bring a certificate from said justice that was the identical money they took for their rates."

1784. At meetings August 9 and October 11, it was voted to "protect or support William Bennet, constable, sued by Rev. Pelatiah Tingley, for cow taken from John Spear to pay taxes, and to pay said Tingley for the cow claimed by him."

1785. March 8. " Voted to give Josiah Norton his rates that is against on account of his losing his house."

1787. On May 14, Major Samuel Nasson was chosen Representative, and a committee of five was appointed to give him instruction.

1788. For the annual town meeting this year, any man that paid twenty-seven shillings tax in 1786 was considered a voter.

1790. Major Samuel Nasson was to have forty shillings for his services. October 4 the voters met at the school-house in the South Parish, to vote for one Representative to Congress.

1793. For the annual town meeting this year, the qualifications of a voter were : Twenty-one years of age, and possessed of three ounds income, or an estate valued at sixty pounds.

1794. October 27. It was voted to appoint a committee of three to act with the selectmen in making a plan of the town, but a week later this action was reconsidered, and " the selectmen to do it or get it done as cheap as they can."

1801. Captain Sheldon Hobbs notified the inhabitants of the annual meeting, March 9, at the Congregational meeting-house. There, for the most part, until 1848, town meetings were held.

1802. It was announced in the warrant for a meeting November 22, that, " At Said meeting the Selectmen intended to Inform their fellow Citizens of the Reason why they agreeable to the good Law of this Commonwealth Did not assemble the freeholders of this Town on the first monday of this Instant to give in their Votes for a Federal Representative, and will ask their favourable Reception."

1803. Qualifications of voters for annual town meeting : Must have an income of ten dollars, or an estate of two hundred dollars. (This may also refer to 1804.)

1804. April 9. " The Treasurer is Directed to supply the Town with Weights and Measures the year ensuing according to Law."

1808. " Voted John Powers turn in to Town Treasurer seven dollars of Tabor Money which he took while it was good, and be allowed for the same." Vote reconsidered.

1811. " Voted to set Powder House on land of Stephen Gowen, between his house and Joshua Batchelder's. The two agreed to give land sufficient for said house."

1820. April 3. Meeting to vote for the first Governor of Maine. William King received one hundred and sixty-four votes, Ezekiel Whitman, nine, and John Holmes and Samuel Merrill, one each.

1822. July 20. "Voted to allow William Butler ten cents for extra services as constable for 1821." September 9. " Voted to purchase burying cloth, and that it be kept at Sanford Corner."

1823. November 3. " Voted to give the sufferers of Wiscasset and Alna $75." The vote was afterwards reconsidered.

1836. April 4. " Voted that the Collector take for taxes small bills of the denominations 1, 2, and 3." The motion to this effect was made by Timothy Shaw. The law against the circulation of such bills was designed to bring specie into circulation. The editor of the Maine Democrat condemned the action of the town. At the " Small Bill " convention in 1836, Timothy Shaw, Thomas Goodwin, Third, and Joseph Hobson were nominated for Senators. Shaw received 2,289 votes. The regular Democratic candidates were elected.

1841. The old powder house was given to Aaron Witham.

1859. June 13. It was voted, thirty-one to nine, against aiding the Aroostook Railroad Company. November 5. Voted, thirty-one to two, " To exempt from taxation all manufacturing establishments hereafter erected in said town by individuals or by incorporated companies, for the manufacture of fabrics of cotton or wool, or of both cotton and wool, and all the machinery and capital used for operating the same, together with all such machinery hereafter put into buildings already erected, but not now occupied; and all capital used for operating the same, agreeable to an act entitled ' An Act to Encourage Manufactures,' approved April 1, 1859." In 1866 and in 1873, similar votes were passed exempting manufacturing establishments from taxation for ten years.

1865. March 13. "Voted to instruct the selectmen and assessors to go over the town and put under oath every person liable to be taxed as to a statement of their valuation. Voted to order the assessors to doom every person liable to taxation in this town ten thousand dollars on their valuation who refuses to be put under oath in regard to their valuation."

1872. December 9. The town officers, for the first time for many years, designated the travelled roads in Springvale on which it should be unlawful for any person to slide with a sled or other vehicle.

1873. Dogs were not to be taxed.

1875. Voted to tax dogs one dollar per head.

1876. January 1. Benjamin F. Hanson was chosen to appear before the next legislature to oppose the petition of Amaziah Whitten and others who wished to be annexed to Alfred. March 13. Voted to authorize John A. Dennett to transcribe the records of the town from the year 1768 to the year 1805. Voted to authorize the selectmen to settle with Ivory Brooks for the building which was taken down to stop the spread of the fire in Springvale, February 20, 1876.

1880. May 19. It was voted to adopt by-laws providing that all dogs that had been bitten or come in contact with a rabid dog should be killed immediately; that it should be the duty of all owners of dogs to keep them shut up four months at least; and any dog found running at large after May 20, 1880, should be killed by the constables.

APPENDIX E.

When the inhabitants of the "Gore" (see page 94) petitioned to the General Court that their grants of lands northwestward of Sanford head-line, eastward of Lebanon line, and adjoining Shapleigh, which were annexed to Sanford by the act of 1785, be annexed to Shapleigh, because they were "fearful that Sanford being an old town was in debt," and they wished to be "taxed in one town," Caleb Emery, Eleazar Chadbourn, and Samuel Nasson were appointed a committee to confer with these petitioners. Their report, presented to the town April 3, 1786, is interesting for its quaintness. It follows, in part:

"It appears to your committee that they (i. e., the inhabitants of the "Gore") are not disposed to be separated from the town of Sanford and what has been done by them was by the influence of some designing men as will more fully appear by the large part of said inhabitants signing a petition to the General Court to be continued to the town of Sanford and those that did not sign declared to your committee their desires to be continued to belong to Sanford and also declared they would be glad to sign to the same petition but they were under embarrassments to some persons. It also appears to your committee that the petition signed and sent last year to the Court by the inhabitants was in a manner forced by hiring some and threatening others. The above is in full what we could collect from the sentiments of the people excepting one Mr. Sam¹ Dinnick who said the reasons which he could give were in his mind sufficient to be set off to Shapleigh which were as follows : that it was his opinion that the taxes in Shapleigh would be very light for ten years to come, but he further said he did not care which town he belonged to. But as to him we can say that it is easily proved that some man to whom he stands indebted in a large sum was heard to say if he did not sign to Shapleigh he should not hold his barn nor the land it stands on. Thus your committee have gone as far as they can concerning the business and leave it to the town's consideration."

The report was received in town meeting and the selectmen were appointed a committee to petition the General Court concerning the matter, but the General Court decided in favor of the annexationists. Again in 1792 there was a petition, signed by Samuel Dennett, Samuel Ricker, William Worster, Simeon Ricker, Gideon Dearing, William Dearing, John Goodwin, Moses Goodwin, Joseph Butler, Hiphsebeth Merifield, Nathaniel Merifield, William Meris (Merifield?), William Ricker, Thomas Worster, and Reuben Ricker, who asked to be set off from Sanford to Shapleigh. After due hearing, on recommendation of the committee of incorporations of the General Court, the house passed the desired bill, and the inhabitants of Sanford were notified to show why the petition should not be granted. This they did through Samuel Nasson and Sheldon Hobbs, selectmen, on November 20, 1792. The remonstrance set forth that about seven years previously the petitioners had sought to have their lands annexed to Sanford, which had been done, the petitioners enjoying the benefit of the expenditure of two hundred pounds or more, part of which had been paid to Sanford, " being so much they had overpaid in Supplying Soldiers in the late war," " they the said Inhabitance living on the Gore" having received " there full proportion of the said money in schooling &c till the whole was spent, although the same was paid by the Town long before the Gore was annexed to us." Remonstrants held that it would be as much to the disadvantage of the petitioners as to the town of Sanford should the desired annexation take place, as would appear, " if your Honours would only Reflect a few moments," and it was emphatically stated that the plan had been " Contrived by Some person or persons who allways wish to Sow discord and Contention among those that have hitherto lived in Perfect Harmony and Love." In conclusion the remonstrance declared :

" Such has ever been the lot of the Peacefull to Encounter and such we are afard are those with whome we have to Contende but we only wish for a full Examination and we are sure and on that we are willing to rest the whole Matter that they Cannot Give one Reason for Being Sett off being asured that after your Honors have fully heard all Parties that you will not be willing to please a few Discontented minds by Cutting of an arme or any other member of the Allready Languishing Town of Sanford but will give the Pertitioners Living on the Gore leave to withdraw their Pertition or rather if you see that it is only ment to blow up the Coals of Strife and Contention you will so far Discharge such procedings for the futer as to Order the pertition to be Dismissed but if Restless minds Cannot be made Easey any other way we wish your Honors would order some futer day for all Parties to be heard and then we rest ourselves Saft knowing that we can in a few words put to Silance those who Can in the absence of the Town of Sanford Say what they Please Resting on this that their is none to answer them."

This appeal was not unavailing. The petitioners were given leave to withdraw.

34

BIOGRAPHICAL INDEX.

INDEX TO REVOLUTIONARY SOLDIERS.

[The lists of Revolutionary soldiers in Chapter VI having been presented in two forms, first by years, and then in part, alphabetically, the following index has been compiled in order to secure completeness in determining a soldier's record].

Adams, Daniel, 55, 61, 72.
John, 52, 53, 72.
Jonathan, 53, 72.

Barnes (Barrons), Abraham, 53, 55, 72.
John, 52, 72.
Thomas, 58, 73.
Batchelder, Joshua, 53, 73.
Bennett, Nathaniel, 52, 56, 58, 73.
William, Junior, 61.
Boston (Baston), Daniel, 53, 73.
Gershom, 61.
Jonathan, 53, 55, 62, 64, 73.
Timothy, 55, 73.
William, 73.
Bridges, Samuel, 58, 60, 66, 73.
Brown (Brawn), Daniel, 58, 59, 74.
Jacob, 66, 74.
Brown (Brawn, Bran), Michael, 57, 63, 65, 66, 68, 74.
Burk (Burks), William, 53, 55, 58, 61, 62, 74.
Burke, Thomas, 70.
Burleigh (Burley), Andrew, 52, 74.
Butler, Nathaniel, 416.
Thomas, 416.

Cane, Joshua, 63, 65, 74.
Chadbourn, James, 56, 65, 74, 423.
William, 70.
Chaney, Joseph, Junior, 67.
Chiffener, Christopher, 70, 510.
Clark (Clarke), John, 53, 57, 74.
Clark (Clerk), Thomas, 64.
Cluff (Clough), Samuel, 53, 74.

Coffin, Bodwell, 70.
Daniel, 54, 70, 75.
Isaac, 53, 75.
Cole, Tobias, 64, 75.
Cram, John, 53, 55, 75.

Davis, James, 55, 56, 61, 62.
Deshon, Moses, 67, 68.

Eastman, Daniel, 54, 63, 75.
Ezekiel, 63, 75.
Emery, Caleb, 42, 61, 434.
Joshua, 55, 75.
Emons (Emmons), John, 53.
Pendleton, 75.
English, William, 61, 64.
Evans, Benjamin, 57, 61, 62.

Faye (Fahy), William, 55.

Garey (Gary, Gare), James, 63, 67, 75.
Getchell, Abel, 58.
Daniel, 64, 75.
Giles (Gile), Daniel, 53, 54, 56, 75.
Ephraim, 53, 76.
John, 57, 69, 76.
Joseph, 53, 76.
Joseph, Junior, 53, 76.
Paul, 52, 54, 56, 61, 76.
Gooding, Jonathan, 61, 76.
Goodrich (Gutterage), Daniel, 63, 76.
Joshua, 64, 76.
Goodwin, Amos W., 76.
———, 76.
Gowen, Ezekiel, 61, 76.
John, 61, 62, 63, 76.

(535)

Ingram Content Group UK Ltd.
Milton Keynes UK
UKHW040757250423
420747UK00004B/262

9 789353 862633